Foundations of Farm Policy

by Luther Tweeten

UNIVERSITY OF NEBRASKA PRESS · LINCOLN

Publishers on the Plains

UNP

Manufactured in the United States of America

To Mom and Dad

Contents

Preface

Foundations of Farm Policy is written to provide the foundation needed to understand, interpret, and analyze farm policy. It can be used as a text, as a reference, or for selective reading. It is especially suited for upper-division undergraduate or graduate courses. Some sections require little economic sophistication and should prove useful to laymen and lower-division undergraduates alike. The necessary background varies by chapters. Chapters 1–5 require little formal economic training. Chapters 7–15 require a knowledge of the principles of economics. Some parts of Chapters 6 and 16 require a knowledge of intermediate economics as well. All readers should be familiar with the meaning of terms such as supply, demand, opportunity cost, and elasticity.

The book follows closely my lecture notes in a three-semester-hour course at Oklahoma State University. At the undergraduate level, some parts, such as Chapter 16, may conveniently be omitted. At the graduate level, I begin with Chapter 16, then follow the normal sequence from Chapter 1 to Chapter 15.

The book is designed for all serious students of farm policy, but it would be disappointing to have it used as a conventional text. Rather, it is intended to be an efficient source of fundamentals. It should be used to build the foundations of policy as quickly as possible so that the student will be free to pursue, in depth, frontier issues and other topics of interest in other publications.

I tell students the first day of class that the three requirements for success in policy study are: "Read, read, read." But to obtain just the fundamentals requires the reading of many books. The purpose of *Foundations of Farm Policy* is to relieve the student of the task of reading several volumes just to learn the fundamentals. Instead he can peruse such references for breadth, depth, and maturity of viewpoint. It is up to the instructor to decide what supplementary topics should be included. Some topics come readily to mind. For example, the material especially needs supplementation in class with timely data on the makeup of congressional agricultural committees and information on current government farm programs.

Foundations of Farm Policy is at once historical and analytical—and more definitive than previous monographs on policy. The book rests on the proposition that farm policy can be studied properly only when it is placed within its social, economic, and political setting. It will challenge the upper-division undergraduate, who is now demanding a richer analytical diet, as his background is upgraded.

The term "farm policy" as used here refers to policies that affect groups and not just individuals. It deals with how farmers influence and are influenced by government policies. The table of contents further clarifies what I define as farm policy. The government policies that will be demanded (and also that will be accepted) by farmers depend heavily on farmers' goals and values, which are discussed in Chapter 1. Farmers do not play the political game in isolation— government farm policies are increasingly subject to what urban America wants. Chapter 2 covers objectives for agricultural policies from an urban perspective. Chapter 3 attempts to complete the picture of farm group behavior begun in Chapter 1 and provides useful lessons from history for farm groups who wish to engage in holding actions, collective bargaining, and other measures to raise income.

Chapters 4 and 5 present the economic history of American agriculture. They illustrate how attitudes, resources, technology, and institutions interact to generate economic growth and to raise the productivity of farming. How economic growth, greater farming productivity, and other factors cause and perpetuate farm problems is discussed in depth in Chapter 6, which deals with symptoms and causes of farm problems. It also deals extensively with the origin of problems of low-resource earnings and why these problems do not disappear.

The cost-price squeeze is a central concept of the farm problem. The "price" side refers to low prices received by farmers through the marketing sector. The structure, conduct, and performance of the marketing sector are examined for clues to farm economic ills in Chapter 7. The "cost" side refers to the nature of input markets and prices paid by farmers. In Chapters 8 and 9, the structure, conduct, and performance of the input markets are examined for clues to farm economic ills. Elasticities of supply, demand, and production that predict farm output, prices, and earnings under alternative policies are also presented in Chapters 7, 8, and 9.

Chapter 10 describes past government policies, emphasizing commodity programs focused principally on commercial farmers. Chapter 11 gives advantages and disadvantages of numerous alternative commodity programs for the future, including bargaining power and free markets. The chapter illustrates how cost-effectiveness criteria can be usefully employed to compare programs.

Chapters 12, 13, and 14 provide the first in-depth discussion of rural poverty in a book of this type. They define the dimensions and causes of poverty (Chapter 12), tell what programs have been tried in the past (Chapter 13), and use systems analysis to set priorities for future programs (Chapter 14).

Chapter 15 cites reasons for foreign trade and describes and evaluates past trade and aid policies. Chapter 16, which is intended to be the first chapter for students who are ready to face the abstractions of welfare economics, develops maturity in economic thinking. Together with Chapters 1–5, it does much to establish favorable mental attitudes in the student so that he is better prepared for the study of current problems of agriculture in Chapters 6–15. Accordingly, some parts of the early chapters challenge the conventional thinking of students. It is not intended that instructors or students agree with everything in these chapters. Rather, it is hoped that the material will often serve as a springboard for discussion of controversial topics.

To Earl Heady and James Plaxico, who have encouraged and stimulated my work; to the typists and reviewers, who have been so diligent and patient; to the Department of Agricultural Economics at Oklahoma State University and the Food Research Institute at Stanford University, whose devotion to scholarship led them to gamble some time on an unknown quantity; and to the Oklahoma Agricultural Experiment Station and the National Science Foundation, which provided considerable financial support for the research—to each of these agencies and individuals I am very deeply grateful. None of them, needless to say, is responsible for any errors or views presented herein.

FOUNDATIONS
OF
FARM POLICY

CHAPTER ONE

Goals and Values for Farm Policy: From a Rural Perspective

It has been said that economists can suggest a half-dozen ways to solve the major farm problems, but progress toward a solution rests on resolution of conflicts in goals and values (Heady, 1961, p. vi). The purpose of this chapter is to articulate the goals and values of major participants in farm policy formulation. The chapter contains a little of the rich and acrimonious dialogue among farm groups as they search for a generally acceptable farm policy based on quite different goals and values.

It begins with a presentation of agrarian goals and values. The positions of the major church groups and farm organizations are presented and evaluated. In the next chapter, the implication for farm policy of living in a dominantly urban-industrial society is examined and interpreted.

GENERALIZED GOALS

Goals are defined as ends or objectives toward which behavior may be directed. *Means* are the ways in which goals are achieved. *Values* are standards of preferences that guide behavior. Values—feelings of what is desirable or what ought to be—can often be interpreted as goals and means held with some degree of intensity. A clear-cut distinction between means, goals, and values is neither feasible nor functional.

GOAL HIERARCHIES AND THE MEANS-ENDS SCHEMA

There is agreement that people individually and collectively are attempting to increase something that may be called welfare, utility, satisfaction, or

1

well-being. This first hierarchy of goals is least controversial because it is so nondescript—almost any lesser goal can be "defined" into this category.

A second hierarchy of goals includes liberty, justice, security, and progress. Stability is another candidate for the second hierarchy, but some instability is inherent in the word "progress." Hence the idea of progress with security subsumes an optimum degree of stability. There is almost unanimous agreement that the items in the second hierarchy are relevant goals, although there is little agreement on which goals society rates most important. Other words—such as freedom (for liberty) and growth (for progress)—might replace those chosen. Politicians who wish to appeal to all and offend no one will campaign on a platform of freedom, growth, justice, and security. Organizations that have a heterogeneous membership also can be expected to stress these lowest common denominators of goals.

The third hierarchy in the means-ends schema are means to the ends defined in the second hierarchy. Democracy might be placed in the third hierarchy, since it is one means to freedom and justice. Economic growth is placed in the third hierarchy because it is one means to progress. And economic efficiency is the means to economic growth. The free enterprise system operating in a capitalistic, profit-oriented economy is one means to efficiency. It also has been interpreted to be formally consistent with justice, security, and freedom. Numerous other ends-in-view, which are in fact means to higher goals, include monogamous marriage, equality of opportunity, patriotism, and humanitarianism.

There is less than general agreement on the third hierarchy of goals; a fourth hierarchy is not presented because there would be little or no agreement about its content.

WHY ECONOMIC GROWTH?

When economists are not occupied with problems of economic growth (defined broadly to include measures to increase income), they seem to be pre-occupied with them. Other social scientists accuse economists of overemphasis on income as a goal.

Data cannot prove that economic growth increases the well-being of society. It is of interest that the suicide rate, one measure of disutility, is highest in other parts of the world in the high-income nations and highest, in the United States, in those states with the highest incomes. Philosophers and psychologists do not contend that people are happier (or unhappier) in more affluent societies than in less affluent societies.

Economists defend their concern with economic growth. One point of view is that, since economic growth leaves the choice open between the new and the old bundle of goods and services, it can be justified on the grounds of offering a wider choice of opportunities or options and can at least leave the individual or society as well off as before. This latter point is invalid, because of the large disutility attending movement back to the former consumption patterns requiring less income. There can be much disutility when a person sees the income of other persons rise while his own does not change. An original bundle of goods and services, like innocence, is one "virtue" to which one cannot return. The simple argument that economic growth is an important goal because people prefer more goods and services to less remains less than fully persuasive.

Some have made the compelling value judgment that an increase in income does raise satisfactions in societies characterized by disease, malnutrition, and the deprivation associated with poverty. This judgment cannot be proved, but it certainly commands a large following among economists.

Economic growth is sometimes justified as essential to confront the dynamic processes of the real world. It may be argued that national income must keep pace with population growth. Also, economic growth is needed in one country to preserve a world balance of power (and hence freedom, culture, and a way of life) so long as growth is occurring in countries with an opposing political and social ideology. Certain goals such as security and justice in some ways complement economic growth. Pursuit of economic growth has been justified to the extent that it falls within this complementary range.

The economist cannot resolve these concerns about the place of economic growth in the hierarchy of goals. For the present, he can be content with the knowledge that individuals and societies give ample evidence in national pronouncements, legislation, and salaries that economic growth and the services of economists that contribute thereto are much in demand. Thus logical positivism currently is perhaps the most defensible apology for the emphasis by economists on the goal of economic growth.

This discussion is not intended to imply that economic motives are dominant in society, even though the "magnificent" economics of Karl Marx, Joseph Schumpeter, and others has given a central role to economic determinants of the social, political, and institutional configuration of nations. It is interesting to note that the peasant in developing nations is increasingly being cast in the image of economic man, while the behavioral theories of the firm reflect a growing disenchantment with that image in developed nations.

It is not very useful to pursue further the taxonomy of goals. The real issues are not over definitions of goals but over the intensity with which they are held and their competitive properties. How much freedom and justice is society willing to sacrifice to secure greater economic growth? How does unmitigated pursuit of freedom for one group affect the freedom and economic growth of another group? How does an increase in farm income affect the income, freedom, and justice of other groups? These are "gut" issues. To analyze them our economic tools are blunt instruments at best, but there is a need to bring the issues into the open.

A discussion of the broad goals listed above gives little emphasis to the goals of American farmers and their subgroups or to the intensity with which these goals are sought. The following discussion of values provides more insight into these issues.

GOALS AND VALUES OF FARMERS

The farm value structure has deep roots. First there is the Judeo-Christian culture of the Western world, which places emphasis on learning and active mastery of the world, in contrast to the more contemplative, ascetic culture of the Eastern world. There is the Reformation, which emphasized the individuality and secular worth of all men and which stimulated the emergence of the Protestant Ethic. There is English democracy, with roots in Greek antiquity, the Magna Carta, and the Reformation. There is capitalism, with its vigor strengthened by the English political stability and institutional structure and the Industrial Revolution.

Then there is *laissez faire*. It has its origins in the philosophy of John Locke, which emphasized that the ideal world lies in the natural order of no collective restraints on individual actions, and in the utilitarian philosophy of Adam Smith, whereby economic man because of his acquisitive instinct is led to Utopia by the invisible hand of the perfect market. There is the eighteenth-century Enlightenment philosophy, which in England emphasized reason, science, empiricism, and individualism and in France supported the view that the government could assume a significant role as servant of an equalitarian democracy. There is the French Physiocratic influence, which emphasized the primacy of agriculture in the total economy.

These influences were felt in the United States and became conspicuous in the moral philosophies of Puritanism and Jeffersonianism. Jefferson stressed the moral values of an atomistic, independent ownership pattern for agriculture and of a limited government role. The latter concept is expressed in the famous maxim: "That government is best that governs least."

America is a melting pot of philosophies as well as of ethnic groups. The amalgam of philosophies in early American life resulted in what may be called agrarian creeds. The ablest statements of the values of our premachine agrarian society have been made by John Brewster (1961) and are paraphrased below. The following four creeds are idealized value judgments which permeated both rural and urban society in nineteenth-century America. They were the chief guides to individual behavior consistent with respect of self and society.

WORK ETHIC

The work ethic contains four component judgments. The *work imperative* is a judgment that the proper way to fulfill one's need for a higher status is to be proficient in one's chosen field. Backward or easy ways are not to be placed above excellence in job performance. A second judgment, the *self-made man ideal*, is that a man who improves his income through honest efforts is worthy of respect and emulation. This judgment precludes dependence on family pedigree for status. A corollary of the ideal is that men and nations alike possess sufficient means to improve the lot of the common man, i.e., to close the gap between present circumstances and aspirations. To be unwilling to strive to close that gap belittles the American Dream. It is apparent that these first two judgments would contribute to a dedicated, hard-working labor force and thereby to high rates of economic growth.

Two final judgments of the work ethic are that society owes to each man (*a*) *commutative justice*, defined as the value of his contribution, and (*b*) *distributive justice*, defined as equal access to the means of developing creative or earning potential (Brewster, 1961, pp. 117, 118). Commutative justice is exactly satisfied with a perfect market, where each factor is paid its value of marginal product—the incremental contribution of the factor to output, multiplied by output price. Of course, there were unresolved arguments about the resemblance between the nineteenth-century economy, as it actually operated, and a perfect market. Distributive justice refers to absence of barriers to entering markets and to equal access to "free and universal" education in basic skills. The latter would violate commutative justice by taxing some of the contribution from the economically advantaged to build the human resources of the economically disadvantaged.

DEMOCRATIC CREED

The democratic creed contains two component value judgments: (*a*) all men are of equal worth and dignity, and (*b*) none, however wise or good, is good or wise enough to have dictatorial power over any other. Included is the idea that all deserve an equal voice in shaping the rules which are deemed necessary for the sake of the general welfare (Brewster, 1961, p. 118).

THE ENTERPRISE CREED

The enterprise creed entails four component value judgments: (1) The individual or his immediate family ought to be responsible for his economic security throughout life; (2) a prime function of the government is to prevent the imprudent from pressing government, business, or any other organization or institution into sharing the burden of an individual's economic security; (3) proprietors deserve exclusive right to prescribe the rules under which their production units operate; and (4) a prime function of the government is to prevent anyone, including the government itself, from infringing upon the managerial freedom of proprietors (Brewster, 1961, p. 119).

CREED OF SELF-INTEGRITY

The self-integrity creed relates to the status of dissenters. Its central judgment is that, in the case of conflict, both the individual and his group are responsible for seeking new modes of thought and practice that will unify the hitherto conflicting views of each. In line with this judgment, the community prizes its dissenting members as its agents for achieving new knowledge and practices. The individual and his group share the common judgment that the highest responsibility of the individual is to follow the dictates of his own exceptional insights (Brewster, 1961, p. 121). The high status of dissenters in agrarian society was afforded primarily to those whose insights were of *practical* significance. The intellectual innovator was relegated to a lower hierarchy of esteem.

The premachine agrarian goals that characterized farm and city people alike left a sizable residue that is apparent today in modern society. The goals lead to substantial positive value for the price mechanism and considerable negative value for the growth of big government and the welfare state.

Technological change and the process of economic growth give rise to numerous conflicts among the agrarian creeds. Emphasis on the creed of self-integrity and efficiency has led to overcapacity in agriculture. Profitable and productive inputs, such as fertilizers, pesticides, and improved seeds and machinery, have raised farm output relative to needs. The price system signals through lower prices that labor is redundant in agriculture and that its contribution to output is less in farming than in other sectors. Since commutative justice holds that labor deserves only the value of its contribution, low labor returns are the "cost" some have to pay for the more general goal of an efficient economy. In a perfect market, employers will advertise and people will seek work until an equilibrium is achieved. An equilibrium here means that comparable resources are earning the same returns in all farm and nonfarm uses or employments. If an apparent disequilibrium exists in the long run, it is only that farm people place a high premium on the farm way of life, and the "social" wage is in equilibrium.

But low labor returns have afflicted a large segment of the farm economy for many years, and certain questions are raised. One is that, although parents may favor the farm way of life, the children have the right of equal opportunity to compete for jobs in either the farm or nonfarm sector. This principle of distributive justice is violated if parents in an economically retarded rural area cannot afford the training and cultural orientation needed for equality of opportunity. Furthermore, market imperfections, such as failure to make job opportunities known and imperfect hiring practices, inhibit mobility.

To stockpile excess production capacity in agriculture for emergencies, to create a more orderly flow of farm migrants to the city, and to bring farm income to a socially acceptable level, let us suppose that a majority of voters in society vote to support farm income by institutional means. This in itself violates the enterprise creed, which states that the household is responsible for its economic security and no outsiders (taxpayers) should accept responsibility for the economic security of farmers. Furthermore, the controls that attend the government programs infringe upon the freedom of the farm operator to make his own production and marketing decisions. Government supports may be consistent with the concepts of individual worth and dignity and with representative voting procedures inherent in the democratic creed, but support programs may conflict sharply with the enterprise creed.

FARM FUNDAMENTALISM

The premachine agrarian values listed above are interpreted primarily on the basis of the English tradition of natural order, democracy, and free enterprise. Agricultural fundamentalism, a related philosophy, as akin to the agrarian creeds but draws more deeply from the French Physiocratic tradition.

Agricultural fundamentalism stems partially from the fact that farming was the major source of the nation's wealth when most of the people lived on farms. But agricultural fundamentalism is much more than that (Fite, 1962, p. 1203). It holds that there is something special and unique about the farm way of life. It holds that farmers are more dependable and stable politically than city-dwellers. It maintains that farmers have a higher moral character, exemplified by honesty, integrity, and reliability. The husbandman is held to be more independent and self-reliant. Agrarian fundamentalism holds that farming is a divine calling and that God and man walk hand in hand to supply the physical needs of mankind (Fite, 1962, p. 1203).

While agrarian fundamentalism dates back to the rural tradition in the Bible, its most articulate and compelling progenitor in America was Thomas Jefferson. He stated:

> Those who labor in the earth are the chosen people of God, if ever he had a chosen people. . . . Corruption of morals in the mass of culti-vators is a phenomenon of which no age nor nation has furnished an example. It is the mark set on those who, not looking up to heaven to their own soil and industry as do husbandmen for their subsistence, depend for it on the casualties and caprice of customers. Dependence begets subservience and venality, suffocates the germ of virtue, and prepares fit tools for the designs of ambition. [Jefferson, 1788, p. 175]

The continuity of fundamentalism is clearly evident from Jefferson to the most recent positions of farm organizations to be discussed later. The continuity was broken by some political leaders, however. Abraham Lincoln stated that "my opinion of them [farmers] is that, in proportion to numbers, they are neither better nor worse than other people" (cf. Fite, 1962, p. 1208). Lincoln displayed no special enthusiasm, motivated by farm fundamentalism or by anything else, for pushing through the great tripartite legislation of 1862: the act that established the Department of Agriculture, the Morrill Act, and the Homestead Act. Rather, Fite contends (1962, p. 1208), passage was the legislative expression of the widely held view that special treatment for agriculture would benefit the nation.

The fundamentalist theme again is apparent in a statement from William Jennings Bryan's "Cross of Gold" speech: "Burn down your cities and leave our farms, and your cities will spring up again as if by magic; but destroy our farms and the grass will grow in the streets of every city in the country."

Paarlberg (1964, p. 3) gives a more current summary of articles in the fundamentalist agricultural creed which has been the basis of our agricultural policy until well into the twentieth century:

1. Farmers are good citizens, and a high percentage of our population should be on farms.
2. Farming is not only a business but a way of life.
3. Farming should be a family enterprise.
4. The land should be owned by the man who tills it.
5. It is good to make two blades of grass grow where one grew before.
6. Anyone who wants to farm should be free to do so.
7. A farmer should be his own boss.

The components of the creed were more or less internally consistent when lack of new technology limited the ability of farmers to grow two blades of grass where one grew before (article 5), but the growth of science, technology, and nonfarm industry changed that, and article 5 began to destroy the basis for the rest of the agricultural creed. Farmers *are* good citizens, but a high proportion of our population cannot be on farms if economic growth is important. Farming is indeed a business, and that leaves little room for it as a way of life. Farming "should" be a family enterprise, but if the family is unable to provide the management and capital to maintain high efficiency, then it will be replaced by a more efficient organization.

Other things being equal, it is desirable to own the land one tills, but the man who *must* own his land increasingly finds his operation restricted to an uneconomic size unit. Few who want to farm can do so. When farming is a business rather than a way of life, then cynics raise the question of what is so unique about farming. A farmer "should" be his own boss, but scientific farming requires that he share his management responsibilities with an electronic computer, his creditors, his landlord, and the government.

Two additional articles could be added to the agricultural creed: (*a*) that food and fiber are the most basic needs of civilization, and (*b*) that farmers must be prosperous if the nation is to prosper. A fundamentalist attitude fostered by the first article is conveniently refuted by the undifferentiated status awarded the waterworks employee, though water is a more immediate necessity for life than food. The "economic leverage" principle grew out of article *b*. It was observed that national income was eight times the farm income. Employing the Physiocratic principle of primary industry generating secondary and tertiary industry, the inference was that one dollar of increase in farm income raised national income by eight dollars. The corollary is that the nation could ill afford a lagging farm income. Confidence in the economic leverage theory has been destroyed as the multiplier has grown absurdly high (in 1968 it was approximately 30). Furthermore, the 1920's and 1950's found the national economy prospering while the farm economy was depressed.

Opinions differ about the contribution of agricultural fundamentalism to farm legislation. One view is that the enduring memory of urban people who have a fond affection for the farm has created the phenomenon of increasing farm aid while the proportion of farm votes has diminished (Brandt, 1961, p. 10). In recognition of this view Brandt (1962, p. 1232) holds that "the extraordinary goodwill which the urban public entertains toward farmers should be treated by them with utmost respect, and nursed by them and their representatives with more care than the treasury's gold reserves in Kentucky are guarded."

Hadwiger (1962, p. 1231) holds a contrary view. He states that "to the extent that agricultural programs depend on urban attitudes, a request for sympathy and willingness to reciprocate in kind will go much farther today than a reliance on fundamentalist attitudes." To explain the rising expenditures on farm programs in recent years, he cites, not urban sentimentality, but the pivotal significance of the farm vote and its demonstrated ability to fluctuate more sharply in response to economic appeals than that of other groups (1962, p. 1223).

RECENT EVIDENCE OF FARMERS' ATTITUDES

Results from a 1964 survey of farmers relate to many of the attitudes discussed above. In the summer of 1964, 500 wheat producers were interviewed in Oklahoma and Kansas (Hines *et al.*, 1965). Two-thirds of the random sample of 500 agreed that "government relief programs have gotten too large." Sixty-three per cent agreed that "present government farm programs are contrary to the free enterprise system." Yet more farmers agreed than disagreed with each of three liberal statements that (*a*) the federal government should be involved in projects such as electric power and housing, (*b*) the federal government should be doing more to help small towns and cities build the schools they need, and (*c*) the federal government ought to see that everyone who wants to work can find a job. Four out of five farmers favored some government program to support farm income. Farmers appeared to be conservative in political philosophy but took a liberal position on specific issues.

The 500 farmers participating in the survey were tested for their perception of the farm problem. Table 1.1 summarizes the results. Reactions to statements about the family farm, bargaining power, and the leverage effect of farm economic conditions are of interest. The table presents the percentage distribution of the farmers' responses to nine statements concerning the farm situation. These statements are listed according to the percentage of "acceptable" responses. The rating of a response as acceptable (meaning a keen perception of the farm problem) is based on the authors' judgment, which is of course fallible. Farmers showed the highest level of understanding of statement 1 (there is apt to be a shortage of food because so many people are moving off the farm). Seventy-three per cent of the farmers disagreed with this statement. Farmers, in general, were aware of the difficulty in organizing U.S. farmers to control production (statement 2).

Just over one-half of the 500 farmers agreed that the United States should consider the effect on other wheat-exporting countries when developing a wheat-export policy (statement 3). Thirty per cent of the farmers indicated they felt that the government should support farm prices, but it shouldn't try to tell farmers what to do (statement 4). This response may reflect strong dissatisfaction (apparent in other parts of the survey) with past acreage controls or failure to understand the enormous problems which would arise with price supports but no controls.

In their response to statement 5 (the wheat price would be higher if farmers didn't use new varieties and fertilizers), farmers showed confusion about the effects of technology on output and, in turn, on price.

Farmers disagreed with the idea that finding new uses for farm products doesn't offer much hope for solving the farm problem (statement 6). Only 18 per cent disagreed with statement 7 (the family farm is rapidly going out of existence). Responses to statement 9 (a depression in agriculture will usually lead the whole country into a depression) indicate that farmers still held to this traditional idea despite the fact that farmers had experienced somewhat depressed incomes over the previous 15 years while the nonfarm sector had experienced general prosperity. Farmers apparently are not aware of the small share (about one-thirtieth in 1968) of farm income in the national income and that fluctuations in farm income may be cushioned by shifts in income of other economic sectors.

TABLE 1.1. Percentage Distribution of Farmers' Responses to Statements about the Farm Situation

	Responses[a]					Acceptable Responses[b]
	SD	D	U	A	SA	
	(per cent)					(per cent)
Statements indicating a high level of farmer understanding						
1. There is apt to be a shortage of food because so many people are moving off the farm.	16	57	8	15	4	73
2. Farmers could easily organize to control production and raise prices.	17	49	15	14	4	66
Statements indicating marginal level of farmer understanding						
3. When developing a wheat-export policy, the U.S. must consider its effects on other wheat-exporting countries.	5	18	19	53	5	58
4. The government should support farm prices, but it shouldn't try to tell a farmer what and how much to produce.	9	45	16	23	7	54
Statements indicating a low level of farmer understanding						
5. The wheat price would be higher than it is now if farmers didn't use new varieties and fertilizers.	12	39	15	30	4	34
6. Finding new uses for farm products doesn't offer much hope for solving the farm problem.	12	52	10	23	4	27
7. The family farm is rapidly going out of existence.	3	15	6	51	24	· 18
8. There's no reason for the U.S. to have so much surplus food while there are hungry people in the world.	1	14	15	48	21	15
9. A depression in agriculture will usually lead the whole country into a depression.	2	5	5	49	38	7

SOURCE: Hines *et al.*, 1965, p. 1191.

[a] SD—strongly disagree; D—disagree; U—undecided; A—agree; SA—strongly agree. The percentage totals do not equal 100, since a few of the 500 farmers interviewed did not respond to the statements.

[b] Responses rated as "acceptable" by Hines *et al.* are underscored.

THE POSITIONS OF MAJOR FARM GROUPS

Goals and objectives of major churches and farm organizations are summarized below. Although much of the following discussion is taken from writings of persons who speak for their respective organizations, it must be recognized that the positions taken are *not* necessarily representative of their organization. Of interest throughout is the way farm groups vacillate between a concern for efficiency (free play of supply and demand) and concern for justice (government or farmer-run organizations to improve bargaining power and raise farm income).

PROTESTANT POSITION

The Protestant representative suggests certain hypotheses about freedom (Greene, 1963, pp. 24, 25). One is that "freedom" in its limited meaning of absence of restraint, can never be the major goal of public policy for agriculture. The exercise of human freedom must be conditioned by a sense of responsibility. Government action may under certain conditions be an unwarranted invasion of freedom but in other circumstances may be the only effective means in a democratic society to promote the rights and freedom of certain groups or individuals. Greene (1963, p. 25) states that traditional economic structures and practices, or newly emerging ones, may pose threats to freedom as great as any programs of the government. He cites as an ethical inconsistency the farm operators' plea for public assistance to cope with problems of low and unstable income while at the same time resisting with violence the efforts of farm employees to organize for collective bargaining (Greene, 1963, p. 28) and adds (p. 30): "As a principle, cooperation has more to contribute to the achievement of a loving community than competition."

The Protestant position concludes with a statement of goals from the National Council of Churches that includes (*a*) equality of opportunity for human development, (*b*) preservation of the family farm, (*c*) encouragement of association and organization, (*d*) conservation and development of resources, (*e*) adequate food supplies, (*f*) fair and reasonably stable levels of farm income, and (*g*) recognition of human interdependence in the world (Greene, 1963, p. 32).

CATHOLIC POSITION

The Catholic representative (Speltz, 1963, pp. 35–36), states: "The natural law principle of the primacy of the person is a surer guide to social policy than the nebulous value of individual freedom. The good of the person is a true end, a goal, whereas freedom is but a means."

A strong note of agricultural fundamentalism is apparent in the following statement:

> The rural values such as reverence for the soil, love of God, love of the fatherland, willing acceptance of honest toil and love of common-wealth are fundamentally spiritual and cannot be maintained for long on any other basis. These qualities should be esteemed above the tech-nological and the economic. They are essential for maintaining an organic social structure based upon freedom and personal responsi-bility. They are part of an authentic rural spirit. [Speltz, 1963, p. 46]

The basic social importance of agriculture is ultimately reflected in Speltz's statement (1963, p. 46) that, "even if this nation could dispense with most of its farmers, there would remain the question of whether it could remain strong without the type of man agriculture produces." If Father Speltz's view is taken seriously, then one would be concerned about the social precariousness of a nation whose population by 1985 will be only 3 per cent rural farm.

The Catholic representative goes on to make a case for development of industry in rural areas and a self-sufficiency in town-country units. He speaks in favor of private ownership and diffuse landholding but favors organized efforts of farmers to promote social justice because "the individual farmer, for example, can do little by himself to establish a just price, but in cooperation with farmers of the region this is possible" (Speltz, 1963, pp. 42, 44, 45).

There is no formal statement of Catholic goals, but within the context of Speltz's statements, the Protestant goals are representative of the Catholic position also. Both are fundamentalist in upholding the virtues of agriculture and the family farm but liberal in their willingness to forgo some *laissez faire* tradition and efficiency to gain more security and justice through group effort. The Protestant position is representative of the established, traditional Pro-testant churches. The position of the theologically fundamentalist Protestant churches would perhaps be considerably more politically conservative.

AMERICAN FARM BUREAU FEDERATION

In 1967 the American Farm Bureau Federation (more often referred to as the Farm Bureau) was the largest of the farm organizations and claimed in its membership 1.7 million families throughout the United States. Most, but not all, are farm families. The proportion of nonfarm families in the Farm Bureau is not made public.

The Bureau's philosophy leans heavily on the side of freedom and efficiency. The following are excerpts from a recent policy statement ("Farm Bureau Policies for 1966," pp. 1–3):

Freedom of the individual versus concentration of power which would destroy freedom is the central issue in all societies.

Property rights are among the human rights essential to the preservation of individual freedom.

Public functions should be performed by the qualified unit of government closest to the people.

We believe in the American capitalistic, private, competitive enterprise system in which property is privately owned, privately managed, and operated for profit and individual satisfaction.

We believe in a competitive business environment in which supply and demand are the primary determinants of market prices, the use of productive resources, and the distribution of output.

We believe in the right of every man to choose his own occupation, to be rewarded according to his contribution to society, and to save, invest, spend or convey to his heirs his earnings as he chooses.

The conservative position of the Bureau is also apparent in the following statement (American Farm Bureau Federation, 1962, p. 7), which recommends that government programs should:

Increase economic opportunity for farm people.
Promote efficiency in farming.
Adhere to the competitive principle.
Be consistent with the law of supply and demand.
Strengthen the free market system.
Stimulate market expansion.
Encourage soil and water conservation.
Insure our ability to feed an increasing population.

The Farm Bureau, despite its strong statements against socialism and interference with the market mechanism, recognized the need for at least temporary government programs to facilitate adjustment of farm production to demand. They favored a voluntary land retirement program with whole farms removed from production of crops. Contracts to retire land would be let on a bid basis and would be of three to five years' duration (American Farm Bureau Federation, 1966, p. 31).

NATIONAL FARMERS UNION

The National Farmers Union claims membership of over 250,000 farm families. Membership is concentrated in the Great Plains and the Southwest. The organization had close ties with the Kennedy and Johnson Administrations, the policies of which coincided closely with those of the Farmers Union. It is not certain whether these close ties came about because the Farmers Union was successful in convincing the two Administrations of the merits of its approach, or because the Administrations independently concluded that policies of the type advocated by the Union were appropriate and then welcomed any organized support available. At any rate, there has been a tendency in the postwar years for the National Farmers Union to identify with Democratic Party policies and for the American Farm Bureau Federation to identify with Republican Party policies.

The Farmers Union has retained certain key elements of agricultural fundamentalism in its philosophy, including the importance to democracy of having a considerable number of people on the land and the spiritual and cultural values of the family farm (Rohde, 1963, p. 80). The family farm is cherished as the most efficient method of food production and as essential to a truly democratic way of life.

The policy statement adopted by the 64th Convention of the National Farmers Union (1966, p. 4) states that "in spite of the phenomenal success of the family-farm system of agriculture, some laymen and some few professional agriculturalists erroneously believe that large scale farming is more efficient and therefore more desirable." The Farmers Union rejects the proposition that large farms are more efficient but is unwilling to accept diseconomies of size as an adequate barrier to growth of large units: "It is mandatory that in order to stop the endless migration of farm people to the cities, limits be placed on commodity loans and payments per producer so that larger-than-family farms will not continue their undue advantage over working farm and ranch families" (National Farmers Union, 1966, pp. 4, 5).

The basic goals of the Farmers Union are: (*a*) parity of returns on labor and other resources for efficient family farmers in conformity with the principle of economic justice, (*b*) preservation of the family farm, (*c*) more bargaining power in the market place, (*d*) expanding food consumption at home and abroad, and (*e*) preservation of rural values and conservation of the soil (Rohde, 1963, pp. 81, 82).

The Farmers Union does not call for parity prices or a socially acceptable income level, but states (1966, p. 3) that federal farm programs should be utilized to the maximum to insure that families who operate family farms can earn "a parity income, defined as returns on family labor, management, capital investment and risk, comparable to returns that similar production resources receive elsewhere in the national economy."

The third goal, bargaining power, deserves special attention because of the interesting interpretation that attends it:

> There is a widespread belief that farmers are the only economic group
> in the country out of step with our free enterprise system. That's why
> we hear so much about returning farmers to the free market. Actually,
> the farm market more closely approaches the free market concept in
> our free enterprise economy than the markets in which other industries

operate. Most industries wield great economic power over the supply and prices of their products. Farmers have little of such control and are essentially "price-takers" in the market place. [Rohde, 1963, p. 81]

The goals of the Farmers Union are translated into a specific policy. The proposal is to determine each year the food and fiber requirements and then restrict production by marketing quotas and land withdrawal to this level. Direct payments would be limited by some formula to a level consistent with the family farm concept. The Farmers Union in 1969 was in the forefront of the effort to obtain legislation forbidding nonfarm corporations from operating farming units.

NATIONAL GRANGE

The National Grange tends to be a middle-of-the-roader and is less doctrinaire than the other three farm organizations discussed in this chapter. The Grange sided with the Farmers Union in the 1963 wheat referendum and was closer to the Kennedy and Johnson Administrations' policy than was the Farm Bureau. The Grange is closer to the Farm Bureau than to the Farmers Union when it comes to stressing the requirement that farm income should come from consumers of farm products rather than from taxpayers.

The President of the National Grange in 1963, pointing to the interaction of various elements of the farm economy, blamed the farm problem on rising prices of farm inputs supplied by the nonfarm sector. Rising prices, he claimed, were "a result of a comprehensive and extensive structure of governmental programs designed to protect the income of those in nonagricultural segments of the American economy" (Newsom, 1963, p. 92). He blamed government protection of the industrial pricing structure and tariffs for the unfavorable pricing of inputs supplied to farmers and favored use of government programs "to give agricultural producers an opportunity to earn and receive for their labor, management, risk and investment a return reasonably comparable to that provided for those same factors in their best nonfarm employments" (1963, p. 88).

The Grange was squarely behind efforts to increase bargaining power: "We must modify agricultural legislation as necessary to permit farm people effectively to regulate their own marketings" (Newsom, 1963, p. 93). The Grange is unique among farm groups in its stress on two-price programs. Its preoccupation with these programs dates back to the McNary-Haugen Bills of the 1920's.

NATIONAL FARMERS ORGANIZATION

The National Farmers Organization, headed by Oren Staley, is the youngest and most militant of the farm groups. Its support is primarily in the Midwest.

It emphasizes that the number-one problem in agriculture is low profit and recognizes that in any business or in any industry a man must be efficient in producing, but "at the same time we must not say that people are inefficient because they are forced to leave the farm due to circumstances beyond their control" (Staley, 1963, pp. 107, 108). Staley's statement may have validity for young farmers who are potentially good managers, but the very essence of the price mechanism is that it operates in a very impersonal way to raise efficiency by weeding out those whose returns are low. Staley's statement also might be more suitable if he distinguished between "social efficiency" and "private efficiency," where social efficiency accounts for the psychic costs experienced by farm people who are forced to find a nonfarm job and move to the city.

The objective of the National Farmers Organization is to secure a successful bargaining front by bringing the producers of 60 per cent of a commodity under contract. The "modest" objective is to secure a fair price to the consumer and middleman but above all to provide a reasonable return to the farmer for his use of land, labor, and capital—including a profit for risk (cf. Breimyer, 1965, p. 199).

The immediate goal of the Organization is bargaining power. "In an organized economy they [farmers] are either going to organize and meet their problems as an organized industry, or they are going to have to relegate themselves to lower and lower incomes and a lower and lower standard of living" (Staley, 1963, p. 111).

The motivation for this view is partly the organized nature of nonfarm industry and the need for countervailing power and partly the view of the farm supply curve held by the National Farmers Organization. According to Staley (1963, p. 110), "past history . . . shows that the greatest increase in agricultural production has been in years of the cost-price squeeze." We shall see in a later chapter that economists have found no empirical evidence to support the proposition that the supply curve for aggregate farm output is backward sloping.

CRITIQUE OF THE ABOVE POSITIONS

There are many similarities among the positions of the foregoing groups. In general all support the need for an equitable return on farm resources. It is interesting that despite the heavy emphasis on parity *prices* in past national programs, the organizations stress parity *income* or parity *resource earnings*. The groups generally support soil conservation, the family farm, and increased bargaining power for agricultural cooperatives. There is stress on efficiency and individual freedom, but it is tempered with economic justice. While the groups would prefer to receive farm income through free market channels, they appear to be willing to accept government intervention in the market if necessary to get equitable returns.

The shifting emphasis over time from parity prices to parity income and from parity income to parity return on resources represents increasing economic sophistication. But none of these objectives is really adequate for agriculture and one is struck by the lack of organized concern for rural poverty. Many farmers have too few resources to earn a socially acceptable income even if resources are paid at parity levels. What these people need is not parity returns or transfer payments but a way to develop their skills, attitudes, and assets so as to compete effectively in the job market. It is parity of access to opportunity that is basic to those who are really disadvantaged, such as operators of un-economic farming units, hired workers, and migrant workers.

Because its philosophy is unique among farm groups, it is well to examine more critically the position of the American Farm Bureau Federation. Breimyer summarizes the writings of newspaper reporters, economists, and political scientists concerning the Farm Bureau position (1965, pp. 195–199). The test of a group is its actions rather than its words. It may be reasoned that the official policy statement of the Farm Bureau necessarily must be broad and emphasize undefined goals, such as freedom, because the membership is so diverse. More specific principles and policy recommendations would be possible from the National Wheat Growers Association, for example, but would lead to conflict among the numerous component interest groups found within the Bureau's 1.7 million member families.

The inscrutability of freedom is clearly stated by Brewster (1961, p. 127): "Unless we pinpoint the specific maladies from which specific individuals or groups seek liberation, there is scarcely a whiff of wind between the teeth so devoid of meaning as the word 'freedom.' One man's freedom is another man's tyranny, just as one man's orthodoxy is another man's heresy."

Protecting group interests may be little more than exploiting all non-members. The beauty of the competitive economic system in its purest form is that pursuit of self-interest is turned to the benefit of all. But the political process, even more than the market economy, is highly imperfect. What is good for one group of farmers is not necessarily good for America—or even for other farmers.

Personal freedom has greatest meaning to those who have power to exercise it. The study of 500 wheat-growers in Oklahoma and Kansas (Hines *et al.*, 1965) revealed that two variables were significantly linked: the preference for a free wheat market and the expectation by a farmer that he would fare better than his neighbor under that market. The free market offers unparalleled freedom, but this freedom may mean crisis to the young farmer who begins with few resources. Since the operators of larger farms tend to be most efficient, to have the most influence in the community, and to be in the best position to reap the benefits of "freedom," the complementarity of freedom, power, and efficiency is apparent. But freedom often tends to be competitive with justice. When confronted with a choice between higher incomes coupled with tighter allotments and no allotments coupled with lower income, higher incomes and tighter allotments were favored by the majority of the 500 wheat-growers. On this test, farmers were clearly willing to sacrifice some freedom in decision-making to gain more justice (income) and security. Thus the term "freedom" to wheat-growers appeared to have no definite meaning until it was applied to specific situations.

The positive concept of freedom means that all deserve an equal voice in making the rules of the economic game. The democratic view of freedom is that men are free from arbitrary power because each individual has the same weight in shaping the collective restraints for the common good. The negative concept of freedom interprets freedom narrowly as the right to operate without restraints, unmolested by collective action.

Because its leaders tend economically to be "haves" rather than "have-nots," the Farm Bureau has been faulted for taking a conservative stance characterized by the negative concept of freedom. To this criticism the Bureau justifiably replies that the political process does much more than merely establish the rules of the game and, in fact, involves activities that profoundly influence income distribution (Hamilton, 1963, p. 72). Furthermore there is such a thing as the tyranny of the majority over the minority. The welfare losses to the minority can exceed the welfare gains to the majority, and "programs which make people dependent on the Federal government certainly impair their freedom to decide how they will use their right to vote" (Hamilton, 1963, p. 72). In refuting the contention that farmers have been amply compensated for any imposition on their freedom, Hamilton (p. 73) asks, "How do we determine the adequacy of compensation for programs that threaten to reduce economic opportunity by permanently destroying the market for a commodity?"

The test of an institution is whether it preserves and extends the basic goals and values of a free society. This test can be failed as readily by group action under private auspices, such as the American Agricultural Marketing Association (AAMA), an affiliate of the Farm Bureau, as by government programs (Breimyer, 1965, p. 197). The AAMA does not now compel participation, does not attempt to raise prices by production controls, and does not engage in holding actions. It does not have the powers of compulsion, as do the federal marketing orders that require participation of the minority who opposed the order, nor is it governed by the checks and balances written into marketing order contracts. Nevertheless, farmers can be expected to have a great desire to raise prices and income through collective action of the AAMA.

The power of the Farm Bureau to make farm policies has declined since the days of Gray Silver (the Farm Bureau's representative) and the Farm Bloc in the 1920's. In the 1960's the Bureau has demonstrated power to veto legislation but it has only limited power to legislate positive policies. One view is that its new position was an effort to do what it could do best—obstruct legislation with attractive but impractical idealistic schemes for which the Bureau need not take responsibility because it could not legislate. This view of the Bureau is unrealistic. A more responsible view is that the Farm Bureau sincerely felt that government influence on farming had gone too far and was in danger of going farther. And a practical political device to moderate an extreme position on one side is to take an extreme position on the other. If the power to legislate were given to the Bureau, its position might have moderated. This view is supported by the fact that the Bureau spoke of the need for a sizable land retirement program operated by the government to restrain production and support prices. It stressed that this program be temporary, however. The Bureau also supported other government activities for agriculture, including research, extension, grading, and marketing orders.

INCREASING THE LEGISLATIVE IMPACT OF FARM ORGANIZATIONS

The weight that a farm organization carries in making legislation depends partly on the extent to which it truly represents its membership. An important question is the extent to which farm groups truly reflect the philosophy of their members. Membership is sustained primarily for fraternal or economic reasons in the major farm organizations. Ability to buy insurance and farm supplies at lower rates or to sell grain to the local elevator overshadows political philosophy as a reason for membership. Analysis of the 1964 survey of 500 wheat-growers in Oklahoma and Kansas revealed no statistically significant association between membership in the major farm organizations and preference for a particular farm program. The conservative (or liberal) viewpoints of a farm organization must be interpreted as the view of the farmers throughout the country who have a conservative (or liberal) economic orientation rather than as the view of members of only that particular organization.

Though organizations may state that they have solicited opinions from the grass roots level, there is a strong tendency for the top officials to influence the outcome. It is very difficult for rank and file members to express opinions in an organization contrary to those of a few strong leaders. If grass roots opinions are at variance with those of the officers, the only way to express them is through a vigorous power struggle that damages the organization.

One way to convince the public that farm organizations truly represent grass roots opinions would be to increase democracy in the system. To improve the public image of organizations, to raise public confidence in the ability of farm groups to express the real preferences and philosophies of their memberships, and to increase the political effectiveness of farm organizations, a significant first step would be for the organizations to establish rules that limit the tenure of officers.

SPECIAL INTEREST GROUPS

Increasing specialization in agriculture has stimulated the organization of commodity interest groups. The goals of organizations representing wool, wheat, dairy, and other interests were not discussed above but have a very important impact on farm legislation. One view (Breimyer, 1965, p. 190) is that the fragmentation of agriculture into commodity groups has heightened the role and influence of interest groups: "In the deliberations over dairy legislation the group most catered to and feared was not the Farm Bureau or the Grange but the National Milk Producers Federation. . . . Organizations of producers of fruits and vegetables and specialty crops of the West Coast have long struck fear in legislators and administrators, and have scarcely bothered to exchange the time of day with national farm organizations."

Another view (Bonnen, 1965) is that fragmentation of agricultural interest groups is destroying farmers' political power: "As a consequence, the level of conflict and disorder is so great at present that it is almost impossible to get agreement within agricultural committees on legislation for many specific commodities." Bonnen goes on to state that "farm-organization leaders and rural politicians, to be effective, must back away from traditional Neanderthal style and from their prepackage ideologies to combine in a politically pragmatic manner with whomever they can." He concludes: "If the agricultural establishment declines or becomes diffuse . . . to survive, it must exhibit more relevance to the broader objectives of society. If the agricultural establishment cannot develop the leadership that is capable of seeing the situation as it really is and adjusting to it, then it not only will fail to survive in any meaningful form but will deserve its death" (Bonnen, 1965, pp. 1125, 1126, 1129).

These words seem to be too strong. The declining political power of agriculture is explained by many other factors including migration from farms, reapportionment, fewer strategic positions in the power structure of Congress, reduced loyalty of Southern voters to Democratic legislators, the growth of Executive relative to Congressional power, and the struggle among farm groups (Hardin, 1965, p. 1097).

The dissension among farm organizations and the growth of numerous interest groups is attributed not only to the growing specialization and heterogeneity of agriculture, but also to the favorable economic conditions in commercial agriculture. If pressed by sharply depressed earnings, farm groups would present a more united front. It would be desirable to iron out internal differences before presenting a common farm front to Congress. This unity was approached only in the darkest days of the Depression of the 1930's. The major future problem will be to make a legitimate case to nonfarm groups that agriculture is in need of legislation and that it is in the interests of nonfarm groups to help.

THE U.S. DEPARTMENT OF AGRICULTURE

This section is devoted largely to the U.S. Department of Agriculture, although other state, local, and national government agencies play a role in formation of goals and values for agriculture. The section will bring out some of the objectives of government agencies and show how these objectives frequently are internally inconsistent. The discussion is confined mainly to the agencies administering commodity programs and soil conservation programs.

The ethos of democratic government is that it is of the people, by the people, and for the people. This suggests that the objectives and values of government have no independent existence and should be discussed only within the context of the goals of society. But the pathos of democratic government is that its agencies develop an independent existence and often have goals that work at cross-purposes. It is not possible here to document the role of all federal agencies. For that, the reader should consult C. M. Hardin's *Food and Fiber in the Nation's Politics* (1967), which I quote frequently below.

The initial goal of a government agency may be to serve the role assigned it by Congress or the President. Once the agency is in existence, it tends to maximize its political base and hence its foundation for existence, subject to the constraints placed on its mission by higher authority. To accomplish this end, the agency is likely to be effective, if not efficient, and to cater to the real needs of groups with political influence. This practice makes it difficult to alter objectives and practices of an entrenched bureaucracy with loyal, though perhaps few, supporters. Yet the bureaucracy may no longer be serving the interests of society. As Hardin puts it:

> The dynamics of our political system forces each bureau to organize its friends, to fix its "base" in the annual appropriations bill, to spread its constituency geographically and then—like street gangs—to defend its "turf." Any Secretary [e.g., of Agriculture] who wants to reorganize a major agency must glue his cards to his chest. If word leaks in the morning, long-distance telephones crackle forth and back, and the afternoon cries of Congressional anguish are deafening. [Hardin, 1967, p. 175]

AGRICULTURAL STABILIZATION AND CONSERVATION SERVICE (ASCS)

The U.S. Department of Agriculture (USDA) in 1966 was composed of 16 program agencies engaged in a wide range of activities. By far the most significant, measured by budget (about two-thirds of USDA expenditures) and political influence, was the Agricultural Stabilization and Conservation Service (ASCS). It traces its lineage back to the Agricultural Adjustment Administration (AAA) of the 1933-45 period, which was succeeded by the Production and Marketing Administration (PMA), which survived to 1953, when it was superseded jointly by the Commodity Stabilization Service (CSS) and the Agricultural Marketing Service (AMS), which were themselves finally superseded by the ASCS.

The major responsibility of the ASCS is to administer payments and allotments of the federal commodity programs. It is administered at the grass roots level by locally elected committeemen; at the state level by committeemen appointed by the Secretary of Agriculture. Many of the state committeemen have gone on to successful careers in the national office in Washington, D.C.

The National Farm Bureau Federation was instrumental in forming the Agricultural Adjustment Administration in 1933. By 1942 antagonism had developed between the two groups, partly from the Farm Bureau's fear that the AAA was a powerful competitor to "bona fide" farmer organizations. While the Farm Bureau has successfully waged war on federal bureaucracies such as the Bureau of Agricultural Economics and the Farm Security Administration, its heaviest guns have been leveled at the AAA and the ASCS. Some of this struggle will be described in Chapter 3. The ASCS has survived largely intact, a credit to its strong political base.

The problem of administering a multibillion dollar program at the local level with some 80,000 community committeemen, many of whom are not sympathetic or loyal to the party in power, is an awesome one. The lines of responsibility and accountability from Washington to local committees are weak at best. Furthermore the President and Congress are elected by and responsive to different constituencies. The result is that "bureaucracies like the AAA–PMA–CSS–ASCS tend to escape control by either President or Congress" (Hardin, 1967, p. 113). Yet after reviewing the record of the ASCS, including the Billie Sol Estes scandal, Hardin concludes:

> ASCS and its predecessors have been remarkably free of graft and corruption, despite the temptations involved in the large sums of money and impressive powers the agency controls—despite, also, the local election of committeemen, and the fact that they rub shoulders in many areas with officials of state and local governments wherein the fifth freedom sometimes seems to be the freedom to suborn public officials. [Hardin, 1967, p. 122]

The reason for the effectiveness of administration and lack of corruption in the ASCS lies in the idealism that pervades the organization and transcends the narrow interests of self and party. The idealism is founded on the goals of equity and justice for farmers which the ASCS believes is its mandate. And the system of allotments and parity prices is guarded jealously as the chief means toward those goals. (It matters not whether commodity programs violate principles of equity and justice; it is only necessary that those who run the system think equity is being promoted.) The conclusion is that the system for administering commodity programs, while bewildering to an efficiency expert, has proved to be workable. But any changes in objectives of farm policy which would mean elimination of the price support and allotment system would be obstructed by the same ideology that makes the system workable.

OTHER GOVERNMENT AGENCIES

It is said that an agricultural economist can find two kinds of jobs—one is to create excess farm capacity by helping farms produce and market more efficiently; the other is to find ways to dispose of the surpluses thus created. The government is in a similar predicament. Vocational agriculture and 4-H programs supported in part by federal monies encourage people to farm, while other government agencies encourage and assist people to leave the farm. Many federal agencies create more production capacity; the ASCS attempts to control it. Activities of government agencies that increase production capacity include conducting research to raise yields of crops and livestock, paying farmers for "conservation" practices that increase output, and adding to cropland by irrigation or drainage. By 1961 Bureau of Reclamation irrigation projects had brought 7 million high-yielding acres into production. Despite surplus production capacity, public programs continue to add thousands of irrigated acres of farm cropland.

Programs of soil conservation under the Agricultural Conservation Program (ACP) and the Soil Conservation Service (SCS) also increase production and work against efforts of the ASCS to control it, although to a lesser extent than the efforts of the Bureau of Reclamation. Emotional appeals have been used with considerable success to justify public investment in conservation of the nation's soil. One would expect that a program motivated by emotional appeals might be overdone. There was some evidence reported in 1967 to support this contention: two-thirds of all farmers refused basic SCS plans; soil conservation practices required sizable subsidies—private owners are unwilling to invest adequately in such practices; soil conservation inputs did not add significantly to the sales value of land; on areas brought to an adequate degree of conservation by subsidies, only a small percentage was maintained in that condition by farmers (Hardin, 1967, pp. 165, 166).

The political base for the SCS is strengthened and broadened by providing a disproportionate share of benefits to large commercial farms and by distributing benefits among areas more nearly according to the number of farms and percentage of total cropland than according to severity of erosion problems. The focus is disproportionately concentrated on white farmers, a characteristic common to many government agencies. The Civil Rights Commission found wholesale discrimination practiced by the SCS, the Extension Service, and the Farmers Home Administration (Hardin, 1967, p. 126). The SCS and other agencies have made substantial progress in overcoming most of the above criticisms.

The efforts to increase farm output while at the same time controlling production is not economically inconsistent in all instances. The criterion is the benefit-cost ratio. Research activities of publicly supported agencies such as the Agricultural Experiment Stations and Agricultural Research Service of the U.S. Department of Agriculture have on the average had high benefit-cost ratios. On the other hand, public programs to irrigate and drain land often have had low benefit-cost ratios.

The Economic Research Service (ERS) and the agencies concerned with program planning and evaluation within the U.S. Department of Agriculture potentially can raise issues of conflicting objectives and inefficiency in use of resources. The ERS has a core of distinguished professional economists and sociologists who have maintained high standards of competence and objectivity in spite of the "power of strategically located individual Congressmen and Senators, many of them from the South, who would not tolerate a strong analytical agency that might probe into problems which they wanted discreetly veiled" (Hardin, 1967, p. 230). This is not to question the sagacity of Congress:

> Most [Congressmen] are keenly intelligent and alert. Nevertheless their responsibility is fragmented. Agricultural policy suffers accordingly. Much of the curse of favoritism in agricultural administration has roots in Congressional politics as does the historical base for acreage allotments, the protectionism that has handicapped our efforts to aid the farm economies of developing countries, and the deep suspicion of study, investigation and teaching in the public policy field. [Hardin, 1967, p. 177]

Because the urban-industrial sector will play a crucial role in the creation of future public policy for agriculture, I defer a summary of the political implications of the issues discussed in this chapter until the end of Chapter 2.

REFERENCES

American Farm Bureau Federation. 1962. Farm Bureau policies for 1962. Resolutions adopted at 43rd annual meeting in Chicago, Ill.
————. 1966. Farm Bureau policies for 1966. Resolutions adopted at 47th annual meeting in Chicago, Ill.

Bonnen, James T. 1965. Present and prospective policy problems of U.S. Agriculture as viewed by an economist. *Journal of Farm Economics* 47:1116–29.

Boulding, Kenneth. 1963. Agricultural organizations and policies. In *Farm Goals in Conflict*, Chapter 15.

Brandt, Karl. 1961. Guidelines for a constructive revision of policy in the coming decade. *Journal of Farm Economics* 43:1–12.

———. 1962. Discussion of farm-fundamentalism—past and future. *Journal of Farm Economics* 44:1231–37.

Breimyer, Harold F. 1965. *Individual Freedom and the Economic Organization of Agriculture*. Urbana: University of Illinois Press.

Brewster, John. 1961. Society values and goals in respect to agriculture. In *Goals and Values in Agricultural Policy*, Chapter 6.

Davis, Joseph S. 1949. Agricultural fundamentalism. In O. B. Jesness, ed., *Readings in Agricultural Policy*, Philadelphia: Blakiston.

Dorfman, Robert. 1965. Introduction. In Robert Dorfman, ed., *Benefits of Government Programs*, Washington: Brookings Institution, pp. 1–11.

Farm Goals in Conflict. 1963. Center for Agricultural and Economic Development. Ames: Iowa State University Press.

Fite, Gilbert. 1962. The historical development of agricultural fundamentalism in the nineteenth century. *Journal of Farm Economics* 44:1203–11.

Goals and Values in Agricultural Policy. 1961. Center for Agricultural and Economic Development. Ames: Iowa State University Press.

Greene, Shirley. 1963. Theology of rural life: a Protestant perspective. In *Farm Goals in Conflict*, Chapter 3.

Hadwiger, Don. 1962. Farm fundamentalism—its future. *Journal of Farm Economics* 44:1218–31.

Hamilton, W. E. 1963. Goals and values underlying Farm Bureau policies. In *Farm Goals in Conflict*, Chapter 6.

Hardin, Charles M. 1946. The Bureau of Agricultural Economics under fire. *Journal of Farm Economics* 28:635–68.

———. 1965. Present and prospective policy problems of U.S. agriculture: as viewed by a political scientist. *Journal of Farm Economics* 47:1901–15.

———. 1967. Food and fiber in the nation's politics. Technical Papers, vol. 3. Washington, National Advisory Commission of Food and Fiber.

Heady, Earl O. 1961. Preface. In *Goals and Values in Agricultural Policy*, pp. v–vi.

Hines, Fred, Delmar Hatesohl, and Luther Tweeten. 1965. Farmers' perception of the farm problem. *Journal of Farm Economics* 47:1190–96.

Jefferson, Thomas. 1788. *Notes on the State of Virginia*. Philadelphia: Prichard and Hall.

National Farmers Union. 1966. 1966 policy of the National Farmers Union. Resolutions adopted at the 64th convention in Denver, Colo.

Newsom, Herschel D. 1963. Goals and values underlying programs of the Grange. In *Farm Goals in Conflict*, Chapter 8.

Paarlberg, Don. 1964. *American Farm Policy*. New York: Wiley.

Rohde, Gilbert. 1963. Goals and values underlying programs of Farmers Union. In *Farm Goals in Conflict*, Chapter 7.

Speltz, George. 1963. Theology of rural life: a Catholic perspective. In *Farm Goals in Conflict*, Chapter 4.

Staley, Oren. 1963. The National Farmers Organization. In *Farm Goals in Conflict*, Chapter 10.

Thompson, Tyler. 1963. Evaluation on an ethical basis. In *Farm Goals in Conflict*, Chapter 14.

CHAPTER TWO

Goals and Values for Farm Policy: From an Urban-Industrial Perspective

In two centuries this nation has been transformed from a society with nearly 19 of 20 people on farms to one with 19 of 20 people living in villages, towns, and cities. The environment in which people live changed radically in this process of economic growth. Notable examples are changes from primary economic activity strongly dependent on man, soil, and nature to secondary and tertiary economic activity dependent more on machines and science. The rise of the city led to increasing mobility, crowding, division of labor, large-scale industry, separation of occupation from family life, and increasing interdependence of man upon man. These environmental factors produced differences between farm and city people in their goals, values, beliefs, and attitudes. And these differences in turn have important future economic ramifications for farmers in a nation increasingly dominated by urban society.

The following section discusses why and how the agrarian tradition depicted in Chapter 1 is giving way to the urban-industrial tradition—a tradition which displays a fundamentalism as surely if not as obviously as farm fundamentalism. The next section is a formal contrast of rural and urban types and provides a forecast of where rural America is headed. The change is already apparent in the contrast contained in this chapter of the urban-industrial "creed" of America today with Brewster's agrarian creed. Sociological research reveals some empirical estimates of rural-urban differences which are recorded in this chapter and support some of the subjective positions taken in earlier sections. Finally, we explore the implications of an increasingly urban-industrial dominated society for public policies affecting commercial farmers, rural poverty, and political lineups.

But first it is necessary to clarify some of the terms used in this chapter. *Urban-industrial* society is used here (and is widely used by social scientists) to depict the dominant U.S. culture. The term is a misnomer if "industrial" refers to "manufacturing." *Industrial* is used in a broader sense in this chapter. Other terms that describe emerging U.S. society are *megalopolitan* (extended city), *technocratic* (technical-scientific), *affluent*, and *rurban*. The last term recognizes the fact that U.S. population growth is taking place primarily neither in the central city nor rural farm areas, but in between.

In general, rural and urban as used here conform to the 1960 U.S. Census definitions. The *rural farm* population is comprised of persons living on farms, where a farm is defined as a place of less than 10 acres yielding agricultural products that sold for $250 or more the previous year or a place of 10 acres or more yielding agricultural products that sold for $50 or more the previous year. The *rural nonfarm* population is comprised of all remaining rural residents not urban. The *urban* population is comprised of all residents of incorporated municipalities of 2,500 inhabitants or more and residents of urban fringe areas and other "densely" populated areas, as designated by census definition.

THE RURAL-URBAN TRADITION

More persons have lived in cities (over 2,500 population) than on farms for approximately a half-century in the U.S., yet a strong agrarian tradition has permeated this society. Agrarian goals and values persist because (*a*) basic values of a once agrarian culture have powerful inertia and yield slowly to pressures for change; (*b*) agrarian values often coincide with values of the growing and influential business interests; (*c*) a large portion of urban dwellers are of rural origin and have not forgotten these roots (over one-fifth of the current nonfarm residents have lived on the farm, and nearly twice as many farm-reared adults are living off the farm as on the farm (cf. Freedman and Freedman, 1956), and (*d*) political representation and power respond slowly to the changing rural-urban proportions.

Goals and values of this nation (including farmers) are increasingly dominated by the urban-industrial sector for several reasons. First, through modern transportation facilities and by sheer magnitude of population and economic activity, the urban sector has a powerful influence. Second, mass communication media such as television, movies, magazines, newspapers, and textbooks are almost universal. These media are largely of urban origin and reflect urban values, but both farm and nonfarm elements are equally exposed to them. A Wisconsin survey showed that, on the average, farmers spent 1 hour and 19 minutes per day listening to the radio and 1 hour and 42 minutes watching TV (Fuguitt, 1963). There was little difference between rural and urban families in this respect.

Third, the dynamic forces of research, education, and industrial growth that underlie many changes in the economic structure of society (and which indirectly influence goals and values) also have their origin in the nonfarm sector. Fourth, farmers interact continually with nonfarm organizations and people that provide farm inputs and market farm products. Only half of all conventional farm inputs are of farm origin. If nonfarm educational and research inputs are included, the proportion is less than half. Two out of five farmers hold part-time nonfarm jobs.

Confrontations between rural and urban political interests are traditional. Resulting compromises depend not only on the size and power of the respective groups but also on the goals, values, and interests of each. Supreme Court reapportionment decisions such as *Baker* vs. *Carr* in 1962 and *Wesbury* vs. *Sanders* in 1964 speeded political adjustments that were perhaps inevitable and shifted the balance of power. To understand and predict what will happen in agriculture, it is essential to examine the structure and attitudes of the urban-industrial sector—of which farming is increasingly an extension or a derivative.

URBAN FUNDAMENTALISM

City and farm are inextricably interdependent in the social and economic growth process. The relationship is clearly a mutually beneficial symbiosis. This fact has not kept one group or the other from taking an occasional funda-mentalist position, maintaining that one sector was inherently superior to the other—that one sector was host and the other parasite. In the words of Con-stance Green (1964, p. 46): "The antagonism of the country bumpkin toward the city slicker mounted from the late 1750's onward, a hostility that would endure for two hundred years until automobiles, telephones, radio, and television largely obliterated basic differences between rural and urban life in America."

Farm people have condemned the city for its slums, race riots, crime, con-gestion, air pollution, business exploitation, secularism, disintegration of the family, corrupt government, and impersonal atmosphere. City people have in turn criticized farm life for being phlegmatic, isolated, uncultured, and unpro-gressive. They have accused farmers of being undemocratic in withholding equal political representation and tax treatment and of being unsympathetic to prob-lems of the city. The rural influence sometimes has been viewed as a bucolic plague. Some urbanites feel that farm groups have been overly concerned with the *family farm* and not sufficiently concerned with the *farm family* and its adjustment problems in the rural-urban exodus.

H. P. Douglass provides one interpretation of urban fundamentalism:

> From the earliest dawn of social life it has been felt that the clash of
> wits, especially in the market place, sharpens them. The mind stagnates

in isolation, is speeded up in association. The man whose business is trade has always felt keenly his sophistication and acumen in contrast with the slower movement of the rustic mind. The typical townsman still implicitly claims this advantage over the farmer. The townsman feels his superiority as the keeper of the ideals of the community and of their peculiar symbols. He has—to paraphrase Prof. Galpin—not only its pantry and shop but also its safe, its medicine chest, its playhouse and its altar. All keepers of ideals tend to hierarchical pride and a sense of class prerogative. It is hard to hold them to the humility of service. [Douglass, 1919, p. 10]

W. Arthur Lewis further elaborates the claims for urban superiority:

The atmosphere of towns is also alleged to be more favorable to the attitudes and beliefs which favor growth. The fact that large numbers of people are thrown together in towns, in a competitive struggle for existence, weakens kinship ties and excessive respect for status; encourages impersonal economic relations and a willingness to trade wherever opportunities are favorable; and sharpens the wits. In addition, the fact that towns develop a great range of arts and entertainments means that the opportunities for spending money are virtually unlimited, that wealth tends to acquire as much prestige as birth, and that ambition is stimulated. Townsmen are also alleged to be more open minded and less superstitious than countrymen, and therefore to be better placed to pursue those scientific enquiries which result in improved techniques. The countryman is impressed by the power of nature, since nature so often frustrates all his work, with its droughts, its floods, its storms, its epidemic diseases of crops, and other signs of its strength. The town, on the other hand, is created by man, who has learnt enough of the secrets of nature to be able to erect great buildings, to trap water in great reservoirs and transport it where he wants it, to summon electricity out of the skies to be his servant, and so forth. So the townsman is more easily tempted to believe that man can do anything he wants to do, if he tries hard enough. [Lewis, 1955, p. 151]

W. L. Slocum states:

It [urbanization] has released great creative forces; for example, most modern technological developments are urban in origin. It has forced the individual from the tyranny of inbred values and close social surveillance; it has brought increased leisure. [Slocum, 1962, p. 233]

Some contend that urban society is the source and vanguard of dynamic forces of science and culture that shape our social and economic environment. According to one observer:

Two philosophies of existence dominate the minds of men: One holds that what has been will always be; the other holds that what man has accomplished is only the beginning, that on the basis of what he has accomplished he will build a bigger and more efficient way of life. . . . The one [philosophy] is agrarian; the other, urban-industrial. [Landis, 1959, p. 114]

Sector fundamentalism is composed of two important elements: superiority and frustration. Incipient urban fundamentalism will grow and provide an enlarged mandate for favored public policies as the urban superiority position described above is combined with frustration over problems of inner-city decay.

Both farm and urban fundamentalist viewpoints contain elements of truth, supported by more objective investigations of rural-urban differences, which we shall examine later. A basis exists for both rural and urban pride, but this should not lead to oversimplification of issues and to valuing one sector as inherently superior to another. Rather, a statement of basic positions is the springboard to greater appreciation of the problems and promises for all society posed by two essential, highly interdependent sectors.

FORMAL CONTRASTS OF RURAL AND URBAN VALUES

Several formal attempts have been made to isolate those social characteristics that distinguish rural from urban living. One approach is the *Gemeinschaft-Gesellschaft* framework suggested by Tönnies (1940) and extended by others (Parsons, 1951; Loomis, 1960; Levy, 1966). Tönnies calls all kinds of associations in which the natural will predominates *Gemeinschaft*; all those which are formed and fundamentally conditioned by the rational will he calls *Gesellschaft*. By means of political and other intellectual organizations promoted by town and city life, the Gesellschaft characteristics gradually permeate the mass of society (Tönnies, 1940, pp. 17, 29).

Polar types are used to distinguish Gemeinschaft from Gesellschaft in Table 2.1, but it is important to stress that the gradient is not dichotomous. It is continuous. Societies are characterized by the profile outlining their position between the polar types. No society is completely Gemeinschaft or Gesellschaft! Rural farm characteristics tend to lie more nearly toward the Gemeinschaft pole, urban society more nearly toward the Gesellschaft pole. Commercial farm areas are closer to the Gesellschaft pole in Table 2.1 than are low-income (poverty) farm areas. In certain attributes, city slums lie closer than commercial farm areas to the Gemeinschaft pole. The process of economic growth is accompanied by movement to the right in Table 2.1. In the following discussion of polar characteristics, keep in mind that the farm community will in the future move toward the right—hence the table is a type of predictive device.

TABLE 2.1. Polar Types Distinguishing Societies

Gemeinschaft	Gesellschaft
Traditional	Rational
Sacred	Secular
Spiritual	Materialistic
Particularistic	Universalistic
Ascriptive norms	Achievement norms
Affective selectivity	Affective neutrality
Functionally diffuse	Functionally specific
Occupation-generalistic	Occupation-specialistic
Responsible	Individualistic
Intimate	Impersonal
Nonhierarchic	Hierarchic
Atomistic	Bureaucratic

SOURCES: Adapted from Tönnies (1940), Parsons (1951), Loomis (1960), and Levy (1966). For a critical evaluation of polar typologies, see the chapter by Oscar Lewis in Hauser and Schnore (1965).

The "man-made" production and consumption process in the city is characterized by terms "rational" and "secular." This is in contrast to the more traditional and sacred orientation of the low-income rural areas in particular. Rational orientation characterizes emphasis on education, research, and application of scientific processes to extend man's knowledge and dominance over nature and to promote economic growth.

The urban-industrial society is characterized by universalist achievement norms. An efficient, smoothly functioning "mass" society requires widely accepted universalist standards of suitability for jobs, evaluation of status, and behavior norms. The impersonal, mobile, urban environment leads to less stress on affective evaluation of individuals based on ascribed status (e.g., family) and emotionally involved criteria, and to more stress on evaluation based on economic achievement and material display.

Intense division of labor in the urban-industrial environment is characterized by functionally specific roles. Occupational specialties often require a high degree of formal training. The result is considerable vulnerability of the individual to changing technology and business fluctuations. Division of labor and mass-production economies are best achieved in an environment of considerable concentration of consumers and workers. Economies of scale lead to industry concentration, bureaucracy, and bargaining power. Bigness and bureaucracy are characterized by hierarchical management echelons in business, government, schools, and other institutions. Increased bargaining power in industry is countervailed by bargaining power in the hands of labor and government. Concentration of people in a small area plus high mobility lead to more impersonal and individualistic relationships, partly to preserve privacy. The breakdown of the extended family unit, interdependence of elements in the economy to satisfy economic wants, and the impersonal human interrelationships in urban society contribute to the demand for government welfare services.

The central cities of the large metropolitan communities are the origin of many of the mass cultural media and exert a large impact on American values, beliefs, and attitudes. The central city is inhabited by larger than average proportions of the highly educated and talented, who congregate there to function in the commercial and cultural centers. A second major group located in the central city consists of the comparatively uneducated and unskilled people from lower socio-economic status groups, who carry on the "housekeeping" chores in the broadest sense. Many Negroes are included in this latter category. These two groups are not identified closely with the middle-class American culture and take a less than sacrosanct attitude toward traditional agrarian goals and values. Pressures of a different environment and a malleable outlook of these urbanites toward cultural change set the stage for adjustments in goals, values, and attitudes that ultimately touch farmers.

SIMILARITIES IN RURAL AND URBAN VALUES

It would be a mistake to view urban values as distinct from farm values. Both rural and urban interests share in what might be called the American Dream—that the best is yet to be, that virtually anything can be accomplished by determined effort, that new is better than old, that forward is better than backward, that life is progress and stalemate is unsatisfactory. All Americans value freedom, justice, progress, stability, and security, though these terms are weighted and interpreted differently.

According to Martindale (1960, p. ix), "All major observers agree that American character tends to manifest great practicality, considerable anti-intellectualism, a strong materialism, a tendency to conceptualize social and political affairs in moralistic terms, a manifestation of great faith in individual initiative and a sense of civic responsibility."

The forces of economic growth and urbanization are causing a profound though gradual change in the values of American society. It is well to review Brewster's agrarian creed from the perspective of a modern urban-industrial society.

WORK ETHIC

The work ethic as stated in the previous chapter has antecedents in the Protestant Ethic and the "liberal" economic philosophy of Adam Smith. These antecedents are characterized by some writers in the U.S. by the Puritan tradition. A *Time* essay ("On Tradition," 1966) states:

> If there is anything left of the Puritan tradition it is hard to detect. Perhaps its strongest remaining element is what sociologists call the "work ethic." . . . At the same time thrift is no longer a virtue—it is, in fact subversive—pleasure is an unashamed good, leisure is the general goal and the subsidized life, from government benefits to foundation grants, is largely welcomed.

Even the work ethic is not as durable a part of the Puritan tradition as the above quote implies. Americans still work hard, but the work ethic is not predominantly the underlying reason. Placing a lower value on asceticism and on postponed gratifications in contemporary society "leads to enjoyment of leisure without the guilt and ambivalence it carried in a 'Puritan' ethos. . . . Recreation may be evaluated as a means for maintaining the capacity for work and achievement" (Williams, 1965, p. 436).

American culture is marked by a central stress on personal achievement. Personal excellence is closely identified with competitive occupational achievement and one's status is influenced strongly by occupation or job—what you are is what you do. But there is growing evidence that performance in consumption is partly replacing performance in work. How one spends his income rather than how he earns it increasingly is the mark of achievement (Williams, 1965, pp. 417, 419). Still, the wealthy and powerful find it desirable to justify their position in the name of service. Our culture values action and mastering of the physical world, but the motive for work is less the metaphysical drive characterized by the Protestant Ethic and more the desire to support the materialistic "good life" and the display of status.

Other value components of the work ethic are found in urban-industrial society, but the emphasis differs from the agrarian tradition. Urban-industrial society is increasingly concerned with distributive justice (providing equal access through education and termination of racial barriers to getting ahead) and is less committed to commutative justice (providing rewards commensurate with contributions). That is, legislation is increasingly concerned with need, not with ability to pay or with productivity. That which enhances the capacity to achieve is accepted. Public programs of health, education, and welfare are legitimized as furthering equality of opportunity. Recreation is "legitimatized" or ethically justified because it increases demand for goods—a blessing in an economy allegedly troubled by automation and underconsumption.

DEMOCRATIC CREED

There is little evidence that urban society is less committed than rural society to the creed that all deserve an equal voice in shaping rules of the economic, social, and political game. In fact, in broad world perspective, the predominantly urban-industrial countries of the world are today more democratic in forms of national government than are the predominantly agrarian countries. However, there is no denial that the transient nature of city life and the indifference toward local government that attends it can be a breeding ground for "boss" or "machine" rule.

Rural people are criticized for unwillingness to recognize the undemocratic nature of rural votes weighted more heavily than urban votes. The unwillingness is not surprising. If the redistribution of population had been from the urban to rural areas, urban people would also in all likelihood have been lethargic in relinquishing their over-representation.

A special concern is rural indifference to the *de facto* isolation from the democratic process of disadvantaged rural groups. Most of the impetus for franchising the Negro has come from urban people. The rural poor have been slow to articulate, either verbally or in the voting booth, their legislative needs. Part of the reason is lack of leaders, organization, education, and information, part is too unswerving a loyalty to one or another party (or person), and part is indifference. The political anomie of *de facto* disenfranchisement is not new but should be of concern to rural people. It is of special significance in an age when the trend increasingly is away from the natural-law, inalienable-rights democracy of the Constitution to the plebiscite democracy of the ballot.

ENTERPRISE CREED

The characteristics of urban-industrial society already discussed increase the vulnerability of the individual to economic circumstances with which he finds it difficult to cope. The result is increased demands on the government for welfare programs. These demands for national policies to avoid or cushion the effect of economic and other disasters can be traced to the urban-industrial process. The call for commodity programs by commercial farmers also stems in part from the industrialization of the farm.

A positive regard for humanitarianism is implicit in our emerging progressive equalitarian democracy. The concern for the underdog and the growth of the welfare state is at odds with the concept of commutative justice and the enterprise creed. Some feel that there is some threshhold income level that should be maintained if necessary by government transfer payments. The opposing view is that guaranteeing individuals at least a socially acceptable income not only cuts off the opportunity for every person to gain the dignity of personal occupational achievement but also impairs the efficiency of the economy. A compromise is reached by enlarging welfare commitments for education that satisfies the concept of distributive justice and "helps the person to help himself" and thus potentially contributes to the efficiency of society through improved earning potential.

Economic affluence leads to increasing emphasis on quality and not just quantity of want satisfaction. Increasing affluence permits Americans to pay more attention to leisure, self-realization, personal adjustment, and mental health. More attention is given to security. Retirement plans, social security, and unemployment and hospitalization insurance are efforts to stabilize and preserve the good life, not only for oneself but also for one's immediate family. Aggressive federal fiscal and monetary policies are designed to stabilize national income cycles. Though a departure from strict adherence to the free enterprise system and to the concept of the family as solely responsible for one's future, there is increasing reliance on government to force savings for old age and misfortune.

According to R. M. Williams (1964, p. 24), the long-term movement toward dominance of large-scale formal organization is perhaps the most dominant single trend in the social structure of the twentieth century. Approximately one-tenth of the U.S. labor force is self-employed. This organizational revolution was made possible by separating the labor, management, and ownership functions. Farming is the one major exception where place of work and residence are the same, where management, labor, and ownership are combined, and where there are no organized barriers to entry. Farming is an island of atomistic competition in a sea of imperfect competition. The paradoxical result is that disadvantaged farmers call on the government to countervail the untrammeled operations of the "agrarian" enterprise creed.

CREED OF SELF-INTEGRITY

There is some evidence that tolerance for dissenters is greater in urban than in rural society. Studies reveal that farm dwellers are less tolerant of nonconformity than town, city, and metropolitan residents (cf. Miller, 1959, pp. 93, 94).

Americans have an increasing respect for science, particularly because it fits into traditional values of active mastery of the physical world, efficiency, and progress. For many years Americans demonstrated a remarkable genius for adapting basic science to practical problems. The high standard of living in the U.S. is a visible monument to this genius.

Realization came slowly that applied research leads to diminishing returns without a regenerating background of basic research. With this realization came increased respect for pure science and basic research. Americans recognize that good basic science must be free from close scrutiny under the price system. To be truly innovative, it must be free to develop along nonconformist, unconventional lines. People who innovate culturally or economically in a dynamic society must have flexible value structures. American society, in spite of a few conspicuous relapses, respects the integrity of the beliefs, values, and attitudinal modes of nonconformist behavior. This tolerance for the new and different is enhanced by constant exposure to the changing environment and heterogeneity found in urban-industrial society.

SOCIOLOGICAL RESEARCH ON RURAL AND URBAN CHARACTERISTICS

Sociological studies and results of opinion-sampling tend to support many of the notions of rural and urban differences noted above. Decades ago, sociologists talked of the rural-urban dichotomy—as if these were two separate and distinct cultures (cf. Tönnies, 1940). The dichotomy later was rejected in favor

TABLE 2.2. Selected Characteristics of U.S. Population, by Residence, 1960

	Urban	Rural Nonfarm	Rural Farm
Total population (millions)	125.3	40.5	13.5
Per cent of total	69.9	22.6	7.5
White population (millions)	110.4	36.5	11.9
Per cent of white	69.5	23.0	7.5
Nonwhite population (millions)	14.8	4.1	1.6
Per cent of nonwhite	72.2	20.0	7.8
Average size of family	3.56	3.81	3.96
Children ever born per 1,000 ever married women (35–39)	2,514	3,034	3,469
Aged 65 and over (per cent)	9.1	8.9	9.3
Median age (years)	30.3	26.7	29.6
Household characteristics. Occupied units with:			
home freezer (per cent)	13.0	26.0	52.7
telephone (per cent)	83.1	67.1	64.2
automobile (per cent)	76.1	83.7	87.3
television (per cent)	89.0	88.0	76.0

SOURCES: U.S. Department of Agriculture (1964a), except data on households with television (from Fuguitt, 1963).

of a rural-urban *continuum* (cf. Dewey, 1960–61, Stewart, 1958–59). Differences in rural and urban society were regarded as differences not so much in kind as in degree. The degree of difference was explained as continuous variables relating goals, values, and attitudes to density of population and economic activity centered on primary versus secondary and tertiary industry. The next step was to admit the existence of the continuum between city and farm but to say that the differences were relatively unimportant. Some social scientists are now asking whether there is any difference at all. The following discussion suggests that the differences are small but important.

Tables 2.2 to 2.5 depict rural-urban differences in racial representation, age distribution, birthrates, size of family, education, communication, transportation, and mobility. The Negro population, once heavily rural farm, is now largely urban (Table 2.2). Currently, a higher percentage of all Negroes live in urban areas than of all whites. In 1920, over half of all whites but only one-third of all Negroes lived in urban areas.

Birth rates are higher in the rural farm than in other sectors, but sizable outmigration of farm youth and of retired farmers washes out differences in the age patterns (Table 2.2). The high proportion of rural farm households with autos, telephones, and television sets demonstrates the considerable communication and transportation potentials of farmers.

TABLE 2.3. Distribution of U.S. Civilian Population 18 Years of Age and Over, by Residence, Farm or Nonfarm Birthplace, and Color, 1958

	Percentage Distribution		
	Total	White	Nonwhite
Total	100.0	100.0	100.0
Farm-born	23.7	22.6	33.8
Nonfarm-born	75.0	76.3	63.5
Birthplace and/or residence not reported	1.3	1.1	2.7
Farm residents	100.0	100.0	100.0
Farm-born	78.5	76.4	94.9
Entire life on same farm	42.9	40.2	63.2
Some moves between farms	20.5	20.4	21.9
Some nonfarm moves	15.1	15.8	9.8
Nonfarm-born	21.5	23.6	5.1
Nonfarm residents	100.0	100.0	100.0
Farm-born	17.2	16.3	25.2
Nonfarm-born	82.8	83.7	74.8
Entire life nonfarm	79.4	80.1	72.4
Some farm moves	3.4	3.6	2.4

SOURCE: Beale *et al.* (1964, p. 2).

Mobility potential also is apparent in Table 2.3. However, rural farm people move around less than other groups: 71 per cent reported living in the same house in 1960 as in 1955, whereas approximately 50 per cent of the urban and rural nonfarm residents so reported. In 1958, 17 per cent of the U.S. civilian nonfarm population 18 years of age and over were farm-born. However, 32 million or 30 per cent of the survey population had either been born on the farm or spent at least one year on a farm. More than one-fifth of the sample farm population in Table 2.3 reported nonfarm origins. A portion of these were nonfarm girls who married farm boys.

Approximately one-fifth of all farm-born farm residents have lived in the nonfarm sector at some time. Combining two categories of farm residents (farm-born with some nonfarm moves and nonfarm-born), it is apparent from the table that 39.4 per cent of white farm adults and 14.9 per cent of nonwhite farm adults have been exposed to nonfarm living. Interaction between the two sectors is indeed great.

ECONOMIC CHARACTERISTICS

The net exodus of farm people to the city is furthered on the one hand by diminishing economic opportunities on the farm and on the other by attractive jobs elsewhere. Some reasons for the shift in employment reported above are apparent from the economic data, reported in later chapters, which show farm income falling far short of urban income. Differences in economic measures between rural and urban sectors are accentuated by a higher proportion of rural people in the South than in other geographic areas. The percentage of female employment is large in urban areas. These factors only partially explain differences in incomes, however. If we include in a "poverty" category all individuals with less than $3,000 annual cash income and unrelated individuals with less than $1,500 annual cash income, 35 million Americans were living in poverty in 1962 (Bird, 1964). Of these, 16 million were rural residents and about 6 million were rural farm residents. Nearly half of all farm families were within the poverty category. The within-sector incidence of poverty was much greater in the farm sector than in the urban sector.

EDUCATION

Migration from the farm has been rapid, and in 1958 substantially more farm-born adults were nonfarm residents (16.3 million) than were farm residents (9.5 million). Still outmigration has not closed the income gap between sectors. This is due at least partly to another characteristic that differentiates farm and nonfarm groups—educational attainment. Whether measured by median edu-

TABLE 2.4. Measures of Education by U.S. Resident Groups

	Urban	Rural Nonfarm	Rural Farm
5-year-olds enrolled in kindergarten, 1960 (per cent)	46.0	23.4	15.8
7 to 13-year-olds enrolled in school, 1960 (per cent)	97.8	97.1	97.2
Age 25–29 with 4 years high school or more, 1960 (per cent)	63.8	53.0	51.4
Median school completed by persons 25 years and over, 1960 (years)	11.1	9.5	8.8
Estimated school dropouts among 16–24-year-olds (per cent):			
1950 Total	35.0	50.4	55.5
Male white	33.8	50.7	54.3
Male nonwhite	63.6	79.7	88.6
1960 Total	27.6	37.6	34.5
Male white	25.8	35.9	32.0
Male nonwhite	47.4	61.3	69.9

SOURCES: U.S. Department of Agriculture (1964a), except dropout data (from Cowhig, 1963, Table 3).

cation completed or by dropout rates, rural farm areas rank low (Table 2.4). Not so apparent are basic rural-urban differences in quality of education. Also not apparent are substantial differences in the quality of schools within rural areas. A study of eastern Kentucky migrants out of rural areas to cities revealed that high school graduates were doing no better than school dropouts (Schwarzweller, 1964). One explanation is that the quality of education was so low that both dropouts and graduates found themselves severely disadvantaged in seeking productive nonfarm employment.

Data in Table 2.5 show a significant association between education and earnings. Farmers stand at the bottom of both the income and education ladders. Persons of farm origin rank low in educational attainment for several reasons. First, many farm youth become farmers and too few of these see the need for higher education. But a college education already appears to be a profitable investment in management skills to operate large commercial farms. Second, more farm youth plan to farm than are able to secure an adequate economic opportunity in farming and belatedly become aware that their educational attainment is too low for successful competition in the nonfarm labor market into which they have been thrust. Third, farm youth who do not plan to farm often have inadequate formal and informal advice and too late realize that their educational background is not adequate for the occupation which they had

TABLE 2.5. Earnings and Education of U.S. Males (25–64 Years Old), by Occupational Groups

Major Occupational Group	Median Earnings, 1959 (*dollars*)	Proportion with 12 or More School Years Completed, 1959 (*per cent*)	Median Schooling, 1962 (*years*)
Professional, technical, and kindred workers	6,978	91	16.2
Managers, officials, and proprietors (except farm)	6,855	66	12.5
Sales workers	5,747	67	12.5
Craftsmen, foremen, and kindred workers	5,444	36	12.5
Clerical and kindred workers	5,216	63	12.5
Operatives and kindred workers	4,645	25	10.1
Service workers	3,799	31	10.8
Laborers (except farm and mine)	3,504	16	8.9
Farmers and farm managers	2,447	30	8.8
Farm laborers and foremen	1,577	12	8.5

SOURCES: Cowhig (1964, p. 13), except median schooling data (from Moore *et al.*, 1964, p. 34).

planned to enter. Again the problem of inadequate counseling and a narrow academic program limits opportunities, especially in areas characterized by rural poverty.

Of more than passing concern is the poor showing of farm-reared elements in adjustment to city life. Schnore (1966, p. 136) concludes, after reviewing previous studies "that the farm reared migrants to the city enter the urban class structure at or near the bottom, whether the measure is education, occupation or income." This appraisal is especially critical because of the heavy out-migration of farm youth to the cities. One study reports:

> For farm males 15–24 years old, it was concluded that: in the north central and northeast [regions] less than one-half of the surviving farm males 15–24 years old in 1960 might be expected to remain in the farm population over the next 10 years. By the same logic, for the West, 1 of 3 may remain. The ratio for Southern whites is 1 in 5. The extreme is found for Southern nonwhites, only 1 in 16 of whom are expected to remain in the farm population. [Bishop and Tolley, 1962, pp. 15–16]

Inadequate education of farm people is of concern to all segments of society. Through migration the problems of rural America become the problems, sometimes intensified, of urban America. There are indications that assimilation and acculturation are rapid for migrants from commercial farming areas (cf. Tweeten, 1965b). But problems of migrants from rural poverty areas, especially of Negroes, are severe and are an important element in the crime and slum conditions of central cities.

Sewell and Haller (1963, p. 166) attribute the problem of inadequate preparation of rural migrants to cities to "relative geographic isolation and its attendant features such as relatively poor schools [and] few occupations visible to the youth." The major concern in rural education is not only the quality of schooling but also the associated problem of finance. The major burden of financial support for local schools in most states is on property taxes in the local community. These taxes are inadequate because the community is poor, and the community may be poor because the schools are inadequate. This cycle of perpetuated rural poverty will continue unless federal and state aid to education becomes a more prominent supplement to local tax support.

PERSONALITY CHARACTERISTICS

There have been a considerable number of comparisons of personality characteristics of farm, village, and urban youth. These studies were made in Michigan (Haller, 1960; Haller and Wolff, 1962), Minnesota (Martinson, 1955; Hathaway *et al.*, 1959), Wisconsin (Strauss, 1964), Iowa (Burchinal and Jacobson, 1963), Florida (Middleton and Grigg, 1959), Ohio (Mangus, 1957), and Oklahoma (Lu, 1969). They generally support the conclusion that farm boys rank lower than nonfarm boys in occupational and educational aspirations and that they are more withdrawn and reserved. They place a lower value on geographic mobility and tend to believe that man has limited control over events. On over-all social adjustment, including lack of nervous tension, farm boys ranked high.

Urban boys had the higher score on occupational and educational aspirations, dominance, aggressiveness, self-confidence, and radicalism. They take a positive attitude toward geographic mobility and tend to believe that man has control over events. They often ranked lower in measures of over-all social adjustment than farm boys. The study of 30,000 Oklahoma high school seniors in 1967 contradicts some of these findings, and suggests substantial progress for farm boys. For example, 77 per cent of the Oklahoma farm boys planned to attend college, whereas "only" 70 per cent of the nonfarm boys planned to attend (Lu, 1969).

A study by Clark and Wenninger reported by Polk (1963) gives some insight into the nature and extent of juvenile delinquency among farm and nonfarm youth. The conclusion from the study of adolescents was that:

> Rural boys differ very little from urban boys in the extent to which they "confess" to minor theft, the telling of lies, loitering, beating up other youngsters without specific reason, the use of narcotics (in all samples rare), and arson (also rare in all groups). In contrast, rural farm youth engage less, according to this study, in such activities as major theft, the consumption of alcohol, taking money on the pretense that it would be repaid, and skipping school. On the other hand, rural youth were inclined to engage somewhat more in trespassing and tampering with another person's car, tractor, or bicycle without permission. These differences are especially pronounced when a comparison is made between the urban working class group and rural youth. [Polk, 1963, p. 223]

MISCELLANEOUS CHARACTERISTICS

Analyses show that in the transition from rural to urban, the extended family gives way to independent nuclear family units, and urbanization leads to "matrimonial asymmetry," with closer ties to the wife's than to the husband's family (Sweeter, 1966, p. 169). Greater economic independence of women in urban areas contributes to the higher divorce rates. Separation of residence from work leads to diminishing presence and influence of the father and, along with growing education and independence of the mother, moves toward a more democratic and somewhat matriarchal urban family structure. Divorce rates are substantially higher among urban than among rural families (Cannon and Gingles, 1956). However, other measures of marital success rate urban marriages higher than rural marriages (Burchinal, 1963, pp. 217, 218).

Sociological studies also indicate that farm people attend church more frequently, are more conservative in their religious beliefs, and are more active in churchwork than nonfarm people (Burchinal, 1961b). Early postwar opinion polls supported the contention that farmers exhibit values of Puritanism, individualism, national loyalty, and traditionalism (Beers, 1953).

LONG-RUN IMPLICATIONS FOR THE FARM ECONOMY

Urban-industrial society, although (poetically speaking) of rural parentage, is now affluent and robust. The personality of urban society is depicted as rational, pragmatic, dynamic, and basically healthy though troubled with crime, slums, race problems, air pollution, and transportation difficulties. It will be increasingly difficult for farm people to convince city people oppressed with their own problems that farm problems are really significant.

The foregoing discussion shows that while rural and urban differences are not large and appear to be diminishing, they are nevertheless important. Many of the differences cited are basically sociological, nevertheless their thrust is also economic and they have important long-term meaning for the farm economy. The emergence of the nonfarm sector as an overriding political, economic, and cultural force has major significance for U.S. agriculture in at least four areas: (*a*) commercial agriculture and commodity programs, (*b*) low-income agricultural and welfare programs, (*c*) the family farm, and (*d*) political alliances.

COMMERCIAL AGRICULTURE

The economic structure of commercial farming is increasingly intolerant of highly unstable economic conditions. In the past, farmers weathered economic crises by diversifying and by deferring returns to equity capital and family labor. As cash production expenses mount as a percentage of costs, as capital requirements become larger, as specialization progresses, and as farm people become psychologically less tolerant of economic crises, the demand for economic stability in farming grows. And this demand comes at a time when much of urban society questions the purpose of farm subsidies and commodity programs designed to stabilize the farm economy.

Apologists for farm programs have in the past stressed that public investment in farm research and technology has vastly benefited the consumer and left the farmer worse off because of the inelastic demand and supply for farm commodities. Thus consumers can (and should, they say) compensate farmers through commodity programs for losses accruing from technological change; the consumers are still better off. This argument has flaws. First, with few exceptions, farm people (even outmigrants) are better off than they would have been without technological change in farming. Of course, society could have better prepared migrants for the transition, but it is possible that ill-conceived policies to cushion adjustments would only have perpetuated uneconomic farming units. Second, the argument implies that society should help those who have contributed to economic efficiency or have been disadvantaged by technological change. The result is subsidies to commercial farmers and lack of concern for poor farm people who have neither been helped nor much hurt by technological change. Instead of building a sophisticated rationale to justify subsidies, perhaps we should first help many farm people just because they are very poor.

A wise course for commercial farm elements is to stress those aspects of commodity programs for agriculture that farm and nonfarm elements find mutually beneficial. Urban-industrial society wants these things from farmers: ample quantity and quality of food at reasonable costs and sufficient reserve production capacity to meet emergencies. Farm commodity programs in the future cannot be forced through by farm political muscle alone, or justified as welfare measures alone, but might be sold to the public on the basis of serving the above objectives.

There is a growing body of evidence that past farm programs have not caused net inefficiency in farming (Tweeten, 1965c; Tyner, 1966). In Tyner's study, the operation of the farm economy was simulated over a thirty-year period both under free markets and under actual commodity programs. Less farm labor was employed with commodity programs than with free markets. The economic stability, security, and capital provided by programs permitted purchase of large labor-saving machines and other improved inputs which substituted for labor. The owner of the larger, more efficient farm found it profitable to purchase (or rent) and operate the farm of his less efficient neighbor who found a nonfarm job or retired. Land prices inflated by capitalized benefits of programs constituted a major barrier to entry into farming. Thus programs did not slow outmovement of labor from agriculture, nor did they increase costs per unit of farm output according to the analysis. Programs helped farmers bear the cost of reserve capacity which society appears to value highly. Farm programs that are administered efficiently with supports designed to stabilize prices in line with production costs (thus avoiding capitalization of benefits into land prices) and to maintain reserve capacity for emergencies in agriculture without undue cost to the government are in the interest of farmers and consumers alike and might be "sold" to society.

In a period when crises of either abundance or scarcity could emerge, it is essential that *flexibility* be maintained in farm programs. The rising call for funds to aid the really poor in cities and farms at home and abroad makes it difficult to justify subsidies to large wealthy farmers. The justification for the lion's share of program benefits going to the large farms (because those who produce the most must be included in programs to control production) will disappear in periods when demand presses supply. More emphasis should be placed on those voluntary farm programs that remove the most production per government dollar. This means a shift away from direct payments to large farmers without requiring maximum acreage diversion. If reserve capacity is to be efficiently maintained, slippage in programs must be reduced so that limited funds for commodity programs will hold more reserve capacity and contribute more to farm income.

The farm community would do well to reappraise critically the whole structure of farm programs. Programs that unduly benefit narrow interests, cause undue inefficiencies, and promote regressive income redistribution need to be revised. Farm programs will need to place more emphasis on society's goals of reserve capacity, efficiency, and flexibility, on streamlined commodity program administration, and on more equitable distribution of benefits.

The growing influence of the urban-industrial sector also has important implications for the market structure of farming, particularly bargaining power. Taking their cue from urban-industrial society, few farmers today adhere to the code of a purely competitive economy for agriculture. The fundamental conflict in agriculture is not over whether farmers should have more bargaining power but rather over who should provide it. The National Farmers Union in the 1960's favored a strong government role to give farmers strength in the market place. The Farm Bureau and National Farmers Organization placed emphasis on bargaining power through a cohesive organization of farmers themselves.

The declining influence of farmers in the voting mechanism and the increasing urgency of city problems suggest advantages in the long run for commercial farmers to become less dependent on precarious government transfer payments. These factors, plus the changing value structure of farmers to less stress on independence and more stress on "urban values" will lead to a struggle for indigenous bargaining power within agriculture. The government's role will be to provide enabling legislation. Antitrust action will not likely interfere with farmers' efforts to organize and bargain collectively with processors as long as plentiful food and fiber supplies are provided at reasonable prices.

WELFARE PROGRAMS

Further departure of urban-industrial society from the early agrarian *laissez-faire* tradition means support will grow for welfare programs in the urban sector. One concern is the adequacy of welfare programs for farm people (cf. Schultz, 1965). Farmers only belatedly secured benefits of Social Security. This is of considerable significance, because it supplements an important past retirement fund—capital gain—which is a highly inequitable source of income. Also increased separation of farm ownership from operation may in the future restrict capital gain to an even smaller group of farmers.

The most important element in welfare legislation is broader financial support for education in rural areas. The foregoing discussion shows clearly that many farm boys and girls are receiving neither the quantity nor quality of education needed to equip them for living in an urban-industrial environment. Yet a majority of farm youth will eventually live and work in the nonfarm sector. To fail to give farm youth adequate education will mean continued exporting of farm problems to the city. Two facts need to be stressed to urban society: that rural poverty problems become more intensified city problems when rural migrants are not equipped in advance for nonfarm jobs and culture and that the economic payoff is potentially large from public policies to improve rural education.

Sizable federal aid to education may be the only feasible way to raise rural education to acceptable levels. There has been little call for federal aid for general education in low-income rural areas which have received welfare grants of other types—many of them federal in origin. Meanwhile urbanites are vocal in calling for federal aid, and pressures now are great for the government to provide more assistance to urban communities. Depressed rural communities need to realize that for economic progress, they too have a stake in education and training in the skills that are a concomitant of the urban-industrial process.

The poor in urban areas and the poor in rural areas have many characteristics in common. Both are "isolated" and both suffer from the anomia of social alienation. The U.S. poor have often been called "invisible" because they have few advocates and have been politically inert. This may once have been true for all poor but it is not now true of the poor in city slums. A riot is a quick way to become visible and obtain aid. The political indifference of the rural poor permitted the "War on Poverty" to be less than a skirmish in the countryside. Unless farm leaders speak out with a louder voice than in the past, aid funds will increasingly pass the rural poor and will go to the vocal urban poor.

The American people have traditionally supported the underdog elements in society. Welfare orientation will provide a reservoir of concern in American society for the disadvantaged and poor in agriculture. Needs must be articulated by farm leaders to draw from this reservoir of concern. It is a kind of perverse agrarian fundamentalism that attempts to retain people in agriculture and preserve rural poverty by refusing to accept federal programs to aid local schools that would better equip rural youth for productive employment elsewhere. It is the rising new generation that pays the cost of this fundamentalism. It is this younger generation also which most surely will perpetuate the problems of rural poverty unless rural elements accept the inevitability of living in a predominantly urban-industrial type of society.

THE FAMILY FARM

A third issue of particular relevance to farm people in an urban-industrial society is the family farm. The family farm can be defined in many ways. One is the nostalgic concept of an economic unit where a family is independent, free from the hustle and bustle of city life, and communes with nature. Here a man has autonomy and freedom from the pressure of the urban world. Here a man is an individualist. With some effort and a minimum of formal training, a hard-working, frugal family can provide sufficient income to lead a complete and wholesome life. Here is the moral and political foundation and sustenance for the democratic, free-enterprise society.

Unfortunately, this nostalgic concept of the family farm is a myth. Today on one hand are the large, hard-headed business operations of the adequate commercial farms which are basically an extension of the industrial system to the countryside. On the other hand are the farms which are classified in the poverty category. A category of farms in between these two groups might conform to the nostalgic concept of the family farm, but this category is small. Society will not long support farm programs to preserve a romantic concept.

A second definition of the family farm is very much to the point, however, and shows vitality and durability: The U.S. Department of Agriculture defines it as a farming unit in which most of the labor and management is provided by the operator and his family. The family farm, so defined, will be preserved as long as it is economically efficient and not just because it provides "the good life." It has proved durable because (*a*) economies of size are not so great but that youth can obtain sufficient financial help for a start from parents; (*b*) apprenticeship has a high value compared with formal training for farming; (*c*) the large requirement for operational as opposed to organizational management provides for a complementarity of manual labor with management; and (*d*) low returns in farming, and in some instances legal restrictions, have discouraged nonfarm corporations from large-equity investment operations. The capital requirements for an efficient, adequate family farm are large and expanding. Efforts of farmers to improve management and efficiency almost invariably contain elements of industrialization and move farmers even closer to the urban-industrial structure. A dilemma facing family farmers in the future is how to increase efficiency (which has been the major barrier of the family farm against inroads of corporate farming and vertical integration) without losing the identity of the family farm.

POLITICAL ALLIANCE

A final relationship of importance is identification of farmers with major power groups in society. Farmers have been traditionally distrustful of "big" business and have attempted to form political alliances with nonfarm labor as in the Populist Party movement. These efforts largely have failed; for example, the close prewar relations have for some time been broken between the American Federation of Labor on one hand and the American Farm Bureau Federation and the National Grange on the other hand.

The cleavage between farmers and the labor movement has grown in recent years for several reasons. The term "farmers" refers to operators and their families, and this group could be classified in either the labor or management camp. However, for at least two reasons farmers increasingly wish to identify with the business community rather than with labor. First, the labor-management struggle is brought close to farming by minimum wage legislation, by intensified efforts of unions to organize hired farm workers, and by the wage-price spiral reflected in rising farm input prices. Second, the management input of the farm operator is rising relative to his labor input. Thus he will lean increasingly to the management position.

The fact that farmers have historically been highly vocal in denouncing big business and have ostentatiously sided with labor on certain issues hides the fact that the basic economic philosophy of the majority of farmers is closer to that of the business community than to that of organized labor. Beers (1953) concluded that farmers' opinions on the economic role of government were more like those of executives, proprietors, businessmen, and white-collar workers than like those of laborers. Similar conclusions were reached in the 1964 Oklahoma-Kansas survey of wheat-growers discussed in Chapter 1.

The voting behavior of farmers and other groups can be predicted on the basis of idealistic and materialistic factors. Materialistic considerations such as wealth, property, status, income, and security are the strongest influences on voting behavior. The farmer, it is said, "votes his pocketbook."

Political theory suggests for farmers a politically conservative position if they are economic "haves"; a liberal position if they are "have-nots." Farm operators who are plagued by unstable product prices and by rising input prices (due to steady cost-push inflation, minimum wage legislation, and unionized hired farm labor) would be regarded as have-nots. Success in forming a cohesive, effective organization of farmers to countervail these forces would make commercial farmers haves and would influence their political philosophy.

But, if his pocketbook is not too pinched, the farmer has more flexibility to vote his political ideology, although "ideology" has little real meaning to most farmers. Several attempts have been made to classify groups by political ideology. One dichotomy is the Platonists—those who hold that only a select elite can understand and interpret truth, and only these should govern—and the Aristotelians—those who hold that all individuals or groups are of equal worth and dignity, and therefore all should have a voice in government.

Political scientists modified the above dichotomy and produced two other categories: qualitarian and equalitarian (Talbot and Wiggins, 1967, p. 5). The equalitarians stress the inherent, intrinsic worth of all men and the fact that differences in economic and social characteristics of persons are explained by the environment, often by chance events of nature or men. The qualitarians stress that the "stuff out of which a man is made," his drive, and his initiative are the factors that explain differences in economic and social characteristics of persons. Legislation to redress social and economic wrongs is justifiable to the equalitarians but is an affront to the natural law of socio-economic Darwinism (survival of the fittest) subscribed to by the qualitarians.

The Farm Bureau, the Republican Party, the National Association of Manufacturers, and the Chamber of Commerce of the United States lean toward the qualitarian pole, while the National Farmers Union (and to a lesser degree the Grange and the National Farmers Organization), the Democratic Party, and the AFL-CIO stand closer to the equalitarian pole. These ideological outlooks help to predict what an organization will say on a particular issue and also what coalitions are most likely to form.

Farmers adopt the liberal position on specific issues when the economic pinch is severe. They face a severe dilemma when it comes to preserving rugged individualism in a society in which bargaining power and public welfare measures are an accepted reality. Also the struggle for bargaining power on the part of a group whose economic structure makes control of output difficult receives more support from labor than from business interests. Thus farmers' philosophic allegiance may be to business groups but political realities frequently dictate the need for support from alliances with organized industrial labor.

The fertilizer, machinery, and other industries supplying inputs to farmers proved an important lobby for extending government food exports in 1966. Business interests are likely to be a continuing part of a coalition composed of large commercial farmers, the Farm Bureau, and other groups that subscribe to the "qualitative" political philosophy.

In summary, commercial farmers are likely to continue to be ambivalent in aligning themselves with either the qualitative or equalitarian interest group. Nevertheless, a sizable element of noncommercial farmers lacking adequate assets and training will continue to be a significant rural element and will constitute a case for farm welfare legislation for many years. The low-income sector of agriculture would seem to find a home with the have-not, equalitarian interest groups. But until low-income agriculture can demonstrate ability to deliver votes, its political interests will not be well served unless someone can make a more convincing case to urban legislators that the farm poor contribute to ghetto problems.

CONCLUSIONS

This chapter is based on the proposition that the future economic structure of farming is best understood in the perspective of our now dominant urban-industrial society. Data and analyses show that differences between rural and urban sectors in demographic characteristics, education, attitudes, and values are small but important. The farm is becoming more urban-industrially oriented.

The increasingly urban-oriented Congress has already pressed for changes, and is expected to press in the future to correct inconsistent farm-related policies, including: stockpiling commodities and paying farmers to restrain production while millions of the nation's disadvantaged go underfed; paying huge subsidies to affluent commercial farmers while doing comparatively little to help the rural poor; speaking of the need to develop poor nations while doing little to support indigenous crop experiment stations and to open U.S. markets to goods produced in these developing countries; advocating freer trade while placing restrictions on imported beef, dairy products, textiles, shoes and other imports; and paying farmers to hold land out of production while subsidizing irrigation and other practices to increase domestic production. Increasingly urban-oriented state legislatures are also expected to block in many instances efforts by farm groups to make corporate farming illegal and to preserve small rural schools.

City people cast the farmer as the underdog. To them he is the last vestige of the early American agrarian culture—independent, thrifty, and Puritanical. One reason why city people have not vetoed sizable public programs for agriculture is that they wish to preserve this farm way of life. It is increasingly recognized that farming is no longer a way of life, however, but a business—an extension of urban-industrial society. Farmers no longer conform to the agrarian image. They might well seek a new image.

Urban-industrial society is affluent and security-conscious. It places a high value on an efficient agriculture that provides adequate food at reasonable prices with sufficient reserve capacity to meet unforeseen difficulties. Some aspects of commodity programs for agriculture have been consistent with these objectives. Programs have not impeded labor outmovement nor increased farm production costs. Programs have maintained reserve capacity—land withdrawn from farm production should not be viewed entirely as a wasted resource by a society which places a premium on flexibility and security but as one having value in "nonuse."

But all is not well with commodity programs. They cost too much—the benefits to farmers and society could be achieved at less cost if some of the more conspicuous weaknesses of farm programs were removed. The intent of the authors and supporters of commodity programs was to promote equity, though it was believed that these programs would cause inefficiency. The opposite result has occurred. As is so often the case we find ourselves doing the right thing for the wrong reasons—the public ordered equity but got efficiency. Programs divert income from the taxpayer who may earn $10,000 annually to one farmer among the top 100,000 (3 per cent of all farmers receive about one-third of the farm program benefits) who earns a net income of $20,000 a year. Urban-industrial society is interested in preserving farming efficiency but is also concerned about equity issues. Program costs might be justified if they are necessary for efficiency and holding reserve capacity in agriculture but can hardly be justified as direct transfer payments that continue even if supply is in line with utilization at acceptable prices in agriculture.

The urban press is largely unsympathetic to commodity programs. Unless the more conspicuous weaknesses of commodity programs are corrected—and unless the public is convinced that programs are consistent with national goals of flexibility, efficiency, and stockpiling for emergencies—programs will be in jeopardy. City people will not dictate future farm programs, but public policies for agriculture will increasingly be those of which urban-industrial society at least does not disapprove.

Farmers too are not entirely happy with federal programs and would like a change. The dilemma is that efforts to gain collective independence—through farmer-controlled, cohesive bargaining groups—means an increasing sacrifice of personal independence. To keep the family farm efficient, farmers must adopt urban-industrial characteristics of self-preservation through larger and more mechanized farms, increased bargaining power, and government welfare legislation. Thus ironically, in the process of attempting to maintain the farm identity, the last vestiges of the traditional agrarian society are lost.

The consumer is becoming a more visible participant in the farm policy milieu. Evidence of this is reflected in the ubiquitous revolts of housewives throughout the nation in 1966 against high food prices. There is talk of renaming the USDA the U.S. Department of Food and Agriculture—apparently to give more recognition to consumers. Also in 1966, the Secretary of Agriculture was severely taken to task by farm groups for allegedly lowering farm prices by reducing government purchases of pork for servicemen. The new feature was not that he was berated for his action, but that the consumer rated that much attention by the Secretary. As a declining political force, the agricultural establishment will frequently find itself on the defensive and will need to learn how a political minority must operate to be most effective.

The rise of consumer bargaining power, coupled with the squeeze imposed by rising costs for hired labor and other farm inputs, puts further pressure and limits on the farmers' economic prerogatives. Supply administration by any farm group needs to be more concerned with stabilizing economic conditions for agriculture than with appreciably or precipitously raising prices.

Farm fundamentalism serves a useful purpose—it contributes to the dignity, self-respect, and well-being of farmers. But like most fundamentalist positions, it sometimes leads to myopia. It often shields farm people from the reality that most farm youth will find their place in a nonfarm environment. Inadequate schooling and other preparation for that environment can only lead to a legacy of socio-economic difficulties that sometimes takes generations to correct.

In conclusion, the farm and nonfarm positions developed in Chapters 1 and 2 provide a foundation for stating society's goals for agriculture. The goals are divided into two parts: (1) what society wants from agriculture and (2) what agriculture wants from society.

1. Society wants from agriculture adequate food and fiber at reasonable cost. This goal implies these subgoals:

a) Food and fiber to meet not only domestic but also foreign demands created by growing population and income levels;

b) Flexibility in production capacity and storage to meet emergencies such as unfavorable weather and war;

c) Growing technical and economic efficiency in agriculture; and,

d) Maximum feasible reliance on the market price mechanism to allocate resources, to determine what and how much to produce, and to distribute income.

2. Agriculture wants from society:

a) Measures to partially compensate farmers for economic losses resulting from a national policy of food abundance and excess capacity in agriculture,

b) Equality of opportunity to share in the fruits of national economic progress, with welfare measures to educate, train, and assist employable rural people to become economically productive; and to transfer income to the unemployable poor so that they can maintain a socially acceptable living standard in disability or retirement,

c) The right of organization to cope with problems of price and production instability; and,

d) Minimum government interference in the economic structure of farming.

Some of the above goals are clearly competitive, and appropriate compromises will have to be made in the political arena. National goals of food abundance and conservation of farm resources require special programs for agriculture. Federal payments to support farm income must not be so high as to promote undue regressive income redistribution, cause undue farming inefficiency, or discourage farm people from making overdue migration decisions.

The highly inelastic domestic demand for farm commodities means that the price mechanism signals a disaster to consumers from not having enough food and a disaster to farmers from having too much. Efforts to eliminate such disasters will likely mean some departure from a freely competitive market. Yet the common goal—1(*d*) and 2(*d*), above—for farmers and consumers alike is to rely as much as possible on the market price mechanism.

REFERENCES

Beale, Calvin, John Hudson, and Vera Banks. 1964. Characteristics of the U.S. population by farm and nonfarm origin. U.S. Department of Agriculture Economic Report No. 66. Washington.

Beers, Howard. 1953. Rural-urban differences: some evidence from public opinion polls. *Rural Sociology* 18:1–11.

Bertrand, Alvin. 1966. Rural communities under confrontation by mass society. In *The World Population Explosion*, Baton Rouge, Louisiana State University, Department of Agricultural Economics, pp. 81–86.

Bird, Alan R. 1964. Poverty in rural areas of the United States. U.S. Department of Agriculture Economic Report No. 63. Washington.

Bishop, C. E. and G. S. Tolley. 1962. *Manpower in Farming and Related Occupations.* Prepared for the President's panel of consultants on vocational education. Washington: U.S. Government Printing Office.

Burchinal, Lee G. 1961a. Differences in educational and occupational aspirations of farm, small town and city boys. *Rural Sociology* 26:107–21.

———. 1961b. Farm-nonfarm differences in religious beliefs and practices. *Rural Sociology* 26:414–18.

———. 1963. Dialogue. In *Farm Goals in Conflict*, Center for Agricultural and Economic Development, Ames: Iowa State University Press, pp. 217, 218.

——— and P. E. Jacobson. 1963. Migration and adjustments of farm and urban families and adolescents in Cedar Rapids, Iowa. *Rural Sociology* 28:364–78.

Cannon, Kenneth, and Ruby Gingles. 1956. Social factors related to divorce rates for urban counties in Nebraska. *Rural Sociology* 21:34–40.

Cowhig, James D. 1962. Early occupational status as related to education and residence. *Rural Sociology* 27:18–27.

———. 1963. "School Dropout Rates among Farm and Nonfarm Youth, 1950 and 1960." U.S. Department of Agriculture Economic Report No. 42. Washington.

———. 1964. Characteristics of school dropouts and high school graduates, farm and nonfarm, 1960. U.S. Department of Agriculture Economic Report No. 65. Washington.

Dewey, Richard. 1960–61. The rural-urban continuum: real but relatively unimportant. *American Journal of Sociology* 66:60–66.

Douglass, H. P. 1919. *The Little Town.* New York: Macmillan.

Freedman, Ronald, and Deborah Freedman. 1956. Farm-reared elements in the nonfarm population. *Rural Sociology* 21:50–61.

Fuguitt, Glen V. 1963. The city and countryside. *Rural Sociology* 28:247–57.

Green, Constance McLaughlin. 1965. *The Rise of Urban America.* New York: Harper & Row.

Haller, A. O. 1960. Occupational achievement process of farm-reared youth in urban-industrial society. *Rural Sociology* 25:321–33.

Haller, A. O., and C. E. Wolff. 1962. Personality orientations of farm, village and urban boys. *Rural Sociology* 27:275–93.

Hathaway, S. R., E. D. Monochesi, and L. A. Young. 1959. Rural-urban adolescent personality. *Rural Sociology* 24:331–46.

Hauser, Phillip, and Leo Schnore, eds. 1965. *The Study of Urbanization.* New York: Wiley.

Landis, Paul H. 1959. *Social Problems in Nation and World.* Philadelphia, Lippincott.

Levy, Marion J., Jr. 1966. *Modernization and the Structure of Societies.* Princeton, N.J.: Princeton University Press.

Lewis, W. Arthur. 1955. *The Theory of Economic Growth.* Homewood, Ill.: Irwin.

Lipset, Seymour M. 1955. Social mobility and urbanization. *Rural Sociology* 20:220–28.

Loomis, Charles P. 1960. *Social Systems.* Princeton, N.J.: Van Nostrand.

Lu, Y. C. 1969. Educational and occupational plans of farm boys in 1967. *Southern Journal of Agricultural Economics*, in press.

Mangus, A. R. 1957. Personality adjustment of rural and urban children. In Paul Hatt and Albert Reiss, Jr., eds., *Cities and Societies*, 2nd ed., Glencoe, Ill.: Free Press, pp. 603–14.

Martindale, Don. 1960. *American Social Structure.* New York: Appleton-Century-Crofts.

Martinson, Floyd. 1955. Personal adjustment and rural-urban migration. *Rural Sociology* 20:102–10.

Middleton, Russell, and Charles M. Grigg. 1959. Rural-urban differences in aspirations. *Rural Sociology* 24:347–54.

Miller, Paul A. 1959. Social, economic and political values of farm people. In *Problems and Policies in American Agriculture*, Center for Agricultural and Economic Development, Ames: Iowa State University Press, Chapter 6.

Moore, E. J., E. L. Baum, and R. B. Glasgow. 1964. Economic factors influencing educational attainments and aspirations of farm youth. U.S. Department of Agriculture Economic Report No. 51. Washington.

Nelson, Lowry. 1957. Rural life in a mass-industrial society. *Rural Sociology* 22:20–30.

On tradition, or what is left of it. 1966. *Time*, Apr. 22, 1966, p. 42.

Parsons, T. 1951. *The Social System.* Glencoe, Ill.: Free Press.

Polk, Kenneth. 1963. An exploration of rural juvenile delinquency. In Lee Burchinal, ed., *Rural Youth in Crisis*, U.S. Department of Health, Education, and Welfare, Washington: U.S. Government Printing Office, Chapter 15.

Schnore, Leo F. 1966. The rural-urban variable: an urbanite's perspective. *Rural Sociology* 31:135–43.

Schultz, Theodore W. 1965. Urban developments and policy implications for agriculture. Investment in Human Capital Series Paper 65:08. Chicago: University of Chicago Press.

Schwarzweller, Harry. 1964. Education, migration and economic life chances of male entrants to the labor force from a low-income rural area. *Rural Sociology* 29:152–67.

——— and James Brown. 1962. Education as a cultural bridge between eastern Kentucky and the Great Society. *Rural Sociology* 27:357–73.

Sewell, William, and Archibald Haller. 1963. The educational and occupational prospectives of rural youth. In Lee Burchinal, ed., *Rural Youth in Crisis*, U.S. Department of Health, Education and Welfare, Washington: U.S. Government Printing Office.

Slocum, Walter L. 1962. *Agricultural Sociology.* New York: Harper & Row.

Stewart, Charles, Jr. 1958–59. The rural-urban dichotomy: concepts and uses. *American Journal of Sociology* 64:152–58.

Strauss, Murray A. 1964. Societal needs and personal characteristics in the choice of occupation by farmers' sons. *Rural Sociology* 29:408–25.

Sweeter, D. A. 1966. The effect of industrialization on intergenerational solidarity. *Rural Sociology* 31:145–70.

Talbot, Ross, and Charles Wiggins. 1967. Political forces in American agriculture. Ames, Iowa State University, Department of History, Government and Philosophy (mimeo).

Tönnies, Ferdinand. 1940. *Fundamental Concepts of Sociology.* Translated by Charles P. Loomis. New York: American Book Co.

Tweeten, Luther G. 1965a. The income structure of U.S. farms by economic class. *Journal of Farm Economics* 47:207–21.

———. 1965b. The role of education in alleviating rural poverty. Background paper for research on rural poverty, Economic Research Service, U.S. Department of Agriculture (mimeo).

———. 1965c. Comparing effects of U.S. and Canadian farm policies: discussion. *Journal of Farm Economics* 47:1152–59.

——— and James S. Plaxico. 1964. Long-run outlook for agricultural adjustments based on national growth. *Journal of Farm Economics* 46:39–53.

Tyner, Fred. 1966. A simulation analysis of the U.S. farm economy. Unpublished Ph.D. thesis. Stillwater, Oklahoma State University.

——— and Luther G. Tweeten. 1966. Optimum resource allocation in U.S. agriculture. *Journal of Farm Economics* 48:613–31.

U.S. Department of Agriculture. 1964a. A summary of selected characteristics of the urban and rural populations by states, 1960. ERS-174. Washington.

———. 1964b. *The Farm Index* 3, No. 11.

———. 1966. *The Farm Index* 5, No. 8.

Williams, Robin M., Jr. 1964. American society in transition. In James H. Copp, ed., *Our Changing Rural Society*, Ames: Iowa State University Press, Chapter 1.

———. 1965. *American Society*. New York: Knopf.

CHAPTER THREE

Farm Organizations and Protest

The traveler is struck by the tranquillity of the rural scene. The reader may also have been impressed. Chapter 1 may have left him with the impression that all farmers are committed to goals and values compatible with democracy, individual independence, and the "orderly" American way of life, but these images do not tell the whole story. American agricultural history is punctuated with discordant notes—by attempts on the part of the farmers to organize and by dramatic, sometimes violent, expressions of protest.

This chapter enumerates various instances in which farmers took extra-marketal measures to deal with pressing economic issues which were part of the commercialization of agriculture, but which at the time were not understood by them. Many of the grievances to which farmers reacted were real, many imagined. Whatever the source of the grievances, they contain real lessons for the current student of farm policy. The roots of several farm organizations lie in the protest movements. The origin and progress of the major farm organizations are also discussed.

Much of early American agriculture was subsistence farming. There were few protest movements until farmers had outsiders to protest against. The outsiders were primarily firms and institutions dealt with by the commercial farmer in his buying and selling activities. As the economy became more complex, and as business and government grew, farmers not only dealt with the local general store and its owner but with the local grain elevator and thus indirectly with the great transportation and marketing industries. Government became larger as it was called upon to perform a wide range of functions. The bigness, complexity, and remoteness of big government and industry often seemed inscrutable and even sinister to farmers. Whether their complaints were justified or not, farmers in fact found the nonfarm sector a ready scapegoat for all kinds of economic ills.

EARLY PROTEST MOVEMENTS

Colonists learned tobacco culture from the Indians and planted the crop as early as 1610. By 1639 they were shipping 1.5 million pounds annually to the English markets. Around 1630, prices of tobacco fell sharply. In response to complaints of farmers, legislative price-fixing and acreage controls were attempted but failed. Farmers organized collective bargaining groups to curtail production by voluntary agreements among themselves but were unsuccessful in stabilizing production or markets. In 1682, rioters engaged in plant-cutting and destruction of tobacco, and their efforts were said to have improved the price in 1683 (Taylor, 1953, p. 21).

Numerous additional attempts were made by tobacco planters' clubs, by merchant organizations, and by legislation to stabilize tobacco prices or control production prior to 1750. Tobacco "wars," often characterized by riots and destruction of tobacco by farmers, were the forerunners of the great farm protest movements that are a part of U.S. history. These efforts of farmers to bargain collectively—and the efforts of the Virginia government to stabilize tobacco prices by destroying the already processed crop and by paying farmers to plant soil-improving crops rather than tobacco—were of some economic success but probably had little long-run influence on tobacco prices, production, or farm income.

SHAYS' REBELLION

Congress was given no control over currency and banking under the Articles of Confederation. Each state was individually responsible for its banking and currency, hence the economy was ill equipped to deal with the deflation in the 1780's that followed the great inflation during the Revolution. Taxes did not decline with prices. Debts incurred in periods of high prices were difficult or impossible to repay. Debtors were imprisoned and mortgages foreclosed. Most of the debtors were farmers; the creditors were merchants and bankers. Debtors first called for settling by arbitration. They later called for induced inflation by issuance of currency so that debts could be repaid more easily. In New England farmers resorted to destruction of produce, market strikes, direct appeals, legislative intervention, and sometimes armed revolt and violence to make their case heard. They burned the barns and haystacks of those who would not participate in the protest. Farmers carried their fight to the newspapers and the legislature. In Rhode Island they succeeded in passing a law which required merchants to accept paper money at face value in place of gold. Merchants responded by closing their doors and the farmers went on strike in 1786. The law was later revoked and farmers lost this fight for cheap money (Taylor, 1953, p. 28).

Politicians and commercial interests said that the unfavorable economic conditions would be alleviated if farmers would just work hard, practice thrift, diversify production, and be more self-sufficient. These suggestions were of little help.

At the height of the rebellion in 1786, there were approximately 5,000 persons, mostly farmers, in open rebellion in Massachussetts, among which was Daniel Shays' contingent. According to Taylor:

> The outcome of Shays' Rebellion was defeat after a number of actual clashes of arms between the rebels and the militia. In March 1787, the leaders were tried and 14 of them convicted of treason and sentenced to death. Governor Bowdoin granted them a reprieve for a few weeks, and Governor Hancock, his successor, pardoned all of them. Thus ended the first formidable insurrection ever to occur in the history of the new nation. Although debtors of all kinds were among Shays' troops, it was primarily a farmers' revolt against debts, taxes and low prices. [Taylor, 1953, p. 36]

Protesting farmers were not strong enough to win their demands. As in so many subsequent protests, direct action accomplished little more than to focus attention on the plight of farmers. The country was ill equipped by theory and resources to legislate favorable economic conditions for farmers, but it did grant the protestors some concessions and treated them with a degree of leniency that prevented an even more serious long-term alienation.

First Farm Organizations

The New England Association of Farmers, Mechanics and Other Working-men is believed to be the first "farmer" political organization (Taylor, 1953, pp. 77–79). Farmers were concerned about low prices, the practice of imprisonment for debt, and compulsory military drill. Many of their sons and daughters were employed in industry, hence farmers were concerned about low wages, long factory hours, and unemployment. The New England group was established about 1830, and many similar groups sprang up in the Northeast and in the Ohio Valley.

Numerous farm groups and societies were organized from 1830 to 1870. Many were local groups which had comparatively few political interests. The Patrons of Husbandry emerged as the first farm organization whose weight was felt in economic matters and farm policy formation.

PATRONS OF HUSBANDRY

Farming was not sufficiently commercial, grievances were too diversified, and overriding national issues such as slavery were too pressing for farm discontent to express itself widely until after the Civil War. The time for organization and protest was ripe. The index of prices received by farmers fell from 119 in 1860 to 93 in 1872 (1910–1914 = 100). Prices continued downward through the 1870's and reached an index of 67 in 1879. Nearly all farmers were antagonistic to the "monopolistic" corporations which asked too much for what farmers bought and paid too little for what farmers sold. They were antagonistic to the railroads, which constantly engaged in rate discrimination and rate wars, and to the bankers, who they thought charged too much interest, foreclosed on mortgages too readily, and created tight money, deflation, and depression. There has never been a period in American history when farm prices were depressed for so long a time as they were in the thirty years following the Civil War; nor has there ever been a period in which so large a percentage of American farmers rose in protest against the conditions in which they found themselves (Taylor, 1953, p. 91). Farmers, Taylor writes,

> welcomed and sought opportunities to produce for the market, but they did not seem to understand that a price and market economy requires finance and credit institutions, transportation and other shipping agencies, manufacturers, middlemen and even additional government services, and thus more taxes. They therefore protested against these and supported public men who were, so to speak, anti-industry, anti-bank and anti-government. [Taylor, 1953, p. 42]

In 1866, Oliver Kelly, as an employee of the recently established Department of Agriculture, toured the South to reestablish statistical reporting after the Civil War. He was a former Minnesota farmer who, because of drought conditions, had sought work with the Department of Agriculture. The deprivation, illiteracy, and lack of social life in the South made a deep impression on him. He resolved to do something about it and, with the assistance of a small group of concerned individuals, founded in 1867 the National Order of Patrons of Husbandry, commonly called the Grange. Because Kelly and some of the other founders were Masons, the new farm Organization was established as a secret social and educational order with a special ritual.

Membership increased slowly at first. By the end of 1871 less than 200 local groups had been formed, mostly in Minnesota and Iowa. But the benign fraternal order was on the verge of becoming the instrument to express farmer discontent. The Grange provided the organization; discontented farmers the membership. In 1872, 1,150 new locals were formed, more than half of them in Iowa. The number of locals numbered 21,697 by the end of 1874. The national leaders were reluctant to make the Grange the tool of agrarian discontent, but the forces of discontent were too strong to oppose. Sharply rising membership, which totaled 268,000 in 1874 and 858,000 in 1875, clearly established the Grange as a political force to be reckoned with. R. L. Tontz estimated its membership to be 451,000 families in 1875 (Table 3.1). The Grange led the farmers' successful fight for reform in the 1870's.

TABLE 3.1. Membership in General Farm Organizations, 1875–1960[a]

	Grange	Farmers Alliance	Farmers Union	Farm Bureau	Total
		(Thousands of families)			
1875	451				451
1880	65	39			105
1885	—	232			—
1890	71	1,053			1,124
1892	—	61			—
1893	—	26			—
1900	99	—			99
1908	—	—	135		—
1910	224	—	117		340
1912	—	—	116		—
1914	—	—	103		—
1916	—	—	107		—
1918	—	—	129		—
1920	231	—	—	317	678
1925	—	—	—	314	—
1930	316	—	—	321	716
1933	—	—	78	163	—
1935	—	—	—	281	—
1938	—	—	84	—	—
1940	337	—	—	444	866
1945	—	—	—	986	—
1950	443	—	—	1,450	2,109
1953	—	—	216	1,623	—
1956	—	—	278	—	—
1959	405	—	—	1,602	—
1960	394	—	—	1,601	2,273

SOURCE: Tontz (1964, p. 147).

[a] Blanks indicate organization not yet in existence. Dashes indicate lack of data, or organization no longer in existence.

THE GRANGER LAWS

Many of the Grange's political activities were aimed at regulation of railroads. Regulations included these features: fixing of maximum rates by a public commission; prohibiting rate discrimination between long and short hauls (the total charge of a short haul could not exceed that of a long haul); forbidding consolidation of parallel rail lines that would reduce competition; and prohibiting the granting of free passes by railroads to public officials.

The single most important goal of the Grange was the public regulation of rail rates. The result was the so-called Granger Laws. The Illinois legislature in 1870 took the lead under the urging of the Grange supporters and established a number of constitutional directives to control railroad rates and warehouses. The following year the legislature passed laws implementing the directives. It also required annual reporting by railroad companies of assets, debts, monthly earnings, and expenses. The courts, however, reacted adversely, so a new act, more carefully formulated, was passed by the Illinois legislature in 1873. Among other features it provided penalties for rate discrimination. The constitutionality of this act was upheld by the State Supreme Court in 1880. "Granger cases," such as *Munn* vs. *Illinois* in 1876, established the right of government to regulate public utilities.

Other states passed laws, often poorly formulated, to regulate railroads. These laws formed a discordant system of regulation. Mercifully, they were short-lived. The U.S. Supreme Court held that states could not regulate interstate commerce in the historic Wabash case of 1886 (Davis *et al.*, 1965, p. 391). The following year, the federal government established a system to regulate freight and passenger service with passage of the Interstate Commerce Act of 1887.

The Grange was also active in national politics. It opposed the single gold standard and redeemable greenbacks. The organization was a major force behind raising the Department of Agriculture to cabinet status and was influential in providing for dissemination of agricultural literature, for agricultural fairs, and for teaching of agriculture in the public schools. It was influential in establishing agricultural experiment stations in 1887 and in obtaining rural mail delivery. It worked for elimination of fraud and adulteration in food processing, against bribery and corruption of public officials, and for resource conservation, women suffrage, and ballot reform. Many of these causes were not immediately successful but later were nationally accepted and enacted into law. The fraternal aspects of the order, though submerged, undoubtedly added much to the quality of rural life.

ECONOMIC PROGRAM

Numerous activities were undertaken of a rather direct economic nature. The Grange engaged in cooperative buying and selling, manufacturing, and banking and even engaged in holding actions to achieve economic objectives. Mutual fire insurance companies were organized in every Grange state. In 1871 members began buying household and farm supplies cooperatively. The operation of cooperative stores organized by county or district Granges was widely practiced. Members would sometimes pool their production and bargain collectively with merchants to receive a higher price for produce. Most of these efforts were without production controls, but "in one instance at least, an attempt was made by the Illinois Grangers in 1878 to influence the price of hogs by withholding them from the market" (Taylor, 1953, p. 157).

Orders of many local Granges were pooled and state agents bargained directly with manufacturers for farm supplies. Sometimes agents were sent or hired abroad to handle exports of farm products such as wheat and cotton. Local Grange cooperatives often handled the buying and storage of wheat. Nearly every phase of "agribusiness" was attempted, including manufacturing of farm machinery. Many of the cooperatives established by the Grange were quite successful. Among these were cooperative elevators, shipping associations, and fire insurance companies (Benedict, 1953, p. 96). However, a large number of business activities failed from too much idealism and too little previous experience, capital, and business acumen. Also unwarranted expectations, intense political involvement, and competition from private firms figured in the demise of Grange business interests. Nevertheless, the Grange provided useful experience and a foundation for business activities of the current farm organizations—including of course the National Grange of today.

The legislative successes of the Grange in the 1870's are a matter of history. Its accomplishments were impressive, and its ideas are still apparent in current farm organizations. But "it had grown too fast, it had attempted too much, and the methods of organization used were better suited to rousing enthusiasm than to maintaining it" (Benedict, 1953, p. 104).

Grange membership peaked at 858,000 in 1875, only seven years after its founding, but dropped rapidly to 124,000 by 1880. It fell slightly lower, but began to recover and by 1900 approached 200,000 members (Benedict, 1953, p. 104). Emphasis on social and educational activities and a few sound economic activities, coupled with a lack of emphasis on political orientation, has given considerable stability to the group in the twentieth century.

THE FARMERS ALLIANCE

The name "Farmers Alliance" was a popular one, and was used by a number of independent farm organizations that began around 1873. Again, the fuel for the movement was farmers' discontent. The index of prices received by farmers stood at 95 in 1882, and fell steadily to 67 in 1886 (1910–1914 = 100). It remained low for several years thereafter. Farmers viewed themselves as a class oppressed by railroads, banks, Wall Street monopolies, government, and the urban-industrial process.

The Southern Farmers Alliance

The first Farmers Alliance is believed to have been formed in Texas in 1873 as an "anti-horse-thief" and "anti-land-grab" farmers organization (Taylor, 1953, p. 194). In other areas, the focus of farmers discontent was government grants to railroads of land already occupied by settlers. One of the accomplishments of the Alliance in Kansas was to win court approval of preemption rights and to set aside the claims of railroads to preempted land (Benedict, 1953, p. 106).

The Agricultural Wheel began in Arkansas as a local debating and discussion group called the Wattensas Farmers Club in 1882. It began innocuously enough. Like other farm groups, it attempted to improve its members in the theory and practice of agriculture and to demonstrate ways to improve rural living. Its humble beginnings hardly foretold its later ambitious objectives: "action in concert with all labor unions or organizations of laborers" to secure legislation beneficial to farmers (Taylor, 1953, pp. 203, 204). At the time of a joint meeting with other farm organizations in 1887, total membership was reported to be 500,000 though it was probably not that high. Membership was mainly located in the south central region but extended as far north as Wisconsin. The Wheel had earlier joined the Brothers of Freedom, another Arkansas group, which included not only farmers but industrial laborers and townspeople. The Wheel opposed mortgages on livestock and crops, "soulless" corporations, and national banks. It proposed reducing crop acreage in order to lower production and raise farm prices (Benedict, 1953, p. 106). It favored a graduated income tax and low tariffs and was much involved in politics.

The Louisiana Farmers Union originated following a discussion between twelve men cleaning a graveyard in 1880 (Taylor, 1953, p. 200). By 1887, it had grown to 10,000 members. Meanwhile the Texas Farmers Alliance had grown to approximately 100,000 members. The two organizations merged in 1887. This merger was joined by the North Carolina Farmers Association early in 1888. Later that year, this group joined with the Agricultural Wheel to form the Farmers and Laborers Union. The name was changed to National Farmers Alliance and Industrial Union in 1889 when the Laborers Union of Kansas joined the organization. The amalgamation is sometimes called the Southern Farmers Alliance. The Southern Alliance claimed membership of up to 3,000,000 in 1890, but less than 250,000 supported the organization financially.

The Northern or National Farmers Alliance

A northern National Alliance was organized at Chicago in 1880. The organization, which stood for protection of farmers from the "tyranny of

monopoly" and the "encroachments of concentrated capital," gained membership in the north-west central states totaling perhaps 400,000 in 1887. Membership was especially large in the Plains states, where low prices and hard times
had increased farmers' discontent.

Numerous other farm groups were closely associated with the Farmers
Alliances. The Farmers Mutual Benefit Association arose in Illinois in 1882 as
an effort to improve wheat marketing. Membership of approximately 150,000
extended from Kansas to North Carolina but was concentrated mainly in the
Midwest. Other groups such as the Alliance of Colored Farmers of Texas,
Farmers Congress, Farmers League, and Patrons of Industry were closely
associated with the Alliance movement, and most had representatives at a 1889
meeting in St. Louis to unite the Northern and Southern Farmers Alliances.
The groups agreed on common objectives but failed to consolidate. The third-
party idea seemed to divert attention from union (Benedict, 1953, p. 109).

ACTIVITIES OF THE FARMERS ALLIANCES

There are many parallels between the Grange and the Farmers Alliances.
The Grange began as a social and fraternal group but was transformed by
agrarian unrest in the 1870's. The Alliance movement—begun in widely separated
localities as a discussion society and anti-horse-thief association (and for other
reasons)—was radically changed in character by agrarian discontent in the
1880's. Both the Grange and Alliance movements were satisfied at first with
comparatively mild measures to treat economic ills. The Alliance moved against
middlemen by wholesale purchasing and manufacturing of farm supplies.
Cooperative selling, insurance of many types, and credit also were provided.
Many Alliance business ventures failed due to poor management, inadequate
financing, or astute (sometimes unfair) competition from private firms (Taylor,
1953, p. 235).

The "subtreasury plan" of the Southern Alliance is significant because,
though never enacted into law, it was similar to the nonrecourse loan used
extensively since the 1930's. The plan was to establish a branch of the U.S.
Treasury in every agricultural county. The owners of farm products would
deposit their commodities in warehouses and receive legal tender for up to 80
per cent of the market value of the commodity. The farmer could redeem the
commodities and sell them as he chose by repaying the advance, plus carrying
charges.

If the farmer did not redeem the commodities in twelve months, they would
be sold at public auction and the money used to cover operation of the system.
The plan was designed to expand the currency and to remove the necessity to
dump farm products on a sagging market (Taylor, 1953, p. 244).

The Alliances were impatient for economic reform, and were dissatisfied with the progress of local initiative and cooperatives, hence they turned increasingly to redress in the political area. This culminated in the joint effort with the Knights of Labor and other groups to support the Populist Party.

SOUTHERN ALLIANCE SUBMERGED IN THE POPULIST PARTY

The Alliances by their political militancy were drifting more heavily into politics. They had substantial success in Kansas in 1890. In 1892, when "in Omaha the Populist Party became a blazing reality, the Southern Alliance was literally buried" (Taylor, 1953, p. 277). The National Peoples Party nominated John Weaver for President. Its platform called for free coinage of silver, a graduated income tax, return of railroad lands to the people, popular election of U.S. senators, secret ballot, an eight-hour workday, public ownership of railroads, and an effective civil service.

The issue that dominated all others was free silver. This was an agrarian issue to the extent that farmers hoped to gain from freer coinage. The Peoples Party did not win a majority of the legislative seats in any state, but it did poll many votes and was not completely discouraged. Weaver received 1.0 million votes, Cleveland 5.6 million, and Harrison 5.2 million (Benedict, 1953, p. 111).

Both Populists and Democrats in 1896 nominated William Jennings Bryan, who was defeated, for President. The farmers' movement had been so thoroughly identified with politics that the setback virtually spelled the end of the Alliances and the third-party idea. One view is that they would have become extinct even if Bryan had won because the leadership had either died or been separated from the membership at the grass roots level (Taylor, 1953, p. 323). Also farm economic conditions were beginning gradually to improve in the last decade of the century, and farmers were finding it more difficult to unite behind a common cause.

The massive Alliance movement, which involved perhaps 4 million farmers, accomplished several important objectives. First, it gave the farmer a sense of worth and a consciousness of class. It reaffirmed, as had the Grange earlier, that the farmer could exert considerable economic and political power if pressed sufficiently by real or alleged wrongs caused by business and other groups. And the Alliance contributed to the experience accumulated earlier by the Grange, showing the need for sound business management and the danger of too heavy involvement in politics. The Alliance provided some of the groundwork for later, more successful farm organizations and their public policies.

NATIONAL FARMERS UNION

The Farmers Educational and Cooperative Union was founded in Texas by Isaac Newton Gresham, a newspaperman and former member of the Farmers Alliance. Gresham and nine of his friends received a state charter in 1902.

The Union absorbed former Alliance and Populist Party members as well as others and grew rapidly to an estimated 50,000 members in 1904. It was plagued by early strife, engendered by rather sizable membership fees coupled with loose accounting procedures and by the issue of whether only farmers could be officers. By 1905 the organization had membership in numerous states of the South. By 1908, membership totaled 135,000 farm families in twenty-three states (Table 3.1). Membership after 1912 shifted westward, and the wheat states by 1920 were the major source of Union support. Unlike the old Alliance, the National Farmers Union grew little from amalgamations although it did increase its membership in the Midwest by absorbing in 1907 a Farmers Union which previously had been formed by combining in Illinois the Farmers Social and Economic Union, the Farmers Relief Association, and the Farmers Mutual Benefit Association.

Whereas the Alliance had focused on politics to attack problems caused by railroads, monopoly, and deflation, the Union emphasized the business approach to problems of buying, selling, middlemen, and credit. The Union never placed a candidate for election or identified closely with one party in its early years. It avoided the political mistakes of the Alliance and the Grange. The Union pressed its political causes on conventions, platforms, and candidates, but did not tie its existence to any one political party or issue. In the 1930's, it was involved in the Farmers Holiday Association, to be discussed later.

The charter of the first Farmers Union group clearly stated that the purpose of the organization was to aid farmers in marketing. The first local, as early as 1903, claimed success in a contract with the cotton ginners in the county to raise cotton prices. The Farmers Union in 1904 sponsored a movement to hold one bale of cotton out of five off the market and to sell the other four slowly. They took credit for raising cotton prices. In 1907 they attempted to limit production and control cotton prices by plowing down 10 per cent of the cotton crop and holding some of the harvested crop off the market (Benedict, 1953, p. 134). Warehouses were built by the Union to facilitate holding and marketing. In 1913, the Union had 1,600 warehouses in the cotton states, and a number in wheat states (Taylor, 1953, p. 353).

The Farmers Union was much involved in business activity. It attempted to produce implements and fertilizers. Its enterprises even included coal mines and banks. Purchasing clubs bought in carload lots to reduce middleman commissions. Some locals negotiated a 10 per cent discount for Union members from retail merchants.

Considerable success was achieved with wholesale and retail cooperatives. These dealt in livestock, grain, insurance, and other items. The local stores handled a large number of items for the farm and household. The Farmers Union was the first farm organization to be really successful in business activities. This success gave continuity to the Union and helped it to sustain membership. Membership in 1967 numbered some quarter of a million farm families.

EQUITY ORGANIZATIONS

The American Society of Equity was founded in 1902 by J. A. Everitt in Indiana. Membership reached a maximum of about 40,000 in 1912. It was not a secret society with fraternal features, nor was it much interested in politics. Its objectives were economic.

Everitt was publisher of a newspaper and author of a book called *The Third Power*. The theme of this book was that farmers should organize in defense of their economic interests just as business and labor had done. The Equity, with its main strength in the upper Midwest, sought early to raise prices by holding farm products off the market.

The first holding action was attempted in 1903 on wheat and was followed by attempted price-setting of other crops. Results were not satisfactory, and many members suggested a reduction in acreage. A large amount of wheat was withheld from markets in the fall of 1906 with some success, but Everitt's vision of a successful holding action supported by several hundred thousand members never materialized. A faction under Everitt later formed the Farmers Society of Equity. It had no success with its price-fixing obsession and ceased to function in 1916.

Following the split with Everitt, the major group, under M. W. Tubbs, established its headquarters in Chicago; its membership eventually was concentrated in Wisconsin, Minnesota, and the Dakotas. It emphasized cooperative marketing rather than price-fixing. The American Society of Equity had lost much of its dynamism through internal dissent, however, and many of its activities and much of its membership were absorbed over time by the Farmers Union and Nonpartisan League. It was not a significant organization after 1917.

Its efforts to merge with the Farmers Union failed in 1910. Out of the attempted merger grew a new group, the Farmers Equity Union, organized by C. O. Drayton, a cooperative business organization with no fraternal features. It had an estimated 65,000 members in 1923. Sound business practices, with local·cooperatives operating in conjunction with central facilities in a nationwide marketing plan, have worked well for wheat, and Equity organizations are still strong in the Great Plains.

Organization of local cooperatives was the great accomplishment of the American Society of Equity and the Farmers Equity Union. In addition to grain-marketing and livestock-shipping, the American Society of Equity sold insurance and operated elevators, warehouses, meatpacking plants, flour mills, creameries, and retail stores. The Equity movement in the first two decades of the 1900's was unique. Unlike previous movements, it grew despite farm prosperity. The holding actions and price fixing schemes were failures, but the business ventures were often financially sound and commanded member loyalty. Because the business ventures were most successful in times of prosperity, it follows that the organization would prosper in these times.

The Equity Cooperative Exchange

Another significant milestone in the farmers' movement was the Equity Cooperative Exchange. It started in 1907 in response to numerous grievances of farmers against the wheat trade. The intent was for the cooperative to own elevator facilities at the local and terminal level and to gain a seat on the Minneapolis Grain Exchange. It failed in the latter but did control marketing of much wheat, about 8,000 carloads in 1915. Spurred on by George Loftus, a fiery and informed business manager, it succeeded in securing many reforms in the grain trade, but the organization grew too fast and could not efficiently finance its operations. It was absorbed by the Farmers Union in 1934 (Taylor, 1953, p. 409).

The Night Riders

Because Everitt's marketing plan appealed to tobacco-growers, Kentucky was the strongest state in the American Society of Equity in 1905. The organization, along with tobacco-growers' associations, attempted to corner enough of the tobacco crop to control supply and to bargain collectively with buyers for a better price. The buyers foiled these attempts by paying a higher price for tobacco to "Hill Billies," who operated independently of the control organization. A small group of growers called the Night Riders operated like goon squads to force the buyers to bargain with the control group and to force the Hill Billies into the cartel. The Night Riders, whose activities were condemned by the Society of Equity, burned barns, destroyed tobacco plantings of growers not participating in holding actions, and destroyed properties of the tobacco companies. There were also cases of beatings and other intimidation.

THE NONPARTISAN LEAGUE

The Nonpartisan League was started in 1915 in North Dakota by Arthur Townley, a former Socialist Party organizer. The grievances of wheat farmers were many, including a deep distrust of grading, storage, transport, and speculation in the grain trade. It was said of wheat that the farmer would sell a bushel and get paid for a peck, and the consumer would receive a peck and pay for a bushel. The middleman and banker were viewed as the cause of farmers' economic ills, and were the common enemy. Encouraged by receptive farmers and enticed by high fees, organizers moved quickly, and the Nonpartisan League swept North Dakota like a prairie fire. It was said to have 200,000 members in 1918, mostly in North Dakota but also in surrounding states. Political power grew, and in 1918 the League elected their man for governor and other executive offices and gained control of both houses of the North Dakota legislature.

Among other accomplishments, the League established a Bank of North Dakota to provide low-cost loans, and a state-owned North Dakota Mill and Elevator Association to engage in processing and marketing of farm products and to establish warehouses and elevators. The legislative program of the Nonpartisan League established the necessary framework for state-operated homebuilding and insurance.

Membership had begun to decline by 1921 for several reasons. Lack of adequate management and financial support in the face of formidable opposition from private enterprise and other groups caused the League's business operations to lose money. The leaders of the League became so involved in politics that the business organization and membership campaigns were neglected. Also World War I brought charges of disloyalty and pacifism against the League and interfered with recruitment of new members. The Nonpartisan League (NPL) was still functioning in North Dakota in 1969. It has often supported Republican candidates in the past, but since the mid-1950's has supported mainly Democrats. Some political candidates in the 1960's ran on the Democratic-NPL Party ticket.

AMERICAN FARM BUREAU FEDERATION

At the close of World War I, farm organizations were not very active. The Grange had a membership of approximately 550,000 persons, but the fraternal, secret approach was losing its ability to attract new farm members. The National Farmers Union had comparatively little influence; its membership was some 140,000. The American Society of Equity had 40,000 members, mainly in Wisconsin, and Nonpartisan League influence was waning as its membership fell from 200,000 in 1918 to 150,000 in 1922. Two decades of prosperity and the identification of the old organizations with past problems, many of which were no longer serious, had taken much of the vitality from the traditional farm groups. The old issues of monopolies and banks had lost some of their appeal. Yet new problems were emerging, and the time was ripe for a new farm organization.

A new organization got its start from an unexpected source—the Cooperative Federal-State Extension Service. Local farm bureaus made up of educated, progressive commercial farmers had been organized to assist the county agent in education and demonstration of improved farming practices. These local groups were concerned not only with more efficient farming but also with the broader problems faced by farmers. These broad problems could best be approached from the state and national level. At a national meeting of county agents in Chicago in 1918 it was resolved that state and national federations of farm bureaus were needed to serve farmers more effectively. State bureaus were organized. At a national convention of these in 1919, Midwest advocates of a national federation that would deal with economic and business functions won out over Eastern and Southern groups who favored a more limited, educational role for a national federation. The convention passed several resolutions including a call for economy in government and an increase in the limit on Federal Land Bank Association loans. These and other resolutions were clear and early evidence that the group would be involved in national issues of public policy.

In 1920 the constitution drawn up at the 1919 meeting was ratified at a national convention in Chicago, and James Howard of Iowa was elected president. By 1921 forty-two state federations were in existence and by 1922 the American Farm Bureau Federation had a paying membership of 315,000 families. From its inception, the Farm Bureau, as it was called, represented commercial, middle-class farmers and, unlike previous groups, did not have the image of an oppressed, underprivileged class. Gray Silver was sent to Washington as a lobbyist and soon made the presence of the Farm Bureau felt in efforts to repeal daylight saving time, to control packers and stockyard companies, and to use government loans to increase farm exports.

The Farm Bureau was not initially committed to the McNary-Haugen Bills, but with a new Bureau president and new Washington lobbyist, the organization supported the third McNary-Haugen Bill in 1926. These legislative proposals were urged by the Bureau in 1932: (*a*) government guarantee of new deposits in all banks, (*b*) monetary reform, (*c*) restoration of price parity for agricultural products, and (*d*) relief for heavily mortgaged farmers in distress. The Bureau supported much of the New Deal legislation in the 1930's. The Farm Bureau claimed pride of paternity in creating the Agricultural Adjustment Administration and reaffirmed their faith in that organization in several national convention resolutions during the 1930's. The Bureau was especially active in securing farm credit legislation and was one of the first farm groups to recognize the folly of high tariffs and the need for reciprocal trade agreements.

POLITICAL TIES

The Grange, the Farmers Union and the Farm Bureau were often united in support of the McNary-Haugen Bills and the New Deal legislation. Farmers could present a united front in times of economic distress. The return of prosperity after 1940 eventually led the organizations down quite different roads, however. The Farm Bureau strongly opposed supply management, acreage diversion, and other programs of the Kennedy and Johnson Administrations.

The Farmers Union and the Grange felt that the Farm Bureau had the undue advantage of support by the Extension Service and land grant colleges. (The ties between the Extension Service and the Farm Bureau were not completely severed until after World War II.) Despite some animosity by competing farm organizations toward the Bureau, the policies recommended by the major farm groups were not unduly different—all recommended legislative measures prior to World War II that were not out of line with traditional thinking. The Farm Bureau maintained a close liaison with business and commercial interests, while the Farmers Union worked more closely with labor unions. The Bureau developed a strong program of education, insurance, and cooperative marketing and by 1967 had a membership of 1.7 million families.

THE FARM BLOC

The index of farm prices fell from 211 in 1920 to 124 in 1921 (1910–1914 = 100) and was never over 156 during the remainder of the 1920's. This acute economic distress of farmers led to a resurgence of farm organization activity. Representatives of all the major farm organizations met with leaders of Congress and the President's Cabinet in 1921. The result was formation of a powerful bipartisan coalition of senators (and later representatives), which soon became known as the Farm Bloc. The Farm Bloc is not treated extensively in this chapter because it was not a farm organization but a coalition of men in Congress concerned with serving farm interests through the national political process.

The outlines of legislation, worked out mainly between the Farm Bureau through its representative, Gray Silver, and the Farm Bloc, soon emerged. Subsequently, laws were enacted in the interest of farmers dealing with packers and stockyards, futures trading, agricultural credit, cooperative marketing, and lower freight rates. With these high-priority measures of the Farm Bloc enacted, and with the loss of the able leadership of Senator Kenyon and some slackening of the unity of farm organizations engendered by the economic crises of the early 1920's, the Farm Bloc began to lose some of its effectiveness by 1923. But the Bloc continued to exist into the 1940's.

THE COOPERATIVE MOVEMENT

The cooperative movement began as early as 1810 when dairy producers in Connecticut attempted to churn and market butter cooperatively (Taylor, 1953,

p. 472). Successful dairy cooperatives were established in Wisconsin in 1841 and in Oneida County, New York, in 1851. Cooperative marketing has since been extended to nearly all farm commodities.

Approximately one-third of farm output is marketed through cooperatives. In the year ending July 1, 1964, business volume of dairy cooperatives was $3.5 billion, grain and soybean cooperatives $2.5 billion, and livestock cooperatives $1.5 billion (U.S. Department of Agriculture, 1966, pp. 464, 465). Total business of marketing cooperatives was $11.2 billion and membership was 3.6 million (some farmers were members of more than one cooperative). Total purchases from farm supply cooperatives were $2.8 billion and membership 3.4 million. Feed purchases alone from the farm supply cooperatives totaled approximately $1 billion in the year ending July 1, 1964.

Establishment of cooperatives was an important activity of all the major farm organizations—the Grange, the Farmers Alliance, the American Society of Equity, the National Farmers Union, and the Farm Bureau. Cooperatives were organized by these groups and independently for two purposes: (*a*) to create a more efficient and orderly marketing system that would reduce middleman margins and (*b*) to control supply and regulate marketing so as to secure a higher retail price. In the former, the record has been spotty, but over-all must be called a substantial success. In the latter objective, the record has not been impressive.

THE SAPIRO MOVEMENT

One of the most successful cooperatives began as the Pachappa Orange Growers Association in California in 1888. Composed originally of eleven growers who pooling their fruit to sell to packers, the Association expanded in size and functions until in 1893 it was supervising the marketing operation up to the wholesale level. This organization led eventually to the California Fruit Growers Exchange (Sunkist) in 1905 and continued to operate under that name. The pattern of organization was repeated for other West Coast fruit cooperatives and eventually became a blueprint for the Sapiro movement. The pattern proceeds as follows: Producers of a commodity enter into an agreement to pool their product for marketing. They incorporate and elect a board of directors which sets up a business organization and hires the management. The management in turn operates the marketing operations of receiving, processing, shipping, financing, storage, advertising, and selling. Members are required to sell only to the organization, and net returns are prorated back to each member according to the products he supplied.

The successful marketing operations of cooperatives on the West Coast led the American Farm Bureau Federation to call a meeting of interested individuals in 1920 to hear Aaron Sapiro, a lawyer for several California cooperatives. He told the 400 delegates, mostly from Midwestern and Eastern co-operatives, that the techniques used to market specialty crops in California could be applied to the major crops. Sapiro advocated a strongly centralized producer cooperative that would issue contracts to members for delivery of a specific volume of commodities, with penalties for noncompliance. Activities of the cooperative were to reach beyond first processing and storage and were to extend to warehousing and terminal markets. Prices were to be set and administered by the board of directors. Commodities which would not bring this price would be "dumped," presumably on the foreign market. He insisted that the monopoly cooperative should gain control of 90 per cent of the entire crop to enable it to administer prices.

Accordingly, attempts were made to organize grain-growers, livestock producers, cotton-growers, tobacco-growers, and others, but the groups were organized too hastily and with inadequate management. Farmers were yet too numerous, too diversified, and too independent for these strong measures. One after another, the groups collapsed, and the Sapiro movement for major farm commodities had failed by 1924 (Benedict, 1953, p. 198). The philosophy lingered, however, and the basic system has continued for a number of specialty crops.

THE CAPPER-VOLSTEAD ACT

The Sapiro movement made it important to clarify the status of cooperatives in the light of the Sherman and Clayton Antitrust Acts. The Capper-Volstead Act, the Magna Charta of cooperatives, became law in 1922. It established the conditions under which an organization might be defined as a cooperative and to a considerable extent exempted cooperatives from the antitrust provisions of earlier Sherman and Clayton Acts. Jurisdiction of matters that dealt with price-controlling activities of cooperatives was placed with the Secretary of Agriculture rather than with the Federal Trade Commission, the Secretary being more congenial toward cooperatives.

THE FEDERAL FARM BOARD

The Republicans answered the 1920's farm problem with the Agricultural Marketing Act of 1929. Its principal attack on the farm problem was to be giant cooperative institutions. The Federal Farm Board, created under the Act, was composed of eight members who were to authorize and support new cooperative marketing associations. Funds of $500 million were appropriated by Congress to be used by cooperatives to buy surpluses and support farm prices. The Farm Board, because of inadequate financing, was overwhelmed by the immensity of the farm problem. Cooperatives serve a useful function of efficient marketing and are loyally supported by members, but at that time they simply were not ready to perform the vast chore of aligning supply with demand at an acceptable, stable price level for agriculture.

NATIONAL COUNCIL OF FARMER COOPERATIVES (THE CO-OP COUNCIL)

The National Council of Cooperative Marketing Associations was liquidated in 1926 and reorganized as the National Cooperative Council in 1929. The name was again changed in 1939 to the National Council of Farmer Cooperatives. The organization—from 1920 to the present—will be simply referred to here as the Co-op Council.

The Co-op Council (like the Grange, Farmers Union, and Farm Bureau) was one of the big four farm groups represented in the Farm Bloc. In 1955 it was composed of farm supply and farm marketing cooperatives that included 116 separate affiliates, representing 5,000 local cooperatives serving a membership of nearly 3 million (McCune, 1956, p. 54). As such it is the largest organized farm group, although it is not ordinarily considered a farm organization as such. While cooperatives have an effective lobby and keep their members well informed, the interests of the many component groups are so diverse that the Council rarely takes a stand on national political issues and partisan politics. The Council has been called a "sleeping giant."

The National Council opposed the McNary-Haugen Bills of the 1920's and the commodity programs and acreage control schemes of the New Deal. The Council's position was motivated by the thinking that cooperatives could better deal with the problems that the commodity programs were attempting to solve. The Co-op Council has been a conservative voice in farm policy, closer to the Farm Bureau position than to that of any of the other major farm organizations. With Ezra Taft Benson as head during World War II, the organization found itself siding with the Farm Bureau, the Grange, and the U.S. Chamber of Commerce to fight Roosevelt's price ceiling policies and his measures to improve the housing and wage standards for migrant workers. Cooperatives had become large employers and were taking the business-management point of view.

The Council adopted a resolution in 1964 that was clearly anti-National Farmers Organization and condemned as self-defeating the group actions of farmers which sought to set the market price above that warranted by competition (Breimyer, 1965, p. 204).

FARMERS HOLIDAY MOVEMENT
We'll eat our wheat and ham and eggs, and
let them eat their gold.—*Iowa Union Farmer*

Farmers consoled themselves through the 1920's by saying, "It could be worse." And sure enough it did get worse. The index of prices received by farmers, which was 211 (1910–1914 = 100) in 1920 and 148 in 1929, fell to 65 in 1932. The slump was no ordinary business recession but a disastrous depression. The number of banks dropped from 30,000 in the early 1920's to less than 15,000 in 1933. In 1931 alone, 2,300 closed and wiped out savings for a large number of depositors. Only the farm economy was depressed in the 1920's; now both the farm and nonfarm economies appeared hopelessly bogged down in a depression. Some farmers burned corn for fuel. Receipts from shipment of livestock to Chicago did not always pay the transport cost. Nearly a million farmers lost title to their farms from 1930 to 1934. The desperate situation led to protests in even the most conservative sections of the country.

The Iowa Farmers Union was the organized core that led to the "Farmers Holiday" rebellion. Union membership was only 9,600 in Iowa in 1932, a far smaller organization than the state's Farm Bureau, but its members were militant. The movement centered in Iowa, but was active also in Nebraska, Minnesota, North Dakota, and other states. Milo Reno, even when not president, dominated the Iowa Farmers Union almost from 1918 when he joined it until his death in 1936. He was the most significant individual in the organization of the Holiday movement. Reno was a charismatic leader with an evangelical style and a strong promoter of a cause that preoccupied major elements of the Farmers Union—cost-of-production pricing. In 1927 Reno introduced a resolution to a corn belt committee, stating, "If we cannot obtain justice by legislation, the time will have arrived when no other course remains than organized refusal to deliver the products of the farm at less than production costs" (Shover, 1965, p. 27). It took five years to realize the mandate of this statement.

He made occasional references to his plan in the *Iowa Union Farmer*, the Iowa Union newspaper edited by H. R. Gross, who much later (in the 1960's) was to be a very conservative Republican representative from Iowa's third district to Congress. Reno and John Bosch of Minnesota presented a resolution to the National Farmers Union convention in 1931 calling for a farm strike. The motion was soundly defeated. The holding action thereupon proceeded as an independent movement. But, "in a real sense, the Farmers Holiday Association was a strong-arm auxiliary of the Farmers Union" (Shover, 1965, p. 35).

In February 1932, 1,500 farmers in Boone County, Iowa, met and pledged to "stay at home—buy nothing—sell nothing." Factions within the Farmers Union continued efforts to organize a strike and in May 2,000 farmers assembled in Des Moines, Iowa, to launch the Farmers Holiday Association as a national movement. Reno was named president. Organizers traveled through farm areas and secured pledges from half a million farmers to support the forthcoming holding action. Plans to begin the strike July 4 fizzled; the strike officially began August 10, 1932. Sporadic action occurred in other places, but the focal point was Sioux City, Iowa. As many as 1,500 farmer pickets on August 11 stalled the movement of milk into the city. The strike was settled on August 20 with somewhat minor concessions from buyers. Picketing continued around Sioux City, however, and the movement became increasingly more violent as it spread to other locations. There were pitched battles between deputies and pickets at the Omaha city limits. A large number of arrests were made. A holding action by the Minnesota Holiday Association began September 21 and ended October 22. At least one picket was shot. The Minnesota action, like that in other areas, achieved very limited direct success.

The Farmers Holiday movement has been regarded by some as a complete failure, and its original objective of cost-of-production pricing was quickly obscured by the violence and turmoil. The movement nevertheless awakened the public to the pressing economic distress of farmers.

Mass protests of farmers against foreclosure sales also brought current economic issues into sharp focus. More farmers were involved in antiforeclosure activity than in any other form of protest in the 1930's. Crowds of from 100 to 2,000 insurgent farmers gathered to block foreclosure sales. These "spontaneous" gatherings, not led by any organized group, dotted the farmbelt. Some were so-called "penny auctions," where the mob forced the property to be sold for a nominal amount so that it could be returned to the former owner (Shover, 1965, pp. 77–81).

The exact impact of the farmer insurgence in the 1930's is difficult to judge, but the proven ability of farmers to use strong measures in pursuit of pressing needs undoubtedly influenced politicians and was a factor in subsequent legislation to relieve the acute economic distress brought on by depression.

NATIONAL FARMERS ORGANIZATION

The farm economic picture was less than dark in 1955. The parity ratio (the ratio of prices received to prices paid by farmers) was 58 (1910–1914 = 100) in 1932 when the Holiday movement occurred; it was 84 in 1955. Nonetheless, prices and incomes were low in a relative, more recent perspective. The parity ratio as recently as 1951 had been 107. Net farm income fell from $14.8 billion in 1951 to $11.2 billion in 1955. But, most important, the price of hogs had dropped from $23.11 a hundredweight in 1953 to $13.10 a hundredweight in 1955. And hogs were very important to farmers in the corn belt where the new movement was to be centered. Thus it was hogs and relative farm recession rather than depression that moved farmers to protest. Drought in southern Iowa and debts accumulated since World War II also played a part.

The National Farmers Organization "started from wonderings aloud between a farmer and feed salesman in an Iowa farmyard one day in the late summer of 1955" (Brandsberg, 1964, p. 4). The feed salesman, Jay Loghry, was the initial leader of a subsequent meeting of 35 farmers at Carl in southwest

Iowa. A week later a meeting was held at Corning, Iowa, and 1,200 attended. The initial aim was to "unionize" farmers, but the term "union" received a very negative response, and the group took the name of National Farmers Organization (NFO) in September 1955. The NFO's only employee was Loghry, and its unpaid adviser was Dan Turner, former Iowa governor, who had called out the state militia to quell violence during the Farmers Holiday movement. Turner, on the basis of his forty years of experience, advised the NFO that they would not achieve their economic goals through strikes and violence but only through action by the U.S. Congress. Though Turner was a charismatic leader and attracted a large membership, the organization later acted entirely out of keeping with his advice.

The first national convention of the National Farmers Organization met at Corning, Iowa (national headquarters) in December 1955 with 750 in attendance. Oren Lee Staley was elected president. The organization listed 55,659 members after only three months of existence. In April 1956, the organization reported 140,000 members (Brandsberg, 1964, p. 70).

The NFO, like the Farmers Holiday Association before it, first sought help in Washington to alleviate economic problems. When visits to Washington and attempts to elect members to Congress failed, the 1957 NFO convention looked to collective bargaining as a more persuasive solution.

Trial "testing" actions—small-scale holding actions of limited duration—were begun in 1959. Another was held in 1960. A final test holding action was held in 1961 with encouraging results.

Some 13,000 members attended a 1961 meeting, and 20,000 attended a 1962 meeting in Des Moines in preparation for the all-out livestock holding action planned for 1962. The action was slated to begin September 1, 1962. Possibly in anticipation of the action, farmers flooded the market, and on the Friday before Labor Day, Midwestern stockyards received the heaviest flow of cattle in fourteen years. Prices, however, did not fall, and the price for prime cattle in Chicago reached $32.50 a hundredweight, the highest it had been since April 1962 (Schlebecker, 1965, p. 208). This was evidence that processors were trying to break the strike.

Initial success of the strike which began after the Labor Day weekend was startling. By September 6, 1962, interior livestock market receipts had fallen 50 to 75 per cent. Livestock market prices rose. Approximately 600 packinghouse workers were laid off by September 7 in Iowa alone (Schlebecker, 1965, p. 208).

Reports of violence soon appeared. Farmers said rifle shots were fired at trucks hauling livestock to market. Tires were slashed. Nails were spread on highways.

NFO membership is secret, but one estimate placed membership at 180,000 or more farm families in the early 1960's (Tontz, 1964, p. 146), too few to have much impact on markets, but the holding in 1962 was supported by a great many nonmembers. Furthermore, it was commonly believed that NFO members had smaller than average farm units. One investigation found that on the average NFO members were better educated and had larger farms than Farm Bureau members (cf. Schlebecker, 1965, p. 212). The membership fee of $25 discouraged very small farmers from joining.

Enthusiasm began to wane in the second week of holding. Nonmembers were the first to sell. In terminal markets for the week ending September 15, cattle and calf receipts were 235,464 compared with 176,048 the week before and 231,658 for a like week a year earlier (Brandsberg, 1964, p. 115). Hog receipts numbered 155,000 during the first week of the strike and 265,000 the second week at Iowa and southern Minnesota markets.

Meanwhile NFO members continued to man their checking stations at crossroads and markets. Considerable peaceful picketing was carried on in stockyards. Oren Staley continued to use his persuasive oratorical powers to maintain member morale. But some members began to sell their livestock. In the fourth week, leaders considered having dairy farmers enter the holding action. The momentum of the strike had been lost, however, and on October 2, the drive was "recessed," with a promise to resume it at a moment's notice. It was not resumed. The action had failed in its goal to sign contracts with enough processors to assure farmers of a market at adequate prices. Nevertheless Staley stated that it was a "breakthrough, the starting to sign contracts with processors . . . because this is the first time that farmers had contracts signed that would determine future price levels" (Brandsberg, 1964, p. 132). Little is known of what contracts were signed with meat packers. The effect on prices and incomes has been insignificant.

The NFO in 1963 turned its attention to collective dairy bargaining. Contracts were signed with some creameries to deliver milk. This was a considerably easier operation than with livestock because the market was localized. The processors were cooperatives with some NFO members and sympathizers on the board of directors, and the numerous dairy processors and producers were already accustomed to operating under federal milk marketing orders. At Annandale, Minnesota, after a creamery had signed a contract with NFO, the dairy processor to whom the creamery delivered its skim milk would not accept any more skim milk unless the creamery legally terminated its contract with NFO. The result was a gathering of 2,000 farmers at which some 40,000 gallons of milk were dumped in the ditch in March 1963.

Subsequent minor holding actions in soybeans, grains, and livestock came and went with little impact on prices or the economy.

The National Farmers Organization was nonpartisan in its politics from the beginning. Nevertheless it had been formed partially as a protest against the policies of Republican Secretary of Agriculture Benson. The NFO received Benson's successor, Secretary Freeman, with much fanfare at one of its meetings and was clearly closer to the Democratic Party than the Republican Party in its philosophy. The term "labor union" was anathema to many Midwest farmers, but the NFO received early inspiration and even some financial support from labor unions. The Farmers Union was clearly in sympathy with the NFO, and an attempt was made to merge the two organizations in Iowa.

Opponents of the NFO included the processors and food chains, the Farm Bureau, the National Livestock Feeders Association, and the American National Cattlemen's Association (cf. Brandsberg, 1964, pp. 224–236). This created some ambivalence among farmers, since numerous farmers were members of both the Farm Bureau and NFO. It cannot be said that the groups mentioned above caused the failure of the holding actions. It was rather the resource and market structure of agriculture that wrecked bargaining attempts. Perhaps the strong measures taken by Secretary Freeman and the Congress to control production and maintain prices were a telling blow, because these measures redirected the attention of the farmers to Washington for alleviating the farm problem in the early 1960's.

The NFO in March and April of 1967, with a reported quarter of a million membership, showed renewed vigor in a twenty-five-state holding action to raise the price received by farmers for milk from 10 to 12 cents per quart. Although thousands of gallons of milk were poured on the ground and the farmers materially reduced the flow of milk to markets, the holding action had less effect on the market than anticipated. A serious shortage of milk was averted by diverting milk formerly used to produce cheese and butter to the fluid milk market. The movement seemed destined for complete failure, but in April the strike was given new impetus when two labor unions, the meat cutters and teamsters, agreed to honor the NFO picket lines in Nashville, Tennessee. The action was so effective that the milk supply was cut off for all but emergency uses. It is interesting to note that the turn of events was made possible by a union group which the NFO had in its earlier days so thoroughly rejected. The holding action, even before it was joined by labor unions, was successful in obtaining contracts which satisfied price demands from processors in some localities. Nevertheless, the NFO had not come to grips with the long-term problem of how to avoid excess supply in a market stimulated by prices above the equilibrium level.

SUMMARY AND CONCLUSIONS

Students of farm policy may remember only the National Farmers Organization holding actions of the 1960's. Yet American history is filled with unsuccessful holding actions of farmers to obtain better prices. American history is replete with legislative measures to control production and improve economic conditions for farmers. This chapter evokes a raft of clichés: "There is nothing new under the sun; history repeats itself; those who do not learn from history are destined to repeat its mistakes."

History teaches that farmers have not always conformed to the basically docile, democratic image of the premachine agrarian creed set forth in Chapter 1. The process of commercialization was unsettling. Neither farmers nor the public understood the exigencies of economic development. They reacted against real and imagined ills that a more enlightened educational and legislative process might have avoided.

Despite the fact that farmers constituted the largest single industry in society, the nation was never in jeopardy from farm insurrection. The fact that only a small percentage of farmers at any one time was engaged in protest supports the fact that the goals and values of farmers presented in Chapter 1 were not totally unrealistic.

A characteristic pattern of each protest movement is apparent: Low farm prices and growing feelings among farmers that they were exploited by nonfarm groups helped create a new organization or commandeer an established one to deal with the issues. The movement was likely to be led by a nonfarmer—a feed dealer, newspaperman, Department of Agriculture employee, Socialist Party organizer, or former grain exchange worker. Formation of cooperative businesses and other efforts to increase efficiency of farming were attempted, but impatience led to seeking legislation as the quickest form of redress for wrongs. When legislative attempts failed, the entire organization including its business interest was stifled and the demise of the organization was as rapid, if not as dramatic, as its rise.

The protest movement has been confined mostly to the major cash crops and dairy and has been in commercial farming areas, primarily the Midwest. Farmers formed marketing organizations to reduce the bite of market middlemen, they formed farm supply cooperatives to reduce costs of inputs, and they sought legislative redress for alleged failure of the economic system. They had a basic faith in the market mechanism, but they sensed a conspiracy against them. In their view it was the bureaucrat and monopolist who had distorted the market rather than the failure of the basic price system and free market structure that was to blame for economic ills.

With increasing economic education and experience, farmers are becoming more sophisticated in dealing with their problems. Since 1961 government programs have demonstrated that supply can be controlled. In certain commodities, cohesive, cooperative organizations of farmers themselves have demonstrated that they can create orderly marketing arrangements and eliminate disastrous supply imbalances and economic chaos. Efforts to extend this system to major crops and livestock have failed in the past. But history is sometimes an erroneous guide. Failure of farm organizations to control production and stabilize markets in the past need not preclude success in the future. Conditions are changing rapidly: increased specialization, fewer farms, larger operations, and increased sophistication of farmers in economic matters continually enhance the probability of future success in attempts of farm groups to run their own programs.

Farmers have found it difficult to form effective organizations to control production for several reasons. First, the atomistic, widely dispersed structure of farming makes it difficult to coordinate activities. Farm products are perishable and, unlike factory labor, either accumulate or deteriorate during a strike. The more effective a holding action is in raising prices, the greater the encouragement for farmers to not participate and to sell their products during the strike. Processors who enter into contracts to take only the products of contracting farmers at prices above the market face a reduction in profits and possible bankruptcy. Contracting processors usually must sell on the same market as firms securing raw materials at lower prices.

Organizations have learned certain lessons. One is that cooperatives are more successful in prosperous times than in depressed times. And legislation has more appeal in depressed times than in prosperous times. Thus, a wise organization will not dissipate its energies in a blaze of politics in good times nor will it seek to solve problems of farm distress with cooperative and other business activities in economically depressed times. A durable farm organization must have as its foundation solid, efficiently managed business enterprises to provide services the farmers demand, whatever the economic and political climate.

A commonly held view is that farmers organizations are most successful when farmers experience distressed economic conditions. This seems to be true for the nineteenth century, but it does not hold in the twentieth. While new organizations may be likely to form as protest movements, the established organizations depend for membership on the success of insurance and other business operations. These succeed best and farmers find membership dues easiest to pay in prosperous times. Membership in the Farm Bureau increased from 440,000 families in 1940 to 1,450,000 families in 1950, a period of unprecedented farm prosperity.

Interestingly enough, the National Farmers Organization movement was not viewed as a protest by all writers in retrospect. It was viewed by one historian as a "carefully planned long ranged effort to change the economic power structure," and it brought a theory that "hope of greater prosperity seemed to motivate farmers to protest, although farmers tend to remain fairly quiet if all is well, or if all is perfectly terrible" (Schlebecker, 1965, pp. 204, 206). Holding actions and other farm protest movements are indeed a tired solution to farmers' economic ills. No one has cried much over the spilled milk, but tired solutions are not dead solutions, and farmers caught between rising input costs, sagging market prices, and an unresponsive government are likely in the future to find market bargaining power a more successful aid to the solution of their problems.

REFERENCES

Benedict, Murray R. 1953. *Farm Policies of the United States, 1790–1950*. New York: Twentieth Century Fund.

Brandsberg, George. 1964. *The Two Sides in NFO's Battle*. Ames: Iowa State University Press.

Breimyer, Harold F. 1965. *Individual Freedom and the Economic Organization of Agriculture*. Urbana: University of Illinois Press.

Davis, Lance E., J. R. T. Hughes, and D. M. McDougall. 1965. *American Economic History*. Homewood, Ill., Irwin.

Fite, Gilbert C. 1954. *George N. Peek and the Fight for Farm Parity*. Norman: University of Oklahoma Press.

Hadwiger, Don F., and Ross B. Talbot. 1965. *Pressures and Protests*. San Francisco: Chandler.

McCune, Wesley. 1943. *The Farm Bloc*. Garden City, N.Y.: Doubleday, Doran.

————. 1956. *Who's Behind our Farm Policy?* New York: Praeger.

Schlebecker, John T. 1965. The great holding action: the NFO in September, 1962. *Agricultural History* 39:204–13.

Shover, John L. 1965. *Cornbelt Rebellion*. Urbana: University of Illinois Press.

Taylor, Carl C. 1953. *The Farmer's Movement*. New York: American Book Co.

Tontz, Robert L. 1964. Membership of general farmers' organizations, United States, 1874–1960. *Agricultural History* 38:143–56.

U.S. Department of Agriculture. 1966. *Agricultural Statistics*. Washington: U.S. Government Printing Office.

CHAPTER FOUR

Economic History of American Agriculture: Attitudes, Institutions, and Technology

Farm policy deals with how farmers affect and are affected by government legislation. This chapter and the next describe how institutions, many created by government, have generated the economic environment in which farmers now live. The current economic environment and current policies to deal with farm problems also have deep roots in the technology and attitudes of earlier decades. It is informative to study the economic history of agriculture to learn how attitudes, institutions, and technologies have led to economic growth and to the economic structure of farming today. The dynamic context of the past contributes much to understanding and interpreting the foundations of present farm policies.

The economic history of American agriculture is a success story of resources, attitudes, organizations, institutions, and technologies interacting to generate economic progress, highlighted, in early years, by the innovative genius of a few mechanics and the organizational genius of a few commercial and industrial magnates. In more recent years the accent has been on team effort in science, education, research, and industry. It is a story of capital accumulation and productivity, and thus of economic growth. Ultimately it is the ironic drama of an economic sector submerged by its own success.

The economic history of U.S. agriculture is inseparable from the economic history of the nation. Hence in this and the following chapter, there are considerable data on what happened outside of agriculture.

This chapter outlines the major attitudes and institutions that led to the development of commercial agriculture. The following chapter will discuss more formal estimates of the contributions of certain of these factors to farm productivity and to national economic growth. As stated above, one purpose of these two chapters is to establish an understanding of the economic forces that brought agriculture to its current economic position with all the promise and problems thereof. Another purpose is to depict a case study in agriculture for developing nations which wish to profit from our experience—from our mistakes and successes.

Three important factors are needed in a nation for economic growth: a marked propensity to save; a marked propensity to invest; and favorable output-input ratios—which includes not only investing funds where marginal returns are highest but also the efficient use of technology. Even more basic elements underlie the above three factors: (*a*) natural resources; (*b*) the attitudes of the population; (*c*) institutions, including government, schools, tenure arrangements, land policies, etc.; (*d*) world conditions, including demand for exports; and (*e*) technological change, including inventions, innovations, and scientific effort.

The United States is endowed with a satisfactory climate and an abundance of natural resources, including coal, iron ore, oil, wood, and soil. Despite this abundance of resources, the country provided a bare subsistence living for the 3 million Indians living in the country when the first white colonists arrived. Most of the resources that now provide high standards of living for more than 200 million Americans clearly had limited meaning to the American Indian, and the abundance of natural resources is inadequate alone to explain economic growth. The attitudes of the people and the characteristics of the institutions that regulate and coordinate activity are important. These in turn are related to inventions and innovations. All are interacting factors that help to explain economic progress.

ATTITUDES

The desire to "make two blades of grass grow where one grew before" (the enterprise creed) and the creed of self-integrity discussed in Chapter 1 were attitudes conducive to economic growth, although they are the grounds for serious value-conflicts in an affluent society possessing excess farm production capacity. Of the fundamental components of economic progress, the role of attitudes has been least understood and articulated by economists. This neglect arises because economists are not adequately trained in the subject, and because attitudes have not been regarded as instrumental variables capable of changing through public policy. If the following discussion of attitudes appears over-extended, it stems from an attempt to compensate partially for serious past shortcomings.

A set of values considered consistent with economic development in America has sometimes been formalized as the Protestant Ethic. To provide a background for later discussion of the Protestant Ethic, and to gain further insight into what underlies economic development and mobility of resources, it is useful to specify certain "ideal" attitudes that, while never fully present in individuals, do serve as a standard of comparison (cf. Tweeten, 1966).

IDEAL ATTITUDES FOR ECONOMIC GROWTH

Given the natural resources, the propensities to save, invest, and be efficient will be high and economic growth most rapid in an area possessing social-psychological characteristics of secular asceticism and functional activism.

Secular ascetism characterizes a populace that is committed to work, either as an end in itself or as the recognized means to an end such as status or material gain. In addition to the shunning of leisure, the ideal encompasses honesty, thrift, market morality, and a drive to accumulate economic goods but with a willingness to defer gratification therefrom to the future. It is apparent that this quality contributes to a high rate of savings and the work efficiency associated with a dedicated, conscientious, disciplined labor force.

Functional activism characterizes a populace that is imaginative, innovative, perspicacious, manipulative, farsighted, mobile, organizationally capable, and willing to take reasonable risks in the use of current assets for future gain. The concept entails the spirit of entrepreneurial zeal but does not stop there. It has several dimensions and applies to public as well as to private enterprise. It is the dynamic quality that gives rise to investment and influences efficiency through development of new opportunities by formal means (e.g., research) and informal means (e.g., individual ideas).

Functional activism can be present in a government agency that seeks new approaches to solve problems and that finds more efficient means of operation. The attitude is present in individuals who seek more remunerative employment and who are efficient "entrepreneurs" of their own manual labor and technical skills. It is entailed in migration decisions. It is also found in "information" entrepreneurs—knowledge brokers who, as individuals, actively contribute to formal and informal information systems that lead to optimum labor and capital allocation.

Functional activism underlies efforts to seek out profitable uses of funds for investment and employment of capital in whatever uses offer greatest returns. It encompasses the need for achievement reflected in the active, functional decisions —both conscious and subconscious—that lead to economic growth. For economic growth, it is important that functional activism be focused on activity that will contribute to economic growth and that it not be dissipated on efforts to "beat" the institutional system.

A certain degree of secular asceticism is necessary for long-term persistence and willingness to forgo current consumption and "save" for an adequate education, but a spirit of functional activism is needed to channel the education into a curriculum that will have a subsequent economic productivity and to subsequently find a position that productively utilizes the investment in education. Thus functional activism is important for education and mobility—two factors of crucial concern especially for low-income rural areas.

The presence of the two concepts of secular asceticism and functional activism underlie the propensities to save, invest, and be efficient; hence they are basic to economic growth. Some degree of secular asceticism within a region is a necessary condition for growth. Functional activism is a necessary condition but need not be strong in a region—it can come from outside—but, if a region is declining and resource mobility is needed, a considerable degree of functional activism must be present to have labor mobility, each person investing his resources in uses where returns are highest.

These two attitudes can be ascribed to individuals or to a collective such as a community. Individuals or communities can rank high in one or both or in neither of the characteristics. A reasonable hypothesis is that the psychological makeup of individuals is such that the two attitudes tend to conflict.

There has been comparatively little scientific analysis of the role of attitudes in American economic growth. The study of the need for achievement (*n* Achievement) is perhaps the closest to any objective analysis available of functional activism. Considerable previous intellectual effort has gone into analysis of the Protestant Ethic, an "attitude" that has many attributes of secular asceticism. Both *n* Achievement and the Protestant Ethic are discussed below.

n ACHIEVEMENT

David McClelland (1961) and his associates examined representative children's stories from numerous countries. The *n* Achievement score was determined by the number of achievement images in these stories. The hypothesis was that a high motivation for achievement in children's stories reflected a high concern for achievement in the society. This preoccupation with achievement would be imparted to the new generation, which would in turn strive for economic success. The success would be apparent in subsequent economic growth rates. The following quote summarizes the findings:

> A concern for achievement as expressed in imaginative literature—folk tales and stories for children—is associated in modern times with a more rapid rate of economic development. The generalization is confirmed not only for Western, free-enterprise democracies like England and the United States but also for Communist countries like Russia, Bulgaria and Hungary, or primitive tribes that are just beginning to make contact with modern technological society. It holds in the main whether a country is developed or underdeveloped, poor or rich, industrial or agricultural, free or totalitarian. In other words there is a

strong suggestion here that men with high achievement motives will find a way to economic achievement given fairly wide variations in opportunity and social structure. What people want, they somehow manage to get, in the main and on the average, though other factors can modify the speed with which they get it.

The results serve to direct our attention as social scientists away from an exclusive concern with the external events in history to the "internal" psychological concerns that in the long run determine what happens in history. [McClelland, 1961, p. 105]

THE PROTESTANT ETHIC

A set of attitudes prominent in eighteenth- and nineteenth-century America has been called the Protestant Ethic. It is examined below for elements that may have created a climate favorable for economic growth. While the Protestant Ethic had its origins in the Protestant Reformation, it should not be viewed as sectarian.

The church is important in creating a climate that influences man's outlook toward his environment and carries over into economic activity. If "the reigning universal of religion assigned to man a predetermined future, an immutable destiny of a judgment by forces superior to him and strong enough to hold him in its chains . . . how could there be a theory of growth other than that already written into the stars?" (Swanson, 1965, p. 60).

The Reformation brought with it several changes important for economic growth. One was the concept of the "Priesthood of all Believers." The result was increased dignity of the common man who no longer was under the authority of a mediator between God and man. Each man had equal access to the means of Grace and the Word. Emphasis on individualistic interpretation of the Bible and on democracy in church affairs undoubtedly contributed to the growing individuality for secular man and carried into a commitment to democracy in government. This ethic in turn has contributed to stability in governments of Protestant countries—a very important part of the environment for economic growth.

This emphasis on individualism and democracy in church affairs was in contrast to the paternal and hierarchical system of the medieval church. It is not surprising that the Protestant tradition found itself highly compatible with capitalism (which appeared before the Reformation) and adaptable to the "liberal" economic philosophy that society owes to each man only the equivalent of his contribution, and equal access to the means of production. W. Arthur Lewis (1957, p. 54) states: "Early medieval theologians thought that the merchant's calling was virtually incompatible with the Christian life, and were even more certain of the sinfulness of moneylending." Max Weber contends that the principal contribution of the Reformation was the new view of a man's calling that turned the religious asceticism of the Catholic church outward into a worldly asceticism that became a powerful force behind the spirit of capitalism.

A mark of status in the medieval period was freedom from work. Dependence on work for livelihood was unequivocal evidence that a person lacked the qualities of mind and character that entitled him to a higher, leisurely, and noble position. "The effect of the Reformation as such was only that . . . the moral emphasis on, and the religious sanction of, organized worldly labour in a calling was mightily increased" (Weber, 1930, p. 83).

Regarding the concept of a calling:

> It is an obligation which the individual is supposed to feel and does feel towards the content of his professional activity, no matter in what it consists, in particular no matter whether it appears on the surface as a utilization of his personal powers, or only of his material possessions.
>
> .   .   .   .   .   .
>
> But at least one thing was unquestionably new: the valuation of the fulfillment of duty in worldly affairs as the highest form which the moral activity of the individual could assume. This it was which inevitably gave the everyday worldly activity a religious significance, and which first created the conception of a calling in this sense. [Weber, 1930, pp. 54, 80]

The Protestant Ethic is most closely associated with the Calvinist sects. The doctrine of Predestination embodied the concept of the Elect, those who are predestined to Salvation. These chosen of God felt a compulsion to reassure themselves and the society of their calling by continuous excellence in worldly affairs.

> When the limitation of consumption is combined with this release of acquisitive activity, the inevitable practical result is obvious: accumulation of capital through ascetic compulsion to save. The restraints which were imposed upon the consumption of wealth naturally served to increase it by making possible the productive investment of capital. [Weber, 1930, p. 172]

There is little doubt that the Protestant Ethic, reflected primarily in the less traditional and less ritual-oriented Calvinism, contributed to the secular asceticism and functional activism that stimulated the Industrial Revolution in England and America. But the exact role of religion is not so clear. In my opinion, it was not until the strict conformity exemplified by Puritanism had begun to disappear that the strong spirit of enterprise emerged. Authoritarianism, not democracy, characterized the Pilgrim leaders. But no systematic succession of ecclesiastic leadership was established, and democratic procedures soon emerged and prevailed in the church.

The stringent puritanical moral requirement and disciplined activity of the early Calvinist groups certainly met the growth requirement of thrift, honesty, and accumulation (secular asceticism). Business activity was one of the few outlets sanctioned by pietistic society for the energies of individuals who wished to be creative and gamble. Tawney (1926, pp. 6–9) reports that the concept of *just price* was prominent among the Puritans and that sanctions against usury and "unfair" pricing were severe. However, the required conformity was initially too great for functional activism. It was not until rationalizing influences of secularization gave members the freedom and the will to exhibit the second ingredient of growth—functional activism—that economic progress was apparent. The Puritan tradition was strongest in America before 1750. The Industrial Revolution came a century later. Ultimately it was flexibility rather than rigidity that was the redeeming quality of Puritanism for economic progress. The dogmatic church was unable to withstand the rationalizing, secularizing forces of income accumulation.

The process of secularization brought entrepreneurship without the loss of secular asceticism. The result was a capitalistic drive among the Puritan New England and Middle Atlantic Quaker elements that gradually played a major role in the U.S. economy and was even conspicuous in Southern commerce and industry. The northeastern U.S., because of its strategic position in geography, culture, and education exerted a strong influence on the attitudes of farmers and other groups throughout all U.S. areas except the Southern states. Boston was the financial capital of the country until it was superseded by New York City about 1850.

The Reformation and attendant Protestant Ethic is useful to explain economic growth in certain areas of the world, but today is more useful as a frame of reference than as an instrumental variable for inducing economic growth. Several stages and many decades are required to transform human values to those conducive to economic growth. The initial period emphasizing evangelism, other worldly goals, forbearance of worldly pleasures, and conformity to a rigid moral code contribute to secular asceticism but not to functional activism. Accumulation is slow but gradually reaches a point where it begins to undermine religious zeal. Increasing secularization and rationalization combined with carry-over of secular asceticism set the stage for the strong entrepreneurial spirit of enterprise that gave the Protestant Ethic its true dynamic properties.

The dignity of labor, the "sin" of leisure, and the virtues of high morals are impressed upon the populace by propaganda in Russia and China with a ubiquity, not to mention fervor, unequaled by our Puritan forefathers. It is no accident that these characteristics of secular asceticism are consistent with economic growth. Communism is explained partially as a revolt against the institutional impediments to growth. It also is a means to foster secular asceticism through a heavy propaganda effort that extols the virtues of hard work and honesty. It also circumvents the problem of low propensities to save and invest by institutionalizing the function in collective farms and confiscating earnings to force savings. Functional activism is thereby bureaucratized but perhaps reduced to levels below those possible in a capitalist economy.

Attitudes conducive to growth seem to have been fostered in Taiwan by the influx of mainland Chinese in the late 1940's and by the earlier Japanese occupation. Attitudes also played a role in the impressive economic growth of Japan. According to Johnston (1966, p. 265), "the influence of Japan's Confucian tradition and other socio-cultural factors" were, for economic growth in Japan, "a 'substitution' or a 'functional equivalent' of—the role of the 'Protestant Ethic' in western Europe as stressed by Weber and Tawney." Many Catholic elements in the U.S. provide more evidence of possessing the Protestant Ethic than do Protestant groups.[1] Thus the Protestant Ethic may be viewed as a particular brand of secular asceticism and functional activism that was widely shared among Americans of various faiths in the eighteenth and nineteenth centuries. And although it may be argued that some degree of secular asceticism and functional activism is essential to initiate sustained growth, the specific forms of these as found in the Protestant Ethic are by no means a requirement.

In early stages of economic growth in a free society, attitudes are important because savings must primarily be the result of individual decisions. As the economy grows, savings come easier as earnings rise above subsistence requirements. Also institutional "internal" investment of the government and corporations come to replace individual savings as a major source of capital accumulation.

GOVERNMENT

In the United States the federal government provided a favorable environment for investment. The government was strong enough to maintain order and avoid dissipation of resources in wars and internal conflicts. There are notable exceptions, such as the Civil War, but the outcome of that war was the reaffirmation of federal superiority. Social and political stability was enhanced by the ability of the masses to identify with the democratic government.

States were not allowed to erect barriers to interstate commerce. The maintenance of law and order created an environment in which contracts could be enforced and long-term expectations for business activity could be formulated with some degree of confidence and usefulness. Laws established rules of business conduct that permitted industry and commerce to function with reasonable efficiency.

1. Father Speltz (1963, p. 38) provides a Catholic position on farming that has the true ring of the Protestant Ethic. Contemporary studies in the United States show that motivation for achievement is as high among Catholic as among Protestant elements (McClelland, 1961). Comparative achievement is also indicated in another study which shows that the proportion of Catholic students who go to graduate schools is higher than that of Protestant students (Greeley, 1965, p. 60).

Yet government was neither very large nor expensive. It had a *laissez-faire* orientation prior to the 1930's and concentrated on establishing rules of the game and creating infrastructure rather than on operating costly welfare programs at a time when the nation could not easily afford these. Many of the faults of social injustice and inequities of income that arose thereby were erased or at least reduced in significance by a high rate of economic growth and opportunity.

LAND POLICIES

Land policies in colonial times varied considerably from colony to colony. Abundance of land led to distribution of land at a nominal fee to settlers. To encourage immigration and settlement, it was not uncommon to grant 50 acres to a settler who came at his own expense, plus 50 additional acres if he brought another settler along.

There was little attempt to establish a feudal system in the northern colonies. The need to raise capital to finance government operations, coupled with an aversion for the British nobility, partly explained why the government did not deed the public domain to a few persons of the political and commercial aristocracy.

Some writers attribute the policies that characterize the family farm to Jefferson and his deep faith in the independent husbandman. In fact, the origins of the family farm predate Jefferson. It is difficult to overemphasize the importance of the method of disposing of the public domain, because it eventually led to the current family farm structure. Institutions of primogeniture (the right of the oldest son to inherit the land) and entail (the system of disposing of land in one piece) were common in eighteenth-century America but did not last long after the Revolution (Krooss, 1966, p. 74).

Of the 2 billion acres that now comprise the continental United States, the federal government at one time or another owned 1.4 billion acres, or 70 per cent (Krooss, 1966, p. 74). Disposition of lands offered the government a sizable opportunity for profit. For example, the land in the great Louisiana Purchase of 1803 was acquired for only 3 cents per acre.

An act of the Continental Congress in 1780 provided for the sale of lands and the creation of new states. The states had considerable surplus lands (despite the fact that states such as Virginia and New York ceded large western claims to the federal government) until after the War of 1812. Federal lands became attractive with the decline of state lands and with the "subjugation" of the Indians and the opening of the Cumberland Road.

LAND LEGISLATION

Some historians ascribe to Jefferson the idea of selling public lands in small tracts at low prices to encourage an equalitarian, agrarian society (cf. Benedict, 1953, p. 5). Other writers say that Hamilton and Gallatin also favored selling land in small parcels at low prices (Krooss, 1966, p. 76). An act of the Continental Congress in 1780, passed while Jefferson was away as Ambassador to France, had a flavor that was more "New England" than Jeffersonian. The act, providing for the sale of land and the creation of new states, was soon succeeded by the Ordinance of 1785, which specified conditions of land sale, and by the Ordinance of 1787, which specified the terms under which new states could be created. Congress chose to sell in quite large tracts. Under the Ordinance of 1785, the government divided the land by survey into townships (Table 4.1). Each township was six miles square and contained 36 sections of one square mile each (640 acres). The township received one section—section 16 (after 1848, section 36 also)—as an endowment for education. Except for certain sections retained by the government, the remainder of the land was to be sold at auction in units of 640 acres for not less than $1.00 per acre.

TABLE 4.1. Terms of Sale under Various U.S. Land Acts

Year	Price per Acre	Terms	Minimum Purchase (acres)
1785	$1.00	Specie, loan-office or debt certificates	640
1796	$2.00	One-half down, one-half due in one year	640
1800	$2.00	One quarter cash; remainder to be paid in three annual installments	160
1820	$1.25	Cash	80
1832	$1.25	Cash	40
1841	$1.25	Squatters who built home and improved land could purchase one quarter section before it was offered for public sale	160
1855	$1.00 12½¢	Land not sold for 10 years offered at $1 per acre; if not sold for 30 years, 12½¢ per acre	40–320
1862	$10.00 (filing fee)	Title could be obtained after 5 years' residence	160
1873		Timber Culture Act granted 160 acres to settlers if they would plant trees on 40 acres (later reduced to 10 acres)	160
1877		Under Desert Land Act, a settler could acquire land if he irrigated it within 3 years (acreage amended to 160 acres in 1890, to 80 acres in 1891)	640
1878		Timber and Stone Act provided for sale of 160 acres at a minimum price of $2.50 per acre (more important for timber interests than farmers)	160
1909		Enlarged Homestead Act, with features similar to original act (1862), except acreage expanded	320
1912		Residence requirement reduced from 5 to 3 years	320

SOURCES: Bolino (1966, p. 101) and Benedict (1953, pp. 3–22, 112 ff.).

Sale of large units for cash precluded most small farmers from buying land directly, and speculators did a brisk business, buying large tracts from the government, dividing the tracts, and reselling the land to farm operators. The Land Act of 1796 again required purchases of large 640-acre units but raised the minimum price to $2.00 per acre and lowered the payment to one-half down, the balance a year later. Since the states were offering land at rates of only 6 to 25 cents per acre, the federal government by 1812 had sold only 3.5 million acres for $7 million (Krooss, 1966, p. 76).

The South and the East initially favored the charging of high prices for the public domain in order to slow settlement, inhibit migration out of the East, and raise revenue. The Western interests gradually prevailed, and the land price and minimum acreage were reduced. Also the rights to land of preemptors (squatters who settled on the land before legal approval was obtained) were increasingly recognized. A major landmark in public land policy was the Homestead Act of 1862. A settler, after paying a registration fee of $10–25 and residing on and working 160 acres of land for five years, would gain clear title to the land. Or he could reside on the land for only six months and gain title to the land for $1.25 per acre.

Several land acts were passed after 1862, many of them designed to make settlement of large farms possible in the arid Great Plains and western mountain areas (Table 4.1).

Between 1868 and 1879, 70 million acres of public land were disposed of through the Homestead Act. From 1898 to 1917, total public land disposal was 100 million acres. In 1935 all federal lands were withdrawn from settlement, but an executive order of the President in 1946 reversed the edict and homesteading was restored, though there was little public land suitable for settlement.

Altogether, the government sold 255 million acres of public lands for cash and gave 256 million acres to individuals, 248 million acres to states, 131 million acres to railroads, and 68 million acres to veterans (Krooss, 1966, p. 82). In 1964, 771 million acres remained in the public domain, and were used for grazing, park, forest, military, and wildlife purposes.

The measures to dispose of the public lands have been criticized for failing to produce much revenue, for encouraging soil exploitation and speculation, and for creating uneconomic-size farms. It was said that the majority of settlers intended to settle, sell, and make a quick profit rather than cultivate the soil permanently. More land was preempted (sold before the five-year residence requirement was met) under the Homestead Act than was given away, and most of the preemption was by speculators. Shannon (1945, pp. 51–75) emphasizes that tenants and hired laborers in agricultural areas of the East could not afford the equipment, livestock, and moving expenses required to homestead in the Midwest and the Great Plains.

Despite these criticisms, government land policies did provide considerable ease of entry and a safety valve for the discontented, who might have caused political and social problems had their energies and talents not been absorbed in the westward scramble. Public policies did make use of an abundant resource—land—to encourage development of transportation and education. The settlement pattern was perhaps as orderly as could be hoped for under the pressure and pace of the westward move. And policies did contribute to a vastly expanded output of farm products to export and to feed a growing domestic urban-industrial sector, which in turn provided capital inputs to improve the productivity of farms.

CONSERVATION OF RESOURCES

The extensive frontier had vanished by 1890 and people began to be concerned about conservation of land resources. The record of exploitation of land and timber in America had no parallel. Undoubtedly much of the "exploitation" was a truly appropriate economic use of abundant resources, but measures to protect land and forests vulnerable to misuse were clearly overdue.

Efforts to establish timberland reserves by President Cleveland and later Presidents were inadequate because of an attitude in Congress represented by Speaker of the House Joseph Cannon's alleged remark, "Why should I do anything for posterity; what has posterity done for me?"

Under the Forest Reserve Act of 1891, Presidents Harrison, McKinley, and Cleveland set aside 47 million acres of forest lands for conservation. The great impetus and leadership for the conservation movement came from President Theodore Roosevelt, who had set aside an additional 125 million acres of forest reserve land by the time he left office (Benedict, 1953, p. 123). Under Roosevelt, many thousand acres of land were reserved for public use as coal lands, phosphate lands, and possible waterpower sites.

During the Administration of Theodore Roosevelt, efforts were made to expand irrigation under public auspices through the Carey Act and the Newlands Reclamation Act of 1902. Under the latter act, giant irrigation projects were initiated and eventually supplied by water from the Roosevelt and Hoover Dams in Arizona, the Grand Coulee and Bonneville Dams in the Northwest, and the Shasta and Friant Dams in California.

Numerous individuals dramatized the serious menace of soil erosion, and under the conservation-conscious President Franklin Roosevelt, the nation was ready for further conservation programs. The Soil Erosion Service was established in 1933 in the Department of the Interior. Numerous Civilian Conservation Corps (CCC) camps were established and operated by the Service. A large number of demonstration projects were established, hundreds of thousands of small check dams were constructed, vegetation was planted on eroded hillsides, firebreaks were opened, and roads were constructed (Benedict, 1953, p. 318).

In 1935 the Soil Erosion Service was transferred to the U.S. Department of Agriculture and became the Soil Conservation Service (SCS). About 450 CCC camps in 1935 broadened and speeded demonstration work. Construction of a large number of check dams and terrace outlets and the planting of 10,000 acres of trees were a few of the CCC accomplishments in that year (Benedict, 1953, p. 318).

Passage of the Soil Conservation and Domestic Allotment Act in 1936 tied soil conservation to acreage control and price support programs. Much emphasis was placed on diverting land from "surplus" crops to soil conserving uses. The Soil Conservation Service continued as a separate agency and was concerned more specifically with problems of conservation. In 1937 the Service began a program of cooperation with soil conservation districts set up under state laws. It provided comprehensive farm plans and technical assistance that included classification of soil and surveying for drainage tile, terraces, and water storage dams. Economic assistance under the Agricultural Conservation Program provided payments for part of the cost of terracing, land-forming, building stock dams, clearing land, and irrigating and draining soil.

More than half of the federal outlays for the Agricultural Conservation Program from 1948 to 1958 were cost-sharing assistance for liming and fertilizer materials and for drainage and irrigation. These output-increasing outlays, which remained at nearly the same level from 1948 to 1965, have run counter to government efforts to control production. They also have run counter to welfare goals, since most of the payments go to farms that are larger than average (Cotner, 1964, pp. 4, 16). Many of the supported conservation practices would be profitable without assistance, and recent attempts have been made with some success to shift government assistance to long-term investments such as mechanical practices to reduce erosion.

In 1934 the Taylor Grazing Act was passed to provide for more orderly use and improvements in grazing lands, mostly located in the West. More than 80 million acres were included in the original grant. Ranchers and stock owners paid to the government a grazing fee for use of public lands. Stocking rates were controlled to avoid overgrazing and consequent problems of erosion and destruction of grass cover.

Other measures have been taken to conserve soil, such as the vast water control projects in the valleys of the Tennessee, Missouri, and Arkansas Rivers. Partially due to the heavy urban requirements for water, there is growing interest in the conservation of water. This interest, stemming from a deep concern in urban as well as rural areas, will in the future give continued impetus to research and action projects to control use of our soil and water resources.

TENURE AND TAXES

The dominant organization pattern in American agriculture has been that of the owner-operated family farm. Hired labor and tenancy were often rungs on a ladder leading to land ownership. Owner-operation of land meant that there was no class struggle between worker, management, and capitalist and that there was a minimum of interference in the process of translating family effort into profits. The majority of farmers had enough "economic man" in them to respond to economic incentives and use efficient farming practices. Competition prodded the most efficient farmers to expand the size of their units.

In the early years, horse-drawn equipment and management requirements limited the size of farm and precluded concentration of farm ownership. Availability of huge machines that permit scale economies for large farms is of comparatively recent origin and is causing a major change in ownership structure. Part-ownership is becoming a more dominant tenure pattern as farmers seek to overcome high costs of real estate—a barrier to forming an efficient economic unit. The percentage of farms in the full-owner, tenant, and part-owner categories were respectively 56, 35, and 8 per cent in 1900 and 57, 20, and 22 per cent in 1959 (U.S. Department of Commerce, 1938; 1966, p. 622). The proportion of land farmed by part-owners increased from 15 per cent in 1900 to 45 per cent in 1959.

The federal government relied heavily on import duties and land sales for revenue in the early days. The federal income tax, now the major source of federal revenue, was not approved until 1913. Propensities to save and invest are known to increase with income. It follows that early imposition of a sizable, progressive income tax might have reduced investment and slowed economic progress.

Road construction and education in rural areas were supported mainly by property taxes. Thus the rural areas made a substantial contribution to infrastructure and intrastructure through the land resource. An advantage of the lump-sum property tax is that it interferes less than some other taxes with output and allocation of resources. Failure to provide an education to the farm populace or taxing of the nonfarm sector to educate farm people would have retarded economic growth.

BANKING AND FINANCE

The federal government, under the influence of Alexander Hamilton and despite the opposition of agrarian spokesmen, established the First Bank of the United States in 1791. Its charter was for twenty years. In 1800 there were only twenty-nine state commercial banks, all located in the East. During the War of 1812, the number of state banks expanded rapidly. By 1815, there were 200 state banks, and the value of the bank notes which they circulated doubled from $23 million to $46 million. Reserves declined, and banks found it difficult to redeem notes for specie payment (gold and silver coins).

After the War of 1812, the federal government, which no longer needed the expansionary money policies that had been used to finance the war, tried to persuade banks to resume specie payments. When this failed, Madison (who, like Jefferson, thought central banking unconstitutional) reluctantly established the Second Bank of the United States in 1816. A policy of the bank, redeeming paper money with specie, was not put into effect until 1819 when, coupled with a drop in demand for foodstuffs in Europe, it was one of the factors that burst the speculative bubble and caused a recession in 1819.

Central banking was opposed by some hard-money supporters, who opposed all banks which could issue paper money, and for a quite different reason by a large number of farmers and other debtor groups who favored easy money. The latter group feared the regulation and limitation of credit imposed by central authority. Thus central banking, though essential for sound banking and monetary policies in the nation, lacked adequate support from either the hard- or easy-money enthusiasts. In 1836 President Andrew Jackson vetoed a bill passed by Congress to renew the bank charter, and central banking did not return for many decades.

With the United States Bank out of the scene, state banks were free to expand operations. By 1837 there were almost 800 state banks, or over twice the 1830 number (Krooss, 1966, p. 228). Their deposits more than tripled in the period. They flooded the economy with money. Jackson issued the Specie Circular in 1836, requiring that land payments be in specie. These factors precipitated an economic contraction, the Panic of 1837. This was one of a long series of economic panics or recessions. Others occurred in 1843, 1857, 1875–79, 1885, 1893, 1908, 1915, 1921, 1932, 1945, 1949, 1954, 1958, and 1960—to list only the major "trough" years (Bolino, 1966, p. 449). The recessions had a growing impact on the rural community as farming became more commercial, culminating in the Great Depression of the 1930's.

The pattern of the Panic of 1837 was repeated in many subsequent recessions. Credit was overextended and insufficiently backed by the liquid assets, deposits, or reserves of richer banks. There was no systematic institutional structure for coordinating borrowing and lending between the capital-rich, creditor economy of the East and the capital-short, debtor economy of the frontier West. For various reasons, farmers and others would lose confidence in the bank and demand their deposits. The banks would then call in loans to pay off depositors, maintain liquidity, and offset the "run" on the bank. This created a general climate of reduced confidence, reduced funds for investment, and lowered prices. Loans could not be repaid and many banks were forced to close. Businesses and farmers whose operation depended on bank loans were forced into bankruptcy. Attempts to institute more sound banking policies and hence avoid such crises were long thwarted. Efforts by states to limit borrowing and increase reserve requirements ran squarely counter to the need for expansion of credit to finance the great economic expansion in boom times.

The New York Stock and Exchange Board was established in 1817, and by the 1850's as many as 71,000 shares were traded in one day (Krooss, 1966, p. 233). The growth of New York as a financial center facilitated investment of foreign and domestic funds in America but also led to pyramiding of bank reserves in New York City and increased the vulnerability of the economy to financial crises.

The struggle between debtors (many of them farmers who wanted easy money and inflationary policies) and creditors (many of them merchants and bankers who wanted hard money) continued into the mid-1800's and was brought to a head by the greenback controversy. To help finance the Civil War, the government authorized issue of $450 million in greenbacks which lacked specie backing. The struggle between easy-money advocates, who wanted the greenbacks to remain in circulation, and the tight-money advocates, who wanted the greenbacks retired and exchanged for specie, culminated in the Resumption Act of 1875 under which greenbacks were to be slowly retired. In 1878, because of depressed economic conditions, greenback circulation was frozen at $347 million (Krooss, 1966, p. 235).

THE SILVER QUESTION

Silver had been underpriced relative to gold since the ratio set in 1834 and was believed by many to have contributed to inflation. In 1873, with few objections, Congress eliminated the silver dollar from coinage. This "crime of '73," as it was later called, became the rallying cry of farmers and Western silver interests for a return to bimetallism and the attendant freer money supply and higher price level.

Silver interests won small victories for bimetallism in the Bland-Allison Act of 1878 and the Sherman Silver Purchase Act of 1890. These measures did not contribute much to inflation because the level of national economic activity and expenditure was not high enough to absorb all the currency. In 1896, the silverites, with agrarian interests strongly represented, gained control of the Democratic Party. Bryan was nominated for the presidency but was defeated by McKinley. This was viewed as a mandate for hard currency and the country returned to the gold standard in 1900.

The National Banking and Currency Act of 1863 established a system of national banks chartered by the federal government. This, coupled with the Acts of 1865 and 1866, which forced state and private bank notes out of circulation, resulted in a more orderly system of banking and currency and provided the federal government with strong though still inadequate tools for the regulation of banking.

Some of the "sound" money policies of the national banks discriminated against providing agricultural credit. The $50,000 minimum capital required to obtain a national bank charter in communities of 6,000 persons or less was too large for country banks to handle. The 10 per cent tax on note issues of state-chartered banks further deprived rural areas of note-issuing banks, since loans were made on notes rather than deposits. The 1863 Act prohibited national banks from making loans on original security of farm real estate. The $300 million limit on national bank notes was inadequate for the nation, and the note issue was too concentrated in the East to provide adequate farm credit. Amendments to the Act between 1875 and 1908 corrected some of these disadvantages but failed to meet all the needs of agriculture. Initially, authority over the Federal Reserve System was quite decentralized, and the system was intended to facilitate commercial banking, not to stabilize the economy. During the 1920's, the Federal Reserve System began to use its monetary powers to influence business activity, but the system was unable to cope with the economic collapse that followed the stock market disaster of 1929.

The Banking Acts of 1933 and 1935 extended the powers of the Federal Reserve Banks and centralized these powers in the Federal Reserve Board of Governors in Washington, D.C. The Board was given control over the rediscount rate, open market operations, and reserve requirements of member banks. By selling government bonds to member banks, by raising the reserve requirements, and by increasing the rate at which member banks could rediscount commercial paper, the Federal Reserve Board could limit the ability of banks to make loans and expand the money supply. By these means, monetary policies could help to cool an overheated economy.

In the 1920's and early 1930's, bank failures were frequent. Some of these resulted from runs on the bank caused by fear among depositors that the banks would fail. In 1933 bank deposits were insured by the Federal Deposit Insurance Corporation. Removal of the fear that deposits would be liquidated by bank runs removed much of the basis for panic that led to bank failures.

In general, farmers favored easy-money policies and weak central banking. They must take much of the blame for failure of the U.S. to establish a sound banking system before the twentieth century. On the other hand, it may be argued that an early strong banking system would have done more harm than good without a comparable breakthrough in economic theory to guide monetary and fiscal policies. Higher tariffs, higher interest rates, and reduced federal spending were the economic prescriptions for fighting a depressed economy in the 1920's. Increasing the effectiveness of these misguided policies might only have increased the magnitude of the economic disaster.

With increasing sophistication in economic theory and education, the American people after World War II had not only the will but the means for devising effective monetary and fiscal policies to eliminate depressions. The extended boom-and-bust cycles—a source of unstable demand for farm products and the attendant farmer discontent—were removed. The greater economic sophistication and improved devices for controlling the money supply, for smoothing business cycles, and for coordinating savings and investment throughout the nation contributed significantly to greater public confidence in the economy, to higher savings and investment, and hence to greater economic growth. These devices have contributed immeasurably to the welfare of farm people. Intelligent use of presently available monetary and fiscal policies can altogether prevent the occurrence of a major economic depression in the future.

AGRICULTURAL CREDIT

The system of agricultural credit prior to World War I was at best inefficient and at worst chaotic. Loans were limited to short periods and renewal charges were large. Widespread mortgage foreclosure and financial disaster often occurred in times of national economic distress. In the traditional capital surplus areas of the East interest rates would be, say, 6 per cent, while in the newer settlement areas they would be 15 per cent. Increasing land values and rising costs of farm equipment increased the need for credit in rural areas. The banking and credit system provided no sound and efficient system for channeling funds between those who had funds to lend and farmers who wished to borrow.

THE COOPERATIVE FARM CREDIT SYSTEM

The Federal Farm Loan Act passed in 1916 created twelve cooperative Federal Land Banks. The twelve district banks were operated under federal charter and were supervised by the Federal Farm Loan Board, a bureau in the U.S. Treasury Department. Local cooperative associations of borrowing farmers, called National Farm Loan Associations, were chartered by the Board. Borrowing farmers held stock in the Loan Associations, which in turn held stock in the land banks. Thus management and ownership of the system rested with farmers, while the federal government provided examination and general supervision of the system. Bonds sold by the Federal Land Banks in national money markets provided funds which were loaned to farmers through the Loan Associations. This land bank system provided long-term farm mortgage credit.

Questions of constitutionality and early lack of acceptance by farmers limited the role of the land bank system until its constitutionality was upheld by the Supreme Court in 1921. This delay turned out to be a blessing, enabling the system to lend on land prices deflated by the 1921 recession rather than on inflated land prices of the early post-World War I period.

The number of loans increased rapidly until 1930. Then high costs of money, falling land values, foreclosures, and delinquencies led to a decline in loans outstanding.

Congress appropriated $125 million in 1932 to bolster the capital structure of the Federal Land Banks and provided other sources of funds to supplement the land bank system loans. The result was a major expansion in land bank system loans. This saved many farmers from foreclosures and improved public relations for the system. The land bank system continues to grow and has become a large and constructive influence in the farm credit structure.

Congress passed the Agricultural Credits Act in 1923 creating twelve Federal Intermediate Credit Banks to operate in conjunction with the twelve district Federal Land Banks. The recent recession had demonstrated that commercial banks were too vulnerable to business fluctuations to provide a dependable, economical source of short- and intermediate-term credit to farmers. The Federal Intermediate Credit Banks were owned by the government, and, like the Federal Land Banks, sold bonds in national money markets. The funds were then loaned to state and national banks and other local lenders but could not be loaned directly to farmers. Commercial banks made little use of the Intermediate Credit Banks, and few local cooperative credit associations were formed. An insufficient number of local lending retailers existed in the Depression of the 1930's to channel to farmers much-needed funds from the wholesalers (the Federal Intermediate Credit Banks).

Consequently, the Farm Credit Act of 1933 established twelve Production Credit Corporations and provided for a country-wide system of local cooperative retail lending agencies called Production Credit Associations. The Corporations were established to organize and provide part of the capital for local Associations, which are now fully owned by farmer borrowers. The Farm Credit Act of 1956 set up a long-range plan for farmer ownership of the Federal Intermediate Credit Banks, which previously were owned by the government. In 1969 the Production Credit Associations bought the last government stock in the Intermediate Credit Banks, thus making the entire production credit system a farmer-owned cooperative.

The Farm Credit Act of 1933 also created the thirteen Banks for Cooperatives with twelve district banks and one central bank in Washington, D.C. As the name implies, each Bank for Cooperatives makes loans to cooperatives, which are comprised mostly of farmers and operate for the benefit of farmers. As with the Federal Intermediate Credit Banks, the plan is to retire government stock and make the thirteen Banks for Cooperatives completely farmer-owned.

The Farm Credit Administration (FCA), created by executive order in March of 1933, brought under one agency all the federally sponsored farm credit agencies and activities existing at the time. Until 1939, the FCA was an independent agency responsible to the President. It was part of the Department of Agriculture from 1939 to 1953. The Farm Credit Act of 1953 again made the FCA an independent agency. Prior to the 1953 Act, the FCA included the Farm Credit Districts, each district made up of a Bank for Cooperatives, a Federal

Land Bank, a Federal Intermediate Credit Bank, local associations, and borrowing farmers. The FCA after 1953 consisted of a Farm Credit Board, a governor appointed by the Board, and personnel who make up the governor's staff. The twelve members of the Board are appointed by the President with the approval of the Senate. The men are chosen from a slate provided by the three principal groups in the cooperative farm credit system: (1) the Federal Land Banks and National Farm Loan Associations, (2) the Federal Intermediate Credit Banks and Production Credit Associations, and (3) the Banks for Cooperatives. A thirteenth member is appointed by the Secretary of Agriculture.

A principal function of the Farm Credit Association is to see that the cooperative banks and associations are operating according to regulations. The FCA is *not* a lending institution and makes no loans. It is supported financially by the cooperative lending institutions over which it exercises its regulatory functions.

OTHER AGENCIES MAKING FARM LOANS

The Resettlement Administration was formed in 1935. One of its programs was to purchase marginal land at "agreed" prices and convert the land into grazing districts or forests or put it to other extensive use. Aid was given to families whose land was acquired to help them rent or purchase land in more productive farming areas. Approximately 12 million acres of land were acquired at a cost of $52 million up to June 1937 (Benedict, 1953, p. 325). From 1918 onward the government had provided loans to farmers who had experienced *natural* disasters, but under the Resettlement Administration and its successor, the Farm Security Administration, this feature was extended along with technical advice to farmers who were in acute distress from *economic* disaster.

The Resettlement Administration also administered a program to develop small homes on plots of land for people who were unable to find their place in the competitive economy. This program, begun earlier under the Subsistence Homestead projects, also entailed teaching of handicrafts so that these people would have supplemental income. In July 1937 most of the programs of the Resettlement Administration were continued by the Bankhead-Jones Farm Tenancy Act. The Secretary of Agriculture in September 1937 changed the name of the Resettlement Administration to the Farm Security Administration.

The Farm Security Administration provided for continuation of earlier policies, including loans, grants-in-aid, camps for migrant farm workers, and various rehabilitation projects. The Farm Security Administration also made efforts to develop cooperative farms on a large scale (Benedict, 1953, pp. 492, 493).

Because some of these features were considered objectionable, the Farm Security Administration was abolished by the Farmers Home Administration

Act of 1946. The new Farmers Home Administration principally carried on the loan activities of its predecessor agency, including the land purchase and loan arrangements of the Bankhead-Jones Farm Tenancy Act of 1937 to help tenants become owners.

The Farmers Home Administration (FHA) remains the major federal agency that grants loans to farmers who cannot obtain credit from commercial sources. Coupled often with technical assistance, FHA loan policies have resulted in a low rate (some argue the rate is too low) of repayment failures. Through the years, the FHA has increased the size and flexibility of its loans, and now also makes loans to small towns for improvement of social overhead.

Major lenders to farmers include (in addition to the cooperative credit agencies and the Farmers Home Administration) individuals, commercial banks, and insurance companies. This impressive credit framework has ample potential for sufficient quantity, flexibility, and security in credit arrangements to American farmers. Problems remain, however, and will be discussed in a later chapter dealing with the resources in agriculture.

TECHNOLOGY

The origins of early American farming technology lie in Europe, especially England. English agriculture was primitive in the early seventeenth century, when the first English settlements were made in America. While the early settlers brought with them many agricultural practices and techniques, they certainly brought no agricultural revolution. In fact, although England was on the threshold of the agricultural revolution that accompanied her Industrial Revolution, the first tools brought from Europe were not unlike those used by the Egyptians four millenniums earlier (Chambers and Mingay, 1966, pp. 6 ff).

One precursor of the agricultural revolution in the United Kingdom according to some authors was the breakdown of the feudal system and the rise of the industrious yeomen class of freeholders. Also the Black Death that ravaged Europe had depleted the population, had temporarily relieved the pressure of population on food supply, and had provided a small surplus of farm output above subsistence requirements that could be used to build production assets. By 1620 clover seed was regularly imported into England. Use of clover in crop rotations and production of turnips intensified feed output. The English Enclosure movement was especially important from 1650 to 1750 and formed the basis for more selective feeding of livestock and intensification of crop production. In England, especially, the farm-business interaction (partly through the business-oriented "landed" aristocracy) was great and created opportunities to obtain capital and provided a rational, broad prospective for agriculture, rarely encountered in the world before.

Legumes to build fertility and intensive crop rotations were not economically suited for wide use in the New World, where soil resources were abundant. From Europe, colonists brought small grains, peas, and other crops, which did well under American soil and climate conditions. Colonists also grew large amounts of indigenous crops—Indian corn, tobacco, potatoes, tomatoes, peanuts, pumpkins, and squashes. The turkey was one of the few indigenous animals; most other poultry and livestock were brought from Europe. Major contributions of Europe to American farm technology were excellent livestock breeds and small-grain varieties. Tools brought from Europe included the hoe, spade, shovel, scythe, harrow, and plow. Plymouth had no plows its first ten years, and Massachusetts Bay had only thirty in 1636 (Krooss, 1966, p. 111). The total cost of tools described as adequate for a farm in 1800 was $20 (Danhof, 1946, p. 136). By 1860, the ordinary investment in plow, cultivator, harrow, drill, and harvesting machinery in the Midwest was approximately $500. In 1969, a typical Midwest farmer had $10,000 or more invested in machinery.

EARLY MECHANICAL INNOVATION IN AMERICA

The first significant American mechanical invention (Table 4.2) was the cotton gin. The long hours required to remove the seed from cotton fiber had made cotton cloth a luxury, out of reach of the average buyer. Eli Whitney in 1793 introduced his cotton gin to separate the seed from cotton. By 1845 the machine had been sufficiently developed so that a gin employing three hands and an investment of $100 could process from 600 to 2,500 pounds of cotton in one day. Without the gin, one man could separate a maximum of only 6 pounds of fiber from the seed in a day (Danhof, 1946, pp. 132, 133). The impact of the invention was to make cotton the cheapest and most-used fiber in the world and to help transform the South into a slaveholding, plantation society.

It also made cotton an important export item and earner of foreign exchange. It contributed significantly in this way to U.S. economic development. Picking cotton required huge amounts of labor. A successful mechanical cotton picker awaited the improved machine tools, materials, and efficient engine power of the twentieth century. Because picking was the bottleneck in cotton production and required large amounts of labor that had essentially zero opportunity cost for the remainder of the year, there was little demand for improving machines to increase output of plowing, harrowing, planting, and cultivating operations. Consequently the South made little technological progress in agriculture until comparatively recent times.

Biological innovations, such as new plant varieties that raise yields, are crucial for raising productivity in a nation such as Japan, which is short on land and long on labor. Mechanical innovations that increase output per man were especially important in a nation such as the U.S., which was long on land and

TABLE 4.2. Milestones in Farm Machinery Development

	Inventor or Innovator	Item	Remarks
1793	Eli Whitney	Cotton gin	Removed seeds from cotton
1797	Charles Newbold	Cast-iron plow	Heavy draft; did not scour in heavy soils
1826	Patrick Bell (Scotsman)	Reaper	Enabled boy with team to do work of 6 men but not widely adopted in U.K. or Europe
1831	William Manning	Reaper	Reapers patented but few machines produced
1833	Obed Hussey		
1834	Cyrus McCormick	First widely used reaper	Had reel as well as cutting bar and platform; a really satisfactory reaper not produced until 1855
1837	Hiram and John Pitts	Thresher	Fanning mill combined with cylinder; concave stacker added; in common use by 1860
1837	John Deere	Steel plow	Broke ground for a new generation of Midwest farmers
1840	John Gibbons	Grain drill	Simultaneously drilled and seeded
1841	Samuel Pennock	Grain drill	Improved drill; small grain, corn, or peas could be sown in covered form
1868	James Oliver	Chilled-iron plow	Chilled outside iron to make it hard so it would scour and wear better
1868	John Lane	Soft-center steel plow	Outer layers of steel for toughness, hardness, and scouring; center layer of soft steel for durability
1878	No one inventor	Combine	Reaper and threshing machine combined; moved through field
1880	William Deering	Grain-binder	Reaper with a Marsh-type platform and Appleby device to tie bundles
1880	E. W. Quincy	Corn-picker	Experiments with mechanical picker began 1820, but Quincy got first important patent

SOURCES: Bolino (1966), Krooss (1966), and Benedict (1953).

short on capital. Although Americans made significant efforts to improve plant varieties, their real genius prior to the twentieth century was mechanical.

The first colonists had only the hoe to till the soil. Wooden plows soon appeared and were pulled first by oxen and later by horses or mules. Wooden plows were used by many farmers until after the Civil War. Early improvement was made in the wooden plow by adding a wrought iron "share" or tip. Charles Newbold patented a cast-iron plow in 1797. Despite subsequent improvements, the cast-iron plows were heavy, wore rapidly, required frequent sharpening, did not properly turn the soil, did not scour in heavy soils, and required much draft power for their size. To turn the heavy prairie soils of the West, a technological breakthrough was necessary. It came with the steel plow produced by John Deere in 1837. Using a new high grade plow steel made at Pittsburg, John Deere manufactured 1,600 steel plows at Moline, Illinois, in 1850, and soon the steel plow was standard in the West. It greatly increased productivity over the old wooden plow, which generally required two men and four oxen to plow an acre per day (Danhof, 1946, pp. 121, 124).

Significant improvements were made in harrows, cultivators, and in seeding and planting equipment, but the most significant advances prior to 1900 were made in harvesting machinery. Harvesting was the bottleneck, the operation that restricted farm output (except for corn). Timeliness was important and all hands were used at harvest, though there might be slack labor available for the operations that preceded harvest. Mechanical devices to mow and reap were known in Europe before they were developed here. Nevertheless these machines were first made practical and popular in the U.S. The first successful grain reapers made by Obed Hussey of Maryland in 1833 and Cyrus McCormick of Virginia in 1834 were little more than mowing machines with a platform. Later William Deering added a device that used wire to bind the grain in bundles. By 1880 a binding device that used twine, much superior to wire, was placed on the market as the Deering harvester.

Though the early McCormick reaper was in many ways crude by modern standards it was used in large numbers and saved a substantial quantity of hard labor. By 1855 quite satisfactory McCormick reapers were produced; in that year some 15,000 reapers were manufactured and sold. By 1860 mechanical reapers were cutting 70 per cent of the wheat in the Midwest.

Although an early model of the combine was patented by Hiram Moore and J. Hascall in 1836, and although combines were said to perform satisfactorily by 1853, the machine in a perfected form did not appear until 1878. After 1878 it was rapidly adopted for use in the dry wheat regions (Danhof, 1946, p. 129).

The first successful American threshing machine was developed by Hiram and John Pitts of Maine in 1837. The first machines were powered either by water, horses, oxen, or, in a few instances, by hand. Steam power, to be introduced later, offered substantial advantages. Improved tillage, harvesting, and threshing machinery reduced the time required to produce one acre of wheat from 75 hours in 1830 to 13 hours in 1880 (Danhof, 1946, p. 137). In 1969, less than two hours were required to produce one acre of wheat on a typical farm in western Oklahoma.

Tractor Power

The practical use of tractor power on farms was an extension of the development of the steam engine, the internal combustion engine, and the automobile—all developed primarily for purposes other than the farm (Table 4.3).

TABLE 4.3. Milestones in Power and Transportation Development

	Inventor or Innovator	Item	Remarks
1678	P. G. Hautefeuille (France)	Internal combustion engine	Burned gunpowder
1705	Thomas Newcomen (England)	Steam engine	Engine not practical until improvements by James Watt (about 1770)
1829	George and Robert Stephenson (England)	Practical locomotive	The same year an English locomotive was brought to America
1830	Peter Cooper	"Tom Thumb" locomotive	First successful locomotives built in America (18 miles per hour)
1830	E. L. Miller	"Best Friend" locomotive	
1830		South Carolina Rail; Baltimore and Ohio	First railroads in U.S. to start regular line service
1849	A. L. Archambault	"Forty-Niner" portable steam engine	Steam engine provided belt power for threshing; pulled between locations by horses or oxen
1855	Obed Hussey	Self-propelled steam engine	"Tractor"; could be used for plowing
1856	Henry Bessemer (England)	Bessemer converter	Iron ore (3–20 tons) poured inside egg-shaped converter; blast of air injected from bottom, removing impurities; provided high-quality, low-cost iron
1859	Edwin Drake	Oil well	First oil well in Pennsylvania began trend that led to cheap, efficient fuel for internal combustion engines
1866		Open-hearth process	Developed in Europe, permitted quality control of iron and use of lower-quality iron ore
1869		Transcontinental railroad	East and west sections joined in Utah
1876	Nikolaus Otto (Germany)	Internal combustion engine	First practical 4-cycle engine
1892	Rudolf Diesel (Germany)	Diesel engine	Burned low-grade fuels with high efficiency
1892	John M. Froelich	First successful gasoline tractor	Forerunner of John Deere tractor
1905	C. W. Hart and C. H. Parr	First business devoted exclusively to making tractors	Forerunner of Oliver tractors

(continued)

TABLE 4.3—*continued*

	Inventor or Innovator	Item	Remarks
1913	Henry Ford	Machine-line mass production	Provided low-cost automobile transportation; mass production made mass consumption possible
1923	John Deere	First "John Deere D"	Rugged tractor, used widely in wheat lands
1924	International Harvester	First McCormick-Deering "Farmall"	First widely used, all-purpose, row-crop tractor
1931	B. F. Goodrich	Rubber tractor tires	Goodrich (and, shortly after, Firestone) developed successful tractor tire

SOURCES: Bolino (1966), Krooss (1966), Dieffenbach and Gray (1960), Davis *et al.* (1965), and Benedict (1953).

Steam engines provided belt power for farm operations, especially threshing. One of the first such engines, pulled from place to place by horses or oxen, was the Forty-Niner, built in Philadelphia by A. L. Archambault in 1849. The machine averaged 1,000 pounds per horsepower (Dieffenbach and Gray, 1960, p. 26). A self-propelled steam engine that could be used for plowing was invented by Hussey in 1855. Wheel and occasionally crawler-type traction were used in the early steam models. Models were slowly improved, and by 1900 more than thirty firms were manufacturing a total of 5,000 large steam traction engines a year. These engines were cumbersome, often weighing more than twenty tons. They required a sizable crew to operate and were primarily practical only to power threshing machines.

The first internal combustion engine burned gunpowder and was invented by a Frenchman, P. G. Hautefeuille, in 1678. The internal combustion engine reached a practical state of development in the four-cycle model of a German, Nikolaus Otto, in 1876. Gottlieb Daimler applied the engine to a motorcycle in 1885 and Karl Benz built a motorcar the same year in Germany. The Packard Company, a French firm, in 1891 was the first to manufacture automobiles commercially (Krooss, 1966, p. 379). Another German, Rudolf Diesel, in 1892 patented the type of engine that now bears his name.

The discovery of petroleum in quantity and the drilling of oil wells (the first by Edwin Drake in 1859 in Pennsylvania) made possible cheap fuel needed for successful use of internal combustion engines in the U.S. By 1899, 100 firms in the United States were making internal combustion engines.

The first successful gasoline tractor, the forerunner of the John Deere tractor, was built by J. M. Froelich in 1892. C. W. Hart and C. H. Parr, forerunners of the Oliver tractor line, established in 1905 the first business devoted exclusively to building tractors (Dieffenbach and Gray, 1960, p. 31).

Techniques of mass auto production were first attempted by R. E. Olds (later of Oldsmobile fame). The highly important concept of precision tools and interchangeable parts was used in auto production by Henry Leland, who built Cadillacs in 1903 in a plant of the Henry Ford Company which had failed. Later, the genius of Henry Ford was the eclectic wedding of mass production and interchangeable parts with a simple, low-cost auto. His company produced about one-third of a million cars in 1915, and over two million in 1923. Substantial internal and external economies of scale generated by the auto industry greatly enhanced the possibility of a practical, low-cost tractor with internal combustion engine. Numerous companies were building tractors, but the financial backing and experience gained from auto-making enabled Ford to emerge as a dominant firm, producing 100,000 Fordson tractors in 1925, 75 per cent of all tractors produced.

Ford fell behind, however, because he failed to keep pace with such engineering advances as were made, for example, in the rugged "John Deere D" of 1923 and the all-purpose, row-crop McCormick-Deering Farmall of 1924.

Following development of rubber tractor tires in 1931 by B. F. Goodrich (and shortly after by Firestone), the advantage of rubber tires for tractors became quickly apparent. By 1940, 85 per cent of wheel tractors were on rubber. Subsequent improvements followed, including electric starting, multigear transmissions, hydraulics, diesel engines, power steering, and introduction of numerous tractor sizes and specialized models. The changes have vastly improved the efficiency, flexibility, and convenience of tractors. From 1920 to 1924, the average number of farms in the U.S. was 6.5 million and the average number of tractors less than 400,000. In 1965 there were 3.4 million farms and 4.6 million tractors. The number of tractors was nearly constant in the decade before 1966, but the total horsepower of tractors increased 50 per cent.

FERTILIZERS

The importance of nutrients for plant growth was known long before commercial fertilizers were widely used. For example, the importance of phosphates for plant growth was shown as early as 1790, and in 1840 Justus von Liebig of Germany showed the way to manufacture superphosphates (Chambers and Mingay, 1966, p. 14).

Edmund Ruffin conducted experiments which demonstrated the value of adding calcareous materials to soils in Virginia in 1820. Eventually he succeeded in influencing farmers to use lime and other calcareous materials so that the fertility of large areas of Virginia soil was restored (Rasmussen, 1960, p. 72).

The total use of principal plant nutrients in 1965 was 4.6 million tons of nitrogen, 1.5 million tons of available phosphorus, and 2.4 million tons of soluble potassium (U.S. Department of Agriculture, 1966, p. 21). Although commercial fertilizers were used earlier, the major increase has occurred since World War II. Fertilizer use in 1939, as a proportion of the 1965 use, was 9 per cent for nitrogen, 22 per cent for phosphorus, and 14 per cent for potassium. Among the reasons for the increase are: (*a*) decline in virgin soil fertility; (*b*) development of new crop varieties that responded well to fertilizers; (*c*) improved techniques for producing fertilizers and economies of scale, which reduced fertilizer costs and kept nutrient prices low for farmers; (*d*) more intensive cropping practices, such as continuous corn that required more fertilizers; (*e*) a program of education to acquaint farmers with the merits of fertilizer use; and (*f*) increasing irrigation.

PLANT VARIETIES

The technological revolution in farm machinery and fertilizers was joined with a third very important ingredient—improved varieties. It is not possible to discuss each of the numerous improvements in seeds. The discussion here will be confined to hybrid corn.

The revolution in hybrid corn can be traced to corn-breeding research by Donald Jones at the Connecticut Experiment Station (Wallace, 1925, p. 244). After several years of persistent effort, he succeeded in developing several inbred lines, the worst of which died and the best of which yielded half as much as ordinary corn. But the important finding, reported in 1910, was that crossing of inbred lines restored vigor and gave yields much higher than ordinary corn. Scientists, such as George Shull of the Carnegie Institution and Edward East of Harvard University, also showed the gains to be made from hybridization, and by 1923 nearly every agricultural experiment station in the corn belt, as well as the U.S. Department of Agriculture itself, was engaged in research on the new idea. In 1925, Wallace reported:

> With this improved seed corn the average corn belt farmer will be able to produce as much corn as he now produces on 80 to 85 per cent as much land, which means a savings in man labor of over 100 hours a year and a saving in horse labor of more than 200 hours.
>
> .   .   .   .
>
> All the corn belt stations are now in possession of hundreds of inbred strains of corn and will soon be in the process of trying out thousands of combinations to discover just which sorts 'nick' best. Within five or 10 years they will have good inbred strains for general distribution. [Wallace, 1925, p. 247]

Farmers did not have to wait that long for hybrid corn. In 1926, hybrid corn was being advertised and made available to farmers. One of the firms so engaged was Henry A. Wallace's own Hi-Bred Corn Company (Rasmussen, 1960, p. 243). Thus began a team effort that persisted, with the agricultural experiment stations providing inbred lines and the private seed corn companies combining these inbreds to form the hybrids that were sold to farmers. By 1940 most corn belt farmers were using hybrid corn. A large number of small grain and other crop varieties have been developed and released to farmers by the agricultural experiment stations.

MISCELLANEOUS TECHNOLOGIES

Although Edison had devised a method of using electricity for illumination as early as 1876, the practical application and use of electricity was slow to reach farms. Only 9.5 per cent of all farms were electrified in 1929. The Rural Electrification Administration (REA) was established in 1935 and in 1936 became part of the U.S. Department of Agriculture. Through REA, low interest, long-term loans were made to local electric cooperatives, which extended lines to farms. By 1965, 98 per cent of all farms were electrified, half by the REA system.

Electricity made practical the use of milking machines, feed-handling equipment, household appliances, and lighting that substantially raised farming efficiency and living levels in rural areas.

Many other technologies had a major impact on American economic development. Among these were the first cotton mills in New England in the 1820's, the Colt revolver in the 1830's, and the development of the refrigerated railroad car, the gang plow pulled by several horses, the mason jar for canning, and barbed wire. A successful method of hog cholera vaccination introduced in 1903 and rust-resistant wheat developed in the 1930's reduced losses to farmers.

After World War II, new technologies came so rapidly it is impossible to document them all. Pesticides such as DDT, developed before the war, became generally available after the war and were used by farmers to control lice, ticks, and corn borers. Feed additives, such as stilbestrol, and antibiotics were used to speed animal growth. Numerous herbicides, such as 2,4-D and pre-emergence weed killers, helped to keep fields clean. Radioactivity was used as a tool to eradicate the screwworm fly.

One of the interesting aspects of technology is the ability of farmers to gain ever greater productivity out of a significant "package" of technology, such as improved seed and fertilizer. By going from an oat-legume-corn rotation to continuous corn and by increasing plant population (many farmers now plant corn rows only twenty inches apart), farmers greatly increase output from a given "technology" over time.

TRANSPORTATION

Development of a commercial agriculture required an efficient transportation system to carry the marketed surplus to consumers and inputs to farmers. The U.S. possessed large river systems that offered access to markets, but these major rivers were often far from the agricultural land and ran primarily north-south rather than in the needed east-west direction.

Most towns in colonial America were located on rivers with access to the ocean. A need existed for east-west transportation to open up the West, hence support developed for turnpikes and canals. With strong assistance from state funds, largely derived from the sale of land, the Cumberland Road was extended from the east coast into Illinois by 1838. The highly successful Erie Canal, from the Hudson River to Lake Erie, was completed in 1825 with heavy financial support from New York state. Numerous other canals were built with state and federal support, but funds were inadequate, competition from American railroads was often decisive, and the ventures were sometimes mismanaged. Douglas North (1966, p. 102) states that of the $102,798 invested by the young nation in canals, $86,434 was invested in canals that were financial failures. It is estimated that 70 per cent of canal expenditures from 1815 to 1860 were by the state and federal governments (Davis *et al.*, 1965, p. 303).

EARLY RAILROADS

The settlement of the great heartland of America was coincidental with the spread of the railroad. This was of tremendous significance, because it made possible more rapid settlement and a more commercialized agriculture. If the settlement technology and transportation had permitted only subsistence farming for several years, farming would have been difficult to transform later into a commercial operation. The character of American agriculture and industry would undoubtedly be quite different today if the locomotive would have come a century later.

The stationary steam engine was developed by an Englishman, Thomas Newcomen, in 1705, but the engine was not practical until the improvements made by James Watt 64 years later. It took 100 years to adapt the steam engine to the railroad. Richard Trevithick is credited with building the first steam engine to pull loaded cars over rails. Improvements made by George and Robert Stephenson made the locomotive practical in 1829. The same year an English locomotive was brought to America. In 1825, a locomotive was built in America, but the first really successful locomotive built in America was the famous Tom

Thumb built by Peter Cooper. It traveled at the unheard of speed of 18 miles per hour.

In 1830 the South Carolina Railroad and the Baltimore and Ohio Railroad were regarded as the first common carriers to begin service. From then on, the growth in U.S. railroad mileage was phenomenal. By the mid-1850's, Chicago, St. Louis, and Memphis were connected with the East. In 1869 the eastern and western segments of the transcontinental railroad were joined in Utah. From the small beginnings in 1830, the spread of railroad is apparent from the following track mileage: 1840—3,328; 1860—30,636; 1880—93,671; 1900—193,321; 1920 —248,700; 1940—235,082 (Davis *et al.*, 1965, p. 306). Railroads extended to Minnesota by 1867, to eastern Nebraska by 1870, and throughout the Great Plains in the 1880's. When the Civil War began, the railroad was a billion dollar industry and the chief single instrument in capital formation, directly accounting for perhaps one-fifth of the nation's capital (Bolino, 1966, p. 149).

Substantial imports of steel and machinery from Europe were providing for growth in American railroads and other industry. Most of these imports were financed by exports of farm products (Davis *et al.*, 1965, p. 300). Thus the railroads not only increased communication and united the country but provided the basis for imports and domestic production of industrial capital goods.

Because railroads needed settlements and production along their routes to aid profits, they encouraged immigration; the Illinois Central did this in Sweden, the Northern Pacific in Germany, and the Union Pacific in Ireland (Bolino, 1966, p. 165).

RAILROAD FINANCING AND FARM DISCONTENT

Government aid was conspicuous in the railroad industry from the beginning. Initially several states either owned or heavily subsidized railroads. State owner-ship was especially prominent in the South.

As early as 1824 the federal government began to subsidize railroads through free engineering surveys of prospective rail routes. A law was passed in 1832 reducing tariffs on imported rail iron. With the Land Grant Act of 1850, federal aid began to be more significant than state aid. A total of approximately 155 million acres were alloted to railroads, but, due to forfeitures, total acreage granted was close to 131 million (Bolino, 1966, p. 155). This was nearly 10 per cent of the land in the states concerned. One land grant of 41 million acres was made to the Northern Pacific Railroad in 1864. The percentage of land patented by railroads in North Dakota was 23.7, in Washington 22, and Minnesota 18.5 (Benedict, 1953, p. 73). In addition, states awarded railroads about 49 million acres. Because the railroads were desperate for capital and settlements, they disposed of the land too quickly to gain large returns. One estimate is that, due to military and mail rate concessions, the government by 1945 had recaptured $900 million in return on the land grants—or about twice the amount the railroads had received for lands sold plus the value of lands they still held (Benedict, 1953, p. 74). The federal government also made loans to railroads, and these were largely repaid.

Despite government assistance, most of the capital for railroads had to come from private sources. As a result of the diligent search for capital, new techniques for financing and management were developed that today are apparent in the equity financing of the New York Stock Exchange, in the "organization man," and in the bureaucratic structure of big business.

Considerable capital also came from outside the U.S. For example, it has been estimated that foreign investors, mainly British, owned half the shares of the Central Pacific, two-fifths of the Pennsylvania Railroad, and one-third of the Union Pacific (cf. Bolino, 1966, p. 159).

Lack of profitability, huge capital requirements, and a tendency to overextend their lines frequently led railroads into bankruptcy and receivership. The result was concentration of roads in a few strong hands. By 1900, five systems (the J. P. Morgan, Hill, Harriman, Vanderbilt, and Rockefeller systems) controlled nearly half the lines in operation.

To cover costs in the generally unprofitable industry, railway companies resorted to numerous devices, including rate discrimination. To ship a tub of butter to New York City cost 65 cents from upstate New York but only 30 cents from Elgin, Illinois. Grain from Chicago was shipped to Pittsburgh for 25 cents per bushel and to New York City for 15 cents (Krooss, 1966, p. 322). Numerous scandals were reported in railroad financing, including watered-down stock and the famous Credit Mobilier case in which several Congressmen received stock, ostensibly to promote favorable legislation in the form of railroad subsidies. Discriminatory rates, financial scandals, stock-watering, "theft" of public lands (land grants) and tie-in of railroads with other companies through financial magnates made railroads the chief scapegoat of farmer discontent for several decades, as reported in the last chapter.

The railroads largely overcame competition from turnpikes and canals in the early days but now receive intense competition from numerous alternative forms of transportation. Trucks, buses, automobiles, barges, pipelines, and airplanes have continually cut into rail traffic.

Federal regulations and competition removed railroads from the "bogeyman" list long ago. Perhaps railroads are now viewed more with pity than scorn. The generally low rates of return on railroad capital should not lead to the conclusion that such investment was always unproductive. It is generally conceded that, at least in the era before good roads and trucks, there were substantial social economies not reflected in the private accounts of railroad companies.

EDUCATION

Education has often been cited as a source of economic growth. Education not only imparts knowledge and skills that are a capital investment in future productivity but also imparts aspirations for higher income and a better way of life. It enhances ability to assimilate into a new environment—an important component of labor mobility and economic growth.

Early stress on literacy to give access to the Bible provided an impetus for mass education that eventually made New England a pervasive force for education in the nation. Harvard, founded in 1636, soon found its ecclesiastical ties too confining for the cultural role it was destined to play in a national setting. In 1647 the Massachusetts Bay Colony required an elementary school in towns of 50 families and a Latin school in towns of 100 families.

As stated earlier, section 16 (640 acres) was set aside in each township as an endowment for elementary education under the Ordinance of 1785. In 1848, a provision was made that section 36 also be set aside for education. Education at the elementary level became free and virtually universal for whites. In time free education was extended to the secondary level as well.

In 1870 only 11.5 per cent of the U.S. white population was illiterate. By 1967 less than 2 per cent of the white population was in that category. Negroes, 80 per cent of whom were illiterate in 1870, have made tremendous advances, and in 1967 less than 10 per cent were illiterate.

EDUCATION FOR FARM PEOPLE

Prior to 1850, formal education centered on the basics: reading, writing, and arithmetic. Few saw the need for application of science to agriculture in schools before that time, although there was considerable effort outside the schools to increase knowledge of agricultural practices and techniques.

Americans early showed an inclination to organize to exchange information, to learn of "scientific" approaches in agriculture, and in general to learn more efficient ways of farming. Societies were formed for promoting agriculture in Philadelphia in 1785, in New Jersey in 1790, in New York in 1791, in Massachusetts in 1792, and in Virginia in 1811 (Krooss, 1966, p. 109). Over 100 of these societies existed in 1820; in 1858 there were 1,000. A substantial number of magazines, newspapers, journals, almanacs, and books were published by these and other groups for improving the lot of farmers. In 1810 private fairs were held in Massachusetts to show farmers better farming methods. By 1850 these fairs had become a rural institution throughout the farming areas and drew large crowds.

The first federal assistance for agricultural technology came in 1839 when $1,000 was appropriated to the Patent Office for importation of foreign plants and seeds and for collection of agricultural statistics (Krooss, 1966, p. 109).

Michigan in 1857 established the first agricultural college in the U.S. Maryland and Pennsylvania established agricultural colleges in 1859. The Morrill Act of 1862 gave each state 30,000 acres of land for each senator and representative it had in Congress to endow colleges in agricultural and mechanical arts. The precedence for use of land to support higher education had already been established. The colonies gave land to encourage education. Harvard, Yale, and Dartmouth received state lands, which put them in the "land grant" college category (Krooss, 1966, p. 80). Under the Morrill Act, 11 million acres were disposed of; altogether the government disposed of a total of 99 million acres to encourage education (Krooss, 1966, p. 81). The land grant colleges included in the Morrill Act have become major contributors to the scholarly activities in the nation. They awarded approximately 40 per cent of all Ph.D. degrees granted in 1967.

AGRICULTURAL RESEARCH

The Morrill Act made low-cost education available at the college level. It was designed to foster application of science to agriculture, and also to enable the sons and daughters of farmers to take their place in an educated, commercial society. The application of science to agriculture could not progress satisfactorily without provision for formal research. This provision came with passage of the Hatch Act in 1887. The Act provided an annual grant of $15,000 to each state for research in agricultural sciences. A system of state experiment stations was established. The stations were generally associated closely with the land grant colleges. The Adams Act of 1906 provided an additional $15,000 per year to each of the states for research on agricultural problems (Benedict, 1953, p. 84). Grants have increased substantially since then, as shown in the next chapter.

AGRICULTURAL EXTENSION

A bill sponsored by Representative Lever of South Carolina and Senator Smith of Georgia became law in 1914. This Smith-Lever Act, as it was called, established the agricultural extension service, which "extended" the results and benefits of the teaching of land grant colleges and the research of experiment stations to farmers. The extension service was established by an initial federal allotment of $10,000 to each state, plus $600,000 of federal funds divided in proportion to the rural population of each state. Funds for extension provided by states and the federal government have increased markedly over the years. The extension program met with considerable early opposition from farmers, who acrimoniously labeled it "book farming" and looked upon it as an effort to increase farm output when what farmers really needed was improved markets. The extension service improved its image as the results of more research from the experiment stations became available, as it divorced itself from the Farm Bureau and politics, and as the professional competence of the county agent and home demonstration agent increased. The U.S. agricultural extension system is now being used as a model throughout the world by nations which wish to extend science not only to agriculture but to homemakers and industry.

VOCATIONAL AGRICULTURE

Congress passed with little opposition the Smith-Hughes Act in 1917, which established federal support for the teaching of vocational agriculture in high schools. The program was given further impetus by the desire to improve farm management and by Franklin D. Roosevelt's back-to-the-land movement in the 1930's. The program has come under increasing attack in recent years for encouraging boys to stay on the farm, when it is recognized that in most farming areas few farm boys will become farmers. The vocational agriculture proponents counter that in most states the number of boys trained are fewer than the number of boys who become farmers, and that training in the Future Farmers of America is useful, whatever a boy's future occupation. In a period of farm depopulation and scientific advance, a case can be made for more general academic training in high school and for a very intensive adult vocational agriculture program for persons after they have become farmers. The share of all federally financed vocational programs was one-third for agriculture in 1940 and 23.2 per cent in 1964. There is some merit in the argument that the share would be best reduced by increasing the expenditures for other vocational programs and reorienting vocational agriculture rather than by decreasing expenditures for agriculture, which totaled $77.5 million in 1964.

Numerous subsequent acts to train veterans and to provide education in nonfarm-oriented vocations for farm youth have been passed. Some of these will be discussed later, but with the passing of the Smith-Hughes Act in 1917 the basic framework for the education of farm youth was complete.

In 1870 only 2 per cent of all 17-year-olds graduated from high school, and the average length of the school term was 132 days—although the average student attended only 78 days! By 1960 the school term had been lengthened to 178 days (the average student attended 160 days), and about two-thirds of all 17-year-olds in the U.S. graduated from high school. The emphasis on education, begun early in rural areas, is a significant factor that has enabled millions of farm people to take their place in urban society with a minimum of friction. It also helps to explain the ability of farmers to read and assimilate information about improved farming practices in newspapers, magazines, and other media. Measures of the economic benefits of education will be discussed in the next chapter.

Education not only has increased the efficiency of farming but has increased the dignity of the farm community. It has removed any fears that the farm community might become a peasant class.

FOREIGN INVOLVEMENT

Foreign nations aided economic growth in the U.S. in several ways. They provided technology, labor, and capital. They served as important markets for American commodities. As indicated earlier, much know-how in the agricultural, steel, textile, and railroad industries came from Europe. An estimated 47 million persons immigrated into the U.S. between 1820 and 1960. Many were just beginning their most productive years of labor, and the dependency rate was low. Some 22 million returned to their homeland, leaving a net inflow of 25 million persons (Krooss, 1966, p. 64). The home countries had invested considerable capital in rearing and educating these immigrants. While the immigrants often sent money home, or returned to their homelands with some of their earnings, still they represented a sizable net inflow of capital and labor into the U.S.

Immigrants not only contributed directly to labor inputs but also made possible external economies of scale. The railroad would not have been profitable without settlers to market products and buy inputs along its lines. The investment in mass production techniques and precision tools to make Model-T Fords or Farmall tractors would not have been feasible without a large commercial market. Total national income in the U.S. would have been substantially lower in 1967 had there been no immigration since the Civil War, but per capita national income would not necessarily have been much different.[2]

Foreign investment, especially from England, was particularly significant in railroads and American foreign trade. Investment by foreign countries reached $4 billion in the early twentieth century and was never more than 3 per cent of all intangible assets (Krooss, 1966, p. 212). Foreign investors preferred securities of the government and a few banks and avoided the more risky investments in industry. Of course the securities purchased from banks often contributed indirectly to financing farms and industry. Foreign investment reached almost $2 billion in 1875, but by the end of the 1870's, Americans were beginning to invest abroad, partially offsetting the rising foreign investment in the U.S.

2. Assume a production function of the form
$$O = aK^bL^c,$$
where O is output, K is capital, and L is labor provided by the populace. Output per capita is
$$O/L = aK^bL^{c-1}.$$
If $b = .3$ and $c = .7$, then a 10 per cent increase in labor *decreases* per capita income (output) 3 per cent. If external economies of scale and stimulants to investment afforded by a rising population are great enough, they will offset the negative coefficient $c - 1$. In a country rich in natural resources such as the U.S. this may be possible, but it is not likely to occur in many underdeveloped areas of the world today.

An important role of foreign countries was to serve as a market for our products. Capital investment and the westward surge of American agriculture would have been impeded by lack of markets for farm output. In 1820 products of the farm and forest comprised over four-fifths of our exports and were therefore substantial earners of foreign exchange (Krooss, 1966, p. 268). In 1900, farm products comprised three-fourths of all U.S. exports. In the early 1960's they made up about one-fourth.

Imports in the early period were predominantly manufactured or semi-manufactured goods. Some proportion of these (rails, locomotives, and machine tools, for instance) were capital goods used to increase the productive capacity of American industry. From 1800 to 1850, foreign trade averaged approximately $200 million annually (Krooss, 1966, p. 275). Trade in merchandise was approximately 15 per cent of the national income. The tariff, initially a device to generate revenue, was favored by the East and Midwest as a device to protect domestic markets for foodstuffs and manufactured goods. The South favored low tariffs partly as a means to reduce costs of imported goods purchased in the South and partly as a device to win tariff concessions from countries importing American cotton.

SUMMARY

Attitudes and institutions as well as natural resources are the stuff out of which capital accumulates. Because of them, economic growth takes place. The process of economic growth in America began long before the U.S. Industrial Revolution. The impressive gains in agricultural productivity, which did not become really apparent until the twentieth century, were made possible by decisions made in earlier decades.

The permissive but orderly policies of a stable government were well suited to a nation with abundant resources of soil, coal, iron ore, and oil, and with attitudes of secular asceticism and functional activism. The favorable environment made capital accumulation possible. Attitudes were especially important in early stages when savings and investment were more personal (that is, individual) and less corporate. Favorable attitudes and the institutional environment were also important when the surplus above subsistence was somewhat limited and it was more difficult to save and invest out of current income.

The whole of economic development is much more than the sum of its parts. Exposition of these parts, as above, is necessarily incomplete, since the inter-relationships were not given the emphasis they deserve. In any attempt to understand our economic environment, developments in credit and technology cannot be separated from the contributions of education and research. The synthesis and evaluation which is properly a part of this summary has been deferred until the next chapter.

REFERENCES

Benedict, Murray R. 1953. *Farm Policies in the United States, 1790–1950*. New York: Twentieth Century Fund.

Bolino, August C. 1966. *The Development of the American Economy*, 2nd ed. Columbus: Merrill Books.

Chambers, J. D. and G. E. Mingay. 1966. *The Agricultural Revolution, 1750–1880*. New York: Schocken Books.

Cotner, Melvin L. 1964. The impact of the agricultural conservation program in selected farm policy pattern areas. Department of Agricultural Economics Mimeo 943. East Lansing, Michigan State University.

Danhof, Clarence H. 1946. Agricultural technology in 1880. In H. F. Williamson, ed., *The Growth of the American Economy*. New York: Prentice-Hall, Chapter 6.

Davis, Lance E., J. R. T. Hughes, and Ducan McDougall. 1965. *American Economic History*, rev. ed. Homewood, Ill.: Irwin.

Dieffenbach, E. M. and R. B. Gray. 1960. The development of the tractor. In *Power to Produce*, U.S. Department of Agriculture Yearbook of Agriculture. Washington: U.S. Government Printing Office.

Greeley, Andrew. 1965. The acculturation process in Catholic education. In E. V. Anderson and W. B. Kolesnik, eds., *Education and Acculturation in Modern Urban Society*. Detroit: University of Detroit Press.

Johnston, Bruce F. 1966. Agriculture and economic development. *Food Research Institute Studies* 6:251–312.

Krooss, Herman E. 1966. *American Economic Development*, 2nd ed. Englewood Cliffs, N.J.: Prentice-Hall.

Lewis, W. Arthur. 1957. *The Theory of Economic Growth*. London: Allen and Unwin.

McClelland, David C. 1961. *The Achieving Society*. Princeton, N.J.: Van Nostrand.

North, Douglas C. 1966. *Growth and Welfare in the American Past*. Englewood Cliffs, N.J.: Prentice-Hall.

Rasmussen, Wayne D. 1960. Editor's comments. In W. D. Rasmussen, ed., *Readings in the History of American Agriculture*. Urbana: University of Illinois Press.

Shannon, Fred A. 1945. *The Farmer's Last Frontier*. New York: Farrar and Rinehart.

Speltz, George H. 1963. Theology of rural life. In *Farm Goals in Conflict*, Center for Agricultural and Economic Development. Ames: Iowa State University Press, Chapter 4.

Swanson, Earl W. 1965. Entrepreneurship and innovation. In *Problems of Chronically Depressed Rural Areas*, Agricultural Policy Institute, API Series 19, Raleigh, N.C., pp. 55–83.

Tawney, R. H. 1926. Religion and the rise of capitalism. In Stanley Coben and Forest Hill, eds., *American Economic History*. New York: Lippincott (reprinted 1966), pp. 6–17.

Tweeten, Luther G. 1966. Socio-economic growth theory. In G. R. Winter and W. Rogers, eds., *Stimulants to Economic Development in Slow Growing Regions*, Edmonton, University of Alberta, Department of Agricultural Economics.

U.S. Department of Agriculture. 1963. Agriculture and economic growth. Agricultural Economic Report No. 28. Washington.

————. 1966. *Changes in Farm Production and Efficiency*. Statistical Bulletin No. 233. Washington.

U.S. Department of Commerce. 1938 and 1966. *Statistical Abstract of the United States*. Washington: U.S. Government Printing Office.

Wallace, Henry A. 1925. The revolution in corn breeding. *Prairie Farmer*. Reprinted in Rasmussen (1960), pp. 244–47.

Weber, Max. 1930. *The Protestant Ethic*. London: Allen and Unwin.

CHAPTER FIVE

Economic History of American Agriculture: Interpretation and Evaluation

The chronology of significant factors underlying economic growth in American agriculture was presented in the previous chapter. The purpose of this chapter is to interpret and evaluate the sources of growth. The opening discussion of farm-industry interaction in U.S. economic development is followed by some measures of growth and efficiency. The chapter contains estimates of agriculture's contribution to national income and the rate of return on investment to raise farm productivity. The final section is devoted to the "knowledge" sector, primarily education and research, which now contributes substantially to the output and productivity of farming.

FARM-INDUSTRY INTERACTION

The singularly most significant element of American economic development was the interaction between agriculture and nonfarm industries. The development of agriculture was inseparable from the Industrial Revolution. Institutions and attitudes established a climate for growth but were primarily passive, rather than active, forces. The direct impetus for the economic takeoff in the mid-1800's was provided by: improvements in agricultural techniques, such as the steel plow, reaper, and thresher; the railroad and attendant efficiency in transportation; the opening of the Midwest for settlement and the subsequent construction of transportation to permit the buy-sell activities of a commercial agriculture; growth in industry made possible by technological advances, such as the reduced cost of steel; immigration; and finally the opening of markets in Europe for our farm products.

Self-Reinforced Growth

The interaction between agriculture and the industrial sector of the economy led to a self-reinforcing upward trend in economic growth. Agriculture provided raw materials and markets for industry. Raw materials supplied by farmers included not only food but basic raw materials for industrial growth, such as cotton for the growing New England textile industry. Thanks to the growing nonfarm population and expanding foreign markets, the commercial demand for farm products was generally strong from 1850 to 1920. Large markets made possible substantial economies of scale in farm production and marketing. Favorable economic conditions enabled farmers to save, but savings would have been sterile without profitable investment opportunities provided in the form of improved capital inputs—especially machinery—from science and industry. And industry would have been much less profitable without growing markets in agriculture. Expansion of agriculture stimulated the farm equipment and transport industries, which in turn expanded demand for steel and coal. The heavy industry made possible by farm equipment and transportation needs later served as the foundation for the automobile industry. Subsequently, the automobile and petroleum industries made possible low-cost tractor power which markedly reduced farm labor requirements, released millions of workers to enter nonfarm industry, and freed millions of acres (formerly producing horse feed) for production of food. Moreover, the sizable middle-class commercial markets, of which farmers were a major component, enhanced opportunities for the mass production of automobiles and farm machinery. Availability of sizable, dependable markets, coupled with efficient transportation, contributed to farming efficiencies through specialization. The dairy industry could concentrate in the Great Lakes states and the Northeast; corn and hogs were specialties in the Midwest, wheat in the Great Plains. Specialization led to increased purchase of improved capital inputs from nonfarm industry, which made possible greater productivity per farm worker and paved the way for subsequent higher output, savings, and investment in agriculture. Thus a large share of the expanding population did not need to move into agriculture to supply the nation's food and fiber needs.

Agriculture in Early Stages of Growth

Economic growth of the nation in early stages was inhibited by the large proportion of the labor force and population in agriculture. Gains in national income depended heavily on progress of agriculture because it was the largest sector. And economic growth in agriculture was inhibited because the dynamic industrial sector, though it was growing rapidly, was not large enough to provide either a sizable amount of capital inputs to increase the productivity of agriculture or an outlet for labor freed from agriculture by rising productivity.

Food demand and supply were closely interrelated in early phases of growth. To some extent, supply created its own demand. The income elasticity of demand for food was comparatively high, and much of the rising output of agriculture was absorbed by increasing per capita consumption of food. Increasing output in agriculture meant rising farm income and hence increasing demand for food products within agriculture. Sizable gains in farm productivity awaited the loosening of these restraints as national income increased; the elasticity of demand for food declined, and agriculture became a smaller part of the economy. Thus the real price of U.S. farm products increased substantially between 1850 and 1920, and was not reduced until the industrial and scientific sectors had reached advanced stages of development.

The working of Engel's law caused agriculture's share of national resources and income to decline. The proportion of all U.S. gainful workers in agriculture dropped from 83.5 per cent in 1800 to 9.5 per cent in 1960 (Table 5.1). Meanwhile

TABLE 5.1. Industrial Distribution of Gainful Workers, 1800–1960, by Per Cent

	Agriculture	Manufacturing and Construction	Transport	Trade	Services	Other	Total
1800	83.5	5.4	3.0	1.3	1.3	5.5	100.0
1840	64.0	18.8	2.1	3.1	1.6	10.4	100.0
1890	42.1	26.1	6.4	8.4	13.5	3.5	100.0
1930	21.5	28.7	10.0	15.2	19.0	5.6	100.0
1960	9.5	32.7	6.7	19.0	30.9	1.2	100.0

SOURCE: Krooss (1966, p. 27).

the proportion of workers in trades, services, manufacturing, and construction rose sharply. Because farmers received lower incomes than other workers, the proportion of workers in agriculture was considerably higher than the proportion of national income originating in agriculture. In 1967 only 3.0 per cent of the U.S. national income of $653 billion originated from farming.

Industrial expansion proceeded rapidly after the Civil War but was frequently interrupted by business recessions. From 1871 to 1964 the average annual increment in the real gross national product was 3.6 per cent, in population 1.7 per cent, and in per capita GNP 1.9 per cent. Steel ingot production increased from 69,000 long tons in 1870 to over 4 million in 1890 (Bolino, 1966, p. 210). Table 5.2 provides a more complete summary of growth in manufacturing in the U.S. between 1849 and 1963. The value added by manufacturing was $464 million in 1849 and $190 billion in 1963. Annual real output of agriculture increased 1.8 per cent on the average since 1870. Real output of the manufacturing industry increased at double this rate (cf. Bolino, 1966, p. 210).

TABLE 5.2. Growth of Manufacturers, 1849–1963

	Number of Establishments	Wage Earners	Capital	Value Added by Manufacture
	(thousands)	*(thousands)*	*(thousands of dollars)*	
1849	123	957	533,245	463,893
1859	140	1,311	1,099,856	854,257
1869	252	2,054	1,694,567	1,395,119
1879	254	2,733	2,790,273	1,972,756
1889	355	4,252	6,525,051	4,210,365
1899	512	5,306	9,813,834	5,656,521
1909	268[a]	6,615	18,428,230	8,529,261
1919	290	9,096	44,466,594	25,041,698
1929	207	9,660	n.a.	30,591,435
1939	174	9,527	51,653,000	24,487,304
1949	n.a.[b]	13,880	114,139,000	75,336,527
1954	287	15,651	167,657,000	116,913,000
1958	298	16,025	n.a.	142,093,000
1959	n.a.	16,662	n.a.	161,315,000
1963	n.a.	17,065	n.a.	190,395,000

SOURCE: Bolino (1966, p. 212).

[a] Excluding hand and neighborhood manufacturing industries and establishments with products valued at less than $500.

[b] n.a. = not available.

INTERACTION IN FINANCE

As financial markets, the farm and nonfarm sectors were quite autonomous. Most of the capital accumulated in agriculture was internally financed out of farm income (Tostlebe, 1957, p. 19). Except for the 1910–19 decade, at least 70 per cent of the new farm capital from 1900 to 1960 was internally financed. In the 1940–49 decade, 91 per cent of the new capital formation in agriculture was financed from farm income.

The capital which farmers have provided the nonfarm sector has been primarily embodied in the human agent—in the education and skills of the migrants to the cities. Because of continued opportunities for internal investments on farms and because farmers were often unaware or suspicious of nonfarm investment opportunities, the bulk of farmers invested only nominally outside of agriculture.

CAPITAL REPLACES LABOR

The growth in nonfarm industry was closely related to the substitution of capital for labor in agriculture. Rising farm productivity is explained in gross terms by the substitution of improved capital inputs supplied by the nonfarm sector for less productive farm labor (Table 5.3). From 1870 to 1965, the proportions of labor and capital reversed in agriculture. In 1870 two-thirds of all farm inputs was labor; in 1965 two-thirds was capital. In 1870 about one-fifth was capital; in 1965 one-fifth was labor.

TABLE 5.3. Changes in Composition of U.S. Farm Inputs

	Labor	Real Estate	Capital[a]	Total
Percentage distribution, inputs based on 1935–39 prices[b]				
1870	65	18	17	100
1920	50	18	32	100
1930	46	18	36	100
1940	41	18	41	100
Percentage distribution, inputs based on 1947–49 prices[b]				
1940	56	14	30	100
1957	31	15	54	100
1960	27	15	58	100
1965	21	15	64	100

SOURCE: Christensen *et al.* (1964, p. 6).

[a] All inputs other than labor and real estate. Real estate includes farm buildings and other capital improvements that cannot easily be separated from the value of the land.

[b] The use of different price weights prohibits exact direct comparison of composition percentages for the periods before and after 1940.

National economic growth, reflected in lower costs and higher productivity of capital along with rising wages in the nonfarm sector, has continually enhanced opportunities to substitute capital for labor in the farm sector. Agriculture now employs more capital per worker than manufacturing. Production capital per worker in 1939 was $5,188 in manufacturing and $3,300 in agriculture. In 1960, the average production capital per worker was $18,227 in manufacturing, and $21,455 in agriculture. The figure for agriculture was $30,457 in 1965 (U.S. Department of Agriculture, 1965, p. 16; Bolino, 1966, p. 215).

The progress of agriculture can be divided into two periods: (1) from colonial times to 1930, when the increase in output was explained largely by expansion of conventional inputs, with productivity expanding on the average no more than one-half of 1 per cent per year; and (2) from 1930 to 1965, when the increase in output was explained largely by expansion of nonconventional inputs. From 1880 to 1930, output expanded 97 per cent and production inputs expanded 83 per cent (Table 5.4). From 1930 to 1965, output expanded 88 per cent and production inputs expanded only 6 per cent.

TABLE 5.4. Index Numbers of Farm Output, Input, and
Productivity, 1870–1965

	Farm Output	Production Input	Productivity[a] (output/input)
	(1957–59 = 100)		
1870	20	41	49
1880	31	53	58
1890	37	63	59
1900	48	73	66
1910	51	82	62
1920	59	93	63
1930	61	97	63
1940	70	97	72
1950	86	101	85
1960	106	101	105
1965	115	103	112

SOURCES: U.S. Department of Agriculture (1966b, p. 36;
also 1964 issue).

[a] For estimates of farm productivity by region see Kaneda
(1967).

Table 5.1 has already illustrated that the share of workers in agriculture has decreased for an extended period. Conditions that determine the number of people in agriculture—availability of capital to substitute profitably for farm labor, opportunities for farm people to obtain jobs in nonfarm industry, and the demand for farm products—were not ripe for an absolute decline in farm population until 1916. Farm population reached a peak of 32.5 million in 1916 and remained near that level for two decades until the alleviation of depressed economic conditions permitted rapid substitution of capital for farm labor and provided nonfarm jobs for farm people. From 1920 to 1965, some 80 million persons moved from farms (U.S. Department of Agriculture, 1960, 1963, 1966a). Some 44.4 million moved to farms, leaving a net migration of 35.6 million. Rearing costs of $10,000 (1965 dollars) per net migrant would place the net capital transfer at $356 billion. One may contend that lower birthrates in agriculture would have reduced rearing costs and freed additional farm capital for investment in machinery and fertilizers, but much of the cost to the farm community of this capital outflow was reduced by work performed on farms by migrants while they were on the farm.

SOURCES AND MEASURES OF EFFICIENCY

Although the depression and bad weather slowed progress and delayed the full impact, the scientific revolution hit American agriculture with force at the beginning of the third decade of the twentieth century. At that time the scientific efforts of the experiment stations founded earlier and the technology of the vast industrial sector made it possible to increase farm output without much increase in real aggregate capital ("capital" here broadly refers to the constant dollar inputs of farm labor, land, and purchased inputs). Improved seed varieties, hybrid corn, low-cost commercial fertilizers, pesticides, tractor power, and electricity were the highlights of the farm technological revolution that took place after 1920.

From 1920 to 1940, the principal source of increased farm output was the replacement of horses and mules by tractor power (Table 5.5). This not only improved timeliness of operations and tillage practices, but also released for other uses, between 1920 and 1965, an estimated 86 million acres formerly providing feed for work animals.

TABLE 5.5. Sources of Increased U.S. Farm Output

	1919–21 to 1938–40	1939–41 to 1949–51	1949–51 to 1959–61	1959–61 to 1980 (est.)
	(per cent)			
Reduction in farm-produced power	51	22	10	0
Change in crop production per acre	34	37	87	73
Change in cropland use	−4	15	−28	−13
Change in net livestock production	19	26	31	40
Change in total farm output	100	100	100	100

SOURCE: Christensen *et al.* (1964, p. 8).

Since 1940, the principal source of additional farm production has been rising crop yields. Of the increase in crop yields between 1940 and 1955, the percentage accounted for by fertilizer is 55 per cent, hybrid corn 12 per cent, and irrigation 7 per cent (Christensen *et al.*, 1964, p. 9).

The forty-eight conterminous states used 8.4 million tons of principal plant nutrients in 1965. If each ton added production equal to 15 unfertilized crop acres, then fertilizer added the equivalent of 126 million acres to cropland. Thus the release of cropland from production of power and the use of commercial fertilizer added production capacity equivalent to 212 million cropland acres. The above factors partly explain our ability to feed twice as many people on 302 million cropland acres in 1965 as were fed on nearly the same acreage in 1910. Over 600 million acres of cropland would be required in 1969 to provide food and fiber needs on land of 1910 productivity.

Several measures of farming efficiency are shown in Table 5.6. The spectacular increases are in output per man-hour and in persons supplied per farm worker.

TABLE 5.6. Selected Measure of Farming Efficiency, 1910–65

	Output per Production Input	Crop Production per Acre	Livestock Production per Breeding Unit	Output per Man-hour	Persons Supplied per Farm Worker
	(1957–59 = 100)				*No.*
1910	62[a]	68	n.a.[b]	24	7.07[c]
1920	63	74	55	26	8.27
1930	63	64	70	28	9.75
1940	72	76	75	36	10.69
1950	85	84	86	61	15.47
1960	105	109	105	115	25.85
1965	112	124	110	153	37.02
Increase 1910–65 (per cent)	81	82	n.a.	538	424

SOURCES: U.S. Department of Agriculture (1966b; also 1964 issue).
[a] See Table 5.4 for earlier estimates.
[b] n.a. = not available.
[c] Persons supplied at home and abroad per U.S. farm worker were 4.12 in 1820, 3.95 in 1840, 4.53 in 1860, 5.57 in 1880, and 6.95 in 1900.

Considering that the number of persons supplied per farm worker increased only 72 per cent in the hundred years from 1811 to 1910, the gains since then are indeed impressive. The measure of efficiency is misleading, however, because about half the farm inputs in 1965 were supplied by the nonfarm sector—the average farm worker received much outside help to feed 37 persons in 1965!

Output per man-hour increased by a spectacular 538 per cent since 1910. This measure too is inadequate, because it imputes to labor the output that arises from capital investment. The way to make labor productive is to use so much capital that the return on the latter is zero. The rising output per man-hour is in one sense a measure of lack of labor efficiency. Low productivity and attendant low returns for labor in agriculture caused capital to replace labor. Because output was maintained or even increased by the process, the gains in output per unit of labor were spectacular. Measured by gross output per horse, think how productive the few remaining farm horses are today! Measuring efficiency by output per unit of all production inputs partially circumvents the problems of one resource being used inefficiently and is the best measure of farming efficiency in Table 5.6.

Another way of measuring efficiency is in the purchasing power of earnings from an average hour of factory labor. This again is a poor measure of farming efficiency because it reflects productivity gains in manufacturing as well as in farming. In 1929 one hour of factory labor bought 6.4 loaves of bread, 1.2 pounds of steak, or 7.8 pints of milk. By 1966, one hour of factory labor bought 12.4 loaves of bread, 2.5 pounds of steak, or 19.6 pints of milk. Consumers spent only 18.2 per cent of their income for food in 1966; 25 per cent in 1950. Had they bought the same market basket of commodities as in 1950, they would have spent only 13 per cent of their income for food in 1965. The farmer received only 40 per cent of the consumer food dollar in 1966, hence the share of consumer dollar that went to the farmer was approximately .4(18.2) = 7 per cent (U.S. Department of Agriculture, 1966d, pp. 7, 55).

Data in Table 5.7 compare labor, capital, and total production input effi-

TABLE 5.7. Efficiency of Labor, Capital, and All Inputs in Farm and Nonfarm Industries to 1962

	Farming	All Nonfarm Industries	Selected Nonfarm Industries			
			Manufac- turing	Trans- portation	Trade	Services
(Per cent of 1929)						
Labor efficiency (output per unit of labor)						
1929	100	100	100	100	100	100
1937	109	116	116	146	114	93
1948	147	144	135	232	144	129
1953	175	168	156	280	157	143
1962	225	170	185	320	160	185
Capital efficiency (output per unit of capital)						
1929	100	100	100	100	100	n.a.[a]
1937	106	108	121	106	74	n.a.
1948	111	148	152	222	120	n.a.
1953	103	149	158	221	144	n.a.
1962	110	155	165	220	130	n.a.
Total conventional input efficiency (output per unit of all production inputs)						
1929	100	100	100	100	100	n.a.
1937	107	114	117	138	114	n.a.
1948	143	144	138	227	141	n.a.
1953	171	164	157	267	151	n.a.
1962	210	185	180	300	170	n.a.

SOURCES: 1929–57 data from Kendrick (1961); recent data from Tweeten and Olson (1964, p. 48). Data are based on value added, not total output.

[a] n.a. = not available.

ciency between sectors from 1929 to 1962. The estimates are based on *value added* by farming rather than *total output*, hence do not necessarily agree with the data in Table 5.6. Labor efficiency (output per unit of labor) averaged 225 per cent of the 1929 level on farms in 1962. This was considerably higher than the increase in labor efficiency of all other industries, which rose to 170 per cent of the 1929 average by 1962. The trends were similar to 1948; then agriculture began to move ahead at a rapid pace.

Agriculture does not come out so well in output per unit of capital, mainly because many farmers have been overzealous in machinery purchases. The last set of data in Table 5.7 shows output per unit of labor and capital combined and is the best measure of efficiency in the table. Again agriculture comes out well, at least in the postwar period. It is above the average of all nonfarm industries in efficiency and is exceeded only by transportation, of all the major industries.

All of the foregoing measures show gains in *relative* efficiency over time rather than absolute efficiency in agriculture. Substantial inefficiency could have characterized the use of resources in all periods. The foregoing data show only that progress has been made.

Considerable savings in the cost of inputs could be achieved by further substitution of capital for labor on farms. Based on a Cobb-Douglas aggregate production function, farm labor was estimated to be in excess supply by two-fifths in the 1952–61 period (Tyner and Tweeten, 1966, p. 613).

Reducing labor by this amount and increasing capital items on the average by 17 per cent would enable farmers to earn opportunity cost returns on all resources. The cost of excess capacity was approximately $2.2 billion, or 6.6 per cent of the resource volume; the cost of a nonoptimum input mix was $2.0 billion, or 5.9 per cent of the resource volume in the 1952–61 period. A more nearly optimum output level and input mix could have saved $4.2 billion, or 12.5 per cent of the actual volume of production inputs.

The above results show overcapacity and input savings from changing the *aggregate* input mix, not from changing the input mix among regions or farms. Based on an income-efficient organization of farm resources in the north central region, income could have been raised an estimated $6.1 billion in 1959 (Kaldor and Saupe, 1966, p. 590). Extrapolating this to the entire U.S., the potential income gain from an efficient organization of all farms would have been $10.4 billion, or approximately one-third of U.S. farm output.

This magnitude is substantial, but inefficiency may be just as large in the nonfarm sector. Excess capacity in the manufacturing sector, measured as the percentage of capacity not utilized, was 9 per cent in 1966 (*Economic Report*, 1967, p. 253). From 1953 to 1961 it averaged 16 per cent. An estimated 25 per cent of the steel industry capacity and 22 per cent of the automobile industry capacity lay idle in the 1953–64 period (Keyserling, 1965, p. 41). The inefficiency would be even larger if the cost of an inefficient resource combination and gains from a recombination of resources were included. There are substantial opportunities to raise efficiency throughout the economy and it is difficult to say whether agriculture is more or less efficient than other sectors from these data.

An alternate measure of efficiency is the relative price level in two sectors. If the demand for farm products is rising less rapidly than the demand for other items in a relatively closed economy and yet farm prices rise relative to other prices, this is evidence of lagging farm efficiency.

From 1889 to 1957, the average annual compound rate of growth in productivity in the private domestic economy was 1.7 per cent and in agriculture only .76 per cent (Loomis and Barton, 1961, p. 28). The relative price of farm commodities doubled from the beginning of the Industrial Revolution to 1920. This record of agricultural productivity is less than impressive. Nevertheless, the conclusion of special importance is not that farm productivity gains were insufficient to forestall an increase in the real price of farm products, but the fact that productivity in nonfarm industry expanded so rapidly and that the real cost of farm products did not rise even more as food needs grew. And the real price of farm commodities has declined substantially since World War II.

AGRICULTURE IN THE SCIENTIFIC AGE

One of the important characteristics of this scientific age is the gradual realization that research to create new products and techniques can be a profitable economic investment. A corollary is that man, through science, has virtually unlimited capacity to amplify the output from the basic raw materials provided by nature. The world's great ultimate resource is the human mind and its ability to shape the materials of nature to improve economic living standards and real income.

In American agriculture, the aggregate food supply expanded to meet a total demand that increased about 1.8 per cent annually with little increase in the aggregate volume of conventional inputs of farmland, labor, and capital from 1950 to 1965. These *conventional* inputs increased in productivity because of the use of *nonconventional* inputs, principally education and research. Similar increases in productivity due to technological and educational advancements took place in many sectors of our economy.

Gains in output per unit of conventional resources in U.S. agriculture are the direct result of adoption of new and improved machinery, fertilizers, seeds, pesticides, feeds, and management techniques. Specialization, large-scale operations, and improved financial, insurance, and transportation facilities have contributed in a quite direct way to farm productivity. These direct sources of rising productivity can ultimately be viewed as the result of nonconventional inputs which have helped considerably to create the environment that made new technologies feasible. Education has shaped the goals and values of farmers and made them more profit conscious and more aware of cost-reducing innovations. Education has created the foundation for the skills, apparatus, and knowledge that make research economically feasible.

Traditionally, economists have concerned themselves with optimum allocation and accumulation of conventional production capital, land, and labor inputs. In a total sense, however, the optimum allocation of inputs cannot be judged without including education and research as production inputs. In other words, just as managers decide to invest in operating capital, machinery, or plants based on expected returns, so managers—or in the case of public funds, society as a whole—can do the same with the cost-returns approach for investments in research and education.

Investment to raise the productivity of conventional farm and nonfarm resources through research and education tends to be a more roundabout process than typical capital investment. But the basic principles of investment still apply. In competitive equilibrium—the point of optimum allocation of inputs—the return on investment equals the discount people place on future versus present consumption. Investments that yield, say, over 8 per cent are exploited, and those that yield less are shunned. This process among many individuals in the market leads to the determination of the interest rate which is a measure of investment yield opportunities and time preference for consumption. Institutional restrictions, indivisibilities, and uncertainties severely distort the process, however.

The earlier conclusion that output per unit of labor is a very inappropriate measure of farming efficiency because capital inputs are omitted (and may be used very inefficiently) applies also to another measure—output per unit of production inputs. Productivity, measured by output per unit of farm production inputs, may be rising rapidly as research and education inputs are applied. But if the latter nonconventional inputs have very low returns, *total* input use may be very inefficient. Efficiency depends in part on how well nonconventional inputs are used. It is possible that agricultural resources in total might be used very *inefficiently* because nonconventional resources are applied in excess to achieve the impressive gains cited in Tables 5.6 and 5.7 of conventional resource productivity. The rates of return on education, research, and knowledge are given below as a basis for evaluating these issues.

EDUCATION

The cost of education can be subdivided into private cost, borne by the individual, and public cost, borne by society, primarily through taxes. Private costs include opportunity costs incurred by individuals (due to earnings forgone while attending school), and costs of books, transportation, and clothing over and above what would have been purchased if the student had not been attending school.

Public costs include repairs, interest and depreciation of capital items, and salaries and operating costs paid by the public. Adding these public costs to private costs, total resource costs in 1956 were estimated to be $280 per elementary student, $1,420 per high school student, and $3,300 per college student (Schultz, 1963, p. 29).

There have been several attempts to compute the contribution of education to national economic growth. Denison attributes 23 per cent of the national income growth in the 1929–57 period to education. The combined categories "education" and "advancement in knowledge," account for 43 per cent of the national income growth in the 1929–57 period (Denison, 1962, p. 125).

From data on school costs, the total capital stock of education embodied in the U.S. labor force has been estimated in 1956 dollars to be $180 billion in 1929 and $535 billion in 1957. Schultz (1961) concluded that growth in education accounted for between 36 and 70 per cent of the increased earnings per worker from 1929 to 1957. His data also indicated that up to one-third of the increase in national income between 1929 and 1957 can be imputed to expanded education per worker. After adjusting data for sex, government service, and internal interest rates, another researcher concluded that education contributed only one-seventh of the national income increment between 1929 and 1956 (Bowman, 1964).

Analysis of education costs and returns for agriculture have been made by Gisser (1965), who derived estimates of the marginal product of education from specifications of the demand and supply of farm labor. Using hired labor wages as a measure of the marginal product for farm labor, he computed the period needed to recover all school costs from added earnings. It ranged from 3.0 to 6.5 years in the north Atlantic area, from 2.7 to 5.9 years in the Great Lakes and Great Plains area, from 2.2 to 4.8 in the Southeast, and from 3.0 to 6.6 in the West and Southwest (Gisser, 1965, p. 46). These "overlapping" results support the hypothesis that the profitability of schooling in agriculture does not vary significantly by area.

Census data on earnings provided the foundation for computing rates of return on schooling for various race, sex, and sector groups (Table 5.8). The rural farm sector includes farm operators, hired farm workers, and unemployed persons. The rate of return may be interpreted as an interest rate that could be paid on outlays for education to make such investment a break-even opportunity —in which case it would be just as profitable to forgo the schooling as to obtain it.

The private rate of return is the decision variable most applicable to the individual, since it includes only costs (mainly forgone earnings) incurred by individuals for schooling. The private rates of return for white males for all sectors were considerably above typical interest rates or returns on nonschooling investment alternatives. Hence, on the average, returns should provide strong

TABLE 5.8. Estimated Private and Social Rates of Return on Investment in Schooling, in Per Cent, United States, 1959[a]

	Elementary School (8 yrs. over no schooling)	High School Dropout (9–11 yrs. over 8 yrs.)	High School Graduate (12 yrs. over 8 yrs.)	College Dropout (13–15 yrs. over 12 yrs.)	College Graduate (16 yrs. over 12 yrs.)
(White males, U.S.)					
Private rate	155.1	20.6	15.8	12.1	13.6
Social rate	17.8	11.9	9.9	8.3	9.7
(White females, U.S.)					
Private rate	37.8	22.7	32.2	6.9	9.9
Social rate	5.6	6.2	9.2	2.3	4.2
(Nonwhite males, U.S.)					
Private rate	78.8	24.9	22.1	2.2	6.0
Social rate	9.7	11.0	11.8	.6	3.0
(White males, urban)					
Private rate	155.9	11.7	11.6	12.9	12.8
Social rate	21.2	7.8	7.9	8.0	9.7
(White males, rural nonfarm)					
Private rate	179.3	—	21.5	—	11.8
Social rate	24.8	—	13.8	—	8.5
(White males, rural farm)					
Private rate	87.9	—	12.2	—	16.0
Social rate	20.7	—	8.4	—	10.2

SOURCES: Preliminary results from Redfern (1969); basic data from U.S. Bureau of the Census (1960).

[a] Private rates of return are estimated from added earnings from education and from costs based on earnings foregone by continuing in school; the internal rate of return makes the present value of benefits and costs equal to zero. Social rates of return are estimated in the same way but also include costs of instruction, facilities, etc., borne by the public. Rates not calculated are indicated by dashes. Rates of return are adjusted for ability and other variables.

economic incentives for schooling irrespective of the benefits from schooling as a consumption good. Four years of college appeared to be only a marginally attractive economic investment for nonwhite males in 1959. Although earnings generated by schooling were lower for farm than urban residents, costs were also lower. Thus rates of return from high school and college were of somewhat comparable magnitudes for farm and urban residents. At the high school level, rural nonfarm residents appear to combine some of the high earnings of urban residents with the low education costs of farm residents; and the result is a high rate of return.

Social rates of return are computed from costs of schooling paid by the public as well as the individual. It is a better measure than private rates of the contribution of schooling to national economic growth. The social rate, like the private rate, trends downward with higher levels of schooling. Social rates of return to white males for college completion in all sectors shown in Table 5.8 tend to be near typical rates of return on business investments and may exceed the rate of return on numerous alternative public investments, except research. White females, because their earnings are frequently cut short by marriage, and non-white males, because of job discrimination and other factors, experienced a low social rate of return on investment in schooling in 1959.

In summary, there appeared to be relatively few uses of capital that would bring greater private or social rates of return to farm and nonfarm male whites than investment in schooling at all levels shown in Table 5.8. And education through at least high school was economically productive on the average for all groups shown in the table, including nonwhites and females.

The quality of education in rural areas varies widely and has an important impact on the output of education. One estimate places the internal rate of return on investment in teachers' salaries to improve the quality of schools at approximately 25 per cent (Welch, 1965, p. 59).

Research

Federal outlays for research and development have shown a spectacular rise since 1940, and in 1965 totaled $15.4 billion. Only 1.5 per cent of these funds were for agriculture in 1965. The majority of funds for research and development are allocated not to specific economic sectors but to general categories of defense, atomic energy, and space. After subtracting funds in these categories from all

TABLE 5.9. Federal Government Expenditures for Scientific Research and Development

	All Federal Expenditures		Agriculture		Nonagriculture	
	Total (1)	Less Defense, AEC, and Space (2)	Total Expenditures (3)	Per cent of (2) (4)	Total Expenditures (5)	Per cent of (2) (6)
	millions of dollars			%	$ *mil.*	%
1940	74	46	29	63.0	17	37.0
1950	1,083	155	53	34.2	102	65.8
1955	3,308	219	73	33.3	146	66.7
1960	7,738	698	132	18.9	566	81.1
1965[a]	15,371	1,677	231	13.8	1,446	86.2
1966[a]	15,438	1,898	258	13.6	1,640	86.4

SOURCES: U.S. Department of Commerce (1960, p. 613; 1966, p. 544). Data include plant expenditures.

[a] Preliminary.

federal outlays, the proportion of federal funds for agricultural research and development was 63 per cent in 1940 and 13.6 per cent in 1966 (Table 5.9). This relative decline occurred despite the large absolute increase in funds for agricultural research.

Private industry allocated considerably more in 1965 to domestic agricultural research and development than the U.S. Department of Agriculture and State Agricultural Experiment Stations combined (Table 5.10). Outlays were primarily to improve efficiency in production and marketing and were directly oriented mainly to crops and livestock rather than to people. Programs oriented most

TABLE 5.10. Agricultural Research and Development Program, by Goal, Fiscal Year 1965

	USDA[a]		SAES[b]		Industry		Total USDA, SAES, and Industry		Relevant to Agriculture Other[c]	
	$ *mil.*	%	$ *mil.*	%	$ *mil.*	%	$ *mil.*	%	$ *mil.*	%
Resource conservation	28.6	17	19.9	9	17.0	4	65.5	8	16.5	5
Protection of forests, crops, and livestock	43.8	26	46.5	21	115.0	25	205.3	24	152.1	42
Efficient production of farm and forest products	25.2	15	98.4	43	115.0	25	238.6	28	148.1	41
Product development and quality	39.0	23	26.6	12	160.0	35	225.6	26	1.3	d
Efficiency in the marketing system	9.4	6	7.2	3	15.0	3	31.6	4	e	e
To expand export markets and assist developing countries	1.1[f]	1	0.5[f]	d	8.0	2	9.6	1	0.6[g]	d
Consumer health, nutrition, and well-being	11.1	7	9.5	4	22.5	5	43.1	5	12.7	3
To raise level of living of rural people	3.1	2	3.4	2	1.5	d	8.0	1	14.2	4
To improve community services and environment	5.6	3	14.7	6	6.0	1	26.3	3	19.5	5
Total	166.9	100	226.7	100	460.0	100	853.6	100	365.0	100

SOURCE: Association of State Universities and Land Grant Colleges and U.S. Department of Agriculture (1966, p. 56).

[a] U.S. Department of Agriculture.

[b] State Agricultural Experiment Stations.

[c] Other universities and federal agencies.

[d] Less than .5 per cent.

[e] No observations in the sample.

[f] Does not include funds to support USDA-SAES research workers located in and working on problems of a foreign country.

[g] Based on only one observation in the sample.

directly to people (the last three categories in the table) utilized less than 10 per cent of the funds for agricultural research and development. The category "Human needs and resources" is more narrowly oriented to problems of rural poverty and accounted for only 3 per cent of total Department of Agriculture, State Agricultural Experiment Stations, and industry research outlays for agriculture. This was too little. But it is also important to improve the efficiency with which crops and livestock are produced in order to raise the well-being of consumers and farmers.

Several estimates have been made of the rate of return on investment in agricultural research and extension in the U.S. (Table 5.11). Several of the rates

TABLE 5.11. Estimated Internal Rates of Return to Investment in Agricultural Research and Extension in the United States

	Rate of Return
	(*per cent*)
Poultry (Peterson)	50
Hybrid corn (adapted by Peterson from Griliches)	37
All research and extension (separate estimates by approaches of Schultz, Griliches, Evenson)	45–53
By regions (Evenson)	
Northeast	110
Lake states	91
Corn belt	152
Northern Plains	50
Appalachian	57
Southeast	38
Delta	34
Southern Plains	36
Mountain	30
Pacific	180

SOURCES: Peterson (1969, p. 28); regional data from Evenson (1969, p. 31).

of return cluster around 50 per cent. It is somewhat surprising that the estimates for two success stories, hybrid corn and poultry, give internal rates of return no higher than the average of all investment in research and extension. The estimated rates of return by regions are subject to considerable error, but suggest that research and extension have been unusually profitable in the Pacific region and east of the Missouri River in the North. Perhaps these areas are best suited by soil, topography, and moisture (either natural or from irrigation) for profitable utilization of improved inputs and techniques.

Estimates of rates of return on research in the nonfarm sector are few. A summary of estimates places typical returns on private capital invested in industrial research at 20 to 100 per cent, with 50 per cent a reasonably representative return (Tweeten, 1969). These high rates of return on research in farm and nonfarm sectors suggest economic inefficiency—more resources should have been invested unless precluded by uncertainties and sharply diminishing returns.

Many of the foregoing estimates are crude. One serious limitation is that they tend to be average rather than marginal rates and are internal to industries. The rates have limited relevance in guiding *ex ante* the next dollar of research investment for a given project, individual or firm. Yet there remains a residue of intuitive feeling that the rate of return on research will remain high in the future when averaged over many firms and projects as above. The problem is to decide how the limited research fund should be allocated for maximum efficiency.

A special task force on agriculture research suggested the needed direction of future efforts (Association of State Universities and Land Grant Colleges, 1966, p. 188). The group recommended a 76 per cent increase in scientist man-years between 1965 and 1977. The major recommended expansion in percentage terms were in efforts to expand export markets and assist developing countries (359 per cent), to raise the level of living of rural people (167 per cent), and to improve community services and environment (163 per cent).

RATES OF RETURN ON NONCONVENTIONAL INPUTS

Table 5.12 contains estimates of the contribution to national income in 1965 from agricultural productivity advances since 1910. National income in 1965 was $556 billion. Only 3.5 per cent of it originated in the farm sector. Assume that in 1965—as was true in 1910—35 per cent of the U.S. population lived on farms. Further, assume that on the average—as in 1965—persons on farms contributed $1,580 per capita to national income and persons not on farms contributed $2,958. Then the national income would have been $75 billion (or 13 per cent) lower in 1965 without the changes in agricultural productivity that accrued from all sources since 1910. Estimates for recent years from Table 5.12 suggest that the changes stemming from greater farm productivity accelerated national income about $1 billion each year from 1962 to 1965. If each annual increment is $1 billion and is permanent, the present value of accumulated future benefits from each annual change in productivity totals $20 billion when discounted at 5 per cent.

The approach used in Table 5.12 was to estimate contributions of agricultural productivity to national income on the basis of employment and the relative earnings of persons in the farm and nonfarm sectors. A second approach was to compute productivity gains as the value of conventional inputs saved through application of nonconventional inputs. From 1950 to 1965 productivity increased 2 per cent annually in agriculture. Based on a farm output of $35 billion, the annual saving in conventional inputs is approximately $35 × .02 = $.7 billion.

TABLE 5.12. Estimated Contribution to the 1965
National Income of Changes in U.S. Agriculture
since 1910

Decade or Year	Contribution to 1965 National Income [a]
	(*billions of 1965 dollars*)
1910–19	12.5
1920–29	13.9
1930–39	4.5
1940–49	21.1
1950–59	15.5
1960	1.9
1961	1.6
1962	1.1
1963	1.6
1964	.8
1965	1.1
Total since 1910	75.5

SOURCES: Income and population data from
U.S. Department of Agriculture (1966c, pp. 43,
45; also 1960 issue, p. 37).

[a] Based on changes in farm population from
April of the previous year to the following
April; changes in nonfarm population are from
July to July.

This estimate includes the net value of all production inputs freed from agriculture and assumes that labor and other resources are mobile. This estimate of the
dollar value of all inputs saved by rising productivity is not far out of line with
the estimates in Table 5.12. In the past, labor has been the major resource
released for alternative uses by application of nonconventional resources.
Farmers cannot long continue to migrate in the numbers recorded for the past
decade, or no one will be left to farm. It follows that future productivity contributions of agriculture to national income will be best measured by total
production inputs freed from agriculture or production inputs that would have
been required in the absence of productivity advances—the second approach
used above—rather than by the approach in Table 5.12.

The cost of nonconventional inputs to raise productivity totaled an estimated
$6.2 billion in 1965 (Table 5.13). If annual benefits of $1 billion are permanent,
and are directly associated with the knowledge input of $6.2 billion, the rate of
return on investment is 16.1 per cent. This crude estimate is by no means the only
possible estimate of the rate of return on investment in farm productivity. View-

TABLE 5.13. Estimated Cost of Nonconventional Farm Inputs in 1965

		Millions of dollars
Education		3,072
Elementary (2,052,000 students at $500/student)	1,026	
High school (834,000 students at $1,500/student)	1,251	
College (220,000 students at $3,500/student)	770	
Vocational education (adult)	25	
Extension		189
U.S. Department of Agriculture	72	
State and local	117	
Research		1,112
U.S. Department of Agriculture	166	
State agricultural experiment stations	227	
Industry	460	
Other	365	
Less timber and forest research	− 106	
Public roads		560
Government services (hospitals, public health, police, fire protection, administration, etc. $75/person)		926
Information (newspapers, magazines, books, etc.)		300
Total		6,159

SOURCES

Education. Primary and secondary enrollment data: Cowhig (1963, p. 12); college attendance data: Nam and Cowhig (1962, p. 14), adjusted to 1965. Vocational education includes only expenditures for adults; other vocational expenditure included in secondary education. Vocational agriculture expenditure is a total of $80 million × 31 per cent for adults (cf. U.S. Department of Commerce, 1966, pp. 140, 141). Cost estimates: U.S. Department of Commerce (1966, p. 104) and Schultz (1961); adjusted to rural areas by Folkman (1961).

Extension. U.S. Department of Agriculture, Economic Research Service, unpublished (for budget costs), and U.S. Department of Commerce (1966, pp. 139, 143).

Research. Association of State Universities and Land Grant Colleges (1966, pp. 56, 58).

Public roads. Outlays for public roads and highways totaled $12.2 billion in 1965 (U.S. Department of Commerce, 1966, p. 423). An estimated $5.6 billion was for purposes other than capital additions. One-tenth of this amount was charged to agriculture. No interest was charged on road and highway capital.

Government services. U.S. Department of Commerce (1966, p. 423).

Information. An allowance of $24 per capita was made for miscellaneous information services.

ing the farming establishment as one large firm, it may be argued that commodity programs have been an inseparable part of the spending for nonconventional inputs and that commodity programs would not have been needed had there been less investment in nonconventional inputs. Furthermore, there is some evidence that farm programs contributed to efficiency by speeding outmigration of surplus farm labor. If the cost in 1965 ($4.2 billion) of programs to support farm prices and income is included, the total annual cost is $10.4 billion. If we use the lower estimate ($.7 billion), presented above as the permanent annual benefit, then the rate of return on investment in nonconventional inputs is reduced to 6.7 per cent.

The assumption is made that annual productivity gains are permanent because increased specialization, scale economies, new techniques, and improved inputs and management are not lost after one year, but persist for a long period until in many cases they become inputs for further improvements in ways of farming. Imputing a shorter life to productivity gains, or some other matching of input to output, would give a different result than that reported above.

There are strong advantages in combining education and research expenditures into a single "knowledge" category as above. Because education and research are complements, it is extremely difficult accurately to separate the aggregate effects of each. Also many education and research expenditures are failures in an economic sense, and it is well to include both the successes and failures in the estimates.

The above rate of return on investment in nonconventional inputs (or "knowledge") in agriculture can be compared with an estimate for the U.S. in all fields. Based on public and private outlays for schooling, research, publishing, radio, television, and other categories, the total cost of knowledge production in the U.S. was $136 billion or 29 per cent of the adjusted gross national product in 1958 (Machlup, 1962, pp. 354–57).

The combined categories of education and knowledge explain 43 per cent of the national income growth in the 1929–57 period, according to one estimate (Denison, 1962). Assume that in the late 1950's, half the annual increment in national income could be attributed to creation of knowledge. Based on a national income of $400 billion and an annual average growth of $20 billion, or 5 per cent, then $10 billion of income growth in the U.S. would be attributed to creation of knowledge. If this gain is permanent and related to the 1958 cost, the rate of return on creation of knowledge in the U.S. is 7.4 per cent.

Equilibrium in use of capital between sectors occurs when rates of return on investment in agriculture and other sectors are equal. The computed rates of return on knowledge (7.4 per cent for the U.S. economy and 6.7–16.1 per cent for agriculture) provide no basis for rejecting the hypotheses that an optimum allocation existed between economic sectors. The rates of return on research, many near 50 per cent in both the farm and nonfarm sectors, provide no basis for concluding that a major reallocation of research between sectors was needed. The high rate of return on research suggests that more capital could have been profitably allocated to that form of knowledge creation. The marked rise in research funds indicates that this allocation has been in process. Available data indicating comparable rates of return on education in the farm and urban sectors provide no basis for expecting a major redistribution of funds for education between the two sectors at this time. In the long run, however, the nonfarm sector will experience an increase in the proportion of investment in education and research.

LOOKING TO THE FUTURE

Research appears to have become more profitable and necessary in many cases in order to meet competition. Thus we can expect a continued rise in private research investment. Because of traditional emphasis placed on private industry and efficiencies therein, private firms will perform an increasing amount of publicly financed research and development. Yet it is an interesting observation that the principal future sources of economic growth—education and research—are not very efficiently allocated by the price mechanism. Allocation of funds for science is based to a great extent on institutional forces. The impact of these trends on our economy and culture is indeed significant.

Long-run trends in funds for investment in education, research, and development between sectors depend on several factors. The rate of return on research is known only in retrospect and hence is not a very efficient allocator. However, expectations of returns are of importance. The fact that agriculture was one of the first major industries singled out for massive research emphasis is only partly explained by expectations of large economic gains from such outlays.

More important reasons for early emphasis on farm research may have been the market structure and size of the farm sector. The public reasoned that the individual farmer could not undertake a program of research. Farmers acting individually possessed neither the capital nor the equity to bear the consequences of uncertain returns on any one undertaking, nor did they have a market and production potential sufficient to reap the gains from research. Where bigness counted, the government of a prosperous society no longer needed to spend all its product on direct, immediate needs. It found itself in a position to support research in agriculture—the nation's major industry.

Undoubtedly, public funds will continue to be a major source of support for research and development in all sectors—including private industry—for some of the same reasons that individual farmers could not undertake the needed extensive research program.

Partly motivated by large payoffs from research in agriculture, private and public focus is now fixed on research as a productive investment of limited capital. This emphasis also is motivated by the improved methodology, trained personnel, and apparatus—electronic computers for example—that reduce the cost of research per unit of findings.

The rate of return on investment in research and development is expected to continue to be high. Other things being equal, initial investments utilize obvious opportunities and in general exploit areas where research returns are high. Further investments would be expected to encounter lower payoffs through the principle of diminishing return and obsolescence of knowledge.

But scale economies are important. In science new investments feed and prosper on old breakthroughs. Bigger, more efficient apparatus and trained personnel can use funds more effectively. The ubiquitous involvement in research ensures that one effort may gain from insights gleaned in another. For these and other reasons, the investment in science probably will not soon reach a stage of diminishing returns and low productivity if growth is balanced. Rather, the age of science is cumulative. It has the potential for a continued vast increase in knowledge and its application with attendant gains in our national welfare. Subsequent chapters will reveal, however, that the investment in research has been a mixed blessing to the farm sector.

SUMMARY AND CONCLUSIONS

It is difficult to conceive of an environment more favorable for economic growth than that which was found in the U.S. Natural resources such as soil, coal, oil, and iron ore were abundant. The land-man ratio was high. The population had know-how and aspirations consistent with economic progress. They were willing to take reasonable risks in pursuit of future gain. Abundance of food sustained the laborer for work in farm and factory. Schooling and material capital formation progressed with income. Each generation had more capital and education than the last, paving the way for more physical and human capital formation in succeeding periods.

The optimism bred of past success provided an impetus for continued investment and expansion. Sometimes a degree of "irrational" entrepreneurship helped. Railroads were sometimes built where there were no settlements and no commodities to transport and were not generally profitable to investors. Nevertheless there were large external economies to transportation, and railroads provided the cutting edge of progress that made subsequent settlement and economic growth feasible.

In the colonial period, income was not much above subsistence levels and saving was difficult. There was little inducement to forgo current consumption in order to invest because rates of return on capital were not particularly high. Growth in national income did little more than keep pace with population until the "take-off" stage was reached the decade before the Civil War. Investment then was raised sufficiently to add significantly to the stock of capital and to output. Once growth in output had well exceeded growth in population, it became easier to save out of income. In the economic milieu, success breeds success.

Expansion of farm output generally has followed the path of least cost. Land initially was cheap, and conventional farm resources were the primary means of expansion until 1930. The land frontier was gone by the late nineteenth century. New frontiers awaited. The internal combustion engine created a "power" frontier which was prominent after 1920. The seed and fertilizer frontiers opened later. After World War II, frontiers opened in chemical pesticides and in feed-handling. The team of agriculture and industry early provided a very basic interaction for economic growth. But this team was not spectacularly successful in raising farm productivity until joined by a third member—science in the form of education and research. Forces of science are continually creating new frontiers. One can only speculate what frontiers await the future (cf. Cochrane, 1965, pp. 45–71).

National economic development imposed price ratios which encouraged substitution of capital for labor. Profitability was not the only impetus for change, however. Farmers often purchased production items as they would consumption items—for comfort, convenience, and prestige.

The impressive advances in farm output in the past two decades have not come from magical new inputs but largely from gains in the quality and quantity of "old stand-bys"—seed, fertilizer, machinery, and pesticides. From more intelligent use of these inputs, farmers have squeezed impressive gains in output. Changes in scale, specialization, timing of operations, intensification, and recombinations of these inputs may be regarded as the product of improved farm management. Even without a major breakthrough in production of synthetic foods, the nation's ability to increase farm output by raising the quality and quantity of conventional farm inputs and farm management is substantial.

EFFICIENCY OF THE FARMING INDUSTRY

Several measures of farming efficiency (including number of persons supplied per farm worker, and output per unit of labor, capital, and conventional inputs) were examined but were considered to be conceptually inadequate for gauging the performance of agriculture.

To make conclusions about the efficiency of American agriculture, it is very important to consider both *static* efficiency and *dynamic* efficiency. The most appropriate measure of static efficiency is the rate of return on resources. Economic equilibrium occurs in a competitive economy when returns are equal for a given resource employed among various uses, adjusted for risk and transfer cost. Although equilibrium is never achieved in a dynamic economy and competitive conditions are not met, still comparable returns suggest a tendency toward economic efficiency. Rates of return, to be discussed more fully in the next chapter, on "conventional" investment to produce goods and services in non-farm industry typically run 10 per cent or somewhat higher. It is of interest that the social rates of return on investment in a college education (the frontier or marginal investment) for white males both in the farm sector and urban sector are near 10 per cent. Rates of return on knowledge creation both for agriculture and the entire economy are also in line with these estimates. These data are consistent with static efficiency and call for no major realignment of investment.

However, rates of return on conventional production capital on most farms (except larger farms) tend to be low, and rates of return on research tend to cluster around 50 per cent. These rates of return reflect inefficiency—too much conventional production input and too little research input. The inefficiency may not be large, nonetheless, because of the adjustment pains that would attend a more rapid reduction in conventional production inputs and because of problems that would attend an increase in research inputs in a farm sector characterized by uncertainty, surplus capacity, and adjustment problems. The payoff from agricultural research, though large, has not been as favorable as some early studies indicated. In some instances, the public may have overinvested.

The above static measures rate agriculture as inefficient in some respects and as no more efficient than other sectors of the economy. Dynamic measures, such as the rate of adoption of new and improved inputs and the attendant freeing of manpower and other resources for other sectors, rate the record of American agriculture as superb. The contribution of agricultural adjustments to national income and the declining real cost of food is a success story, unparalleled anywhere in the world. If farmers had not responded to economic incentives and had not migrated to nonfarm jobs in huge numbers, the investment in agricultural research and education would have had a small economic payoff. This is not to say that the adjustments were easy. Later chapters will consider how public policy might have better served the needs of outmigrants and others called to bear the cost of greater farming efficiency.

The above paragraphs highlight the conflict between static and dynamic measures of efficiency. A farm economy in static equilibrium is likely to demonstrate little dynamic efficiency. Very low or very high rates of return are static measures of needed adjustments. A dynamically efficient sector will adjust resources and production in response to these signals. Despite substantial adjustments, however, in a really dynamic economy it is impossible to fully catch up and completely erase differences in rates of return.

Lessons from Development

Several lessons for economic growth of developing nations can be learned from the American experience. The basic principle of growth—that resources in plentiful supply be used to remove restraints on those of short supply—is universal. Developing nations have two important advantages not enjoyed by the U.S.: (1) Developed nations can provide them with considerable capital.

(2) Developing nations can draw from the large store of accumulated knowledge and techniques (they can also profit from our mistakes).

But developing nations have several handicaps that hinder progress. Time, cost, and knowledge are required to transfer and apply techniques developed elsewhere. The culture, institutions, and attitudes in these nations are often old, well-established, inflexible, and inimical to growth. Class prerogatives, bureaucracy, inefficient landholding patterns, and political instability are but a few of the factors that create a growth environment quite unlike that in the U.S. Nations with people and institutions which make it difficult to save part of their output, and which lack investment opportunities and entrepreneurs who can rise above the growth-inhibiting environment, may need to seek other paths to progress than the somewhat unstructured approach used in the U.S.

With favorable attitudes, institutions, and abundant resources, the gross national product of the U.S. grew 4 per cent annually from 1871 to 1964. This would little more than keep pace with population growth in some countries of Latin America. The U.S. experience counts population growth as a favorable or neutral force for economic progress (defined as income per capita), but unless effective measures are taken to reduce population growth, many developing nations are destined to experience a growing divergence in income per capita between themselves and developed nations. The high man-land ratios found in many developing nations mean that instead of concentrating efforts to raise farm output per unit of labor, as in the U.S. experience, they must emphasize gains in output per unit of land. This means concentration on improved seeds, irrigation, and fertilizers rather than on machinery. Here the experience of Taiwan, Israel, and Japan may be more instructive than the U.S. experience.

While the U.S. record is indeed impressive, it is not particularly outstanding when ranked beside the growth rate of Japan (Johnston, 1966, p. 305). This observation is partly explained by the fact that per capita income in Japan began at a lower level and, despite impressive gain, is today considerably short of that in the U.S. But considering the fact that economic development in Japan was superimposed on an old culture with comparatively few resources and that the U.S. development took place in a dynamic new environment, the Japanese experience appears even more impressive. The experience in Japan—and in Taiwan, South Korea, and Mexico—proving that traditional societies with higher man-land ratios than in the U.S. can achieve economic development provides some basis for optimism.

REFERENCES

Association of State Universities and Land Grant Colleges and U.S. Department of Agriculture. 1966. A national program of research for agriculture. Washington.

Becker, Gary S. 1964. *Human Capital*. National Bureau of Economic Research. New York: Columbia University Press.

Bolino, August C. 1966. *The Development of the American Economy*, 2nd ed. Columbus: Merrill Books.

Bowman, Mary Jean. 1964. Schultz, Denison and the contribution of "Eds" to national income growth. *Journal of Political Economy* 72:450–64.

Christensen, R. P., W. E. Hendrix, and R. D. Stevens. 1964. How the United States improved its agriculture. ERS Foreign-76. Washington, U.S. Department of Agriculture.

Cochrane, Willard W. 1965. *The City Man's Guide to the Farm Problem*. Minneapolis: University of Minnesota Press.

Cowhig, James D. 1963. Age-grade school progress. U.S. Department of Agriculture Economic Report No. 40. Washington.

Denison, Edward F. 1962. Education, economic growth and gaps in information. *Journal of Political Economy* 70 (Suppl.):124–28.

Economic Report of the President. 1967. Washington: U.S. Government Printing Office.

Evenson, Robert. 1969. Economic aspects of the organization of agriculture research. In Fishel (1969).

Fishel, Walter, ed. 1969. *Resource Allocation in Agricultural Research*. Minneapolis: University of Minnesota Press.

Folkman, William S. 1961. Rural problem areas need better schools. *Agricultural Economic Research* 13:122–30.

Gisser, Micha. 1965. Schooling and the agricultural labor force. Unpublished Ph.D. thesis. University of Chicago.

Griliches, Zvi. 1958. Research costs and social returns: hybrid corn and related innovations. *Journal of Political Economy* 66:419–31.

————. 1964. Research expenditures, education and the aggregate agricultural production function. *American Economic Review* 54:961–74.

Johnston, Bruce F. 1966. Agriculture and economic development. *Food Research Institute Studies* 6:251–312.

Kaldor, Donald and William Saupe. 1966. Estimates and projections of an income-efficient commercial farm industry in the north central states. *Journal of Farm Economics* 48:578–96.

Kaneda, Hiromitsu. 1967. Regional patterns of technical change in U.S. agriculture, 1950–1963. *Journal of Farm Economics* 49:199–212.

Kendrick, John W. 1961. *Productivity Trends in the United States*. Princeton, N.J.: Princeton University Press.

Keyserling, Leon H. 1965. Agriculture and the public interest. Conference on Economic Progress. Washington.

Krooss, Herman E. 1966. *American Economic Development*. Englewood Cliffs, N.J.: Prentice-Hall.

Loomis, Ralph A. and Glen T. Barton. 1961. Productivity in agriculture. ARS Technical Bulletin No. 1238. Washington.

Machlup, Fritz. 1962. *The Production and Distribution of Knowledge in the United States*. Princeton, N.J.: Princeton University Press.

Nam, Charles B. and James D. Cowhig. 1962. Factors related to college attendance of farm and nonfarm high school graduates: 1960. Series Census-ERS (P-27) No. 32. Washington, U.S. Department of Agriculture.

Peterson, Willis. 1969. The returns to investment in agricultural research in the United States. In Fishel (1969).

Redfern, Martin. 1969. Unpublished data on rates of return on education. Stillwater, Oklahoma State University, Department of Agricultural Economics.

Schultz, T. W. 1961. Education and economic growth. In Nelson B. Henry, ed., *Social Forces Influencing American Education* (60th yearbook, part II), National Society for the Study of Education. Chicago: University of Chicago Press.

————. 1963. *The Economic Value of Education.* New York: Columbia University Press.

Tostlebe, Alvin S. 1957. *Capital in Agriculture.* Princeton, N.J.: Princeton University Press.

Tweeten, Luther G. 1969. The search for a theory and methodology of research resource allocation. In Fishel (1969).

———— and Carl Olson. 1964. Efficiency: the aggregate result of managerial action. *Oklahoma Current Farm Economics* 37:43–52.

Tyner, Fred H. and Luther G. Tweeten. 1966. Optimum resource allocation in U.S. agriculture. *Journal of Farm Economics* 48:613–31.

U.S. Bureau of the Census. *U.S. Census of Population, 1960* (subject reports, educational attainment, final report PC (2)-5B). Washington: U.S. Government Printing Office.

U.S. Department of Agriculture. 1960. Farm population estimates for 1950–59. AMS-80. Washington.

————. 1963. Farm population estimates for 1910 62. ERS-130. Washington.

————. 1965. The balance sheet of agriculture. ERS Agricultural Information Bulletin No. 290. Washington.

————. 1966a. Farm population estimates for 1965. ERS-286. Washington.

————. 1966b. Changes in farm production and efficiency.

————. 1966c. Farm income situation. ERS, FIS-203. Washington.

————. 1966d. Handbook of agricultural charts, 1966. Agricultural Handbook No. 325. Washington.

U.S. Department of Commerce. 1960. *Historical Statistics of the United States.* Washington: U.S. Government Printing Office.

————. 1966. *Statistical Abstract of the United States.* Washington: U.S. Government Printing Office.

Welch, Finis. 1965. The determinants of the return to schooling in rural areas. Unpublished Ph.D. thesis. University of Chicago.

CHAPTER SIX

Farm Problems

This chapter is devoted to the symptoms and causes of farm problems. Four possible symptoms of farm problems are (*a*) high consumer food cost, (*b*) price and income instability, (*c*) involvement of the government or organized farm groups in farm economic activity, and (*d*) low farm income. The real cost of food has fallen substantially in the last two decades in the U.S. and happily is not a symptom of U.S. farm problems. Thus the discussion of symptoms is focused on farm income and government involvement in agriculture. The presentation of symptoms is followed by an analysis of factors which cause and perpetuate farm problems. The causes of low rates of return on farm resources receive emphasis in this chapter; causes of rural poverty will be examined in a later chapter.

FOOD COST

The most ubiquitous evidence of farm problems in world perspective is the high relative cost of food. Consumers in many nations spend more than half of their income for food, while U.S. consumers spend less than one-fifth of their income for food, including marketing services. The cost of farm food in the U.S. may be defined as the outlays by consumers for the farm-produced ingredients of food plus the federal budget for agriculture (including half of the amount spent for Food for Peace). This combined cost of farm foods and agricultural programs was $20.5 billion in 1947 and $31.1 billion in 1965. Some inflationary element is present in these figures, hence the data must be deflated by the implicit price deflator of the gross national product (1958 = 100). The result shows that real spending for farm foods and agricultural programs was the same, 30 billion constant dollars, in 1947 as in 1965. And farmers were feeding 50 million more people in 1965! The real cost of farm foods and agricultural programs was $191 per capita in 1947, and $144 per capita in 1965. The reduction in the real cost of food is a truly remarkable achievement. Outlays for farm foods and agricultural programs comprised only 6 per cent of U.S. disposable income in 1965. Unfortunately, this unprecedented success datum has a less favorable side—low farm income—which will be discussed later.

ECONOMIC STABILITY

The variability and not just the level of farm prices and incomes was long a major symptom of farm economic problems. The historical record of fluctuating farm prices and incomes has been cited in previous chapters and needs little further documentation. This instability has been dampened but not eliminated by government policies. It has been caused by business cycles which lead to variation in domestic demand, by unstable world markets, and by factors which affect the supply of farm products such as weather and commodity cycles. Judicious use of monetary and fiscal policies and the secular decline in the income elasticity of demand for farm commodities have removed business cycles as a serious source of variation in domestic aggregate demand for farm products. The supply of farm commodities continues to fluctuate because of commodity cycles and weather, but the impact on the farm economy has been lessened by crop insurance and, what is more important, by government commodity programs.

In the decade preceding 1965, total net farm income ranged from a high of $13.5 billion to a low of $11.3 billion (U.S. Department of Agriculture, 1966b, p. 40). This period was characterized not only by the most intense government involvement in the farm economy up to that time but also by the greatest relative stability of farm income.

Some price and income changes are necessary to induce adjustment of resources and commodities to economically efficient uses. Yet price variation from 1950 to 1966 was greater than explained by this factor alone. The annual average index of prices received by farmers (1957–59 = 100) from 1950 to 1966 ranged from 80 to 133 for meat animals, from 97 to 118 for dairy products, and from 90 to 144 for poultry and eggs (*Economic Report*, 1967, p. 300). Variation in prices for individual components of these series was much greater. Price fluctuation caused by imperfect expectations, apparent in cycles of livestock production, is a social cost to society and a continuing source of frustration to farmers.

In the absence of government programs, price and income instability would be large and would be a very serious long-term frustration for commercial farmers. It would be caused especially by unstable foreign demand and unstable output of farm products. It would be compounded by high cash production costs and by the rising price flexibility of demand for farm products. The price flexibility of long-run domestic demand for food at the farm level increased from −4 in the 1922–41 period to −10 in the 1948–65 period (Tweeten, 1967a). This means that, on the average, in the domestic market a 1 per cent increase in quantity depressed prices by 4 per cent in the prewar period and by 10 per cent in the postwar period.

GOVERNMENT IN AGRICULTURE

A third symptom of farm problems is the involvement of the government in controlling farm production and supporting farm income. Value judgments in our society are that each farmer should be free to make his own production and marketing decisions and that income from the market is unequivocally superior to income from the U.S. treasury.

FEDERAL COST OF FARM PROGRAMS

From 1932 to 1966, the federal government spent nearly $50 billion to support and stabilize farm income. Federal outlays for such purposes (including half of Food for Peace) averaged $3.9 billion from 1961 to 1966 (Table 6.1). During this period, programs to support farm income were clearly the largest component of the federal budget for agriculture.

Direct government payments to farmers totaled $3,277 million in 1966, an average of $1,012 per farm (U.S. Department of Agriculture, 1968a, p. 46).

TABLE 6.1. Federal Budget for Agriculture, 1961–66

	1961	1962	1963	1964	1965	1966
Federal budget for agriculture	*Millions of dollars*					
Farm income stabilization	2,176	2,871	3,693	3,798	3,236	1,925
Land and water	347	367	324	324	341	346
Rural electrification and telephone	301	303	342	342	392	373
Farming and rural housing loans	349	234	300	251	268	160
Research and other services	324	341	391	414	457	503
Total	3,498	4,116	5,050	5,129	4,694	3,307
Food for Peace	1,823	1,947	2,040	2,049	1,843	1,784
Farm income stabilization plus half of Food for Peace (Total)	3,088	3,844	4,713	4,822	4,158	2,817
(Per cent of gross income)	7.7	9.2	11.0	11.6	9.1	5.7
(Per cent of personal taxes)	195	223	267	283	246	151
Personal taxes paid by farmers[a]	1,585	1,727	1,768	1,702	1,689	1,863

SOURCES: U.S. Bureau of the Budget (1967, pp. 66, 67) and U.S. Department of Agriculture (1968a).

[a] Taxes and nontax payments to local, state, and national government.

Government transfer payments to farmers have sometimes been justified by the claim that all sectors are subsidized by the government. Farmers in 1966 paid $1,863 million in income taxes and other personal taxes to local, state, and national governments (Table 6.1). This was substantially less than federal outlays to support farm income. If other industries were subsidized at similar rates, the federal government would incur very large deficits indeed.

Yet the word "subsidy" has a negative emotional connotation that is not entirely appropriate. To some extent, treasury costs are a substitute for market receipts. The latter would by no means be called a subsidy. Low-income consumers spend a higher proportion of their dollars for food than high-income consumers. The progressive structure of income taxes that support the federal budget for agriculture falls heaviest on persons with high income. To the extent that the utility of money is higher on funds spent for food than for taxes—and that tax dollars are a substitute for consumer dollars as a source of farm income —government subsidies to support farm income are a social gain rather than a social cost. Studies cited in previous chapters have shown that government farm programs have not reduced farming efficiency, and that outlays for agricultural research have been a most rewarding economic investment.

EXCESS CAPACITY

The federal outlays for agriculture are closely related to another symptom of the farm problem—excess capacity—defined as the surplus of production capacity over market utilization at socially acceptable prices. Three measures of farm excess capacity are given in Table 6.2 for 1955 to 1962. The first measure is net stock accumulation of the Commodity Credit Corporation plus probable production on land withdrawn from production by government programs, divided by anticipated farm output in the absence of farm programs. These programs might be the first to be terminated under free markets; they would have increased commercial marketings by an average of 3.5 per cent for the 1955–62 period.

If 40 per cent of government-subsidized exports are also included with excess capacity, then excess capacity as a percentage of probable production was approximately 7 per cent from 1960 to 1962. And finally, if all net Commodity Credit Corporation stock acquisitions, exports under government programs, and production withdrawals are included, then excess capacity was approximately one-tenth of probable farm output in the last two years shown in Table 6.2.

Data in Table 6.1 permit a crude estimation of excess capacity in more recent years. Assuming each dollar spent on programs to stabilize farm income (plus half of the Food for Peace outlays) represents removal of one dollar of farm production capacity, then excess capacity as a percentage of gross income ranged from 6 to 12 per cent from 1961 to 1966. The more carefully formulated estimates

TABLE 6.2. Excess Capacity in U.S. Agriculture, Measured by the Percentage of Production Diverted from Price-Setting Markets by Government Programs

| | Government Diversions as Per Cent of Potential Production at Existing Prices under Three Conditions[a] | | |
	A	B	C
1955–56	3.8	6.4	8.1
1956–57	.0	5.3	8.9
1957–58	4.4	9.1	12.3
1958–59	7.7	11.2	13.5
1959–60	4.3	9.1	12.4
1960–61	1.8	7.1	10.6
1961–62	2.8	7.4	10.4

SOURCE: Tyner and Tweeten (1964).

[a] A—Net purchases of farm commodities by the Commodity Credit Corporation plus estimated production on land diverted from production by land withdrawal programs, divided by actual farm output plus anticipated production on diverted areas.

B—Same as A, but including as government diversion 40 per cent of subsidized exports with net stock accumulation by Commodity Credit Corporation and land withdrawal.

C—Same as B, but including as government diversions *all* subsidized exports, net stock accumulation by Commodity Credit Corporation, and land withdrawal.

in Table 6.2 are not conceptually comparable to the crude estimate of excess capacity in Table 6.1. One reason is that inclusion of direct payments in Table 6.1 (which have increased markedly since 1961 and which do not necessarily represent production withdrawals) leads to overestimation of excess capacity. Comparison of overlapping data in Table 6.1 with the second estimate (considered to be the most reasonable) in Table 6.2 supports the conclusion that excess capacity has been 5–10 per cent of farm output from 1956 to 1966.

Presence of excess capacity need not necessarily imply a serious problem. As stated previously, reserve capacity has been useful in national emergencies, and private enterprise may not provide the socially desirable stockpile of reserves because of uncertainties and high capital costs.

FARM INCOME

The final and most convincing symptom of a farm problem is low farm income. Income has many dimensions including size and type of farm, race, time, and location. It also has price and output dimensions. Perhaps the most frequently used measure of economic health in agriculture is the parity ratio, the ratio of prices received to prices paid by farmers (Table 6.3). The index of prices

TABLE 6.3. Index of Prices Received and Prices Paid by Farmers; Parity Ratio as Per Cent of 1910–14 Average.

	Prices Received for Crops and Livestock	Prices Paid (Parity Index) Including Interest, Taxes, and Wage Rates	Parity Ratio	
			Excluding Government Payments	Including Government Payments
		(1910–14 = 100)		
1910	104	97	107	n.a.
1920	211	214	99	n.a.
1930	125	151	83	n.a.
1940	100	124	81	88
1950	258	256	101	102
1960	238	300	80	81
1961	240	302	80	83
1962	244	307	80	83
1963	242	312	78	81
1964	236	313	76	80
1965	248	321	77	82
1966	266	332	80	86

SOURCE: U.S. Department of Agriculture (1966c, p. 14).

received by farmers has increased substantially since the 1910–14 period. The index of prices paid by farmers increased even more. Hence the parity ratio was only 80 per cent of the 1910–14 average in 1966. It has remained somewhat stable since 1960. Because direct government payments comprise a growing proportion of farm income, these payments are included in a second measure of the parity ratio in Table 6.3. This adjustment raised the "effective" parity ratio from 77 to 82 in 1965.

IMPROVEMENTS IN FARM TECHNOLOGY REDUCE THE PARITY RATIO NEEDED FOR A GIVEN INCOME

While parity price standards may have been designed originally to associate a given parity price ratio with a specified farm income, this relationship continues to change. The parity price ratio needed to obtain a specified net farm income falls as farming efficiency rises. Competitive equilibrium and constant returns to scale specify that

$$P_y Y - P_x X = 0,$$

where P_x is prices paid, X is aggregate production input, P_y is prices received, and Y is aggregate farm output. Rearranging terms,

$$\frac{Y}{X} = \frac{P_x}{P_y}.$$

Thus in equilibrium, the output-input ratio equals the inverse parity price ratio, and all costs of production are covered by receipts. Assume an average index of productivity Y/X of 100 and a parity price ratio P_y/P_x of 100 in 1910–14. If the productivity index rises to 171, as it did in 1960, the parity index could drop to 58 in 1960 and give resource returns comparable to those in the 1910–14 period under the above assumptions. These results show why many farmers prefer the parity price ratio to measures of parity income. With 100 per cent of parity prices, farmers can obtain a higher real net income in 1965 than in 1910! Nevertheless, the productivity index is an imperfect guide to parity prices needed to cover all costs of production because of structural changes in the farm and nonfarm sectors not included in the simple model, market disequilibrium, and imperfections in the price and productivity indices. Thus we must examine farm income trends for more reliable measures of farm economic health.

AGGREGATE FARM INCOME AND PRODUCTION EXPENSES

Total gross farm income, $49.5 billion, less production expenses of $34.8 billion, left a net farm income of $14.6 billion in 1967 (Table 6.4). This net was not substantially below the all-time record of $18 billion set in 1947. The purchasing power of farm income had fallen, however, and created a larger gap in real income between 1947 and 1967. Net income was deflated by the index of prices paid by farmers for family living items to show purchasing power in the last column of Table 6.4. In real terms, net farm income in 1967 was one-third below the immediate postwar level.

The real economic position of farmers must take into account off-farm earnings of farm people, trends in farm population, and the income of nonfarmers. The impact of these factors was not discernible from Table 6.4, but is apparent in Table 6.5. Farmers in the 1960's received substantial personal income from employment and other earnings in the nonfarm sector. This added much to income but still left it lower than nonfarm per capita income. Farmers have

TABLE 6.4. Total Gross Income, Production Expenses, and Net Income from Farming, 1910–67

	Cash Receipts from Marketing[a]	Govern-ment Pay-ments	Total Non-money Income[b]	Total Gross Farm Income	Produc-tion Expenses[c]	Total Net Income	
						Current dollars	1957–59 dollars
	Millions of dollars						
1910	5,780	0	1,909	7,689	3,531	4,158	11,983
1920	12,600	0	4,032	16,632	8,837	7,795	9,744
1930	9,055	0	2,148	11,203	6,944	4,259	8,518
1940	8,382	723	2,235	11,340	6,858	4,482	10,671
1950	28,461	283	4,339	33,083	19,410	13,673	15,899
1960	34,154	702	3,574	38,431	26,352	12,079	11,842
1967	42,788	3,079	3,597	49,464	34,820	14,644	12,959

SOURCES: U.S. Department of Agriculture (1968a and previous issues).

[a] Includes crops and livestock.

[b] Includes commodities consumed in home, rental value of dwelling, and net change in farm inventories.

[c] Includes current operating expenses, depreciation and consumption of capital, taxes on farm property, interest on mortgage debt, net rent, and government payments to nonfarm landlords; does not include the opportunity cost of family labor and equity capital.

TABLE 6.5. Average Per Capita Farm Personal Income and Farm and Nonfarm Disposable Personal Income

	Farm Per Capita Personal Income		Per Capita Disposable Income		
	From Farm Sources	From Nonfarm Sources	Farm Population, All Sources	Nonfarm Population, All Sources	Farm as Per Cent of Nonfarm
	Dollars		*Dollars*		%
1940	158	91	245	671	36.5
1950	612	272	841	1,458	57.7
1960	737	458	1,100	2,017	54.5
1961	824	509	1,226	2,050	59.8
1962	856	573	1,308	2,127	61.5
1963	906	637	1,410	2,191	64.4
1964	875	718	1,462	2,340	62.5
1965	1,096	812	1,772	2,477	71.5
1966	1,235	901	1,976	2,637	74.9
1967	1,203	992	2,037	2,784	73.2

SOURCE: U.S. Department of Agriculture (1968a).

improved their income position relative to nonfarmers since 1940. The drastic decline in farm population has not been sufficient to offset the income disparity between sectors, and per capita disposable farm income was nearly $1,000 less than that in the nonfarm sector in recent years. The discrepancy between income in the two sectors is even larger based on average income of workers. "Farm workers" include hired laborers, farm operators, and family labor (except those doing housework). By this standard, the average annual income of farm workers was $2,567 below that of factory workers in 1965.

One aim of public policy is to achieve comparable real labor income in the farm and nonfarm sectors. The factory wage, often used as the standard of comparison, is inadequate. Gale Johnson (1958, p. 164) estimated for 1956 that per capita farm income should have been 68 per cent of per capita nonfarm income if labor of comparable earning ability were to receive the same real returns in the two sectors. Dale Hathaway (1963, p. 37) concluded that "the returns for comparable labor would be about equal if the median income of farm families were 86 per cent of nonfarm families." Vernon Ruttan (1966, p. 1107) concluded that "a valid analysis . . . would indicate substantially lower real purchasing power for rural than urban families with similar money incomes."

The gap in income between sectors would have to narrow through time to represent comparable real income, but not necessarily at the trend in the estimates cited by the authors above. As farm income rises, families increasingly prefer to spend their income for entertainment and other cultural activities, which are quite costly to farmers far from urban culture centers. The importance of food grown and consumed at home declines with rising farm income. There is also some doubt whether the estimates by Johnson and Hathaway adequately accounted for the cost of transportation, equivalent schools, and other social services in rural areas.

In their calculation of the farm-nonfarm income ratio needed for comparable real income, Johnson and Hathaway adjusted for differences in age, sex, education, and purchasing power of farm income. An exact evaluation would also need to include psychic satisfaction of farm versus city employment and living. Some contend that the farm way of life gives greater satisfaction than city life and hence that real farm income with the same buying power for economic goods should in "social" equilibrium be less than nonfarm income. That is, the difference in real-money income is due to the satisfactions farmers receive from rural living. Evidence for this proposition is provided by Bellerby (1956, p. 270) and Hagen (1958, p. 501), who show that nonfarm income tends to be greater than farm income throughout the world. What appear to be "psychic" earning differentials are explained in part by the process of economic development, with higher wages necessary to attract people to growing industry and by lack of knowledge. These factors will be discussed in more detail later.

ASSETS AND EQUITY

The asset position of farmers is another measure of financial health. Production assets per farm increased from $17,378 in 1950 to $65,960 in 1966 (U.S. Department of Agriculture, 1966c, p. 22). Debt as percentage of assets increased from 9.4 to 16.3 per cent in the same period. Debts averaged 41 per cent of assets over all manufacturing firms in 1966; thus, by this measure, the farming industry is in a favorable financial position. While farmers had unusually high assets per farm and had sizable equity, their equity percentage is declining according to these figures.

Heady (1967, p. 15) published data showing farmers with an average net worth per family of $43,973, compared with an average net worth per family in the entire nation of $22,588. Median net worth of farm families was only $26,250, indicating a highly skewed distribution. Farmers have accumulated a high net worth through a high propensity to save, through capital gains on farm real estate, and through a family farm structure wherein parents pass considerable equity to children who farm. It will become apparent later that a favorable average net worth for the farm industry has comparatively little meaning for the income of many farmers. The above data hide essential information on the distribution of assets and equity among farms.

FARM INCOME BY ECONOMIC CLASS

Economic classes of farms, grouped by sales volume, illustrate that farm net income is closely related to farm size (Table 6.6). Output, measured by cash receipts, was heavily concentrated on large farms. The farms with gross sales over $40,000 in 1967 comprised 6 per cent of all farms but accounted for 47 per cent of all farm output measured by receipts. Farms with sales under $5,000 in 1967 comprised 54 per cent of all farms but produced only 7 per cent of farm output.

Wide differences exist in net income among classes of farms. This inequality is partly explained by the resource structure. In general, cash production items such as fertilizer, high-protein feeds, and pesticides are highly productive, while machinery, labor, and real estate are relatively less productive per unit of cost. The output of larger farms tends to be produced with cash operating inputs (costs) in excess of the sales percentage. The situation is reversed for the categories of smaller farms. The more nearly optimum input mix on large farms helps to explain some of the differences in efficiency and net income.

High land quality is one hypothesis that potentially explains the efficiency of large farms. To the extent that land value reflects quality, 1960 data provide no

TABLE 6.6. Number of Farms, Farm Income, and Farm Expenses, by Economic Class of Farms, 1960 and 1967

Sales		I $40,000 and over	II $20,000– $39,999	III $10,000– $19,999	IV $5,000– $9,999	V $2,500– $4,999	VI and Noncommercial Farms (less than $2,500)
		Economic Class of Farm					

Sales		I $40,000 and over	II $20,000– $39,999	III $10,000– $19,999	IV $5,000– $9,999	V $2,500– $4,999	VI and Noncommercial Farms (less than $2,500)
Number of farms							
Total number	1960	113	227	497	660	617	1,848
(thousands)	1967	183	318	492	446	360	1,347
Per cent of total	1960	2.9	5.7	12.5	16.7	15.6	46.6
	1967	5.8	10.1	15.6	14.2	11.5	42.8
Cash receipts from farm marketings							
Dollars per farm	1960	101,327	28,551	14,835	7,750	3,959	1,079
	1967	117,749	30,006	16,100	8,350	4,258	1,187
Per cent of total	1960	32.8	18.6	21.2	14.7	7.0	5.7
	1967	47.0	20.8	17.3	8.1	3.4	3.4
Realized gross farm income							
Dollars per farm	1960	102,796	29,806	15,829	8,564	4,681	1,785
	1967	119,481	31,506	17,254	9,260	5,050	2,034
Farm production expenses							
Dollars per farm	1960	83,841	21,154	10,461	5,259	2,720	935
	1967	95,727	21,714	10,988	5,676	3,031	1,016
Per cent of total	1960	35.9	18.2	19.7	13.2	6.4	6.6
	1967	50.3	19.8	15.5	7.3	3.2	3.9
Realized net farm income							
Dollars per farm	1960	18,955	8,652	5,368	3,305	1,961	850
	1967	23,754	9,792	6,266	3,585	2,019	1,018
Per cent of total	1960	18.3	16.7	22.7	18.6	10.3	13.4
	1967	30.5	21.9	21.7	11.2	5.1	9.6
Total income, including off-farm income and nonmoney income [a]							
Dollars per farm	1960	21,132	10,330	6,626	4,878	3,810	3,581
	1967	28,781	12,679	8,975	7,394	6,138	6,699

SOURCE: U.S. Department of Agriculture (1968a, pp. 68–72).

[a] Includes income from food grown and consumed on farm and rent on farm dwelling.

support for this hypothesis (Tweeten, 1965, p. 209). The value per acre, excluding the farm dwelling, was highest for class III commercial farms and noncommercial farms and was nearly as low for class I as for class VI farms. Class I farms averaged $302,000 of productive assets and 2,491 acres per farm. The "modal" commercial farms, class IV, averaged $45,000 productive assets and 282 acres in 1960.

Off-farm income made up a sizable proportion of income of small farms, and in 1967 raised average income per farm above $6,000 for each class of farms shown in Table 6.6. Subtracting the opportunity cost of equity capital would reduce the net income by a considerable amount, however.

RATES OF RETURN ON FARM RESOURCES

The symptom of a farm problem referred to as low farm income is composed of two fundamental components. One is low absolute net income to pay living expenses. This welfare issue of farm poverty will be treated in considerable detail in later chapters. The other component consists of low rates of return on farm resources. The latter component is sometimes called the commercial farm problem, although farms in poverty even more frequently experience low rates of return on their resources.

Low rates of return are defined as earnings below opportunity costs on farm resources. There are problems in allocating returns among owned resources such as family labor and land and in selecting a suitable opportunity cost. If an opportunity charge is made for all farm resources except farm real estate, and this charge is subtracted from gross farm income, the residual is the return to farm real estate capital. From 1950 to 1957, the annual average residual rate of return on investment based on income earnings of farm real estate was 3.2 per cent and capital gain averaged 4.9 per cent for a total average rate of return of 8.1 per cent (U.S. Department of Agriculture, 1968b, p. 33). For the 1958–67 period, the income rate of return was 3.6 per cent and capital gains 5.5 per cent, providing a total annual average rate of return of 9.1 per cent on investment in farm real estate.

Common stock may be taken as an alternative investment of comparable risk. Dividends plus capital gains on common stock averaged a 17.6 per cent rate of return annually on investment in the 1950–57 period and 11.8 per cent in the 1958–67 period. This means that farm real estate capital was earning less than its opportunity cost on the average. If farm real estate would have been costed at this opportunity cost of common stock, included with other nonlabor expenses, and subtracted from gross farm income, then farm labor would have showed an average return in the above periods lower than its opportunity cost.

The above data suggest that farm resources were earning low returns *on the average*. But averages can be misleading, and it is necessary to disaggregate the data. The U.S. Department of Agriculture compiles budgets for farms of various types, sizes, and locations throughout the country (U.S. Department of Agriculture, 1966a, p. 4). Subtracting all costs, including hired labor and the opportunity cost of equity capital from gross farm income, the residual left a negative return per hour of operator and family labor on cattle ranches and sheep ranches in the Southwest in 1965. The residual labor return was 50 cents or less per hour on ten farms and was less than $1 per hour on twenty typical farms. The hourly return was less than the average hourly earnings of factory workers ($2.61 in 1965) on 36 of the 42 farms. Yet 1965 was a reasonably typical year for farm income.

Farm families with low incomes are found in all parts of the U.S. but tend to be most concentrated in the South and among minority groups (see Chapter 12). Median income of nonwhite farm families in the South was only about half that of white farm families in the region in 1964. Since Negroes are leaving agriculture at a more rapid rate than whites, the racial dimension will become less important in explaining low average farm income in the future.

Table 6.7 is taken from a comprehensive study of the parity-returns position of farms, by economic class of farms (100 per cent of parity returns would mean that farm resources would be earning their opportunity cost). The results indicate that *average* returns on farm resources were low compared with their opportunity cost in 1959, 1964, and 1966 but were improving. The results differ substantially according to farm size. Farms with gross sales over $20,000 earned more than opportunity costs of their resources in 1964 and 1966, but smaller farms earned less than opportunity costs on the average.

TABLE 6.7. Number of Farms, Returns from Farming, and Returns from Farming as Percentage of Parity Returns, 1959, 1964, and 1966

Class (by sales) and Year	Number of Farms		Cash Receipts plus Government Payments (percentage of total)	Returns from Farming per Farm			Returns from Farming as Percentage of Parity Returns (stockholder standard)	
	Total	Per-centage of Total		Realized Net Farm Income	Capital Gain	Total	Excluding Capital Gain	Including Capital Gain
	Thousands	%	%			*Dollars*	%	%
All farms								
1959	4,097	100.0	100.0	2,773	1,042	3,815	67	47
1964	3,472	100.0	100.0	3,747	1,588	5,335	81	69
1966	3,252	100.0	100.0	5,049	2,013	7,062	96	82
$20,000 and over								
1959	325	7.9	49.1	11,506	4,489	15,995	129	61
1964	424	12.2	61.2	14,979	5,521	20,500	158	101
1966	527	16.2	68.3	17,539	6,298	23,837	167	112
$10,000–$19,999								
1959	503	12.3	21.5	5,091	1,521	6,612	83	54
1964	488	14.0	18.8	5,984	1,980	7,964	90	76
1966	510	15.7	17.1	6,869	2,173	9,042	98	84
$5,000–$9,999								
1959	693	16.9	15.5	3,160	1,061	4,221	62	46
1964	530	15.3	10.7	3,434	1,387	4,821	64	60
1966	446	13.7	7.9	3,989	1,527	5,516	70	67
Under $5,000								
1959	2,576	62.9	13.9	1,114	509	1,623	39	35
1964	2,030	58.5	9.5	945	726	1,671	32	39
1966	1,769	54.5	6.7	1,071	813	1,884	35	43

SOURCE: U.S. Department of Agriculture (1967, p. 22); data for 1966 are preliminary.

In an earlier study, the opportunity cost of all farm resources except operator and family labor was subtracted from all farm income including off-farm income (Tweeten, 1965, p. 211). The average income in 1960 per worker (excluding hired labor) was found to average $14,487 on farms with gross sales over $40,000. It was $1,991 per farm worker on farms with gross sales from $2,500 to $4,999. This estimate did not include capital gains. If average annual capital gains from 1950 to 1960 were included with gross farm income, then the larger farm class averaged $27,782 per worker and the smaller class averaged $3,012 per worker in 1960. The factory wage averaged $4,665 per worker in 1960. If this is chosen as the opportunity cost of farm labor, then only farms with gross sales over $20,000, comprising 10 per cent of all farms, received labor incomes on a par with factory worker earnings in 1960, with capital gains excluded. Inclusion of farm capital gains brought the earnings of farmers with gross farm sales over $10,000 up to the factor worker standard. If farm incomes need to be only 89 per cent of factory worker incomes to be a comparable real income, then farms with gross sales over $5,000 per year tended to receive a satisfactory return for their labor with capital gains included. A serious limitation of this analysis is that capital gains and income are by no means evenly distributed among farms, even within a given economic class.

PARITY PRICE RATIO REQUIREMENTS BY CLASS OF FARM in 1960

Price ratios required to pay all farm resources an opportunity return provides further insight into the income position of farms by size classes. The required parity price ratio in Table 6.8 is defined as that price level (1910–14 = 100) needed for gross farm income to cover the cost of all farm inputs, including the opportunity cost of equity capital and all labor. The labor cost is man-hour requirements in farming multiplied by the urban wage rate adjusted for age, education, and sex. In 1960, the median age of all farm operators was 51 years and median education was 7.8 years. For operators of class VI farms, median age was 54 years and education was 7.0 years; hence their parity labor income was reduced accordingly. The opportunity cost for farm operator labor was set at $2.20 per man-hour of farm employment on class I, II, and III farms, $1.94 per hour on class IV farms, $1.86 per hour on class V farms, and $1.80 per hour on class VI farms. Each man-hour of unpaid family labor was set at $1.60 per hour and each man-hour of hired labor at $1.54 per hour. The average factory wage was $2.61 per hour in 1960.

Conditions A, B, and C in Table 6.8 differ because of the charge for real estate capital. In condition A, the opportunity cost for farm real estate was the dividend rate plus capital gain on common stock, arbitrarily considered a comparable investment risk to farm real estate. Condition B includes only a 5 per cent interest charge on farm real estate. Condition C includes a 5 per cent charge for

TABLE 6.8. Parity Price Ratio (1910–14 = 100) Required to Earn a Parity Resource Return under Selected Assumptions in 1960 and 1966

	Economic Class of Commercial Farms						Non-commercial Farms
Condition[a]	I	II	III	IV	V	VI	
				1960			
A	94	105	119	142	173	258	330
B	74	77	89	109	137	217	236
C	64	65	75	92	119	197	190
				1966			
	—— 73 ——			86	103	——— 167[b] ———	

SOURCES: For 1960 data see Tweeten (1965). The parity ratio was computed as follows: costs of land, capital, and labor were totaled and divided by all farm receipts (excluding off-farm income and including receipts from farm products sold plus government payments plus value of farm products consumed on the farm), then multiplied by the parity ratio (including government payments) which was 81 in 1960. In all cases the cost of nonreal estate durable capital was 5 per cent interest plus depreciation. The cost of all farm labor was man-hour requirements multiplied by the wage rate of factory workers, corrected for the age, education, and sex of all farm-hired, operator, and family workers.

Data for 1966 from U.S. Department of Agriculture (1967, p. 25). The opportunity cost of real estate was based on a landlord standard that is somewhat comparable in concept to the B estimate for 1960.

[a]A—Parity ratio required to cover *all* farm production costs, including a 16.5 per cent opportunity cost on farm real estate in 1960 (common stock dividend yield of 4.8 per cent and capital gain of 11.7 per cent, the 1950–60 average). Common stock yield and capital gain data from *Economic Report* (1967, p. 297).

B—Parity ratio required to cover *all* farm production costs, including a 5 per cent return on farm real estate with no capital gain. Real estate and other costs valued at 1960 prices.

C—Parity ratio required to cover *all* farm production costs with real estate cost as in B but with farm real estate capital gain of 5.5 per cent (1950–60 average added to receipts in 1960).

[b]Average for farms smaller than class IV.

farm real estate and deducts farm capital from costs because some may wish to regard it as a form of income which offsets part of farm costs.

The parity ratio, including government payments, was 81 in 1960 and 82 in 1965. Under condition A, even the large farms did not cover all costs in 1960. Class I farms required 94 per cent of parity and class VI farms required 258 per cent of parity. Only 74 per cent of parity would have covered all production costs of class I farms in 1960 under condition B, so a parity ratio of 81 meant that some farmers received a positive economic rent.

The estimate C in Table 6.8 highlights the potential importance of capital gains but has important limitations. First, it is from a period of unusually high capital gain, and future appreciation of real estate may not be as large. Second, it is impossible to forecast capital gains and hence it is not an operational concept to use for establishing future parity price ratio standards. Third, as stated before, capital gains are not a perfect substitute for labor income and are by no means distributed equally among farmers.

The conclusion to be drawn from Table 6.8 is that cost-of-production pricing is bedeviled by numerous pitfalls, and implementation of the concept by supporting farm prices at a level that will give all farmers a parity return on resources is simply not feasible. The level at which farm prices would need to be set to cover the cost of production is highly arbitrary—it all depends on which size of farm is chosen to establish the standard. In addition to the differences among farm sizes, there is a problem of how to charge for farm real estate. The price of land is in fact determined partly by prices received by farmers. Increasing commodity prices to pay the cost of farm real estate will lead to higher land prices and the need to support commodity prices at even higher levels. Nevertheless, the income parity standards can be a useful initial basis for setting direct payments.

In summary, the foregoing analysis of symptoms provides considerable documentation that economic problems exist in agriculture. The presence of low average earnings on farm resources is apparent. Yet it is very easy to oversimplify the issues. The difference between the economic structure of large and small farms is so great that it is impossible to view farming as a homogeneous low-return industry. From an economic standpoint, efficient large farms are doing very well and small farms on the average are doing poorly. Yet without government programs, it appears that even the large farms would have serious economic problems.

The analysis supports the traditional view that the problem of many commercial farms is low rates of returns on resources. The analysis also supports the contention that commodity programs primarily are for large farms, and separate poverty programs are needed to deal with problems of small farms.

RESOURCE DISEQUILIBRIUM

Low resource returns imply resource disequilibrium. A formal estimate of the aggregate farm production function has been used to compute optimum levels of nine farm resources, consistent with economic equilibrium (Table 6.9). The least-cost input combination to produce the *actual* average 1952–61 output would have reduced the annual input dollar volume by $1.9 billion, or 5.6 per cent. Actual output exceeded the equilibrium output, however. Adjustment of farm resources to an equilibrium input and output level, with all resources earning an opportunity-cost return, would have entailed a reduction of 4.2 billion 1947–49 dollars, or 12.5 per cent of the actual input volume. The cost of excess capacity

TABLE 6.9. Estimated Equilibrium Annual Aggregate Input Levels for 1952–61

Inputs	Actual Annual Average Input	Equilibrium Annual Input	Actual Input as Percentage of Equilibrium Input
	Millions of 1947–49 dollars[a]		%
Fertilizer and lime	1,364.7	1,431.9	95
Feed, seed, and livestock	2,698.0	2,932.0	92
Labor (millions of man-hours)	11,782.2	7,009.7	168
Machinery	2,642.4	3,112.4	85
Real estate (fixed)	3,742.8	3,742.8	—
Machinery operating expenses	2,502.4	3,394.0	74
Miscellaneous current operating expenses	2,100.7	2,578.1	81
Crop and livestock inventory (interest)	1,441.4	1,360.2	106
Real estate taxes	902.2	1,171.9	77

SOURCE: Tyner and Tweeten (1966, p. 624). Real estate is fixed at the 1952–61 average volume. All inputs except real estate are assumed to be variable and perfectly elastic in supply. All variable inputs are valued at opportunity-cost levels. Labor is valued at 85 per cent of the average hourly factory wage.

[a] All farm inputs are in 1947–49 constant dollars except labor, which is in millions man-hours.

was approximately $2.2 billion or 6.6 per cent of the resource volume; the cost of a nonoptimal input mix was $2.0 billion or 5.9 per cent of the resource volume. Two-fifths of agriculture labor was estimated to be in excess supply in the 1952–61 period. Capital inputs purchased by farmers needed to increase on the average by 17 per cent to reach an equilibrium. The finding that the optimum allocation called for a major reduction in farm labor and an increase in items supplied by the nonfarm sector is instructive in the discussion later of fixed resource theory.

The above results apply to all of U.S. agriculture, not just to commercial farms. Also, the above analysis applies only to the optimum levels of *aggregate* inputs in farming and does not show the potential gain in efficiency from redistribution of inputs among farms and regions. Research reported in the previous chapter shows that the possible economic benefits are larger from a more complete redistribution of farm resources.

CAUSES OF ECONOMIC DISEQUILIBRIUM

The focus on resource disequilibrium rather than on low product prices, low gross incomes, or low resource returns signals some progress toward explaining farm economic problems. Issues remain, however, of why labor is redundant and why farm resources do not adjust to an equilibrium. Stated in other terms, two important relationships underlie low returns in agriculture: factors which create the need for adjustments in farm resources and factors which inhibit adjustments at the needed rate.

FACTORS WHICH CREATE DISEQUILIBRIUM

Forces of technology, economic growth, and inflation continually generate disequilibrium in farming. Heady (1967, Chapter 1) stresses that economic growth in the nonfarm sector increases the amount of capital in relation to labor and reduces the capital-labor price ratio. This dynamic process, now largely exogenous to the farm sector, continually calls on farmers to adjust to the new price ratios by using more capital and less labor.

Inflation, some of it caused by the wage-price spiral in firms supplying production and consumption items to farmers, increases not only prices of capital inputs but also the opportunity cost of farm labor. There is no immediate means by which farmers can pass higher input costs to consumers, as can many firms producing farm inputs, and the resulting cost-price squeeze calls for adjustments in farm resource use.

OUTPUT-INCREASING TECHNOLOGY

A major cause of disequilibrium in agriculture falls under the broad heading of "technology." Technology is defined here to include those forces that increase farm output with a given dollar volume of production inputs (production inputs include farm land, labor, and purchased inputs). It includes new and improved inputs and changes in farm management, specialization, farm size, and institutions serving agriculture. These forces of technology increased the output from a virtually stable total dollar volume of farm inputs by nearly 2 per cent per year from 1947 to 1958. Since demand for farm output often increased less than 2 per cent annually, the result was a tendency to create disequilibrium in the form of low product prices and low returns on farm resources.

Profitable and productive inputs such as improved seeds, fertilizers, and pesticides are continually made available to farms through science and industry. The supply of these inputs is highly elastic—farmers can purchase virtually all they want without raising the price of these inputs. As these inputs are introduced, the output of farm commodities expands. This would cause no serious price problems if the demand for farm products were moving rapidly to the right, or if demand were highly elastic so that larger marketing would bring greater revenue. But these demand conditions do not characterize agricultural products—the price elasticity of aggregate demand is very low in the short run; it is $-.5$ in three or four years, and is unitary only in the long run. The result is depressed prices and incomes for farmers as output expands at a greater rate than demand. Depressed economic conditions would be temporary if supply were highly elastic, and if low prices led farmers immediately to cut back production. But supply is inelastic—about .1 in one to two years, .3 in three to four years, and exceeds 1.0 only after many years (see Chapter 8).

Because of the perfectly elastic demand faced by individual farmers and because of lags in the response of farm product prices to increased farm output, early adopters profit from introduction of technology. Late adopters find they must join the technology bandwagon to maintain income as the macro effects become apparent in falling farm prices. The cycle of introduction of new technology, adoption by farmers, increased output, depressed prices, and further search for new technology to maintain farm income in the face of falling prices has placed farmers on a treadmill (cf. Cochrane, 1958). Farmers must tread fast just to keep up, and those who do not keep up experience low returns, poverty, or bankruptcy. There seems to be no end in sight to the treadmill because science and industry continually create new technologies.

While the treadmill theory helps to explain why farm economic problems arise, it is not able to explain why problems persist despite the slowdown in output-increasing technology. The aggregate productivity index for farms was the same magnitude in 1966 as in 1961 and was only 4 per cent greater in 1968 than in 1960. The farm economy was expanding—the volume of production inputs increased 11 per cent from 1960 to 1968. Despite slowing of productivity growth, a strong national economy that grew steadily from 1961 to 1969, comparatively low rates of national unemployment, and expansion of the aggregate farm plant, the farm economy continued to be depressed as measured by low returns on resources. Depressed returns persisted despite shifting of supply to the right at a slower rate than demand.

The supply of farm products depends on the level and productivity of farm inputs. Since not much can be done about the structure of demand, it is to the input structure of agriculture that we must look for the basic causes, and perhaps cures, of the farm problem. To maintain or increase resource returns in the face of declining farm prices and incomes, a reduction in conventional farm resources, primarily labor, is required. Why don't resources move out of agriculture at a rate sufficient to bring equilibrium returns? Three theories that explain this phenomenon are: (*a*) the fixed resource theory, (*b*) the decreasing cost theory, and (*c*) the imperfect competition theory. Less convincing are theories which depict the supply curves for farm output and labor input as backward bending.

PERVERSE BEHAVIOR THEORIES

A discredited view is that farmers supply a greater quantity of products in response to lower prices. This theory is grounded on three assumptions: (*a*) the correct assumption that the demand curve faced by individual farmers is perfectly elastic; (*b*) the correct assumption that farmers have certain fixed obligations in the form of living expenses and payments on mortgages and other loans; and (*c*) the incorrect assumption that farmers can raise income to meet these fixed obligations by increasing output in response to falling prices (demand). If farmers had no variable costs and chose only to attain a gross income equal to their fixed obligations, then they would in fact expand output as prices fall and decrease output as prices rise. This behavior would lead to a backward-bending aggregate supply curve, a rectangular hyperbola with a price elasticity of -1.0. This specious reasoning ignores variable (marginal) costs, diminishing returns, and the profit motive. The concept is supported neither by economic theory nor empirical results, which show that the farm aggregate supply curve has a positive slope.

A similar line of reasoning has been applied to the farm labor supply curve. Laborers, it is said, adjust employment in inverse proportion to the wage, thus providing a fixed labor income to meet given living expenses. The supply curve for labor would be backward sloping with an elasticity of -1.0 under these assumptions. Again this conclusion is not supported by empirical evidence, which shows that the labor supply quantity rises in response to higher wage incentives (cf. Heady and Tweeten, 1963, Chapter 8). These two theories of the perverse behavior of product supply provide no satisfactory explanation of farm problems.

FIXED RESOURCE THEORY

Classical economic theory stipulates that an efficient allocation occurs when the value of marginal product of a given resource is equal to its market price in all uses. The concept must be revised considerably when applied to the dynamic environment of the actual agricultural economy. Not one price but four prices are relevant for the farm labor resource in Figure 6.1. P_A is the acquisition price for labor (Hathaway, 1963, Chapter 4). It may be regarded as the return needed to attract farm operators into agriculture from the nonfarm sector, or the wage rate necessary to attract hired labor to farms from employment elsewhere. The optimum employment of labor in agriculture would be X, given P_A and MVP_1.

The second price P_0 in Figure 6.1 is the opportunity cost of farm labor. It is what labor currently employed in agriculture would earn in the nonfarm sector. Farmers tend to have less formal education and tend to be older than nonfarm workers. If farmers were employed in the nonfarm sector, their average earnings would be below that of nonfarm workers.

General education imbues skills that are somewhat readily transferable between occupations. It is quite true that farmers have unusually high management skills that could not easily be learned by outsiders. But when considering

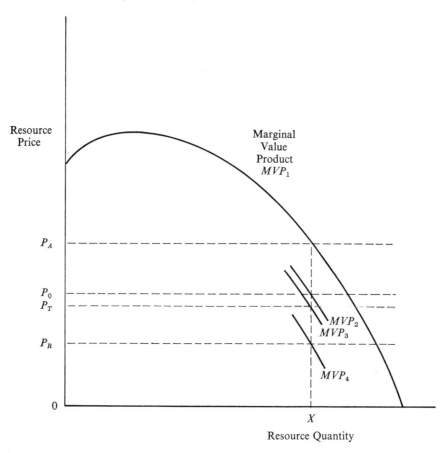

FIGURE 6.1. The marginal value product of labor in agriculture.

the salvage price of farm labor, it is the value of these skills in the nonfarm sector that is important. Unfortunately, these skills have rather limited value outside of agriculture. For farm workers who have few transferable skills, the alternative to farm employment is often urban unemployment. For them the opportunity price P_0 either is zero or the value of unemployment compensation.

The age distribution of farmers limits mobility. The fact that farm employment is characterized by a relatively high proportion of very young and very old workers who have relatively low earnings and few opportunities for outside employment contributes to a low opportunity price at which to salvage farm labor. The median age of farmer operators was approximately 51 years in 1960. In the same year, 5.3 per cent of the total farm labor force was between 14 and 17 years of age, and 14.7 per cent 60 years and over. The respective percentages for the same age groups in urban employment were 3.0 for younger group and 9.7 for the older group.

Data presented earlier showed that the farming industry received a low return on resources when all farm resources were valued at their opportunity price. Gross farm income did not cover all costs of farming when farm resources were valued at their opportunity price—what they would likely earn if employed elsewhere. The problem of low returns on farm resources appears to be real. We must look beyond the opportunity price to explain the difference between actual returns and the acquisition price of farm resources.

THE TRANSFER COST HYPOTHESIS

Wage rates in economic equilibrium differ because of transfer costs. The wage rate in agriculture must drop below the opportunity value less transfer cost to justify economically the transfer of labor from agriculture. The opportunity price P_0 less transfer cost is designated P_T in Figure 6.1. Transfer costs are unlikely to be a large part of potential earnings in the nonfarm sector. If moving costs are $500 and the migrant will earn $5,000 for 20 years in new employment, moving costs are only .5 per cent of future earnings. Thus monetary transfer costs appear to be too small to explain the discrepancy between the earnings of comparable farm and nonfarm resources. Transfer costs may loom large, however, for individuals who because of old age will have few years of productive employment ahead or who must search long and perhaps unrewardingly for a new job or who have little capital or credit base on which to support the transition.

THE ENDODERMAL HYPOTHESIS

The price that induces outmovement of labor from agriculture may be considerably lower than P_T for workers who value highly the farm way of life. Brewster (1961, pp. 129 ff.) labeled this the "endodermal" hypothesis explaining the farm problem. If alternate employment means leaving the community, the farmer may accept a low return for his labor rather than leave relatives and friends. The reservation price of farm labor is labeled P_R. It is the price below which the farm labor earnings must fall before alternative employment will induce release of labor from agriculture, given potential earnings in nonfarm employment, transfer cost, psychic satisfaction from farming, and expectations of future farm earnings and of living in the city.

Given favorable economic conditions such as immediately followed World War II (indicated by MVP_1), farm employment (X), and labor earnings (P_A), suppose that prices received by farmers fall because supply is increasing faster than demand. This can occur because government supports are curtailed, because of favorable weather for crops, or because demand contracts due to a depressed national economy or declining farm exports. If farm labor responded strictly to opportunity costs in the absence of transfer costs and special values on farm employment, then outmovement of farm labor would begin with the drop of the marginal value product just below MVP_2 (Figure 6.1). Reduction of farm employment would begin with a drop in the marginal value product to just below MVP_3 if transfer costs are included. And the marginal value product would need to fall below MVP_4 to induce lower farm employment when the psychic satisfactions of the farm way of life, imperfect knowledge, and other factors reflected in P_R are considered. The marginal value product could range from MVP_1 to MVP_4 without changes in farm employment. The farm economy would be in "equilibrium" in a period requiring fewer resources only if all farm labor were valued at its reservation price, P_R. Use of any other price, P_A, P_0, or P_T, would show that the gross income in agriculture would not cover all farm costs.

EFFECTS OF RESOURCE FIXITY ON FARM OUTPUT AND EARNINGS

Before appraising the actual role of fixed resource theory in explaining persistence of low returns, it is necessary to examine the fixity of farm production resources in addition to labor. How fixed are farm resources? To answer this question it is useful to divide farm resources into five categories: (*a*) financial resources, (*b*) operating capital, (*c*) durable capital, (*d*) real estate, and (*e*) labor. It is also necessary to consider two basic dimensions of fixity—durability of resources and the relationship of the marginal value product to the four prices listed in Figure 6.1.

Financial resources such as currency, bank deposits, and bonds are quite readily transferable to nonfarm investments and should cause no extended problems of fixity and attendant low returns.

Operating capital such as fertilizer, fuels, seed, repairs, pesticides, and hardware supplies have generally low opportunity prices for salvage once they are committed to farming. These supplies, purchased on the basis of an expected product price, are likely to be used even if the product price falls sharply during the production period. But the inputs are consumed quickly, most in one production period. Hence the farmer can correct his error by purchasing fewer operating capital inputs in the next production period. Furthermore, the farm MVP's for these inputs have tended to lie above acquisition prices. It follows that operating capital poses no real problem of input fixity.

Durable capital items such as farm machinery give off services over an extended period, and have low salvage value outside of the farming industry. Estimates (U.S. Department of Agriculture, 1968a) show an annual depreciation rate for farm machinery of about 10 per cent, although the services given off fall less than 10 per cent per year from a given stock. Even if services decline at half this rate, without adding to the stock of machinery the machinery input would fall nearly one-fifth in four years—hardly a serious degree of fixity. Again the data conflict on where the marginal value product of machinery lies in relation to acquisition price. Table 6.9 indicates that machinery is not in excess supply. Farm-produced durables such as breeding stock would seem not to create serious problems of fixity because the acquisition price varies proportionately with farm economic conditions and because they can be salvaged at slaughter prices.

The fourth input category, farm real estate, is durable and has a low opportunity price for salvage in nonfarm uses (except around cities). Its degree of fixity is so great, however, that its price is largely determined by economic conditions within agriculture. Because the land price does not determine farm output, it would be unwise to blame excess capacity and associated low returns in farming on the land price. It will become more apparent later that low returns on farm land arise because farmers pay "too much" for land.

Because the input life is short or the *MVP* exceeds the acquisition price—or because of the pricing structure—the above nonlabor resources accounting for about three-fourths of all farm inputs do not support the asset fixity theory as an explanation of low farm returns over an extended period of time.

We must return to labor as the "problem" resource if fixed-resource theory is to provide an explanation of low farm resource returns. Labor is a durable resource, and, thanks to high birth rates, unlike other resources, it increases in supply even though farmers do not purchase more from the nonfarm sector. Because a change in the labor input itself has little effect on farm output, it would appear that resource fixity would not explain excess capacity in agriculture. Labor is more important that its contribution to output might suggest, nevertheless, because capital inputs are often used in fixed proportions to labor on family farms, and because labor is very important as a *denominator* in expressing returns per *unit* of labor.

In short, there are indications cited earlier that farm labor is in excess supply and its marginal value product lies not only below its acquisition price but also below its opportunity price less transfer cost P_T. This suggests that many farmers could increase their earnings by employing their labor resource elsewhere. Questions remain of whether earnings below P_T represent inefficiency and a cost to individuals and society, and whether in fact the disequilibrium ascribed to fixity of labor even exists.

Whether earnings below P_T represent economic disequilibrium depends on the source of the gap. Given no disassociation of private and social costs (or returns), earnings of labor below P_T would indicate economic inefficiency, and the product of society could be raised by closing the gap. If the gap arises because of reasonable inertia in making adjustments to dynamic forces that constantly generate disequilibrium, and the inertia can be overcome only with great trauma to workers, the gap may not represent a social cost. If the gap arises only because farmers, though fully informed of alternatives, place a high value on farming as way of life, then the gap measured by usual economic yard-sticks does not represent a social cost. If the gap arises only because farmers are not informed about employment opportunities elsewhere or about the city way of life, then the gap is a social cost as well as a private cost unless the cost of providing such knowledge is prohibitive. And if the gap arises because of racial discrimination and labor unions that inhibit mobility, then it may represent a private and social cost but no disequilibrium. That is, farm workers may not close the earnings gap because they cannot obtain the higher-paying nonfarm jobs which they are able to perform.

THE FLIP-FLOP ANTITHESIS—THE PROBLEM OF HIGH RETURNS

Fixed resource theory explains the secular problem of low return through the labor resource. Even this last beachhead of alleged fixity is threatened. The challenge to the fixity of farm labor is raised by several findings: that farm operators and hired laborer earnings are consistent with the schooling-earnings relationship over several occupations (Tweeten, 1967b, p. 16); that rates of adjustment to equilibrium for farm labor and other resources is comparatively rapid (Tyner and Tweeten, 1965); and, most significantly, that farmers engage in much experimentation—a considerable number actually try nonfarm jobs but nine return to farming for each ten who leave, presumably because they find it is the "best" alternative for use of resources (Hathaway and Perkins, 1968).

Some have interpreted these data to mean that there is no problem of low resource returns in farming, with factor markets operating efficiently to hold farm labor earnings to opportunity cost levels. Of course, there is dynamic resource disequilibrium which is alleviated quickly enough by outmigration to keep farm earnings nearly on a par with nonfarm earnings. If farm resource earnings appear low, it is only because economists have imputed to farm labor too high an opportunity cost. And what was considered to be the major economic problem of commercial farms, low resource returns, evaporates; its only "reality" is an illusion created by economists. Fixed resource theory then helps to explain the lack of annual variation in farm input in the face of fluctuating prices but does not explain the "nonexistent" secular low returns on farm resources.

Acceptance of the antithesis would place farm problems in an entirely new perspective. The problem would become one of low absolute returns rather than low relative returns on farm labor. Raising the opportunity price of farm labor through education and training would take even greater priority. The problem of disequilibrium would remain, but it would be the high return on schooling investment (much of it financed from nonfarm sources) rather than the low return on farm production resources that would become the focus of attention. The shortage of schooling rather than the excess of production resources would gain prominence. The new interpretation, emphasizing shortage and high returns rather than surplus and low relative returns, would be indeed a flip-flop.

Nevertheless, strong evidence in addition to that cited above contradicts the conclusion that resource markets are efficient. An alternative interpretation is that "back-movement into agriculture [which] offsets 90 per cent of the mobility out of the industry" (Hathaway and Perkins, 1968, p. 351) reflects a serious lack of job information indeed, and that factor markets must be working very inefficiently. Only a small proportion of farm workers move to nonfarm jobs each year, and there is no reason to suppose that even these are efficient in locating the best jobs available to them.

Support for the proposition that much redundant labor in fact remains in agriculture can be found from numerous sources in addition to those cited earlier. Ninety per cent of all farm output is produced on farms that account for half of farm labor man-hour requirements. Since 5 to 10 per cent of farm production capacity is surplus, release of farm labor from units that produce one-tenth of farm output would cause no food and fiber shortage. In fact, output could expand as better managers took over the smaller farms. In all likelihood, the marginal product of the above farm workers is negative, allowing for reorganization of farms. If this half of all farm labor has a marginal product greater than zero in the nonfarm sector, it could contribute more to society there. The conclusion that more than half of farm labor is redundant is consistent with the production function results presented earlier. It is also supported by micro-economic results aggregated to area levels (Walker *et al.*, 1964). Also, doubts have been raised about the validity for mobility studies of the Social Security data on which the "efficient-labor market" contention rests heavily (Beale, 1968; Reinsel, 1968).

Rejection here of the flip-flop antithesis as premature should not be interpreted as belittling the massive and monumental accomplishment of factor markets. Nearly 40 million net migrants have left farming in four decades since 1929! What is at issue is whether considerable redundant labor still remains in farming and whether factor markets need to be improved. The answer to both questions is "yes." It is not within the scope of this chapter to list needed improvements in factor markets, but greater investment in education certainly complements such improvements.

The thesis and antithesis can partly be reconciled. The farm labor market works most efficiently for the young, and outmigration of this group has enabled agriculture to dissipate much of the dynamic disequilibrium generated each year by output-increasing technology, inflation, and other factors. For reasons discussed above, operator labor and associated family labor do not so readily adjust out of agriculture, and it is this group which constitutes a sizable reservoir of redundant labor, which in so many cases could be employed more profitably elsewhere.

The problem of surplus farm labor will diminish in the future, and the above antithesis will gain greater validity. The pressures are now great to force excess labor from farms: these pressures come from high land costs and other capital costs, large know-how requirements, and other barriers to entry. Also, the farm population is becoming such a small portion of the national population that a sizable percentage of the farm population can take nonfarm jobs without turning the economy upside down. In fact, a simple linear projection of farm employment indicates no workers in farming by the early 1980's. This of course is an unrealistic projection, but it means not only that rapid progress is being made in reducing the number of workers but also that the annual absolute number of outmigrants will be able to decline considerably in the future. Signs of a slowdown were already apparent in 1968 and 1969.

INCREASING RETURNS TO FARM SIZE

Numerous studies have documented the existence of decreasing average costs and increasing returns to size of farm firms (cf. Madden, 1967). But the concept has not been related to farm problems. The term "size" rather than "scale" is used. Returns to scale refer to the impact on farm output of a given change in the level of all resources in fixed proportion. Expansion of the farming units does not entail an equal percentage expansion in all resources, and the pure concept of returns to scale is academic, with little relevance to farm policy. The expansion in the farm firm is generally characterized by increasing the proportion of capital to labor, and of variable capital to fixed capital. These changes result in a sizable reduction in cost per unit of production.

Evidence of decreasing costs per unit (increasing returns to size) is readily apparent in Figure 6.2 and Table 6.10. Figure 6.2 is called a "unit" cost curve because it lies somewhere between the concepts of a long-run "average" and a "marginal" cost curve. The curve is an average within an economic class of farm but is a marginal curve among classes. The output-input ratio is defined as gross income from farming divided by the cost of all farm inputs, including the opportunity cost of equity capital and all labor. The labor cost is man-hour requirements in farming multiplied by the central city wage rate adjusted for age, education, and sex. The cost of all inputs (including the opportunity cost of equity capital and of operator and family labor) per unit of output (including receipts from farm commodities, nonmoney income, and government payments) average 2.67 on class VI farms and .91 on class I farms. Most of the economies of size appear to be achieved by class II farms, and unit costs decline very slowly beyond an annual output of $30,000 per farm.

The marginal and average revenue curves are indicated by the horizontal dotted line at $1 in Figure 6.2. The intersection of the revenue curve with the

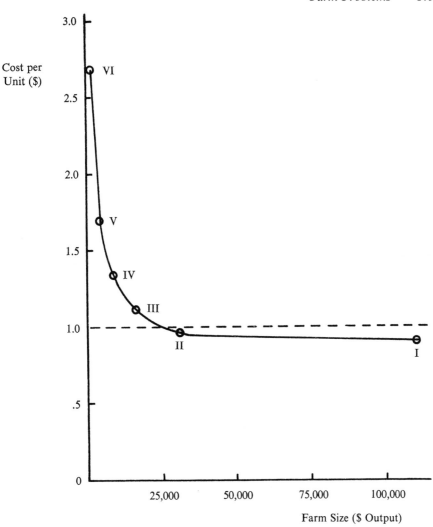

FIGURE 6.2. Long-run unit cost of farm production, by economic class of farms in 1960 (see Table 6.10 for data).

unit cost curve means that farms with sales under $25,000 on the average lost money and did not cover all production costs in 1960. Farms with sales over $25,000 received an economic rent per unit of output equal to the difference between the cost and revenue curves.

It may be said that small farms earned low returns because they paid too much for their land. Land tends to be a complementary input with farm size. There is constant pressure to expand farm acreage to achieve the economies of size so apparent in Figure 6.2. The savings through greater efficiency are bid into the price of land. The actual price of land tends to be that price which will make

TABLE 6.10. Output, Input, and Efficiency, by Economic Class of Farms

	Economic Class of Commercial Farms						Noncom-mercial Farms
	I	II	III	IV	V	VI	
1960 input per output (unit cost) *in dollars*[a]	.91	.95	1.10	1.34	1.69	2.67	2.91
1960 output per input (efficiency) *in dollars*	1.10	1.05	.91	.74	.59	.37	.34
1960 output if all farm resources would have been used with respective farm-class efficiency: *in billions of dollars*	46.9	44.9	38.8	31.8	25.4	16.0	14.7
Per cent of all inputs in respective class of farm[b]							
1960		24.8	15.5	20.6	16.4	10.0	3.5	9.2
1965		33.5	19.1	18.6	11.3	6.2	3.9	7.4

SOURCES: See Tweeten (1965); 1965 data are based on U.S. Department of Agriculture (1968a).

[a] The input-output ratio was computed as follows: costs of land, capital, and labor were totaled and divided by all farm receipts (excluding off-farm income and including receipts from farm products consumed on the farm). In all cases the cost of nonreal estate durable capital was 5 per cent interest plus depreciation. The cost of all farm labor was man-hour requirements multiplied by the wage rate of urban wage earners corrected for the age, education, and sex ratio of all farm-hired, operator, and family workers.

[b] The 1960 and 1965 estimates are not strictly comparable. The farm dwelling interest charge and 60 per cent of the auto interest and depreciation are excluded in 1960 estimates to arrive at production inputs. These costs are included in the 1965 estimates because data were inadequate to remove them. Since dwelling and auto inputs tend to be relatively large for small farms, this at least partly explains the incongruously larger per cent of inputs on the small class VI farms in 1965 than in 1960.

all costs, including real estate interest, equal to the value of all farm receipts *on an economic size unit*.

Competition in the land market tends to bid the land price to the point where the return on land will be equal to the return on capital in other uses. A potential buyer who is unwilling to pay this price will find land bid away from him by the investor who wished to maximize returns. And investors will not pay more than this price because a greater return can be achieved on nonland investments. The residual return to land tends to be greatest on large farms. The law of one price and the large potential number of investors will ensure that the "high" price for land on large, efficient farms will be the market price of land applicable to all farms.

The small farmer must pay this price or land will be bid away from him by an investor who has or can achieve an economic size unit. Thus the small farmer tends to actually incur losses if he paid the current land price. And the small farmer who has full equity in land is losing money if a charge is made for the opportunity cost of his owned land valued at the current price of farm real estate. The tendency in some localities to bid up the price of farmland for potential nonfarm uses also contributes to apparent persistent low returns on resources assumed used only for farm purposes.

Table 6.10 and Figure 6.2 suggest that land was *not overpriced* at the margin because large farmers were earning returns greater than needed to hold capital in farming. But land was clearly overpriced for an average farmer who had gross sales under $25,000.

The struggle to obtain an economic unit leads to further problems, apparent in Table 6.10. Output per unit of input is the reciprocal of the long-run cost curve in Figure 6.2 and is essentially the aggregate production function for farming units. Output per input is 1.10 on class I farms and only .37 on class VI farms. The actual total volume of inputs was $42.8 billion and the average output per input over all farms was .85 in 1960. Had all inputs been used on farms of class I efficiency, total output would have been $46.9 billion at 1960 prices.

Class I farms require a substantial input of feed and livestock provided by other farms. Their atypical structure means that if all farms were organized in this manner there would not be sufficient intermediate farm inputs. Class II farms are somewhat more typical and provide a more meaningful measure of the potential gain in efficiency obtainable by a more nearly optimum farm size and combination of inputs. If all farms were organized as class II farms, the actual 1960 total input would have produced an output of $44.9 billion—24 per cent above the actual level. If all farms had been organized like those in class II, only 1.2 million farms could have produced the 1960 output with $34.5 billion of inputs—19 per cent less inputs than the actual total 1960 inputs of $42.8 billion. Even discounting the shortcomings of this approach, the results clearly point to large potential efficiency from reorganization of farms into more nearly economic units.

And because most size economies were achieved by class II farms in 1960, there would have been few economic advantages in having a system of superfarms that would have reduced the number of farms much below 1.2 million. This conclusion applies only to 1960 conditions. In the future the unit cost curve will move to the right, decreasing the number of farms compatible with maximum production efficiency.

The heterogeneous size structure of farms helps to explain why farm land is overpriced for most farmers and why returns are low on farm resources of most farmers. It also is a partial explanation of why farm product prices tend to be low. The continued trend toward larger farms, apparent in the 1960 and 1965 distribution of inputs in Table 6.10, increases farm output. Based on the distribution for these two years and the output-input ratio by class of farm in 1960, output would increase 6 per cent, or 1.2 per cent annually, from 1960 to 1965 due to the change in size distribution with the same total volume of farm resources as in 1960. Other things being equal, this depresses the revenue line in Figure 6.2 as supply presses demand and creates new pressures for farms to expand in size. However, the decreasing cost theory depends more on labor-saving technology and differing efficiency among farms than it does on output-increasing technology to explain low resource returns in farming.

The decreasing cost theory is especially instructive in pointing out the permanency of the problem of low returns. An increase in the product price results in a larger residual return to land. The higher land return causes land prices to rise to the point where farm and nonfarm investors can realize a "parity" return on their investment. This land price is determined at the margin for adequate size units. It follows that small farms, which constitute a large majority of all farms, will receive a low return on all resources when valued at their imputed opportunity costs, even with higher farm product prices. The majority of commercial farmers will be underpaid for their resources, whatever the parity ratio, as long as the distribution of farms and the cost curve remain similar to the pattern discussed above.

IMPERFECT COMPETITION AND LOW RETURNS ON FARM RESOURCES

Econometric studies show that the farm-nonfarm wage ratio is completely overshadowed by the national unemployment rate in explaining the net out-migration of farm labor (Heady and Tweeten, 1963, Chapter 9). One conclusion is that there has been a persistent earnings differential attracting farm workers to nonfarm jobs. But employment of farm workers in nonfarm jobs is inhibited by discrimination, union hiring, and other elements of imperfect competition. Minimum wage laws also cause a departure from a market orientation and undoubtedly have inhibited the ability of many farm workers to find nonfarm jobs.

The markets in which farmers purchase inputs and sell commodities are generally characterized as some form of imperfect competition. The actions of a single firm can influence the market price. Whereas the sales of any one farmer have no apparent impact on total output of the farming industry, the sales of one firm supplying farm inputs or buying farm output often can perceptibly influence industry output and price. An industry characterized as *monopolistic competition* has a large number of individual firms; but each firm, through promotion and research, has differentiated its product from the product of other firms. An industry characterized as *oligopoly* has just a few firms and the actions of one firm are felt by the other firms; hence pricing and output decisions are interdependent. An industry in which there is just one firm which can adjust industry price and output at will and can keep other firms from entering the industry is called *monopoly*. A market characterized by one firm which is the sole seller of a product or resource is called monopoly; and a market characterized by a single firm which is the sole buyer of a product or resource is called *monopsony*.

Most industries which sell farm inputs and market farm products are oligopolistic. There are no neat analytical models to predict the behavior of oligopolistic industries, and these industries are best analyzed in the framework of market structure, conduct, and performance presented in later chapters. Nevertheless, the "neat" models of monopoly and monopsony suggest hypotheses and illustrate *tendencies* characterizing pricing and output under imperfect competition, and hence are the point of departure in this section. The implications of imperfect competition for farm prices and quantities, both for resources and products, are examined.

Effect on Farm Labor of Monopoly Selling of Farm Products

Farm resources potentially can produce either farm products or nonfarm products. For example, in Figure 6.3 the national labor force is considered to be the resource. Its derived demand, or value of marginal product VMP, is assumed to be the same in the farm and nonfarm sector. Total labor supply S is assumed to be perfectly inelastic. Total labor demand is the sum of the demand in each sector, or $\sum VMP$ in Figure 6.3. The equilibrium wage W_{cc} and employment L_{cc} (equal in each sector when both sectors sell products in a perfectly competitive market) are indicated by the intersection of supply curve S and the total demand curve $\sum VMP$.

Now assume that the nonfarm sector sells its product as a monopolist. Its demand for labor then is the marginal revenue product curve MR. The farm sector continues to sell its products in a perfectly competitive market, and its demand for labor is the VMP curve. The total demand for labor in the economy is then $MR + VMP$. Total demand intersects supply at a wage rate W_{mc}. While labor receives the same wage in each sector, the allocation of labor is only L_m to the nonfarm sector and L_c to the farm sector. Labor is exploited by the nonfarm industry, because its contribution to the value of output M considerably exceeds the wage W_{mc}. A reallocation of some labor from agriculture to nonfarm industry would increase the total value of output. Hence monopoly pricing and output represents a social cost.

Next assume that farm products also are sold monopolistically. The demand for farm labor then becomes the marginal revenue product MR in Figure 6.3.

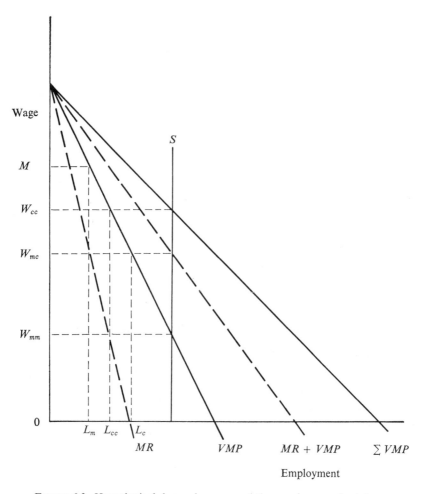

FIGURE 6.3. Hypothetical demand curves and the supply curve for labor.

Total labor demand in the two sectors is $MR + MR$, which is the VMP curve. The curve intersects S at a wage rate W_{mm} received by labor in both sectors. Allocation of labor to each sector L_{cc} is the same as when both sectors sold their output competitively. Thus there is no malallocation of labor based on the competitive norm, but the wage rate W_{mm} is considerably below both W_{mc} and the value of marginal product W_{cc}, hence labor in both sectors is exploited to the extent that it receives less than its marginal contribution to the value of output.

In summary, the example illustrates that monopoly selling of products in the nonfarm sector does not lead to relatively lower wages in agriculture, but does lead to generally low wages and to malallocation of labor between sectors.

EFFECT ON FARM LABOR OF MONOPOLY SELLING OF LABOR

We now examine the effect on farm wages and employment of selling labor monopolistically. The national labor supply is assumed to be S. The demand for labor in the farm sector VMP is assumed to be the same as the labor demand in the nonfarm sector (Figure 6.3). Total labor demand is therefore $\sum VMP$. If labor is sold competitively in both sectors, supply intersects demand at W_{cc} giving a wage rate W_{cc} and employment L_{cc} in each sector.

Suppose that a single labor union gains monopoly control over the sales of labor in the nonfarm sector.[1] Its effective demand for labor then is indicated by the marginal revenue of labor MR. With labor sold competitively in farming, the total labor demand from the two sectors is $MR + VMP$. This intersects supply at W_{mc}, the wage in the farm sector. However, M is the wage and L_m is the employment in the unionized sector. Based on the competitive norm, the wage is too low and the employment too large in agriculture. The opposite holds for the unionized nonfarm sector.

Again assume that the demand for labor is VMP in each sector but that labor is unionized into a monopoly seller in both sectors. The marginal revenue curve in each sector is MR. Optimum allocation for maximum wage income occurs where $\sum MR = VMP$ intersects S at W_{mm}. While the marginal revenue is W_{mm}, the wage in each sector is W_{cc} and the employment is L_{cc}. The interesting result is that wages and employment are the same as under perfect competition. Having both sectors as monopoly unions is clearly preferred to having only one sector so organized. This result provides support for countervailing power. However, the lack of social cost with monopoly labor control in both sectors occurs only when supply is perfectly inelastic. In the real world, supply is not perfectly inelastic. This fact weakens the justification for countervailing power.

Figure 6.3 also can be used to infer the implications of various combinations of imperfect competition in labor sales and product sales, but such inferences are not drawn here.

EFFECT ON FARM LABOR OF MONOPSONY

In certain isolated rural communities, a single large firm may be the only significant employer of labor. Figure 6.4 provides an analytic framework for

---

1. The assumption is that labor is allocated between sectors to maximize returns to all labor. It is as if one large labor allocator sold in a competitive structure in one market and as a single seller in the other market. If the nonfarm market were completely separated and operated independently of the total labor supply, the results would not necessarily be those above because the total "demand" would not be the sum of the marginal revenue curves. This comment also applies to other parallel cases examined in the text.

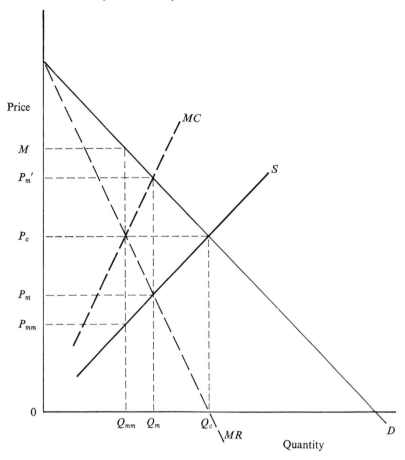

FIGURE 6.4. Hypothetical supply and demand curves.

exploring the economic implication of this market structure. D is labor demand
and S is labor supply. The equilibrium wage is P_c and employment is Q_c under
competitive conditions. The monopsonist firm maximizes profit where marginal
revenue product MR equals the marginal resource cost MC. If the single buyer
could perfectly discriminate among laborers, paying only the minimum wage to
a worker that would induce his employment, the firm's marginal resource cost
would be the supply curve S. But if the firm must pay the same wage to all
workers, then it must pay the higher wage for the incremental labor input to
all workers. Hence MC lies above S. Assuming that the monopsonist firm sells
on a competitive market, it maximizes profit by employing labor Q_m at the point
where MC intersects D. The wage is P_m; the marginal value product P_m'. If the
monopsonist is also a monopolist selling on an imperfect market so that its
marginal revenue is MR, it maximizes profits by employing Q_{mm} labor, a point
indicated by the intersection of MR and MC.

Assuming that the demand for labor by a monopsonist firm is D and that rural workers form a strong union to sell their services as a monopolist, then the situation becomes one of bilateral monopoly—a monopsonist facing a monopolist. Both the union and the firm want employment Q_m. But the labor union wants a wage P_m' and the monopsonist employer wants a wage P_m. The model specifies no unique wage. Where the wage would settle between P_m' and P_m would depend on the relative bargaining power of the two opposing groups.

The model in Figure 6.4 does not show if wages are high or low in the isolated environment in relation to outside employment. If the monopsonist firm is mobile and rural labor is not, the firm is likely to pay lower wages than it would pay outside the area. If the monopsonist firm is tied, say, to a mineral resource found only in the area and if the labor supply is low, even wages under a monopsonist market structure may exceed wages outside the area.

EFFECT ON FARM PRODUCTS OF MONOPOLY AND MONOPSONY

Many farm commodity markets are isolated from a large number of buyers by high transportation costs. A single processor may buy the entire area output of fruits and vegetables for example. The possible effect on farm pricing and output is apparent in Figure 6.4. The demand for the commodity by the single buyer is D, and the supply is S. Under competitive conditions in buying and selling, the equilibrium price is P_c and the quantity is Q_c. If the single buyer could perfectly discriminate between producers, paying only the supply price for each unit of production, the marginal cost curve would be S. But if the monopsonist must pay one price for the entire quantity purchased, then the marginal resource cost is MC. The monopsonist firm which buys from many farmers and which sells in a competitive market maximizes profits at that quantity where demand equals MC. The quantity purchased from farmers is Q_m and the price paid farmers is P_m. The effect is a lower price, lower quantity, and lower income to farmers than under competitive conditions.

If the monopsonist firm is also the single monopoly seller of the processed commodity, the firm's profit is maximized at the point where marginal revenue MR is equal to MC. The result of monopoly and monopsony in the firm buying the commodity is to reduce the quantity to Q_{mm} and the farm price to P_{mm}, hence to reduce farm income even further than in the previous case.

Next consider the situation where farmers form a cohesive bargaining group to sell their output as a monopoly, given the demand D for their output Q. The marginal revenue for farmers is MR. If they were to maximize profit, they would market that quantity Q_m where MR intersects S. They would receive a price P_m' for the commodity and would make a greater profit than at the competitive equilibrium price P_c and quantity Q_c.

Finally, assume that the demand for farm production is D and that farmers have a bargaining group which pools production to sell as a monopoly. Also assume that there is a single buyer of the commodity, a monopsonist firm which faces the supply curve S and marginal resource cost curve MC. With this bilateral monopoly, the monopsonist processor wishes to buy Q_m and pay P_m; the monopolist farmer-group wishes to market Q_m and receive a price P_m'. While there is agreement on quantity, the model stipulates no unique price. Where the price will settle between P_m' and P_m depends on the bargaining power of the two antagonists. This indeterminateness could be eliminated either by farmers integrating into the processing business or by the processor integrating into the growing operation. If the integrated firm's marginal cost curve were S and it sold its product in an imperfect market with a marginal revenue MR, its output would be Q_m. However, if the integrated firm were confronted by a market situation where competition kept the price equal to marginal cost, then the price and output would be the competitive result, P_c and Q_c. The analysis shows that integration can conceivably improve market performance.

It should be pointed out that with much imperfection in the market, represented, for example, by P_{mm} and Q_{mm} pricing and output, farm resources will not receive low relative returns per unit if they are mobile. But from a social standpoint, too few resources would be in farming. However, an exploitative monopsonist firm may encourage investment in farm resources and greater output with initially high product prices and then later reduce prices, thereby exploiting farmers by paying low returns to durable resources "trapped" in farming.

THE EFFECT OF MARKETING MARGINS ON THE FARM ECONOMY

The effect of marketing margins on farm and retail markets is depicted in Figure 6.5. The quantity is defined as the ingredients provided by farmers for items purchased by consumers. The supply of farm commodities at the farm level is S_F. The supply S_R of farm ingredients at the retail level is the farm supply plus marketing margins. The demand by consumers for farm output at the retail level is D_R. The derived demand D_F at the farm level is D_R less marketing margins. Marketing margins include transportation, processing, wholesaling, and retailing costs. With constant margins, the demand curves (and supply curves) at the farm and retail levels have the same slopes. Then the price elasticity at the farm level will bear the same ratio to the elasticity at the retail level as the farm price bears to the retail price at a particular quantity. This means that the price elasticity of demand for farm products is lower at the farm level than at the retail level. If margins rise per unit as quantity expands, this tends to make the demand for farm products even more inelastic. If margins decrease per unit as the quantity expands, this tends to make the demand for farm output less

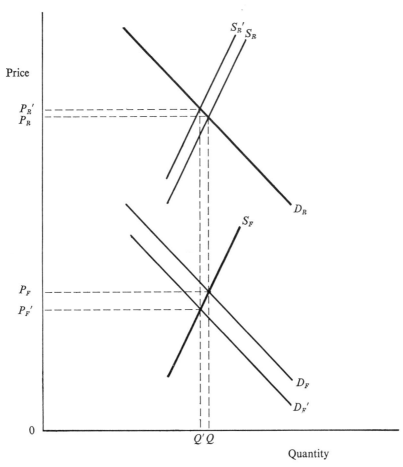

FIGURE 6.5. Marketing margins; farm and retail supply and demand for farm commodities Q.

inelastic. In fact, marketing costs tend to remain somewhat stable as farm output expands and contracts.

The market initially is in equilibrium at quantity Q, farm price P_F, and retail price P_R. Now assume that elements of imperfect competition are introduced in the form of excess profits or advertising costs that neither educate consumers nor raise the demand for farm commodities. These "costs" are assumed to raise the marketing margin by a fixed amount for all quantities and therefore to reduce demand at the farm level to D_F' and to reduce supply at the retail level to S_R'. The result is a lower equilibrium farm quantity Q', lower farm price P_F', and a higher consumer price P_R'. Conversely, viewing D_F' and S_R' as an initial position, part of the gains from removing wasteful advertising and excess profits from the marketing sector are passed on to farmers and part to consumers.

The distribution of benefits depends on the supply and demand elasticities. With marketing margins reduced by a given amount at all farm quantities as in Figure 6.5, the following are the guidelines for distribution of benefits: (*a*) if demand is perfectly inelastic, all benefits go to consumers, and the quantity Q is unchanged; (*b*) if supply is perfectly inelastic, all benefits go to farmers, and Q is unchanged; (*c*) if demand is perfectly elastic, all benefits go to farmers, and the farm quantity Q is increased; and (*d*) if supply is perfectly elastic, all benefits go to consumers and the farm quantity Q is increased.

In fact, the actual distribution is somewhat indeterminate because both supply and demand for farm output are highly inelastic but not perfectly inelastic. Thus it is not possible to say exactly whether farmers or consumers gain the most benefits from increased marketing efficiency. However, aggregate supply and demand elasticities have been found to be somewhat comparable in magnitude (but opposite in sign, of course) in the short and intermediate run at the farm level. A crude inference therefore is that farmers and consumers share somewhat equally in the benefits of marketing efficiency—as depicted in Figure 6.5. However, farm supply becomes more elastic in the long run and benefits eventually pass in majority to consumers as specified by guideline (*d*) above.

Some measure of the impact of technological change on the farm and retail sectors is also apparent in the figure. As farm resources become more productive, supply S_F moves to the right, and the farm price is depressed. With a fixed marketing margin, the benefits of the lower farm price are completely passed on to consumers. While benefits of improved farming technology go to consumers, farm prices and resources returns tend to be depressed.

Finally, the effect on the farm economy from variation in supply due to weather and commodity cycles is also apparent from Figure 6.5. The stability of marketing margins means that the effect of supply pressing demand is not absorbed or cushioned by lower marketing *margins*, and the result is fluctuating farm prices. The burden of adjusting supply and demand falls heavily on the farm sector.

SUMMARY AND CONCLUSIONS

Data presented in this chapter document the prevalence of excess production capacity, high costs of government programs, economic instability, and low earnings in farming. These are symptoms of a more basic problem of excess resources. And excess resources are the symptom of an even more basic problem—the lack of resource mobility. Improved technology and other factors continually generate economic disequilibrium in agriculture. Three theories were advanced to explain why farm resources do not adjust to an allocation that would make returns comparable among sectors, and reduce the total cost of farm resources to equal the level of farm income.

THEORIES OF LOW RESOURCE EARNINGS

The resource fixity theory singles out the low reservation price for labor as one primary perpetuator of farm economic problems. More effective public policies are clearly needed to raise the salvage value and reservation price of all types of farm labor. The decreasing cost theory advances the hypothesis that farm land, labor, and other resources are in equilibrium at the margin. Large farms are earning an adequate return on resources. Because prices are determined at the margin (by large farms) it follows that resources are priced too high for the majority of farmers who operate small, inefficient farming units. The marginal cost of farm output tends to be equal to marginal revenue. But with a decreasing cost structure, marginal cost lies below average cost. It follows that average costs exceed average (and marginal) revenue. Thus when the average costs are multiplied by output, total cost exceeds total revenue in the farming industry. In 1960, the 90 per cent of farms with gross sales below $20,000 per year tended to make low returns on resources, while larger farms on the average were making an equilibrium return.

Imperfect competition offers several hypotheses explaining low farm returns. Labor unions in the nonfarm sector and monopsony purchase of labor in relatively isolated rural areas can contribute to low labor returns in agriculture. Monopsony in purchase of farm products or monopoly in sales of farm products does not directly lead to low farm returns, but when coupled with resource fixity in agriculture can create economic problems.

PERMANENCY OF FARM PROBLEMS

The three theories advanced to explain persistent low returns in agriculture help to gauge the permanency of farm problems. The resource fixity theory implies that low returns would disappear if the rate at which output-increasing technology is released to farmers would slow, or if demand would increase sufficiently fast in relation to supply so that all farm resources would be valued at their acquisition cost. By this measure, the farm problem is somewhat "temporary."

The decreasing cost theory takes into account the size structure of farms and the valuation of real estate at the margin. Because the slack between returns and nonland costs tends to be absorbed by the land price, it follows that land prices will adjust to make returns equal resource costs at the margin on the efficient size units. As land values adjust to changing conditions, economic size farms will tend to receive an equilibrium (opportunity-cost) rate of return on resources within a considerable range of prices received by farmers. It follows that whether product prices are high or low, roughly 90 per cent of all farms will receive low returns when the opportunity cost of all resources are taken into account. This points to low returns even on most commercial farms over a long period until farms reach the "flat" portion of the unit cost curve. Farm bargaining power and government income-support programs only temporarily change the picture in Figure 6.2—these programs raise both total cost and total revenue so that the unit cost and revenue curves remain somewhat stable as the benefits become capitalized into the control instruments.

The third theory, imperfect competition, depicts the farm problem of low returns as virtually permanent, given racial discrimination and the economic structure of resource and product markets. Some forms of imperfect competition lead to relatively low earnings on farm labor, even if all the forces tending toward economic equilibrium work their full effect. Only a change in the structure of markets will alter the result as long as agriculture acts on a residual claimant of the labor force that cannot be used by the nonfarm sector.

The decreasing cost theory of farm problems is related to technology, imperfect competition, and fixed resources. The ability to expand farm size is linked to the ability of farmers to purchase more land. And the ability to buy land and consolidate farms is linked to the rate at which a neighbor can find employment outside of agriculture. The process of adjustment to economic farming units is slowed if operators of inefficient units are unaware of better alternative uses for their resources, if education is inadequate to equip farm people for the exodus, if low-income farmers prefer farming as a way of life, and if labor unions and high national unemployment inhibit mobility. Technology, reflected especially in farm machinery and farm management, has given the shape to the unit cost curve in Figure 6.2, and is continually changing the shape. In contrast to Cochrane's treadmill theory the decreasing cost theory does not depend on an inelastic demand and output-increasing technology to explain low resource returns. It derives its substance from labor-saving technology, economies of buying and selling in larger quantities, and labor and machine indivisibilities that give rise to economies of size.

In 1960 only about 9 per cent of all farms were in the somewhat flat portion of the cost curve above $25,000 annual output. Public policy must be concerned with getting more of the remaining 91 per cent of farms into that category. An unanswered question is how sensitive is the shape of the unit cost curve in Figure 6.2 and the distribution of farms along the curve to changes in the number of workers in farming. A preliminary conclusion, based on work with 1960 and 1965 data, is that the shape is not highly sensitive to outmovement of workers. Outmovement per se places more farms on the flat portion of the curve. But this tendency is offset to a considerable extent by a shift of the unit cost curve to the right. These problems of low returns on resources are likely to plague agriculture for some time, although workers are moving from agriculture at a rapid rate.

The decreasing cost theory shows how adequate size farming units can be profitable while the farm economy is generally depressed. These profitable firms can be the "mouth" to feed new inputs to an industry that is already over-satiated and can lead to problems of resource fixity.

Because all the various theories explaining the persistence of low returns are highly interrelated, it is difficult to pinpoint in fact the portion of the problem of low returns that can be imputed to each causal factor.

Finally, the antithesis of the persistency theories contained in this chapter is that virtually no disequilibrium in the form of low resource returns exists in agriculture. Labor markets function efficiently and quickly to eliminate earning disparities and dynamic disequilibrium which are continually generated and quickly dissipated. The result is no latent excess labor, measured by low resource returns. If there appear to be measurable low resource returns, it is only because those who are doing the measuring assign too high an opportunity cost to farm labor. While some evidence supports this antithesis, most of the evidence contradicts it. The prematurity of this antithesis suggests that efforts be continued to improve the efficiency of factor markets. If the antithesis is true, then the major economic problem of commercial operators in a growing farm economy is the price and income instability. Even if problems of low average returns are overcome, some form of supply control may be necessary to stabilize farm prices.

REFERENCES

Beale, Calvin. 1968. The rural to urban population shift (statement to National Manpower Conference). Senate Committee on Government Operations, 90th Congress, Washington.

Bellerby, J. R. 1956. *Agriculture and Industry: Relative Income*. New York: St. Martin's Press.

Brewster, John M. 1961. Society values and goals in respect to agriculture. In *Goals and Values in Agricultural Policy*, Center for Agricultural and Economic Development. Ames: Iowa State University Press, pp. 114–37.

Cochrane, Willard. 1958. *Farm Prices: Myth and Reality*. Minneapolis: University of Minnesota Press.

Economic Report of the President. 1967. Washington: U.S. Government Printing Office.

Hagen, E. E. 1958. An economic justification of protectionism. *Quarterly Journal of Economics* 72:496–514.

Hathaway, Dale E. 1963. *Government and Agriculture*. New York: Macmillan.

——— and Brian Perkins. 1968. Farm labor mobility. *American Journal of Agricultural Economics* 50:342–52.

Heady, Earl O. 1967. *A Primer on Food, Agriculture and Public Policy*. New York: Random House.

Heady, Earl O., E. O. Haroldsen, L. V. Mayer, and L. G. Tweeten. 1965. *Roots of the Farm Problem.* Ames: Iowa State University Press.

———— and Luther G. Tweeten. 1963. *Resource Demand and Structure of the Agricultural Industry.* Ames: Iowa State University Press.

Johnson, D. Gale. 1958. Labor mobility and agricultural adjustment. In Earl O. Heady *et al.*, eds., *Agricultural Adjustment Problems in a Growing Economy.* Ames: Iowa State University Press, Chapter 10.

Madden, J. Patrick. 1967. Economies of size in farming. Economic Report No. 107. Washington, U.S. Department of Agriculture.

Paarlberg, Don. 1964. *American Farm Policy.* New York: Wiley.

Reinsel, Edward. 1968. Labor mobility. *American Journal of Agricultural Economics* 50:745–47.

Ruttan, Vernon W. 1966. Agricultural policy in an affluent society. *Journal of Farm Economics* 48:1100–20.

Tweeten, Luther G. 1965. The income structure of the U.S. farms by economic class. *Journal of Farm Economics* 47:207–21.

————. 1967a. The demand for U.S. farm output. *Food Research Institute Studies* 8:343–69.

————. 1967b. The role of education in alleviating rural poverty. Economic Report No. 114. Washington, U.S. Department of Agriculture.

————, Earl O. Heady, and Leo V. Mayer. 1963. Farm program alternatives, farm incomes and public costs under alternative commodity programs for feed grains and wheat. *Oklahoma State Journal* No. 911 and CAED Report No. 18, Ames, Iowa.

Tyner, Fred. 1966. A simulation analysis of the U.S. farm economy. Unpublished Ph.D. thesis. Stillwater, Oklahoma State University.

———— and Luther G. Tweeten. 1964. Excess capacity in U.S. agriculture. *Agricultural Economics Research* 16:23–31.

———— and ————. 1965. A methodology for estimating production parameters. *Journal of Farm Economics* 47:1462–67.

———— and ————. 1966. Optimum resource allocation in U.S. agriculture. *Journal of Farm Economics* 48:613–31.

U.S. Bureau of the Budget. 1967. The budget in brief. Washington: U.S. Government Printing Office.

U.S. Department of Agriculture. 1966a. Farm costs and returns. Agricultural Information Bulletin No. 230. Washington.

————. 1966b. Farm income situation. FIS-203. Washington.

————. 1966c. Handbook of agricultural charts. Agricultural Handbook No. 325. Washington.

————. 1967. Parity returns positions of farmers. Washington: U.S. Government Printing Office.

————. 1968a. Farm income situation. FIS-203. Washington.

————. 1968b. Farm real estate market developments. CD-71. Washington.

Walker, Odell, Luther Tweeten, and Larry Connor. 1964. Potential economic and social adjustments. *Proceedings, Southwest Social Science Quarterly.*

CHAPTER SEVEN

The Economic Structure: Farm Product Markets

The cost-price squeeze and imperfect competition were introduced as part of the foundation for farm problems discussed in the previous chapter. The "cost" side of the squeeze refers to rising prices for what farmers buy. Accordingly, the structure of farm input industries is examined in Chapters 8 and 9 to determine whether farmers are victimized by abuses in markets characterized by imperfect competition.

The "price" side of the squeeze refers to the low (or lowering) prices received by farmers for what they sell. We hardly need to be reminded after reading Chapter 3 that farmers have felt exploited by the marketing sector and after reading Chapter 6 that a cost-price squeeze has existed. The issues to be examined in this chapter are not these, but rather whether elements of unfair competition exist in the marketing sector which absorb funds that should have gone to farmers. What appears diabolical to farmers (e.g., the falling proportion of farm income in national income) may in many instances be the normal, expected workings of the market in an industry characterized by low price and income elasticities. These elasticities and their expected impact are examined in this chapter, and help to explain the behavior of the farm economy.

Few products are sold by farmers directly to consumers. Commodities are purchased, stored, transported, processed, and sold by numerous firms between farmers and consumers. The demand for farm products is derived from retail consumer demand for food but is directly dependent on marketing firm demand for raw materials. Of the $78 billion spent by consumers for food in 1965, the marketing system absorbed $52 billion. Farmers have viewed this as a cost—often as an unnecessary cost! Recognizing that the marketing sector creates place, form, and time utility, it is more useful to view the margin not as a cost but as value added. In this chapter, I review the nature of demand for farm commodities and the structure of industries that market farm products. An analysis of profits, advertising, pricing practices, and market integration in the marketing sector is included to help answer the question "Are farmers exploited by the food industry?"

THE AGRIBUSINESS SECTOR

The agribusiness sector is composed of livestock and crop producers (farming); suppliers of agricultural services, chemicals, fertilizers, petroleum, rubber, farm machinery and equipment, and motor vehicles (agricultural supply business); and processors of food and kindred products, tobacco manufacturers, and manufacturers of fabrics, miscellaneous textile goods, and apparel (agricultural processing). Numerous other activities of the marketing sector are included in the "other" category in Table 7.1, which comprises all intermediate

TABLE 7.1. Agribusiness Interindustry Transactions, 1958

Producing Sector	Purchasing Sector					Total Output
	Farming	Agri- culture Supply	Agri- culture Processing	Other	Consumers	
	(Millions of dollars)					
Farming	13,166	780	23,551	3,692	8,528	49,717
Agricultural supply	4,571	14,258	1,346	29,151	32,689	82,016
Agriculture processing	3,050	1,142	24,529	5,847	66,515	101,084
Other	8,084	35,363	22,743	248,602	339,602	654,394
Value added	20,846	30,473	28,915	367,100	—	447,334
Total input	49,717	82,016	101,084	654,394	447,334	—

SOURCE: Latest available data (see Blaich and Hermann, 1966, p. 4). Data are based on producer prices.

sectors in the U.S. economy exclusive of the agribusiness sector. Total output of the farming sector was $50 billion in 1958—of which farmers themselves purchased $13 billion in "interfarm sales," the processing sector purchased $24 billion and consumers (many of them farmers) purchased directly $8.5 billion (first row, Table 7.1). The farm output purchased by farmers was also an input. This input was supplemented by an input of $4.6 billion from agricultural supply firms and by $3.0 billion from firms whose primary activity was processing farm commodities. Firms not classified as primarily agricultural supply or processing organizations supplied a substantial input of $8 billion to farming.

The value added by farm labor, land, and capital resources was $21 billion and is a guide to the size of industry. By this measure, farming was 68 per cent as large as the agricultural supply industry and 72 per cent as large as the agricultural processing industry. Total value added by the agribusiness complex was $80 billion, or 18 per cent of the value added by all industries.

A high degree of interdependence among sectors is apparent in Table 7.1. If the final demand for farm products is increased $100, the farming sector would have to increase its output by $141 (this output includes many "double-counted" intermediate products such as livestock feed), agricultural supply by $19, agricultural processing by $12, and other industries by $54 (Blaich and Hermann, 1966, p. 4). A $100 increase in final demand for processed agricultural products will require an increase in farm output of $44, in agricultural supply of $11, in processing of $137, and in other industries of $69. Farming, however, is not greatly influenced by a $100 increase in the demand for "other" industries in Table 7.1; it is required to increase output only $2 (Blaich and Hermann, 1966, p. 4).

PRICE AND INCOME ELASTICITIES OF DEMAND

Certain parameters often expressed as elasticities determine the impact on farming of changes in consumer disposable income and other nonfarm variables. Chief among these important parameters are price and income elasticities.

INCOME ELASTICITIES OF DEMAND

The income elasticity shows the percentage change in the demand quantity of a commodity associated with a 1 per cent change in consumer income. An income elasticity of zero for a commodity means that its use is not influenced by income, and a growing demand for the commodity will depend on rising population and on favorable trends in preferences. An income demand elasticity greater than one means that the share of consumer income spent for the commodity rises with income. And the sector (measured by sales) producing the commodity will grow as a proportion of all industries as consumer income rises. The weighted average of income elasticities over all items in the consumer budget is one. The income elasticities of demand at retail for all items in Table 7.2 are less than one; many are near zero. This means that as consumer income grows, consumers will spend a declining proportion of their income for these foods and an increasing proportion for nonfood items.

The retail-level elasticities contain some elements of marketing services along with farm ingredients. Because the marketing-service ingredients have a higher income elasticity than the farm raw material ingredients, it follows that income elasticities at the farm level are lower than at the retail level.

TABLE 7.2. Price and Income Elasticities of Domestic Demand at Retail and Price Elasticities at the Farm Level for Selected Commodities

	Retail Level		
	Income	Price	Farm Level Price
Beef	.47	−.95	−.68 (cattle)
Veal	.58	−1.60	−1.08 (calves)
Pork	.32	−.75	−.46 (hogs)
Lamb and mutton	.65	−2.35	−1.78 (sheep and lambs)
Chicken	.37	−1.16	−.74
Turkey	.49	−1.40	−.92
Butter	.33	−.85	−.66
Margarine	.00	−.80	$\left\{\begin{array}{l}-3.99 \text{ (soybean oil)[a]} \\ -6.92 \text{ (cottonseed oil)[a]} \\ -7.04 \text{ (other food oil)[a]}\end{array}\right.$
Eggs	.16	−.30	−.23
Fluid milk and cream	.16	−.28	−.14
Cheese	.45	−.70	−.53
Ice cream	.35	−.55	−.11
Fruit	.40	−.60	−.36
Vegetables	.15	−.30	−.10
Cereals, baking products	.00	−.15	[b]
Sugar and syrups	.18	−.30	−.18
Beverages	.23	−.36	n.a.
Potatoes	.08	−.20	−.11
Dry beans, peas, nuts	.12	−.25	−.23
Nonfoods	1.22	−1.03	n.a.[c]

SOURCE: Brandow (1961, pp. 13, 59).

[a] Not necessarily for use in margarine.

[b] The price elasticity at the farm level for corn is −.03, for wheat −.02, and for barley −.07. These are not comparable to the "cereals, baking products" category, however.

[c] Not available.

The income elasticity for a weighted aggregate of all farm products consumed in the U.S. is approximately .15 (cf. Tweeten, 1967). This means that a 1 percent increase in consumer disposable income raises the demand for farm products only .15 per cent. If the population is growing 1.5 per cent annually, and per capita real income is growing 2 per cent annually, then the domestic demand for farm products will increase about $1.5 + (.15)(2) = 1.8$ per cent per year. It also means that the farm share of the national income will fall and in this sense farming will continue to be a "declining industry."

All food expenditures as a proportion of consumer disposable income were 22.2 per cent in 1950 and 18.2 per cent in 1966. The proportion of civilian expenditures for marketing services declined only from 12.6 per cent in 1950 to 10.9 per cent in 1966. Meanwhile, the proportion of civilian expenditures on the farm-produced food ingredients (farm value of food) showed a more substantial decline from 8.7 per cent to 5.6 per cent in the same period.

The change in the proportion A/Y of income spent on farm food as consumer income rises is given by

$$\frac{d(A/Y)}{dY} = \frac{A}{Y^2}(E_y - 1), \tag{7.1}$$

where A is food expenditures at the farm level, Y is consumer disposable income, and E_y is the income elasticity of demand for food. Using 1965 as the base, $A = \$26$ billion, $Y = \$469$ billion, and $E_y = .15$. Then the farm share of consumer income declines .01 percentage points with each $1 billion rise in consumer disposable income according to Equation (7.1). An annual $20 billion rise in consumer income reduces the farm share by .20 percentage points. The farm share of consumer income was 5.6 per cent in 1966. If consumer income rises $20 billion per year, the farm share would fall to 5.4 per cent in one year and to 3.6 per cent in ten years. While Equation (7.1) is inexact for extended projections, the results clearly foretell the lessening importance in the future of farm-produced ingredients in consumers' budgets. This is consistent with the past trend.

PRICE ELASTICITIES OF DEMAND

The price elasticity of demand E shows the percentage change in the quantity purchased of a commodity resulting from a 1 per cent change in its price. If demand is elastic (E is greater than 1 in absolute value), then a decrease in the price leads to a more than compensating increase in the quantity taken and total receipts for the commodity rise. On the other hand, if demand is inelastic (E is less than 1), then a decrease in the price is not compensated by an increase in quantity sufficient to maintain receipts from the commodity. According to Table 7.2, the demand for most farm commodities at the retail level is price-inelastic. Demand is even more inelastic at the farm level. The price elasticities at the farm and retail levels would be the same only if the marketing margins were a fixed proportion of the retail price, whatever the quantity sold. If the marketing margin were constant at all quantities sold, then the farm price elasticity would be the same proportion of the retail price elasticity as the farm share is of the food dollar at that quantity. For example, if the marketing margin were an absolute constant, if the retail elasticity were $-.30$, and if farmers received half of the consumer food dollar at that given quantity, then the farm level demand elasticity would be $-.15$.

Numerous public policies for agriculture have regulated market supplies as a means to influence price and income. It follows that policies to raise farm income by reducing the quantity marketed will be most effective for commodities for which demand is price-inelastic. For analyses of the impact of supply management on prices and income, it is useful to employ the concept of price flexibility F, which for our purposes may be defined as the reciprocal of the price elasticity. With a 1 per cent change in quantity, the associated percentage change in price is $F = 1/E$ and in gross receipts is $1 + F$. Thus if the price elasticity is $-.5$, a 1 per cent decrease in quantity will increase prices 2 per cent and receipts 1 per cent. This consideration suggests that income from the major agricultural commodities shown in Table 7.2 can be increased by restricting the quantity sold with marketing quotas or production controls. If good substitutes are developed for the commodity, this conclusion may not hold, however.

Larger marketings will lead to higher gross income for commodities with elastic demands. It does not necessarily follow that farm *net* income can be increased by expanding sales of commodities for which the demand is elastic. Incremental production costs may exceed market prices although E is large. It is emphasized that the price elasticities in Table 7.2 are at the farming *industry* level. The demand curve faced by individual farmers tends to be *perfectly elastic* —the sales by any one farmer have no perceptible influence on the market price.

The Price Elasticity of Demand for Farm Output

Public policy is concerned with the income of all farmers as well as with the income of those who produce a particular commodity. Efforts of the government to raise the price of one farm commodity by curtailed marketing are eroded when consumers substitute other items for the high-priced commodity. A similar interrelationship is apparent in supply as well as in demand. Efforts to restrict the quality of one commodity often result in diversion of resources to the production of other farm commodities. This leads to lower prices for commodities not under controls. The government has implemented programs requiring cross compliance, acreage diversion, and purchase of excess commodity supplies either to store or to dispose outside of markets through foreign aid, school lunch, and welfare programs. The ability of programs that divert production from markets to raise income of the farming industry depends on the market elasticity of demand for farm output in aggregate.

The results of a study of the elasticity of demand for farm output are presented in Table 7.3. The elasticity of demand at the farm level for domestic food was estimated (Tweeten, 1967) to be $-.25$ in the short run (1–2 years), $-.18$ in the intermediate run (3–4 years), and $-.10$ in the long run (a large number of years). The elasticities were estimated by least squares from time series. The results reflect the historical response of the market to changing economic conditions. But because there has been no extended period of high prices and short supplies of food in the U.S., the equations fail to show the impact of efforts to develop

TABLE 7.3. Intermediate-run and Long-run Price Elasticities of Demand for Farm Output and Its Major Components

	Domestic			Foreign			Total Demand Elasticities $\sum E_i \dfrac{O_i}{O}$
	Food and Feed	Cotton	Tobacco	Food and Feed	Cotton	Tobacco	
(Elasticities E_i)							
Intermediate run	−.18	−.65	−.10	−1.91	−1.8	a	—
Long run	−.10	−1.84	−.50	−6.42	−3.7	a	—
(Weights: component O_1 as proportion of all output O)							
	.762	.048	.025	.131	.024	.010	—
(Contribution $E_1 \dfrac{O_1}{O}$ of component market to total output elasticity)							
Intermediate run	−.137	−.031	−.002	−.250	−.043	a	−.46
Long run	−.076	−.088	−.012	−.841	−.089	a	−1.11

SOURCES: For data sources and details, see Tweeten (1967).

a Not estimated. Its weight is so small in the total output demand elasticity, $\dfrac{dO}{dP}\dfrac{P}{O} = \sum E_i \dfrac{O_i}{O}$, that it is omitted.

fish, petroleum, and synthetic substitutes for farm-produced foods. Thus the long-run elasticity for domestic food shown in Table 7.3 is likely to be under-estimated, and the price elasticity plotted against length-of-run on a horizontal axis would be expected to display a U shape.

The elasticity of demand for food and feed is considerably higher in the export market than in the domestic market. The long-run export demand elasticity for food and feed in Table 7.3 is a weighted average of the domestic demand and supply elasticities in foreign countries and is adjusted for market imperfections including variable levies, quotas, tariffs, and lack of foreign exchange.

The total elasticity of demand for farm output is an average of the demand elasticities for food and feed, cotton, and tobacco; weighted by the respective shares of farm output going to each market. The elasticities, multiplied by their respective shares, show the contribution of each market to the total demand for farm output in Table 7.3. The contribution of domestic markets to farm output demand elasticity is −.17 in the intermediate run and −.18 in the long run. Export elasticities contribute −.29 to the output elasticity in the intermediate run and −.93 in the long run. Hence the total elasticity of demand for U.S. farm output is −.46 in the intermediate run and −1.11 in the long run.

These results can be used to estimate the impact on farm prices, total revenue (excluding government payments) and net income associated with government programs to divert farm output from markets by acreage diversion and other forms of supply control not directed at specific products. The price flexibility F is approximately -2 in the intermediate run and -1 in the long run. Thus a sustained 1 per cent decrease in farm output will increase prices received by farmers 2 per cent in 3–4 years and 1 per cent in many years. It will increase total revenue 1 per cent $(1 + F)$ in 3–4 years and not at all in many years. The effect on net farm income is indicated by

$$E_N = \frac{TR}{NR}(1 + F) - \frac{TC}{NR}E_S, \tag{7.2}$$

where E_N is the elasticity of net farm income with respect to output, TR is total revenue, NR is net revenue (total revenue less production cost), TC is total production cost, and E_S is essentially the supply elasticity of farm output (cf. Tweeten and Plaxico, 1964, pp. 54, 55). If the elasticity of supply is zero, if the ratio TR/NR is three, and if F is -2, then a 1 per cent decrease in output increases net income 3 per cent. This example illustrates that net income is more highly sensitive in the short run to exogenous changes in marketings than are either prices received by farmers or gross receipts. The sensitivity wears off to some extent in a longer period as the supply response becomes prominent. Because the ratios TR/NR and TC/NR are difficult to predict over a long period, the long-run elasticity of net farm income with respect to changes in the quantity of farm products placed on the market is difficult to judge from Equation (7.2). It seems reasonable to speculate, however, because $1 + F$ is near zero in the long run (gross farm income is not much affected by supply management) that net income also would not be influenced to a marked extent. Net income might be slightly higher with less output and attendant lower costs.

The conclusion that public programs to control production do not raise farm income in the long run because demand is elastic does not signal a major change in policy recommendations. The conclusion was valid even assuming an inelastic long-run demand because the benefits of the programs are capitalized into the control device and are lost to the new generation of farmers—hence net income is not raised by controls.

The estimates lead to additional conclusions about farm policy. One is that public policies to expand farm output through research and other means have not depressed farm gross receipts as much as many economists have supposed. It means that research and other efforts to raise farming efficiency have kept the U.S. competitive in foreign markets, and without these efforts export volume and export earnings would have been much lower.

The results (in Table 7.3) support the assumption inherent in the McNary-Haugen Bills and other multiple-pricing programs that farm income can be raised by price discrimination among markets. Charging higher prices in domestic markets and in portions of the foreign market made inelastic by institutional measures and charging lower prices in free trade export markets can raise U.S. farm income. This conclusion is subject to limitations including the ability to discriminate among markets and the reaction of foreign countries to "dumping" of our farm commodities in export markets.

The exact magnitude of the elasticity of demand for farm products is unlikely ever to be known with a high degree of certainty, especially because of the difficulties in estimating export demand. The above estimates are highly controversial. Total demand remains inelastic for most time periods that might be considered, and in other chapters is sometimes referred to as inelastic for this reason.

CHANGING FOOD CONSUMPTION

Consumption patterns in Table 7.4 in part are explained by income elasticities shown earlier in Table 7.2. The income elasticities for bread, flour, and potatoes were low, and per capita consumption of each of these items declined accordingly. The income elasticities of demand for beef and ice cream were comparatively high, and consumption of these items increased. But other factors such as technology (which changes food costs and services embodied in retail foods) and changes in tastes and preferences were also important. The increased consumption of margarine and decreased consumption of butter was more a reflection of changes in preferences, laws, dietary recommendations, and technology than of income elasticities. Total pounds of food utilized per capita have decreased—from an annual average of 1,533 pounds in 1937–39 to 1,420 pounds in 1963–65 (National Commission on Food Marketing, 1966, p. 9).

The pounds consumed fail to indicate the relative importance of foods in the marketing bill. Table 7.5 reveals that the proportion of consumer expenditures among commodity groups changed comparatively little from 1929 to 1963. The importance of meat products and fruits and vegetables increased slightly; and the importance of dairy products, poultry and eggs, and baking and cereal products declined in the consumer food budget.

THE MARKETING BILL FOR
FARM-PRODUCED FOOD PRODUCTS

Table 7.6 shows several major changes in the structure of farm markets since 1929. Because marketing costs do not vary greatly from year to year, the farm share of the consumer food dollar tends to be lowest when farm output is large

TABLE 7.4. Per Capita Consumption of Major Farm Products, United States, Selected Years, 1929–65

Product and Group	1929	1939	1949	1959	1965[a]
Decreased consumption		(*Pounds*)			
Potatoes (except canned and frozen), farm weight	159	122	110	101	89
Citrus fruit, fresh	40	61	48	33	29
Apples, fresh	40	31	25	23	20
Lard	13	13	12	9	6
Wheat, flour	177	158	136	120	116
Cotton	28	28	26	24	23
Butter	18	17	10	8	6
Little change in consumption					
Dry beans	8	9	7	8	7
Pork (no offal or lard), carcass weight	70	65	68	68	59
Eggs	42	39	49	46	40
Sugar	97	101	96	96	96
Whole milk, fluid	272	266	296	292	270
Rice, milled	6	6	5	5	8
Wool	3	3	3	2	3
Increased consumption					
Beef (no offal), carcass weight	50	55	64	81	99
Shortening (other than lard and margarine)	10	11	10	13	14
Chickens, ready to cook	14	14	20	29	33
Nonfat dry milk	1	2	3	6	6
Ice cream	11	11	18	19	18
Margarine	3	2	6	9	10
Canned soup	4	6	10	15	16

SOURCE: Bird *et al.* (1966, p. 38).
[a] Preliminary.

relative to needs. The farm share of the consumer's food dollar was 42 per cent in 1929, dropped to 35 in 1939, and was 46 in 1947. It has trended downward since, and in 1965 was 33 per cent. Consumer expenditures for food rose 85 per cent from 1947 to 1965. The value of farm ingredients rose by one-third, and the value of the marketing bill rose 130 per cent in the same period. The income elasticity of demand for food, approximately .15 at the farm level for farm ingredients and .6 for food processing, helps to explain the relative rates of increase. The income elasticity of demand for food in restaurants and other eating places is high and is reflected in the sharp rise in the "eating places" component of the marketing bill in

TABLE 7.5. Distribution of Consumer Expenditures for Farm Foods, by Commodity Groups, Selected Years, 1929–63

Commodity Group	Percentage of Total Consumer Expenditures							Average Farm Share[a]
	1929	1935	1939	1947	1954	1958	1963	
	(Per cent)							
Meat products	24.6	22.1	24.4	30.5	28.6	28.6	27.8	50
Dairy products	21.1	20.7	20.0	19.0	19.1	18.8	17.7	44
Poultry and eggs	10.6	10.0	8.8	9.5	8.8	8.4	7.3	61
Fruits and vegetables	19.7	20.4	22.0	18.1	20.1	21.2	21.9	29
Bakery and cereal products	17.1	19.0	16.4	14.1	14.5	14.4	15.0	20
Miscellaneous products	6.9	7.8	8.4	8.8	8.9	8.6	10.3	21
Total	100.0	100.0	100.0	100.0	100.0	100.0	100.0	39

SOURCE: Gale (1967, p. 7).

[a] Farm value as a percentage of consumer expenditures. The percentages shown are simple averages of farm shares for the selected years 1929–58.

Table 7.6. Foods served in public eating places typically carry a margin of 65 per cent above the wholesale food price (Blaich and Hermann, 1966, p. 8). Margins for the same foods in retail stores have averaged about 20 per cent for many years. It is estimated that one out of four consumer food dollars in 1966 was spent for food away from home.

The desire to have a built-in maid service has proved irresistible to housewives who prefer to spend less time preparing foods. Processing costs, which exhibit a marked upward trend in Table 7.6, do not always add to food costs, however. In a list of 115 convenience foods, 38 were found to cost less than in fresh form because processing costs were offset by savings in transportation and other inputs (cf. Blaich and Hermann, 1966, p. 9).

FARM SHARES OF FOOD GROUPS

The farm share of the retail cost of food differs among commodities and displays a downward trend in Table 7.7. Farmers receive a greater share of consumers' outlay for meat products than for crop products. Some crop products such as breakfast cereals are processed extensively before they reach consumers. For other crops such as fresh fruits and vegetables, the high costs of spoilage and transportation partially explain the low farm share. The fact that in some instances the container costs more than the farm ingredients of processed fruits and vegetables partly explains why farmers received only 23 cents of each dollar spent by consumers for these items in 1965.

The fact that marketing margins are high and have increased through the years for most of the categories in Table 7.7 has led to the proposition that the

TABLE 7.6. Components of Consumer Expenditures, All Farm Food Products, Selected Years, 1929–65

	Consumer Expenditures[a]	Farm Value[b]	Total Marketing Bill	Marketing Bill Components						Farm Share of Consumer Expenditure[f]
				Assembly[c]	Processor[d]	Transportation[e]	Wholesaler	Retailer	Eating Places	
	(Billions of dollars)									*(Per cent)*
1929	18.0	7.5	10.5	.7	3.5	.6	1.1	2.8	1.7	42
1935	13.8	5.2	8.6	.5	3.0	.6	.8	2.4	1.2	38
1939	15.3	5.4	9.9	.6	3.4	.7	1.0	2.5	1.6	35
1947	41.9	19.3	22.6	1.3	8.2	1.2	2.2	5.0	4.8	46
1954	51.1	18.8	32.3	1.6	12.3	1.7	3.0	7.1	6.6	37
1958	61.0	21.4	39.5	1.5	17.0	1.9	3.7	8.6	7.9	35
1963[g]	71.5	22.6	48.9	1.7	19.0	2.1	4.4	11.5	10.2	32
1965[g]	77.6	25.5	52.1	n.a.[h]	n.a.	n.a.	n.a.	n.a.	n.a.	33

SOURCE: Gale (1967, p. 45). Detail may not add to total because of rounding.

[a] Civilian expenditures for domestic farm food products; excluded are imported foods, seafoods, and other foods of nonfarm origin.

[b] The farm value is the payment to farmers for the products equivalent to those sold to consumers. The imputed values of inedible by-products are not included.

[c] Assembly margin includes some transportation from farm to processor, packing of fresh fruits and vegetables, and other handling charges for the raw farm products.

[d] Includes cost of materials, supplies, containers, and minor food ingredients—also distribution charges (including transportation) between manufacturers for intermediate products such as flour used in bakery products.

[e] Transportation charges are only for the finished products destined for consumers.

[f] Other frequently used estimates of the farmers' share of the consumers' food dollar are based on food sold through retail stores and give a higher estimate of the share, e.g., 39 per cent in 1965. The estimates in this table include additional marketing charges incurred for food purchased at eating places and the lower cost of food sold through channels other than retail stores; hence they give a lower estimate of the farm share.

[g] Data for 1963 and 1965 are preliminary.

[h] Not available.

TABLE 7.7. Farm Share of Retail Cost of Selected Food Groups, 1947–65

	Meat Prod-ucts	Dairy Prod-ucts	Poultry and Eggs	Bakery and Cereal Products	Fruits and Vegetables Fresh	Fruits and Vegetables Proc-essed	Sugar	Fats and Oils
				(Per cent)				
1947–49 (average)	66	54	70	31	37	n.a.[a]	51	41
1950	65	50	66	26	35	n.a.	46	38
1951	66	52	68	27	35	n.a.	48	42
1952	62	52	67	25	37	n.a.	48	34
1953	59	49	69	25	33	19	47	38
1954	59	46	64	25	33	19	46	39
1955	53	46	66	23	33	19	45	33
1956	51	46	64	23	33	20	46	36
1957	53	46	62	22	31	19	45	34
1958	57	44	62	20	32	19	44	28
1959	53	44	57	19	31	19	43	27
1960	52	44	61	19	33	18	43	29
1961	52	44	58	20	31	19	42	35
1962	53	43	57	20	32	18	44	28
1963	50	43	57	20	32	18	41	30
1964	48	44	56	20	33	21	43	29
1965	54	44	57	21	33	23	42	31

SOURCE: Blaich and Hermann (1966, p. 25).

[a] Not available.

performance of the marketing sector has been less than satisfactory. Much research has been focused on testing the validity of this proposition and will be reported in the remainder of the chapter.

MARKETING COSTS

Tables 7.8 and 7.9 provide some preliminary answers to the perennial question "Why is the food marketing bill so high?" The marketing bill increased 65 per cent from 1953 to 1965. The hourly cost of labor, the major component of the marketing bill, increased 59 per cent during the same period. The total cost of labor increased only 50 per cent; thus labor efficiency appeared to increase. The "other" category in Table 7.8 shows the largest increment, $10.3 billion, from 1953 to 1964. It includes depreciation, fuel, packaging material, interest on borrowed capital, and other items for which more detail would be desirable.

TABLE 7.8. Labor, Transportation, Corporate Profits, and Other Costs for Marketing Farm Food Products, United States, 1947–65

	Labor[a]	Rail and Truck Trans- portation[b]	Corporate Profits[c]		Other[d]	Total Marketing Bill
			Before Income Taxes	After Income Taxes		
			(Billions of dollars)			
1947	10.2	2.0	1.5	1.0	8.9	22.6
1948	11.2	2.2	1.3	.8	10.2	24.9
1949	11.7	2.3	1.3	.7	10.7	26.0
1950	12.2	2.7	1.6	.9	9.5	26.0
1951	13.0	2.7	1.3	.6	11.7	28.7
1952	13.8	3.1	1.4	.6	12.2	30.5
1953	14.6	3.3	1.5	.7	12.1	31.5
1954	15.3	3.4	1.5	.7	12.1	32.3
1955	15.7	3.4	1.8	.9	13.5	34.4
1956	16.3	3.8	1.9	.9	14.3	36.3
1957	16.8	3.9	1.9	.9	15.3	37.9
1958	17.1	4.2	1.9	.9	16.3	39.5
1959	17.8	4.5	2.1	1.0	17.8	42.2
1960	18.7	4.6	2.1	.9	18.8	44.2
1961	18.8	4.9	2.2	1.0	19.2	45.1
1962	19.7	4.9	2.2	1.0	20.1	46.9
1963	20.3	5.0	2.4	1.2	21.2	48.9
1964	21.0	5.1	2.7	1.4	22.4	51.2
1965[e]	21.9	n.a.	2.9	1.5	n.a.	52.1

SOURCE: Gale (1967, p. 14). Data are for domestic farm foods bought by civilian consumers in this country. Beginning with 1960, estimates in this table are for 50 states.

[a] Labor cost includes imputed earnings of proprietors, partners, and family workers not receiving stated remuneration. It also includes supplements to wages and salaries, such as Social Security and unemployment insurance, taxes, and health insurance premiums, but it does not include the cost of labor employed in for-hire transportation.

[b] Includes charges for protective services, heating, and refrigeration; does not include local hauling. Charges for intercity transportation by water and air are a part of the "other" (or residual) component of the marketing bill.

[c] Does not include profits of unincorporated firms or transportation firms.

[d] Residual component; includes other costs such as advertising, depreciation, fuel, electric power, containers, packaging materials, air and water transportation, interest on borrowed capital, taxes other than those on income, and noncorporate profits.

[e] Preliminary.

TABLE 7.9. Costs and Profits in Marketing Farm Products

Net Profits of Leading Food Companies

	Percentage of Stockholders' Equity			Percentage of Sales			Advertising Expenditures
	48 Food Processing Companies	5 Wholesale Food Distributors	8 Retail Food Chains	43 Food Processing Companies	5 Wholesale Food Distributors	8 Retail Food Chains	by Corporations Marketing Food
	(Per cent)						*(Millions of dollars)*
1947–49 (average)	11.7	15.8	16.6	2.3	1.7	1.4	n.a.[a]
1950	11.5	10.0	14.0	2.5	1.2	1.3	560
1951	8.5	9.4	10.1	1.7	1.1	.9	609
1952	8.2	5.8	10.0	1.6	.7	.8	673
1953	9.2	7.6	11.4	1.9	1.0	1.0	729
1954	8.9	7.5	11.3	1.9	1.0	1.0	796
1955	10.2	6.7	11.2	2.2	.9	1.0	899
1956	10.3	7.6	13.1	3.3	1.0	1.1	976
1957	9.6	7.6	14.2	2.1	.9	1.2	1,038
1958	10.1	9.7	13.8	2.3	1.2	1.2	1,063
1959	10.7	8.1	12.9	2.4	1.1	1.2	1,201
1960	10.3	9.9	12.5	2.4	1.2	1.2	1,398
1961	9.7	8.6	11.3	2.3	1.1	1.2	1,488
1962	9.9	5.5	11.0	2.4	.7	1.2	1,671
1963	10.5	9.1	10.8	2.5	1.2	1.2	1,888[b]
1964	11.3	9.2	10.7	2.7	1.2	1.2	2,172[b]

SOURCE: Blaich and Hermann (1966, p. 26).
[a] Not available.
[b] Preliminary estimate.

Profits before taxes increased $1.4 billion between 1953 and 1965 (Table 7.8). After-tax profits were about half the total profits of corporations. Table 7.9 contains estimates of net profits as a proportion of stockholders' equity and a percentage of sales for a number of food processing companies, wholesalers, and retailers. Profits as a percentage of equity have averaged about 10 per cent in recent years and as a proportion of sales have averaged about 2.5 per cent for processors and 1.2 per cent for food wholesalers and food chains. These profits are high by farm standards but are not out of line with profit rates in the industrial sector.

Estimated advertising expenses nearly tripled from 1953 to 1964. The total advertising expenditures by corporations marketing food, $2.2 billion in 1964, comprised 4 per cent of the marketing bill of $51 billion. Before-tax corporate profits in the same year comprised 5 per cent of the marketing bill. Thus the two components, advertising and profits, account for nearly one-tenth of the cost of food marketing.

In short, the marketing bill for farm products has increased for several reasons including (*a*) a substantial increase in the volume of products handled, brought on by growth in income, population, and the movement of farm people to cities; (*b*) changing costs of marketing services, especially labor; (*c*) shifts in consumption patterns brought on by housewives' demand for more processing of foods; and (*d*) rising profits and advertising expenses. Before evaluating this conclusion further, it will be useful to examine in greater detail the performance of the major sectors of the food marketing industry.

ANALYTICAL FRAMEWORK

The classical analytical frameworks of pure competition, monopolistic competition, oligopoly, and monopoly have traditionally been used to study farm markets. These rigid models have given way to the concept of workable competition, which is a more meaningful if less rigorous orientation. The existential philosophy of market structure, conduct, and performance is an attempt to operationalize the concept of workable competition with analytical concepts that provide a more adequate yardstick for the analysis of farm markets. Market *structure* refers to characteristics of the market, including the supply and demand parameters, number and size of buyers and sellers, differentiation of products, barriers to entry, and extent of market integration. Market *conduct* is the behavior of enterprises, methods of determining price, sales promotion, efforts to vary products, and incidence of predatory or exclusionary practices. Market *performance* is the economic efficiency of the market. It is measured by efficiency in procurement, plant utilization, and distribution, by the amount and type of sales promotion, innovative activity, and quality of product, and by the level of profits. A market that is characterized by a single large firm and high advertising costs may *not* be viewed as "bad" or inefficient if economies of size are so large relative to the market that only one firm can produce at an efficient level and supply the market, if it is innovative, if it does not charge unreasonable prices, and if its advertising is educational and its profits in line with risk and capital costs.

Net sales of farm products for food use totaled $26.1 billion in 1964. Of these sales meat animals constituted 34.2 per cent, dairy products 19.2 per cent, fruits and vegetables 15.3 per cent, poultry and eggs 12.7 per cent, and grain for food 9.2 per cent (National Commission on Food Marketing, 1966, p. 7). These products constituted 91 per cent of farm food sales, hence it is the structure of these markets that is especially important and which will be discussed below. Most farm foods reach consumers through grocery stores; thus some attention will be given to food retailing.

FOOD RETAILING

The number of grocery stores in the U.S. declined from 378,000 in 1948 to 245,000 in 1963. Most of this decline was in stores with annual sales under $100,000. A "supermarket" is defined as a grocery store with annual sales of one-half million dollars or more. A food "chain" is defined as a firm operating eleven or more stores. In 1962, 27,125 supermarkets comprised 11.5 per cent of all grocery stores but accounted for 68.2 per cent of all grocery store sales. This proportion was up significantly from the 48 per cent of grocery store sales by supermarkets in 1953 (Garoian, 1966, p. 5).

A major increase in the share of grocery store sales by corporate chains and affiliated independent chains (which purchase some 20 per cent of their products from affiliated voluntary and cooperative wholesalers) has come at the expense of unaffiliated independent grocers. The share of grocery store sales by corporate chains increased from 34.4 per cent in 1948 to 47.0 per cent in 1963. Affiliated independents increased their share in the same period from 35.4 per cent to 43.9 per cent of total grocery store sales. Meanwhile the unaffiliated independent stores, although comprising the largest number of stores (173,600 in 1958), saw their share of the market decline from 30.2 per cent in 1948 to 9.1 per cent in 1963 (National Commission on Food Marketing, 1966, p. 70).

High concentration is sometimes defined as a situation where the four largest firms account for over 50 per cent of the sales. Based on this criterion food retailing is not characterized by a high degree of concentration. Sales of the four largest chains comprised only one-fifth of all grocery store sales in 1963, and the 20 largest comprised only one-third of all sales. The situation at the local level was different, however. In 218 local markets, the four largest firms in each market accounted for half of all sales and the 20 largest accounted for two-thirds of all sales.

Concentration on the buying side of food retail markets increased more rapidly than concentration on the selling side. The 20 largest chains and whole-sale groups increased their share of the food store purchases from 32 per cent in 1948 to 52 per cent in 1963 (National Commission on Food Marketing, 1966, p. 73). For example, the ten largest chains purchased 61 per cent of all frozen fruit and vegetables sold under private label in 1959.

Market Integration

There are incentives for large retailers to produce their own products and to sell under private labels either to reduce procurement costs or to use as a bargaining base for lowering prices of items purchased from other suppliers. This is one facet of vertical integration defined as coordination in one firm of various stages of the food-marketing process. The value of food manufactured in retailers' facilities increased over one-half billion dollars from 1954 to 1963. However, the value of supplies produced in their own plants by retailers fell from 9.8 per cent of business done in 1954 to 8.2 per cent in 1963. The extent of retailer integration into any one industry was small. Plants owned by retailers accounted for 10 per cent of the baking and coffee roasting industries' output in 1963. For other industries it was much less.

Grocery manufacturers and wholesalers are also integrating vertically into grocery retailing. These grocery suppliers in 1958 controlled grocery retail outlets with sales of 8 per cent of the total sales of chains with eleven or more stores. The trend toward vertical integration is clear, and does cause concern because it increases market power.

Horizontal integration, defined as obtaining a larger per cent of sales at a specific market level under one organization, is considered to be even more effective in gaining market power. Most mergers for horizontal integration have been in the twenty largest retail chains. From 1954 to 1959, sales of these firms grew 58 per cent. About 73 per cent of this growth was from internal expansion and 23 per cent from mergers (National Commission on Food Marketing, 1966, p. 71).

Mergers can increase efficiency of firms operating below the optimum scale. A firm with one-half billion dollars of retail sales was large enough in 1963 to achieve most significant size economies. Grocery store sales of $52.7 billion in 1963 meant that a firm needed only one-hundredth of the market to achieve these scale economies. All of the twenty largest chains in 1965 had market shares well above this level.

There are some indications of diseconomies of size in large firms, but these diseconomies may not be sufficient to preclude high concentration in food retailing. Profits as a proportion of net worth for food chains exhibited a downward trend from 18 per cent in 1947 to approximately 12 per cent in 1965. The profit level and trend is very similar to that in total manufacturing and in the trade industries. Profits of the ten largest food chains averaged 11.1 per cent of net worth in 1964 and 1965. Profits of chains ranking 41st to 50th in size averaged 12.0 per cent in 1964 and 12.8 per cent in 1965. It is of interest that the share of grocery sales of the four largest chains declined from 23.0 per cent in 1940 to 20.0 per cent in 1963. The top twenty, however, increased their share of sales from 26.9 in 1948 to 34.0 in 1963. Most of the growth in local markets was among firms with less than 15 per cent of the market.

Barriers to entry into grocery retailing are becoming greater as firms find it increasingly difficult to secure capital for a half-million-dollar investment for a supermarket and overcome the losses that are likely to occur until a market is established in the now highly competitive business. Yet there is evidence that a large number of firms enter the industry each year (National Commission on Food Marketing, 1966, pp. 74, 75).

ADVERTISING AND PROMOTION

Between 1947 and 1952, advertising as a proportion of sales remained relatively stable. Corporate food retailers' advertising expenditures rose rapidly from .54 per cent of sales in 1952 to .92 per cent in 1957. This rate is considerably below that for food processors, who spent $808 million, or 2.03 per cent of their sales, on advertising in 1957. Advertising outlays of food processors and retailers totaled approximately $1.3 billion in 1963. It is not known what proportion of this performed a useful educational or entertainment function or what proportion was devoted only to maintaining market shares.

Trading stamps, like advertising, are a cost of sales promotion. In 1962, 47 per cent of all grocery store sales were made by retailers using stamps. Four-fifths of all chain supermarkets gave trading stamps in 1964. Gross margins of food chains rose from 18.12 per cent in 1955 to 22.48 per cent in 1964–65. Up to one-third of this increase was due to trading stamps. A U.S. Department of Agriculture study published in 1958 showed that food stamps cost about 2 per cent of sales, but food prices in stores using stamps were increased only .6 per cent over stores without stamps. Prices were not increased as much as stamp costs because of economies of larger sales promoted by food stamps and because the stores absorbed some of the cost. Because stamps were worth about 2 per cent of sales when redeemed, it follows that consumers would save approximately 1.4 per cent by patronizing stamp stores. Size economies fostered by trading stamps have tended to decline as more stores have adopted stamps. Thus it would appear that food retailers rather than housewives would provide the principal impetus to ban all trading stamps.

Another measure of economic performance is innovative activity. The supermarket (and its attendant cost economies in buying, transportation, and processing made possible by chains) can itself be regarded as a major innovation. In 1960, food manufacturers spent $96 million on research, or .2 per cent of sales, as compared with $1 billion on advertising.

There remains much room for innovation in quality control, procurement, and sales. Much of food retailing could be automated. The housewife may one day stand in a single spot without clerks but with many buttons which she will press, or IBM cards which she will feed into a machine, and have her order immediately packaged and delivered. Her bill will immediately be charged against her bank account by electronics. The entire operation may be controlled by high-speed computers. To increase marketing efficiency at a satisfactory pace, food firms will likely raise their research budgets considerably above current levels.

SUMMARY

In summary, the food retailing industry performance must be rated as very satisfactory. There is some cause for concern in the trend toward concentration. The largest firm in 1963, the A&P chain, accounted for about one-tenth of industry sales, hence was not in a position to exercise much monopsony or monopoly power. Profit rates were not high by nonfarm industry standards. Analysis of scale economies and profit rates pointed to no great pressures for increased concentration or monopoly profits in large firms. But average profit rates can be misleading, since a large firm may accrue high profits in a market where it has a dominant position and may sell below costs and have negative profits in a market where it desires to drive out competition and eventually gain dominance. Occasionally, such practices have been found. But existing legislation, such as the Robinson-Patman Act and antitrust legislation, appears adequate to stop such practices and halt mergers that would give large firms undue market power. Price leadership seems to be effective in food retailing only to the extent that it reflects competitive forces such as changes in labor costs, supply, and demand. Increasing costs of food retailing appear not to be caused by growing profits and inefficiency, but rather by the growing demand for more food services and by rising labor and other input costs.

LIVESTOCK AND MEAT

Changes in transportation and slaughter plant technology have led to decentralization of the livestock slaughter industry. The traditional pattern of livestock marketing involved shipment of livestock to concentration points or terminal markets where they were sold and slaughtered, usually in plants in large cities. The trend has been to construction of slaughtering plants in the livestock-producing areas, and to direct selling to packer buyers or sale through auction markets. The proportion of cattle purchased in terminal markets by packers fell from 75 per cent in 1950 to 36 per cent in 1964.

Terminal market purchases of hogs by packers declined from 40 to 24 per cent in the same period. Selling in terminal markets has performed the useful function of establishing prices. These prices have been reported by the Department of Agriculture's market news service, and the quoted prices for grades and classes of livestock have been used to price livestock in other markets as well. The decline of the terminal market raises questions about the relevancy of prices determined therein for other markets, and the Department of Agriculture has had difficulty extending its coverage to include prices outside terminal markets.

Another important development in the livestock industry is grade and yield selling. The grade and yield are determined from the carcass by the packer in the case of hogs. An estimated 8–10 per cent of cattle and 3 per cent of hogs were sold on grade and yield in 1964. Many producers feel that a third party should determine the grade and yield, and ensure that the carcass identity is maintained.

Another important element in livestock selling has been the growing activity of the cattle and hog futures market. This enables the producer to shift part of the price risk to professional speculators.

Meat imports have risen in the past decade and have caused considerable concern to livestock producers. Imports of red meats totaled 2.0 billion pounds in 1963, or 6.9 per cent of commercial production. Legislation was enacted in 1964 which established import quotas but left the Secretary of Agriculture considerable leeway in imposing restrictions on imports. Imports "voluntarily" dropped to 4.5 per cent of domestic production in 1963 and 1964 and were below the import quota level. Imports of live cattle, primarily for U.S. feedlots, numbered over 1 million head in 1962 and 1965. Although these imports also depress domestic meat prices, U.S. producers have not objected and called for quotas. Exports of red meat averaged approximately .5 per cent of national production from 1962 to 1965, thus were not a major market for U.S. meat output.

INTEGRATION INTO FEEDLOTS

The number of cattle fed in commercial feedlots increased rapidly in recent years. Feedlots with a capacity of 1,000 or more head in thirty-two states marketed two of every five cattle sold in 1962. Cost studies show feed cost economies of 2 cents per pound as capacity is raised from 200 to 5,000 head. With these economies, more feeding in large commercial feedlot operations can be expected (National Commission on Food Marketing, 1966, p. 24).

Three large food chains operated packing plants and commercial feedlots in 1964. Cattle fed by these chains comprised only .4 per cent of fed cattle marketed in 1964. Nearly 200 meat packers fed cattle amounting to 3.4 per cent of total commercial production of slaughter cattle in the same year. Packers and other marketing firms controlled 12 per cent of feedlot capacity, but feedlots were principally owned by farmers, ranchers, and specialized cattle feeders. Custom feeding is increasing by feedlot owners for packers and others who take title to the cattle before they are marketed and who specify feeding standards and marketing dates. Nearly half of all cattle marketed by commercial feedlots in fifteen Western states was owned by packers for eight days or longer. The increased ownership of cattle by packers, either in their feedlots or in feedlots of custom feeders, has caused concern about possible manipulation of market prices.

CONCENTRATION

The four largest packers, measured by red meat sales in 1963, accounted for 39 per cent of the meat production in 1947 and 29 per cent in 1964. For commercial beef and veal, the eight largest packers were responsible for 39 per cent of the production in 1947 and 28 per cent in 1964. The share of hog slaughtering by the eight largest firms declined from 51 per cent to 48 per cent between these years (National Commission on Food Marketing, 1966, p. 25). Intermediate-size firms increased their share at the expense of large firms. The trend toward decentralization apparent in the above figures may not continue, however.

PRICING

Highly advertised brands of meat sell at higher prices than brands which are not advertised. Advertising and promotion expenses of the eight largest packers rose from .5 per cent of sales in 1947 to 1 per cent in 1964.

A considerable amount of meat is sold by formula-pricing. An estimated 41 per cent of the beef sold by packers to their major customers in 1964–65 was priced by formula. The formula was usually tied to prices quoted in the *National Provisioner* "Yellow Sheet." The formula, which takes into account transportation costs, tends to remain stable for extended periods and may not reflect changing supply-and-demand conditions. The growing use of formula pricing means that fewer prices are negotiated in a manner to reflect economic conditions. Two large food chains negotiate purchases and do not report the results to the *National Provisioner* (National Commission on Food Marketing, 1966, p. 27). For these and other reasons, there is some doubt whether the prices quoted in the Yellow Sheet reflect actual conditions well enough to promote a high degree of market efficiency.

The margin between farm and wholesale prices, reflecting transport, slaughter, and processing costs, remained stable from 1955 to 1964 at approximately 10 cents per pound for beef and 13 cents per pound for hogs and lambs. Retailing margins increased, however.

PERFORMANCE

Packer profits average lower than profits of other food processors, and suggest diseconomies in large-size operations. Average return on net worth after taxes of the four largest packers was 5.5 per cent from 1948 to 1964. In the same period the average return for packers ranking from fifth to eighth in size was 9.2 per cent. Profits in 1964 as a proportion of net worth after taxes were 8.6 per cent and were the highest for the 1948–64 period for the four largest packers.

Partly due to the seasonal nature of meat production, packing plants are often operated at less than capacity. The average annual utilization rate from 1950 to 1960 varied from 53 per cent to 86 per cent for cattle and from 57 per cent to 71 per cent for hogs (Williams, 1966, p. 66). To increase efficiency by more complete utilization of capacity (by filling seasonal gaps in supply) and to satisfy demands for grades and classes of meat, there is pressure for packers to integrate into feedlot operations. Also there is pressure for large retail food chains to integrate into packing and feeding operations to counter efforts of packers to raise wholesale meat prices. The result of these pressures will likely be increased vertical integration in the meat industry.

The over-all performance of the meat industry has been quite satisfactory. The industry is highly competitive and has made numerous adjustments that have increased efficiency.

DAIRY PRODUCTS

Numerous changes have been made in the dairy industry. Despite a 40 per cent reduction in the number of farms selling milk and a 15 per cent decline in dairy cow numbers between 1959 and 1964, total milk production increased slightly. Two-thirds of the milk sold in 1964 in fluid-milk markets was in some way connected with cooperative or producers' bargaining associations. Federal milk marketing orders established minimum prices for milk to be used in different end uses. Where prices encouraged oversupply, the government purchased excess stocks and sold them later when supplies were slack or disposed of them through school lunch and other programs.

The market for milk has been localized because of transport costs and sanitary regulations. These sanitary regulations are sometimes used to protect a market from milk shipped from outside areas, and milk price differentials are greater among areas than can be justified by transport costs alone. Some sanitary regulations can be regarded as an unnecessary restriction on interstate commerce. As transport costs decline, the regulations fostered by local governments and localized milk marketing orders will eventually need to recognize the regional and national structure of the milk market.

CONCENTRATION AND INTEGRATION

The number of milk processing plants declined 55 per cent from 1950 to 1961, although the number of plants processing over 40,000 quarts per day rose 57 per cent.

The number of plants manufacturing dairy products such as ice cream, cheese, and butter fell 37 per cent, while average plant size increased 83 per cent from 1944 to 1961. Farmer cooperatives were very active in processing manufactured dairy products. In 1964 they manufactured three-fourths of all dried milk and two-thirds of all creamery butter.

The proportion of shipments of fluid milk handled by the four largest firms was 23 per cent in 1963 and had changed little since 1954. Market concentration in local areas tended to be high, however, and was increasing. In seventy-eight federal order markets, the market share of the four largest firms in small markets increased from 67 to 87 per cent between 1950 and 1964, but in the large markets increased only from 52 to 53 per cent.

Concentration in the processed cheese and ice cream industries was quite high in 1963. In each, the eight largest firms accounted for nearly half of all shipments. Concentration rates in the butter and natural cheese industries were low.

Large dairy firms frequently diversified their operations into nondairy lines. Motives for this included the greater profitability of nondairy operations and protection against loss of wholesale dairy accounts.

Vertical integration of dairy processors into dairy farming has been nominal, but chain stores have become heavily involved in processing and distributing fluid milk and its manufactured products. This action of chain stores has been motivated by the desire to circumvent regulations in some states that establish minimum prices which retail stores must pay for milk and to use delivery men paid by the hour rather than on a commission basis. Fourteen of the forty largest food chains in 1963 produced in their own plants 53 per cent of their sales volume of fluid milk (National Commission on Food Marketing, 1966, p. 45). Milk-processing plants owned by chain stores sold one-third of their dairy product output to other food retailers and wholesalers in 1963.

To balance the power of chain stores and to raise sales and efficiency, dairy firms have merged at a rapid pace. From 1922 to 1964, over 2,000 dairy companies were absorbed by eight large dairies. The mergers led to several antimerger cases by the Federal Trade Commission. The result was a ten-year proscription against the four largest dairy companies merging with other dairy firms.

PROFITS AND PRICES

Profits from dairy manufacturing have been low. Four large dairy firms in 1964 reported that their after-tax profits on manufacturing operations were most frequently in the range of from zero to 2 per cent of sales (National Commission on Food Marketing, 1966, p. 46). Low profits tended to result from competitive dominance of cooperatives, which made no attempt to gain sizable profits.

Profits on fluid-milk operations have been greater than on manufacturing operations and have tended to increase the average rate of profit of dairy firms. Dairy company after-tax profits were similar to those of other food industry firms, ranging from 10 to 12 per cent of net worth for large dairy companies from 1959 to 1964. Economies of size were apparent. After-tax profits of dairy firms with over $250,000 of annual sales averaged 9.1 per cent of net worth in 1963 while those of firms with under $50,000 of annual sales averaged − 1.2 per cent.

Evidence of price leadership and lack of active competition was apparent in some local markets. Nonprice competition in the form of concessions to retail stores was frequent. These practices included free store equipment, advertising allowances, financial backing for store operators, and free gifts of automobiles to store operators. Through the use of private labels and their strong bargaining position as major outlets, retail food chains secured cost concessions on milk and increased competition in the dairy industry. Consumers benefited from this competition.

The trend toward concentration and vertical integration in the dairy industry must be watched, but the current dairy market structure and measures available to the government to restrain unfair practices and monopoly power appear to be adequate to maintain a workable degree of competition and efficiency in the dairy industry. Nevertheless, J. R. Moore (1966, pp. 121–22) states that "both the structure and conduct of the fluid milk industry is in need of improvement." He suggests amending the Clayton Act and requiring premerger notification as ways to accomplish this improvement.

FRUITS AND VEGETABLES

The fruit and vegetable industry has two major divisions, one concerned with fresh products, and one with processed products.

FRESH FRUITS AND VEGETABLES

The market for fresh fruits and vegetables is dominated by the urgency engendered by the perishable nature of the product. Before World War II, the usual practice was for growers to deliver their crops to shipping points. The shipping firms graded, packed, and shipped the product to wholesalers and auction markets in large terminal markets in urban centers. This procedure changed, and in 1966 only half the product was traded in terminal markets. Big buyers from large corporate chains started the trend to buy directly at shipping points and by-pass the terminal market. The result was a decline in the significance of the establishing of prices by terminal markets. Since large buyers reveal neither volume nor purchase price, direct selling has made price discovery more obscure. The insensitivity of prices at the retail level to changing supplies makes it difficult to clear a market of excess supply without major price changes at shipping points (National Commission on Food Marketing, 1966, p. 50).

The shipper is limited in bargaining power with buyers because of the large volume purchased by big buyers such as chain food stores and by the possibility of merchandise rejection and attendant need for price renegotiation. The effect is that the shipper is in a stronger position to bargain with growers than with buyers. Shippers have also improved their bargaining position by growing some of their supplies. The shipper handles the crop for the grower for a fee in some instances, with the grower bearing the market risk.

Growers have attempted to improve their position by forming cooperatives which integrate production, packing, and selling operations. Cooperatives marketed one-fourth of all fresh fruits and vegetables in 1964. Marketing orders have also been used to improve the bargaining position of growers. In 1965, eighty-two orders were in operation, sixty of these in the three Pacific coast states. Few marketing orders exercise control over the production and flow of products to the market and consequently the orders have not materially strengthened the market power of growers.

PROCESSED FRUITS AND VEGETABLES

The fruit and vegetable processing industry has two principal components—canned products and frozen products. The four largest firms in the canning industry accounted for 24 per cent of the production in 1963; the twenty largest accounted for 50 per cent. The percentages in the frozen-products industry were nearly the same. Concentration in the canning industry has increased slowly while that in the frozen-products industry has declined.

High costs for facilities, distribution, and advertising make entry into the processing industry difficult. There has been comparatively little vertical integration, either of food chains into processing or of processors into the grower operations. The average plant in 1964 obtained 10 per cent of its raw materials from land owned or rented by the company. Because processors desired additional assured sources of supply, 70 per cent of the supply requirements for freezers and canners were obtained through contractual arrangements with growers in 1964.

Packers and distributors of national brands have a comparatively strong bargaining position with food retailers. Packers of unadvertised brands and private-label brands for retailers are in a weaker position, especially with large chains which use a central purchasing agency. The use of private labels and lower prices on these private-label brands by food retailers undermines the market power of even the large processors who market nationally advertised brands and intensifies competition.

The rate of return on net worth after taxes in sixty-one fruit-and-vegetable-canning firms averaged only 1.4 per cent from 1960 to 1964. The average is misleading, because there is large variation in returns. Canning has tended to become more concentrated in the large operations found on the West Coast, but firms in the Midwest (which are smaller than firms in the West) had higher profit rates. Profit rates generally did not appear to be associated with size of operation. For 61 firms surveyed, less than half had a profit in each of the years from 1960 to 1964. It has been of some concern to growers that the containers cost on the average almost as much as the raw product that goes into them. Cost, as a proportion of sales for the raw product, was approximately 29 per cent; and for containers, cases, and labels was 25 per cent in 1963 and 1964.

There were seventy cooperative bargaining associations in 1964, but only forty-three were active in negotiating prices, and twenty-four of these were located on the Pacific coast, which provided approximately 90 per cent of supplies for canned fruits and vegetables. The impact of bargaining associations on the market was small because they did not limit production and usually did not control a large share of the supply.

POULTRY AND EGGS

The factory system has been extended to the farm in poultry operations. This was made possible by improved techniques of disease control, breeding, nutrition, housing, and marketing. It now requires about two pounds of feed to produce a pound of broiler meat. Spurred by low prices and good quality, the consumption of chickens has doubled since 1948. Commercial broiler output in 1965 was eight times as large as in 1940.

VERTICAL INTEGRATION

Feed is the major expense of poultry production. Poultry producers were anxious to increase production but lacked capital. Feed manufacturers were anxious to expand feed sales and could provide capital but were afraid of the risk. The impasse was overcome through contracts by feed companies with growers which provided for feed payments when the poultry were sold. The feed companies increasingly assumed the organizational management decisions while the grower provided the operational management. Generally, growers furnished the land, building, equipment, electricity, water, and labor. The contracting firm provided the chicks and feed. This vertical integration of the broiler industry has been accompanied by a shift in geographic location to the South, where farms are characterized by excess of labor and shortage of capital. Excess labor on farms made contracts a cheaper form of integration than outright ownership of production facilities by integrating firms. About 95 per cent of broiler production is under some type of economic integration (Roy, 1966, p. 70).

A smaller share of total production is integrated for turkeys and eggs, but there is an increase in contract arrangements in which growers receive a base guarantee payment plus an incentive increment for efficiency. There is growth of large-scale, specialized egg-producing units using much automatic equipment, which reduces unit cost and raises quality control. These units are owned and operated by specialized egg-producing firms, by feed manufacturers, and by food retailers.

Firms specializing in poultry production and processing typically operate a feed mill, a hatchery, and a processing plant. Most of the large firms in the broiler industry are feed companies or meat packers with subsidiaries or divisions to handle poultry. The feed companies that were initially involved in broiler production found advantages in owning hatcheries and in processing and marketing dressed poultry rather than live broilers. Integrating firms did not extend their activities to grocery retailing because it is a complex, specialized business involving many other products and because retail margins were not sufficiently high to justify alternative ways of retail marketing.

CONCENTRATION

Concentration in poultry processing is not high but is rising. The proportion of federally inspected slaughter by the four largest firms increased from 12 per cent in 1960 to 18 per cent in 1964. The four largest turkey slaughterers accounted for about the same percentage of federally inspected slaughter in 1960 as in 1964 (24 per cent).

Economies-of-size studies show that all intraplant efficiencies are attained in a plant that produces only 2 per cent or less of U.S. production. However, selling economies of size are significant, and this has hastened the growth and merger of firms. Between 1960 and 1964, the number of poultry slaughtering plants declined from 286 to 201 firms for chickens and from 249 to 189 for turkeys (National Commission on Food Marketing, 1966, p. 33). Concentration is low in egg handling. There were 9,000 egg handlers in 1965. Thirteen firms handled 10 per cent of U.S. table eggs in that year.

ADVERTISING AND PROMOTION

A large proportion of mature chickens are used as ingredients in soups, frozen dinners, and other highly differentiated items. Advertising and promotion expenses for firms producing such products ranged up to 9 per cent of their sales dollar in 1964. In contrast, young chickens are essentially undifferentiated in the retail store, and chicken processors who sold most of their product ice-packed or frozen spent less than 1 per cent of sales for advertising and promotion.

Three-fourths of the chickens and half the eggs sold at retail were government-graded in 1964. The improvement in quality and freshness of eggs has been significant.

PRICING

Buyers usually depend on certain regular customers for most of their poultry and egg needs. The twenty largest processors of young chickens and turkeys account for a larger proportion of industry volume than the volume purchased by the largest twenty retailers. This fact might suggest bargaining advantages for processors, but broilers are produced throughout the year, and ice-packed, perishable supplies often accumulate to levels that erode the bargaining power of processors. Most turkeys are marketed frozen and can be stored over slack seasons, but eventually must be sold. Egg handlers frequently make concessions to retailers for the privilege of becoming regular suppliers. The strong bargaining position of buyers is evidenced by the usual flow of concessions and allowances from seller to buyer—not from buyer to seller. Allowances are in the form of quantity discounts, advertising allowances, and price reductions. Some instances of bribery, cash payments, and gifts from sellers to buyers have come to the attention of government regulatory agencies (National Commission on Food Marketing, 1966, p. 35).

Formula-pricing was widely practiced in the poultry industry. Firms processing chickens reported in 1964 that 42 per cent of sales to their most important customers was tied directly by formula to a specific market quotation. The figure for egg distribution was 72 per cent. The difficulty is that the spread of vertical integration, other forms of market coordination, and formula-pricing reduce the number of genuinely negotiated prices. The burden of price formation falls on a few markets, and prices become more sensitive to manipulation and other factors not associated with industry supply and demand.

In 1952, the farm value of eviscerated frying chicken was 40 cents per pound and the retail price was 60 cents per pound. By 1962, the farm value had declined to 21 cents and the retail price to 41 cents per pound (Roy, 1966, p. 90). The farm-retail spread remained virtually constant throughout the period. The processing and distribution cost was 9 cents per pound and the retail margin was 8 cents per pound in 1964. Though retail chains and other marketing firms possess superior marketing power, it was not this factor but rather the adoption of modern technology (which made it possible to expand broiler production much faster than demand) that explains the precipitous price decline. The retail price of eggs was 51.5 cents per dozen and the farm value was 29.1 cents per dozen in 1964. This left a margin of 8.8 cents for retailers and 13.6 cents for wholesalers.

PROFITS

After-tax profits on net worth from 1948 to 1964 ranged from 4 to 14 per cent for chicken processing firms, and from 9 to 26 per cent for turkey processing firms. The financial returns for ten leading firms specializing in each of three categories—chickens, turkeys, and eggs—showed that earnings after taxes on net worth averaged 13.3 per cent for turkey processors, 18.0 per cent for egg handling and processing firms, and 6.2 per cent for chicken processors in 1964. Broiler growers producing under contract ordinarily received 5 to 7 cents per bird. After subtracting nonlabor costs, this provided a return on labor of $.25 to $2.00 per hour to grower-labor (National Commission on Food Marketing, 1966, p. 38).

Roy (1966, p. 96) states that the "overall performance of the broiler processing-retailing segments has been satisfactory in supplying consumers with an abundant, wholesome product at low cost." He continues: "That economic integration in the broiler industry has reduced cost is verified by research experience and observations. Horizontal and vertical integration have eliminated many smaller, inefficient firms with high costs and much instability in operation."

GRAINS AND OTHER PRODUCTS

Three components of the grain-processing industry are discussed below: (*a*) milling, (*b*) baking, and (*c*) breakfast cereals, crackers, and cookies.

FLOUR MILLING

New techniques have made it possible for fewer farmers, millers, and bakers to meet domestic requirements for food grains. More than half the flour mills operating in 1948 had closed by 1964. Grinding capacity was reduced only 8.7 per cent, however, and attrition was heaviest among smaller mills. The twenty largest milling firms accounted for 58 per cent of capacity in 1951 and 61 per cent in 1966 (National Commission on Food Marketing, 1966, p. 56). Vertical integration has been prominent. Many flour millers produce cookies, crackers, and prepared foods. Since General Mills closed nine of its seventeen plants in 1965, it uses practically all its flour to produce consumer items. On the average, the twenty largest firms use one-fifth of their processed flour for further processing in their own plants.

The large investment required to achieve size economies and provide specialized equipment gives large, established firms an advantage. But smaller firms often have advantages of flexibility and nearness to customers or growers. Economies of operation were greatest in plants of 7,500 hundredweight of daily flour milling capacity in 1964.

Profits after taxes of flour millers averaged 7.6 per cent of net worth from 1955–56 to 1964–65 and were never as high as 10 per cent.

Mills purchased 4.5 per cent of their wheat from farmers, 29.9 per cent from country elevators, 53.8 per cent from terminal or subterminal elevators, and 11.8 per cent from mill-owned country elevators in 1964. Loans offered by the federal government to farmers for wheat have established a floor under prices. Domestic demand is somewhat stable, but foreign demand, which was 55 per cent of utilization from 1963 to 1965, is volatile. Futures markets are maintained for wheat, which enables millers and grain companies to hedge risks arising from price fluctuations.

Flour is not a differentiated product, and competition is keen in selling. Millers usually negotiate flour prices with their largest customers and post comparable listed prices for smaller buyers. The price structure is therefore strongly influenced by a few large millers and bakers.

BAKING

Bread and bread-type rolls account for approximately two-thirds of the value of bakery products. Wholesale bakers produce 77 per cent of the total value of all bread and related products. Grocery chains produce 11 per cent. Three cooperatives are included among the 12 large bread-baking firms and account for 24 per cent of bread production. The share of bread shipments by the four largest bakeries was 33 per cent in 1963. This had remained nearly stable since 1958. There is evidence that profits as a per cent of sales are higher in large bakeries, and a gradual trend toward concentration is anticipated. Profits of wholesale bakeries averaged 10 to 12 per cent of stockholders' equity from 1952 to 1964.

More than half of all bread sold by chain stores in 1964 was private label. This was partly to reduce the margin between retailer and wholesaler. It costs nearly as much to move bread from the baker's platform to the consumer as it does to grow the wheat, mill the flour, and bake the bread. The farmer receives 3–4 cents for the ingredients he contributes to a loaf of bread. The bread costs 11 cents on the baker's dock and sells for about 21 cents retail. There is considerable evidence of inefficiency in deliveries to supermarkets. Each day, driver salesmen from several wholesale bakeries deliver bread, restock the shelves, and remove stale items in a supermarket. The salesmen have attempted to maintain their commission of 7 per cent or more of the wholesale value of bakery products distributed in their territory.

GROCERY MANUFACTURING

Grocery manufacturing, defined here as the production and sale of highly processed packaged foods, tends to be characterized by high concentration, advertising, promotional activity, innovation, and profits. The four largest firms in the respective grocery-manufacturing categories in 1965 sold 95 per cent of the baby food, more than 90 per cent of the soups, more than 55 per cent of the coffee, 75 per cent of the cake mixes, and 65 per cent of the shortening. A sample of twenty-two firms selling these and related products showed that their sales increased 5.9 per cent annually from 1951 to 1964 while the food industry sales as a whole grew 4.7 per cent annually. In 1964, the after-tax profits of the 22 food manufacturers averaged 13.2 per cent of net worth (National Commission on Food Marketing, 1966, p. 63).

Manufacturers of breakfast cereals tend to sell highly differentiated products. Private labels are uncommon. In 1964, 99 per cent of cereals were sold under the producer's own brand name or trademark. Cereal manufacturers spent approximately 15 per cent of their sales dollar for media advertising—more than 80 per cent of it on television. Sales promotion, marketing research and other advertising expenses were 5 per cent of sales, bringing total advertising and promotion costs to 20 per cent of sales in 1964.

Cereal manufacturers have concluded from marketing research that variety and novelty in breakfast cereals attract customers. Each of the four largest cereal firms offered an average of fifty-eight items in 1964. The ten best-selling items comprised nearly 60 per cent of sales. Thus a large number of items sold in relatively low volume.

Net income after taxes was 7.5 per cent of sales and 18.0 per cent of stockholders' equity in 1964. Data for 1947, 1950, and 1956 showed profits of 15–16 per cent of stockholders' equity, hence breakfast cereal manufacturing is one of the most profitable food industries. The strong tendency for profit rates to increase by size of firm and the barriers to entry (such as the cost of establishing a widely accepted product line) suggest a tendency for greater concentration in the industry in the future. On the other hand, the high profits may encourage other food processors and retail food chains to expand their activities into the breakfast cereal line and to reduce concentration.

NATIONAL COMMISSION ON FOOD MARKETING

Many characteristics of the food industry reported in the previous pages were taken from the results of the extensive study of food marketing made by the National Commission on Food Marketing (1966). The Commission was virtually unanimous in praising the research reported in the technical studies, but the characteristics of the food industry were by no means interpreted with unanimity by members of the Commission. There were separate majority and minority reports. Both groups agreed that great progress has been made and will continue to be made in the processing and distribution of food. The food industry received high marks for efficiency—for moving a high volume of quality food to consumers at reasonable cost. The majority report concluded, however, that private industry, which has responsibility for seeking efficient methods of processing and distributing food and for developing superior methods and products, needs additional surveillance by the government to ensure a competitive environment and fair business dealings.

CONCENTRATION

The Commission was disturbed by the trend toward concentration in the food industry beyond levels needed for efficient operation. The changing market structure has transferred market power from processors and manufacturers to retailers. Increasing concentration, according to the Commission, restricts the alternatives open to suppliers, stimulates concentration among suppliers, and weakens the effectiveness of competition. However, the Commission did not regard concentration as sufficiently high to justify divesture of current holdings nor restraint of internal growth. The principal danger was viewed as the impairment of competition by merger and acquisition by dominant firms. The Commission majority stated in its report (1966, p. 106) that:

> It is our conclusion that acquisitions or mergers by the largest firms in any concentrated branch of the food industry, which result in a significant increase in their market shares or the geographic extension of their markets, probably will result in a substantial lessening of competition in violation of the Clayton Act.
>
> We conclude that legislation requiring some form of premerger notification is desirable.
>
> In order to accomplish this purpose, we consider it necessary to give the regulatory agencies power to issue temporary cease and desist orders, to be effective for a limited time and from which appeals can be taken to the courts.

Conglomerate and vertically integrated firms presently publish financial data only for their total activities and do not disclose information about particular fields of operation. The Commission felt that firms will be less likely to engage in activities contrary to fair competition if information is made available about their operations in various fields of business. The Commission (1966, p. 107) wrote:

> We conclude that each public corporation having annual sales in excess of a specified amount should be required to report annually to the Securities and Exchange Commission, for publication, its sales, expenses, and profits in each field of operations in which the annual value of shipments is larger than a given minimum.

Some regulatory functions of government agencies are made obsolete by changes in the structure of food marketing. As for emerging regulatory needs, an up-to-date appraisal of changes in the industry was deemed necessary. The Commission majority recommended in its report (1966, p. 107):

> In order that the Congress, the executive branch, and the public will be fully informed, we believe that the Federal Trade Commission should be charged with making a continuing review of market structure and competition in the food industry and report annually thereon to the Congress.

The Robinson-Patman Act was designed to ban favoritism and unfair discrimination in buying and selling. The Commission majority considered that there were loopholes in the Act that reduce its effectiveness and recommended that it be reappraised for possible revision in light of current economic conditions and over-all antitrust policies. They recommended that regulatory jurisdiction over transactions in meats, dressed poultry, and products processed from these commodities be removed from the U.S. Department of Agriculture and be exercised only by the Department of Justice and the Federal Trade Commission (National Commission on Food Marketing, 1966, p. 108).

SERVICES TO CONSUMERS

Several recommendations were made to provide consumers with choices and unbiased information needed to get more satisfaction from their food dollar. The Commission (1966, p. 109) made the following suggestions:

> Consumer grades should be developed and required to appear on all foods for which such grades are feasible, that are sold in substantial volume to consumers, and that belong to a recognized product category.
>
> Packages and their labels should assist consumers in gaining an accurate impression of the contents and in making price comparisons.
>
> A centralized consumer agency should be established in the executive branch of the government by statute.

The consumer agency would assume consumer protection roles now held by other government agencies. The agency would be involved in legislative matters and would make a major effort to help the consumer play a more intelligent role in purchasing food.

MARKET POWER OF FARMERS

The Commission majority noted economic problems of farmers stemming from the large and uncoordinated number of producers, lack of product differentiation, frequent oversupply arising from difficulties in forming price expectations, and uncertainties of weather and technology. Three approaches to these problems were suggested: (*a*) greater reliance on producers' marketing cooperatives and bargaining associations, with government assistance to these groups where possible, (*b*) federal marketing agreements and orders to be authorized for any agricultural commodity produced in a local area or regional subdivision of the U.S., and (c) legislation to be enacted enabling agricultural marketing boards to be brought into existence upon the vote of producers for the purpose of joining in the sale of products as they first enter into channels of trade (National Commission on Food Marketing, 1966, p. 110).

The boards would have powers granted under federal marketing orders and, in addition, power to regulate production or marketing and to negotiate prices and other terms of trade. The purpose would be to strengthen the bargaining position of farmers. Regarding the right of farmers to form bargaining associations, the Commission (1966, p. 111) stated:

> We believe that specific legislation should be enacted providing that all processors, shippers, and buyers of farm products, engaging in or affecting interstate trade, are prohibited from obstructing the formation or operation of a producers' bargaining association or cooperative, and from influencing producers' understanding of or voting on marketing orders or similar programs, by disseminating false or misleading information, discriminating among producers in any manner, boycotts, or other deceptive or coercive methods.

OTHER CONCLUSIONS

Concern was expressed about state and local regulations that were obstructing the movement of farm products, particularly fluid milk, and the need to establish uniform regulations among states was stressed. The Commission (1966, pp. 112, 113) called for increased efforts by the U.S. Department of Agriculture and other agencies to collect and interpret new data on advertising costs and discounts, prices, farm-retail price spreads, profits, futures trading, and other aspects of the food industry.

It is not possible here to summarize all of the minority reports. In general, the minority contended that the food industry had performed more responsibly and efficiently than reported by the majority and that the recommendations of the majority were ill advised, too strong, puzzling, inconsistent, and unsupported. The following quote catches some of the flavor of their spirited objection:

> In this exuberant spirit sundry antitrust and other nostrums, interred long ago, have been exhumed. But there has been no examination of their likely impact on the food marketing industry. There has been no attempt to relate them to any other business complex. The staff did not even present to the Commission the pros and cons of these proposals, as extensively developed in the hearings and reports of Congress.

To all of this the minority protested again. We maintained that a preoccupation with issues beyond the charge and competence of the

Commission, together with cursory examinations of proposals of vast import to all American enterprise, would weaken the credibility of the Commission's entire effort. [National Commission on Food Marketing, 1966, p. 128]

The minority reached quite different conclusions than did the majority from examination of the data. In general they felt that current antitrust and control legislation is adequate and that measures recommended by the majority would only create inefficiency. They further argued that Congress, after due deliberation and consideration of more data and analyses of the food industry than were gathered by the Commission, should make any recommendations and actions they deemed necessary.

SUMMARY AND CONCLUSIONS

Studies of the market structure, conduct, and performance of the food industry are designed to circumvent the impasse of classical economic theory when confronted with markets such as dynamic bilateral oligopoly. These studies provide few "pat" answers, however, and must be interpreted with circumspection.

The goal of the food industry is to provide adequate volume, quality, and variety of foods to consumers at reasonable prices. In general the imperfect competition predominant in the industry is characterized by a high degree of innovation and promotional activity. It is constantly seeking new products and more efficient methods of production and distribution. The high volume and quality in American food products are without precedent.

Serious problems remain nevertheless. The public is concerned about tendencies to concentrate ownership, about high advertising and promotion costs, and about the impact of the food industry market structure on farmers. These problems are discussed below.

IMPROVING MARKET PERFORMANCE

There are two ways of interpreting the data on size economies, which, for food retailing for example, show few economies for large firms. The food chains say that the presence of size diseconomies for very large firms means that market forces preclude tendencies for high concentration, and the public need not be concerned. Certain public agencies argue that mergers and increasing concentration are in fact taking place in spite of the observed diseconomies in very large firms and that mergers are motivated by the desire to obtain an inordinate amount of market power. They contend that in the absence of clear economies of large size, the public is not benefited by increasing concentration. The public would appear to have nothing to gain and perhaps much to lose by mergers and acquisitions by large firms.

Merger activity of a large firm in many instances increases workable competition, as, for example, when a large food chain absorbs a small firm about to go bankrupt in an area where the large chain has no stores. It also may be argued that profit rates, promotional activity, and other measures of market performance give unconvincing evidence of predatory behavior or other objectional practices of larger firms. Furthermore, it can be said that potential public regulations of operating practices can ensure high performance in an industry where concentration is very high. On the other hand, the pressure of effective competition is a much more reliable goad to efficiency than reliance on federal regulation of pricing or reliance on the "altruistic" desire of firms lacking competition to act in the public interest. Maintaining an environment of effective competition among firms is perhaps the most satisfactory public policy. In industries where economies of size are not large, antimerger and other public policies to preclude high concentration seem appropriate.

IMPLICATIONS FOR FARMERS

The proposition that the farm problem is due to a conspiracy in the market sector and can be eliminated by improving the performance of the marketing sector is a myth. There simply is no giant rathole in the marketing sector absorbing money that should go to farmers. Some feel that the solution to farm problems is to make the marketing industry atomistic. This is not possible. And, if it were possible, it would not be desirable. Economies in production and sales are large enough so that costs would rise if the industry were atomized, and consumers would end up paying more for a lower quality of food.

Profits in the food industry comprise about 5 per cent and advertising about 4 per cent of the marketing bill; together they totaled $5 billion in 1965. Could these be eliminated, and could farm income be raised $5 billion? The answer is "No!" Contrary to the view of some spokesmen, the marketing industry is more closely akin to other industries than to farming. It must compete with nonfarm industries for labor and capital. While profit rates and wage rates in the marketing industry appear very high by farm standards, they are not high for nonfarm industries, and the food sector must pay comparable rates to acquire and hold its resources. Advertising is prominent in most nonfarm industries, but this does not resolve the issue of its worth in the food industry. Some advertising performs a very useful function of informing buyers of new or cheaper products, of helping the housewife plan her menu, and sometimes of providing entertainment. In some cases, advertising increases sales and reduces costs. On the other hand, much advertising is of no social value and is designed only to preserve market shares. If the excess profits and socially unproductive advertising were eliminated in the food industry, even the most optimistic estimate would place the reduction in the food marketing bill at $2 billion. Perhaps half of this might be passed on to farmers in higher product prices—the rest would accrue as savings to consumers. A billion-dollar increase in farm income would be no solution to the farm problem.

Although there are no large, unreasonable inefficiencies in the marketing sector, farmers might be exploited by the monopsony pricing of farm products. Some such exploitation undoubtedly occurs in situations where there is one or a very few buyers for a commodity, but research data on this issue are limited. Even if monopsony pricing exists, it does not explain the low return on farm resources. Firms purchasing farm commodities must pay the variable cost of production or farmers will not supply the commodity. In the long run, all production costs are variable and it follows that purchasers must pay the full cost of farm output. If farm resources are mobile, this full cost of production means a return on all resources equal to what these resources could obtain in employment outside of farming. If resource returns are low in the long run, it is because farm resources are not mobile rather than because of monopsony exploitation by marketing firms.

The market structure of the food industry does lead to marketing costs that are quite stable despite variation in the volume of products handled. This places on farm prices the burden of adjustment to changing demand and supply of farm products. The result is substantial annual and long-term variation in prices received by farmers in the absence of government programs. This is the most serious problem for farmers stemming from the structure of food marketing. The solution to this problem is government farm programs and increased bargaining power for farmers rather than forced atomization of the food industry.

Estimates for 1968 showed that about 95 per cent of the U.S. broiler output was produced under contract, as were 95 per cent of the broiler-type hatching eggs, nearly 35 per cent of the table eggs, 85 per cent of the turkeys, 10 per cent of the hogs, 30 per cent of the beef cattle, 25 per cent of the lamb and mutton, nearly all of the citrus fruits, and 90 per cent of the vegetables for canning and freezing. Farmers are concerned with the vertical integration of the food industry into farming. There is considerable evidence that this integration, though unsettling to farmers, has resulted in greater efficiency. Whether the social gain from laws to stop the trend would be more than offset by the social loss in terms of efficiency sacrificed is a sociological and political as well as an economic question and cannot be answered by economists alone. The best defense against vertical integration into farming appears to be alert management and efficient use of resources by farmers.

REFERENCES

Bird, Kermit, P. B. Dwoskin, and M. E. Miller. 1966. Marketing innovations. In *Agricultural Markets in Change*, Agricultural Economics Report No. 95, Washington, U.S. Department of Agriculture, pp. 28–57.

Blaich, O. P. and L. F. Hermann. 1966. Perspectives on farm product marketing. In *Agricultural Markets in Change*, Agricultural Economics Report No. 95, Washington, U.S. Department of Agriculture, pp. 2–27.

Brandow, George. 1961. Interrelationships among demands for farm products and implications for control of market supply. Agricultural Experiment Station Bulletin 680. University Park, Pa.

Buchholz, H. E., G. G. Judge, and V. I. West. 1962. A summary of selected estimated behavior relationships for agricultural products. Department of Agricultural Economics Research Report AERR-57. Urbana: University of Illinois.

Cook, Hugh L. 1966. The ice cream industry. In Moore and Walsh (1966), pp. 123–49.

Daly, R. F. 1958. Demand for farm products at retail and the farm level. *Journal of the American Statistical Association.* (Page reference is to a mimeo version of the paper.)

Economic Report of the President. 1967. Washington: U.S. Government Printing Office.

Farris, Paul L. 1966. The grain procurement industry. In Moore and Walsh (1966), pp. 249–65.

Fowler, M. L. 1966. The cotton industry. In Moore and Walsh (1966), Chapter 12.

Gale, Hazen F. 1967. The farm marketing bill and its components. Agriculture Economic Report No. 105. Washington, U.S. Department of Agriculture.

Garoian, Leon. 1966. Grocery retailing. In Moore and Walsh (1966), pp. 3–37.

Heady, Earl and Luther G. Tweeten. 1963. *Resource Demand and Structure of the Agricultural Industry.* Ames: Iowa State University Press.

Helmberger, P. G. and Sidney Hoos. 1966. The vegetable processing industry. In Moore and Walsh (1966), pp. 172–91.

Moore, John R. 1966. The fluid milk industry. In Moore and Walsh (1966), pp. 101–22.

———— and Richard C. Walsh, eds. 1966. *Market Structure of Agricultural Industries.* Ames: Iowa State University Press.

National Commission on Food Marketing. 1966. *Food from Farmer to Consumer.* Washington: U.S. Government Printing Office.

Roy, Ewell P. 1966. The broiler chicken industry. In Moore and Walsh (1966), pp. 68–100.

Tweeten, Luther G. 1965. Commodity program for wheat. Agricultural Experiment Station Technical Bulletin T-118. Stillwater, Oklahoma State University.

————. 1967. The demand for U.S. farm output. *Food Research Institute Studies* 7:343–69.

———— and James S. Plaxico. 1964. Long-run outlook for agricultural adjustments. *Journal of Farm Economics* 46:39–55.

U.S. Department of Agriculture. 1966. *Agricultural Statistics.* Washington: U.S. Government Printing Office.

———. 1966. Farm income situation. FIS-203. Washington.

Walsh, Richard G. and Bert M. Evans. 1966. The baking industry. In Moore and Walsh (1966), pp. 192–224.

Waugh, F. V. 1964. Demand and price analysis. Agriculture Technical Bulletin No. 1316. Washington, U.S. Department of Agriculture.

Williams, Willard F. 1966. The meat industry. In Moore and Walsh (1966), pp. 38–67.

CHAPTER EIGHT

The Economic Structure: Product Supply and Farm-Produced Inputs

In the previous chapter, the marketing sector was cleared of causing the share of farm income in the national economy to decline and of causing the parity ratio to be depressed. Rather, these companions of the cost-price squeeze are manifestations of low-price and low income elasticities of demand characteristic of all affluent societies.

We next look more closely at the cost and input side of the cost-price squeeze. Some attention will be given to an overview of the resource structure, including a consideration of family and corporate farms as the basic units of farm firm organization. Input demand and input production elasticities will provide additional overview of the resource structure and provide the foundation for one of several estimates of the aggregate supply elasticity in this chapter. The supply elasticity, which is determined by the level and productivity of farm resources, tells how long it takes for farm inputs, output, and income to adjust to a parity price ratio depressed by inflation, a slack demand, or other factors.

It was apparent in Chapter 6 that farm labor and land are key elements of farm problems, and in this chapter these resources will be analyzed. The following chapter (Chapter 9) will focus on the market structure of inputs purchased from the nonfarm sector. It will help answer the question: "Are farmers exploited by firms supplying inputs?"

THE BROAD PICTURE

This chapter begins with a broad view of farm input levels, assets, and liabilities. Major changes in the structure of farm inputs have included a shift from inputs of farm origin, such as real estate and labor, to purchased inputs of

TABLE 8.1. Index Numbers of Total Farm Inputs and Inputs in Major Subgroups, United States, Selected Years, 1910–65

	Total Inputs			Farm Real Estate	Mechanical Power and Machinery	Fertilizer and Liming Materials	Feed, Seed, and Livestock Purchased[c]	Miscellaneous
	All	Nonpurchased[a]	Purchased[b]	Farm Labor					
					(1957–59 = 100)				
1910	82	162	44	212	88	20	12	16	56
1920	93	174	55	226	92	32	16	23	67
1930	97	170	62	216	91	40	21	26	76
1940	97	142	72	192	92	42	28	45	73
1950	101	119	91	142	97	86	68	72	85
1960	101	96	103	92	100	100	110	109	106
1965[d]	103	86	113	75	100	101	163	124	124

SOURCES: U.S. Department of Agriculture (1966b, p. 35, and earlier issues).

[a] Includes operator and unpaid family labor, operator-owned real estate, and other capital inputs.

[b] Includes all inputs other than nonpurchased inputs.

[c] Nonfarm portion.

[d] Preliminary.

nonfarm origin (Table 8.1). Since the volume of farm real estate has remained nearly stable, the major adjustment has been substitution of fertilizer, machinery, and other capital inputs purchased from the nonfarm sector for farm labor. The total volume of all farm production inputs has remained nearly stable since 1942, but because a given dollar volume of purchased inputs was more productive than a given dollar volume of farm labor which was replaced, output increased 40 per cent from 1942 to 1965. Total inputs increased 3 per cent, and output per unit of all farm inputs increased 37 per cent, or 1.4 per cent per year. Productivity is largely the product of nonconventional inputs including education and research. These inputs were discussed in Chapter 5; this chapter and the next are confined to conventional farm inputs.

QUANTITIES

The volume of nonpurchased inputs declined by nearly one-half from 1910 to 1965 (Table 8.1). Meanwhile the volume of purchased inputs more than doubled. Labor declined drastically, and all other input categories shown in the table increased.

While the real volume of all inputs in agriculture increased only 6 per cent from 1940 to 1965, the current dollar value of inputs and assets rose substantially. During this period, farm operating expenses increased from $4.9 billion to $21.5 billion, and total production expenses from $6.9 billion to $30.7 billion. These changes reflect increasing cash requirements in agriculture, and the growing reliance on the nonfarm sector for farm inputs.

Farm assets increased 384 per cent in value from 1940 to 1966 (Table 8.2). Proprietors' equities increased 400 per cent in the same period, and liabilities as a proportion of equities decreased from 23 per cent in 1940 to 19 per cent in 1966.

TABLE 8.2. Comparative Balance Sheet of Agriculture, United States, January 1, Selected Years, 1940–66

	1940	1950	1960	1965	1966[a]
ASSETS	*(Billions of dollars)*				
Physical assets					
Real estate	33.6	75.3	129.9	159.4	171.1
Nonreal estate:					
Livestock	5.1	12.9	15.6	14.4	17.5
Machinery and motor vehicles	3.1	12.2	22.3	25.7	27.5
Crops stored on and off farms	2.7	7.6	7.8	8.9	9.6
Household furnishings and equipment	4.2	8.6	9.6	8.7	8.6
Financial assets					
Deposits and currency	3.2	9.1	9.2	9.6	10.0
United States Savings Bonds	.2	4.7	4.7	4.2	4.1
Investments in cooperatives	.8	2.1	4.8	7.0	7.4
Total	52.9	132.5	203.9	237.9	255.8
CLAIMS					
Liabilities					
Real estate debt	6.6	5.6	12.1	18.9	21.2
Nonreal estate debt to:					
Commodity Credit Corporation	.4	1.7	1.2	1.5	1.4
Other reporting institutions	1.5	2.8	6.7	10.0	11.1
Nonreporting creditors	1.5	2.3	4.9	7.1	7.9
Total liabilities	10.0	12.4	24.9	37.5	41.6
Proprietors' equities	42.9	120.1	179.0	200.4	214.2
Total	52.9	132.5	203.9	237.9	255.8

SOURCE: Allen *et al.* (1966, p. 1).

[a] Preliminary.

FARM INPUT PRICES

With the notable exception of feed and livestock, all farm input prices displayed an upward trend from 1950 to 1965 (Table 8.3). The former inputs have a large component of farm origin. The fact that prices received by farmers for crops and livestock fell during the period restrained the rise in prices of feed, seed, and livestock purchased by farmers.

TABLE 8.3. Prices Paid by Farmers: Index Numbers, by Groups of Commodities, United States, 1940–65

	1940	1950	1960	1965
		(*1910–14 = 100*)		
Feed	100	210	194	207
Livestock	143	402	358	344
Motor supplies	100	149	175	176
Motor vehicles	163	320	420	464
Farm machinery	153	277	382	426
Farm supplies	146	247	262	270
Building and fencing materials	146	312	393	391
Fertilizer	98	144	152	152
Seed	101	228	211	237
All commodities bought for use in:				
Production	123	246	265	276
Family maintenance	121	246	290	306
Production and family maintenance	122	246	275	288
Interest payable per acre	102	89	220	377
Taxes payable per acre	189	320	578	774
Wage rates for hired farm labor	129	425	631	728
All commodities bought, including interest, taxes, and wage rates	124	256	300	321

SOURCES: U.S. Department of Agriculture (1966a, p. 476, and 1962 issue).

The falling index of prices received by farmers and the rising index of capital input prices would on face value suggest that farmers reduce the use of these inputs. Yet Table 8.1 clearly showed that farmers increased the use of capital inputs. This by no means implies perverse economic behavior. The use of inputs depends not only on the product-input prices ratio but on the ratio among input prices and the productivity of inputs. Wages have tended to increase more than other input prices, encouraging substitution of capital for labor. Furthermore, the rising productivity of nonlabor inputs would have stimulated the substitution of purchased inputs for labor even if price ratios had remained unchanged.

FARM SIZE AND TENURE

Changes in the composition of inputs have been accompanied by major changes in farm size and tenure patterns (Table 8.4). While total land in farms has changed little since 1940, the number of farms declined by 3 million, and farm size increased from 167 acres to 328 acres between 1940 and 1965. Production assets per farm were a very sizable $60,000 in 1965. The number of farms in the lower sales and acreage categories will continue to decline, and assets per farm will continue to rise.

TABLE 8.4. Changes in Farm Acreage, Numbers, Tenure, and Size, 1940–65

	1940	1959	1965
Number of farms (millions)	6.35	4.10	3.37
Land in farms (millions of acres)	1,061	1,120	1,106
Cropland used for crops (millions of acres)	368	358	335
Tenure[a]			
Full owner (per cent of all farms)	50.6	57.1	n.a.[b]
(per cent of all land in farms)	35.9	30.8	n.a.
Part owner (per cent of all farms)	10.1	22.5	n.a.
(per cent of all land in farms)	28.2	44.8	n.a.
Tenants and croppers			
(per cent of all farms)	56.8	27.2	n.a.
(per cent of all land in farms)	35.7	15.9	n.a.
Farm size			
Production assets per farm			
(current dollars)	6,158	40,400	59,691
(1947–49 constant dollars)	13,118	23,120	n.a.
Acres per farm	167	273	328
Percentage of all farms:			
Less than 100 acres	59	46	n.a.
100 to 499 acres	37	45	n.a.
Over 500 acres	4	9	n.a.

SOURCES: U.S. Department of Agriculture (1966a, p. 435; 1966c, p. 41); Allen *et al.* (1966, p. 17, and earlier issues); U.S. Department of Commerce (1966, p. 616).

[a] Excludes managers.

[b] Not available.

THE CORPORATE FARM

A U.S. Department of Agriculture study (Scofield and Coffman, 1968) revealed that in 1968 corporate farms made up the following percentages of all commercial farm numbers (and percentages of all land in farms): Great Lakes states, .42 (1.34); corn belt, .33 (1.10); and northern Plains .42 (2.18). Corporations comprised over 1 per cent of all farms and accounted for over 5 per cent of all land in farms only in the Mountain and Pacific regions. Seventy-one per cent of all the corporations were family corporations, which are not ordinarily considered a threat to the family farm. Total gross sales of farm products of all corporations in the twenty-two survey states comprised only 4 per cent of total farm receipts from all farms in the states. It is apparent that corporations not of the family type accounted for less than 2 per cent of all receipts and only about .2 per cent of all farms in 1968 and thus could not *yet* be considered a threat to the family farm. But the number of farm corporations grew 7 per cent in 1967, while total farm numbers dropped 3 per cent.

A short discourse on advantages and disadvantages of a corporate farming organization helps to judge future trends in the structure of farming. Since family farm corporations are not generally considered major threats to the traditional family farm, the following discussion relates to the more industrial types of corporate farms.

The chief advantage of corporate farms can be said to be economies of size. The corporate farm may be a vertical, horizontal, or conglomerate firm, in many instances with huge farm and nonfarm assets, with access to national money markets, and with limited stockholder liability. It need not be restrained by the life-cycle problems of the family farm, which typically is refinanced and begun anew each generation. Its size may permit purchase of inputs in large lots, by-passing retail outlets. Its size may also permit sales in large lots, with attendant bargaining advantages and higher selling prices. The vertically integrated corporate firm may reduce costs by carefully coordinating production and marketing operations to obtain the optimum timing, quantity, and quality of commodities from the soil to the consumer. Large farming units may enable operation of big labor-saving machines at efficient capacity levels. The firm may utilize specialized and sophisticated management personnel, techniques, and apparatus.

Many of the advantages of the big corporation can also be disadvantages. Corporations of the type discussed here cannot long accept low resource returns or they will lose their credit and the hired or salaried labor on which they depend for existence. They are likely to have to pay more for labor than family farms, because a larger number of workers within a firm tends to lead to an impersonal owner-worker relationship, to unionization, and to higher costs of social programs for workers. The limited liability of corporations can raise the risk and cost of credit, since the personal assets of the stockholder no longer back the credit. (Some creditors require stockholders to pledge their personal assets as security on farm corporation notes.) Large farm corporations, especially those horizontally integrated, can also generate countervailing power at other levels in the market structure, raising input prices and lowering returns to the corporation. If corporations by-pass the local community in buying and selling, the community can retaliate with higher property taxes. Farm corporations also face the risk of state legislation making them illegal. Such laws already exist in some states. Corporate income taxes, minimum wage laws, commodity program payment limitations, and tax-loss write-off limitations for "hobby" farming also may inhibit the corporation. Finally, many crop and livestock enterprises continue to require close personal supervision. The personal management "art" of the proud owner-husbandman may elude the corporate farm and raise production costs.

Absence of substantial economies of huge size and willingness of family farms to accept low returns on resources have been effective barriers to corporate farming in the past. The future may be different. Some commodities, such as perishable fruits and vegetables for canning and fed-out livestock for slaughter, are required in a sizable, assured, and well-coordinated supply as raw material for processing plants. The operations often are particularly suited for a vertically integrated corporate structure. States that outlaw corporate farming may be disappointed to find these operations locating in other states.

The Family Farm

The expanding size of farms and the contracting number of farms have led to fears that the family farm is disappearing. Several circumstances would seem to support this hypothesis. If family farms were really on the decline, (*a*) family farms would account for a decreasing proportion of all farm numbers and all production, (*b*) family farms would be underrepresented in the expanding sector of agriculture—farms with annual sales over $10,000, (*c*) hired labor and hired managers would increase relative to family labor, and (*d*) tenure patterns would show a declining importance of ownership by farmers.

If the family farm is defined as a unit where less than 1.5 man-year equivalents are hired, none of the above circumstances by 1964 supported the hypothesis that the family farm structure was being replaced (Nikolitch, 1965). In 1949 family farms accounted for 95 per cent of all farms and for 66 per cent of all farm marketings. The respective percentages had increased to 96 and 73 per cent by 1964. Furthermore, in 1949 family farms accounted for 68 per cent of all farms and 42 per cent of all marketings in the expanding sector of agriculture (farms with annual gross sales over $10,000). The respective percentages had increased to 88 and 67 per cent in 1964 (Nikolitch, 1965). Results also show that family farms increased in relative importance among units with over $40,000 of annual sales from 1949 to 1964.

Data show that hired laborers have remained a remarkably stable one-fourth of all farm workers since 1910; thus family workers are not being replaced with hired workers.

Finally, we might expect the demise of the family farm to be heralded by a growing importance of corporate, factory farms operated by paid management, but from 1900 to 1920, only about 1 per cent of all farms was under paid management, and, while there was slight increase in the proportion of all farms under paid management from 1950 to 1959, the proportion was only .6 per cent in 1959. The trend toward vertical integration and contract farming has not yet made great inroads into family farming (cf. Tootell, 1965).

The conclusion is that the family farm not only continues to be the mainstay of the farm economy, but its dominance has increased in recent years. This does not mean that the trend will continue. The family farm organization will encounter increasing competition from large "industrialized" farms. The future viability of the family farm depends on several factors, especially the ability of a single family to deal with future capital and management hurdles. Family farms have adopted various financial strategies to cope with the huge capital requirements for an economic unit. The traditional life cycle of hired worker, renter, part owner and full owner is obsolete, and new starts must often be made by inheriting or "marrying" a farm. Part ownership is used more and more as a way to achieve some tenure security and an economic unit with limited capital (Table 8.4). Full ownership is not a meaningful goal for new entrants into farming. Strategies such as leasing of equipment, perpetual mortgages, etc., are discussed in the next chapter. Enlightened credit policies will be important if the family farm is to be preserved.

The second major barrier to family farming is management. More sophisticated and specialized management, operating economies, and enhanced bargaining power in the market are some of the advantages of large units. Some market economies in purchase and sales can be obtained through banding together of family farmers in cooperative businesses and bargaining associations. Electronic record keeping, help from the extension service and other management aids from feed, fertilizer, and other input dealers can aid the family farmer to compete successfully with large factory farm units. Corporate organization can be a help and need not be a threat to the family farm. Corporate legal arrangements can be used to ease family farm life-cycle problems and thus will aid in preserving the continuity between generations. Nevertheless, one can only conclude that the family farm will find it increasingly difficult to compete with "industrial" expansion into agriculture, and the trend toward family farms in all likelihood will be reversed.

ELASTICITY OF SUPPLY

The elasticity of supply is closely related to the level and productivity of farm resources. The supply elasticity is the core around which to provide additional overview of the structure of input markets and input production and demand elasticities. The discussion of supply elasticity will be followed by an analysis of the structure of individual input markets. The elasticity of supply shows the percentage change in output associated with a 1 per cent change in product price. It also shows the speed and magnitude of output adjustments in response to changes in product price. This parameter is especially important for public policy because it measures the ability of farmers to adjust production to the changing economic conditions that continually confront them.

The elasticity of supply tends to be highest for commodities that comprise a small part of farm production, that can be produced under a wide range of resource conditions, that have alternatives that are readily substitutable in production, and that have a short production period.

Output of eggs and poultry meat, which have a short production period, is considerably more responsive to price than is milk production (Table 8.5). The components of any one category in the table tend to have a higher elasticity than the total. Because milk can be used for many purposes, the supply elasticity for fresh fluid milk may be .6, while the total milk supply elasticity is .3.

TABLE 8.5. Estimated Short-run Elasticities of Supply for Selected
Agricultural Products

Crops	Elasticity	Livestock Products	Elasticity
Potatoes	.8	Eggs	1.2
Soybeans	.5	Poultry meat	.9
Feed grains	.4	Hogs	.6
Cotton	.4	Beef	.5
Tobacco	.4	Milk	.3
Vegetables	.4		
Wheat	.3		
Fruits	.2		

SOURCES: Data interpreted from numerous estimates (Cochrane, 1955; Heady *et al.*, 1961; Buchholz *et al.*, 1962). Estimates are for an adjustment period of approximately two years.

Although the supply elasticity for fruits in total is only .2, one estimate places the elasticity for fresh apples at 13 (cf. Brandow, 1956).

Farmers have considerable latitude to substitute one commodity for another in production over a long period. Eventually, this should lead to adjustments among commodities until each is earning a somewhat comparable profit. Public policies concerned with the earnings of all farm products and total farm income must consider the aggregate response of farm output to changing economic conditions. The aggregate response of output to price depends on total resource adjustments in agriculture. Farm resources can be adjusted much more easily among farm commodities than between farm and nonfarm commodities. It follows that the aggregate supply response, which influences total resource earnings in agriculture, will be less than the supply response for the individual commodities shown in Table 8.5.

Three approaches are used to estimate the aggregate supply elasticity. The first is a direct least squares estimate of the supply function with total farm output a function of prices, technology, and other variables. This resulted in a supply elasticity of .1 in 1–2 years, .2 in 3–4 years, and .6 in many years (Heady and Tweeten, 1963, Chapter 16).

The second approach is to separate the yield and basic production unit components of supply. For all crops, the acreage response to price is quite low in both the short and long run (Table 8.6). The yield response is considerable in

TABLE 8.6. Estimated Aggregate Supply Elasticity of Farm Output, with Crop and Livestock Components

	Elasticities	
	Short Run (2 years)	Long Run (many years)
Crops[a]	.17	1.56
Acreage	.04	.10
Yield per acre	.15	1.50
Livestock[b]	.38	2.90
Animal units (stock)	.12	1.80
Yield per animal unit	.26	1.10
Aggregate supply elasticity[c]	.25	1.79

SOURCES: Data interpreted from Heady and Tweeten (1963, Chapter 16) and Buchholz *et al.* (1962).

[a] The elasticity of crop production C with respect to farm price P is E_{CP}. Given the elasticity of acreage with respect to price E_{AP}, the elasticity of yield with respect to price E_{YP}, and the elasticity of yield with respect to acreage $E_{YA} = -.4$, then

$$E_{CP} = E_{YP} + E_{AP}(1 + E_{YA}).$$

[b] Computed as for crops, above, with the elasticity of livestock yield with respect to animal units E_{YA} equal to zero.

[c] Computed by the formula

$$E_{OP} = E_{CP}\frac{C}{O} + E_{LP}\frac{L}{O} + E_{LC}E_{CP}\frac{L}{O},$$

where O is total farm output, C is crop output, L is livestock output, and P is the index of prices received by farmers. E_{OP} is the supply elasticity of O with respect to P. Other elasticities E_{ij} are interpreted accordingly. E_{LC} is assumed to be $-.4$ in the short run and $-.6$ in the long run.

the long run, however. The total elasticity of supply of farm crop production with respect to prices received by farmers is the acreage elasticity plus the yield elasticity corrected for the negative effect of higher acreage on yields as production moves to lower yielding land.

The production period for livestock such as poultry and hogs is comparatively short, and animal units of livestock show a greater response than acreage to higher farm prices (Table 8.6). While output per animal unit is more responsive to price than is the number of animal units in the short run, the reverse is true in the long run. That is, there is greater potential for expanding livestock production by increasing the number of animal units than by increasing yield per animal unit over an extended period. Empirical results do not show that increasing the number of animal units depresses the yield per unit, hence the supply elasticity of total livestock output is the simple sum of the unit and yield components.

The total elasticity of farm output with respect to product price is a weighted sum of the livestock and crop components. There are opportunities to substitute livestock for crops by feeding. Part of this interaction at least is included in the term E_{LC}, which is the elasticity of livestock output with respect to crop output (see footnote *c*, Table 8.6). With a given supply of crops, an increase of livestock means less crops for final sales to consumers—hence E_{LC} is negative. The elasticity of total supply computed from data in Table 8.6 is .25 in approximately two years and 1.79 in many years. This implies that a sustained 10 per cent increase in prices received by farmers raises farm output 2.5 per cent in two years and 17.9 per cent in many years. Some estimates in the table are based on weak data and must be interpreted with reservation.

The final estimate of the elasticity of aggregate supply is determined from the elasticities of production and the elasticities of input demand with respect to prices received by farmers. In other words, output is a function of the productivity of an input and its level of use. And the level of use is a function of farm product prices.

TABLE 8.7. Estimated Elasticities of Production, Input Demand, and Product Supply for U.S. Agriculture

| Inputs | Elasticity of Production | Elasticity of Demand[a] | | | | Contribution to Aggregate Supply Elasticity[a] | |
| | | Own Price | | Product Price | | | |
		SR	LR	SR	LR	SR	LR
Fertilizer and lime	.06	−.6	−1.8	.5	2.4	.030	.144
Machinery operating expenses	.11	−1.0	−1.5	.5	2.5	.055	.275
Feed, seed, and livestock	.09	−.8	−1.5	.7	2.0	.063	.180
Miscellaneous current operating expenses	.09	−.3	−.5	.3	2.5	.027	.225
Crop and livestock inventories	.04	−.2	−1.0	.2	2.5	.008	.100
Machinery inventory	.10	−.2	−1.0	.2	2.6	.020	.260
Labor	.25	−.1	−.5	.1	1.0	.025	.250
Real estate	.28	b	b	.1	.3	.028	.084
Total elasticity	1.02					.256[c]	1.518[c]

SOURCES: Data based on Heady and Tweeten (1963), Tweeten and Nelson (1966), and Tyner and Tweeten (1965 and 1966).

[a] SR refers to a short run of two years; LR refers to a long run of many years.

[b] Nearly zero.

[c] The total price elasticity of supply of farm output E_{OP} is

$$E_{OP} = \sum E_{Oi}E_{iP},$$

where E_{Oi} is the production elasticity of the farm output O with respect to input quantity X_i, and E_{iP} is the demand elasticity of input X_i with respect to product price P.

A 1 per cent increase in the use of fertilizer increases farm output .06 per cent, whereas a 1 per cent increase in farm real estate increases farm output .28 per cent (Table 8.7). Because farm real estate tends to be quite fixed, its large impact on output is offset by its low response to farm product prices—hence fertilizer contributes more to the aggregate supply elasticity than does farm real estate. The total elasticity of supply is .25 in two years and 1.52 in many years, according to results in Table 8.7. If only operating inputs are variable when prices fall, then the short-run elasticity is reduced from .26 to .18, and the long-run elasticity is reduced from 1.52 to .82 in Table 8.7.

More recent estimates of the aggregate supply function allowed for a different response of output to price in the pre- and post-World War II periods and for increasing and decreasing prices (Tweeten and Quance, 1969). There was no evidence that the supply elasticity increased in the postwar period over the prewar period. Greater specialization and a lower ratio of price to output tended to reduce the elasticity in recent years and offset the tendency for a higher proportion of cash-operating inputs to raise the elasticity.

There was evidence, though weak, that the supply elasticity was greater for price increases than for price decreases, in conformity with fixed resource theory (Tweeten and Quance, 1969). However, all the point estimates were in the 0–2 range—certainly not high elasticities or a wide range in total perspective. Based on results already described and the more recent estimates by Tweeten and Quance, it appears that the supply elasticity is 0.10 in the short run and 0.80 in the long run for decreasing prices. But the supply elasticity is 0.15 in the short run and 1.5 in the long run for increasing prices. According to these estimates, a once-for-all *decrease* of 10 per cent in prices received by farmers would decrease output 1 per cent in two years and 8 per cent after many years. But a once-for-all *increase* of 10 per cent in prices received by farmers would increase farm output 1.5 per cent in two years and 15 per cent after many years.

FARM-PRODUCED INPUTS

The two principal farm-produced inputs are labor and real estate. These inputs are responsible for producing nearly half of the total farm output. They also account for approximately half of farm expenses, when valued at opportunity cost levels. Most farm labor is provided by the family and most real estate is owned with high equity by farmers. Hence, these inputs tend to earn a residual return out of farm income after cash costs are paid. As income fluctuates, the returns to these resources varies more than returns to other resources. These inputs bear much of the impact of risk in farming. While there is some basis for setting the price of farm family labor at the amount it would earn if transferred to nonfarm employment, this calculation is difficult for real estate. Land price is determined largely by forces within agriculture, and this raises issues of why the land price is so high that an inadequate return is left for labor. Following the discussion below of the farm labor input, the forces that determine land prices are analyzed.

FARM LABOR

In Chapter 6, changes in technology, inflation, and the demand for farm products were blamed for the emergence of economic problems in agriculture. But farm labor was the resource singled out to explain the persistence of problems for an extended period. Tables 8.8 and 8.9 show that people have left farming at a rapid rate, yet outmigration has not been sufficient to raise earnings and alleviate poverty. Gross migration from farms has averaged over 1 million persons per year since 1920. This gross outflow has been partly offset by the excess of births over deaths and a high rate of migration back to agriculture. Some of the inmigration is explained by farm boys who marry nonfarm girls. Few nonfarm males choose farming as their vocation.

Inadequate preparation for nonfarm jobs is probably the single most important reason for the high rate of migration back to agriculture of farm-reared people who have held nonfarm jobs. This phenomenon is treated in other chapters and will not be discussed in detail here.

TABLE 8.8. Farm Population[a] and Employment, 1910–66

	Farm Population (April 1)		Farm Employment[b]		
	Number	As Per Cent of Total Population	Total	Family Workers	Hired Workers
	(*Thousands*)	%	(*Thousands*)		
1910	32,077	34.9	13,555	10,174	3,381
1920	31,974	30.1	13,432	10,041	3,391
1930	30,529	24.9	12,497	9,307	3,190
1940	30,547	23.1	10,979	8,300	2,679
1950	23,048	15.2	9,926	7,597	2,329
1960	15,635	8.7	7,057	5,172	1,885
1965	12,363	6.4	5,610	4,128	1,482
1966[c]	11,500	5.8	5,259	3,902	1,357

SOURCE: *Economic Report* (1967, p. 301).

[a] Farm population as defined by Department of Agriculture and Department of Commerce, i.e., civilian population living on farms, regardless of occupation.

[b] Includes persons doing farm work on all farms.

[c] Preliminary.

TABLE 8.9. Annual Average Components of Farm Population Change and Rate of Net Migration, 1920–65

	Natural Increase			Migration			Annual Rate of Net Migration
	Births	Deaths	Total	To Farms	From Farms	Net	
	(Thousands)						%
1920–30	796	−311	485	1,314	−1,944	−630	−2.0
1930–40	713	−328	385	1,076	−1,458	−382	−1.2
1940–50	644	−254	390	n.a.[a]	n.a.	−1,139	−4.4
1950–60	436	−165	271	n.a.	n.a.	−1,013	−5.3
1960–63	293	−139	154	316	−1,226	−910	−6.3
1963–64	248	−127	121	283	−816	−533	−6.1
1964–65	234	−121	112	275	−978	−703	−5.4

SOURCES: Banks *et al.* (1963, p. 20, and later supplements), based on April 1 population. The estimates for 1964–65 for example are from April 1, 1964, to April 1, 1965.

[a] Not available.

The farm population comprised one-third of the national population in 1910 (Table 8.8). By 1966, only 5.8 per cent of the U.S. population resided on farms. The farm population was only half as large in 1966 as in 1950. The net migration rate was over 5 per cent per year from 1950 to 1965 (Table 8.9). It is interesting to note that the highest migration rate was in the 1955–65 decade of massive farm programs. These programs appear not to have impeded mobility.

Annual farm net migration rates from nine geographic divisions from 1960 to 1965 were quite similar, ranging from a low of −5.0 per cent in the middle Atlantic division to a high of −8.1 in the New England division. Rates were −5.7 in the south Atlantic division and −5.4 in the east south central division—rates too low to close the gap between the low farm income in these two divisions and the relatively higher farm income in other geographic areas.

If the 1964–65 annual net migration of 700,000 persons is maintained for sixteen years (to 1982), there will be no one left in farming! The absolute rate of outmigration must decline. The current migration rate from commercial farms appears to be sufficiently high to satisfy reasonable adjustment goals for commercial farmers. Policy need not be concerned with pushing people out of farming—economic forces are now exerting considerable pressure for outmovement. In commercial farming, the capital barriers to entry of new farmers are almost overwhelming. Furthermore, the farm population is such a small part of the national population that massive outmovement of farm people no longer would disrupt the national economy.

AGE COHORTS

The study of age cohorts contributes considerably to understanding the pattern of migration. In 1910 there were 419,000 farm operators between 15 and 24 years of age (Tolley and Johnston, 1966). Additional entrants to the labor force increased this cohort so that in 1920 there were 1.33 million farm operators between 25 and 34 years of age. The cohort increased to 1.42 million in 1930. Thereafter, the effects of retirement, death, disability, and change of occupation began to be apparent. In 1950, when the cohort was in the 45–54 age category, the number was 1.43 million and by 1960 the number of age 64 and over operators was 620,000.

In 1950, only 164,000 farm operators were in the 15–24 age group. This cohort had increased to 403,000 by 1960. Only 62,000 farm operators were in the 15–24 age group in 1960. The cohort analysis indicates that most farm operators enter farming when they are between 25 and 34 years of age. The number of farm operators in a given cohort tends to increase slightly beyond the 25–34 age group and tends to be highest in the 35–44 group, then a gradual decline begins. The principal reduction in number of operators occurs because fewer young people enter farming and not because of outmigration of established farmers. The results show that there is little tendency to withdraw from farming, even under considerable pressure, but, on the other hand, many potential farmers are restrained from entering farming by adverse economic conditions.

The fact that there were only 15 per cent as many farmers of age 15–24 in 1960 as in 1910 indicates that there are substantially fewer operators entering farming. The average age of farm operators tends to be high. So even if current rates of entry are maintained, there will be a sizable reduction in farm population as older farmers retire. Still, by 1970 there will be many fewer farms made available by death, retirement, and disability than there are potential operators.

In 1960 there were 1.4 million farmers 55 and over. This was not significantly less than the 1.7 million farmers 55 and over in 1950. Hence, the potential decline in farm numbers from this "retiring" category has not changed much, and past experience would indicate a reduction in farm operators of about 1 million in the 1960's from the 55 and over age group. Many of the farming units released by these operators will be consolidated with existing farms and hence will not provide opportunities for new starts in farming.

Of rural youth under 15 years of age in 1960, about two out of three will have migrated to nonfarm residences by 1970 (Tolley and Johnston, 1966). Results are similar for all regions. The expected declines are most pronounced for non-whites in the South. The average age of farm operators will continue to rise, and in 1970, 47 per cent of all operators will be 55 years or older. In 1960, 39 per cent were 55 and over.

UNEMPLOYMENT AND MIGRATION

Past studies have shown that national unemployment and not the ratio of farm to nonfarm earnings is the single most important variable regulating the outmovement of farm people (Heady and Tweeten, 1963, Chapters 8 and 9). The long-run elasticity of farm operator and family labor employment with respect to nonfarm income was computed to be $-.2$ if national unemployment is nominal and $-.1$ when national unemployment is 10 per cent of the labor force. National unemployment will not have such a large impact in the future, because farm labor will be a considerably smaller part of the national labor force. Furthermore, the burden of farm labor adjustments is on youth, and youth from commercial farming areas where education is adequate will be able to "filter" into the national employment stream. Nevertheless, in areas characterized by rural poverty, problems of labor mobility are likely to remain for an extended period.

It would be a mistake to conclude that ridding commercial agriculture of excess labor, which seems to be an attainable goal, will solve the major commercial farm problem of price and income instability. The declining importance of labor means that farmers will have fewer "owned" resources whose returns can vary to absorb income fluctuations. The rising importance of capital inputs implies more fixed financial obligations which cannot easily be postponed, and the vulnerability of farmers to economic instability will increase. Of course, the rising proportion of cash operating inputs also means that the elasticity of supply will probably rise. Farmers will have more leeway to adjust output to changing economic conditions.

MARGINAL PHYSICAL PRODUCT OF LABOR

Currently, about half of farm labor is not needed on farms. Most of the redundant labor force is not unemployed—it is underemployed. That is, much of the excess farm labor may be working full-time at physically demanding jobs. But this labor could be replaced efficiently by machines and could be employed to produce commodities more favored by society.

This raises issues of what is the marginal physical product (MPP) of labor in agriculture, i.e., what is the effect on output of removing labor from farms? Ordinarily, economists have too much terminology. But in the case of MPP there appear to be too few terms, and confusion has been created by employing the same concept (MPP) to different things.

The effect of labor input on farm output can be viewed in a positivistic and normative framework, with and without adjustments in farming organization. First consider the effect of removing a marginal quantity of labor with a deliberate normative goal of increasing farm efficiency. With no reorganization of farms, a careful selection would eliminate many workers from agriculture with no decrease in output, implying MPP = 0. With a reorganization of farms to larger units, numerous workers could be released, and the result would be a substantial increase in farm output, implying that the normative MPP of labor is highly negative.

The positivistic concept of MPP here refers to the actual outmovement of farm workers—not a carefully chosen group that has the lowest efficiency. If no change in farming organization occurred, it is likely that the workings of the price system would result in outmovement of some workers whose labor was somewhat productive and would not be replaced by other inputs already on farms. Hence, the MPP by this measure is slightly positive.

Finally, the positivistic concept of MPP with farm reorganization is the actual effect of labor outmovement on farm output. In general, farms are enlarged and old farms are taken over by established operators who possess better management and a more efficient input mix than migrating farmers. The result is that in actual practice, the migration of farmers has tended to increase farm output, implying a negative MPP of labor. Thus, depending on which definition of MPP is used, one can conclude that the marginal physical product of farm labor is negative, positive, or zero. The marginal physical product of labor estimated in least squares production functions does not adequately account for the changes in farm size and efficiency associated with consolidation. The functions "erroneously" show a positive MPP for labor. More detailed studies show that a substantial quantity of labor can leave agriculture while farm output is increased (cf. Tweeten and Walker, 1963; Hoffman and Heady, 1962).

HIRED LABOR

Hired farm labor comprises about one-fourth of all farm labor, and has been declining in use at about the same rate as operator and family labor. The number of hired laborers dropped over 1 million from 1947 to 1966. Yet expenditures for hired labor were $2.8 billion in each of these years. This means that the decrease in labor input was exactly offset by the rise in wages. Still, wages of farm workers are low by nonfarm standards. Average annual earnings of male hired farm workers from farm and nonfarm sources were $1,280, based on a 1961 survey (Cowhig, 1963, p. 7). Average earnings of factory workers were $4,802 in the same year. While hired farm workers' earnings seem unreasonably low, it is especially disturbing that earnings per unit of operator and family labor have been lower than earnings of hired labor in some years (Plaxico, 1966).

The age distribution, education, job categories, and mobility of hired farm laborers suggest that low wages are the result of low salvage value (opportunity cost) rather than a lack of awareness of nonfarm jobs or a low reservation wage (high preference for farm living). Median school completed by farm wage earners surveyed was 6.9 years compared to 10.6 years in the U.S. population in 1961. Among farm workers, 29 per cent had completed four or less years of school; 14 per cent had completed twelve or more years. In the U.S. population, the respective percentages were 8 and 41. For male hired farm workers 25 years and over, annual earnings averaged $2,266 from farm and nonfarm sources for those with nine or more years of education, $1,532 for those with five to eight years, and $1,225 for those with four years of education or less (Cowhig, 1963, p. 7). Most farm jobs called for relatively little skill. One-third of hired farm work required stoop labor, and one-third required tractor- or truck-driver skills.

Seasonal hired labor is prominent. Of 2.0 million individuals who worked twenty-five days or more on farms in 1964, 1.3 million were seasonal workers who averaged sixty-four days of farm work (Plaxico, 1966, p. 8). Of 3.4 million persons who worked on farms in 1964, 71 per cent were men or boys and 69 per cent were white; 11 per cent were migratory workers. Of 1.3 million who worked on farms and elsewhere, the average work on farms was forty-nine days and on nonfarm employment was ninety-eight days.

An increasing number of hired farm workers have nonfarm residences and commute to farm work. Of all hired farm workers, the proportion of persons who worked on farms but lived elsewhere increased from one-fourth in 1960 to one-third in 1966. The seasonality of employment led to considerable unemployment during off-seasons. This was partially offset by the fact that many hired workers were students in the off-season. The hired farm work force was relatively young. Over one-fourth were from 14 to 17 years of age, and median age for the entire group was only 25.3 years.

Migration rates from 1950 to 1960 show that hired farm laborers were relatively mobile while farm operators and family workers were relatively immobile. The migration rates during this decade for all employed persons over 14 years of age in the U.S. was 16.3 per cent (White House, 1965, p. 271). Rates for farmers and farm managers averaged only 6.3 per cent, while farm laborers and foremen averaged 16.8 per cent. Professional, technical, and kindred workers had an average mobility of 30.4 per cent. Of ten occupational categories, farm operators had an average mobility less than half that of the least mobile nonfarm occupation, laborers, who had a mobility of 13.6 per cent. Of particular interest is the low mobility of nonwhite farm people. The mobility rate of employed nonwhite farmers over 14 years of age from 1950 to 1960 was only 4.9 per cent.

Farm Labor Unions and Minimum Wages

Extension of minimum wages and labor union organization to farm labor raises new issues. The effect is to raise wages and improve the living conditions of *employed* workers. However, such actions create inequities—the benefits go to workers who are employed but leave more farm workers unemployed. For those who cannot find adequate employment elsewhere, the result of minimum wages and union activity is to make them worse off. The net result of efforts to raise wages is to discourage farm hiring and to speed the substitution of machines for labor. Thus the income effect is regressive among workers. It is by no means clear that the net welfare gains to society are positive.

Few farm workers are now members of labor unions. Labor unions are likely to focus membership drives where hired labor concentration is high, especially in fruits and in vegetable crops where migrant labor is prominent. High concentration of workers reduces the cost of organizing and increases the feasibility of control and administration of workers by unions. Progress will be slow in unionizing hired workers on diversified, dispersed family farms producing feed and livestock. There the problems of organizing and coordinating unions will be difficult to overcome.

NONFARM LABOR UNIONS

A factor potentially explaining farm labor immobility and low earning is race discrimination and union restraints on hiring in the nonfarm job market. The discrimination of employers against hiring of Negroes for nonfarm jobs and the failure of some unions to accept Negro members in a union shop undoubtedly explains some of the inability of Negroes to leave farming at a more rapid rate for employment elsewhere. Labor unions have been accused of retarding employment of workers of all races. Unions have reduced total employment in industries for which skill requirements are probably not very high—nonfarm industries with jobs most attainable for unskilled farm workers. This has created the greatest problems for workers from rural poverty areas, where lack of education inhibits movement into higher-status occupations, where unions are weakest. The exact impact of racial discrimination and of nonfarm unions on farm earnings and employment is unknown. However, unions also contribute to farm problems in other ways. By raising wages in nonfarm firms marketing farm products and providing goods to farmers, unions have raised marketing margins, farm input prices, and the cost of living. Unions have thus contributed to the cost-price squeeze.

The contribution of labor unions to the cost-price squeeze should not be exaggerated, and imperfect competition in nonfarm industry and government deficit-spending have contributed substantially to higher farm costs. Furthermore, the strength of labor unions by some measures is diminishing. Total union membership, 18,117,000 in 1960, fell slightly by 1964 (U.S. Department of Commerce, 1966, p. 246). Membership in labor unions as a percentage of the national labor force fell from a high of 24.4 per cent in 1955 to 21.9 per cent in 1964.

FARM REAL ESTATE

From World War II to 1969, capital gains from farm real estate appreciation provided many farmers with funds for retirement or for investment in a home freezer, tractor, fertilizer, or more land. In the 1930's, real estate depreciation wiped out an equity base and caused mortgage foreclosures for numerous farmers. Changing land prices obviously have had an important impact on real income and resource returns in agriculture. This section will depict the magnitude and selected effects of changes in land prices.

Rising land values in recent years have prompted several questions: What is the role of the nonfarmer in the real estate market? Is he gaining control of farm land resources? Are government-administered allotment and land retirement programs the principal source of land price increments? Is the U.S. in danger of exhausting its land supply to provide food and living space for an expanding population? To what extent was the 1950–63 land price spiral based on pure speculation, unfounded in prospective earnings—hence in danger of "overheating" and collapse with consequent heavy capital losses to farmers and others? This section will attempt to answer these and other questions.

Magnitude of Capital Gains from Farm Real Estate

The average per acre value of U.S. farmland and buildings increased 337 per cent from 1940 to 1964. This is a substantial rise in relation to other prices in the farm and nonfarm sectors. The implicit price deflator of the gross national product, a measure of the general trend (inflation) in all prices in the economy, increased only 148 per cent from 1940 to 1964. In agriculture, the index of prices paid by farmers for items used in production (excluding land but including interest, taxes, and wage rates) rose 152 per cent in the same period. The index of prices received by farmers for all commodities was up 136 per cent from the 1940 level. It is apparent that, by several standards, farm real estate prices displayed a substantial advance from 1940 to 1964. Meanwhile, land by some measures declined in importance as a factor of production. Cropland used for crops decreased 9 per cent and land in farms increased only 5 per cent from 1940 to 1964. Net capital improvements totaling 11.4 billion 1964 dollars from 1940 to 1964 justify no more than a one-third increment in land values. Clearly, capital gains were an important element in the farm real estate price trend.

Changes in farm real estate prices are especially important because of the attendant capital gains (losses) and redistribution of income. Measures of capital

TABLE 8.10. Total Value and Estimated Annual Capital Gains from U.S. Farm Land and Buildings, 1910–63

	Value of Farm Real Estate	Value of Annual Capital Gains		Value of Farm Real Estate	Value of Annual Capital Gains
	(*Billions of current dollars*)	(*Billions of 1957–59 dollars*)		(*Billions of current dollars*)	(*Billions of 1957–59 dollars*)
1910	34.8	2.8	1937	35.2	.0
1911	36.0	2.8	1938	35.2	−2.5
1912	37.3	2.5	1939	34.1	−1.0
1913	38.5	2.4	1940	33.6	1.5
1914	39.6	−.7	1941	34.4	6.7
1915	39.6	6.6	1942	37.5	7.6
1916	42.3	7.3	1943	41.6	11.2
1917	45.5	8.2	1944	48.2	9.2
1918	50.0	6.8	1945	53.9	10.8
1919	54.5	15.8	1946	61.0	9.5
1920	66.3	5.6	1947	68.5	5.1
1921	61.5	−12.5	1948	73.7	2.1
1922	54.0	−1.9	1949	76.6	−2.9
1923	52.7	−3.6	1950	75.3	12.4
1924	50.5	−1.3	1951	86.6	8.3
1925	49.5	−1.5	1952	95.1	.6
1926	49.0	−2.9	1953	96.5	−2.4
1927	47.7	−.9	1954	95.0	2.7
1928	47.6	.0	1955	98.2	4.5
1929	48.0	−.8	1956	102.9	7.2
1930	47.9	−8.2	1957	110.4	5.1
1931	43.7	−15.2	1958	115.9	8.0
1932	37.2	−17.2	1959	124.4	5.0
1933	30.8	3.7	1960	129.9	1.0
1934	32.2	2.5	1961	131.4	5.5
1935	33.3	2.4	1962	137.4	5.5
1936	34.3	2.3	1963	143.6	—

SOURCES: See Tweeten and Nelson (1966, p. 7).

gains in Table 8.10 are defined as the consumption items that the hypothetical owner of all U.S. farm real estate could purchase at the end of the year with funds remaining from the beginning year real estate investment—after repaying the purchase price and capital improvements. The annual gains are accounting (or "paper") profits never fully realized. The estimates are a general measure of changes in U.S. farm financial conditions stemming from annual farm real estate price fluctuations. An attempt by all owners simultaneously to sell farmland and realize the large capital gains for any year in Table 8.10 would depress land values and cause capital losses.

Three periods of major capital gains and losses are shown in the table. An apparent association existed between capital gains and net farm income in the first two periods. The first period, 1910–20, was one of substantial capital gains and increasing net farm income. Net farm income rose from a $11.2 billion (1910–14 average) to $16.4 billion in 1917, then began to decline (1957–59 dollars). The sharp income break from $9.7 billion in 1920 to $5.8 billion in 1921 marked the beginning of a protracted period of capital losses through 1932. The year 1932 was significant not only for the lowest net farm income of the 1910–63 period ($5.5 billion) but also for the largest capital loss ($17 billion).

Then began a period of capital gains that has persisted except for small losses in 1938, 1939, 1949, and 1953. Gains were nominal from 1933 until the war involvement in 1941. The period since 1941 has been one of generally substantial capital gains. Real net farm income reached an all-time peak of $21.5 billion in 1946, then gradually declined to about $12.5 billion in 1955. Income fluctuated near that level from 1955 to 1964. Yet capital gains continued to be sizable, reflecting a tendency to depart from the past association between income and capital gains.

EFFECTS OF CAPITAL GAINS

Rising land values influence farm income. In 1950, the average residual income was $1,300 per farm family worker (including operator) after paying all real and opportunity costs except family labor out of gross income (Tweeten and Nelson, 1966, p. 9). This estimate is based on 1950 costs with land and other assets valued at 1950 prices. With a land cost reduced to the 1940 value, the income residual is $1,512. The implication is that if land prices were fixed (bought and sold) at the 1940 instead of the 1950 price, income per farm family worker would have averaged $212 higher in 1950. In 1962, if land were bought and sold at the 1940 rather than the 1962 price, residual labor income would have been nearly double. Stated in other terms, the beginning farmer who purchased an "average" farm in 1962 must pay $1,369 more annual interest because of land appreciation since 1940. The hypothetical former owner who purchased the farm in 1940 receives the gains.

It is possible that the new owner will experience similar capital gains of course. The factor share can give some insight into future feasible trends in land values. The factor share is defined as the opportunity interest cost on the total U.S. farm real estate value divided by all U.S. farm receipts. The share declined substantially until the early 1940's, then began a consistent rise and was .18 in 1965. The postwar trend cannot be sustained indefinitely, or all farm receipts will not cover land costs. The implication is that the tendency for land prices to rise relative to other prices and income in agriculture will not persist in the long run. The "long run" may be very distant, however, and the 1960's trend could continue for several more years.

In an environment of rapid capital gains, such as that near large cities, liquidity problems can stem from land appreciation. In spite of favorable long-run net worth, current earnings may be hard pressed to cover operating and living expenses after paying property taxes expanded by rising real estate values. This problem can be minimized by informed lenders who will accept growing real estate equity as security for loans.

Impeding farmland adjustment to recreational, forest, or other uses with higher "true" marginal value products and other consequences of inflated farm real estate values detract from economic efficiency. Other aspects of high land values contribute to economic efficiency. Land value appreciation can provide incentive for retirement from uneconomic units, an important equity base for purchase of additional land necessary to achieve size economies, or can provide funds for technologically improved inputs. To illustrate, consider the hypothetical owner of 100 acres valued at $200 per acre, who has been extended all possible credit but wants to purchase an additional 20 acres to realize scale economies. Appreciation of land price to $250 per acre increases equity by $100 \times \$50 = \$5,000$, or enough to purchase the 20 acres at $250 per acre.

Between 1940 and 1963, the value of all U.S. farm real estate rose from $33.6 billion to $143.6 billion, an increase of $110.0 billion. Some of the land price appreciation reflects investment in capital improvements through irrigation, buildings, drainage, and conservation. The value of these improvements tends to be offset by land losses through leaching, erosion, and cropping attrition. A correction for capital improvements on real estate (as was done in Table 8.10) would reduce this capital gain below $110 billion. But it may be argued that a correction (precluded by lack of data) for land attrition through cropping and erosion would offset the capital improvement correction. Much of this capital gain remains as paper profit, has been realized and spent for consumption items, or has been invested in the nonfarm sector. However, some capital gains have been directly invested in farm machinery, fertilizers, etc., or have provided the credit base for such purchases by initial landowners. Land price increments have been a form of saving for many owner-operators who realized that capital gains were providing security for emergency use or retirement, and hence current income could be used to purchase operating inputs which raised farming efficiency.

High land values have become an important barrier to entry in farming. Average real estate investment per farm, only $5,518 in 1940, rose to $37,266 in 1963. After allowing for depreciation and interest plus all other costs except family labor, the residual income per family worker in 1940 was $509; in 1962 it was $1,065. Arbitrarily assuming that one-half of this residual is applied to the real estate investment, then twenty-two years are required to repay the 1940 investment and seventy years are required to repay the 1963 investment out of the respective year's farm receipts alone. The 1963 duration is longer, not only because land prices are higher but also because farms are larger. If capital gains occur in the future as in the 1940–63 period, the 1963 principal will be easier to repay than indicated. Many young farmers have been "encouraged" to learn new skills and obtain nonfarm jobs because of high entrance requirements in farming—a decision they may not have regretted and would have eventually made even at lower land prices—but only after an unsuccessful tenure on an inadequate farming unit.

The incidence of capital gains from farm real estate and other fixed assets depends on who the debtors and creditors are. Periods of capital gains redistribute real wealth from creditors to debtor-owners. Some would consider this redistribution of real income—often from the older, financially adequate, nonfarm creditor to the younger, less prosperous farmer debtor—consistent with increased welfare of society. Boyne (1964, p. 62) found that farm operators were net debtors at the beginning and end of the 1940–60 period but were net creditors from 1943 to 1948. Capital gains during that period represented real wealth losses to operators as net creditors. Estimated net real wealth losses to farm operators was 4.42 billion 1960 dollars ($175 for each member of the farm population) during the 1940–60 period.

It was apparent in Chapter 3 that farmers traditionally have favored easy-money policies and inflation as net debtors. But inflation affects economic conditions in more ways than the net asset position. It has been reasoned that prices received by farmers are flexible and that input prices lag behind the general advance of prices. An untested hypothesis is that inflation is no longer financially advantageous to the large majority of farmers because they are renters or creditors, because prices received are inflexible due to government programs, and because nonfarm firms supplying farm inputs quickly raise prices to cover higher labor and other costs.

SOURCES OF RECENT U.S. LAND PRICE TRENDS

Knowledge of the sources of the recent trends in farmland values is important. For example, if the land price increments are generated by competition for future *speculative* gains without any basis in land earnings—then the foundation for current land prices would be weak. The speculative price trend would need to be arrested by informing investors of risks involved in a market held up by unwarranted expectations.

Should it be found that current prices are justified by productive earnings gained from control of the land factor, the conclusion and recommendation might be to encourage rather than restrain the market mechanism—a system prized for allocating factors toward a Pareto optimum and for rewarding factors according to their contribution to value of output.

If capitalization associated with farm commodity programs is found to be the major source of recent price increments, then a reappraisal of farm commodity programs may be in order. An emphasis on programs minimizing inflation of land values could mean more income for the beginning farmer or new owner to spend on household and operating items rather than on real estate interest and principal.

On the other hand, if it is found that farm consolidation and urban expansion rather than commodity programs have contributed to land price increments, policy inferences might be quite different.

The above inferences would not necessarily be those of policy-makers but are intended to illustrate some of the potential value of knowing the sources of land price change. The remainder of this chapter is focused on sources of land price trends. Hypotheses potentially explaining the formation of land prices are presented below.

Net Farm Income

Theory suggests that land prices are closely tied to net farm income. Land prices reflect expected future earning power of land, and such expectations would likely be formulated from past and present earnings.

The relationship between net farm income and land prices is apparent from cross-sectional data. Scofield (1964) used state data to estimate the elasticity of land price with respect to net farm income per acre for three time periods. A 1 per cent increase in net income per acre resulted in an .84 per cent increase in land price in the 1936–40 period, an .82 per cent increase in the 1951–53 period, and a .75 per cent increase in the 1961–63 period. These coefficients statistically were highly significant. While net farm income does have an impact on land prices according to these data, the effect appears to be declining secularly. Scofield's analysis using cross-sectional income data explained 86 per cent of the variation in land prices among states in the 1961–63 period.

But farm income data are less effective in explaining historical land price variation over an extended period. Income effects are confounded with many other factors (discussed subsequently) through time. Also it is not current net income but expected earnings from ownership of land that motivates buyers.[1]

---

1. The value V of a perpetual annual income flow I discounted to the present at rate r is $V = I/r$, where V is called the present, discounted (or capitalized) value. If annual income *increments i* are anticipated, the formula becomes

$$V = \frac{I}{r} + \frac{i}{r^2}.$$

V is highly sensitive to i since the denominator r^2 is very small. For example, if r is .05, the value of i/r^2 is $400 if $i = \$1$. Thus even an anticipation of small annual income increments such as $1 per acre can have a very significant impact on land price. The value of i may be based on expected gains from productivity, inflation, or supply-demand conditions.

Many considerations are involved in formulating these expected earnings, and not all can adequately be quantified or otherwise included in a statistical model.

Whether the trend in land values is speculative or is tied to production earnings can be judged, at least in part, from rents. Rents can be expected to reflect earnings or value added by control of the land resource. Rents would not be expected to contain the speculative element built into land prices.

The ratio of net rents to the market value of U.S. rented land decreased from 4.4 per cent in 1955 to 3.6 per cent in 1962 (U.S. Department of Agriculture, 1957–66; August 1963, p. 22). Another measure of land return, the ratio of cash rent per acre to land value in Midwest farms, has trended upward since 1940. Cash rent, as a proportion of land value, annually averaged approximately 7 per cent from 1961 to 1966 in twelve Midwestern states (U.S. Department of Agriculture, 1957–66; July 1966, p. 22). In the last decade the rent-to-value ratios remained nearly stable. The conclusion is that recent land price trends appear to have considerable economic foundation stemming from improved technology, from size economies through consolidation, and from other earnings factors which are reflected in rents. The presence of some purely speculative element cannot be ruled out, however.

FARM PROGRAMS

Control of the land resource has been used in recent years as a public instrument to raise farm prices and incomes. Output restrictions, coupled with an inelastic (except in the long run) demand for farm commodities, effectively raised farm income. Economic theory and observed behavior suggest that the monetary benefits of federal programs controlling land would be capitalized into land values over time. This tendency has been cited as a hypothesis explaining the rise of land values in recent periods of falling or nearly stable farm commodity prices and net income.

Regression analyses of individual farm sales reveal large estimated values for allotments: $1,139 per acre for tobacco, $669 for peanuts, and $463 for cotton in northeastern North Carolina (Hedrick, 1962, p. 1751); and up to $2,500 per acre of tobacco allotment in east central North Carolina (Maier *et al.*, 1960, p. 39). Analysis of Virginia data from 1956 to 1960 showed that an additional acre of peanut allotment added $565 to the sale value of a farm (Boxley and Gibson, 1964, p. 22). The same study revealed that one additional acre of flue-cured tobacco allotment in Pittsylvania County, Virginia, contributed $2,040 on the average to the farm sales price. Even sizable per acre values for peanut and tobacco allotments would not make a substantial contribution to total U.S. land values because relatively few acres are involved.

Linear programming studies have also indicated sizable marginal income potentials from the acquisition of allotments. The annual value of one additional acre of corn allotment on fifteen southern Iowa farms averaged $10 and on four northern Iowa farms $20 (Heady and Butcher, 1965). An additional acre of cotton allotment in southwest Oklahoma averaged $17 on six representative farms under 1961 conditions (cf. Sobering and Tweeten, 1964; Sobering, 1965). If capitalized in perpetuity at 5 per cent, the value of these allotment acres would be twenty times as large.

From U.S. Department of Agriculture data on numerous representative farms, it is apparent that farms characterized by allotments have experienced greater land price appreciation since 1950 than have ranches which are not directly involved with allotments (Goodsell and Jenkins, 1963). Appreciation of land prices from 1950 to 1963 ranged from 20 to 44 per cent on five typical ranches and from 60 to 147 per cent on twelve typical farms. The data support the hypothesis that the allotment system has tended to inflate land prices, although the differential impact of technology on farms and ranches may also be a factor.

If farm benefits of commodity programs are soon lost through land value appreciation, then inflated land values and income of original land owners are indirectly sustained through transfer payments from current net farm income, higher consumer food bills, or public taxes—from funds that new farmers, consumers, and taxpayers might prefer to use elsewhere. The redistribution of income stemming from capitalization of commodity program benefits into land prices is not likely to be consistent with the goals of society. The owner of farmland at the time a government income support program tied to land is initiated tends to receive the entire expected monetary benefits of the program. The benefits are received in two parts: (*a*) annual income from price supports or provisions to grow crops while the initial owner retains title, and (*b*) the discounted value of all expected future earnings that will accrue from the support program through land ownership. Sale of the land brings the latter benefits (*b*) to the initial owner since the new owner will receive the same net income whether he pays the discounted value of future earnings from allotments or buys a similar farm without allotments. These benefits largely elude the hired farm worker and tenant.

If annual benefits from allotments are A and the interest rate is r, the discounted value of allotment acres in perpetuity is A/r. The interest on this value is $r(A/r)$, or the annual allotment benefit A per year. It follows that the buyer can pay the seller as much as the discounted value of future benefits and still have as high a return as purchase of similar land without an allotment. The seller receives a substantial "reward." But, since the buyer pays real or opportunity interest equal to annual benefits, the intended income benefits are lost to him. In a perfect market with complete knowledge, this type of income redistribution occurs. With future land price appreciation, the new owner discussed above can later sell and also reap rewards. But this process cannot continue indefinitely, at least not without accelerating transfer payments to farmers at public expense to maintain artificially high land prices.

The capitalization of program benefits into land prices redistributes income in at least two directions. First, the *seller* who realizes the benefits of the support program often is the older farmer with high equity and income. The *buyer* who must pay the interest on inflated land prices often is young and possesses limited equity. The young farmer's income is needed to purchase operating inputs and pay living expenses. Second, the seller very often either is moving off the farm or is already living in town. The income redistribution from government support programs (through real estate appreciation) is likely to be regressive in both of the above instances. Of course in many instances expectations are incorrect or the initial owner bequests the land (or sells at very low prices) to his heirs so that the income benefits of the support program are not lost to farmers after the first generation. Also, many farm buyers are established farmers with a large equity who purchase land for consolidation from farmers with less equity.

FARM CONSOLIDATION

The proportion of all farm purchases made for farm enlargement varies among regions, but has consistently increased in all regions of the U.S. in recent years. This proportion nearly doubled in a decade, rising from 26 per cent in 1950–54 to 48 per cent in 1963 for the forty-eight contiguous states (U.S. Department of Agriculture, 1957–66; April 1964, p. 12). In the wheat areas, the increase was from 48 to 74 per cent in the same period, indicating above-average pressures for consolidation.

Farm consolidation has been especially pronounced during the recent period of real estate price increases, suggesting a relationship between the two phenomena. The farmer investing in labor-saving equipment usually buys a larger or more efficient machine than he owned previously and eventually finds that he has excess machine capacity and family labor supply for the land he operates. Already owning the machinery and controlling the labor, he budgets the buying price he can afford to pay for additional land at a higher rate than the "whole-farm" buyer who does not have an existing unit to absorb the fixed costs of equipment and labor.

The tendency for individual farm demand for land to stimulate prices can be illustrated with a simple example. Suppose a farmer operates 200 acres at average operating costs of $30 per acre and nonland overhead (machinery, other inventories, operator and family labor) of $10 per acre. Assuming gross returns of $55 per acre, the $15 remaining residual to land capitalized at 5 per cent suggests a $300 land price per acre. Suppose the farmer has the opportunity to purchase a contiguous 40 acre unit. He can farm it with little increase in family labor, machinery, and buildings; hence his overhead on the new unit is reduced to, say, $5 per acre. The income residual to land on the marginal unit is $20. Capitalized at 5 per cent, the land is worth $400 per acre—one-third more than the "home" unit per acre.

Average costs per acre decline as more land is farmed. These size economies not only justify a higher land price on a consolidated unit, but also mean that farmers who currently have adequate size units may be making sizable profits to be used for land investment despite low average returns for the farming industry. The home farm also is a useful credit base, giving the consolidating farmer even more impetus in the land market.

EXCESS LABOR IN AGRICULTURE

Excess labor in agriculture provides another explanation of rising land values. This theory is based on land scarcity relative to the number of people who want to farm. Accumulation of excess labor and consequent competition for available farming units forces those who remain to pay more for control of land and, therefore, to accept lower residual returns to their labor and management. If all males born on farms "demanded" a farming unit upon reaching age 20, these youths would not find sufficient farming opportunities. The ratio of total farm transfers to potential farm operators decreased from .39 in 1955 to .23 in 1963, accelerating competition for available units.

Transfers for consolidation do not represent opportunities for new starts in farming. Approximately half of all farm transfers are single farm units not for consolidation. This rate implies that about 20 per cent of potential farmers can acquire single units in 1969. Considering the fact that many of these acquired units are uneconomic and that the trend is to fewer transfers for single units, only about 15 per cent of farm youths can be expected to find *adequate* farm opportunities in the future. The result will be continued competition for available units.

CAPITAL GAINS

Capital gains can be a self-generating mechanism underlying land price appreciation. A negative residual income to real estate from farm production need not *necessarily* concern the speculative buyer—not if the sale price is sufficient to cover the purchase price plus operating losses and still leave a satisfactory return for risk and capital. Current capital gains can establish speculative expectations of future gains irrespective of earnings from production.

The estimated average residual income return to farm real estate was 3.5 per cent between 1950 and 1967. This is well below opportunity-cost investment returns. Combining the average land appreciation of 5.3 per cent with the income from production results in a total land return of 8.8 per cent for the same period. Investors conceivably might compete in the market for such returns.

Speculative investment of this type is hazardous since a change in farm programs or some other shock could reverse land price trend expectations. The result could be further regressive income redistributions as the equity of heavily indebted beginning farmers and other vulnerable groups is eroded and assets are acquired by more financially adequate survivors.

One point of view holds that farmland (and other durable capital assets) are attractive investments as a tax haven and as a "store of value" against the effects of inflation. Long-term capital gains are taxed at one-half the rate on ordinary income, but numerous other investments including common stocks receive similar tax treatment.

The average annual compound rate of increase in appreciation of 500 common stocks (Standard and Poor Index) was 10.3 per cent from 1950 to 1967. The average dividend on these stocks was 3.5 per cent, hence total returns were 13.8 per cent. Average income returns to farmland plus average land capital gains in the same period gave a total return of 8.8 per cent. Thus the total return on investment in farm real estate was less than on common stocks, and it may be argued that the investment risk was no greater with common stock than with farmland. The low down-payment requirement gives real estate one advantage over common stock. Real estate can give a higher return on *equity* while it earns a lower return on total investment.

POPULATION PRESSURE

A growing population expands demand for land indirectly through increased food requirements and directly through conversion of farmland to urban housing, airports, roads, etc. Population growth at the rate of 1.5 per cent annually can be expected to increase food requirements at least by a similar rate. Other things being equal, greater food requirements would be expected to increase land demand and farm real estate values.

A comprehensive study of land resources and anticipated needs has predicted that 15.8 million acres will be shifted to urban and built-up uses between 1958 and 1975 (U.S. Department of Agriculture, 1962). This is equal to more than the combined areas of Rhode Island, Delaware, Hawaii, Maryland, and New Jersey.

The long-run urban requirements are impressive. Assuming a 1.5 per cent annual growth rate, the U.S. population would multiply 1,000 times to 200 billion people in 464 years (approximately the same time span that has elapsed since the first Spanish settlement in the U.S.). Assuming .1 acre per person (a reasonable current standard for urban housing, working space, recreation, etc.), land in the U.S. (including Alaska and Hawaii) totaling 3.5 billion acres is enough to support direct urban land requirements of 35 billion people (land needs for food production are not included). Assuming an annual population growth rate of 1.5 per cent and direct urban land requirements of .1 acre per person, all U.S. land would be utilized in 393 years. These proportions are disturbing but not imminently meaningful. Direct urban growth requirements will absorb no more than 2 million acres of land per year for some time and will not soon have a significant impact on the national demand for land. Also, birth rates will decline in the long run.

CHANGING FARM TECHNOLOGY

Farm technologies have opposing effects on land prices. Mechanical innovations such as specialized, expensive machines often require large farming units to achieve size economies. Efforts to secure sufficient acreage to achieve size economies tend to raise land prices.

Biological innovations on the other hand cause a secular decline in land prices, other things being equal. Direct and indirect population pressures for more farmland and higher land prices are offset by substitution of fertilizer, irrigation, and other capital inputs for land. Use of fertilizer and replacement of horses by tractor power has already added production capacity equivalent to over 200 million cropland acres (see Chapter 5). The use of fertilizer, irrigation, improved seed varieties, and pesticides can increase the effective land supply and more than compensate for rising land demand—thus inhibiting increases in land prices.

The effect on land prices of decreasing production costs through scale or innovation can be quite different at the micro (firm) and macro (national) level. The land buyer, likely to visualize only the short-run micro impact of increased farming efficiency, can easily be misled into overpricing land.

The impact of output-increasing technology can be seen from the following formula,

$$E_L = \frac{TR}{NR}\left(1 + \frac{1}{E}\right),$$

where E_L is the elasticity of land price with respect to farm output, E is the price elasticity of demand for farm output, TR is total farm revenue, and NR is the income residual to land. If technology increases output from land by 1 per cent without an increase in total farm cost, and if the ratio $(TR/NR) = 5$, then an average farmer who faces a perfectly elastic demand ($E = \infty$) could pay 5 per cent more for land. As many farmers adopt the new technology and raise output, the macro response becomes apparent. If the aggregate price elasticity is $E = -.5$, then the 1 per cent increase in output of all farms would lead to a 5 per cent *decrease* in income residual to land and in land price.

These macro effects become increasingly important as technology becomes generally adopted. The implication is that farmers acting individually view increasing productivity as justification for considerably higher land prices. But as many farmers follow this pattern, improved technology results in lower rather than higher prices, other things being equal. Farmers who do not recognize this macro relationship, and especially late adopters who are unable to reap their income gains before the macro effects become important, may endanger their equity by paying too much for farmland. Farm income support programs to some extent have cushioned this macro effect of technology.

NONFARM INVESTORS

The nonfarm investor is a possible factor in the rising farm real estate price structure. Nonfarmers become owners of farm real estate through inheritance, gift, or mortgage default so that a change in the nonfarm ownership of farmland does not necessarily reflect competition for farmland or profitability of farm real estate to nonfarmers. When farm migration is high and especially when it accelerates, a substantial amount of farm property is passed to nonfarmers who are: (*a*) sons and daughters of farmers, and (*b*) retired farmers or other owner-operators who leave the farm for a nonfarm job. During periods of farm depopulation, nonfarm ownership is likely to rise, other things being equal.

Real estate dealer reports on the farmland market have indicated reduced activity in farm real estate by nonfarm investors. Between 1955 and 1963, acquisitions by nonfarmers dropped from 38.2 per cent to 31.0 per cent of the farms transferred (Table 8.11), and their participation in sales increased from 14.6 to 24.9 per cent of all sales. The *Census of Agriculture* reports an increase in owner-operated acreage from the Depression low of 49.0 per cent to 59.7 per cent in 1954 and only a slight decline to 59.5 per cent in 1959 (U.S. Bureau of the Census, 1959, p. 1042). Average annual net investment by nonfarmers in farm real estate fell from $312 million (1950–54) to $232 million in the 1955–61 period (Scofield, 1963, Table 4). It is apparent from Table 8.11 that the owner-operator

TABLE 8.11. Percentage Distribution of Farm Real Estate Buyers in U.S. Transactions, 1955–63

Buyer	1955	1956	1957	1958	1959	1960	1961	1962	1963
					(*Per cent*)				
Tenant	24.1	21.7	19.9	20.0	18.4	16.2	16.6	17.0	14.9
Owner-operator	38.7	37.9	39.9	39.8	41.4	46.9	48.1	47.9	51.0
Retired farmer	4.4	4.9	4.3	5.2	4.0	3.1	3.2	2.9	3.1
Nonfarmer	38.2	35.5	35.9	35.0	36.2	33.8	32.1	32.2	31.0
Total	100.0	100.0	100.0	100.0	100.0	100.0	100.0	100.0	100.0

SOURCE: U.S. Department of Agriculture (1957–66).

was becoming the dominant force in the land market at the expense of the tenant farmer and nonfarmer.

Reasons for reduced participation of nonfarm investors in the farm real estate market include (*a*) the fact that rates of returns on farmland have not been lucrative in relation to returns from other investments, and (*b*) uncertainty about farm programs and the duration of inflationary trends in land values. The above trends will most likely be reversed in the future, and the nonfarmer will probably play a larger role in the farmland market.

CHANGING FINANCIAL STRUCTURE

The equity position of farmers places restraints on their ability to finance land purchases. Farm real estate debt as a percentage of farm proprietors' equities was high in the 1930's and stood at 15 per cent in 1940 (*Economic Report*, 1967, p. 305). It declined sharply with favorable terms of trade for agriculture in the 1940's and reached a low of 4.3 per cent in 1949.

This favorable debt position could be expected to ease credit restraints and promote competition for farming opportunities through land purchases. Land prices increased and farm real estate debt as a percentage of proprietors' equities increased to 10 per cent by 1967. This equity position is considerably more favorable than in 1940, but it undoubtedly puts some restraints on land purchases and prices.

Farm real estate debt as a proportion of total farm debt dropped from 66 per cent in 1940 to a low of 45 per cent in 1950. The proportion then remained nearly stable for several years. It is notable that in 1965 real estate had increased to 49 per cent of all farm debt despite the substantial growth of nonreal estate capital and nearly stable physical volume of farm real estate.

Changes in financial structure to broaden asset ownership per unit of income or equity include an increasing proportion of land sales for credit. Less than half of all transfers were credit-financed in the early 1940's. From 1955 to 1961, a stable two-thirds of all land transfers were credit-financed. The balance—one-third of all transactions—were cash transactions. In the year ending March 1, 1962, 71 per cent of all transactions involved credit. The following year ending March 1, 1963, 73 per cent were credit-financed (U.S. Department of Agriculture, 1957–66: April 1964, p. 17).

Major adjustments have been made in the form of credit-financed transfers— notably the shift to land contracts. In 1956, 37 per cent of all credit transfers were financed by sellers. This increased to 43 per cent in 1958 and 1959, then declined to 38 per cent in 1963. Seller financing was principally under land contract. The use of land contracts rose in all regions. The percentage of farm sales made under installment land contracts has increased almost every year since U.S. Department of Agriculture estimates of the variable were started in 1946 (1957–66: August

1964, p. 28). It was the instrument of transfer in 29 per cent of all sales in the year ending March 1, 1964.

Possible reasons from the seller's standpoint for expanded use of land contracts as opposed to conventional mortgages include (*a*) tax savings, (*b*) more security in the event the buyer cannot meet obligations, (*c*) higher land prices, and (*d*) higher interest rates. Results of a U.S. Department of Agriculture survey (1957–66: August 1964, pp. 19–22) tend to be consistent with (*c*) and (*d*). Respondents indicated that land prices averaged 10 per cent higher when sold under land contracts. Lower down-payment requirements increased the potential number of buyers and attendant competition for land.

The advantage to the buyer is low down payment, thereby extending his opportunity to control larger holdings of land to achieve size economies with less equity. Down payments in the year ending March 1, 1963, averaged 23 per cent under land contract and 32 per cent under mortgage transfers.

INCOME DISTRIBUTION

One hypothesis cites a widening distribution of income and equity in agriculture as an important source of demand for land. The argument is that early innovators and farmers in a position to obtain windfall gains from commodity programs and land appreciation have prospered and improved their financial condition despite falling *average* income for farmers as a group. Data reveal that income among farm operators is distributed more inequitably than is income in the entire U.S. economy. The above hypothesis is not supported by a 1965 study which showed that the inequality in income among farm operators has been declining (Boyne, 1965).

Nonetheless, it is well to recall the significant size economies in agriculture discussed in Chapter 6. In 1960 the average residual farm income on class I farms to cover the cost of family and operator labor, management, and risk was a substantial $17,000. Farmers in classes I and II comprised only 10 per cent of all operators but sold 53 per cent of farm products and had 40 per cent of productive farm real estate. In a land market where about 2 per cent of the land is sold each year, these few farmers with a positive economic rent can be an important force.

OTHER FACTORS DETERMINING LAND PRICE

The extent to which farmers impute income to their own labor and nonland equity and how much they attribute to land cannot be directly determined. Income data usually reported do not account for the cost of family labor and owned real estate except for taxes and interest on farm mortgages. Imputing a cost to all farm real estate is an arbitrary process. Only by making assumptions can we separate returns to farmland and other resources. In a period of falling gross farm income, the farm income imputed to land and the level of land prices may be rising because of structural changes affecting efficiency of farm production and marketing and affecting the marginal product of land.

A five-equation econometric model was used to determine the sources of the increase in land price from 1950 to 1963 by Tweeten and Nelson (1966). The model, supplemented by other approaches, led to the conclusion that approximately one-third of the land price rise from 1950 to 1963 was from pressures from consolidation to achieve size economies, one-third was from capitalization of commodity program benefits into land, one-sixth was from speculative elements, and 5 per cent was from the use of installment land contracts. The remaining portion (about one-tenth of the land price rise) was attributed mainly to demand for land for nonfarm uses. The increasing demand for food was largely offset by increased farm productivity, so that the net effect of these factors was small.

The econometric model predicted that the 1963 level of factors that influence farmland prices would eventually raise land prices one-sixth above the actual 1963 prices. The validity of the prediction was borne out by continued land price gains to 1970; and 1963 prices appeared to be based on a foundation of relatively sound factors. Government commodity programs likely will contribute less and urban land demand will contribute more to land price gains in the future.

SUMMARY AND CONCLUSIONS

The level and productivity of farm resources determine farm output. Much of the so-called "technology" in agriculture is embodied in new levels and combinations of resources. Farmers have made many changes in farm size, tenure, and the use of resources, and the result has been increased efficiency of production. The family farm has been an efficient organization to absorb technology and continues to be the mainstay of the farm economy. But it is increasingly threatened by alternate forms, such as the large industrial-type corporation.

Pressure of increased output on an inelastic demand has led to lower prices and income for many farmers. The ability of farmers to reduce supply in response to falling prices depends on the response of inputs to changing prices. The analysis in this chapter showed that resources are generally not highly responsive to product price, and the elasticity of aggregate supply (output) was found to be .1 in the short run, .3 in the intermediate run, and .8 to 1.5 in the long run. The trend toward use of fewer farm-produced resources and use of more capital resources produced by nonfarm industry suggest that the aggregate supply elasticity could increase in the future but that farmers will become more vulnerable to product price fluctuations. They will have fewer postponable resource-cost commitments.

The two major resources of farm origin, farm labor and real estate, were examined in some detail. Input of farm labor has declined substantially in recent years. Alleviation of problems of low returns and poverty in agriculture awaits the outmovement of much farm labor to other employment. Approximately half of the 1966 farm labor force was not needed in farming. The farm labor force was reduced by half from 1950 to 1966, hence the adjustment goal seems attainable. The goal seems even more possible since the barriers to entry into commercial farming are becoming greater, many farmers are reaching retirement age, and the nonfarm job market is larger. It is much easier to reduce 1966 farm employment (5 million workers) by half, than it was to reduce 1950 farm employment (10 million workers) by half. These factors suggest that excess labor in *commercial* agriculture is not likely to be a serious problem of farm policy in the future. The trend is well on the way toward 1 million large commercial farms, providing all but a nominal part of the nation's food and fiber needs, with perhaps 2 million farm workers.

Problems will remain, however. New technology is continually released which alters farm labor requirements and tends to open new adjustment gaps as old ones are closed. Numerous farm people will lack adequate training and background for productive employment elsewhere. Problems of economic instability in the commercial farm sector and of low income in the poverty farm sector will plague agriculture for many years.

Land price is an important variable in public policy, because it tends to be a residual claimant on farm income. Long-term fluctuations in farm income tend to be absorbed by land values. Raising the level of farm income by government programs of the type used from 1955 to 1969 tends to result in capitalization of program benefits into land. The resulting income redistribution is not necessarily consistent with the goals of society and the intended purpose of the programs. While land prices on the larger, well-organized farms tend to adjust to farming income, leaving a parity return on resources, it does not necessarily follow that any level of farm income is equally satisfactory to farmers. A reduction in farm income can wipe out equities, raise mortgage foreclosures, and cause other financial hardships, while the market adjusts the land price down to a lower equilibrium level consistent with less farm income.

REFERENCES

Allen, Philip *et al.* 1966. The balance sheet of agriculture. Information Bulletin No. 314. Washington, U.S. Department of Agriculture.

Banks, Vera, Calvin Beale, and Gladys Bowles. 1963. Farm population estimates for 1910–62. ERS-130. Washington, U.S. Department of Agriculture.

Boxley, Robert, Jr., and W. L. Gibson, Jr. 1964. Peanut acreage allotments and farm land values. Technical Bulletin No. 175. Blacksburg, Va., Agricultural Experiment Station.

Boyne, David H. 1964. Changes in the real wealth position of farm operators. Technical Bulletin No. 294. East Lansing, Mich., Agricultural Experiment Station.

————. 1965. Changes in the income distribution in agriculture. *Journal of Farm Economics* 47:1213–24.

Brandow, George. 1956. A statistical analysis of apple supply and demand. A.E. and R.S. No. 2. University Park, Pa., Agricultural Experiment Station.

Buchholz, H. E., G. G. Judge, and V. I. West. 1962. A summary of selected behavior relationships for agricultural products in the United States. Department of Agricultural Economics, AERR-57. Urbana, University of Illinois.

Center for Agricultural and Economic Development. 1961. *Labor Mobility and Population in Agriculture*. Ames: Iowa State University Press.

Cochrane, Willard. 1955. Conceptualizing the supply relation in agriculture. *Journal of Farm Economics* 37:1161–76.

Cowhig, James D. 1963. Education, skill level and earnings of the hired farm working force in 1961. Economic Report No. 26. Washington, U.S. Department of Agriculture.

Economic Report of the President. 1967. Washington: U.S. Government Printing Office.

Goodsell, Wylie, and Isabell Jenkins. 1963. Costs and returns on commercial farms. Statistical Bulletin No. 297. Washington, U.S. Department of Agriculture.

Heady, Earl O., and Luther G. Tweeten. 1963. *Resource Demand and Structure of the Agricultural Industry*. Ames: Iowa State University Press.

———— and Walter Butcher. 1965. Effects of feed-grain output control on resource use and values. Research Bulletin No. 531. Ames, Iowa, Agricultural Experiment Station.

———— et al., eds. 1961. *Agricultural Supply Functions*. Ames: Iowa State University Press.

Hedrick, James L. 1962. The effects of the price-support program for peanuts on the sale value of farms. *Journal of Farm Economics* 44:1749–53.

Hoffman, Randall, and Earl Heady. 1962. Production, income and resource changes from farm consolidation. Research Bulletin No. 502. Ames, Iowa, Agricultural Experiment Station.

Maier, Frank H., James L. Hedrick, and W. L. Gibson. 1960. The sale value of flue-cured tobacco allotments. Technical Bulletin No. 148. Blacksburg, Va., Agricultural Experiment Station.

Nikolitch, Radoje. 1965. The adequate family farm. *Agricultural Economics Research* 17:84–89.

Plaxico, James S. 1966. Farm labor and commercial farming. A.E. 665. Stillwater, Oklahoma State University, Department of Agricultural Economics (mimeo.)

Schuh, G. Edward. 1963. The agricultural input markets. Production economics Paper 6302. Lafayette, Ind., Purdue University (mimeo).

Scofield, William H. 1963. Investment in farm real estate. *Journal of Farm Economics* 45:396–406.

————. 1964. Land prices and farm income relationships. *Agricultural Finance Review* 25:13–22.

Scofield, William H. and G. W. Coffman. 1968. Corporations having agricultural interests. Agricultural Economic Report No. 142. Washington: U.S. Department of Agriculture.

Sobering, Fred. 1965. Unpublished work sheets from S-42 regional economic study of cotton production. Stillwater, Oklahoma State University, Department of Agricultural Economics.

────── and Luther G. Tweeten. 1964. A simplified approach to adjustment analysis. *Journal of Farm Economics* 46:820–34.

Tolley, G. S., and W. E. Johnston. 1966. Policy implications of farm operator age adjustments. Raleigh, North Carolina State University, Department of Economics (mimeo).

Tootell, R. B. 1965. The future of the family farm. *Agricultural Policy Review* 5:8–9.

Tweeten, Luther G., and Ted R. Nelson. 1966. Sources and repercussions of changing U.S. farm real estate values. Technical Bulletin T-120. Stillwater, Okla., Agricultural Experiment Station.

────── and Leroy Quance. 1969. Positivistic measures of aggregate supply elasticities. *American Journal of Agricultural Economics* 51:342–52.

────── and Odell L. Walker. 1963. Estimating socioeconomic effects of a declining farm population. In *Regional Development Analysis*, Agricultural Policy Institute, Raleigh: North Carolina State University, pp. 101–19.

Tyner, Fred H., and Luther G. Tweeten. 1965. A methodology for estimating production parameters. *Journal of Farm Economics* 47:1462–67.

────── and ──────. 1966. Optimum resource allocation in U.S. agriculture. *Journal of Farm Economics* 48:613–31.

U.S. Bureau of the Census. 1959. *Census of Agriculture: 1959.* II:X.

U.S. Department of Agriculture. 1957–66. *Farm Real Estate Market Developments.* Washington.

──────. 1962. Basic statistics of the national inventory of soil and water conservation needs. Statistical Bulletin 317. Conservation Needs Inventory Committee. Washington.

──────. 1963. Farm population. ERS-130. Washington.

──────. 1966a. *Agricultural Statistics.* Washington: U.S. Government Printing Office.

──────. 1966b. Changes in farm production and efficiency. Agriculture Statistical Bulletin No. 233. Washington.

──────. 1966c. Farm income situation. FIS-203. Washington.

──────. 1966d. Handbook of agricultural charts. Agricultural Handbook No. 325. Washington.

U.S. Department of Commerce. 1966. *Statistical Abstract of the United States.* Washington: U.S. Government Printing Office.

White House and U.S. Department of Labor. 1965. Manpower report of the President. Washington: U.S. Government Printing Office.

CHAPTER NINE

The Economic Structure: Purchased Inputs

Data in the previous chapter clearly showed that farmers are increasingly dependent on purchased inputs. The growing importance of purchased inputs raises issues for public policy as well as for the farm firm. Farmers saw the price they paid for inputs (parity index) increase 82 per cent from 1950 to 1966. The cost increments of the cost-price squeeze continually subtract from farm receipts; they prompt farmers to ask, "Are we being taken advantage of by the firms that produce and sell farm inputs?" Some deem that public policies are needed to protect farmers from unfair business practices of nonfarm firms. One of the purposes of this chapter is to examine the economic structure and performance of major industries supplying purchased inputs to farmers. Emphasis is given to the credit, fertilizer, feed, and machinery industries.

Growing use of purchased inputs also confronts farmers with important management decisions which influence firm efficiency and survival. The family in the future will find it increasingly difficult to cope with complex business decisions while simultaneously providing the principal source of operating labor on the farm. Issues of credit and farm business organization discussed in this chapter include strategies to preserve the family farm.

FARM CREDIT

A farmer's ability to secure credit is one of his most important resources. Financial management is often the key to obtaining a viable economic unit. In his search for credit, the farmer faces several possible sources of funds in a diversified structure of lending agencies.

FARM MORTGAGE LOANS

Real estate assets totaled $184 billion and constituted two-thirds of all farm assets in 1966 (*Economic Report*, 1967, p. 305). Much of the real estate was owned with full equity by farmers, and the real estate debt was only $23.5 billion in that year. Real estate debt more than doubled from 1959 to 1966.

The Federal Land Bank Associations had $4.2 billion in outstanding mortgages in 1966, or about one-fifth of all farm mortgage debt. The Associations are cooperative lending agencies owned by farmers (see Chapter 4). The Farmers Home Administration, a federal loan agency designed to grant low-interest loans to farmers who cannot obtain sufficient commercial credit, held $631 million in farm mortgages in 1966 (U.S. Department of Agriculture, 1966c, p. 505). The other major institutions providing real estate credit to farmers are the life insurance companies, which held $4.8 billion of farm mortgage debt, and commercial banks, which held $2.9 billion of farm mortgage debt in 1966. Approximately $9 billion of real estate debt was held by individuals and agencies other than those listed above. A considerable amount of the "other" category was held by individuals who financed farm land sales through installment land contracts.

TABLE 9.1. Commercial Farm Operators with Major Real Estate Debt, by Source of Such Debt, 1960

	Debt				Total Debt as Percentage of	
	Total		Average per Farm			
	All Types	Major Real Estate	Total	Major Real Estate	Land and Buildings Owned	Total Net Cash Income
	(Millions of dollars)		*(Dollars)*		*(Per cent)*	
Source of major real estate debt						
Federal Land Bank Associations	3,043	2,147	14,778	10,428	30	248
Farmers Home Administration	798	617	14,972	11,582	53	n.a.
Insurance companies	3,157	2,343	30,025	22,287	41	402
Banks	1,995	1,529	11,274	8,642	31	212
Other lending institutions	515	368	14,410	10,307	38	n.a.
Individuals from whom part or all of farm was purchased						
Under mortgage	2,394	1,723	20,904	15,044	42	340
Under land purchase contract	2,062	1,564	26,849	20,356	57	417
Other individuals	432	319	13,289	9,830	39	254

SOURCE: Board of Governors (1964, p. 48).

Judging by the magnitude of loans per farm, the ratio of debt to owned land and buildings and the ratio of debt to income, insurance companies and individuals who financed land purchase contracts held real estate debt with the most risk in 1960 (Table 9.1). The Federal Land Bank Associations had smaller loans with less risk, as based on the measures in Table 9.1.

There has been a tendency for Federal Land Bank Associations, the Farmers Home Administration, and holders of installment land contracts to increase their share of farm real estate loans. These and other sources of credit are available to most farmers and supply credit at highly competitive interest rates. The structure of the credit market for farm real estate has improved considerably since the 1930's. Competition has been sufficient to ensure adequate performance, and farmers are certainly not now exploited by the farm real estate loan industry. Still, the performance can be improved, and numerous adjustments will have to be made in lending policies to cope with emerging financial needs.

NONREAL ESTATE DEBT

Nonreal estate farm debt totaled $22.3 billion in 1966. From 1950 to 1966, there was a tendency for nonreal estate debt to nearly equal real estate debt. Commercial banks are the largest single source of nonreal estate credit and had outstanding loans of $8.2 billion on January 1, 1966 (U.S. Department of Agriculture, 1966c, p. 510). The Production Credit Associations, cooperative lending agencies owned by farmers, had $2.6 billion in loans outstanding on January 1, 1966. Merchants and dealers increasingly are extending credit along with sales of production inputs and consumer items to farmers. Systematically reported data on the amount and terms of such credit are limited (cf. Board of Governors, 1966).

Data in Table 9.2, from a 1960 survey of farm debt, highlight the major role of merchants, dealers, and banks in the provision of short-term credit to farmers. However, the average debt of commercial farmers to the Production Credit Associations was larger than to merchants, dealers, or banks, indicating that the Associations tend to make larger but less numerous loans. Based on debt as a per cent of land and buildings and as a per cent of total net cash income, the Farmers Home Administration holds nonreal estate debt with the most risk.

The large number of commercial banks and the availability of Production Credit Association and Farmers Home Administration loans to farmers mean that a good deal of competition exists in the market for short-term credit. There appears to be little room for excessive interest charges on the part of these organizations, but the merchant and dealer credit sources bear watching. Research is needed to determine what interest farmers are paying for credit from the latter sources and to what extent the interest rates are hidden in installment payments and other practices.

TABLE 9.2. Commercial Farm Operators with Nonreal Estate and Related Debt, by Source of Such Debt, 1960

Source of Nonreal Estate and Related Debt	Debt				Total Debt as Percentage of	
	Total		Average per Farm			
	All Types	Major Real Estate	Total	Major Nonreal Estate	Land and Buildings Owned	Total Net Cash Income
	(*Millions of dollars*)		(*Dollars*)		(*Per cent*)	
Production Credit Associations	2,648	1,475	16,592	9,241	47	324
Farmers Home Administration	598	329	13,769	7,590	69	350
Insurance companies	639	455	14,961	10,668	40	263
Banks	6,720	3,714	12,252	6,771	41	232
Other lending institutions	1,119	623	12,589	7,016	42	262
Merchants and dealers	7,761	3,748	10,596	5,116	41	225
Other individuals	2,298	1,385	11,666	7,032	48	269
Miscellaneous	2,978	1,342	13,440	6,056	45	281

SOURCE: Board of Governors (1964, p. 53).

FARM DEBT BY AGE AND ECONOMIC CLASS OF FARMS

Judicious use of credit is one way to secure an adequate size farming unit. Based on the 1960 data in Table 9.3, a substantially higher proportion of operators of large farms had debts than did operators of small farms. Debts as a per cent of total net cash income were much greater on large farms than on small farms. Debt per operator was twenty-five times as great on class I farms as on class VI farms.

In 1960, the average age of farm operators was 51 years. On the average, operators of large farms were younger than operators of small farms. And operators with debts were younger than operators without debts. Table 9.4 presents a more complete picture of the relationship between age and indebtedness of farm operators; 78 per cent of farm operators under 35 years of age had debts in 1960, while only 42 per cent of operators over 64 years of age had debts. Total debt as a percentage of owned land and buildings, and as a percentage of total net cash income declined with increasing age of operators. On the one hand, this represents a favorable picture of young farmers effectively using their credit resources to expand income. Young farmers appear to be well represented in large farming units of an economically adequate size. On the other hand, the data in Table 9.4 show that young farmers are considerably more vulnerable than older farmers to unfavorable economic conditions that would jeopardize their ability to meet financial obligations.

TABLE 9.3. Farm Debt by Economic Class of Farm, 1960

| | Economic Class of Commercial Farms[a] | | | | | | Noncom-mercial Farms |
	I	II	III	IV	V	VI	
Operators with debt (per cent)	76	75	73	66	55	47	46
Average age of all operators (years)	46	48	46	49	52	51	56
Average age of operator with debt (years)	45	47	44	47	50	50	50
Total debt per operator with debt (thousands of dollars)	49	18	11	7	4	2	4
Total debt as percentage of land and buildings owned (per cent)	23	26	28	21	16	15	12
Total debt as percentage of total net cash income (per cent)	215	157	149	114	69	91	44

SOURCE: Board of Governors (1964).
[a] See Chapter 6 for definition of farms by economic class.

TABLE 9.4. Debt Status, by Age of Commercial Farm Operator, 1960

| | Age of Operator | | | | | |
	Not Reported	Under 35	35–44	45–54	55–64	Over 64
Number of operators (thousands)	209	269	488	591	507	197
Operators with debt (thousands)	126	209	362	387	273	83
Total debt of operators with debt As percentage of owned land and buildings (per cent)	38	62	41	31	24	19
As percentage of total net cash income (per cent)	253	230	219	198	192	153

SOURCE: Board of Governors (1964, pp. 16, 17).

OBJECTIVES OF FARM CREDIT POLICY

The direct, micro goals of farm credit agencies include flexibility and adaptability in lending practices to meet changing technical and economic conditions. Credit institutions should provide a stable and dependable source of loans for farmers with "legitimate" needs at terms consistent with the risks involved and with costs associated with administration, alternative returns on money, and "wholesale" money market discount rates (Baker and Tweeten, 1965). Macro objectives are closely tied to national fiscal and monetary policies and emphasize stability in income and employment and support for economic growth. Macro considerations also include organizational efficiency and the distribution of farm income and assets.

The current excess capacity in agriculture, immobility of labor, and high equity point to plentiful aggregate credit reserves to meet the needs of agriculture in the future. The potential ability of cooperative and private credit sources to extend funds is large. Tootell (1961) stated that Federal Land Bank Associations, Banks for Cooperatives, and Production Credit Associations could double their loan volume if necessary. Although future capital requirements *per farm* are very large, capital requirements for agriculture *in total* appear modest except possibly for operating inputs. Ties to the national money markets for loanable funds give great potential volume for the farm credit structure. Country banks also are often connected to larger money suppliers through branch and corresponding banking. Increased mobility of commercial farmers, who can travel to large city banks if necessary, also ensures adequate loan potential. The fact that the growing nonfarm sector has an increasing share of the nation's wealth and capital reserves means that agriculture can draw more heavily from nonfarm money markets. Close liaison with the U.S. Treasury for funds in national emergencies prevents gross instability. The impact of a sudden unfavorable change in agriculture's economic health will not now, in contrast to the nineteenth century, cause a national financial crisis.

A major effort to expand the aggregate volume of credit to agriculture by subsidies and liberalized credit terms might well generate a major conflict arising from the dual goals of efficiency and equity (equality) in an "ideal" credit structure. Farm income could be depressed in at least two ways: (*1*) by increasing aggregate farm output, benefiting initial users with productive capital opportunities but depressing incomes to agriculture in aggregate, and (*2*) by dissipating initial benefits through inflated land values. Any credit policy to slow the trend in land prices would also need to consider the impact on the beginning farmer. Higher land prices hurt him by requiring greater interest and principal payments. But policies to restrain land prices through more tightly controlled lending could put him at a relative disadvantage in relation to established farmers who depend less on borrowed funds for land purchases. Of course, in some instances, barriers to land purchase might also encourage the younger generation to make needed labor adjustments to favorable off-farm opportunities.

DISTRIBUTION OF FARM CAPITAL AND CREDIT

A basic capital problem in U.S. agriculture is to improve the distribution and mobility of capital among alternatives within agriculture. Distribution problems arise (*a*) within the farm firm, (*b*) among farmers within regions, e.g., for large, efficient, established farmers versus low-income and beginning farmers, (*c*) among general uses and geographic areas, and (*d*) over the farm firm life cycle (Baker and Tweeten, 1965).

ALLOCATION OF CAPITAL WITHIN THE FARM FIRM

Better financial coordination might improve allocation of capital within the firm. Efficiency and equitability would be served by making loans less available for real estate (to restrain relative increases in land prices) and relatively more available for highly profitable operating inputs such as fertilizer, feeds, and pesticides. Credit restraints on operating inputs may have been partially prompted by the fact that they are used up in the production process, with no tangible assets remaining for loan security. Greater awareness of the potential returns from operating inputs, additional finance from input dealers, contract production, and vertical integration, will increase funds for such uses.

A greater loan volume per farm will permit more supervision and possible coordination with commercial or cooperative record-keeping agencies that monitor financial health and reveal opportunities for expanded investment. There may be a trend toward credit "supermarkets." A supermarket structure would provide a favorable environment for coordinating long-term and short-term credit. Long-term credit at lower rates for a continuing series of short-term farm capital needs would not be restricted to real estate financing. Private local banks, working on a branch or correspondent basis with larger banks tied to city money markets and with life insurance companies (for long-term loans), already are able to provide a sizable volume of loans to individual borrowers. Similar cooperation in long- and short-term loans is possible between the Production Credit Associations and Federal Land Bank Associations.

Careful coordination of management and credit also is useful in appraising where perpetual debt and open-end mortgages might be best used. With perpetual debt, the farmer would not be required to repay the entire mortgage during the life cycle of the farm firm and hence would avoid some of the large principal payments. The future owner in some instances would merely continue the mortgage, as is often done now with home purchases in urban areas.

ALLOCATION AMONG FARMS WITHIN REGIONS

Approximately 95 per cent of farm loans are made to commercial farmers. This allocation is expected to continue and is consistent with economic efficiency criteria but can conflict with welfare goals. What of the small farmer trapped in agriculture by skills with little value outside of farming, and what of the farm youth with large management capabilities but not enough equity from parents or other sources to form a viable economic unit? The Farmers Home Administration can continue to perform an essential role in working with these people.

It will not be performing a useful function if it simply allows farmers to hold on to a marginal unit predestined to a subsistence income. Rather, the Farmers Home Administration might more intensively direct credit to help farmers obtain an economic size unit, which means consolidation of farming units for some farmers and migration to alternative employments for other farmers. Its perspective might be broadened to include more financing to train farmers for nonfarm jobs and to help them relocate at distant points if jobs are not available in the vicinity.

ALLOCATION TO OVERHEAD INVESTMENTS

The farm firm requires "overhead" investments as well as on-farm investments. Possible alternative investments include capital allocations to local government, education, electricity, drainage, local area development, soil conservation, watershed protection, and research. The welfare of farmers and nonfarmers alike depends on the efficient allocation of capital among these uses as well as among uses on the farm itself. The allocative means are different as are the terms in which to compare payoffs. Hence, many of these uses are outside the traditional sphere of the farm capital structure described earlier.

In two of the above areas—education and research—returns on capital appear to be higher than on most farm enterprises, and further capital allocation to these uses seems justified (see Chapter 5). Education performs at least two important functions: (*1*) it raises the managerial ability of the farmer, allowing him to realize a greater return on capital invested in farming enterprises, and (*2*) it increases the working skills and adaptability of human resources to a wide range of employment, thereby increasing the mobility of labor. In both of these ways, education can perform an important role in raising farm earnings relative to nonfarm earnings, particularly in low-income areas. Many of the foregoing capital and credit allocation problems among enterprises, farms, and regions will become amenable to solution only with additional investment in farm overhead capital.

ALLOCATION OVER THE LIFE CYCLE

The single proprietor firm is peculiarly subject to factors associated with the biologic cycle of the operator and family. If no way is found to remedy credit problems associated with this cycle, the family farm is seriously disadvantaged relative to a corporation. In the typical productive life span, the farmer commences with a labor surplus and a deficit in management and capital. He progresses through a period of growth financed from income or credit use. He reaches, in later life (if successful) a period when, after reaching his maximum in managerial skills and capital access, he looks forward to retirement with or without an heir for the farm organization he has generated. With an heir, he must begin considering the operational characteristics of the farm organization for the next generation. Without an heir, he must consider the marketability of the organization or its properties as a source of rental income in his retirement.

Both borrower and lender face a changing array of problems through such a cycle. An early problem for the borrower is to identify managerial aptitudes and market opportunities and to gain access to capital at a rate commensurate with his ability to grow in managerial skills. The lender's problem at this stage is to identify the young farmer capable of meeting these demands successfully. In a period of accelerating change in technology and markets, it is increasingly difficult to base projections on the farm itself. Success is becoming less land-related and more management-related.

Problems no less urgent occur in the middle period. Having established a going organization, the farmer now faces alternatives in the rate and direction of firm growth. He also must choose among alternatives in financing growth. Relying on growth from current income, he risks letting managerial skills go underused. If they are substantial, or are the type with high payoff, it becomes feasible for him to lease or to use credit or other financial strategies. Opportunity costs become important. He must develop an acute sense of timing for seasonal problems in finance and for the life-cycle problems of which he finds himself increasingly aware. The lender's problem again is one of identification. For the overcautious farmer, encouragement may be needed; for the plunger, a defensive role is required.

Some of the more urgent and difficult problems arise in preretirement years. In this period, even the moderately successful farmer may have attained an equity and credit position that allows him access to more capital than he can use profitably with his managerial and labor resources. Because of declining labor resources, he is all the more tempted to mechanize, even at a considerable outlay, to reduce labor requirements, and to avoid the problems of managing hired labor. Often, however, such an organizational move can be treacherous. To exploit economies generated by mechanization means an increase in livestock (in case of materials-handling investments) or cropland. If the increase is in livestock, the organization is usually made more specialized than before and hence more difficult to sell, should the occasion to do so arise. Equally important, should the farmer have an heir, the heavily mechanized, specialized organization may not be appropriate for a young manager, who has a surplus in labor but a deficit in management and capital.

The lender is unlikely to suffer loss from the moderately successful farmer we have characterized. He has a pressing problem, however, in the case of the less successful farmer who has emerged from the "growth period" without substantial growth and with no appreciable financial progress. Faced with no particular past deterioration in the recorded quality of loan, it is easy for the lender to continue until the loan does become undesirable because of the opera-tor's age and income requirements. At the other end of the scale, the lender may have plungers who continue financing operations in postretirement years that would have been questionable even in earlier periods.

In the early postwar period we have seen that U.S. farmers were in a highly favorable financial position. In recent years, returns (excluding capital gain) to real estate have been low. But for many farmers with a high equity in land, this posed no problem. Rising land values and high land equity permitted returns to equity in real estate to be imputed essentially to labor, and the returns were used to pay household expenses. Problems created were those of liquidity. Lower commodity prices, high operating costs, and inflated land prices left farm owners with a satisfactory net worth but low annual income. Assets have tended to be tied to land while liquid assets were exhausted to pay household and production expenses. For many, the principal problem becomes one of holding out long enough to sell the farm and retire on capital accumulated in land. Increases in farm mortgage debt as a percentage of total farm debt suggest that in recent years farmers may be using real estate credit for operating capital partly to alleviate such a condition. A major future difficulty may arise if farm profit margins become narrower and if capital gains (which have provided retirement income and made almost any loan policy look good) are not forthcoming.

FARM FINANCIAL STRATEGIES

Farm gross output of $42 billion in 1965 was produced with farm production assets of about $202 billion, implying a capital (asset)-output ratio of 4.8. It seems likely that by 1970 an output of $40,000 of gross sales per farm will be required to earn a farm income equivalent to a factory wage (see Chapter 6). This implies that an economic-size farm unit in 1970 will require production assets of $192,000. When household furnishings and equipment are added, it is apparent that, on the average, by 1970 an investment of $200,000 will be needed by the farm operator if he is to earn a reasonable return on his resources. This finding is broadly consistent with numerous other studies based on linear programming analysis of minimum resources required to pay all farm costs and leave a $5,000 return to the operator for his labor, management, and risk (cf. Baker and Tweeten, 1965; Strickland *et al.*, 1963).

How to gain control of assets required for an economic farming unit is a major problem facing future farmers. If an equity of 25 per cent were required to gain title to $200,000 of assets, ownership would require that a farmer acquire $50,000 of equity. Many farmers will inherit or marry this equity, but for other farmers this equity is clearly impossible.

With improved management devices such as electronic record keeping, financial institutions will undoubtedly move somewhat farther in the direction of making loans on the basis of earning power and away from their past tendency of tying loans closely to equity. A study of farm debt in 1960 showed that the average size of farmers' debts was more closely related to the value of the land and buildings they owned than to their earning capacity (Garlock, 1966, p. iv).

It has long been recognized that internal credit rationing by the farmer himself is often a greater restraint than the credit limitations imposed by lenders. An Oklahoma study attempted to determine whether credit was available to form an "economic unit" on representative farms (Collins, 1965). An economic unit was the minimum farm size and organization computed by linear programming that would pay all costs of farming, including interest on all assets, and leave a $3,000 return to the operator and his family for their labor, management, and risk. In all instances, a considerable increase in capital was necessary to enlarge the current actual farm size to an economic unit. A number of commercial banks, Federal Land Bank Associations, Production Credit Associations, and other lending agencies were presented with the current and needed farm capital structure and asked whether they could loan funds required to reach an economic unit. In nearly all instances, they could not. The nonreal estate credit requirements could be met more easily than the real estate credit needs. But it is of interest that the net worth of representative farmers was not sufficient in most instances to obtain even a modest size economic unit; and the fact that the earnings potential was fairly large did not overcome the equity restraints on loans. The implication is that full ownership is not now a feasible way to achieve an economic unit—other financial strategies must be employed to gain control of necessary resources for an adequate-size farm firm.

Several financial strategies are available to the farmer assembling capital consistent with his managerial skills. They include leasing of real property and capital assets; borrowing on open note (with or without specific pledge of real or personal property), or conditional sales contract for either real or personal property; contractual arrangements associated with vertical coordination; or incorporation of the farm firm. When financing terms are taken into account, these various financial alternatives are far from neutral in their effects on farm output and earnings. The size of the aggregate that can be acquired varies by choice of financing strategy. As will be seen below, the size of the farmer's credit reserve also is affected (Baker and Tweeten, 1965).

LEASING

Farm leasing has long been viewed as a rung on the tenure ladder, a stage in the progression of the successful farmer from a hired worker to a debt-free owner. To an increasing degree, however, farmers are leasing, on a permanent basis, part of the land needed to make an economic farming unit. There appear to be substantial economic reasons for projecting increased part-tenancy. The farmer growing in managerial skills can thus finance expansion to exploit size economies. Part-tenancy also provides the means for later "retreat" associated with a decline in the labor and managerial capacity of the farm operator. In fact, part-tenancy may well be an important means of maintaining viability of the single-proprietor firm in agriculture. It may also contribute, along with part-time farming, to a reduction in barriers between the farm and nonfarm economies. The modern successful farm operator no more confines his investments to farming in general or to farm land in particular than he does his labor. Investment alternatives of farmers in the future will broaden still further for an increasing percentage of commercial farm operators.

Heretofore limited mainly to farm land (and associated buildings), a considerable activity has been generated in leasing various capital items: machinery and equipment items, certain kinds of materials: handling and storing facilities, and even livestock. That capital leasing is an important alternative is attested to by the rapid growth of contractual arrangements. The explanation of such growth, despite higher cost of leasing relative to owning in many situations, may be found in tax advantages and in the value of credit reserve thus left unused by the farmer dependent on external finance for expansion.

BORROWING AND CREDIT RESERVES MANAGEMENT

Among resources valuable to the farmer is his "credit"—his ability to borrow. Though not listed in a conventional balance sheet as an asset, credit provides a reserve that can be drawn upon much like cash. Unused, it provides a degree of liquidity that enables the farmer to undertake uncertain ventures unacceptable to the indebted individual. Growth in unused credit reflects financial growth in an important sense. Moreover, it can be used to generate economic growth as well.

A credit reserve is subject to growth or decline through financial as well as production decisions. A resource allocation that raises income clearly increases credit, other things being equal. But credit also grows through increased liquidity in the asset structure—conserving credit for use in loans relatively attractive to lenders. There is significant evidence to suggest that, at least in the short run, the farmer can increase total credit available by splitting it among primary and secondary lenders. This may also increase financial management problems. But many farmers *have* found total credit expanded by using machinery and feed dealers as well as the bank or Production Credit Association.

In recent years the conditional sales contract has come into increasing use. As was discussed in the previous chapter, it frequently is more costly than a conventional farm mortgage loan. Also, it leaves the borrower more vulnerable, since many legal protections available to the farm mortgagor are not available to the installment loan contract borrower. What then accounts for its increased use? The most obvious answer is that it reduces the minimum down payment. Either a larger land base can be financed out of given capital, or capital is left with which to finance nonland resources.

VERTICAL COORDINATION

Processors of farm products and suppliers of farm inputs not only lend to farmers but also invest directly in the farm sector. The consequence is to radically alter the structure of the farm firm. Particularly in the case of processors, investments tend to relate specifically to individual enterprises—a specialty crop or a livestock enterprise. Also, the investments typically are accompanied by managerial services. In many cases the whole structure of the farm firm is altered and bears little resemblance to the individual-proprietor farm firm that existed prior to the structural change. Since the nonfarm firm typically is much larger in resources and in ability to acquire capital, it is relatively easy for the farm firm to be dominated in the structural change. Easier access to markets and capital are incentives for farmers to participate in integrated operations. The incentives for input supply firms include development of outlets for products and services; for processing firms they include development of a supply of farm products controlled as to timing, quality, and to a degree, quantity. Investment from nonfarm sources is promoted by a lag in farmers' response to changes in market or technical opportunities, by lenders' failure to respond to lending opportunities, by the presence of a large supply of underemployed labor, or by combinations of such factors.

FARM INCORPORATION

The outstanding financial advantage of the corporate firm is in its chartered privilege to acquire capital through the sale of stock with limited liability for stockholders. Additional advantages for farm families are flexibility in estate planning and, in certain instances, reduction in the tax on inheritance and income. In contrast with vertical coordination, incorporation may often be a means of preserving the family structure of the farm firm.

In the proprietor firm, profits and losses remain with the operator. Returns to a lender are limited to a dollar-fixed sum that depends only on the interest rate. Thus it can matter but little to the lender whether a financed venture is expected to yield a 5 or a 50 per cent return. It is difficult to see how a commercial lender can be expected to make loans in which any appreciable *predictable* risk in principal payment is involved—at least at interest rates common on farm loans.

Incorporation may provide a convenient means for heirs migrating from the family farm to retain an investment in the farm and at least a potential voice in control of the farm business. The operator who remains escapes the sudden burden of financing the whole of an economic-size farm organization. As he develops financially, he may be able to buy at a more modest pace an increasing share of the business he operates. But he is at no time forced to "revolutionize" his financial organization to preserve access to the farm and the base thus afforded for growth and development. Given these advantages, the incorporation on a "family" basis may well increase in future years. Such a trend has much to recommend it.

One factor that may retard the development is the borrowing capacity generated by a family-incorporated farm firm. Limited liability has accounted for vast capital accumulations outside agriculture, *through sale of stock*. The market for farm-based stock is not likely to generate anything comparable in magnitude. Meanwhile the farm operator may find less credit available per dollar of corporate equity than previously was available per dollar of equity in the single-proprietor firm. In the case of family-incorporated farm organizations, Federal Land Bank and Production Credit Associations sometimes request personal signatures on loan documents in addition to corporate evidence of obligations. Loan guarantees by the government might be justified for a limited period to finance the organization of an incorporated farm under certain conditions. Such conditions would be analogous to those in which the Farmers Home Administration loans are made to farmers. That agency might well be the appropriate one to entrust with such a program. In addition to the supervisor-client relation so successfully used in its present program, the Farmers Home Administration could assist and instruct all parties to the incorporation on the requirements, opportunities, and peculiarities of the corporate form of business enterprise. Such help would be far from negligible for families that might "qualify" for incorporation financing.

CONCLUDING OBSERVATIONS

Adaptability of financial intermediaries servicing farmers to the credit goals indicated earlier is impressive. Since World War II, Production Credit Associations and commercial banks have established effective programs in intermediate-term loans. Considerable experimenting continues and is wholly understandable in view of the complexities involved in nonreal estate loans that extend beyond a single cycle of production. Financing beginning farmers is a perennial problem in a sector with high initial capital requirements. However, the array of leasing arrangements, the flexibility of local lenders, and the formal programs of the Farmers Home Administration combine in a program that seems reasonably effective in financing new farming entrants.

Farm mortgage lenders can neatly tailor a farm mortgage loan to the repayment capacity of a qualified borrower. A considerable fraction of the loan often can be left unamortized. Earnings from off-farm sources, an increasingly important part of the income of many farm families, are often taken into account in appraising the applicant for farm mortgage as well as nonreal estate loans. All these are welcome adaptations and realistic responses to change in the environment of the farm firm.

Despite these favorable adaptations, credit use is not well distributed among farmers. Lender-decisions for credit-dependent farmers can lead to difficulties, and serious intergeneration problems exist. Lender preferences for asset-generating and self-liquidating loans often are inconsistent with optimal allocations implied by marginal analysis. For the farmer, two alternatives are open. The first is to minimize credit use for those purposes in relative disfavor of lenders and to otherwise generate such growth in his credit as seems feasible. The second alternative is to use merchants and dealers in a split line of credit. This latter alternative is frequently adopted. Thus the machinery dealer is increasing his share in machinery loans (often not self-liquidating). So also are feed and fertilizer dealers in loans that are not asset-generating. The borrower is left with a complex financial organization to manage.

The use of merchant and dealer loans will continue to grow. The machinery and equipment dealers have several advantages in competition with the primary lenders. With a stake in merchandising returns, the dealer can often afford to finance more liberally than can the primary lender with his fixed interest returns. Moreover, the dealer is necessarily better equipped to judge the payoff from new and sophisticated inputs. Unfortunately, he also is biased in his judgment. Successful credit policies require policies and personnel not always found in firms selling fertilizers, feed, and machinery to farmers. Thus the farmer is faced with a judgment problem that is different from the one he faces when he borrows from a relatively neutral primary lender.

A large percentage of the nation's 14,000 commercial banks are located in rural areas, most organized at the outset more or less specifically to finance farmers. Banks in such areas suffered a 50 per cent attrition during the depressions of the 1920's and 1930's, a factor that to this day conditions lending practices in a large number of country banks. More important, however, is the fact that a large number of country banks are capitalized at a level too low to permit them to finance a substantial fraction of commercial farm applicants. A common loan limit has been 10 per cent of paid-in capital and surplus for the nonlivestock (Baker and Tweeten, 1965). Finding it unprofitable, unpleasant, or simply "out of character" to use a city correspondent for the overline, the banker watches the most profitable farm borrower shift to the Production Credit Association or split his line of credit with one or more merchants in the community.

Clearly this is an undesirable situation. One alternative is to expand branch banking. For the foreseeable future, however, this will be an unacceptable solution in a large number of unit-banking states. An alternative to this is an educational campaign on the use of correspondent banking facilities. A considerable effort along this line already is in progress. Another alternative is the development of legislation in which interbank compacts might be developed. Under such an arrangement a single bank would be entirely responsible for any given loan but would be able to add to its reserves some fraction of the combined reserves of all banks in a given compact. Banks might be grouped along geographic lines to foster similarities in the environment and outlook of bankers. Such a grouping of banks might eventually gain additional benefits—perhaps some specialization in lending, and joint hiring of personnel.

From the banker's point of view, a relative decline in direct financing need not be unsettling. The bank will become less a retailer and more a wholesaler of loan funds. The bank may provide funds to merchants and dealers who then extend credit to farmers. How seriously this will impair the regulatory character of the banking system is difficult to judge. The effect may be slight. A tight money policy that affects banks will be transmitted quickly throughout the whole of the financial and commercial sectors.

It seems likely that Production Credit Associations will expand as a "complete-line" lender, with budgeting facilities and a "neutral" source of financial advice. It is important, however, to keep their possibilities in proper perspective. They possess no magic in obtaining loan funds cheaply for farmers in periods of monetary and credit contraction. Nor can they be expected, with their member-wise responsibilities, to lend on other than self-preservation criteria. They are, however, chartered to deal with farmers and can entertain no other investment alternatives for the use of funds available to them.

Continuation of the trend to closer cooperation of Production Credit Associations and Federal Land Bank Associations is desirable. As a matter of fact, it might be defensible to accelerate the merger of the two lending institutions at the local lending level under single management. In the future, a similar move might be useful at the district level of the Production Credit Associations. Economies from size, greater efficiency in use of reserves, and the possibility of better serving the needs of individual farmers are some possible advantages of merger. Components of the cooperative farm credit system (the Federal Land Banks, Federal Intermediate Credit Banks, and Banks for Cooperatives) currently market their securities separately in the wholesale money markets. However, there is now some coordination between agencies, with one borrowing from another which has floated a new bond issue and which does not immediately need all the funds obtained. There would be advantages in efficiency and flexibility if the cooperative credit agencies sold their bonds as a single agency. Potential buyers would have fewer agencies to investigate in determining the quality of the bonds, and funds from bond sales could be more efficiently allocated among the component agencies.

THE FERTILIZER INDUSTRY

Use of the three principal plant nutrients—nitrogen, available phosphorus, and soluble potassium—doubled in tonnage in the decade preceding 1965 (U.S. Department of Agriculture, 1966a, p. 21). It is estimated that farmers received an average return of $2.50 for each dollar spent on fertilizer from 1960 to 1964 (Ibach, 1966, p. ii). In 1964 farmers spent $1.6 billion for fertilizer. This implies that $4.0 billion or about one-tenth of the total farm output in 1964 was imputed to use of fertilizer. It is estimated that one-third of the increase in crop output in recent years resulted from increased application of fertilizers (U.S. Department of Agriculture, 1967, p. 8).

If farmers had been willing to settle for a $2 return on each dollar spent for fertilizer in the 1960–64 period, they could have produced the 1960–64 crop output on an estimated 259 million acres—80 million acres less than actually used (Ibach, 1966, p. ii). Fertilizer required would have been 13.3 million tons of nitrogen, phosphorus, and potassium, or double the average 6.7 million tons used from 1960 to 1964. Farmers *could have more than doubled* crop production per acre in the mid-1960's if they would have applied fertilizers for maximum economic efficiency—so that the last dollar spent on fertilizer earned one dollar of return (Ibach, 1966).

Use of fertilizers will be a key factor in meeting future demands for crop output. If crop output requirements increase 3 per cent annually, a 45 per cent increase over 1965 in crop output will be needed by 1980. Even if Ibach's estimate cited earlier of prospects for doubling crop output is discounted considerably for possible error, the prospects are indeed favorable for meeting 1980 crop needs, even with current prices and technology. New sources of fertilizer supplies and new technologies are expected to reduce the prices of nitrogen, phosphorus, and potassium. The most spectacular change is for nitrogen, which is projected to fall from the current price of 11.6 cents per pound to 5.1 cents per pound by 1980 (Ibach, 1966, p. 17). Based on a marginal return of $2 per dollar invested, 1980 crop requirements can be met with expenditures of $3.7 billion for fertilizer at projected prices (Ibach, 1966, p. 20).

These data elicit mixed reactions. They show that there need be no panic about the ability of farmers to meet future food needs. But the data also show that output is likely to press demand for farm commodities for some years as farmers move toward more profitable input levels. Low fertilizer prices are a boon to food consumers but are a mixed blessing to farmers as the macro effects from increased farm output become apparent in lower prices received by farmers.

We now turn to an analysis of the market structure, conduct and performance of the fertilizer industry. It is somewhat ironic that, while fertilizer has been singled out as one of the great wellsprings of rising farm productivity, the performance of the industry has not always rated high marks. We shall observe, however, that performance has improved in recent years. This improvement helps to explain the large gains in farming efficiency since 1955.

THE MARKET STRUCTURE

The fertilizer industry is here defined as producers, processors, and mixers of fertilizer nitrogen, phosphate, and potash. Farmers traditionally have purchased more than half of their fertilizer as mixtures containing two or more of the three principal plant nutrients. In the 1962–63 fertilizer year, 32 per cent of the elemental nitrogen (N), 91 per cent of the phosphorus (in the form of P_2O_5), and 86 per cent of the potassium (in the form of K_2O) used in fertilizer were sold to farmers as mixtures (Markham, 1966, p. 362). A large proportion of the mixing industry is vertically integrated with the production and distribution of phosphate rock. Producers and processors of sulphur might also be included in the fertilizer industry because sulphuric acid is one of the most important sources of superphosphate, produced from approximately equal parts of phosphate rock and sulphuric acid.

Phosphate production for fertilizers consists of three stages: mining and preparation for smelting of phosphate rock, manufacture of phosphate fertilizer materials, and manufacture of mixed fertilizer. The market concentration declines with each successive stage, reflecting in part the declining cost of entry. The five largest phosphate rock producers accounted for 70 per cent of total domestic output in 1950 (latest available data). The four largest superphosphate producers accounted for 47 per cent of total domestic production in 1958. And in the same year the four largest mixed fertilizer producers accounted for 24 per cent of total mixed fertilizer shipments (Markham, 1966, p. 362).

A German cartel supplied nearly all the potash consumed in the United States before World War I. This picture has changed radically, and in the mid-1950's foreign companies supplied about 10 per cent of the domestic consumption of potash, and three large and three small domestic companies supplied the remaining 90 per cent.

A Chilean nitrate cartel supplied most of the nitrogen before World War I. Only two domestic synthetic nitrogen producers and imported Chilean sodium nitrate supplied 90 per cent of nitrogen consumed by U.S. fertilizer manufacturing firms just before World War II. Following a Department of Justice investigation of cartel arrangements and other practices in restraint of trade, five federal grand jury indictments were issued against the leading members of the nitrogen industry and the major importer of Chilean nitrate in 1939. The defendants entered pleas of *nolo contendere* and, after payment of fines, the five cases were disposed of in three civil complaints which resulted in a consent decree covering most of the allegations made by the government in the original indictment (Markham, 1966, p. 372).

Partly because of the way the government disposed of its nitrogen plants built during the war, the level of concentration in nitrogen production declined after World War II. In 1962–63, the four largest companies accounted for only 30 per cent of production, and the number of independent domestic competitors had increased to 51 (cf. Markham, 1966, p. 363). While the structure changed from concentrated oligopoly to effective competition, and marketing margins declined appreciably, Walsh (in Markham, 1966, p. 374) states that competition was not sufficiently effective at the manufacturers' level to eliminate monopoly profits and to force producers to operate at optimum scale and output rates.

Vertical integration is prominent in the fertilizer industry. The six largest integrated firms produced 70 per cent of the phosphate rock, 47 per cent of the output of superphosphate, and 24 per cent of the output of mixed fertilizers in 1958. The key position of phosphate producers in the fertilizer industry and their involvement in an international cartel led to charges of artificially high and inflexible rock phosphate prices. Partly because of World War II and investigations by the Federal Trade Commission, the cartel activities were ended. Lower prices suggested a greater degree of competition in the industry by the 1950's.

Cartel pricing was also practiced in the potash industry. After World War I, domestic producers entering the field adopted the prices quoted by the German-French potash cartel. The system of selling in the U.S. at cartel prices and at uniform prices among producers ended in 1940 with a consent decree permanently enjoining large potash producers from agreeing, combining, or conspiring among themselves or with other potash producers (Markham, 1966, p. 373).

Potash producers have earned high rates of return. Rates of return on investment in the three major companies averaged 34 per cent, 24 per cent, and 10 per cent from 1936 to 1951. Profit rates have declined, however, and in the three years from 1960 to 1962 the three companies earned rates of 8.3 per cent, 5.3 per cent, and 8.2 per cent, respectively.

The mixed fertilizer industry has had a somewhat spotty record. Simple technology and low capital requirements have resulted in a large number of firms—a total of 671 in 1958. Plants tended to be market oriented, most plants selling half of their output within a radius of fifty miles from the plant. Nonetheless, through wholesale merger, a few large integrated phosphate fertilizer firms acquired a significant share of the mixing capacity from 1900 to 1913, which they continue to hold. The largest eight firms, seven of which were phosphate fertilizer companies, accounted for 39 per cent of the mixed fertilizer shipments in 1958.

ECONOMICAL SOURCES OF FERTILIZER

The fertilizer industry has been responsive to more economical sources of plant nutrients and has substituted them for less economical sources on a large scale. But it has transmitted the gain from such technology only slowly to farmers. According to Markham (1966) the industry has, over most of its history, lacked that creative entrepreneurship that constantly seeks to improve the product and techniques of production. Until recently, entrepreneurs engaged in the manufacture of mixed fertilizers not only failed to innovate, they even failed to transmit to the farmer the benefits of innovation in industries that supplied their raw materials. For example, in 1910, mixers relied heavily on such raw materials as cottonseed meal, castor pomace, animal tankage, fish scrap, low-grade potash salts, and 12 per cent to 16 per cent superphosphate. Almost any balanced combination of such materials yielded a mixed fertilizer containing a maximum of about 15 per cent plant nutrients. The average plant nutrient content of mixed fertilizers in 1910 was 14.8, or very close to the maximum. Over the next fifty years, the chemical industries developed fertilizer materials having from four to ten times the plant nutrient content of those used in 1910. In 1950 the average plant nutrient content was still only 22 per cent. And 16 per cent of the average bag of mixed fertilizer was nonnutrient-bearing filler. In 1963, the average plant nutrient content had climbed to 34 per cent, registering a greater increase in the previous thirteen years than had occurred over the previous century. The gap between optimum and actual plant nutrient content was closing (Markham, 1966, p. 375).

It has been estimated that the social cost of farmers purchasing less economical sources of plant nutrients than were available on the market amounted to $61 million in 1949 and $45 million in 1958 (Markham, 1966, p. 377). This cost is partly due to imperfect knowledge and irrational buying practices of farmers. Fertilizer buying practices of farmers have improved slowly under an extensive program of education by the Agricultural Extension Service, the Tennessee Valley Authority, and other groups.

The index of fertilizer prices remained virtually constant from 1949 to 1965 while prices of other farm capital inputs displayed a marked upward trend. Yet the fertilizer industry receives low marks for its economic performance. It has been the frequent focus of antitrust and price fixing charges by federal agencies and has been lethargic in passing improved technologies to farmers. In 1906, 1926, 1941, and 1964, the Department of Justice brought antitrust actions against a number of fertilizer firms for conspiring to fix prices and engaging in other restraints of trade (Markham, 1966, p. 375). The industry structure has become more competitive and now appears adequate to ensure a workable degree of price competition, but the industry undoubtedly will be watched for performance in the public interest.

Cooperatives are growing in some phases of the fertilizer industry and will help to improve some aspects of industry performance. As of early 1966, cooperatives owned 11 ammonia plants, which accounted for 14 per cent of the total domestic capacity. The proportion of all fertilizers bought by farmers that was retailed by cooperatives increased from 9 per cent in 1943 to 15 per cent in 1951 and to nearly 30 per cent in the year ending June 30, 1965 (Gale, 1968, p. 35).

Future supplies of the three basic fertilizer elements are adequate. About 90 per cent of the domestic production of potassium came from mines in the Carlsbad, New Mexico, area in 1965, where seven firms were in operation. Quality deposits in the area are depleting rapidly; by 1965, 25 firms had acquired rights to huge potash deposits in Saskatchewan, Canada, that exceed domestic reserves by an estimated 70 to 100 times (Gale, 1968). With three firms in production in Saskatchewan, the United States had become a net importer of potash in the year ending June 30, 1966.

Phosphate rock supplies are also adequate, and are located in the Southeast and in the Mountain states. Florida alone accounted for 80 per cent of the national mine production in 1966, with twelve firms engaged in mining operations.

Nitrogen can be obtained from several sources, including the air, and potential supplies are virtually unlimited. An increasing proportion of nitrogen fertilizers comes from synthetic ammonia derived from petroleum or natural gas. The sharp rise in production of nitrogen from ammonia has been accompanied by the entrance of many petroleum firms into the fertilizer industry and to problems of excess capacity in nitrogen fertilizer production.

THE MIXED FEED INDUSTRY

The value of shipments of prepared animal feeds was nearly $4 billion in 1963 (Allen and Hodges, 1968). The number of firms in the industry increased from 2,379 in 1958 to 2,587 in 1963. The rate of concentration increased gradually from 1947 to 1958 but was less in 1958 than in 1935 (Padberg, 1966, p. 269). The proportion of shipments of the four largest firms in 1958 was 22 per cent. Cooperatives play a major role in feed manufacturing and distribution. Cooperatives in 1959 manufactured 90 per cent of the feed, which they sold through 5,310 local retail outlets. In that year nearly one-fourth of the feed industry output was manufactured by cooperatives.

VERTICAL INTEGRATION

Excess capacity characterizes the feed industry and partly explains its involvement in vertical integration. Research conducted in the north-central region indicated that excess capacity was 52 per cent in 1954–55 and 53 per cent in 1960 in feed manufacturing (Padberg, 1966, p. 278). Manufacturers found some outlet for their capacity through vertical integration into the poultry industry. Feed manufacturers assumed some of the services formerly supplied by feed dealers and added other services, often by-passing dealers in the distribution channel. The result was a reduction in distribution costs and probably in margins (Padberg, 1966, p. 278). Also the certainty of outlets was increased. An estimated 18 per cent of feed industry sales in 1959 were affected by some type of contract arrangement in six north-central states. Results of one study indicated that feed manufacturers on the average sustained a loss of 87 cents per ton on contract programs as compared with other feed sales (cf. Padberg, 1966, p. 279). Thus the motive for integration appears to be the desire to expand sales, utilize excess capacity, and lower production costs rather than obtain higher returns per unit of volume. Ability to extend the assembly line production process is one important element determining the future trend of feed manufacturers to integrate into cattle feeding, hog feeding, and other farm enterprises. The comparative advantage of large feed manufacturers in extending integrated feeding operations also depends on the ability of manufacturers to combine their capital advantage with low-cost labor in agriculture. As new cultural practices in feeding come into importance, especially those requiring specialized know-how and extensive capital investment, the role of feed-manufacturing firms in livestock feeding is likely to increase.

There are significant economies of size in plant operation, research, selling, and transport in feed manufacturing. These economies suggest competitive advantages for large firms, and some trend toward consolidation is expected. Nonetheless, the bulky nature of feed and attendant high transport costs preclude extensive centralization of manufacturing facilities.

PERFORMANCE

The feed industry utilizes the results of abundant state and federally supported nutrition research and also conducts much research itself. The results of this research are incorporated into the product. Results that relate to farm feeding practices are provided as services to farmers who buy feed. Farmers have indicated that the promotional efforts of feed companies often provide more timely nutrition information than other sources. Padberg (1966, p. 283) concludes that "this industry is characterized by good performance in product quality, the availability of appropriate quality variations, and a high degree of progressiveness concerning the improvement of product quality over time." The presence of cooperative firms and aggressive price competition among manufacturers substantially reduces the feasibility of large firms using their position to exploit the market. Analysis of profit rates shows no tendency toward chronic excess profits (Padberg, 1966, p. 284).

THE FARM MACHINERY INDUSTRY

MARKET STRUCTURE

The farm machinery industry is dominated by a few large full-line firms. In 1922 the International Harvester Company alone was responsible for 44 per cent of the farm machinery sales. Its share of machinery sales has declined steadily, although in 1965 it still had the largest farm machinery sales of any firm in the industry. In the 1950's, International's domestic sales were exceeded by those of Deere and Company (John Deere). Its foreign sales are exceeded by those of Massey-Ferguson, a Canadian firm. From 1922 to 1948, the number of full-line farm machinery manufacturers in North America increased from three to nine. This trend reversed and the number was reduced to seven by the early 1960's. Oliver Corporation, Minneapolis-Moline, and Cockshutt Farm Equipment (a Canadian firm) were acquired by the White Motor Company. The percentage of the value of tractor shipments accounted for by the four largest companies was 69 per cent in 1958, approximately the same as in 1947. The concentration rate for the four largest firms making farm machinery remained stable from 1947 to 1958 at approximately 38 per cent of all machinery shipments.

MARKET CONDUCT AND PERFORMANCE

In an industry of high concentration, issues of conduct and performance are of particular interest. The industry is characterized by constant product improvement over and above the major technological breakthroughs which have periodically occurred. Recent emphasis on frequent tractor model changes, patterned after the automobile industry behavior, creates some costs that are of questionable economic value.

Purchases of tractors are sensitive to farm income. Perhaps to minimize losses, firms have not lowered prices to maintain sales as farm income falls. The result is considerable fluctuation in sales from year to year. Because of the large cost and durability of production facilities, firms maintain plants in slack periods and operate them considerably below capacity. There are substantial economies of size in a large, diversified output. The Oliver plant, which had previously run six months a year and then virtually shut down, was reported after merger running full-speed for six months and at 70–80 per cent of capacity the other six months (cf. Phillips, 1966, p. 336). The higher overhead of smaller firms is partly reflected in total costs as a share of the value of goods sold which from 1959 to 1962 averaged 73.7 per cent for Deere and Company, 80.4 per cent for International Harvester, and 91.8 per cent (1961–1962 only) for J. I. Case (Phillips, 1966, p. 336).

The conclusion that overhead and selling costs per unit of output are substantially higher in the small firms than in the large firms producing tractors does not necessarily carry into other items of farm machinery. Firms such as New Idea and New Holland have had considerable success in entering the industry and holding a share of the market.

International Harvester was the recognized price leader in the farm machinery industry for several decades until World War II. The company dominated the industry in many respects, including research and engineering advances, in tractor and harvesting machinery production, and in production of a number of tillage machines. Other companies followed International's price leadership for several reasons, including fear of retaliatory action. They also followed suit because International, by its superior resources, its generally progressive policies, and its mature judgment born of wisdom (gained from twenty years of fighting federal antitrust suits in court), was accepted by the industry as best fitted to make price changes in the industry (Phillips, 1966, p. 343).

In 1947 International attempted to reassert its price leadership by lowering prices. Other companies did not follow suit. Improvements in the product-line, large imports (the industry is not protected by tariffs), and strength in the market position of other firms left the industry with no price leader after World War II. The more evenly divided strength of the large firms has stimulated price competition. Yet price competition is not great for reasons presented by a representative of Deere and Company in 1960:

> It is sometimes said that our industry could make the same or higher profits by reducing prices, thereby gaining greater sales volume and lower unit costs. This is a tempting idea. Unfortunately, it is an illusion when applied to our industry. For it to work for the industry, decreasing prices would have to result in a very much larger total market for farm machinery. For it to work for any one company, all other companies in the industry would have to maintain their present prices. The end result of such action would be little or no profits with business failures resulting in fewer manufacturers in the industry. The conclusion is distasteful but nonetheless realistic. [in Phillips, 1966, p. 338]

Farm machinery manufacturers in early years favored having a large number of local dealers throughout the country to give maximum exposure to their line to farmers. Problems arose, however, because small dealers could not provide parts and other services for customers, and because they could not finance needed inventories of machines for sale. The result was a decline by about half in the number of dealers after 1940. Machinery manufacturers have become heavily involved in dealer financing. This covers not only financing of new machines until they are sold by dealers but also financing of used machines taken in trade. On the shipment of new machines to dealers, no payment is required for a year, unless the dealer sells the machine. Manufacturers say they have become involved reluctantly in dealer financing, because commercial banks could not meet the needs of the industry. The practice is of concern, nevertheless, because it gives the dealer less independence, makes entry into manufacturing more difficult, and makes manufacturers more sensitive to changing economic conditions affecting sales.

Profit rates of farm machinery firms are highly variable but do not appear to be excessive over the long term. After-tax returns on investment from 1919 to 1946 averaged 6.9 per cent for International Harvester, 9.7 per cent for Deere and Company, and substantially less for other major firms in the industry. From 1957 to 1960, net profit per dollar of total assets averaged, for all U.S. manufacturers, 6.5 cents, for Deere and Company 6.1 cents, for International Harvester 4.8 cents, and for other major farm equipment firms less than 3.6 cents (Phillips, 1966, p. 353). Advertising rates are not known for the industry, but Deere and Company expenditures for advertising were 1.0 to 1.5 per cent of net sales from 1954 to 1960.

In summary, the performance of the farm machinery industry in recent years rates mainly plus marks. Any attempt to break up firms to increase competition would likely raise costs of production and lead to higher machinery prices to farmers. And a large reduction in prices would drive more firms from the industry and increase the concentration of sales among the few remaining firms.

SUMMARY AND CONCLUSIONS

Traditionally, farmers have relied heavily on internal financing out of farm income to build capital assets. Changing farm technology has a hearty appetite for capital, and an efficient farm economy must rely increasingly on external credit sources. Growing requirements for financial management is placing more and more burden on the family farm structure. To preserve the family farm, public policy will need to devote more attention to provision of education and sophisticated management techniques for use by farmers. Feed, fertilizer, and machinery dealers, along with credit institutions, will become more deeply involved in providing farm management services and are likely to participate in a growing number of farm management decisions even in the absence of increasing vertical integration.

The performance of industries that supply purchased inputs to farmers as reported in this chapter has been generally high and is improving. The large number of firms and the many cooperative organizations provide workable competition, and there has been little evidence of exploitation of farmers by input suppliers in recent years. The farm machinery industry of necessity is highly concentrated, but its record of innovation is impressive and profit rates show little evidence of exercise of monopoly power.

The conduct of the farm machinery industry and certain other industries supplying inputs to farmers is consistent with the widely held view that farmers are "price-takers" and not "price-makers." The supply of farm inputs produced in the nonfarm sector is very highly elastic—the farming industry can vary purchases within a reasonable range without markedly changing the industry price.

Wages in firms supplying purchased inputs to farmers will continue to rise. The structure of these firms suggests that rising labor costs will be passed on to farmers and will not be absorbed by the input industry. This means that the cost part of the cost-price squeeze will continue to press upward with attendant problems for farmers. An exception is the fertilizer industry, where low prices and improved marketing techniques will continue to make fertilizer a very good buy for farmers. The resulting increase in farm output precludes the need for fear of serious food shortages but will contribute to some future problems on the product-price side of the cost-price squeeze.

Inflation in prices of items purchased will continue to distress farmers. If the causes are labor unions, oligopolistic firms, and government deficit spending, then what are the cures? While farmers perhaps give too much weight to deficit spending as a source of inflation in prices paid, there clearly exists a need for sound monetary and fiscal policies.

Public policies must continue to reduce undue concentration of power in labor unions and industry. Unfortunately there is little hope of creating enough atomized competition to stop the wage-price spiral. Countervailing farm bargaining power may be the only answer.

REFERENCES

Allen, George, and Earl Hodges. 1968. Livestock feeds. In *Structure of Six Farm Input Industries*, pp. 55–64.

Baker, C. B., and Luther G. Tweeten. 1965. Financial requirements of the farm firm. In *Structural Changes in Commercial Agriculture*. Center for Agricultural and Economic Development Report 24, Ames: Iowa State University Press, pp. 27–52.

Board of Governors of the Federal Reserve System. 1964. Farm debt. Washington, Federal Reserve System.

————. 1966. Merchant and dealer credit in agriculture. Washington, Federal Reserve System.

Collins, G. P. 1965. To what extent can farm capital needs be met by conventional credit? In *Financing Oklahoma's Agriculture*, proceedings, Farm Business Training Conference, Stillwater, Oklahoma State University.

Economic Report of the President. 1967. Washington: U.S. Government Printing Office.

Gale, John. 1968. Fertilizers. In *Structure of Six Farm Input Industries*, pp. 26–41.

Garlock, Fred L. 1966. Farmers and their debts. Agriculture Economics Report No. 93. Washington, U.S. Department of Agriculture.

Ibach, D. B. 1966. Fertilizer use in the United States. Agriculture Economics Report No. 92. Washington, U.S. Department of Agriculture.

Markham, Jesse W. 1966. The fertilizer industry. In Moore and Walsh (1966), Chapter 14.

Moore, John R., and Richard G. Walsh, eds. 1966. *Market Structure of the Agricultural Industries*. Ames: Iowa State University Press.

Padberg, Daniel I. 1966. The mixed feed industry. In Moore and Walsh (1966), Chapter 11.

Phillips, W. G. 1966. The farm machinery industry. In Moore and Walsh (1966), Chapter 13.

Strickland, P. L., Jr., J. S. Plaxico, and W. F. Lagrone. 1963. Minimum land requirements and adjustments for specified income levels. Oklahoma Agricultural Experiment Station Bulletin B-608. Stillwater.

Strickler, Paul. 1968. Farm machinery and equipment. In *Structure of Six Farm Input Industries*, pp. 14–25.

Structure of Six Farm Input Industries. 1968. ERS-357. Washington, U.S. Department of Agriculture.

Tootell, R. B. 1961. Adequacy of our agricultural credit structure. In E. L. Baum *et al.*, eds., *Capital and Credit Needs in a Changing Agriculture*. Ames: Iowa State University Press, pp. 255–63.

U.S. Department of Agriculture. 1966a. Changes in farm production and efficiency. Statistical Bulletin No. 233. Washington.

―――. 1966b. Farm income situation. FIS-203. Washington.

―――. 1966c. *Agricultural Statistics*. Washington: U.S. Government Printing Office.

―――. 1966d. The balance sheet of agriculture. Agricultural Information Bulletin No. 314. Washington.

―――. 1967. The farm index. Economic Research Service. Washington.

CHAPTER TEN

Commodity Programs: A Short History

To understand the current structure of farm programs and what form legislation is likely to take in the future, it is well to examine history. This chapter reviews briefly the major commodity legislation of the four decades preceding 1970. Sometimes programs that were advanced but not enacted into law are as instructive in understanding farm policy as are the programs in effect. Thus this chapter will include a discussion of the McNary-Haugen, the Brannan, and the Cochrane proposals.

The chapter deals primarily with programs of the federal government to alleviate commercial farm problems described at some length earlier, especially in Chapter 6. Later chapters will examine past federal programs to alleviate problems of rural poverty.

The excitement and drama of political infighting are sacrificed to brevity in the following pages. This is unfortunate, and the reader is encouraged to read such able presentations as *Pressures and Protests* (Hadwiger and Talbot, 1965) and *The Policy Process in American Agriculture* (Talbot and Hadwiger, 1969).

PROGRAM OF THE 1920's: A HISTORY OF FAILURE

The McNary-Haugen plan was originated by George Peek and Hugh Johnson of the Moline Plow Company. The plan was publicized by the slogan "Equality for Agriculture." It was a two-price plan, relatively simple in principle. A government export corporation was to be set up to "buy" farm commodities that would not sell on the domestic market at a price (later called "parity") that bore the same relationship to prices paid by farmers as those in the pre-World War I period. The government corporation would dispose of excess supplies in the foreign market at the world price. Tariffs would be maintained to keep the commodities from being imported into the U.S. at the higher domestic price.

The farmer would receive an average price made up of the parity price for the domestic portion and the world price for the excess.

FIVE DEFEATED BILLS

The first McNary-Haugen Bill was introduced in 1924 and was defeated in the House of Representatives. Southern and Eastern sections were unified in their opposition. The second McNary-Haugen Bill in 1925 never came to a vote. The third, even with new support from the American Farm Bureau Federation and amendments to make the bill more palatable, was defeated in both House and Senate in 1925. A fourth bill was passed by both houses of Congress in 1927 but was vetoed by President Coolidge with strong objections that the bill would aid farmers in certain sections at the expense of other farmers, that it was price-fixing, that it was impossible to administer, and that some portions of the bill were unconstitutional. A fifth bill was passed by Congress and vetoed by Coolidge in 1928. The principal features of the McNary-Haugen Bills were not dead, however, but became part of the New Deal legislation of the mid-1930's.

THE FEDERAL FARM BOARD

Herbert Hoover took office as President in 1929. The Agricultural Marketing Act of that year established the Federal Farm Board. With a revolving fund of $500 million, the Board was to make loans to cooperatives to control surpluses by acquiring excess supplies, by constructing new storage facilities and other buildings, and by making advances to growers for their crops. The Board attempted to stabilize prices by purchasing stocks of wheat, cotton, and other commodities. Its limited finances were soon exhausted, and farm prices continued to fall. In 1932 the Federal Farm Board stated that its efforts had failed and recommended to Congress that legislation was needed to control production or quantities going to market.

Much effort of the Board was erroneously predicated on the assumption that the problems of agriculture could be solved with a more efficient marketing system. When the woes of a farm economy that had been depressed throughout the 1920's were compounded with the slack in demand evolving from nationwide depression and lagging foreign demand for farm commodities in the early 1930's, the farm problem was obviously much larger than the Farm Board. The Board was unable to support market prices and cope with existing excess production capacity without production controls. In May 1933 President Franklin Roosevelt abolished the Board by presidential order.

PROGRAMS OF THE 1930's

THE AGRICULTURAL ADJUSTMENT ACT OF 1933

The Agricultural Act of May 1933 created the Agricultural Adjustment Administration and authorized strong measures to raise the level of farm prices. Among these were authorizations (*a*) to enter into voluntary agreements whereby farmers were paid to reduce acreage of "basic" crops, (*b*) to store crops on the farm with advance payments to producers for the crop, (*c*) to enter into voluntary marketing agreements with farmers and middlemen, (*d*) to levy processing taxes, (*e*) to license handlers and processors for the purpose of enforcing provisions of the marketing agreements, and (*f*) to use the proceeds of processing taxes to pay costs of adjustment operations and to expand markets (Benedict, 1953, p. 283). The "basic" commodities were cotton, wheat, corn, rice, tobacco, hogs, and milk. Acreage allotments were applied to the five crops listed above plus sugar and peanuts. Portions of cotton and tobacco acreage were plowed down as an emergency measure in 1933. "Nonrecourse" loans were made for corn and cotton in 1933. The term nonrecourse meant that the advance loan made to farmers on corn at 45 cents per bushel (60 per cent of parity) and on cotton at 10 cents per pound (69 per cent of parity) need not necessarily be repaid. If the market price were above the loan price, the farmer could sell on the open market and repay the loan. If the loan rate was above the market price, the farmer could turn in the commodity (as full payment of the loan) to the Commodity Credit Corporation, a government financed corporation created by executive order in October 1933.

Marketing quotas were introduced by the Bankhead Cotton Control Act and by the Kerr Tobacco Control Act, both passed in 1934. Two-thirds of the producers of cotton had to approve the allotment before it would go into effect. The required proportion was three-fourths before the tobacco allotment program would become effective. The quota was introduced by alloting to each producer certificates which, when accompanying the crop, would exempt it from "sales" tax. The tax was set high to prohibit sales not accompanied by certificates. Other processing tax proceeds were used to pay farmers to reduce production and to purchase commodities for distribution to persons unemployed and on relief.

Marketing agreements attempted to raise prices by controlling the timing and volume of marketing fruits, vegetables, milk, and other commodities. The first marketing agreement covered handling of milk in the Chicago market and became effective in August 1933.

The production control features, including payments for taking land out of production, coupled with dry weather, materially reduced production. Farm prices and incomes gained markedly from 1932 to 1936. The Agricultural

Adjustment Administration program was halted by the Hoosac Mills decision of 1936 in which the production control and processing tax features of the program were declared unconstitutional by the Supreme Court.

SOIL CONSERVATION AND DOMESTIC ALLOTMENT ACT OF 1936

The Soil Conservation and Domestic Allotment Act of 1936 combined conservation with production controls. Farmers were paid to voluntarily shift acreage from soil-depleting crops (which just happened to be those in excess supply) to soil-conserving legumes and grasses. For the first time the goal of income parity rather than price parity was introduced into the legislation. Although income parity was the stated goal in this and subsequent programs, price parity remained the operating concept. Income parity was defined as the ratio of purchasing power of the net income per person on farms to that of income per person not on farms which prevailed during the August 1909 to July 1914 period, a very favorable one for farmers.

Production was down because of the severe 1936 drought, but the large crop in 1937 showed that the program inadequately controlled production.

AGRICULTURAL MARKETING AGREEMENT ACT OF 1937

The Hoosac Mills decision had not invalidated the marketing agreement provisions of the 1933 legislation, but Congress saw fit to reaffirm certain provisions in the Agricultural Marketing Agreement Act of 1937. The 1937 Act disclaimed authority to levy processing taxes and redefined the machinery for establishing marketing orders. Under provisions of the 1937 legislation and subsequent amendments, a large number of marketing orders have been established under the authority of the Secretary of Agriculture.

The act specified the terms for example for milk-marketing orders. Each order established minimum prices which handlers must pay for milk purchased from producers or associations of producers. Generally a minimum price was established for class II milk to be used to produce butter, cheese, evaporated milk, and other manufactured products. A higher minimum price was usually established for class I milk to be used in fluid products, principally to be sold to consumers as fresh milk. The terms of the order were developed through public hearings prior to issuance of the order. The role of the federal government was to hear all arguments and proposals, to evaluate proposals and resolve differences in the public interest, and to enforce provisions of the order.

Federal milk orders do not control production but increase farm income by the multiple price features. Because production is not controlled, prices can be established above equilibrium levels, causing overproduction and attendant need for the government to dispose of the excess outside the market. Due in part to overproduction generated by marketing orders, the government purchased for example 8.4 per cent of all milk produced in the U.S. in 1953, 7.3 per cent in 1954, and 8.4 per cent in 1961. The tendency to overproduce was caused to some extent by the use of a "blend" price, giving producers an average of the prices for class I and class II milk. This practice obscured and distorted the marginal price in the two-price plan and gave the wrong economic signals to producers. Had farmers actually received the manufactured milk price for their added production, they would have been somewhat restrained from supplying more than the market would absorb.

AGRICULTURAL ADJUSTMENT ACT OF 1938

The Agricultural Adjustment Act of 1938 became the pattern for subsequent farm commodity programs. It contained the conservation provisions of the 1936 legislation. New features included (a) nonrecourse loans for producers of corn, wheat, and cotton under specified supply and price conditions if marketing quotas were approved in referendum, (b) crop insurance for wheat, and (c) payments, if funds were available, to producers of corn, cotton, rice, tobacco, and wheat in amounts which would provide a return as nearly equal to parity as the available funds could permit.

The Secretary of Agriculture had discretion in establishing the nonrecourse loan rate between 52 and 75 per cent of parity for wheat and cotton. A specific formula regulated loan rates on corn. The loan rate was to be 75 per cent of parity if the supply was not expected to exceed a year's domestic consumption and exports and 52 per cent of parity if supply was expected to exceed by 25 per cent a year's domestic consumption and exports. There were several gradations between these extremes. The plan was to maintain an "ever-normal granary" to provide reserve stocks for possible emergencies.

Rice and tobacco referendums failed to obtain the necessary two-thirds approval for marketing quotas for the 1939–40 marketing year. A record-breaking crop was produced. The increased supply coupled with a decline in foreign demand brought lower prices, and growers approved tobacco marketing quotas for the 1940–41 crop year. Marketing quotas were in effect for cotton, peanuts, and wheat in 1941.

Marketing quotas and acreage allotments for wheat, tobacco, and cotton reduced acreage in the years they were in effect. Wheat acreage for example was 81 million in 1937 and dropped to approximately 63 million acres from 1938 to 1944 under the influence of controls. However, yields rose to partially compensate for acreage reduction in crops. Acreage allotments reduced corn acreage, but hybrid seed contributed to a sharp rise in yields. Surpluses accumulated, and farm prices fell 20 per cent from 1938 to 1940. The government programs helped to avert a drastic drop in farm income, however.

Meanwhile efforts were made to expand demand for farm commodities. Section 202 of the 1938 legislation provided for establishment of four regional laboratories for scientific research to develop new uses and outlets for farm products. In addition to direct distribution to the needy of surplus farm commodities, a school lunch program, low-cost milk program, and a food stamp plan were initiated by the government. The food stamp plan reached 4 million people in 1941, was discontinued in 1943, and was revived later.

FEDERAL CROP INSURANCE

A federal all-risk crop insurance bill was introduced in Congress in 1922. The proposal did not become reality until 1938 when the first Federal Crop Insurance Act was passed. It was signed by President Roosevelt as Title V of the Agricultural Adjustment Act of 1938. The original intent was to make the crop insurance bureau self-supporting. This feature was later changed to the requirement that premiums need only be sufficient to pay the indemnities. Coverage was closely associated with yields, although the intent was to cover cash production cost or investment in the crop. Coverage was to be low enough to avoid deliberate neglect of crops by farmers to collect insurance.

The coverage was first extended only to wheat, but in 1939, after one year of wheat crop insurance, a bill was passed to extend the program to the 1942 cotton crop.

A number of weaknesses in the program were apparent by 1943. Over $17 million had been lost on capital appropriated to operate the wheat program, and administrative costs of $20 million on wheat alone had accrued. Only one-third of wheat farmers and one-tenth of cotton farmers were participating. It is of interest that the largest net losses had accrued in the Midwest, while net surpluses had built in the Great Plains. The program was temporarily suspended in 1943 (Myrick, 1967, p. 14).

The program was revived in 1945. The number of counties in the program was reduced from 2,400 in 1947 to 375 in 1948. The crop coverage has gradually extended to more counties and to a large number of grains, vegetables, and fruits. Through 1947, the ratio of losses to premiums was 1.48. From 1948 through 1963 the ratio was .93, hence the program was on a sounder financial basis.

In 1963, the total value of protection under crop insurance was $497 million, with premiums of $30 million and indemnities of $23 million. This half-billion dollar coverage is a small portion of total U.S. net farm income or production expenses. Thus all-risk crop insurance, though useful for many farmers, is not a large enough program to materially reduce risk in the farming industry. The program is most heavily concentrated in the Great Plains, Midwest, and Southeast. The program has reduced the risk from natural hazards such as drought, wind, and hail but does not protect farmers from market uncertainties such as unstable prices.

AGRICULTURE IN A WAR ECONOMY

The burdensome "ever-normal granary" stocks accumulated by the Commodity Credit Corporation proved a blessing in World War II. The emphasis changed from restraining production to encouraging production with high price guarantees that were to dominate farm legislation until the 1950's.

Congress passed legislation in 1941 to raise the loan rates for cotton, corn, wheat, rice, and tobacco to 85 per cent of parity on the 1941 crop. This legislation was followed by the "Steagall Amendment" later in 1941, which directed the Secretary of Agriculture also to support the prices of nonbasic commodities at 85 per cent of parity if he found it necessary to increase their production.

In the Stabilization Act of October 1942 the support rate was raised to 90 per cent of parity for corn, cotton, peanuts, rice, tobacco, and wheat, and for the Steagall nonbasic commodities. However, the rate of 85 per cent of parity could be used for any commodity if the President deemed that a lower rate was in the interest of reduced feed and livestock costs for the national defense. Section 8 of the 1942 legislation provided that the prices of basic commodities would be supported at 90 per cent of parity for two years immediately succeeding the first day of January following a presidential or congressional declaration that hostilities had ceased. Loans were to be limited to cooperators, i.e., farmers operating in accordance with acreage or marketing quotas announced by the Secretary of Agriculture and accepted by the growers. Section 9 extended the two-year postwar guarantees to the Steagall nonbasic commodities (Benedict, 1953, pp. 415, 416).

The price support on cotton was raised to 92.5 per cent of parity by a June 1944 law, and was raised to 95 per cent of parity by an October 1944 law. The Commodity Credit Corporation paid 100 per cent of parity for cotton in 1944 and 1945.

Marketing quotas were retained throughout the war on burley and flue-cured tobaccos. Marketing quotas were retained to February 1943 on wheat and to July 1943 on cotton (Rasmussen and Baker, 1966, p. 74).

THE PAINFUL TRANSITION

The provisions of the Stabilization Act were to terminate December 31, 1948. Price supports for basic commodities would then drop back to the range of 52 to 75 per cent of parity as provided by the Agricultural Adjustment Act of 1938.

However, new legislation, the Agricultural Adjustment Act of 1948, was approved. It established mandatory price supports at 90 per cent of parity for 1949 crops of wheat, corn, rice, peanuts, cotton, and tobacco if producers had not disapproved marketing quotas. Price supports at 90 per cent of parity were also provided for a substantial number of other crops and livestock, including hogs and chickens marketed before December 31, 1949.

Title II of the 1948 legislation was an amended version of the Agricultural Adjustment Act of 1938 and contained provisions for a new parity formula and sliding scale of price supports between 60 and 90 per cent of parity. The sliding scale slated to begin in 1950 never became effective because the 1948 legislation was superseded by the Agricultural Act of 1949.

If producers approved necessary quotas and allotments, basic commodities were to be supported at 90 per cent of parity for 1950 and from 80 to 90 per cent for 1951 crops under the 1949 Act. Cooperating producers were to receive price supports of 75 to 90 per cent of parity, depending on supply, for 1952 and succeeding years if producers approved marketing quotas. The price support for tobacco was to continue at 90 per cent of parity.

Price supports generally from 60 to 90 per cent of parity also were made available for wool, mohair, tung nuts, honey, Irish potatoes, whole milk, and butterfat.

Price supports were in fact maintained for basic commodities at 90 per cent of parity through 1950. Supports for nonbasic commodities were maintained at lower levels where possible under the 1949 Act. In 1950, price supports were discontinued for hogs, chickens, turkeys, long-staple cotton, dry edible peas, and sweet potatoes (Rasmussen and Baker, 1966, p. 75). Prices of chickens, turkeys, and sweet potatoes fell, but not so far that severe economic hardship resulted for producers. Any unfavorable long-term economic impact of removing price supports was obscured by the Korean War.

THE BRANNAN PLAN

A farm program was advanced by Secretary of Agriculture Charles Brannan in 1949 that was a considerable departure from past programs. A key feature of the Brannan Plan was a shift to an income standard rather than a price standard as a measure of a "fair" return to farmers. The moving base period for income would initially be 1939–48, with the earliest year to be dropped and a new one added each year. The price support standard would be the level of prices for individual commodities necessary to raise farm income to that in the base period. The same relationship would be maintained among prices as in the base period. A second feature was that prices of perishable commodities would not be supported in the market. All commodities would be sold at prices that would clear the market, and the difference between the market price and the support price would be made up by compensatory (direct grant) payments to farmers. A third important feature was that supports would be limited to 1,800 units where a unit was defined as ten bushels of corn, eight bushels of wheat or fifty pounds of cotton. It was estimated this would exclude 2 per cent of the farms from full coverage. The program was strongly opposed by all major farm organizations except the National Farmers Union on grounds that it discarded the "comfortable" price parity tradition, that it would entail great government expense, that it would obtain farm income through the Treasury rather than through the market, that it would be too difficult to administer, and that if Treasury costs were to be held down then production and marketing would have to be stringently curtailed to raise market prices to proposed levels. The Brannan Plan received little support from the Republican controlled Congress and was not enacted.

Secretary Brannan maintained price supports on basic commodities at 90 per cent of parity to 1952. The Korean War strengthened demand for farm products, and led to continued efforts to maintain fixed supports at high levels, and to postpone flexible supports. Legislation in 1952 stipulated that price support loans for basic crops be at 90 per cent of parity or higher through April 1953 unless producers disapproved marketing quotas. Mandatory supports at 90 per cent of parity were extended to 1953 and 1954 crops by legislation approved in July of 1952.

Toward Lower Prices and Higher Surpluses

Secretary of Agriculture Ezra Taft Benson continued the high price supports and marketing quotas to 1954, although quotas were not imposed on corn. Surpluses began to mount after the end of the Korean War in 1953. The Agricultural Trade Development and Assistance Act, Public Law 480, was approved in 1954. This Food for Peace Act provided substantial financial assistance for farm exports and was of major importance in providing for disposal of farm surpluses in foreign countries.

The Agricultural Act of 1954 established flexible supports for basic commodities. Supports were to range from 82.5 per cent of parity to 90 per cent in 1955, and from 75 to 90 per cent thereafter, except for tobacco, which was to be supported at 90 per cent of parity.

The Agricultural Act of 1956 established the Soil Bank, the first large scale effort since the 1930's to bring production in line with the utilization. Under one provision, the Acreage Reserve, farmers were paid to reduce below allotment levels the plantings of allotment crops—wheat, cotton, corn, tobacco, peanuts, and rice. Under a second feature of the 1956 Act, the Conservation Reserve, farmers were paid to divert all or part of their cropland to soil-conserving uses under long-term contracts. The Conservation Reserve was a general cropland retirement program and was not directed at specific crops.

The Agricultural Act of 1958 made price supports for most feed grains mandatory. Changes were made in the cotton and corn programs. Farmers producing corn were given the option in a referendum of either (*a*) terminating allotments for the 1959 and subsequent crops and receiving supports at 90 per cent of the average price of the preceding three years, or (*b*) keeping acreage allotments and receiving supports at 75 to 90 per cent of parity. They chose the former alternative in a 1958 referendum.

Two basic approaches to commercial farm policy are workable: one is to adequately control production and support prices, the other is to leave production uncontrolled and let prices fall to levels that will clear the market. A Democratic Congress and Republican Secretary of Agriculture Benson concocted an unworkable combination: price supports with ineffective controls at an inopportune time when the technological revolution had struck agriculture full force. The result was unconscionable levels of stocks. The carry-over of wheat in July 1960 was 1.4 billion bushels; of corn in October 1961 it was 2.0 billion bushels. A major shift in policies was clearly needed.

COMMODITY PROGRAMS SINCE 1960

Soon after John Kennedy was inaugurated President in 1961, Secretary of Agriculture Orville Freeman was directed to expand the distribution of food to needy persons. Other measures taken to increase utilization of food included initiation of a food stamp plan, and expansion of the school lunch and Food for Peace programs.

The emergency Feed Grain Act was approved in March 1961. It was designed to divert corn and sorghum acreage to soil-conserving uses. Producers were eligible for price supports at 74 per cent of parity if in 1961 they diverted to soil-conserving uses 20 per cent of the average acreage they had devoted to corn and sorghum in 1959 and 1960. The national average support rate for corn was $1.20 per bushel and for grain sorghum $1.93 per hundredweight. Payments for reducing the minimum acreage were equal to 50 per cent of the support price times the normal yield of the farm. Additional reductions of 20 to 40 per cent of the base were paid at 60 per cent of the county support rate. The program was voluntary, but the payments were so generous that farmers were strongly induced to enter the programs. The government released Commodity Credit Corporation stocks to hold prices below loan levels and discourage farmers from staying out of the program. The program was expensive to the government, but it did restrain production and reduce the burdensome carry-over. It was also popular with farmers. For these reasons it remained the basic form of feed grain program for the remainder of the 1960's.

THE FIGHT FOR MANDATORY CONTROLS

Willard Cochrane of the University of Minnesota was chosen to be Secretary of Agriculture Orville Freeman's chief economic adviser. Cochrane had argued forcefully and persuasively that burgeoning agriculture production induced by the technological revolution would bring huge commodity surpluses and chronically low farm prices and would ultimately destroy the family farm (cf. Cochrane, 1958). The only feasible solution according to Cochrane was mandatory supply management.

President Kennedy, Secretary Freeman, and Congressional leaders of the agricultural committees agreed with this approach and proceeded to sell it to Congress. The Administration sent to Congress in late 1961 an omnibus farm program called the Cochrane Bill. One provision of the Cochrane Bill was that Congress would establish the broad guidelines for programs, but the decisions regarding allotment levels and price supports would be made by the Secretary of Agriculture. Congress could, however, veto a commodity program sixty days after it was submitted, but the delay likely would mean no program for that commodity for the coming year. The Cochrane Bill would also have strengthened the Department of Agriculture-affiliated Agriculture Stabilization and Conservation Service committee system which administered programs at the local level. Under the new plan the Service was to be given a strong voice in formation of policies.

The procedural aspects of the Cochrane Bill were designed to pave the way for mandatory supply-management programs. Although this satisfied many liberal spokesmen who felt, like Cochrane, that it was the only feasible way to get income protection to farmers, the 1961 procedural bill did not pass Congress. And the supply-management programs themselves had not yet been submitted (Hadwiger and Talbot, 1965, pp. 46–71).

The original version of the Food and Agriculture Act of 1962 was introduced into Congress in early 1962. The bill was designed to establish a comprehensive but flexible system of supply control for the major farm commodities, including feed grains and dairy products. The Secretary of Agriculture would establish allotment and quota levels. Producers of a particular commodity would vote in national referendum whether or not to approve the quotas and price supports. If no more than one-third disapproved, the quotas would become mandatory, and producers who violated the provisions would be penalized. The Administration saw the Cochrane mandatory program as the only alternative. It would at one and the same time maintain farm income, stop the growth of stocks, and hold down government cost. President Kennedy, who was strongly urban-oriented, felt pressure to cut the farm budget and release funds for other uses.

The bill was under the very able leadership of Congressman Harold Cooley,

Chairman of the House Agricultural Committee, and Senator Allen Ellender, Chairman of the Senate Agricultural Committee. It was supported by strong pressures from President Kennedy and Secretary Freeman, the National Farmers Union, and other farm organizations with the notable exception of the Farm Bureau. The bill was passed in the Senate 42 to 38 but was defeated in the House 205 to 215. A shift of six votes would have brought an extensive program of supply management. The vote was principally along party lines, although a sufficient number of Democrats defected to defeat the bill. The Farm Bureau and cattlemen's organizations effectively lobbied to defeat the bill. They were motivated not only by their ideological position but also by public opinion polls and wheat referendum votes, which showed that farmers were increasingly unwilling to accept mandatory programs.

Following the congressional defeat, the Administration was not yet ready to settle for expensive voluntary programs and pressed for amendments that would make the mandatory program acceptable. The interesting result was that the Republicans pressed for continuation of the costly 1961 feed grain program, which they had opposed in 1961. The Administration opposed its continuation, though they had pressed for its enactment in 1961. The 1962 act, when finally enacted in amended form by Congress, contained an extension of the 1961 feed grain program but made provision to submit to wheat growers in 1963 the opportunity to accept in referendum essentially the mandatory wheat program that was included in the original Food and Agriculture Act of 1962, which had earlier been defeated in Congress.

THE 1963 WHEAT REFERENDUM

Wheat-growers prior to 1963 had approved quotas annually in a national referendum. But surpluses accumulated because the minimum national acreage allotment, established by law, produced more wheat than could be utilized. The 1962 act continued the mandatory 55 million acre allotment and referendum features. In addition, growers were paid to divert some of their allotment to soil-conserving uses. The law stipulated that in 1964 the 55 million acre minimum national allotment would be abolished, and the Secretary of Agriculture could set allotments as low as necessary to keep production in line with utilization. Farmers were to choose in referendum between two alternatives. One provided for the payment of penalties by farmers who overplanted acreage allotments, and provided for issuance of marketing certificates based on the quantity of wheat to be used for domestic human consumption and a portion to be used for exports. The amount of wheat on which farmers received certificates would be supported between 65 and 90 per cent of parity, the remaining portion would be priced at its value for feed. The 15-acre exemption from wheat controls that had been in effect was to be eliminated. The second alternative provided that the wheat of growers complying with allotments would be supported at 50 per cent of parity, about $1.25 per bushel. There would be no penalty for overplanting, but noncomplying growers would not be eligible for price supports. The first alternative was defeated in a national referendum held in May 1963.

The Administration and the Farm Bureau, which had highly conflicting views on farm policy, chose the 1963 wheat referendum as the battleground for the farmer to decide which direction to take. The Farm Bureau mounted an extensive campaign to defeat mandatory controls. The economic implications of the two alternatives proposed were clear: wheat would be priced at approximately $2.00 per bushel with the supply control "yes" alternative; at $1.10 to $1.25 per bushel with the "no" alternative. The second alternative would mean economic disaster for farmers who had to pay for land they had bought with the expectation of higher wheat prices. But economic issues were not all-important. The Farm Bureau said the issue was "freedom to farm" and "who would control agriculture, the bureaucrats or the farmers." Max Cooper interpreted the Farm Bureau information to mean "that a 'yes' vote [for mandatory controls] is a vote for slavery, bureaucrats and big government. . . . If he [the farmer] votes 'yes' he'll start the whole country down the road to slavery. . . . One little 'yes' vote too many could throw the constitution out the window, overthrow the Supreme Court and make Congress useless" (Hadwiger and Talbot, 1965, pp. 300, 301). This was an exaggerated but colorful appraisal of the tenor of the campaign.

The advocates of the mandatory program—the Democratic Administration, the Agricultural Stabilization and Conservation Service, the National Farmers Union, and other groups—also mounted a strong, if less well-organized, campaign. Max Cooper summarized their views thus: "that a 'no' vote is a vote for depression, disaster and big farmers. . . . If he [the farmer] votes 'no' he'll put us on a toboggan slide to a horrible depression. . . . And if we ever get into another depression, a dictator will take over, they warn" (Hadwiger and Talbot, 1955, pp. 300, 301). Over a million farmers and their wives voted, five times the number who had participated in the referendum of the previous year. Only 48 per cent voted for the mandatory program. It was a stunning defeat for the Administration. The Farm Bureau had successfully captured the resentment that farmers had built up in past years toward the faulty administration of wheat programs. This resentment was apparent in the 1964 survey of 500 wheat producers, which has been cited in Chapter 1.

The "no" alternative would indeed mean economic disaster to a great many farmers. The Farm Bureau had argued throughout the campaign that farmers would get a better program than the "no" alternative if they turned down the Administration proposal. The campaigners for the Administration program urged just as strongly that farmers would in fact be stuck with the "no" alternative if they voted for it.

The Farm Bureau did not have sufficient influence to get a better program after the referendum. Ironically, Democrats in Congress and the Administration realized that they could not live with the "no" alternative. They put forth a new program in 1964, which I will describe later, that was remarkably similar to the one wheat farmers had rejected. The new program was voluntary, however. The Farm Bureau, which had been so effective in defeating the program in referendum, could not stop the new program in Congress despite vigorous efforts.

Farmers had made a momentous decision, reversing the trend toward mandatory programs. Advocates of mandatory programs had argued that the public would not stand the high cost of voluntary programs needed to maintain farm income at satisfactory levels. They were wrong—the taxpayer was more tolerant of high Treasury costs than was the farmer of tight controls.

In retrospect, the issue of mandatory controls was poorly timed. Continuation of Benson-type programs would likely have created an environment whereby the original 1962 act easily would have passed the more heavily Democratic Congress of 1965. High Treasury costs of farm commodity programs continue to burden the federal budget. With declining voting power of farmers, a future administration may see fit to present with sincerity to farmers the alternatives of voluntary controls with a low farm income versus mandatory controls with high farm income. Or the mandatory program could be offered to farmers under the guise of "bargaining power."

1964 LEGISLATION

The Wheat-Cotton Act of 1964 established a certificate program for wheat. It, like the alternative rejected by farmers, was a two-price plan. But unlike the rejected alternative, it was voluntary. Complying farmers received $2.00 per bushel for 45 per cent of their normal production, 70 cents of which was from purchase of certificates by processors. Another 45 per cent was supported at a price of $1.55 per bushel. The remaining portion was supported at $1.30 per bushel. In subsequent years the domestic (40–45 per cent) portion was supported at parity and the remainder at $1.25 per bushel. Processors paid 75 cents per bushel on the domestic or certificate portion.

Complying farmers were required to divert land from wheat to soil conserving uses. In addition, land diversion payments were used to reduce production below allotment levels. The program effectively reduced production and carryover. The 1964-type wheat program with modifications was used during the remainder of the 1960's.

Under the 1964 act, the Secretary of Agriculture was authorized to make subsidy payments to domestic handlers or textile mills to reduce the effective price of cotton consumed domestically to the export price level. Each farmer complying with his regular allotment was to have his cotton crop supported at

30 cents per pound. Farmers reducing acreage to a smaller domestic allotment were to receive a support price of 33.5 cents per pound (Rasmussen and Baker, 1966, p. 77).

FOOD AND AGRICULTURE ACT OF 1965

The Food and Agriculture Act approved in November 1965 extended to 1969 the wheat and feed grains programs. The 1965 act was extended to 1970 by legislation enacted in 1968.

Cotton surpluses had continued to mount under the 1964 act, which called for a new policy. The market price of cotton under the 1965 act was to be supported at no more than 90 per cent of the world price, thereby eliminating the necessity to subsidize cotton used in domestic mills and exports. Participation in the program was voluntary although the monetary incentives of the program made participation overwhelmingly attractive. A minimum acreage diversion of 12.5 per cent of effective allotment was necessary if a farmer was to be eligible for supports. Provisions were also made for participation at higher levels. The program was effective in reducing cotton production and carry-over.

The 1965 act also established a long-term, general land retirement program called the Cropland Adjustment Program. The Secretary was authorized to enter into five- to ten-year contracts to retire cropland to conservation uses. Payments were to be not more than 40 per cent of the value of probable crop production on the land, and new agreements were not to obligate more than $225 million per year.

SLIPPAGE AND PAYMENT LIMITATIONS

The following data on cropland diversion, government costs, and the distribution of payments provide an over-all view of commodity programs. Slippage, defined as the tendency of a given acreage or budget outlay to remove less output over time, is apparent from some of the data. With growing awareness of the slippage has come deeper concern among urban legislators over the equitability of programs—if programs are not efficient in removing production, they at least need not subsidize the wealthy.

Cropland diverted from production by government programs reached a peak of 65 million acres in 1962 (Table 10.1). A significant portion of this was land retired under the long-term Conservation Reserve. This land was of lower productivity than land diverted by the feed grain program. Hence the 61 million acres diverted in 1966 represented a larger amount of production avoided by control programs than in 1962.

TABLE 10.1. Cropland Diversion: Acreage Diverted under Specified Programs Annually, 1956–66

	Acreage Reserve	Con-servation Reserve	Feed Grain	Wheat	Cotton	Cropland Con-version	Cropland Adjust-ment	Total[a]
			(Millions of acres)					
1956	12.2	1.4	—	—	—	—	—	13.6
1957	21.4	6.4	—	—	—	—	—	27.8
1958	17.2	9.9	—	—	—	—	—	27.1
1959	—	22.5	—	—	—	—	—	22.5
1960	—	28.7	—	—	—	—	—	28.7
1961	—	28.5	25.2	—	—	—	—	53.7
1962	—	25.8	28.2	10.7	—	—	—	64.7
1963	—	24.3	24.5	7.2	—	0.1	—	56.1
1964	—	17.4	32.4	5.1	0.5[b]	.1	—	55.5
1965	—	14.0	34.8	7.2	1.0[b]	.4	—	57.4
1966[c]	—	13.3	32.0	8.2	4.7	.4	2.0	60.6

SOURCE: U.S. Department of Agriculture (1966a, p. 541).
[a] Total diverted including acreage devoted to substitute crops.
[b] Not required to be put to conserving uses.
[c] Represents enrolled acreage except for Conservation Reserve.

SLIPPAGE

A major concern is the tendency for farmers to offset the acreage control programs by diverting inferior acres, by conserving moisture on land "fallowed" under government acreage controls, by increasing crop acreage on uncontrolled land and by otherwise avoiding the production control features of government programs. Allotments contributed to higher yields, but it is notable the yields of nonallotment crops increased more than yields of allotment crops (Christensen and Aines, 1962, p. 19).

Table 10.2 shows that the reduction in cropland acres harvested since 1956 was considerably less than the total cropland diversion. Considering that yields of diverted acres would average perhaps 20 per cent lower than average yields on acres in production and that many diverted acres would not return to crop production if controls were eliminated, the expected production on diverted acres may be only 60 per cent of that on a comparable number of average acres already in production.

FEDERAL EXPENDITURES FOR AGRICULTURE

The agricultural budget was 8.3 per cent of the total federal budget in the 1932–39 period (Table 10.3). The absolute amount spent on farm income

TABLE 10.2. Total Cropland Harvested in the U.S. and Deviation
from 1950–54 Average[a]

	Cropland Harvested	Deviation from 1950–54 Average (346 million acres)	Cropland Removed per Diverted Acre
	(Millions of acres)		*(Acres)*
1955	340	−6	—
1956	324	−22	.79
1957	324	−22	.79
1958	324	−22	.81
1959	324	−22	.98
1960	324	−22	.77
1961	303	−43	.80
1962	295	−51	.79
1963	300	−46	.82
1964	301	−45	.81
1965	298	−48	.84
1966	295	−51	.84

SOURCE: U.S. Department of Agriculture (1966b, p. 16).
[a] Area in fifty-nine principal crops plus fruits, tree nuts, and
farm gardens.

stabilization was a total of only $2.2 billion from 1932 through 1939. Expenditures in 1959 alone and 1964 alone were more than double this amount. The apparent lower cost of farm programs in 1966 was caused by sales of Commodity Credit Corporation stocks and failure to restore that agency's losses in the Department of Agriculture budget. Unrestored losses in 1966, which did not appear in the budget, were approximately $1.5 billion. Stabilization expenditures, including this amount, were $4.3 billion in 1966 and the total agricultural budget $5.7 billion.

Total federal outlays to stabilize farm income from 1932 to 1966 were $49.8 billion (excluding unrestored Commodity Credit Corporation losses). The total agriculture budget of $2.8 billion in 1950 was a higher proportion of the federal budget than the proportion in any year of the 1960's. Since World War II, total federal expenditures for all purposes as a percentage of the gross national product showed no apparent trend. The federal budget for agriculture was 1.5 per cent of the GNP in 1940 and .6 per cent in 1966. Thus the relative cost of farm programs has declined.

PAYMENT DISTRIBUTION

In 1967 387 producers received Agricultural Stabilization and Conservation Service payments of over $100,000 each (Wilcox, 1969). This very exclusive set, call them the "400 Club," has been one reason for the disenchantment apparent in the "bad" urban press and in Congress toward commodity programs for farmers.

TABLE 10.3. Federal Expenditures for Agriculture and Total Budget, 1932–66

	Agricultural Expenditures			Federal Expenditures	
	Income Stabiliza-tion[a]	Total Budget[a]	Proportion of Federal Budget	Total Budget	Proportion of GNP
	(Billions of dollars)		%	*($ Bil.)*	%
1932–39 (Total)	2.2	4.5	8.3	54.2	9.0
1940	.7	1.5	17.0	9.1	9.1
1941	.8	1.3	9.9	13.3	10.6
1942	.6	1.5	4.4	34.0	24.4
1943	.5	.6	.8	79.4	44.7
1944	.4	1.2	1.3	95.0	47.1
1945	b	1.6	1.6	98.3	45.3
1946	b	.7	1.2	60.3	29.9
1947	−.1	1.2	3.2	38.9	17.7
1948	.1	.6	1.7	33.0	13.5
1949	.3	2.5	6.4	39.5	15.2
1950	.5	2.8	7.1	39.5	15.0
1951	.5	.7	1.5	44.0	14.2
1952	.3	1.1	1.6	65.3	19.4
1953	.3	2.9	4.0	74.1	20.7
1954	.8	2.6	3.8	67.5	18.7
1955	3.1	4.7	7.3	64.4	17.0
1956	3.2	4.9	7.4	66.2	16.2
1957	2.5	4.2	6.0	69.0	16.0
1958	2.1	3.9	5.5	71.4	16.2
1959	4.7	6.2	7.5	80.3	17.1
1960	2.9	4.3	5.6	76.5	15.5
1961	3.1	4.4	5.4	81.5	16.1
1962	3.8	5.1	5.8	87.9	16.2
1963	4.7	6.1	6.6	92.6	16.2
1964	4.8	6.2	6.3	97.7	16.0
1965	4.2	5.6	5.8	96.5	14.8
1966	2.8	4.2	3.9	107.0	15.0

SOURCES: U.S. Bureau of the Budget (1967), *Economic Report* (1967, p. 283), and unpublished worksheets, Economic Research Service, U.S. Department of Agriculture.

[a] Includes half of Food for Peace outlays.
[b] Less than $50 million.

Fifty per cent of the producers received only 9 per cent of these payments in 1967 (Table 10.4), and 50 per cent of the payments went to only 8 per cent of the producers. It appears that in 1967, such payments were only slightly less concentrated among large producers than were cash receipts from farm marketings (see Chapter 6 for the latter distribution).

TABLE 10.4. Number of Producers by Size of Agricultural Stabilization and Conservation Service Payments, 1967

Size of Payments	Producers	Portion	Total Payments	Portion
			(Millions of	
(Dollars)	*(Number)*	%	*dollars)*	%
Less than 100	388,166	15.7	16.5	.6
100–499	858,171	34.6	238.0	8.0
500–999	528,309	21.3	379.5	12.8
1,000–2,999	511,498	20.6	841.6	28.5
3,000–4,999	98,424	4.0	375.9	12.7
5,000–7,499	41,918	1.7	253.3	8.6
7,500–9,999	18,272	.7	157.4	5.3
10,000–14,999	15,341	.6	185.4	6.3
15,000–24,999	9,793	.4	185.0	6.2
25,000–49,999	4,796	.2	160.0	5.4
50,000–99,999	1,271	.1	83.7	2.8
100,000–499,999	373	[a]	61.3	2.1
500,000–999,999	14	[a]	8.8	.3
1,000,000 and over	5	[a]	10.9	.4
Total	2,476,351	100.0	2,957.3	100.0

SOURCE: Wilcox (1969, p. 4).
[a] Less than .05 per cent.

Representative Silvio Conte proposed an amendment in July 1968 to the bill extending the Agricultural Act of 1965 for one year. The amendment would have limited aggregated payments to $20,000 per year to any one recipient. The amendment was approved by the House of Representatives but a comparable amendment proposed in the Senate was defeated.

Payment limitations have been used for smaller-scale programs. There is no cutoff of payments to sugar producers, but a sliding scale of support has been used. Agricultural conservation payments to any one producer have been limited from time to time; in 1969 they were limited to $2,500. Payment limitations were included in the Soil Bank of the 1950's and the Cropland Conservation Program of the 1960's.

The principal arguments against payment limitations are that they are not enforceable and that the large farms must be included if production controls are to work. A scale-down rather than a cutoff of payments might reduce efforts to break up units (at least in name) in order to receive benefits.

A $20,000 cutoff would not seem to jeopardize production controls, except possibly in the case of cotton. The cutoff would have limited the 1967 payments of 10,000 producers (Wilcox, 1969). Of these, 8,157 were in the cotton program, 3,304 in the wheat program, and 4,878 in the feed grain program. (Some producers were in more than one program.) Farms affected by the payment limitation in 1967 grew 34 per cent of the cotton, 5 per cent of the wheat, and only 2 per cent of the feed grains. The payment limitation would have reduced payments by only $206 million. This is a small proportion of program costs. The principal benefit of such a cutoff appears to be better public relations rather than Treasury savings.

SUMMARY

Farm legislation has chronically been at a crossroads. In the 1920's the issue was direct intervention in the market versus improved credit, storage, and marketing efficiency to raise farm income. In the 1930's the issue was not whether, but to what degree, the government should be involved in supporting farm income. In the 1940's the issue was flexible versus fixed levels of price support. In the 1950's the issue was continued controls and supports or transition to a market orientation. In 1962 and 1963 one branch of the crossroads led to voluntary controls, the other to mandatory controls. The result of the directions taken in farm legislation has been a growing commitment of the federal government to support farm income. The direction has been to voluntary programs and direct payments, hence the Treasury costs are high. The Employment Act of 1946 committed the federal government to policies that would secure full national employment. The government since the 1930's has committed itself in a less formal (though effective) way to support farm income.

Some lessons are apparent from history. In the absence of effective controls, prices supported above free market equilibrium do lead to a crisis of abundant stocks. Second, history has demonstrated that production can be controlled with voluntary programs, although the Treasury cost is high. The problem becomes even more difficult as land, the focus of controls, is increasingly replaced in the production process by fertilizer and other nonfarm-produced inputs.

Third, the economic problems of agriculture are not solved by controlling the acreage or marketing of one crop. Cross compliance is necessary to keep farmers from planting grain sorghum, for example, on land removed from corn production by allotments, thus depressing the price of crops not supported by the government. Farm production capacity behaves like a balloon filled with water. Compressing one part causes the volume elsewhere to expand. The volume can only be reduced by letting water out of the balloon. Controlling only one crop without cross compliance is like pushing in one part of the balloon; removing resources from production is like letting water out. Only the latter is really effective in controlling production and raising income in the farming industry. Individual allotments without diversion of land to soil-conserving uses do little to raise the total income of farmers. Programs to improve the efficiency of markets and reduce marketing margins have been unable to cope with the more basic problem of too many resources in agriculture.

A final lesson to be learned from history is that it is very difficult to change the direction of policy. The Brannan Plan, the Cochrane Bill, and the policies of Secretary Ezra Taft Benson represented a considerable departure from previous directions and were failures. The farm commodity programs since 1933 have been remarkably similar in structure, though different in style and emphasis. This is not meant to imply that the trend in farm policy should not be changed but that a strong program of economic education must precede changes.

REFERENCES

Benedict, Murray. 1953. *Farm Policies of the United States, 1790–1950*. New York: Twentieth Century Fund.

———, and Oscar Stine. 1956. *The Agricultural Commodity Programs*. New York: Twentieth Century Fund.

Christensen, Raymond, and Ronald Aines. 1962. Economic effect of acreage control programs in the 1950's. Agriculture Economics Report No. 18. Washington, U.S. Department of Agriculture.

Cochrane, Willard W. 1958. *Farm Prices: Myth and Reality*. Minneapolis: University of Minnesota Press.

Economic Report of the President. 1967. Washington: U.S. Government Printing Office.

Hadwiger, Don, and Ross Talbot. 1965. *Pressures and Protests*. San Francisco: Chandler.

Hardin, Charles. 1946. The Bureau of Agricultural Economics under fire. *Journal of Farm Economics* 28:635–68.

Myrick, Dana. 1967. Background of the Federal Crop Insurance Program. In *Crop Insurance in the Great Plains*, Bulletin No. 617, Bozeman, Mont., Agricultural Experiment Station, pp. 6–27.

Rasmussen, Wayne, and Gladys Baker. 1966. A short history of price support and adjustment legislation and programs for agriculture. *Agricultural Economics Research* 18:68–79.

Shepherd, Geoffrey. 1964. *Farm Policy: New Directions*. Ames: Iowa State University Press.

Talbot, Ross, and Don Hadwiger. 1969. *The Policy Process in American Agriculture*. Chicago: Chandler.

U.S. Bureau of the Budget. 1967. The budget in brief. Washington, Executive Office of the President.

U.S. Department of Agriculture. 1966a. *Agricultural Statistics*. Washington: U.S. Government Printing Office.

———. 1966b. Changes in farm production and efficiency. Statistical Bulletin No. 233. Washington.

Vermeer, James. 1963. An economic appraisal of the 1961 feed grain program. Agriculture Economics Report No. 38. Washington, U.S. Department of Agriculture.

Wilcox, Walter W. 1969. Large farm program payments. Washington, Legislative Reference Service, Library of Congress.

CHAPTER ELEVEN

Commodity Programs: The Choices

This chapter is about farm commodity programs, some alternatives to programs we now have, and some "costs" and "returns" of each for farmers, taxpayers, and consumers. To discipline and systematize our thinking, a maze representing the labyrinth of program alternatives is shown in Figure 11.1. The maze provides the conceptual framework and outline for much of this chapter. It helps to clarify just what the decision is at each crossroad and illustrates the fact that a particular decision opens a vista of further decisions. Arrival at the farthest point by choosing preferred directions may not necessarily imply a realization of a best choice but may represent an unacceptable dead end. It is then necessary to backtrack to a single program or a combination of programs that are a more realistic compromise of farm policy goals and values. The following pages contain a discussion of the decisions that must be made at each crossroad in Figure 11.1, stressing some of the pros and cons of following a particular path. The chapter concludes with a suggested program and with numerous recommendations for commercial agriculture made by the National Advisory Commission on Food and Fiber.

INVESTMENT IN TECHNOLOGY (DECISION A)

In broad perspective, farm commodity programs are one result of a gigantic public program of investment in education and research. The public decision to invest in measures to increase farm resource productivity is not for us to initiate—only to review and perhaps to renew. One of the first decisions to encourage farm productivity was through public investment in elementary education. Public support for increased productivity in farming gained momentum through several pieces of legislation: the Morrill Act, which established land grant colleges; the Hatch Act, which established the state experiment stations; and the Smith-Hughes and Smith-Lever Acts, which broadened education in applied agriculture. The evidence compiled in Chapter 5 backs

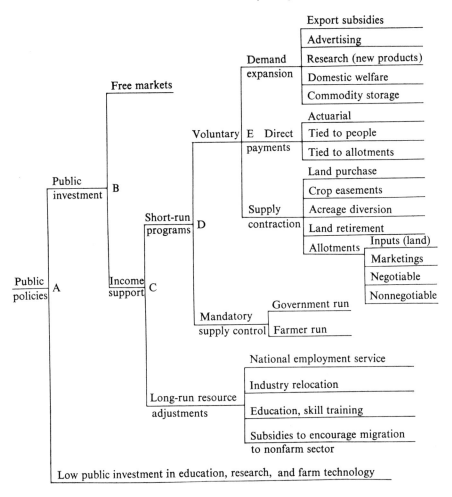

FIGURE 11.1. Maze, showing selected public policies for commercial agriculture.

the conclusion that the decision to encourage technological change and capital accumulation in agriculture was wise. Our standard of living would be lower without gains in farm productivity because the inputs (primarily labor) no longer needed for farming have helped supply the cars, home appliances, food processing, etc., that we now enjoy.

Today's tide of technology cannot be stopped because (*a*) society wants it to continue, (*b*) private industry would provide a steady flow of new, improved inputs even if the public sector stopped its contribution, and (*c*) the economic structure of farming would not permit any braking of technological change. The fact that early adopters find new technology profitable and late adopters find it essential to maintain income ensures that improved farming techniques will be used. Although farmers as well as nonfarmers have favored public investment in increased technology, farmers have gotten the short end of the deal. It is likely that farmers suffered only in a relative sense, however, as farm income declined in relation to nonfarm income. Farmers benefited in an absolute sense, and their standard of living is higher than it would have been without farm productivity gains.

The public policy of investing in more agricultural productivity while at the same time restricting farm production appears inconsistent. However, if the decision is between (*a*) investment in technology and income support versus (*b*) no public investment in technology and free markets, the former alternative has proved more profitable. The gains from farm productivity since 1910, largely attributed to public and private investment in education and research, were estimated to be $75 billion in 1965 alone and outweigh the public investment in both creating and controlling productivity (see Chapter 5).

FREE MARKETS OR INCOME SUPPORT FOR AGRICULTURE (DECISION B)

While commodity programs undoubtedly are one result of public measures to expand farm productivity, it does not necessarily follow that society must support farm income with federal programs during an adjustment period. The decision then is at B in Figure 11.1: free markets or farm supports? The decision in favor of federal support of farm income or free markets depends on at least three considerations: (*a*) the magnitude of the overcapacity in agriculture, (*b*) the net "cost" to agriculture of adjusting to this overcapacity, and (*c*) the net "cost" to society of maintaining excess resources in agriculture.

OVERCAPACITY

Excess capacity in agriculture, measured as probable production in excess of market utilization at socially acceptable prices, was 5–10 per cent of farm output in the 1955–66 period (Chapter 6). Termination of production controls and other government programs during this period would have released excess capacity on the market and confronted farmers with serious economic problems.

Numerous studies clearly establish that farm prices, farm receipts, and net farm income would have been lower in the 1955–66 period in the absence of government support programs.[1] In summary, these studies show that prices received by farmers would have been 10–20 per cent lower in recent years without support programs. Gross receipts would have been 5–15 per cent lower and

1. These studies include Brandow (1960, 1961), Heady and Tweeten (1963, Chapter 16), Herendeen (1965), Legislative Reference Service (1965), Robinson (1960), Shepherd *et al.* (1960), Tweeten *et al.* (1963), Tyner and Tweeten (1964), and U.S. Department of Agriculture (1960).

net farm income 20–50 per cent lower. There is a surprising degree of agreement among the studies, despite the fact that many were performed independently by economists with a considerable range of approaches. This consistency lends credence to the results.

The implications of a free market can be judged from the data on excess capacity presented in Chapter 6. Based on the intermediate-run price elasticity of demand of $-.5$, if costs remain unchanged, each 1 per cent increase in farm output released on the market depresses prices 2 per cent, gross receipts 1 per cent, and net farm income approximately 3 per cent. If excess capacity of 7 per cent is placed on the market, prices would be expected to fall 14 per cent, gross receipts 7 per cent, and net receipts 21 per cent. Government payments to farmers totaled \$3.3 billion in 1966 or 20 per cent of the net farm income of \$16.3 billion. Including this figure in the effect on farm income following release of excess capacity on farm markets, net income would be expected to fall 40 per cent. It follows that termination of farm commodity problems in the 1955–66 period would have placed a severe hardship on the farm economy. And because commodity programs benefit commercial farmers primarily, these farmers would have incurred the greatest losses.

LONG-RUN IMPACT OF FREE MARKETS

What the above analyses fail to establish is the long-run market and price situation under free markets. Price supports do not raise the long-run income of farmers for three reasons: (*a*) the long-run demand for farm commodities is probably price elastic (see Chapter 7), (*b*) the income benefits of supports are capitalized into land values, and (*c*) farmers reduce the use of production inputs over time in response to falling prices.

That a downward adjustment in resource use would occur in response to lower prices is apparent from one study of farm inputs, based on a demand elasticity for farm output of $-.25$ (Heady and Tweeten, 1963, Chapter 16). In four years farm prices, gross income, and net income would recover, respectively, to 90, 93, and 88 per cent of the initial level that held before release of 5 per cent more commodities on the market. Net income to pay labor would fall farther than labor input, hence earnings per worker would be lower after this period of adjustment. A longer adjustment period, which would take account of the increasing demand elasticity and changing farm land prices, would show little net monetary gain from commodity programs.

Production controls on land have been the principal instrument used to raise farm income. A farmer can afford to pay additional interest on land equal to the monetary benefits of allotments and be just as well off as the farmer who has no allotment. As land changes hands over time, the intended income benefits of farm programs are lost through this method of capitalization. Estimates from Chapter 8 indicate that up to one-third of the land value gains from 1950 to 1963 were due to farm programs. Discounted at 10 per cent, this $30 billion represents a perpetual income stream of $3 billion per year. The latter figure may not be an unreasonable estimate of the long-term annual contribution of programs to net farm income. In the long run, the benefit goes to the past generation of landowners and is lost to the new generation of farmers. Government programs thus lose their intended income effect over time.

Then why have government support programs? There are several reasons why farm programs are beneficial even if, as argued above, they are not effective in raising farm income over the long pull. Government programs stabilize income and remove some of the risk and uncertainty that farmers are unwilling and unable to absorb. This uncertainty stems especially from variations in weather and demand, which give rise to annual market instability.

Government programs contribute in some ways to efficiency and for several years cushion the effect of a sizable shift in demand or supply. From 1950 to 1965, productivity of agriculture increased approximately 30 per cent. The increased productivity meant that demands for food and fiber could be met with fewer resources, and the price mechanism signaled this through product price reductions. Farm programs bought time for farmers to make necessary adjustments and find jobs elsewhere. Programs reduced acute economic pressures for immediate labor outmovement but appeared not to have reduced total outmovement of labor in a more long-term perspective. The farm population and labor force were cut nearly in half between 1950 and 1966! Tyner's (1967) simulation study of the farm economy indicates that there would have been slightly more workers in agriculture between 1933 and 1961 in the absence of the government programs in actual operation during that period. In many instances, price supports gave farmers the security they needed to increase efficiency through specialization and large-scale production and through purchase of highly productive new capital inputs. The forward pricing that attended commodity programs removed some of the uncertainties that frustrate farmers and create an unstable food supply. The security and income from programs provided capital which substituted for farm labor (Tyner, 1967). And higher land values stimulated by government programs constituted a barrier to entry into farming, thus reducing the number of farmers.

A final reason for government programs is insurance for national emergencies. Excess production capacity in agriculture and excess Commodity Credit Corporation commodity stocks have been highly valuable emergency stockpiles in time of war and drought in the past—and may be again in the future—but the economic structure of agriculture places a heavy burden on farmers if they are to carry the strategic reserve in the form of excess production capacity with no government assistance.

If reserve capacity is 7 per cent greater than market utilization at current prices, then, based on a 2 per cent annual increase in utilization, this reserve capacity is enough to provide food needs at stable prices if agricultural resources and productivity remains static for about three years. In other terms, the reserve capacity is sufficient to provide annual food needs at current prices without depleting stocks despite a 7 per cent drop in production due to drought. Current technology may preclude such a drastic drop in production except over a weather cycle of several years, but in 1934 and 1936 production fell 14 and 10 per cent respectively below that of the previous year. It seems, however, that the federal cost of farm programs, $4 billion per year, is an unduly high cost of maintaining strategic reserves.

While it would be desirable precisely to match food needs and farm production at prices acceptable to farmers and consumers, this precision is difficult to achieve. First, society cannot accurately judge how much investment in education and research is needed to get the proper advance in production. Secondly, even if the rate could be predicted, society likely would want a faster increase in production than farmers could gracefully absorb. The highly profitable and productive new inputs such as hybrid seeds and pesticides are introduced at a rapid rate despite falling farm commodity prices. Conventional farm labor and land resources, which must move out to maintain per unit income, respond sluggishly to falling returns. The result is depressed farm income over an adjustment period.

The Social "Cost" of Farm Commodity Programs

Under very restrictive assumptions, it can be shown that a perfectly competitive economy operating without production controls or income supports maximizes the social product or public good (see Chapter 16). Some of the underlying assumptions are that the initial distribution of assets is satisfactory, that resources are mobile, that knowledge of alternatives is complete, and that competition is atomistic (many buyers and sellers so no one has a perceptible influence on the national price). Many argue that the initial asset distribution is not satisfactory in agriculture. Many farmers have too few resources to earn an acceptable income even with favorable prices. Also because many farmers lack necessary skills and knowledge of alternative opportunities, or are excluded from nonfarm jobs because of national unemployment, the assumption of resource mobility is strongly violated. Because these and other assumptions do not hold, free markets for agriculture do *not* necessarily maximize the total good, especially in the short run.

A TRANSITION PROGRAM

Since farm programs are short-run expedients that do not raise farm net earnings over the long run, there is little point in permanently holding farm prices above the free market equilibrium level. The effect is only to create higher land prices. Transition programs have been proposed to help farmers bridge the gap between current price levels and those under a free market. The Committee for Economic Development (1962) proposed that direct payments be tied to farm people. These payments would continue whether the people stayed on the farm or moved to the nonfarm sector so that labor adjustment would not be discouraged. Payments would be scaled down each year and would terminate in five years, after which farm labor would presumably be adequately adjusted. The farm economy would be a free market.

For the early 1960's, the period for which the plan was proposed, there were approximately 14 million farm people and 7 million farm workers. The analysis in Chapter 6 showed that approximately half of this labor was redundant. With a target date of five years for adjustment, net farm employment would need to fall by 3.5 million workers. Each year approximately 700,000 would need to find employment elsewhere to close the current gap, 100,000 to close the emerging gap as new technologies were introduced and an additional 100,000 to keep down the number of farm workers due to the natural population increase. Thus a total of 900,000 farm workers would have had to find employment in the nonfarm sector each year. With less than 1.5 million new nonfarm jobs created annually in the early 1960's, this would have left few jobs for new nonfarm workers seeking employment. The example is somewhat overdrawn but is included to illustrate that a satisfactory transition to a free market for agriculture cannot be accomplished in five years. Also, the transition program does not cope with the farm price and income instability problem that would emerge.

A solution to problems of low returns in agriculture awaits the outmovement of enough farm families so that a large proportion of all farm firms are producing in the flat portion of the unit cost curve (see Chapter 6). An effort to make the adjustment rapidly would place many farm people in cities where they would be unprepared to compete in the job market and would cause social problems that attend unemployment and low income. Farm commodity programs do not slow the outflow, but they do make it more orderly.

LONG-RUN VERSUS SHORT-RUN PROGRAMS (DECISION C)

Two general approaches can be used to raise farm income above free market levels: (*a*) speed farm resource adjustments or (*b*) support income through commodity programs. Education of farmers (particularly youth) in nonfarm employment skills, provision of outlook information on job availability through a national employment service, subsidies to encourage migration, and measures to locate industry in depressed rural areas can be used to improve farm labor mobility. These measures to move labor to employment with greater productivity are consistent with economic efficiency. Many years will be required to solve farm income problems with these long-run measures. Many contend that short-run commodity programs for agriculture are necessary to supplement the essential long-term programs.

VOLUNTARY VERSUS MANDATORY COMMODITY PROGRAMS (DECISION D)

The term "mandatory controls" can refer to programs including supply management, marketing quotas, acreage allotments, and production controls. The common element is that the producer is penalized by extramarketal arrangements if he does not comply with controls. Yet the term "mandatory" perhaps unduly overemphasizes the restrictions on freedom. In the past, controls have become binding on all producers only if approved by a substantial majority, usually two-thirds of all producers, in referendum. Even then, the penalties for producers who have not conformed to regulations approved by the majority have not been severe. There have been so many loopholes that mandatory programs have been less than effective. Imposing of quotas on sales rather than on acreage would be the first step toward improving the effectiveness of supply control.

Increments in total net farm income can come from (*a*) reduced marketing margins, (*b*) increased efficiency in farming, (*c*) larger consumer outlays, or (*d*) larger Treasury outlays. Alternative (*a*) is not feasible because marketing firms pass increased raw material costs to consumers. Alternative (*b*) is not feasible because a concerted attempt by farmers to raise income through greater efficiency raises output and *depresses* commodity prices and aggregate farm income. Thus, for all practical purposes, increments in farm receipts above free market levels must come either from consumers or the U.S. Treasury. Farm income can be raised above free market levels either by voluntary or mandatory programs. Mandatory controls tend to increase farm income through the market; voluntary controls emphasize the role of the Treasury.

GOVERNMENT MANDATORY PROGRAMS

Using mandatory controls, farm income can be increased at low Treasury cost. This is a very desirable feature based on the public outcry against heavy government spending on farm programs. Disadvantages of mandatory controls are (a) a regressive "tax" on consumers, (b) high administrative costs, (c) restrictions on the freedom of farmers to market and produce, and (d) the freezing of production patterns that are inefficient. Mandatory control programs tax the public regressively; increasing food expenditures "tax" low-income consumers who spend a high percentage of their earnings for food. Voluntary programs compensate farmers from the Treasury, which is replenished by progressive income taxes. Hence, a shift from voluntary to mandatory programs shifts the "tax" burden to persons with relatively lower ability to pay. But we must remember the basic accounting identity suggested above. Whether from consumers or taxpayers, whether a voluntary or mandatory program, the total dollars required to raise farm income a given amount remain unchanged.

Allotments have been made negotiable to a limited extent for cotton and tobacco. While allowing sale and transfer among farms of allotments helps to circumvent the criticism that mandatory programs freeze production in inefficient patterns, it does not avoid the criticism that the value of allotments is capitalized into the control instrument. The benefits of allotments go to former allotment holders and are largely lost to the new generation of farmers.

FARMER BARGAINING POWER

Bargaining refers generally to negotiated outcomes between two or more parties. The party on the one hand here is made up of farmers (or their chosen representatives) and on the other hand of processors, distributors, food chains, or the government. Farmers generally think of higher prices and incomes as the focus of negotiations, but the bargaining is likely to be over issues of volume, grade, and time and place of delivery as well. *Bargaining power* may be defined as the ability of a party to influence the outcome of negotiations to its own advantage.

Farmers have observed the wage gains of labor through collective bargaining and the orderly markets achieved by nonfarm industry through internal supply control. Farmers have concluded that through market power and collective bargaining they too can achieve similar advantages.

There is no doubt that more bargaining power is coming to the farm. The question is how much will be provided and when and who will provide it: the National Farm Organization, the Farm Bureau, the AFL-CIO, the U.S. Department of Agriculture, Safeway, General Mills, or perhaps General Motors? There are several directions that farming could go in the future. One direction might be corporate farming, with equity capital provided by General Motors, say, and Du Pont. In this case, the bulk of "farmers" will be hired laborers and the AFL-CIO might provide the organization to bring bargaining power to farmers. Another direction might be vertical integration, with equity capital provided, for instance, by Safeway, Purina, General Foods, and Armour. Another direction would be to maintain the family farm structure but for farmers to become renters of land owned by nonfarmers. In this case the current farm organizations would likely be the bargaining nucleus for farmers. And a combination of the above is possible, with hired workers organized by labor unions to bargain with farmers represented by the farm organizations. Simultaneously farm organizations might, in the vertically integrated broiler industry, be bargaining with Purina, and Purina in turn bargaining with the retail food chains over broiler prices. There is likely to be no single bargaining agent for agriculture, and the growing strength of one agent is likely to lead to growing strength of opposing agents through the principle of countervailing power.

One can foresee a situation of bargaining between feed producers and beef and pork producers, between hired workers and farm operators, between farmers and processors. A corn group might battle a grain sorghum group for the feed grain market. Midwest soybean producers might battle Southern soybean producers for the soybean market. It is apparent that this could be a discordant, if not chaotic, situation. Who become the bargaining agents for agriculture is a moot question, and the answer seems to be "the fewer the better."

Issues of bargaining have been treated extensively in other chapters, especially Chapter 3, where the repeated attempts of farmers to achieve bargaining power were documented. Repeated failures have not killed interest in bargaining. Specialization, large-scale operations, fewer farmers, fear by farmers that the increasingly urban-based Congress will by-pass them, and increased sophistication in economic matters hasten the coming of self-help success in the market. Furthermore, commercial farmers seem increasingly disenchanted with government programs, partly because of political uncertainty and partly because major monetary advantages have already been lost through capitalization of benefits into land. Farmers experience feeling of anomie—alienation and lack of confidence in their environment—as they view themselves as individually helpless in the hands of big government, big business, big labor, and "big" nature. The way to overcome anomie is to increase economic understanding and personal involvement in economic decisions. Although self-help bargaining suffers from the same economic limitations as government programs, the best case for it seems to rest on the sociological grounds of overcoming anomie.

Three questions will be answered below: What conditions are necessary to gain an advantage in the market? How should farmers go about strengthening their bargaining position? What will farmers gain from greater bargaining power?

Several conditions generate power in the market. In general, the larger the number and the greater the extent to which the following conditions are met, the greater will be the bargaining power of the group possessing them:

1. A homogeneous, easily identified product produced under controlled conditions.

2. A small geographic area and few producers.

3. All producers willing to accept discipline of elected or appointed leaders (no noncompliers).

4. Producers able and willing, either individually or through group action, to bear the cost of adjusting the time, volume, and grade of marketing, even up to the point of withholding supplies, cutting production, or diverting land to soil-conserving uses.

5. The condition that buyers with which producers are bargaining either are inefficient and have excess profits which can be "bargained" away, or that they face a market structure which can absorb higher prices (without reducing sales to the point where net returns are reduced).

6. The existence of an inelastic demand for the product (substitutes and foreign competition will not make the demand elastic and will erode the long-run gains).

Many of these points resolve to issues of member discipline and protection from farmers who do not comply. The image of the farmer as a rugged individualist has enough truth in it to raise serious doubts about the success of any extensive farmer-run program to withhold supplies and control production. The more successful the holding action, the greater the incentive for noncompliers to sell and reap the benefits of higher prices. After the holding action, the strikers may have to sell damaged, overripe, or overfat items on a market glutted by items produced but not marketed during the strike. The farm production process, once started, tends to run inexorably to a conclusion. And high farm overhead costs continue, even when nothing is being sold.

Many farm leaders feel that their economic gains from a successful holding action are often exceeded by the economic pains of holding actions, and that reduction of production through government programs is a wiser action than trying to hold a crop already produced away from the market. Many also recognize that without adequate police powers and built-in safeguards, farmers might turn in a much less satisfactory performance than the government in setting allotments and administering production controls.

Some are also concerned about whom farmers will bargain with. Bargaining with a few processors in a competitive processing industry is likely to be unsuccessful, because the processors can neither absorb the loss themselves nor pass the higher raw material prices on to consumers. The illusory success of farm bargaining will then be reflected directly in the demise (through bankruptcy) of the hapless firms with which the price-raising contracts are signed.

The way out of this dilemma is (*a*) to bargain with processors who have excess profits that can be bargained away—an example being the bilateral monopoly situation depicted in Chapter 6—(*b*) to pursue industry-wide bargaining with a competitive processing industry so that all processors will be equally disadvantaged and hence can pass higher costs on to consumers, or (*c*) to set more modest bargaining objectives with goals such as stable and efficient markets rather than significantly higher prices. A safe conclusion is that bargaining can be successful with modest goals.

It is useful here to distinguish degrees of market power. The two lowest degrees described below employ the "market gain" approach. This approach relies heavily on convincing a cooperating processor that he will increase profit and hence receive economic benefits by cooperation. First-degree bargaining is also a "social gain approach" because it relies on greater efficiency rather than curtailment of production as an inducement for closing a bargain. The higher degrees of market power entail increasing member discipline and production controls. These succeed by convincing the processor he will incur "market pain" if he does not agree to desired terms. Thus higher degrees of bargaining entail greater social cost (production controls) and are more difficult to organize and administer. The degrees of bargaining power are classified below according to opportunities to (*a*) gain production and marketing efficiency through contractual arrangements, (*b*) direct supplies among markets and thereby practice price discrimination, and (*c*) control production.

First-degree bargaining is defined as use by producers of potential production and marketing efficiencies to induce processors to sign contracts. This was the approach used by the American Agricultural Marketing Association in the 1960's. There were no production controls nor attempts to significantly raise prices above equilibrium levels.

Opportunities for such agreements between farmers and processors arise because of imperfections in the price system. That is, the "free" price system, because of time lags, lack of genuinely negotiated prices, inadequate opportunities for price discovery, or for other reasons, does not adequately regulate the volume, grade and timing of the commodity desired by the processor. In a contract negotiated between processor and producers, the producer agrees to supply the volume and grade at the time specified by the processor. The processor in turn guarantees a market for that volume at a price specified in advance. The price is little (if at all) above the free market level, but the forward pricing and guaranteed volume reduce some of the uncertainty and may raise profits for the contracting parties.

Second-degree bargaining is defined as securing income advantages to producers through price discrimination. No production controls or efficiency gains are required, but processors must agree to pass some of the economic gains on to farmers. This is because the price discrimination is often practiced on consumers—and supplies are often allocated to markets—by processors rather than by producers at the farm gate. Many farm commodities cannot benefit from price discrimination because of inadequate administrative machinery, an inability to separate markets, or small differences in demand elasticities among markets. Price discrimination has been used extensively by milk producers using the federal administrative machinery provided by milk marketing orders. Milk producers reap some economic gains through the high administered price in the inelastic fresh fluid milk market. Excess production can be disposed in manufactured milk markets at a lower price. The advantages to processors are adequate supplies and an orderly market—their competitors will have to pay the same price for the raw product—and processors are more certain to obtain adequate supplies.

Bargaining above the second degree entails various types of control over supplies. Third-degree bargaining may be defined as efforts to gain greater income for producers by withholding supplies from the market. There are no production controls. Unlike industrial labor bargained by unions, farm commodities tend to deteriorate or accumulate during the time supplies are withheld. This does little to enhance the farmers' bargaining power. Third-degree bargaining, as practiced extensively by the National Farmers Organization, has had almost no success.

Fourth-degree bargaining power seeks economic gains to producers through production controls administered by an organization of producers. Marketing quotas announced before the start of production can accomplish the same purpose. Such bargaining seeks to raise prices by reducing output of the commodity. The success of these efforts depends heavily on the discipline of members, protection from nonmembers, and an inelastic demand. While more difficult to manage than first- or second-degree bargaining, fourth-degree bargaining offers the only real opportunities for income gains among commodity groups that cannot develop greater marketing efficiency or market discrimination. The price objectives may be modest. A wise policy for many commodity groups is to merely use production controls to stabilize marketing from year to year and not to cut supplies and thereby raise prices appreciably above the long-run, average, free market level.

The volume of farm resources is not reduced in fourth-degree bargaining, and resources diverted from producing the controlled commodity are used to produce other commodities. The gains to the in-group producing the commodity come partly at the expense of producers of that commodity who are denied access to the market, and partly at the expense of producers of other commodities who find their market oversupplied by production from farm resources diverted from the controlled commodity. To be successful and of much benefit to the total farm economy, this and other types of bargaining should be accompanied by government programs to reduce excess production capacity through, for example, long-term land retirement. In fact, successful bargaining in some ways may only compound farm problems. The in-group of successful bargainers is benefited, but the burden of excess production capacity becomes focused even more heavily on the farmer outside the bargaining groups.

In fifth-degree bargaining, producers seek economic gains from processors and consumers through diversion of farm resources from production. Under this form of bargaining, producers might agree to leave some of their resources idle. This is a little like across-the-board withholding, since the production controls do not focus on any one commodity. The approach is appealing, because it is the only one that reduces the "water in the balloon," and does not just squeeze water from one end to another. No serious attempt has been made by the farm groups to employ fifth-degree bargaining nor are such attempts likely for some time. Farmer bargaining groups might well focus on lesser degrees of bargaining and rely on government to take some of the water out of the balloon with long-term land retirement programs.

Farmers recognize that their bargaining leeway is limited not only by the discipline they can muster among their own members but also by such unpredictable factors, on the one hand, as "girlcotts" by housewives who refuse to pay high food prices, by substitute commodities, by imports, and by threats of antitrust legislation and, on the other hand, by input suppliers and rising land values that absorb the gains. Furthermore, success in farmer bargaining is likely to speed vertical integration by the food industry into farming, with processors and food chains owning and operating their own farm production facilities.

Some government legislation is required to make virtually any type of bargaining feasible for farmers. For even first degree bargaining, some exemptions from the Clayton and Sherman Antitrust Acts are necessary. The next line of legislation required for almost any degree of bargaining is protection of participating producers from boycott, intimidation, and discrimination by processors.

Marketing order legislation, setting the terms and conditions for second-degree bargaining, has already been established in the Agricultural Marketing Act of 1937 and subsequent legislation. In addition, a combination of third- and fifth-degree bargaining could be encouraged where marketing orders now exist by allowing minimum prices to become effective if approved by (say) 60 per cent of producers and the U.S. Department of Agriculture. Concurrently, the Department of Agriculture or a producer group might be enabled to establish the production base for the commodity among producers, perhaps using past history. Police power would be granted so that producers who violated the agreement would be subject to fines or other penalties.

A third line of enabling legislation would allow producers of a particular commodity to elect a committee to represent them in negotiations with processors. The committee would negotiate market-wide price and nonprice terms of sale with a committee representing buyers and consumers. If an agreement were reached, the terms would be submitted to producers for approval in a commodity-wide referendum. If no agreement could be reached by bargaining groups, the President could appoint a compulsory arbitration board whose decision would be binding on all parties.

The producers' bargaining committee could establish a system of production and marketing controls. A national agricultural board appointed by the President and supported by federal funds or a tax on the commodity might be necessary to conduct referendums and administer controls. A gradual extension of such a system to many farm commodities might lead to fifth-degree bargaining. It would be somewhat like the current government programs, but with major decisions made by farmer bargaining agents.

It is instructive to examine some "successful" efforts at bargaining by farmers. Two organizations in the West, the California Cling Peach Association and the California Canning Pear Association, have had some success because (a) the two crops involved were highly specialized and local in nature, (b) the marketing channels from grower to processing plant were simple and direct, (c) all buyers (processors) were engaged in performing similar marketing functions and hence shared similar interests, and finally (d) grower-owned processors (cooperatives) provided a useful yardstick for negotiations with private processors. Outside the fruit and vegetable industry, the success story in bargaining in the 1960's appeared to be in dairy products. Large organizations of producers, building on the system of milk marketing orders, gained considerable bargaining power. The above examples are instructive in that the most successful operations entailed only the lower degrees of bargaining and resulted in only modest price gains to farmers. The principal gains were more orderly markets and greater dignity of farmer members.

Considerable progress has been made in extending bargaining arrangements in fruits, vegetables, and dairy products. Poultry may be next in line. It is of interest that extensive vertical integration in the broiler industry has not enhanced bargaining appreciably, and prices and profit rates for the integrators between farm and supermarket have been low. It is horizontal rather than vertical integration that is the greater source of market advantage.

Another commodity likely to experience considerable bargaining in the future is red meat. Increased bargaining power in beef and pork production will lead to the need for countervailing bargaining power in feed grains. Wheat-growers can achieve only very limited economic benefits from bargaining because the public is unlikely to tolerate domestic wheat prices much above parity (which farmers received on domestic wheat in the late 1960's) and because higher export prices will lose foreign markets. Cotton also offers few gains from group bargaining by producers. The scope for action is limited because any attempt to charge a higher price will be offset by substitution of synthetics for cotton and by loss of foreign markets. Thus cotton and grains, the major focus of government subsidies in 1968, have little to gain economically by using farmer-run market power as the means to escape government commodity programs.

In short, there are severe limitations on any bargaining efforts. About all the economic benefits that can be hoped for are some short-term income gains and price stability. The long-term gains, as with government control programs, are lost through greater output stimulated by higher prices, by loss of markets through foreign competition or through substitution of synthetics for farm-produced products, and finally by capitalization of benefits into the control device. The major advantage that farmer-run bargaining power has over current government programs is sociological—farmers at least feel that they are involved in the decision process. Also the groups chosen to bargain for farmers must learn the market realities and educate farmers to them or the process breaks down. This involvement, economic education, and economic stability are no small gains.

Past government programs have removed some of the pressures that would lead to effective collective bargaining by farmers. It is not entirely unreasonable to classify the cost of government farm programs as the price society pays to keep farmers from forming cohesive bargaining groups that would entail higher social costs than do government programs.

CHOOSING AMONG VOLUNTARY PROGRAMS (DECISION E)

In 1962 and 1963 the trend toward mandatory programs was at least temporarily reversed. Awareness that farmers were not willing to accept mandatory programs on major farm commodities led to the search for satisfactory voluntary programs. Numerous types of voluntary programs are available, and the choice of the "best" program is based on criteria such as (*a*) the cost to the Treasury of raising farm income a given amount, (*b*) the economic inefficiency fostered by the program, (*c*) the flexibility of the program, (*d*) its impact on the rural nonfarm community, and (*e*) the administrative burden. These criteria are not always explicitly stated below but are useful in judging the desirability of voluntary programs.

LONG-TERM LAND RETIREMENT

Programs in this category include Conservation Reserve, Cropland Conversion, and Cropland Adjustment. Whole or part farms are retired from crop production by long-term contracts. The advantage of the method is that, if run "efficiently" (through use of sealed bids, whole farms, 10-year contracts, etc.), it potentially removes more farm production per government dollar than any other voluntary program. Without unduly stimulating land prices, it makes government dollars go far to raise farm income. The U.S. Department of Agriculture has estimated that under the Conservation Reserve program each $100 of rental payments reduced production $292 from 1957 to 1960 (Christensen and Aines, 1962). The program also increases farming efficiency by encouraging movement of farm resources, including workers, marginal land, and operating capital to uses more favored by society. It leaves to farmers a high degree of freedom in production and marketing decisions. Disadvantages arise when this long-term land retirement program is administered efficiently, however. Its concentration in marginal farming areas creates large adjustment problems not only for farmers but also for people who formerly supplied inputs to the retired farms. It is estimated that up to 80 million acres would need to have been retired in the 1960's to bring supply in line with demand at acceptable prices. Another disadvantage is that long-term contracts are inflexible, since the contracts cannot be changed rapidly to correct for a new supply-demand balance. Also, a farm operator finds it more difficult to acquire land necessary to achieve an economic unit if his neighbor's farm has been retired from production.

Several alternative long-term programs for withdrawing land from production could be used. One is outright purchase of land by the government. The total cost of U.S. Department of Agriculture programs to stabilize farm prices and incomes was $50 billion from 1933 through 1966. For half this amount ($25 billion) 100 million acres could have been purchased by the government at $250 per acre to bring production into line. While this control approach would have greatly reduced government cost, it has the same disadvantages as the Conservation Reserve program and, in addition, is in disfavor by farmers. Land purchase would not have alleviated annual problems of instability in commodity prices and farm income.

Crop easements and related devices have been suggested to reduce crop production. One approach would be for the government to grant farmers a loan in return for cropping rights on a farm (cf. Aines, 1964). No interest would be charged on the loan by the government unless the loan were paid back. Cropping rights could be regained by repaying the loan plus interest. In many instances the land would be permanently placed in grass or trees and the loan would never be repaid. The easement would accompany the title to real estate with changes in ownership. The loan would compensate the landowner for the lower land price that would attend removal of cropping rights. This would cushion the impact on landowners of removing production allotments on land where prices had been inflated by previous farm programs. With this and other long-run programs, the government could introduce flexibility in production by temporarily terminating the control features in emergencies when greater farm output is needed. Contract payments would not be reduced and the farmer would not lose income—he would gain. Terms of the contract would again become binding when production of farms under contracts would no longer be needed.

The loan-easement contract would ordinarily be open-ended and of indefinite duration, although the farmer could elect to repay the loan plus interest and to crop the land at anytime. Variations of the program might include easements forbidding grazing as well as cropping, or contracts carrying a specific termination date. The restrictions on cropping would be terminated at the end of a fixed-term contract, and land could again be placed in production without repaying the loan. Much acreage would likely remain in grass or trees after termination of contracts.

Nebraska researchers estimated from a farm survey that easement purchase programs would cost the government less than either Conservation Reserve or land purchase programs, although a higher recovery of the initial investment could be expected with land purchase than with easements (Griffing and Fischer, 1965). According to another study, an easement program would cost the government less than a ten-year land retirement (rental) program; and most production would be removed per government dollar by forbidding grazing as well as cropping (Bottum *et al.*, 1961).

Short-term Land Retirement

Acreage diversion and related programs in recent years have been effective in curtailing production of specific crops such as corn and wheat. These were the "bread-and-butter" programs of the Johnson and Kennedy Administrations. Like the land retirement program, they have a double-barrel effect on farm income and can make government dollars go farther than would direct payments to raise farm earnings. Farmers increase their income, first, by receiving a cash payment to remove land from production. Second, by reducing national production, they reduce the aggregate supply quantity and get better prices in the market. The U.S. Department of Agriculture has estimated that each $100 spent on the feed grain program in the 1961–63 period increased farm income $186 (cf. Legislative Reference Service, 1964).

Because acreage diversion is oriented to better land than long-term land retirement, it reduces output with a smaller acreage withdrawal. In the 1960's, 50–60 million acres under short-term acreage diversion programs would have brought production in line with utilization.

Disadvantages of acreage diversion are that farmers learn to reduce the effectiveness and increase the cost of the control program by substituting fertilizer for land and by diverting inferior acres. Also, the program is not as effective as the whole-farm land retirement program in inducing movement of farm workers, operating capital, and marginal land to uses higher in the public interest.

COMMODITY STORAGE PROGRAMS

One way to raise farm income is for the Commodity Credit Corporation to purchase and store commodities. The advantages of storage are that it gives flexibility to price support programs, stabilizes farm prices, and provides insurance against unforeseen droughts, war, and foreign needs. The disadvantage is that strong political pressures exist to raise stocks above reasonable needs. The socially desirable carry-over may be approximately 600 million bushels of wheat and 40 million tons of feed grains. A free market carry-over might be little more than half these levels on the average, hence a goodly portion of the former estimates represent a strategic stockpile (cf. Gustafson, 1958). The government finds it politically very unpopular to release reserves to stabilize rising prices. Yet the stabilization function is the most important reason for commercial farm programs and can only be effective if stocks can also be released.

MULTIPLE PRICING

Multiple pricing has been used for several farm commodities including feed grains in recent years but its principle application has been to dairy products and wheat (Tweeten, 1965). It uses the principle of market separation, with the higher price in the market where quantity is unresponsive to price and the lower price in the market where receipts are expanded by a low price. Overproduction can be discouraged by giving producers the lower of the prices on their marginal output. The system effectively raises farm income above free market levels at minimum Treasury cost where (*a*) markets are markedly different in elasticities, (*b*) markets can be separated, and (*c*) no good substitutes in the high priced market will erode the gains over time. The voluntary two-price approach has had many backers since the McNary-Haugen era in the 1920's, but it can be applied usefully in domestic markets to few farm commodities. This is because there are good substitutes for most farm commodities, because consumers or processors in the high-price market resist the program, or because the needed administrative mechanisms are not available to divide markets. Demand elasticities presented in Chapter 7 suggest opportunities for greater use of multiple-price plans in our foreign markets. With higher prices charged in the inelastic domestic market and lower prices in the export market, farm income can be raised but the scheme leads to charges of dumping and unfair competition to other exporters.

DIRECT PAYMENTS WITHOUT CONTROLS

Direct payments or grants to farmers have considerable appeal to economists because they potentially provide free market pricing, output, freedom, and efficiency while at the same time they correct some of the inequitable income distribution within farming and among farm and other groups. These advantages, plus the flexibility of direct payments, have led to an increasing use of the method. From 1964 to 1969 it was an important component of major commodity programs, including wheat, cotton, and feed grains.

There are several disadvantages to direct payments. Direct transfer payments do not get the double-barrel income effect described earlier for control programs. Hence they are costly to taxpayers. If free market net income were $7 billion (a frequent estimate in the studies cited in footnote 1), then farm income can be brought to $13 billion by a government payment of $6 billion. Government costs of income supports averaged about $4 billion annually in the early 1960's, the period to which these income data apply. Taxpayers are not pleased with the high cost of a direct payment program, but consumers do get abundant, low-priced food.

A second disadvantage is that direct payments without controls stimulate farm production even beyond the free market level because of the security and capital that farmers get from the program. One way to partly avoid this problem is to limit payments to some fixed proportion of production on some historic period. Also the payment per farm might be limited to a maximum fixed amount that would keep large farmers from receiving a big subsidy. A third disadvantage is that farmers do not like outright subsidies. This drawback can be avoided by making the payment contingent on the farmer doing something (even though his contribution is small) to "deserve" the payment.

Another disadvantage is the difficulty of establishing equitable payment procedures. If payments are proportional to sales, the big farmers receive the lion's share and the income transfer is often from a low-income taxpayer to a more well-to-do farmer. If the payment is tied to land, the benefits are capitalized into land values and eventually lost to farm operators. If it is a flat payment per person in farming, then it may be argued that the small farmer is encouraged to stay in farming when he might have otherwise improved his economic position with a nonfarm job. If he can continue to receive these payments when he leaves agriculture, the nonfarm worker asks why he too does not receive similar benefits. If the payment is cut off for the large producer, it is said that "he is penalized for being efficient." Also direct payments are highly vulnerable to the moods of politicians and therefore create income uncertainties.

To a considerable extent, direct payments have masqueraded as a two-price plan or as acreage-diversion payments for grains and cotton since 1960. This tends to make direct payments proportional to sales and erodes one great potential advantage of direct payments—a more equitable distribution of benefits among farmers. Also the public does not understand that these are direct payments, and this makes payments highly vulnerable to political expediency when acreage diversion is not needed. The practice can contribute to the uncertainty of farm income, which farm programs should alleviate instead.

DEMAND EXPANSION

Raising farm income through demand expansion is the solution perhaps most widely accepted by laymen to the problem of low farm income. Three areas of possible demand expansion include (*a*) domestic expansion through food stamp plans, advertising, school lunch programs, etc., (*b*) finding new uses for farm products through research, and (*c*) expansion of export markets for U.S. farm commodities. While (*a*) and (*b*) may have some success in the long run, they do not offer immediate hope for closing the gap in farm demand (cf. Wetmore *et al.*, 1959).

Food aid is one form of commodity program to support farm income. Farm production can be removed from the market by paying farmers not to produce or by using the commodity as foreign aid. Government foreign aid can be given in food or other forms. Much food aid has been predicated on the assumption that the presence of excess capacity in agriculture means that our food has no cost to the U.S. government. Another assumption is that a dollar (market value) of food aid is equal to a dollar of aid in any other form. These assumptions are not valid, and a mechanism is needed to allocate optimally the combination of (*a*) food versus nonfood foreign aid, and (*b*) food aid versus domestic production control as a means to handle excess capacity in U.S. agriculture. A simple augmented market mechanism can do this. The proposal is that all foreign aid be given in unspecified (cash or credit) form, or at least in a form that would give recipient nations considerable choice among several goods and services that would be consistent with economic development (Tweeten, 1966b). A discount would be given on cash aid when used by recipient countries to purchase U.S. farm commodities. The discount per dollar (market value) on our food would be equal to the cost to the U.S. Department of Agriculture of inducing our farmers not to produce a dollar of output.

MISCELLANEOUS PROGRAMS

Numerous approaches to farm income and adjustment problems in addition to those listed above are possible. One method is to support farm income on an actuarial basis. With a plan patterned somewhat after the insurance concept of Social Security, farmers would pay into a fund in favorable financial years and draw out of it in years of depressed earnings (Swerling, 1961). The government might match the input of farmer dollars into the fund to induce more farmers to participate. A negative income tax is a related alternative but has its primary application to low-income farms rather than to commercial farmers.

As stated earlier, many contend that more direct policies aimed at farm resources rather than at commodities are necessary to encourage and smooth farm adjustments. Examples are government-subsidized programs of vocational training and general education to equip farm youth for alternative employment. Another possibility would be government grants to help farmers pay moving expenses and to settle in new employment.

Proposals have been made to reduce farm output and hence raise farm income by slowing the rate of technological advance in agriculture. These proposals, such as curtailing scientific effort or placing a tax or limit on fertilizer use, have received little support because of the high social cost of reduced farming efficiency and because farmers see higher input costs as a perverse method of raising net farm income.

The major long-term problem of *commercial* farms is not labor mobility, low resource returns, or low income but rather economic instability. One solution to this problem is hedging of losses from unpredictable price changes in the commodity futures markets. Some farmers are now using the futures market for major crops and livestock. This approach to farm problems is currently underutilized by farmers but it offers many advantages not yet widely understood. It also has disadvantages. First, it is questionable whether a large proportion of commercial farmers can be educated to hedge their production. Second, use of the futures market does not provide security against variation in prices stemming from changes in world markets and in domestic supply that are caused by trends in technology and weather cycles lasting several years.

RANKING OF PROGRAMS BY CRITERIA

Groups concerned with farm policy do not judge programs by the same criteria. Farmers want high income and minimum restriction on production and marketing decisions. Consumers want abundant and high-quality food and fiber at low prices. The government (and taxpayers) want low Treasury cost and low administrative burdens. They want flexibility in programs to meet world food problems. These interests often conflict and lead to inconsistent, piecemeal legislation. This section reviews some considerations discussed previously and ranks several programs according to their acceptability in fulfilling some of the criteria for a desirable commercial farm program.

Treasury Cost to Raise Farm Income

The cost of commodity programs to the U.S. government is high, and there are pressures to reduce Treasury cost without curtailing farm income. The Department of Agriculture, faced with a mandate to maintain or raise farm net income, might wish to choose a program on the basis of cost-effectiveness, i.e., one giving the greatest farm income per government dollar spent on the program.

Mandatory control programs minimize government costs and can maintain farm income. Farmers have, in general, objected to mandatory control programs. Consequently, production controls in agriculture are now for the most part obtained by voluntary programs.

The number of possible voluntary programs is large, and they are not all equally efficient in use of public funds to reduce production and raise farm income. Which of these programs are most efficient in use of government funds to control production and raise farm income?

Programs that are most efficient in removing production also contribute most to farm income because the aggregate demand for farm commodities is inelastic except in the long run. At the farm level, it is useful to estimate the value of production removed per government dollar (rather than increase in income per government dollar) as a measure of efficiency in use of federal funds, because the aggregate price effects are not immediately apparent. On farms where substitution among crops is likely, the aggregate production removed can best be measured by value reflected in price-weighted quantities. A bushel of wheat and a bale of cotton, for example, cannot be directly added.

If the value of production removed per program dollar spent is E, if C is variable production cost per acre, P is product price, and Y is yield, then

$$E = \frac{1}{1 - \dfrac{C}{PY}} \qquad C < PY \quad \text{and} \quad 1 < E < \infty.$$

The equation is based on the assumption that the government must pay "rent" equal to the difference between receipts PY and variable costs C to remove land from production (Sobering and Tweeten, 1964, p. 829). The farmer then makes the same net income whether he farms the land or rents it to the government. E increases (the ratio C/PY becomes larger and approaches 1) as land becomes more marginal in quality (lower Y), as product prices fall (lower P), and as variable costs become larger (higher C). It is apparent that as variable costs approach the gross value of production PY, efficiency becomes large and approaches infinity. The lower limit of E is 1 as variable costs become small, i.e., as C/PY approaches zero. This theoretical lower limit ($E = 1$) means that government programs concentrating on the best land have the lowest efficiency and that a government dollar should, in theory, remove at least \$1 of production even under the "worst" conditions. The practical limits are much more restrictive than the theoretical limits stated above.

A greater proportion of costs become variable when the time period is extended and when whole farms are dealt with so that labor and machinery assets become variable costs. Thus the theoretical efficiency of voluntary land retirement programs is highest with long-term, whole-farm programs that concentrate on land of marginal quality. Also, sealed bids to obtain the minimum payment to remove production on a given piece of land (rather than use of a uniform payment per acre over a given area) would theoretically increase the efficiency of program dollars.

Because of administrative difficulties and other reasons, efficiency as defined above is not obtainable in practice. Landowners require more than the theoretical payment to divert land from production. This premium may be greatest for long-term, whole-farm contracts. A need exists to determine the actual as well as theoretical efficiency of alternative production withdrawal programs.

Several studies include estimates of the efficiency of government programs. The U.S. Department of Agriculture estimated that in the 1957–60 period, long-term land retirement under the Conservation Reserve program removed nearly $3 of production for each dollar of "rental" payment made by the government to farmers participating in the program (Christensen and Aines, 1962). Iowa State University economists estimated that the 1961 feed grain program, a short-term acreage diversion program, removed $1.14 of corn production per dollar of government cost (Shepherd *et al.*, 1963, p. 22). Robinson (1966, p. 24) estimated that average annual production of feed grain was reduced 30–40 million tons by acreage withdrawal programs in the 1963–64 period. The cost to the government averaged $1.4 billion, and (with corn at $1.10 per bushel) the value of production removed ranged from $0.86 to $1.14 per dollar spent on the program. Other estimates of the efficiency of short-term acreage division and long-term land retirement range from 1.1 to 1.6 (cf. Tweeten *et al.*, 1963).

In another study, the U.S. Department of Agriculture estimated that, on the average, each $100 spent on feed grain programs in the early 1960's increased farm income $186 (cf. Legislative Reference Service, 1964). Direct payments without production controls increase farm income $100 for each $100 spent by the government. Hence they have an efficiency of 1.0. This efficiency is eroded, however, to the extent that payments encourage unwarranted farm production. The estimates of program efficiency in this paragraph are based on net farm income and hence are not comparable with the above estimates based on the value of production removed.

Commodity storage programs directly remove $100 of farm production for each $100 spent by the government, hence their immediate efficiency is 1.0, but efficiency declines as storage costs are incurred. Storage costs are likely to equal the purchase price in about five years, hence efficiency is reduced to zero. However, storage costs to some extent are offset by the value of having reserves for unforeseen emergencies. The efficiency of multiple-price plans and export subsidies depends on the structure of farm product markets. One study shows that the efficiency of these programs in wheat markets can be high (Tweeten, 1965).

In summary, the ranking of programs from most to least efficient in use of government dollars to raise farm income is: mandatory supply control, long-term land retirement, short-term land retirement, direct payments, and finally commodity storage. Among long-term general land retirement programs, the ranking from most to least efficient is land purchase, loan easement, and land rental.

ECONOMIC EFFICIENCY

Two types of economic inefficiency are of interest. One is the social cost of a farm output that deviates from that of a perfect market. The second is inefficiency that results in high production costs and a nonoptimum combination of farm resources. The two concepts are discussed separately but are related.

The concept of net social cost is defined in Chapter 16. It is the value of production (and consumption) forgone by output that deviates from that of a perfect market. Net social cost perhaps comes closest of any criterion to measuring the aggregate welfare of farmers, consumers, and taxpayers alike and thus transcends to some degree the dilemma of consumers wanting low food cost, farmers wanting high income, and taxpayers wanting low Treasury costs. The net social cost concept assumes equal marginal utility of dollars for all persons. This assumption does not hold in reality. The following rankings give insight into the economic efficiency of programs, disregarding the distribution of benefits from greater efficiency.

In general, programs which are most effective in controlling farm production and marketing entail the highest social cost. Thus mandatory supply management is least efficient, and the free market is most efficient. Market quotas are more efficient than acreage allotments because the former permit a more nearly optimum combination of resources. Direct payments and price supports without allotments are less efficient than free markets because they result in too much farm output. Long-term voluntary land retirement entails less social cost than mandatory controls and, because it encourages resource adjustments, entails less social cost than short-term land retirement. Storage programs that accumulate stocks above reasonable reserve requirements entail a high social cost. Allowing a surplus to be produced and stored dissipates not only redundant fixed farm resources (which do not represent much social cost because they have little value in other uses) but also variable resources that could be used to produce farm or nonfarm commodities valued by consumers.

Total average production costs of the farming industry change little over a considerable range of output. It follows that farm production costs per unit are not influenced much by programs that restrain farm output within the range experienced under past programs.

It also may be useful to judge the economic efficiency of a program by its contribution to farm resource adjustments apart from the output effect. By this criterion, long-term land retirement may rank above free markets. The full benefits to society of technologically improved inputs adopted by farmers cannot be reaped until the labor and other surplus resources are moved to uses having higher economic value.

As stated earlier, research indicates that farm labor adjustments have not been materially slowed by farm commodity programs. Farm labor mobility is more strongly influenced by nonfarm job availability than by an increment in farm income due to program benefits. It appears that farm income has been low enough to pressure farmers to seek outside employment at an orderly pace. Even a small improvement in their financial position does not restrain them. What restrains them is the availability of suitable jobs—and their suitability (training) for available jobs.

While free markets undoubtedly would release labor from farming (because of resulting low income and mortgage foreclosures), it is possible that the released labor would not be quickly or "gracefully" absorbed into other industries. It may be more prudent for social efficiency to encourage out-migration at a slower rate, more consistent with reliance on the economic adjustment of young people.

IMPACT ON RURAL NONFARM COMMUNITIES

Programs of direct payment or demand expansion to maintain farm income (and farm numbers) would require the fewest economic adjustments from rural nonfarm business and social groups. Farm programs, such as long-term land retirement, that are most successful in adjusting farm resources (mainly people) to nonfarm uses tend to have the greatest impact on local towns. To maintain farm income with a Conservation Reserve type program of 80 million acres concentrated in marginal areas would cause a severe impact on local towns because production items would no longer be purchased for retired acres. Furthermore, many farmers would use the opportunity to move out of the small local communities. This would affect schools, churches, and grocery stores as well as farm production input dealers (cf. Tweeten and Walker, 1963).

MISCELLANEOUS CRITERIA

Free markets rank high measured by criteria of minimum government administrative burden and freedom of farmers to make their own individual economic decisions. Direct payments based on need rather than output rank high as an income support program if equality of income is the goal. Free markets and direct payments rank low in desirability if having output flexibility and reserve capacity is a useful goal. These goals are largely self-evident in programs and need no further elaboration.

In concluding this section, I emphasize that there is no one program that satisfies all participants in the farm policy milieu. No program at the same time gives farmers high income and complete freedom, gives consumers plentiful food at low prices, and gives the government good reserves for emergencies, a low administrative cost, and a low tax burden. We must recognize that farm policy is made out of compromise and hard choices.

FARMERS' PREFERENCES FOR PROGRAMS

The acceptability of commodity programs to farmers depends not on the economic implications discussed in detail above but on how farmers weigh the economic factors in their system of values. In the summer of 1964, 500 wheat farmers in Oklahoma and Kansas were interviewed and asked to state their preference for specific programs. This study was unique in that, for the first time, farmers were informed of the economic consequences of programs when asked to make their choices. The results are tabulated in Table 11.1.

When asked to specify their first choice of several programs before being informed of the economic implications, 42 per cent of the wheat-growers chose the voluntary acreage diversion program of the type used for feed grains. The second preference was the free market program. Mandatory programs of the type used for wheat prior to 1964, and the two-price 1964 program ranked low in preference.

Later in the questionnaire, farmers were asked to state their preferences for the set of programs with a price, income, and (where appropriate) allotment tag placed on each. Under a free market, farmers were told that economists had estimated the wheat price would be $1.20 per bushel, and net income from wheat would be 50 per cent below the 1962 and 1963 wheat income.

With a voluntary acreage diversion program, farmers were told that the estimated wheat price would be $1.30 per bushel and that there would be no allotments but that they would be paid to divert acres and that net income would average 88 per cent of 1962 and 1963 income. Except for the two-price and free market programs, which entail nominal government cost, the remaining programs were each set to cost the government approximately $500 million.

Farmers rated mandatory controls and the two-price programs highest when asked to choose the best-liked of the five programs submitted with economic implications attached. In general, there was a strong tendency for farmers to rank programs in proportion to farm income. In this and other parts of the survey it was apparent that farmers were willing to accept some administrative nuisances and tighter production controls to obtain a higher income. Awareness of probable price and income led 39 per cent of the farmers to rank free markets

TABLE 11.1 Preferences of 500 Oklahoma and Kansas Farmers for Commodity Programs for Wheat, Before and After Being Informed of the Program's Economic Implications

	Before Being Informed of Economic Implications		After Being Informed of Economic Implications	
	Liked Best	Liked Least	Liked Best	Liked Least
	%	%	%	%
Mandatory controls (all farmers would be required to comply with allotments if approved in a national referendum)	11	27	29	16
Two-price plan (wheat used in U.S. supported at a parity level; all wheat beyond that needed in U.S. sold on the world market at the world price)	11	8	20	8
Voluntary acreage division program (each individual farmer is free to decide each year if he wants to receive payments to divert land from wheat production and be eligible for price supports)	42	2	19	1
Free market (no acreage allotments, no price of income supports)	20	24	16	39
Direct payments (no production controls, no marketing controls; a direct government payment would be made to farmers to raise farm income)	1	20	3	16
No reply or undecided[a]	15	19	13	20
Total	100	100	100	100

Source: Tweeten (1966a).

[a] A long-term land retirement program was included where farmers were asked to state preferences before being informed of implications. Only 8 per cent liked it best; 5 per cent liked it least.

as "liked least." The percentage who rated free markets as "liked best" fell from 20 to 16 when the farmers were informed of its implications.

The programs discussed above are conventional programs to which most farmers have been exposed in the past or with which they have become familiar in educational literature or at meetings. The programs described below were outside the recent experience of wheat farmers. The 500 wheat-growers in Kansas and Oklahoma were asked to react to each. The farmers used a scale of 1 to 5 to indicate their approval or disapproval. If they strongly approved of a proposal, they marked it 1; if they disapproved, they marked it 5. If they could not make up their mind, they marked it 3, a neutral position. Thus a rating above 3 means farmers disapproved of the proposal.

The six proposals, just as they were stated to the farmers, and the average rating of each are as follows:

1. The government would buy whole farms and combine several farms to be used for public recreation or leased for grazing.

Average rating: 4.2

2. The government would buy the rights to raise wheat on a farm. Then this farm could not grow wheat, thus reducing total production. Other crops could be raised as desired.

Average rating: 4.0

3. Wheat allotments would be bought and sold among farmers so that allotments would eventually end up in the hands of those who could make the best use of them.

Average rating: 4.2

4. The government would pay a $5,000 grant to train and move to some nonfarm job those farmers who had income problems.

Average rating: 3.7

5. An organization of farmers themselves (independent of the government) would control production and raise farm prices and income.

Average rating: 2.7

6. Allotments would be based on bushels rather than acres.

Average rating: 2.4

Farmers disapproved quite strongly of proposals 1, 2, and 3. The average ratings on these were 4 or above. Farmers also disapproved of proposal 4, but not as strongly as the first three proposals.

The last two proposals received some degree of approval. However, the average rating of 2.7 on proposal 5 was very near the neutral or undecided rating of 3. Many farmers said they would favor a workable organization of farmers to run wheat programs but put down "undecided" because they thought such an organization would not be feasible.

Greatest approval was given to proposal 6, the idea of basing allotments on bushels rather than acres. A number of farmers stressed unfair or arbitrary acreage allotment decisions under the past farm programs as one of their main criticisms. Many farmers felt that the fairness of present government programs would be improved if allotments per farm were based on bushels only.

In the mid-1950's, several economists sampled the reaction of farmers to wheat programs of that period (Hemphill and Anderson, 1958; Schnittker *et al.*,

1957; Smith *et al.*, 1956). In each of these studies, the majority of farmers stated that their net farm income was raised by price supports and acreage allotments. Despite a general dissatisfaction with the method of establishing the wheat base, a sizable majority of farmers either favored the allotment program or expected it to continue.

A New York study found, as did a Michigan study, that many farmers opposed production controls (Moe, 1952; Hathaway *et al.*, 1952). Thirty per cent of the New York farmers opposed production controls and 52 per cent of the Michigan farmers felt production controls were unneeded. However, New York farmers overwhelmingly favored surplus removal programs, such as export subsidies or grants to underdeveloped nations. Later studies in Minnesota and Ohio reported a generally favorable attitude toward the 1961 feed grain program (App and Sundquist, 1963; Sharples and Tompkin, 1963).

Studies are lacking in most areas of the nation on attitudes toward government programs when farmers are educated to the probable consequences of their choice. Some tentative conclusion can be drawn from the less sophisticated studies, however. In general, producers of major crops favor government supports more than do producers of livestock. Farmers of the Midwest, Great Plains and South are more favorably inclined toward government programs than are farmers of the East and West. This result can be explained in part by the degree of protection offered by past programs. Robinson (1965) estimates that farm income in Oklahoma would drop 48 per cent without support programs, while farm income in New York would drop only 12 per cent.

In short, the sampling of farmers' opinions revealed that farmers tend to favor government programs to support farm income. But they do not rally strongly around one program. Price support benefits tend to concentrate most heavily in the hands of landowners and farmers with largest production. Yet tenure, farm size, income, and equity appeared to have little to do with the farmers' choice of programs in the 1964 Oklahoma and Kansas study.

SUGGESTED ELEMENTS IN A TRANSITION PROGRAM

This chapter would be incomplete without some attempt to combine into one government program for commerical agriculture the desirable features of the programs listed above. The program presented below is *not* a recommendation. It is a suggested outline only, containing elements useful in such a farm program.

It was argued earlier that government support programs do not have much impact on the long-term level of net farm income. It does not follow, however, that farmers could quickly or easily adjust to the lower farm income that would immediately attend removal of government programs. A transition program is needed to help farmers adjust to a more permanent government program that would be primarily concerned with stabilizing farm income rather than with holding it above the free market level. Policies should be designed to forestall a sizable drop in farm receipts. Nevertheless, prices should not be supported at levels so high that much of the gain from rising farm productivity would not pass to consumers in the long run, or so high that land prices would be unduly inflated. The key provisions of the suggested program include (*a*) an Agricultural Board removed one step from politics to administer programs, (*b*) a long-term, loan-easement, land retirement program, (*c*) immediate expansion of market pricing and multiple pricing, (*d*) phasing out of these multiple-pricing programs over a ten-year period, leaving only long-term land retirement and commodity storage as a government stabilization program, and finally (*e*) encouragement of farm bargaining groups to eventually take over and phase out all the government income stabilization programs.

Long-term Land Retirement

To reduce government cost, the program would entail only long-term general land retirement, with loans made to farmers for the cropping rights on their farms. Contracts would be for whole or part farms for an indefinitely long (infinite) period. The government would take sealed bids, accepting for loans only that farmland that removed the greatest amount of production per dollar of the loan. Owners would retain title to the land, continue to pay taxes on it, and grazing would be permitted. The tendency to concentrate production withdrawal in marginal areas and on whole farms would be consistent with economic efficiency, but safeguards in the form of limiting production withdrawal to one-third of the land in any one county would cushion the impact on the rural nonfarm sector. The new program would be introduced and phase out current acreage diversion programs over a five-year period. This would reduce the immediate capital cost of the program. A total of 60–80 million acres eventually would be included. Loans would have no interest, but, if at any time the owner wished to place the land in crop production, he could repay the loan plus interest. This would provide flexibility in the long-term program. Times of pressing food and fiber needs would lead to a considerable amount of loans being repaid and lands again being placed in crop production.

Market, Marginal, and Multiple Pricing

Research reported in Chapter 7 strongly supported the conclusion that the export demand for U.S. farm products is price elastic. To expand export markets and export earnings, it is important to keep the prices of our farm commodities competitive in foreign markets. To reduce charges by competing exporters that we are dumping surpluses, in order to lower the cost of U.S. government export subsidies and in order to use prices to restrain U.S. farm production, it is recommended that U.S. farmers actually receive the world market price for their marginal production.

The following general recommendations are deliberately framed to avoid a major shift in policies.

The two-price system would be extended. The higher domestic price would maintain and stabilize farm income; a lower export price would help to expand world markets. The plan would supplement the long-term land retirement program to give stability to the farm economy in a transition period. The two-price program would avoid a sharp drop in farm income and would avoid serious problems for young farmers who have paid "too much" for land. But the trend would be to a greater role of market demand and supply in establishing price and output. All allotments would be eliminated, but the historical production pattern would be retained as the basis for setting payments on the "high-price" portion of the output of each farm. To discourage overproduction, these payment bases would not expand with higher yields. Instead the payment bases would be completely phased out over a ten-year period, declining by 10 per cent of the original amount per year.

Domestic policies consistent with goals of maintaining the stability and level of farm income, holding food prices at reasonable levels, holding some reserve capacity, utilizing foreign markets, and giving farmers maximum feasible control over their production and marketing decisions require a commodity-by-commodity approach. In all cases, the marginal price would be determined by the commercial market forces—of which world markets would be a major factor.

For individual commodities, these are some suggestions:

1. Soybeans, livestock, poultry, fruits, and vegetables would have no production controls and no special price or income supports.

2. *Dairy products:* A two-price system would be used, with a higher price for class I milk paid on a fixed historic base of production. Other milk would be priced at market levels, with farmers paid the market price on production above the fixed class I base. There would be no production controls and milk would be free to move into any use consistent with sanitary regulations.

3. *Cotton:* The market price would prevail for cotton. A direct payment from the government would be used to maintain a higher price on a fixed proportion of the historic allotment. There would be no production controls, and any farmer who wished could produce and sell at the market price. If deemed necessary, however, the direct payments would be used temporarily to divert land to soil-conserving uses.

4. *Wheat and feed grains:* These commodities would essentially become part of a single market. Farmers would receive the market price for feed grains and

wheat. They could grow any grain, and there would be no acreage allotments or marketing quotas. A certificate plan would be continued on wheat, with the entire cost paid by processors. The certificate payment would be based on a fixed proportion of the historic allotment allocated to domestic use of wheat. If necessary, the certificate payment could be used temporarily to induce farmers to convert some land to soil-conserving uses. It would be gradually reduced and finally eliminated after a ten-year period.

For feed grains, the government would provide a direct payment to farmers to give stability and avoid a sharp drop in farm income. The payment would be related to the historic feed grain base.

All of the above programs would be voluntary. There would be a scaling down of payments to large farmers, with an absolute annual limit of $20,000 from all programs to anyone receiving payments. A scaling down rather than a lower absolute limit is recommended to reduce deception—breaking up large farming units on paper only. As stated before, the government would gradually eliminate the direct payments and the two-price system, leaving only long-term land retirement and commodity storage programs to stabilize fluctuations in farm income. As farm bargaining groups gained strength and assumed the stabilization function, the government storage program would be eliminated.

MANAGEMENT OF COMMODITY STOCKS

A long-term land retirement program alone is too unwieldy to stabilize the farm economy. While some feel that a supplementary short-term acreage-diversion program is needed for flexibility, simulation analysis at Oklahoma State University of the farm economy indicates that a combination of long-term general land retirement, coupled with commodity stock adjustments, can give adequate stability at low government and social cost. The proposal is that guidelines for commodity stock operations be carefully specified in advance by the government with the advice and consent of farm interest groups. The decision guidelines might even be stored in an electronic computer, which would spell out stock buy-sell activities after being fed information on current prices, production, and stocks. While average carry-over would, by design, be larger than under a free market, there would be no special strategic reserve insulated from the market. The entire commodity stock would be available to stabilize supplies and prices in any year.

FOREIGN AID AND FOOD DISCOUNTS

Efforts to remove export barriers, including tariffs, quotas, and variable levies, should be vigorously pursued. Reciprocal trade agreements, barter, and other measures should be used to expand farm exports. All economic aid to foreign countries would be given in unspecified form with a discount offered on U.S. commodities in surplus—a program described earlier in this chapter.

The most effective means to increase U.S. farm exports in the long run is to promote economic development, especially in less developed countries that now lack effective demand and the foreign exchange necessary to purchase our products. To promote development, total aid (and especially our nonfood aid) should be increased to improve industry and agriculture in foreign countries.

AN AGRICULTURAL BOARD

Narrow political interests have contributed to the inadequacies of current farm policies. To overcome this problem, farm programs would be administered by a nonpartisan Agricultural Board, similar in structure to the Federal Reserve Board. Board members would be appointed by the President with the approval of Congress for long terms, staggered to give continuity. The purpose would be to remove the Board from the immediate political exigencies of partisan politics. The Board would have the mandate to make decisions on production controls, prices, and stock levels that would be a reasonable compromise of farm, consumer, and taxpayer interests.

Politics neither can nor should be separated from farm policy. But placing the administration of farm programs in an Agricultural Board composed of members with various geographic and policy backgrounds and operating within guidelines and budgets established by Congress and the President would be a step away from narrow politics.

NATIONAL ADVISORY COMMISSION ON FOOD AND FIBER

The National Advisory Commission on Food and Fiber was appointed by the President and charged with a mandate to investigate all aspects of U.S. farm policy. A report, intended as a guide and focus for future decisions and policies, was issued in July 1967. The Commission's major recommendations for commercial farm policy are outlined below (page references are to the 1967 report):

1. The majority (16 out of 29 members) recommended that modified government programs be retained until problems of excess capacity in farming are alleviated, and farmers are able to earn incomes from the market that are comparable to nonfarm incomes (p. 17). The minority (13 of 29 members) recommended, as did the majority, that farming should be market-oriented but recommended that the transition to a free market be more positive and prompt (p. 16).

2. The majority recommended that the parity price concept be replaced

with a parity income concept, based on what farm resources would earn if employed outside of farming (pp. 17, 18).

3. The majority recommended that direct commodity payments be used to enable efficient, commerical farmers to receive parity of income. The minority endorsed the use of direct payments but only on a temporary basis (p. 17).

4. The majority recommended that price supports be set modestly below a moving average of world market prices. The minority stated that price supports should not be above 90 per cent of the five-year average of world market prices, and should be gradually phased out in favor of temporary income supplements or price deficiency payments (p. 18).

5. The Commission claimed that payments based on "projected" yields have encouraged farmers to increase yields to receive higher payments. To avoid encouraging overproduction, the Commission suggested that the bases for payments be set once and for all (p. 20).

6. The majority recommended that supply management programs be voluntary; the minority stated that supply management is inconsistent with the market orientation and would interfere with resources moving to their most profitable use (pp. 16, 20).

7. The Commission recommended that acreage allotments and marketing quotas be made negotiable or transferable and that allotments be in quantities (pounds or bushels) rather than in acreage (pp. 19, 20).

8. The Commission recommended that public subsidies through the Agricultural Conservation program for capacity-increasing farm practices be discontinued (pp. 21, 22).

9. The Commission recommended establishment of a strategic reserve for national security. The reserve would be isolated from the market except for offsetting purchases and sales to maintain the quality of the reserve stock. The majority recommended that a program of stocks for major storable farm commodities be used to maintain reasonable stability of supplies and to avoid extremely high or extremely low prices. The minority considered the latter to be ill-advised, and instead recommended that direct payments be used to cushion farm price changes (pp. 22–24).

10. The Commission recommended that a long-term land retirement program be expanded to cover all marginal cropland areas of the country (p. 28).

It may be noted that the National Advisory Commission was almost equally divided between a program that in many ways resembles past policies and a program that would, after a transition period, resemble a free market.

SUMMARY AND CONCLUSIONS

Commodity programs have become a significant part of the agricultural establishment in recent years. They have been highly controversial, and the advantages and disadvantages of the programs have been well documented. Proponents argue that the the programs have removed the great instability in farm prices and incomes, have provided a strategic reserve of production capacity to meet unpredictable emergencies such as wars and droughts, have provided an orderly outmovement of surplus farm labor, and have conserved farm resources for future generations.

Opponents argue that the programs have cost taxpayers too much money, have benefited only large producers, have regressively distributed income from taxpayers of modest means to prosperous farmers, have diverted public attention and support from real problems of rural poverty, have interfered with freedom of farmers to produce and market as they please, have lost their effectiveness through capitalization of benefits into land or through slippage (bringing in new cropland, using more fertilizer, etc.), have interfered with commerical exports of farm products, and have caused inefficiency through freezing of production patterns and idling of land resources which have little value for anything but agricultural uses.

A number of suggestions to improve farm programs have been offered. It has been suggested that allotments be made negotiable, that acreage allotments be shifted to bushel or poundage quotas, that "normal" yields be set once and for all so farmers are not encouraged to expand yields to get more payments, that a farmer not be allowed to move allotments from a poor farm which he purchases to the good land on his "home" farm, that the farmer actually receive the market (rather than a blend) price for his marginal production so as to constrain output expansion in a two-price program, that long-term land retirement be expanded so as to remove marginal land from production and to reduce government costs, that program administration be streamlined at the local level, that payments be cut off or graduated for large farmers, and that program formulation be placed in the hands of an Agricultural Board patterned after the Federal Reserve Board.

Many of these changes in programs have much merit, but changes in commercial farm policies come slowly. A review of history suggests that crisis is the major impetus for major policy adjustments. Crises took the form of extremely low farm income in the 1930's, war in the 1940's, large surpluses in the later 1950's, and farmer revolt against mandatory programs in the early 1960's. Factors that could cause changes in farm programs in the future include a major shift in the world supply-demand balance for food, unwillingness of farmers to accept current type programs, and serious erosion of farm political strength.

In formulating realistic policies, it is well to recognize that commodity programs do not raise the net income of farm people over the long run. The principal purposes of commodity programs are to create an orderly economic environment for agriculture and to hold a strategic reserve of farm production capacity. The stability function is so important that a free market is now mostly an academic exercise and is unlikely to become an actual policy for agriculture. Yet there appears to be little point in holding farm prices above the free market equilibrium level over extended periods. The benefits of higher prices will be capitalized into land or other control instruments and will eventually be lost to farmers anyway.

REFERENCES

Aines, Ronald O. 1964. Farm land valuation and farm programs. *Journal of Farm Economics* 46:1253–59.

App, James L., and W. B. Sundquist. 1963. The feed grain program in Minnesota. Bulletin 464. St. Paul, Minn., Agricultural Experiment Station.

Bottum, J. Carroll, *et al.* 1961. Land retirement and farm policy. Bulletin 704. Lafayette, Ind., Agricultural Experiment Station.

Brandow, George E. 1960. Direct payments without production controls. In *Economic Policies for Agriculture in the 1960's.* U.S. Congress, Joint Economic Committee, 86th Congress, 2nd Session. Washington: U.S. Government Printing Office.

———. 1961. Interrelations among demands for farm products and implications for control of market supply. Bulletin 680. University Park, Pa., Agricultural Experiment Station.

Christensen, Raymond P., and Ronald O. Aines. 1962. Economic effects of acreage control programs in the 1950's. Economic Report No. 18. Washington, U.S. Department of Agriculture.

Committee for Economic Development. 1962. An adaptive program for agriculture. New York.

Griffing, M. E. and L. K. Fischer. 1965. Government purchase of crop limiting easements as a means of reducing production. *Journal of Farm Economics* 47:60–73.

Gustafson, Robert. 1958. Carryover levels for grain. Technical Bulletin No. 1178. Washington, U.S. Department of Agriculture.

Hathaway, Dale E., E. E. Peterson, and Lawrence Witt. 1952. Michigan farmers and the price support program. Technical Bulletin 235. East Lansing, Mich., Agricultural Experiment Station.

Heady, Earl O., and Luther G. Tweeten. 1963. *Resource Demand and Structure of the Agricultural Industry.* Ames: Iowa State University Press.

Hemphill, Parry V., and Donald E. Anderson. 1958. The effects of wheat support programs on North Dakota agriculture. Report No. 11. Fargo, N.D., Agricultural Experiment Station.

Herendeen, James. 1965. Effects of national farm programs on farm prices and incomes in the United States and the northeast. Bulletin No. 716. University Park, Pa., Agricultural Experiment Station.

Legislative Reference Service, Library of Congress. 1964. Farm program benefits and costs in recent years. U.S. Senate Committee on Agriculture and Forestry, 88th Congress, 2nd Session. Washington: U.S. Government Printing Office.

———. 1965. Farm programs and dynamic forces in agriculture. U.S. Senate Committee on Agriculture and Forestry, 89th Congress, 2nd Session. Washington: U.S. Government Printing Office.

Moe, Edward O. 1952. New York farmers' opinions on agricultural programs. Extension Bulletin 864. Ithaca, N.Y., Cornell University.

National Advisory Commission on Food and Fiber. 1967. *Food and Fiber for the Future*. Washington: U.S. Government Printing Office.

Robinson, K. L. 1960. Possible effects of eliminating direct price support and acreage control programs. In *Farm Economics*, Ithaca, N.Y., Cornell University, pp. 5813–20.

———. 1965. The impact of government price and income programs on income distribution in agriculture. *Journal of Farm Economics* 47:1225–34.

———. 1966. Cost and effectiveness of recent government retirement programs in the United States. *Journal of Farm Economics* 48:22–30.

Schnittker, John A., J. O. Bray, and B. J. Bowlen. 1957. Kansas farmers' views on the wheat price support and acreage control program. Economic Report 77. Manhattan, Kan., Agricultural Experiment Station.

Sharples, Jerry A., and J. Robert Tompkin. 1963. The effect of the 1961 feed grain program on west-central Ohio farms. Research Bulletin 947. Wooster, Ohio, Agricultural Experiment Station.

Shepherd, Geoffrey, *et al.* 1960. Production prices and income estimates and projections for the feed-livestock economy. Special Report 27. Ames, Iowa, Agricultural Experiment Station.

——— *et al.* June, 1963. Controlling inputs. Bulletin B-798. Columbia, Mo., Agricultural Experiment Station.

Smith, Mervin G., *et al.* 1956. An analysis of Ohio wheat growers' views and responses in 1956 to federal agricultural policies. Bulletin AE 270. Columbus, Ohio, Agricultural Experiment Station.

Sobering, Fred D., and Luther G. Tweeten. 1964. A simplified approach to adjustment analysis. *Journal of Farm Economics* 47:820–834.

Swerling, Boris. 1961. Positive policies for American agriculture. In *Goals and Values in Agricultural Policy*. Center for Agricultural and Economic Adjustment, Ames: Iowa State University Press, pp. 310–22.

Tweeten, Luther G. 1965. Commodity programs for wheat. Technical Bulletin T-118. Stillwater, Okla., Agricultural Experiment Station.

———. 1966a. Commodity programs for agriculture. Situation paper prepared for National Advisory Commission on Food and Fiber. Washington.

———. 1966b. A proposed allocative mechanism for U.S. food aid. *Journal of Farm Economics* 48:803–10.

———, Earl O. Heady, and Leo V. Mayer. 1963. Farm program alternatives; farm incomes and public costs under alternative commodity programs for feed grain and wheat. *Oklahoma State Journal* No. 911. Center for Agricultural and Economic Development Report No. 18. Ames, Iowa.

——— and Odell L. Walker. 1963. Estimating the socioeconomic effects of a declining farm population. In *Regional Development Analysis*, Agricultural Policy Institute, Raleigh, North Carolina State University, pp. 101–19.

Tyner, Fred H. 1967. A simulation analysis of the economic structure of U.S. agriculture. Unpublished Ph.D. thesis. Stillwater, Oklahoma State University.

——— and Luther G. Tweeten. 1964. Excess capacity in U.S. agriculture. *Agricultural Economics Research* 16:23–31.

U.S. Department of Agriculture. 1960. Projections of production and prices of farm products for 1960–65 according to specified assumptions. U.S. Congress, Senate, Report from the U.S. Department of Agriculture and a statement from the Land Grant Colleges Advisory Committee on farm price and income projections. 86th Congress, 2nd Session. Senate Document 77. Washington: U.S. Government Printing Office, pp. 3–24.

Wetmore, John M., Martin E. Abel, Elmer W. Learn, and Willard W. Cochrane. 1959. Policies for expanding the demand for farm food products. Technical Bulletin 231. Minneapolis, Minn., Agricultural Experiment Station.

CHAPTER TWELVE

Rural Poverty: Dimensions and Causes

National views on poverty have changed markedly. Decades ago, many considered that some of the populace must be poor to avoid consuming what was produced. The consequent savings would be invested, leading to capital accumulation and national economic progress. A widely held current view is that poverty is not only unnecessary for savings and economic progress, but that the poor represent wasted human resources and forgone buying power. Poverty thereby retards national income. It is also recognized that private charity is capable of reaching only a few of the people who lack resources to compete effectively for jobs and wealth. A person can be unemployed for reasons beyond his control.

Americans are disillusioned with treating poverty symptoms. These symptoms include relief rolls and public assistance; in the cities they include riots, looting, destruction, and violence. These symptoms have causes. The modest size of the public investment to eliminate poverty is attributable as much to inadequate understanding of the problem and of effective cures as to public apathy.

Many of these causes can be traced to the rural origins of many of the city rioters or their parents. The obvious need to deal with the roots of the symptoms requires an understanding of what causes poverty and what public program will efficiently and effectively eliminate its causes.

This chapter documents, first, the dimensions of rural poverty and explains why it exists. A general theory of socio-economic stagnation follows the opening section containing considerable statistical data on the magnitude and incidence of poverty. Chapter 13 will describe past public programs to raise incomes of the disadvantaged, and will outline some of the strengths and weaknesses of these programs. Chapter 14 will suggest priorities for future efforts to alleviate poverty.

DIMENSIONS OF POVERTY

Poverty in one sense is a product of affluence. The terms "poor" and "poverty" are often used in a relative sense, identifying individuals or groups who have income well below the income of the mass of society. If everyone in this country had the same low income, it is unlikely that we would be discussing poverty or having programs to alleviate poverty. It is the contrast of affluence that makes poverty visible and provides the public revenue spent on poverty programs. Much of the alienation of the poor stems from a grim realization that they have no share in the affluence which surrounds them.

U.S. POVERTY

Measures of the magnitude of poverty are subjective. The poor are those who have a socially unacceptable level of income. Economic development is continually reducing the number of persons below any given level of income. Meanwhile, the socially acceptable income threshold continues to climb.

If we base poverty on the number of consumer units with personal income under $3,000 (at 1954 prices), the number of all consumer units in poverty fell from 47 per cent in 1941, to 35 per cent in 1947, and to 24 per cent in 1962. Depending on which of four measures of poverty are used, in 1957 the incidence of U.S. poverty ranged from 13 to 26 per cent (Lampman, 1966, p. 31). There is some agreement among the measures used that the incidence of poverty has been declining by about one percentage point per year, with the poverty income threshold unchanged. Based on Table 12.1, the incidence of national poverty was 24 per cent in 1959 and 18 per cent in 1966. Whites outnumber nonwhites (mostly Negroes) 3 to 1 in poverty but 10 to 1 in the population. Hence the incidence of poverty is substantially higher among nonwhites than whites.

The poverty income gap, the difference between the income of those in poverty and the socially acceptable threshold income, was a total of $11 billion in 1965, or 1.6 per cent of the gross national product. In 1959 the poverty gap was 2.8 per cent of the GNP. It appears that elimination of poverty is now within the financial means of the nation.

The foregoing estimates do not adjust for changing public concepts over time of a socially acceptable income. President Franklin Roosevelt spoke of one-third of the nation as economically deprived in the 1930's, yet by current measures, 60 per cent of the nation was in poverty at that time. This means that Roosevelt was using a lower income threshold than current standards.

It has been many decades since the starvation level was considered the socially acceptable poverty threshold by most people. In the future, the poverty

TABLE 12.1. Number of Poor Households and Incidence of Poverty,
1959 and 1966

	Poor Households[a]		Incidence of Poverty[b]	
	1959	1966	1959	1966
	(Millions of households)		*(Per cent)*	
Total	13.4	10.9	23.9	17.8
Nonfarm	11.6	10.3	22.5	17.6
White	9.0	7.9	19.6	15.3
Male head	5.0	3.9	13.4	9.4
Under 65	3.3	2.4	10.2	6.8
65 and over	1.7	1.5	34.0	24.7
Female head	4.0	4.0	45.2	37.7
Under 65	2.2	2.0	37.8	30.5
65 and over	1.8	2.0	59.3	48.9
Nonwhite	2.6	2.4	48.9	37.5
Male head	1.4	1.2	39.7	26.9
Under 65	1.2	.9	36.7	23.3
65 and over	.2	.3	64.4	51.4
Female head	1.1	1.2	69.4	60.8
Under 65	.9	.9	68.1	58.8
65 and over	.2	.2	76.3	69.9
Farm	1.8	.6	40.9	20.8
White	1.3	.5	34.7	16.9
Nonwhite	.4	.2	85.0	69.7

SOURCE: Economic Report (1968, p. 143).

[a] Defined here as the total of families and unrelated individuals. Poverty is defined by the Social Security Administration poverty-income standard, which take into account family size, composition, and place of residence. Poverty-income lines are adjusted to take account of price changes during the period. With some modifications, a household is classified as poor if its total money income falls below $1,570 for an unrelated individual, $2,030 for a couple, and $3,200 for a family of four.

[b] Number of poor households divided by all households within the specific category.

threshold income will increase and partly offset the reduction in the number of persons below a given income level brought about by economic development.

The "elasticity of poverty" may be defined as the percentage increase in the poverty threshold associated with a 1 per cent increase in median, real, per capita personal income in the nation. If this elasticity were equal to 1, the incidence of poverty would remain virtually stable. Most measures of poverty, such as those in Table 12.1, assume that the elasticity is zero. In fact, the elasticity is greater than zero, hence the usual measures of poverty overestimate progress in reducing poverty.

RURAL POVERTY

The declining incidence of farm poverty is dramatic according to Table 12.1. Two of five farm families in 1959 were poor; in 1966 only one of five was poor. The incidence of farm poverty, almost twice the national average in 1959, had fallen to nearly the national average in 1966.

An alternate classification system, based by Mollie Orshansky on the food budget, gives a completely different picture of rural poverty (cf. Tweeten, 1968, p. 5). By this system (considered by many to be inferior to the Social Security classification used in Table 12.1), there were 3.5 million more persons in urban than in rural poverty in 1965. In the same year, there were twice as many poor persons in rural nonfarm residence as in rural farm residence. Many poor farm people, of course, retire to nonfarm rural residences. But most interesting is the rising incidence of persons in farm poverty—36.5 per cent were poor in 1960, 43.5 per cent in 1965. The corresponding estimate from the Social Security classification was 24 per cent for 1965.

The National Advisory Commission on Rural Poverty (1967, p. 3) listed 14 million rural poor in 1965, 11 million of them white. The incidence of poverty (and the number of persons in poverty) was as follows: rural farm 29.3 per cent (3.9 million), rural nonfarm 23.6 per cent (9.9 million), and urban 14.8 per cent (19.9 million). While central city problems have generated the major concern over poverty, the incidence of poverty in central cities was 18.2 per cent in 1965, eleven percentage points below that on farms.

The above data indicate that rural poverty is sizable by any definition—but that the science of formulating definitions is primitive.

FURTHER CLASSIFICATIONS OF THE POOR

The data given so far only grossly present the anatomy of poverty. The classification ignores such factors as assets, particular family needs, and variability of income. Of the 11.0 million poor households in 1966, only 3.7 million had a male head under 65 years of age (Economic Report, 1968, p. 146). Of these 3.7 million households, 400,000 male heads were ill or disabled and 2.4 million worked at full time jobs. This left only 900,000 poor households with male heads who worked either part-time or were chronically unemployed. If we were to somewhat uncharitably and arbitrarily classify this group as the "indolent" group, it would mean that only 8 per cent of U.S. poverty is due to this factor. The remaining 92 per cent is comprised as follows: 39 per cent by the aged (65 years and over), 27 per cent by households with female heads under 65 years of age, 4 per cent by illness or disability of the male head, and 22 per cent by male heads who do not earn an acceptable income, even with full-time employment.

The breakdown of poverty into categories indicated that 2.4 million households headed by males and 1.0 million headed by females were poor in 1966, despite the fact that the head was ablebodied, under the age of 65, and worked at a full-time job. This category of the "fully" employed, accounting for nearly one-third of all U.S. poverty, is often outside of existing programs to alleviate poverty. New data are needed to determine how many of the "poor" have considerable wealth (assets), are in the military (e.g., privates and corporals), and have high future earning expectations (e.g., students).

The above data are for the entire nation and are only rough measures of conditions in rural areas. Of 1,583,000 low-income rural farm family heads in 1959, an estimated 1,000,000 were boxed in; that is, they had limited ability to attain adequate earnings (U.S. Department of Agriculture, 1966, p. 43). Many of the boxed-in families were those with older heads whose potential for retraining and migration to other communities was limited. In the boxed-in group were an estimated 343,000 farm families with heads over 65 years of age, 505,000 families with heads 45 to 64 years of age and eight years or less of schooling, and 152,000 families with heads 25 to 44 years of age with generally less than eight years of formal schooling. Low-income families with heads under 25 were not considered to be boxed-in despite low education and assets. This latter group had a sufficient planning and learning horizon to justify investment in training to escape from low income. This left 583,000 families, or 37 per cent of low-income farm families, whose heads were not boxed in by the age factor and by lack of education. Provisions of training and more jobs will effectively reduce low income among the group that is not boxed in. Public efforts to reduce the number of boxed-in poor will require expensive educational efforts for some. For others, the most efficient way to alleviate poverty will be through transfer payments and early retirement.

POVERTY AMONG REGIONS AND MINORITIES

In addition to the breakdown of poverty given above, two additional dimensions are highly important: race (or ethnic group) and geography.

Four groups—rural Negroes from the South, southern Appalachia (mainly whites), Spanish Americans, and American Indians—comprised less than 20 per cent of the rural population in the United States in 1950. But in the 1950–60 decade, they contributed, because of their very high migration rate, about 50 per cent of the net migration out of the rural and predominantly rural counties of the United States into the predominantly urban counties (Beale 1968, p. 14).

In these four groups, one-fourth of the persons who were living in rural areas in 1950 (or who were born in rural areas during 1950–60 and survived to the end of the decade) were living in predominantly urban areas in 1960 (Beale, 1968, p. 14). But even with this very high outmigration rate, they had only a 10 per cent decline in their total rural population in the decade. This low efficiency, 25 per cent outmigration to acheive a 10 per cent reduction in population, was the result of high birthrates in the areas of origin.

In 1959, 58 per cent of the poor rural nonfarm families and 53 per cent of the poor rural farm families lived in the South. A substantially lower percentage (38 per cent) of the poor urban families lived in the South. Approximately 41 per cent of all rural nonfarm families and 46 per cent of all rural farm families lived in the South in 1959, hence, the incidence of poverty was higher in the South than in other areas of the nation. The major extended region of rural poverty is the southern U.S., bounded by eastern Texas and eastern Oklahoma on the west, by the Ohio River and Maryland on the north, by the Atlantic Ocean on the east, and by the Gulf of Mexico on the south. Much rural farm poverty outside of this region tends to be widely dispersed within the commercial farming areas. The latter type of poverty has different causes and requires different remedial action than does poverty in sections where it is the dominant pattern.

Negroes

Negroes are by far the largest of the racial minority groups in the U.S. According to Table 12.1, the incidence of poverty among farm households headed by nonwhites (mainly Negroes) was 70 per cent in 1966. In that year the incidence of poverty was 37.5 per cent among nonfarm families with nonwhite heads. While the latter was high by white standards, it indicates considerably better economic conditions for nonwhites off the farm. Negroes have responded to shrinking farm opportunities and expanding urban job opportunities with massive migration from farms to cities outside the South. In 1890, 60 per cent of all employed Negroes were farmers or farm laborers. Approximately 8 per cent were so employed in 1960. By 1965, only 11 per cent of the farm population was Negro. Over 90 per cent of the rural Negroes but only half of all urban Negroes were in the South in 1965. The low income of Negro farmers pulls down the average farm income of all Southern farmers.

The Negro rural population is characterized by high birthrates, inadequate education, and low income. Each 1,000 nonwhite farm women 40–44 years old in 1960 had borne an average of 5,618 children. In the same year nonwhite urban women and white rural women in the same age group had borne 2,361 and 2,873 children, respectively. In addition to high birthrates, a distinctive feature of Negro households is the large number headed by women. A 1962 survey of farm workers showed that 26.6 per cent of Negro households had female heads compared with 8.5 per cent among their white counterpart (U.S. Department of Agriculture, 1966, p. 51). Two-thirds of the Negro farm workers performed only hand labor, while the majority of white workers performed more skilled work.

In 1959 only one-fifth of the rural Negro men age 25 to 29 in fourteen Southern states had completed high school. Numerous measures of economic, demographic, education, and housing characteristics indicated that the gaps between whites and nonwhites increased rather than decreased from 1950 to 1960 in rural farm sectors of 14 Southern states. Meanwhile, the education and housing gaps between the two racial groups in urban areas tended to narrow (U.S. Department of Agriculture, 1966, p. 122).

Problems stemming from racial discrimination, poor housing, high birthrates, family disintegration, inadequate education, and low skills will make Negroes a focus of poverty for many years in both rural and urban areas. Between 1920 and 1965, the Negro farm population dropped from 5.1 to 1.4 million. Mechanical cotton pickers and other changes have virtually eliminated the once numerous sharecropper. Mechanization of tobacco production would result in another large drop in the Negro farm population. Freeing of poor Negro farmers from cotton or tobacco production by no means signals the end of Negro poverty—which is often only transplanted to the city. Roughly, the probability of a rural Negro migrating to a city of over 500,000 is about seven times that for a rural white born in the same area (Hathaway, 1968, p. 8).

Lester Thurow (1967, p. 42), in an article entitled "The Causes of Poverty," concluded that the percentage of farm families in the population was associated with high incidence of area poverty. He also showed that reduction of the number of farmers in poverty by a given amount does not result in an equivalent increase in urban poverty. Education was found to be significantly related to poverty in Thurow's regression model. This is supported by other data, which show that the incidence of poverty is 44 per cent among households with family heads who have less than eight years of schooling. The incidence of poverty is only 5 per cent among households with family heads with four years or more of college (cf. Thurow, 1967, p. 46).

Regression results indicated that being a Negro per se had little impact on the incidence of poverty. However, socio-economic factors such as low educational attainment, unemployment, and part-time job holding, frequently associated with Negroes, had a major influence on the incidence of poverty. Whites with similar socio-economic characteristics had nearly the same incidence of poverty as Negroes. This conclusion does not rule out the presence of racial discrimination; it only implies that racial discrimination shows up in variables such as education and employment. Since low education was such an important factor in explaining Negro poverty, it might be reasoned that a massive effort to improve the education of Negro youth would materially reduce Negro poverty—although the result would take several years to be felt.

A 1968 study used the "trickling down" hypothesis to analyze the change in the incidence of poverty among farm families under various assumptions of national unemployment (Madden, 1968). With 4 per cent national unemployment from 1966 to 1975, the incidence of poverty among farm white families was projected to fall from 28 per cent in 1966 to 20 per cent in 1975. The incidence of poverty among nonwhite farm families was projected to fall from 75 per cent in 1968 to 67 per cent in 1975 under the same national unemployment percentage. The incidence of poverty by 1975 was nearly the same assuming a 6 per cent national unemployment rate. Farm nonwhite families in 1966 were so far below the poverty threshold that considerable economic progress moved very few above the $3,000 threshold used by Madden.

SPANISH-SPEAKING PEOPLE

White persons of Spanish surname in five Southwestern states numbered 3.5 million in 1960. This population, though once largely rural, is now 80 per cent urban, and only 5 per cent live on farms (U.S. Department of Agriculture, 1966, p. 53). The Spanish-speaking population is characterized by very low income and education and by poor housing and living conditions. The median income of these people in rural areas of each of five Southwestern states was less than $2,000 in 1949 and 1959. Educational attainment of Spanish-speaking residents of the Southwest was even lower than among Negroes in the South. Farm men averaged only 4.6 years of schooling. Birthrates were high—two-fifths of the farm families in 1960 had six members or more. But unlike Negro families, the Spanish-speaking families were stable. There is considerable evidence that the younger generation is accommodating to a culture and way of life more nearly consistent with economic progress.

AMERICAN INDIANS

There are over one-half million Indians in the U.S. They are the most rural of all ethnic groups in the nation. The rurality of Indians ranges from a high of 95 per cent in North Carolina to a low of 47 per cent in California. Two-fifths of all Indians live in three states: Arizona, New Mexico, and Oklahoma.

The Indian population, like the Negroes and Spanish-speaking groups, is characterized by high birthrates, low income, inadequate education, poor housing, and frequent health problems. In 1960, 70 per cent of all Indian farm families had incomes under $3,000. The median income of all employed Indian farm males was just over $1,000. Some of the most abject poverty anywhere in the U.S. is found among the Navaho. Yet, the average population increase on Navaho reservations may be more than 4 per cent per year. On a Navaho reservation in Utah, the median education in 1960 was less than one year. Median education of all farm male Indians 14 years of age and over ranged from 3.7 years in New Mexico to 8.6 years in California and South Dakota in 1960 (U.S. Department of Agriculture, 1966, p. 57).

OTHER ETHNIC GROUPS

Additional ethnic groups in the U.S. include the rural French-speaking people in Louisiana, the Japanese, the Chinese, and Puerto Ricans. There are comparatively few Japanese and Chinese in farming, and those who are constitute no low-income problems. There are a substantial number of French-speaking rural residents in Louisiana. Their income and education levels are low. In two counties in Louisiana, 60 per cent of the French-speaking families had an income of less than $1,500 in 1959, and those who spoke French in their homes averaged only 5.2 years of schooling (cf. U.S. Department of Agriculture, 1966, p. 61).

CONVENTIONAL THEORIES OF POVERTY

Classical economic theory stresses that economic growth in a region is determined by rates of return on capital, which attract capital to regions where returns are high, and by wages, which draw labor to regions where wages are high. But this theory begs the question why capital and labor earnings are higher in some regions than others and why differences do not disappear over time. Three reclassified conventional theories of regional economic development are presented, but they are not very helpful.

Economists have recognized the unique properties of rural poverty and have concocted a separate bag of theories to cope with the pathology of regional economic growth. Two hypotheses, the settlement hypothesis and the matrix-location hypothesis, have largely preoccupied economists. Following a discussion of these, I advance a liminal concept of economic stagnation, which attempts to incorporate past explanations into a general theory.

SOME TRADITIONAL THEORIES OF REGIONAL GROWTH

Numerous theories have been proposed to explain regional economic growth. The export-base, staple, and trade theories emphasize comparative advantage and the growth-generating properties of an export industry (Perloff *et al.*, 1960, p. 57; Berry, 1967, pp. 12–20), but do little to explain why or how a region can develop an export industry, or why rates of return on investment are higher in some regions than others. Location theory provides a rationale—usually cost-minimization—for location of industry and other economic activity, given the location of markets and resources (Berry, 1967, p. 12), but does not adequately account for external economies and the nonmonetary factors of location.

The above theories have considerable overlap, and some of their elements are included in the following reclassification of conventional theories of regional growth.

Basic Resources Theory

The basic resources theory implies that the economic growth of a region depends on the presence and development of indigenous basic resources—land, water, minerals, climate, and locational advantage. Primary industry that depends on basic resources in turn creates secondary and tertiary industries. The fundamental employment and output linkage among primary, secondary, and tertiary industries can be quantified and expressed as multipliers.

Internal Combustion Theory

The internal combustion theory of area growth stresses that economic growth can be generated by internal forces other than the presence of basic resources. Among such sources of economic growth are technology, specialization, division of labor, economies of scale, and a well-developed infrastructure.

For example, many industries require little transportation cost or natural resources. The fundamental requirement is often skilled labor and techniques. The technology-oriented electronics industries of California and New England are examples.

The attractiveness of the internal combustion growth theory is that, unlike the basic resource theory, the requirements for growth are not written in the stars. Growth can occur in any area or region and depends largely on the will of indigenous individuals and society to themselves create the kind of environment that attracts capital and labor. Much of the effort is likely to be geared toward creating export industries. If the region is large enough, however, the growth can largely occur internally, without major exports to finance imports from other regions.

External Combustion Theory

The external combustion theory places the stimuli for growth outside the natural resources or man-made efforts of the region. Growth is generated by stimuli from outside the region. Examples are such factors as luck or an increase in outside demand for goods produced in a region. It is likely, for example, that the economic configuration of regions in the U.S. would look quite different today if settlement had first been made in the West and then followed by a movement East. The regional economic pattern in the U.S. would also look quite different today had there been no Civil War, no automobile, or no cotton gin. The trouble with the external combustion theory is its fatalism—a region can find few internal instrumental variables to self-determine its growth. However, the theory does point to a role for an "outsider" such as the federal government in development of areas or regions that lack impetus for growth from unstructured market forces.

In summary, regions are finding that growth is less tied to natural resources and is more dependent on technology and on the attitudes and skills embodied in people. Also it is recognized that the chance factor is highly important, with economies of size sufficiently prominent so that a region may possess a comparative advantage simply because it was developed first. The service industries tend to have high-income elasticities of demand, tend to be market-oriented, and are relatively free from ties to a natural resource base. Regional science suggests that future area economic activity will be less tied to the natural resource and export base but will be more dependent on luck, nearness to markets, conglomerate (size) advantages, and investments in education and research.

The above theories are fragmentary, have a large tautological element, and give little insight into the factors that explain rural poverty. The problems of a depressed area are not brought much closer to solution by concluding that there is too little basic or tertiary industry, or that demand from outside has diminished for products currently being produced in the region. Thus, we must turn to theories more centrally focused on depressed areas.

SETTLEMENT PATTERN HYPOTHESES

History offers some clues why incomes in certain areas have lagged over extended periods. One set of historical explanations is based on settlement patterns. Caudill states that the U.S. was settled in three waves (Caudill, 1965, pp. 3–9). In the foremost wave were the frontiersmen—the trappers, hunters, traders, and adventurers. Following them were the "scratch farmers," who built crude cabins, cleared the land, and plowed the earth. They felt no real attachment for the land, however, and intended to move to a new frontier after the topsoil was eroded and the land began to lose its productivity. The third wave was composed of farmers and town-builders, who formed permanent settlements, built schools and churches, and were concerned with conservation of resources. They had a long-term perspective.

But at every stage in the scramble westward, some groups of frontiersmen and scratch farmers were engulfed by the third wave. "Out of tune with the dominant society and culture . . . the frontiersmen and scratch-farmer . . . fell

behind a generation or two in their own lifetime. . . . [They] were largely un-
schooled. They were addicted to direct action and simplicity of thought . . .
were magnificent specialists, but their specialty had vanished" (Caudill, 1965,
p. 4). Caudill goes on to state that, while the dominant culture was based on the
wealth it created, the heirs of this marooned subculture tended to fall farther
behind their compatriots. The cultural gap widened because the homelife and
psychology of the dominant culture differed radically from those of the subculture, which, according to Caudill (1965, p. 54) is similar to the backwards
subculture predominant today in Appalachia and the Ozarks.

Galbraith (1956) cites the settlement pattern—the way land was initially
divided and occupied—as the factor which gave rise to a whole set of rural
institutions inimical to growth. Early homesteaders, and sometimes the laws
under whose jurisdiction they settled, gave too little attention to the productivity
of the land, to climate, and to topography. The result was oversettlement, which
led to underemployment and low income, which in turn led to the privations,
enforced idleness, inadequate diet, and limited perspective associated with
subsistence living.

A third settlement pattern hypothesis is that the more educated, progressive,
and vigorous pioneers settled in what today are the commercial farming areas.
Another class of settlers who lacked education and capital, often because they
were former indentured servants or sons of renters, were unable to compete
with other pioneers for better lands and were forced by economic realities to
settle on lands of lower productivity, which today are the low-income rural
areas. Inertia traced to initial lack of physical assets and education continues to
provide a barrier to economic progress, and the income level continues to lag
behind that in other areas.

Several studies have tested the ability of the settlement pattern hypotheses
to explain current poverty. Nicholls, whose analysis of the Upper Tennessee
Valley (1957, p. 313) tended to support the hypothesis, found that "today's more
industrial counties have historically had somewhat superior 'original' natural
resources for financing education." However, the currently more industrialized
counties appear to have had no economic advantage over other counties in
1900 because of the economic stagnation that followed the Civil War.

Financial support of schools in the 1850–1900 period was closely related to
the wealth in agriculture, which was greater in what are today the more industrialized counties. Emphasis on education and lower fertility rates in these
counties eventually led to industrial development. Nicholls (1957, p. 314) concluded that basic differences in cultural attitudes and agricultural wealth among
counties resulted in industrial development rather than the other way around.
This finding—that industrial development and economic growth stemmed from
basic initial differences among counties—is generally consistent with the settlement pattern theory of growth.

Booth's (1961) study of eastern Oklahoma showed that the current income pattern is directly correlated with initial farm settlement patterns. Early farms in that area were too small. The area was, into the late nineteenth century, under the control of Indians, who displayed little interest in constructing and improving schools. Furthermore, white settlers were interlopers in Indian territory for a number of years and had little to say about establishment of schools and about spending for other social overhead. Many of the white settlers were from the Southeast and Appalachian areas, with less interest in education than persons from the Midwest, who more frequently settled on the plains of western Oklahoma.

The ranking of counties by income in eastern Oklahoma remained substantially the same from 1910 to 1950. Booth's results were generally consistent with the settlement theory hypothesis. It is interesting to note that income per farm worker in eastern Oklahoma *declined* relative to the rest of the state between 1910 and 1950. It accomplished this considerable feat while starting at an income level per farm worker of only 59 per cent of the state average in 1910.

Numerous examples can be used to support the settlement theory. It may be said that the Negro is poor because he was a slave and a sharecropper who never really recovered from the economic disadvantage of this "settlement" pattern.

On the other hand, numerous examples can be cited of instances where areas, currently poor, were not always so. Tang's (1958) analysis of the Southern Piedmont demonstrated that current differences among counties could not be explained by differences in settlement patterns or land quality. Many areas of the rural South, urban slums, parts of the Upper Great Lakes region, the Ozarks, and the Appalachians, though now chronically depressed, were not always so. The settlement pattern explanation of poverty applies in a sufficient number of cases to justify its usefulness, but there are so many exceptions—cases of poverty not explained by settlement patterns—that it is necessary to look for a more general explanation.

THE MATRIX-LOCATION HYPOTHESIS

T. W. Schultz (1953, p. 157) states that differences in level of living are basically the consequence of the way the economy of the U.S. has developed and are not primarily the result of original differences in cultural values, capabilities of the people, or man-land ratios. Low-income areas, once nearly at the same economic level as areas that are now developed and prosperous, did not progress as fast economically because resource mobility was hindered by a disadvantaged position in the location matrix. Schultz (1953, p. 147) argues that economic development occurs in a specific location matrix, that each matrix is primarily urban-industrial at the core, and that factor markets and forces of economic development operate best near the core.

Numerous studies have tested Schultz's matrix-location hypothesis. Tang (1958) found substantial support for the hypothesis in the Southern Piedmont; Booth (1961) rejected the hypothesis in its application to eastern Oklahoma. Diehl (1966) found no support for the hypothesis based on cross-sectional data for the Southeast between 1950 and 1960. Bryant (1966, p. 569) found that "For the nation as a whole, the closer a county is to an SMSA [Standard Metropolitan Statistical Area] and the larger the SMSA, the lower are the earnings of farmers." He did find support for the matrix-location hypothesis in the divisions east of the Mississippi River, with factor markets in proximity to urban centers functioning significantly to raise farm income levels. This relationship was not found for divisions west of the Mississippi River, however.

The matrix-location hypothesis is logically compelling and would appear to be as "intuitively obvious" as the widely accepted principles of classical microeconomic theory on which it rests. The hypothesis in all likelihood is sound. Then why is it not more roundly supported by empirical evidence? The reason is that it, like the settlement pattern hypothesis, has been often wrongly applied as *the* theory of poverty, when in fact it is a very partial theory. It is like saying that only demand or only supply determines pricing and output. The matrix-location hypothesis has not been proven wrong, but it is overshadowed by other more important forces in the many instances where data do not support it.

The Great Plains, by many reasonable predictive standards of the location-matrix theory, should be a rural poverty area. Most farms are hundreds of miles from an urban-industrial center. Biological innovations and fertilizers need water for economic application. The vast majority of Great Plains farmers are dryland farmers, and they have been by-passed by many of the chemical-biological innovations that have substantially raised yields in more humid areas. The downward adjustment required in the labor force and farm numbers in the Great Plains to reach the level of an economic unit is stupendous.

There are four principal reasons why the Great Plains region is not now a poverty area: (*a*) it is very difficult to subsist on an uneconomic unit, because noncommercial sources of livelihood are rare, and weather uncertainties are large and will literally starve out laggards in unfavorable years; (*b*) Great Plains farmers have not lagged seriously in providing education for their children; (*c*) people migrated into the Great Plains in a comparatively recent period and were thus accustomed to mobility and did not have the ossified structure of values and institutions that severely limits mobility; and (*d*) transportation and other communication networks were maintained so that people separated from an urban-industrial complex by 1,000 miles of paved road were less isolated than persons separated by only a few miles of "trails" from the industrial complex on the other side of a mountain.

Because of large machinery, well-suited for the Great Plains topography, the cost per unit of production there can be reduced more by expanding farm size than in most areas. Part of the savings of the buyer who consolidates units is passed on to the seller, and hence constitutes an opportunity cost of maintaining an uneconomic unit for the farmer who does not sell out and leave the area to secure nonfarm employment. The Great Plains example shows that the problem of development is complex and that no one simple theory is capable of explaining every situation.

A GENERAL THEORY OF ECONOMIC STAGNATION

The simplicity that characterizes the foregoing hypotheses is sacrificed to gain more realism in the following theory of economic stagnation. The theory contains three basic elements that apply to individuals, regions, or groups: (*a*) they are confronted by factors which require adjustments in resources, products, and technology; (*b*) they have identifiable characteristics which give rise to differences in ability to adjust to factors in (*a*); and, finally, (*c*) when the forces requiring adjustments are large relative to the ability to adjust, a liminal level of adjustment is reached at which the environment develops anomie and other dysfunctional syndromes inimical to rapid change. The area environment then becomes less rather than more conducive to satisfactory economic adjustments to changing conditions.

Forces that Require Adjustments

Changes in the economic, social, technical, and political environment continually require adjustments in resources, products, and techniques. A mistake in settlement pattern is only one reason why changes are needed. Even without an error in settlement, nearly all regions experience the need for major adjustments at one time or another from dynamic sources, including (*a*) a decline in demand for products produced, (*b*) depletion of natural resources through mining or erosion, (*c*) technical obsolescence, and (*d*) a social upheaval.

Examples of each can be illustrated for agriculture in the Southeast. Irrigated cotton in the Texas High Plains and the West reduced the effective demand for Southeast cotton. Erosion severely depleted fertility of upland slopes, making some former cotton land unsuited for cash crops. What erosion failed to do, the boll weevil, other insects, and disease often accomplished. Mechanical cotton-pickers released many workers from the cotton fields. Development of large tractors greatly expanded the farm size required for optimum efficiency. But because of rough terrain and fragmented fields, this opportunity to reduce unit costs and adjust to lower prices stemming from aggregate excess supply eluded many areas now in poverty. The legacy of slavery, the Civil War, and racial discrimination also have been major factors in the economic and social upheavals that underlie rural poverty.

ABILITY TO ADJUST TO CHANGING ECONOMIC CONDITIONS

All individuals, groups, and areas have some capacity to adjust to changing economic conditions, but some have greater capacity than others. This capacity to adjust is highest, and the limen is least likely to be exceeded, in areas where (*a*) birthrates are low, (*b*) educational levels are high, (*c*) transportation and communication are adequate, (*d*) people have a "mobility ethic" fostered by past migration and willingness to change, (*e*) the culture of the area is malleable and compatible with that in growth areas to which people must migrate, (*f*) there are no "institutional" barriers such as racial discrimination within the region receiving migrants to preclude mobility, and (*g*) the area is in reasonable proximity to an urban-industrial complex.

Thus, the matrix-location concept is one subset of this general hypothesis, whereas the settlement pattern concept is one subset of the previous general hypothesis that identifiable forces cause the need for economic adjustments.

RESOURCE MOBILITY AND THE LIMEN

The important feature of rural poverty is not that the settlement pattern or other dynamic forces listed above resulted in low incomes but that incomes have been so slow to recover. These chronically depressed areas have not developed or attracted new industries and jobs at a pace sufficient to replace declining industries. Market incentives have not induced sufficient outmigration to eliminate differences in wages.

For political reasons and to minimize social cost, it would be most desirable to have economic progress within the region that lags economically so that the specter of outmigration need not be confronted. It would seem more advantageous to bring jobs to people than to bring people to jobs. This solution requires substantial *economic growth*, defined as an increase in real output of goods and services. Potentially the two most appealing solutions in this context are to increase the productivity of farms and to industrialize.

The most optimistic target would be to expand the productivity of farms so that the existing farm operators could achieve a satisfactory income. Even this unrealistic target of maintaining the current number of farms would require outmigration of nearly half the farm youth. The realistic conclusion, however, is that there is no feasible way to make current-size farms and villages sufficiently productive to provide a satisfactory net farm income. Farms must be expanded in acreage. Part-time farming offsets expanding farm size and outmigration, but it also has distinct limitations. Thus, in addition to the new jobs required by the excess of births over deaths in a static farm structure, there are also substantial dynamic adjustments required to correct past disequilibrium and accommodate new factors. In serious problem areas, only one in sixteen farm youths will find adequate opportunities in farming.

Local industrial development potentially could create sufficient new jobs so that rural youth need not leave the home community. This alternative will be discussed in more detail later; only a few of the limitations of this solution are mentioned here. Many industries have not found the specialized resources, including skilled labor, or the large markets needed to attract them to depressed rural regions. Some industries which potentially can locate in depressed regions must be excluded because they are themselves declining industries, pay low wages, or have a footloose history of high mobility. The most favorable prospects for industry have been in core cities with populations of 25,000 or over, and many farmers are too distant from these cities to be influenced.

From the above discussion it is clear that every farm and community does not have the potential for indigenous economic development. But income growth can nevertheless occur through labor mobility. It is in the lack of labor mobility that we must seek many of the basic causes and cures to chronic poverty. Labor mobility is a key issue in economic development in rural areas. *Economic development*, meaning an increase in per capital real income, is a felicitous concept because income per person can increase if outmigration is sufficient to counterbalance lack of economic growth.

Low incomes in underdeveloped nations in Asia, Africa, or South America can be explained by institutional restraints, including inadequate credit and marketing mechanisms, poor transportation, the caste system, incentive-depressing tenure arrangements, and uncertainties and waste fostered by government bureaucracy. Political instability in developing countries has also created problems. Illiteracy and the attendant lack of information required to improve efficiency—and an industrial and research sector too small to turn out sufficient amounts of improved capital inputs or to absorb excess farm labor—can also be blamed. But institutional restraints, such as immigration restrictions, do not limit mobility among U.S. areas and regions. Economically stagnant rural areas in the U.S. have not been troubled with political instability or isolation from efforts to improve production technology. Also lagging areas are continually exposed to the dominant goals and attitudes of the economically progressive elements of U.S. society through mass media.

In isolated underdeveloped countries, poverty can be explained by an understandable lack of savings and investment and absence of entrepreneurship. Language and geographic barriers and institutional impediments preclude high mobility of resources and techniques. However, capital and credit are readily available to a U.S. region from outside regions if returns are adequate. Lack of natural resources may impede economic progress in India for example but not necessarily in the Ozarks, from which the individual can move to a region well endowed with "natural" resources and jobs. The outlook for economic development can be bright for any U.S. area that possesses resource mobility. The enigmatic and frustrating property of rural poverty in the United States is that it can exist as an island in a progressive economy despite the economic pressures for it to disappear. Mobility has not been great enough to overcome the friction in the markets and to equalize resource returns among all U.S. areas. One of the principal reasons is the development of certain poverty syndromes that emerge as the required economic adjustments exceed the limen. The poverty syndrome is apparent in the goals, values, and institutions found in poverty areas.

GOALS, VALUES, AND INSTITUTIONS IN CHRONICALLY DEPRESSED RURAL AREAS

Factor markets in the U.S. have generally operated efficiently to allocate labor and capital to uses where wages and returns are highest. Purely economic behavior would lead to individual decisions that would eliminate pockets of poverty. This has not occurred in areas of chronic rural poverty for reasons rooted in the values of the people and in the institutions of the areas.

Values reflect the intensity of feelings with which means or ends are held and are the personal criteria that determine what behavioral response will follow economic or other stimuli. Institutions refer to family, school, church, and government (including the tax structure). Properties of values are: (*a*) they often have a functional origin in the need of society to operate effectively in maintaining its welfare and identity; and (*b*) they result from the dominant striving of individuals to create a favorable image of themselves in the eyes of others as well as themselves.

In the long run, values and institutions are flexible and accommodate to dynamic features of economic growth and decline. All areas have considerable potential capacity to adjust to a changing economic environment. If the liminal rate of adjustment is not exceeded, then adjustment takes place smoothly and the ability to adjust may increase as institutions such as schools and family learn to prepare people for the transition. The family accepts mobility as a way of life, and local leaders are flexible and constructive in setting policies.

But if the economy calls for a rate of adjustment in excess of the limen, then reactionary forces set up cultural and other barriers to forestall adjustments. The adjustment gap then may grow larger rather than smaller. General pessimism is apt to pervade the area. Often the young, educated, industrious, and optimistic elements migrate and leave local leadership, which is responsible for establishing the value climate, in the hands of persons with the opposite attributes. Pessimism is infectious and colors the outlook of the community toward efforts to make changes consistent with growth.

The gap between the values held in the depressed community and the values required for success in modern society widens rather than disappears. As the income and culture gap grows between poverty areas and the remainder of society, then boundary-maintaining conditions must be accentuated or the community will lose its pride and identity. The functional objective of the community, and hence the focus of value formation, becomes one of maintaining community cultural boundaries rather than making economic adjustments. The fact that these means are successful, in spite of mass communication media and other pressures to conform with urban-industrial values, testifies to the strength of the boundary-maintaining devices. These cultural barricades will be discussed later in more detail.

There are numerous examples of the self-generating forces that emerge when the rate of economic decline exceeds the liminal level. The property tax base may decline little or not at all, but there is likely to be a decline in tax base in comparison to other growing regions, and the schools, the roads, and the local government are a "fixed plant" difficult to maintain—much less to improve. The dependency ratio of children and retired persons to the productive age groups will be high because of the outmigration of the productive groups. This raises school and welfare costs in relation to the earnings of those in the productive age categories, and the quality of education declines because the local tax base is not able to support the ever-growing outlays required for well-trained teachers and a diversified curriculum.

Also important is the unwillingness to utilize the tax base that exists (cf. Welch, 1965). The depressed community is likely to be apathetic about tightening its tax belt to provide better schools, because many people who absorb the taxes through education leave the community. The benefit-cost ratio from education for the depressed area itself may be low, and the growing community to which migrants move is benefited by the taxes of the depressed community. Schools of the poverty areas are sometimes so poor that migrants lacking education and ability to compete for city jobs become part of the legacy of crime and rioting found in our large cities (cf. Tweeten, 1967). Schnore (1966, p. 136), after reviewing previous studies, concludes that "farm reared migrants to the city enter the urban class structure at or near the bottom, whether the measure is education, occupation or income."

IDEAL ATTITUDES FOR ECONOMIC PROGRESS

Before examining the attitudes and institutions found in depressed rural areas, it is useful to review briefly certain elements of socio-economic growth theory presented in Chapter 4. Given the natural resources, then the propensities to save, invest, and be efficient will be high and economic development will be most rapid in an area possessing social-psychological characteristics of *secular ascetism* and *functional activism*. While never fully present in individuals, these ideal attitudes serve as a basis of comparison with existing attitudes.

Secular asceticism characterizes a populace that considers work either an end in itself or the recognized means to some end such as status or material gain. In addition to the shunning of leisure, the ideal encompasses honesty, thrift, market morality, and willingness to defer consumptive gratification from accumulated economic goods to the future. It is apparent that this quality contributes to a high rate of savings and work efficiency associated with a dedicated, conscientious, and disciplined labor force.

Functional activism characterizes a populace that is imaginative, innovative, perspicacious, manipulative, farsighted, mobile, organizationally capable, and willing to take reasonable risks in use of current assets to pursue future gain. The concept entails the spirit of enterprise and entrepreneurial zeal, but does not stop there. It applies as well to public and private enterprise. It is a dynamic quality that gives rise to investment and influences efficiency through development of new opportunities by both formal means (e.g., research) and informal means (e.g., individual ideas).

Functional activism is an attitude that underlies efforts to seek out profitable uses of funds for investment, and the employment of capital and labor in whatever uses offer greatest returns. It encompasses the need for achievement reflected in the active, functional decisions that lead to economic growth. A certain degree of secular asceticism is necessary for a long-term perspective and the willingness to forgo current consumption and to "save" for an adequate education. But functional activism is needed to channel the education into a curriculum that will have subsequent economic productivity and to find a position that productively utilizes the investment in education. Thus, functional activism is important for education and mobility—two factors of crucial concern for low-income rural areas. The presence of the twin concepts of secular ascetism and functional activism underlie high propensities to save, invest, and be efficient, and hence they also underlie economic progress.

Low-income areas do not possess these two characteristics in sufficient degree to promote local area growth or permit sufficiently rapid outmigration to compensate for declining local income. I discuss below how attitudes are influenced by the local culture, including status evaluation, family structure, religion, economic and political institutions, and level of economic growth already achieved.

U.S. Value Orientation

Olaf Larson (1955, p. 1422) lists the following significant value systems in the U.S. It is apparent that they are quite consistent with the secular asceticism and functional activism needed for economic progress.

Among the several major value-orientations in American culture that serve as guides to choices that people make individually and collectively are listed (1) a central stress upon personal achievement, especially secular occupational achievement, (2) efficiency and practicality, (3) progress, (4) material comfort, (5) external conformity, and (6) belief in science and secular rationality. To the extent that these values are shared by the low income group, motivation would be expected for an improvement in status. Thus, knowledge of new agricultural techniques to improve income would lead to adoption. Or knowledge of alternative opportunities would lead to occupational shifts or migration.

Attitudes in rural poverty areas can be contrasted with those for the U.S. listed above by Larson. Poverty in the U.S. tends to be disproportionately concentrated in the South, in rural areas, and among Negroes. Thus the following discussion of Southern attitudes seems apropos.

SOUTHERN ATTITUDES

Nicholls (1960) lists five principal elements in the Southern way of life that have hampered economic progress.

1. *The persistence of agrarian values embracing work on the soil as the best and "most sensitive" of vocations, deserving of the maximum number of workers.* This view encouraged farming as a way of life, irrespective of economic returns, and diverted energy from industrial development which is such an important part of economic progress. The South, settled prior to the Civil War, was alienated from the remainder of the nation by its unique subculture and by the Civil War and Reconstruction. The South relied heavily on cash crops of cotton and tobacco, which required extensive labor. Landowners favored policies to maintain cheap farm labor. One such policy was to avoid industrialization. The above factors were the seeds of a self-reinforcing momentum for economic retardation which led to disparity of income between the South and non-South.

2. *The undemocratic nature of the political structure.* Large landholders held political power out of proportion to their numbers. Negroes and poor whites were not proportionately represented. This was reflected in tax policies and in the reduced allocation of public funds to roads, schools, and other social overhead necessary for development of a productive rural farm economy as well as industry.

3. *The rigidity of the social structure.* Discrimination limited job mobility and incentives to improve employment potential through education.

4. *The weakness of social responsibility.* A rigid social structure emerged which was often preoccupied with preserving white supremacy. The social conscience, manifested by a desire to improve the lot of the Negroes and poor whites, was narrowly restricted.

5. *Conformity of thought and behavior.* As mentioned above, there was little tolerance for dissent for the existing social structure, and formal law enforcement agencies and informal groups (ranging from Ku Klux Klan to press and radio) helped to maintain the tradition. One would expect functional activism to be severely retarded in this social climate.

The above factors do not provide an adequate explanation of current problems of rural poverty, even in the Southeast. Status valuation, religion, attitude toward education, and outlook on life are more relevant and have a broader geographic base.

ATTITUDES ASSOCIATED WITH INDIVIDUAL ECONOMIC PERFORMANCE

Most studies of individual economic behavior are predicated on the assumption that this behavior is rational and goal-oriented and that a person does in fact work toward achieving his needs and goals. The goals and needs are conditioned by the cultural environment, by the biological makeup and personal experience of the individual, and by expectations of success which are conditioned by accessibility of goals in the social and physical environment. The limitations of the environment mean that all needs cannot be achieved immediately, and a hierarchy of needs may help to predict behavior. The following is a suggested hierarchy of needs, from basic to higher-order, the basic needs ostensibly being fulfilled first.

1. Security needs (self-preservation, protection from immediate physical danger to life)
2. Physiological needs (hunger, thirst, body warmth)
3. Belonging (acceptance by others)
4. Self-realization (freedom, justice, stability, independence)
5. Self-gratification (recognition, prestige, success)

The entrepreneurial function is concerned with more than provisions of goods and services to meet basic physiological needs. Rather it falls in a higher order, the self-gratification category listed above. A subsistence economy, limited in perspective and conditioned to a niggardly environment that provides only basic needs, might not be expected to afford the "luxury" of functional activism, which may rank high in the above hierarchy. Latent functional activism may also be repressed in economically retarded areas for lack of ready capital, a complement of functional activism.

Hobbs, Beal, and Bohlen (1964, p. 153) have analyzed the association between the attitude of farm operators and their economic performance. The most significant attitudes influencing economic performance were found to be independence, economic motivation, and risk preference. The single most significant factor was willingness to make independent economic decisions on the basis of functional relevance and not necessarily in conformity with the norms of the local culture. According to Merton (1957), the innovator may be defined as an individual who accepts the culturally defined goals of the neighborhood while rejecting the culturally defined means. In contrast the ritualist is defined as an individual who rejects the culturally defined goals and adheres too rigidly to the culturally defined means. The findings of Hobbs *et al.* at the firm level are consistent with the contention of Nicholls that pressures for conformity have inhibited innovation and other aspects of functional activism needed for economic progress.

The above finding (that attitudes favorable both toward making money and taking risks are positively associated with earnings) appears to be inconsistent with McClelland's study (1961, p. 238), which found that persons with a strong need for achievement preferred neither very high nor very low risk, but rather preferred manageable levels of risk. McClelland found that persons motivated to achievement valued money not for itself but as a yardstick of success. The seeming inconsistency is largely explained by differences in the way terms and attitudes were defined and measured.

Orientation to science and a relative emphasis on mental over physical activity have been found in some instances to give rise to successful economic performance, but the research of Hobbs, Beal, and Bohlen revealed little association of these attitudes with economic performance. Their study of individual behavior, however, may have limited relevance for low-income areas, where collective rather than individual behavior is the focus of interest.

STATUS VALUATION

As stated earlier, behavior tends to be directed to activity that earns high esteem in the eyes of oneself and others. From the standpoint of economic growth, it is important to examine what type of behavior elicits esteem. If it is the belief that dependence on economic employment is indisputable evidence that one lacks capacities of mind and character that entitle one to a higher position (one that provides leisure to hunt, fish, commune with neighbors, or pursue social graces), then economic growth is inhibited (Brewster, 1961). But if proficiency in economic behavior is the appropriate way of earning a high valuation in the eyes of others, then economic growth is enhanced. The question of what constitutes economic behavior needs elaboration.

The masses try to emulate the activities of those highest in status and to avoid participating in the activities pursued by those lowest in status. The behavior of the upper classes and their habits of work and thrift have an important bearing on economic activity of the populace. This fact, according to W. Arthur Lewis (1957, p. 37), has influenced the attitude toward work in the South. His specualation, of dubious relevance, is that "in the slave communities of the New World, the plantocracies were much given to going on picnics and to having good times and there was much absentee ownership. The middle and working classes of these communities to this day show a greater propensity to consume lavishly than they do to work, and this may plausibly be explained by saying that they have inherited the idea that work is fit only for slaves."

The hierarchy of prestige attached to occupations tends to be associated with power and wealth. It has been postulated that behavior is motivated and activity directed toward those occupations which are accorded the highest status. If so, economic growth tends to be greatest where the highest status is accorded economically productive occupations, such as running a successful business, rather than being a priest, absentee landlord, sportsman, or society patron. If traditional occupations, such as the professions of medicine and law, are ranked in status well above business-oriented occupations that have higher rates of economic return, then economic growth is retarded as the most capable people are attracted to the professions with the higher status. Fixation on the high status of professional entertainers and athletes *vis à vis* merchants and skilled workers may give unattainable occupational aspirations to large numbers of Negro youth. Even the farming occupation can be too attractive in the sense that the demand for farming opportunities exceeds the supply of economic units. If a stigma is attached to renting land or being a debtor, this can limit the potential for growth in farm acreage, investment, and income.

Additional research is needed to determine the place of labor and status valuation in the poverty milieu. Operators of low-income farms probably perform as much physically demanding labor as operators of commercial farms. Operators of farms with low returns are underemployed in the sense that off-farm work or farm reorganization and expansion would bring higher labor returns, but they are not unemployed.

There is considerable evidence to indicate that too many farm youth are attracted either to farming or to high prestige professions (cf. Cleland *et al.,* 1965; Burchinal *et al.,* 1962; Horner *et al.,* 1967). As a consequence, their aspirations are often unrealizable because of few opportunities and high entrance requirements. Entrance requirements as to schooling, special aptitudes, IQ, or capital may be too high. In the case of farming, huge capital requirements are a sizable barrier to forming an economic unit. Failing to realize their intended goals, these youths find too late that they are not trained for nonfarm occupations in which the demand for workers is great and for which the resources within their reach could have qualified them.

Anomie

Anomie is social alienation—a lack of confidence in the social environment. Ford (1965) discusses the "being" orientation found among rural people. It is fostered by a subsistence agriculture, where members of society feel subjugated by nature. Appalachian attitude surveys revealed that among the poor, the supernatural is viewed as punitive, and man is viewed as unable to control his own destiny. This outlook can foster three symptoms of anomie: demoralization, fatalism, and pessimism. Behavior then may become spontaneous and directed toward filling immediate ends because "long-run plans don't work out anyway." This is in contrast to the "doing" orientation of the urban-industrial middle class and commercial farmers, who have greater belief in the power of man over nature and have had their confidence in long-term plans reinforced by successful past activity.

The reinforcing aspects of success are apparent in the statement of Ford (1965, pp. 41–42):

> But in the experienced world of the very poor, the probabilities of success in almost any major achievement endeavor are relatively low regardless of the effort put forth. To the middle class, the fact that the success chances of the poor are lower may appear irrelevant, for the members of this group are seen as having everything to gain and nothing to lose from seeking to improve their situation. The loss of self-esteem that inevitably attends failure, however, represents a good deal to those who have little else but pride. For many, the stakes are too high and the odds too poor in this middle class, whether it is called the pursuit of success, self-betterment, achievement, or community development. There is only one sure way not to lose, and that is not to play.

Universalist norms of achievement, success, and high-mass consumption are amply advertised by mass media and reach all members of society, rich and poor. To protect the ego, persons trapped in poverty by low education and limited assets and skills often form protective barriers. Either they do not identify themselves with this mass culture or they compensate by various means.

COGNITIVE DISSONANCE

Cognitive dissonance refers to situations in which noneconomic rewards such as the community environment, family, and religion are elevated to superior status to compensate for inadequate conventional rewards such as money and material possessions. People in chronically depressed rural areas elevate the values and goals which they are able to realize to greater prominence relative to the achievement-success norms of commercial society. Persons interviewed in Texas rated the family and religion above job or work as the source of greatest satisfaction in life (cf. Cleland *et al.*, 1965). Persons also can be expected to lower needs gradually to levels which can be reached in a community of limited opportunity. This becomes a poverty-perpetuating device if these limited motivations and economic needs are passed on to the next generation.

To some extent, local attitudes are shaped by contrasts with the standard of living in other parts of society. Standards of living and earnings in many areas of poverty in the U.S. are greater than that of the masses in Taiwan or Japan. Yet the values are quite different as measured by the morale of the individuals. The poverty state, one of mind as well as of pocketbook, is determined to a great extent by *relative* income levels. Some gap between aspirations and present circumstances leads to creative tensions and motivates escape from poverty, but too large a gap leads to anomie and explosive tensions that are sometimes released in socially unacceptable behavior. If opportunities for improvement are not forthcoming, this state can lead only to despair and elevation of other non-monetary factors (such as religion and family) to higher status—or lead to riots and demonstrations. Welfare programs that involve direct subsidy and free distribution of food commodities without a reciprocal requirement of some work or job-training to deserve them can be criticized for reducing the feeling of worth and dignity of the individual and for fostering disrespectful attitudes toward work. In short, symptoms of anomie generated by some forms of public assistance are not conducive to the secular asceticism and functional activism needed for economic progress.

RELIGION

The role of religious culture in economic development has been discussed at length by Max Weber and others. The Protestant Ethic has been analyzed as a set of quasi-religious attitudes that simultaneously embodied secular asceticism and functional activism (Tweeten, 1966). W. Arthur Lewis (1957, p. 105) summarizes:

> If a religion lays stress on material values, upon work, upon thrift, and productive investment, upon honesty in commercial relations, upon experimentation and risk bearing, and upon equality of opportunity, it will be helpful to growth, whereas in as far as it is hostile to these things, it tends to inhibit growth.

The dominant religious tradition in many areas characterized by rural poverty is that of the fundamentalist Protestant sects, who place much emphasis on the merits of work, thrift, and high moral standards and on the evils of conspicuous consumption. Of these groups, Loomis (1960, p. 192) has written:

> It is likely to be a small homogeneous sect with strong emphasis on emotionalism and evangelism. It is likely to extol the virtues of self-discipline, hard work, thrift and industry, and to deplore the "sinful" (and costly) indulgences of worldly and high-living pleasures. Although these choices are made in the name of religion, their selection and pursuit are consistent with economic rise.

The attitudes fostered by these religious groups are virtually the epitome of secular asceticism, and hence are compatible with one facet of economic growth. But the emphasis on other worldly goals and conformity and the lack of emphasis on education are too binding on the innovative, imaginative spirit required for functional activism. Thus this type of religion is hypothesized to inhibit the spirit of enterprise and mobility needed for economic progress.

THE FAMILY

Another institution which is found in rural poverty areas is the extended family system. The meaning and functional origin of the system are discussed by Okun and Richardson (1961, p. 335):

> Under the kinship system, all family members, however distant, claim the right of support from the group, as well as the right to advise and pass judgments on each other's activities, regardless of their individual contributions. The advantage of such a system lies in the economic security it provides to individuals living at or near subsistence levels. But to the extent that individual effort is motivated by personal economic reward, the extended family system offsets market incentives to labor mobility, and to increased effort more generally, because of the obligation of the individual to share his rewards with the family.

The reference is not to the family farm structure which permeates agriculture and which has demonstrated a high degree of efficiency compatible with our industrial society. The issue is rather the situation found frequently in low-income rural areas where there is strong dominance of family and kinship groups over other groups. Priority of the family group limits mobility to economic employment where pay is highest. The family confers status, provides security against old age and misfortune and rewards and punishes individual members. The familistic culture provides work opportunities on an ascriptive basis. The individual is accorded status without demonstrating ability to achieve economic success. This contrasts with industrial society which is affectively neutral in providing jobs (to those most qualified) and gives status on the basis of economic achievement.

The extended family culture may have served a vital function of providing security in traditional society, but for a depressed area to grow, people must be cognizant of universalist norms (they must trust outsiders and not feel themselves to be aliens in mass society), must respond to economic incentives (they must not be tied to the family but be willing to migrate to obtain better work opportunities), and must place some value on organizations outside the family (they must attend meetings, school, etc., to become acquainted with values and requirements for productive economic roles in commercial society). Many programs to eliminate poverty and speed resource adjustments operate through institutions such as schools and local committees. Strong reliance on family to the exclusion of outsiders can stifle organized efforts to raise income and living standards.

EDUCATION

Farm people may adjust to either distant or nearby nonfarm employment, but they must adjust. Only a small minority of farm youths can expect to remain on the farm in some depressed regions. There are few factors more crucial for mobility than proper skills and attitudes. Education plays a part in both.

Attitudes of poverty areas toward education are especially important because education imparts productive skills which affect income; it imparts attitudes to the new generation. It provides one of the few opportunities to intervene in the cycle of parent-child attitude formation, even though studies show that the family is dominant over the school in forming aspirations. Education is one of the few socially acceptable ways of altering attitudes inimical to economic growth. It is the major cultural bridge between a poverty area and the mass, achievement-oriented society.

University of Michigan researchers constructed a measure of the need for achievement based on the ratings by individuals of the prestige of nine occupations (Morgan *et al.*, 1961, Appendix C). The hypothesis was that a person with a sizable need for achievement would place an unusually high value on succeeding in a high prestige occupation and an unusually low value on succeeding in a low prestige occupation. Results were consistent with the hypothesis; it was found that persons who were most educated had the highest measured need for achievement. Statistical significance was not high, however, and questions of causality remain.

In a later study, an "index of concern for progress" was constructed. It can be considered a measure of functional activism (Morgan *et al.*, 1966, p. 351). A sample of 2,214 household heads revealed a positive and consistent relationship between education and concern for progress. Other data to be presented later show that greater educational attainment is associated with higher labor force participation, lower unemployment, greater mobility, and higher income. There is little doubt that education in some way contributes to these positive forces for economic progress. It is therefore especially disturbing to note the following, frequent problems affecting the quality and quantity of education in low income areas (cf. Tweeten, 1967):

1. Local schools are not adequate to invest in the individual the productive assets needed to earn an acceptable income level. Both the quality and breadth of the curriculum are at fault. High school graduates are poorly equipped either for higher education or for immediate competition in the nonfarm job market.

2. Persons are simply uninformed of job opportunities outside of their restricted environment. Students do not face occupational decisions while in school, partly because of inadequate formal counseling but mainly because the local environment provides little first-hand evidence of opportunities and entrance requirements in growing occupations. Many students drift along without direction until they become dropouts. They belatedly realize their inadequacies of training, but deficiencies are too large to be made up by a return to school.

3. Youths with high occupational aspirations are unaware of training and the initial financial assets required for the occupations to which they aspire. By the time they learn what the requirements are, it is too late, and (to their way of thinking) too costly, to correct past mistakes in preparation. An Arkansas study found that 70 per cent of high school students in selected low-income counties of the state overaspired significantly for their capability level (Jordan *et al.*, 1967). This was partly because the quality of basic education was not adequate—lack of reading skills reduced their capability-test scores—but it was also because the environment was not conducive to progression from the fantasy to the reality stage of formulating aspirations. Nearly 42 per cent of the students aspired to professional, technical, and kindred occupations. The gap between aspirations and capability was less in large high schools than in small.

4. Youths plan for an occupation such as farming and obtain "appropriate" education for it. After completing their education, they find that opportunities are few and disappointing in their chosen field, but they have too little preparation to transfer to, and better their economic position in, another promising field of employment.

5. People see opportunities for labor transfer, but the personal "social" costs are too high. They wish to take a better-paying job, but the difficulty of separating from family and friends and of adjusting socially to a new environment is too great. This attitude reduces their interest in education. The direct monetary costs of labor transfer are comparatively low. That the social cost is large is evidenced by very high rates of migration back home after holding jobs in other areas. Researchers found that for every ten workers who left agriculture in the Tennessee Valley in 1958–59, thirteen returned to the farm sector. (This year was not typical because the economy was weak.) Studies of the U.S. economy also reveal high rates of movement of farm-reared people back to farms after holding nonfarm jobs (cf. Perkins and Hathaway, 1966).

The limited perspective afforded by parents and peers in the isolated rural environment can lead to little value being placed either on higher education or on a job outside the community; and the opposing forces of mass communication media, teachers, school counselors, and other aspects of school environment often are not sufficient to compensate. Concentration of educationally deprived children in certain schools tends to reinforce pupils' inadequacies.

Data show conclusively that education levels are lower in poverty areas than in other areas of the U.S. (cf. Schultz, 1968, pp. 145–71; Tweeten, 1968, pp. 33–35). Not only is the median schooling completed lower—and dropout rates higher—but the quality of education is below national standards.

The more serious areas of rural low income have pupil-teacher ratios comparable to those in more prosperous areas, but, measured by teacher salaries and annual expenditures per student, poverty areas rank low.

In rural farm areas of the South in 1960, only 23.3 per cent of the white and 5.7 per cent of the nonwhite adults had completed at least four years of high school. This means that 76.7 per cent of the white and 94.3 per cent of the nonwhite adults had either not attended or not completed high school. Dropout rates in 1960 among 19-year-olds were over 50 per cent for farm youth in the South Atlantic and East Central regions, where low incomes are frequent.

Low educational attainment can be partly explained by two economic factors: (*a*) opportunity costs of education are high in rural poverty areas where the earnings of youth are needed to help support the family; and (*b*) a considerable portion of education is supported from local tax revenues, principally property tax, and the local tax base is too low to support an adequate educational system. Furthermore, because many of the benefits of education are lost to the local community through outmigration, the local benefit-cost ratios are low and do not motivate the community to increase outlays.

Several sociological studies document the attitude toward education in areas of the South where income levels are low (cf. Cleland *et al.*, 1965). In Texas, researchers found that interviewed homemakers cited "relations with family" and "religion" as the source of their greatest satisfactions in life. "Job or work" and "education" received an insignificant response. Louisiana researchers found that respondents with low educational attainment tended to view their work more favorably than did those with higher education, indicating perhaps that greater educational attainment motivates high job aspirations, which persons who stay in the area are unable to fulfill. However, high-prestige occupations were universally desired for sons of respondents. These aspirations were unrealistically high in many instances, as was cited earlier for Arkansas children (Jordan *et al.*, 1967). The forming of aspirations progresses from fantasy to tentative and realistic phases. Many individuals in depressed communities do not seem to advance much beyond the fantasy stage of aspiration formulation. Further research is needed to determine not only the level of aspirations for children, but also the depth of motivation for realizing these aspirations, for attaining a knowledge of job requirements (education, migration, and capital funds required for training and getting started in occupation), and for evincing a willingness to overcome obstacles to reach occupational goals.

Sociologists in Kentucky found that a highly important variable in explaining escape from poverty was the homemaker's education which, if sufficient, seemed to provide adequate awareness of alternatives and conflict with present circumstances to create a desire for mobility. Other research repeatedly points to the mother as a highly important source of motivation for achievement in the child (cf. Horner *et al.*, 1967).

An Alabama study found that farmers ranked lower than other occupational groups in aspiration levels. The study found little value-orientation toward education among persons who, currently at low income levels, needed it most to enhance mobility and earnings (cf. Cleland *et al.*, 1965).

Multivariate analysis based on a U.S. sample of 939 families was used to account for the variance in completed education of youth based on characteristics of their parents and environment (Brazer and David, 1962). The mean education level was 11.82 years. Having an uneducated father, other things being equal, reduced the completed education of the children 1.60 years (Table 12.2).

TABLE 12.2. Estimated Impact of Parental Characteristics Prevalent in Rural Poverty on Educational Attainment of Children

	Years of School Completed
Over-all group mean for children	11.82
Adjustments for parental characteristics often found in farm poverty areas	
Uneducated father	−1.60
Farmer	−.13
Always lived on farm	−.06
Large family	−.54
Low success drive	−.26
Fundamentalist religion	−.55
Young father	−.92
South	−.54
Negro	−.52
Total	−5.12
Group mean for children adjusted to above characteristics of parents found in poverty areas	6.70

SOURCE: Brazer and David (1962).

Children who grew up in a household where the breadwinner was a farmer and had always been a farmer received .19 years less education than the average. Being from a large family and from the South each reduced education .54 years. If the family head possessed little motivation for achievement and believed that hard work was less important than luck, educational attainment of children dropped .26 years. Being from a fundamentalist church background lowered the education level another .55 years. If the father was very young when the youth was born, the youth on the average tended to lose another .92 years from the educational level. And if the family was Negro another .52 years of school had to be subtracted.

It is obvious that the member of a family possessing these characteristics faces several serious obstacles to educational attainment. Summed over all categories, the total educational deficit is 5.12 years. Subtracted from the group mean of 11.82 years, the result suggests that a child in these circumstances would receive only 6.7 years of education. The above-listed characteristics are often found in rural poverty areas. Thus, it is not surprising to find that this result is not inconsistent with actual median education levels reported for some poverty areas. Yet there is no one "poverty" or "income" variable in Table 12.2. Perhaps poverty and attendant low educational attainment is the result of a concentration in one family or area of negative factors such as those listed in the table. Even being from a white family outside the South but possessing the other characteristics would raise the educational level a little over one year, bringing the total to approximately eight years.

The relatively small impact on the children's education of being from the farm gives some basis for optimism in raising educational levels in farm poverty areas. The fact that education of parents is such a large factor in the child's education means that progress may be slow, however.

Characteristics (mainly of parents) listed in Table 12.2 explained 44 per cent of the variation in educational attainment of the youth. Attitudes and other factors associated with each youth apparently are confounded with the regional, family, and religion factors listed and also account for some portion of the unexplained variation in attainment. The attitudes of the individual may be more readily influenced by corrective policies than the factors listed in Table 12.2. Although income was not explicitly included, many of the factors are influenced by income.

SUMMARY AND CONCLUSIONS

The greatest *number* of persons in poverty are in households with the following characteristics: white; nonfarm; family head under age 65; family head a male; and outside the South. But the greatest *incidence* of poverty is in the South, in rural areas, among Negroes, and in households with a head over 65 years of age or with a female head. Only a small porportion of the nation's poverty is found in families with an able-bodied male head under 65 who is unemployed or only sporadically employed. Much poverty is characterized by disintegration of the family, high birthrates, and by failure to earn a satisfactory income even though the male head is working full time.

The incidence of poverty has declined for all major U.S. groups since 1959, based on the income threshold set by the Social Security Administration. The number of farm households in poverty declined two-thirds from 1959 to 1966. On the other hand, the Orshansky classification places the number of farm poor at nearly the same level in 1965 as in 1960. These conflicting data reveal the ambivalence of classification schemes. Nevertheless, it is clear that millions of poor continue to be a major problem in rural and urban areas alike.

The worst of the farm-urban exodus is over, though much is yet to come. From 1929 to 1965, 80 million persons moved from U.S. farms. Many persons moved to farms, leaving a net outmigration from the farm of 36 million. Contrast this with an estimated 47 million persons who migrated to the U.S. from foreign shores from 1820 to 1960. Some 22 million returned to their homeland, leaving a net inflow of "only" 25 million foreigners into the U.S.

Despite the fact that public policy seemed preoccupied with preserving the family farm and was little concerned with preserving the farm family during the great farm-urban exodus, there is considerable evidence that the movement was a success. The incidence of poverty and other measures of economic well-being clearly show that migrants as a group, even the Negro, are better off in the city than on the farm. Still, too often farm underemployment was traded for urban unemployment. In the next two chapters, public policies to deal with such problems are discussed.

Poverty is no longer considered to be functional—most Americans now view it as a social cost. There is a desire by many Americans, rich and poor, to eliminate poverty. This desire has not been matched with efficacious prescriptions by economists. The theory explaining poverty was examined to provide a foundation for establishing the means to eradicate poverty.

A liminal theory of poverty was advanced. The theory embodies three concepts: (*a*) that there are forces originating from settlement patterns, depletion of resources, obsolescence of production techniques, changes in product demand, and other sources that confront regions with the need for economic adjustments; (*b*) that there are factors such as proximity to an urban-industrial complex, adequacy of transport and communication facilities, and education which determine the ability of a region to adjust to forces for change; and (*c*) that the need for adjustments leads to creative tensions and may actually facilitate area adjustments up to a liminal point. Once the limen is reached, however, reactionary forces—apparent in goals, values, and institutions—set in which are inimical to rapid and smooth adjustments. Economic adjustments do not stop, but they become more painful as the environment of the area begins to lag seriously in preparing people socially, psychologically, and educationally for the adjustments. It is the anomie and cognitive dissonance permeating area-wide poverty that separates the subculture of poverty from the merely "low-income" people and separates the "poor in spirit" from those who merely lack material possessions.

Gestalt psychology emphasizes that individual behavior can only be understood within the context of the environment in which it occurs. The valuation of education by people is strongly influenced by their local perspective. And the perspective in rural areas is strongly influenced by agriculture. Many farm operators in a depressed agriculture are likely to have realized little economic return on higher education. It follows that community-wide indifference toward the value of education can be fostered by this poor payoff from education in the home community. The momentum of indifference and low incomes caused by a declining industry in a large city can be offset by the optimistic outlook and higher incomes of growing industries in that city. Progressive farmers can support favorable attitudes and institutions, such as good schools, in commercial farming areas in which only a few farmers are poor. Thus, area-wide rural poverty is a different problem than poverty interspersed with plenty. There are fewer opportunities within area-wide poverty to lift the poor by the communities' somewhat frayed bootstraps. The liminal theory of rural poverty is based on the premise that economic decline adds fuel to further decline. The faltering tax base can only maintain existing mediocre roads and schools. The community would be better off with fewer but higher-quality roads and schools, but the location of farms and community attitudes preclude such changes. A declining tax base also cannot support an able, aggressive local government that can be a factor in economic growth. Consolidation of counties to support such a structure also has little chance of approval.

Inadequate funds for local social overhead such as schools, libraries, recreation facilities, police, fire protection, water, and sewage disposal make the area unattractive compared to other areas and reduce chances of industry locating there. The families from other areas who might provide initial high-level management for industry are not attracted due to lack of cultural attractions, good schools, and progressive attitudes in the depressed area.

Often more important in industry location than nearness to markets or access to resources is the climate of optimism based largely on the success of earlier industries in a location. In the minds of businessmen a depressed economic area can be prima facie evidence that there are factors present which are not conducive to future success. This state of mind is self-reinforcing. There are large economies in growing markets. A generally optimistic climate for plant location in an area can lead to sufficient jobs and people to create economic advantages for all firms in a market that grows to make the plants profitable. Depressed rural areas will find industry subsidies necessary to attract industry against the inertia of pessimistic expectations and inadequate infrastructure.

REFERENCES

Beale, Calvin. 1968. Statement to Senate Subcommittee on Government Research. In *The Rural to Urban Population Shift*, National Manpower Conference, 90th Congress, 2nd Session, Stillwater, Okla., pp. 6–11.

Berry, Brian. 1967. Strategies, models and economic theories of development in rural regions. Agricultural Economic Report No. 127. Washington, U.S. Department of Agriculture.

Booth, E. J. R. 1961. Economic development in eastern Oklahoma until 1950. Unpublished Ph.D. thesis. Nashville, Tenn., Vanderbilt University.

Brazer, Harvey E., and Martin David. 1962. Social and economic determinants of the demand for education. In *Economics of Higher Education*, Education and Welfare, OE-50027, Washington, U.S. Department of Health, Education, and Welfare.

Brewster, John M. 1961. Beliefs, values and economic development. *Journal of Farm Economics* 43:779–96.

Bryant, W. Keith. 1966. Causes of inter-county variations in farmer's earnings. *Journal of Farm Economics* 48:557–77.

Burchinal, Lee G., Archibald Haller, and Marvin Taves. 1962. Career choices of rural youth in a changing society. Bulletin No. 458. St. Paul, Minn., Agricultural Experiment Station.

Caudill, Harry. 1965. Reflections on poverty in America. In Arthur B. Shostak and William Gomberg, eds., *New Perspectives on Poverty*, Englewood Cliffs, N.J.: Prentice-Hall, pp. 3–9.

Cleland, Charles L., *et al.* 1965. Review of findings of the S-44 southern regional research project and selected other regional and state rural research projects. Athens, Ga., Agricultural Experiment Station.

Diehl, William D. 1966. Farm-nonfarm migration in the Southwest: a costs-returns analysis. *Journal of Farm Economics* 48:1–11.

Economic Report of the President. 1968. Washington: U.S. Government Printing Office.

Ford, Thomas R. 1965. The effects of prevailing values and beliefs in the perpetuation of poverty in rural areas. In *Problems of Chronically Depressed Rural Areas*, Agricultural Policy Institute Series 19, Raleigh, N.C.

Galbraith, J. K. 1956. Inequality in agriculture—problems and program. Unpublished lecture. Guelph, Ont., Ontario College.

Hathaway, Dale. 1968. Statement to Senate Subcommittee on Government Research. In *The Rural to Urban Population Shift*, National Manpower Conference, 90th Congress, 2nd Session, Stillwater, Okla., pp. 6–11.

Hobbs, Daryl J., George M. Beal, and Joe H. Bohlen. 1964. The relation of farm operator values and attitudes to their economic performance. Rural Sociology Report No. 33. Ames, Iowa State University, Department of Economics and Sociology.

Horner, James T., James Buterbough, and J. Judith Carefoot. 1967. Factors relating to occupational and educational decision making of rural youth. Report No. 1. Lincoln, Nebr., Department of Agricultural Education, Agricultural Experiment Station.

Jordan, Max, James Goldin, and Lloyd Bender. 1967. Aspirations and capabilities of rural youth. Station Bulletin No. 722. Fayetteville, Ark., Agricultural Experiment Station.

Lampman, Robert J. 1966. Population changes and poverty reduction 1947–75. In Leo Fishman, ed., *Poverty Amid Affluence*, New Haven: Yale University Press, Chapter 2.

Larson, Olaf. 1955. Sociological aspects of the low-income farm problem. *Journal of Farm Economics* 37:1417–27.

Lewis, W. Arthur. 1957. *The Theory of Economic Growth*. London: Allen and Unwin.

Loomis, Charles P. 1960. *Social system*. Princeton, N.J.: Van Nostrand.

McClelland, David C. 1961. *The Achieving Society*. Princeton, N.J.: Van Nostrand.

Madden, J. Patrick. 1968. Poverty by color and residence. *American Journal of Agricultural Economics* 50:1399–1412.

Merton, Robert K. 1957. *Social Theory and Social Structure*. Glencoe, Ill.: Free Press.

Morgan, J. N., M. H. David, W. J. Cohen, and H. E. Brazer. 1961. *Income and Welfare in the United States*. New York: McGraw-Hill.

———, I. S. Sirageldi, and Nancy Baerwaldt. 1966. *Productive Americans*. Survey Research Monograph 43. Ann Arbor, University of Michigan, Institute of Social Research.

National Advisory Commission on Rural Poverty. 1967. *The People Left Behind*. Washington: U.S. Government Printing Office.

Nicholls, William H. 1957. Human resources and industrial development in the upper east Tennessee valley, 1900–1950. *Quarterly Journal of Economics* 71:289–316.

———. 1960. *Southern Tradition and Regional Progress*. Chapel Hill: University of North Carolina Press.

Okun, Bernard, and R. W. Richardson. 1961. *Studies in Economic Development*. New York: Holt, Rinehart and Winston.

Perkins, Brian, and Dale Hathaway. 1966. Movement of labor between farm and nonfarm jobs. Station Research Bulletin No. 13. East Lansing, Mich., Agricultural Experiment Station.

Perloff, Harvey S., *et al*. 1960. *Regions, Resources and Economic Growth*. Lincoln: University of Nebraska Press.

Schnore, Leo F. 1966. The rural-urban variable: an urbanite's perspective. *Rural Sociology* 31:135–43.

Schultz, T. W. 1953. *The Economic Organization of Agriculture*. New York: McGraw-Hill.

———. 1968. *Economic Growth and Agriculture*. New York: McGraw-Hill.

Tang, Anthony. 1958. *Economic Development in the Southern Peidmont, 1860–1950*. Chapel Hill: University of North Carolina Press.

Thurow, Lester. 1967. The causes of poverty. *Quarterly Journal of Economics* 71:39–57.

Tweeten, Luther. 1966. Socio-economic growth theory. In G. R. Winter and W. Rogers, eds., *Stimulants to Economic Development in Slow Growing Regions*, Edmonton, Department of Agricultural Economics, University of Alberta, Chapter 1.

———. 1967. The role of education in alleviating rural poverty. Economic Report No. 114. Washington, U.S. Department of Agriculture.

———. 1968. Rural poverty. Process Series P-590. Stillwater, Okla., Agricultural Experiment Station.

U.S. Department of Agriculture. 1966. Rural people in the American economy. Economic Report No. 101. Washington: U.S. Government Printing Office.

Welch, Finis. 1965. Schooling versus education. Chicago, University of Chicago, Department of Economics.

CHAPTER THIRTEEN

Rural Poverty:
Past Programs

This chapter describes past poverty programs: their content, advantages, and shortcomings. Politicians increasingly recognize the relationship between rural poverty and urban slums and accordingly have declared war on all poverty. The ensuing programs have come too late—millions of rural people with inadequate investment in the human agent have already migrated. But millions more will migrate from rural areas to cities in the future, and the mistakes of the past can be averted in the future. An analysis of past programs is a point of departure for analyzing improvements that can be made in future programs.

In the realm of poverty programs, rural programs cannot be entirely separated from urban. Any serious public policy to increase the income of farm people entails off-farm education and off-farm jobs. Schooling and jobs mean government programs to support education and maintain national employment. For these and other reasons, much of the discussion of poverty programs in this chapter is concerned with the entire economy, not just the farm sector.

GENERAL RURAL POVERTY PROGRAMS

The first significant public efforts specifically to help the rural poor were initiated in the 1930's under the New Deal. Programs languished during the 1940's as a full employment economy and the demands of war blunted demands to help the economically disadvantaged. Strong commodity programs and 100 per cent of parity, though of benefit only to commercial farmers, also diverted attention from the rural poor in the 1940's.

The Eisenhower Administration recognized the problems of the rural poor in the 1950's, but its programs had a nominal impact on the problem. Programs for the poor multiplied during the Kennedy and Johnson Administrations, but the impact of these programs was not proportional to their number.

PROGRAMS OF THE 1930'S

The Resettlement Administration was established as a separate agency in 1935 and operated for two years. Its activities included (a) purchasing very large farms and dividing them into modest size units; (b) purchasing small farms, consolidating them, and reselling them as economic units; (c) resettling farmers from whom it had purchased farms; and (d) "rehabilitating," with loans and grants, farmers who lacked resources to earn a satisfactory living. The Resettlement Administration made loans and grants of nearly $300 million to needy farm families.

The Farm Security Administration, established by the Bankhead-Jones Farm Tenancy Act passed in 1937, carried on many of the Resettlement Administration's activities. These included (a) loans to tenants to purchase farms, (b) "rehabilitation" loans to farm families who could not obtain commercial credit at reasonable terms to purchase farm production supplies, and (c) submarginal land retirement. Many poor farm families were reached by the program, an estimated 232,000 in 1943 alone (Cochrane, 1965, p. 195). The program was too radical for conservative groups in Congress and was reorganized out of existence by 1946 legislation.

The programs of the two agencies were the first to focus specifically on alleviating farm poverty and helped many farm people but were much too small to deal with the whole enormous problem. The programs foreshadowed future public programs that suffered from the same malady.

The Farmers Home Administration replaced the Farm Security Administration in 1946. It continued only the less controversial features of the Farm Security Administration and more carefully specified limitations on loans and operating policies. The act of 1946 specifically forbade activities in cooperative farming and the operation of farm labor camps. The agency was established to finance farmers unable to obtain adequate credit from commercial sources, and it continues to operate under the basic framework established in 1946. Technical management assistance is often provided with loans. In 1967 the principle indebtedness of the farmer who was borrowing could not exceed $60,000. The maximum term was 40 years; interest was approximately 5 per cent. The federal subsidy to support farm and rural housing loans from 1961 to 1966 ranged from $160 million to $349 million per year. One view is that a comparatively small portion ($50 million of Farmers Home Administration loans or grants annually) benefited the poor in rural society (Bonnen, 1966b, p. 454).

The agency is authorized to make loans to public and nonprofit organizations in "rural" towns (up to 5,500 population) to develop domestic water supplies and waste disposal facilities.

Fifty-year loans up to $200,000 could be made by the Farmers Home

Administration in 1967 to private nonprofit corporations and cooperatives to construct housing for low-income senior citizens. The agency could also make loans to public agencies and nonprofit organizations in rural renewal areas for the purpose of stimulating the economy. These loans could be made for feasibility and engineering studies, for purchase of land tracts for flood control or soil conservation, for improving water supply, recreational facilities, and timberland, for building access roads, or for purchase and development of grazing areas.

The Rural Electrification Administration was established in 1935, a time when only 11 per cent of the farms in the U.S. had electricity. By 1966, 98 per cent of all farms were electrified. Electricity has contributed much to the quality as well as to the economic productivity of farm life. By improving communication and raising the level of rural living, electrification has done perhaps as much as any federal program to alleviate rural poverty.

THE EISENHOWER PROGRAM

Economists had long recognized problems of poverty in agriculture, but their efforts and analyses did not begin to reach a telling pitch until the mid-1950's. Partly as a result of these analyses, the Rural Development Program was started by President Eisenhower in 1955. To develop agriculture's human resources, a number of lines of action were proposed. The general approach was to be primarily educational and developmental. Local people would be urged to form rural development committees in selected counties for outlining and guiding the local development program.

Research, extension, and technical assistance were to be focused to a greater extent than in the past on the problems and opportunities of low-income rural areas. The number of private, cooperative, and government loans was to be increased. Nonfarm employment information was to be disseminated, and the necessity of outmigration confronted. Industrialization, vocational education, and health services for rural areas were to be expanded.

Congress allocated only $2 million to operate the Rural Development Program, but it gave the FHA some additional lending authority to operate under the program. In 1960 it was reported that 210 counties participated in development programs and that 18,000 new full-time jobs were created in the year as a result of industrial growth and new business. Nevertheless, in the judgment of Cochrane (1965, p. 202), "the Rural Development Program never really moved out of the pilot stage. . . . In general [it] barely touched the hard-core underemployment-poverty problem in rural areas."

Providing farm operators with low interest capital through the Farmers Home Administration, for example, and with know-how through the extension service to expand their farming units is an attractive solution to low-income problems but has important drawbacks. For the marginal operator who needs special help, it is difficult to determine whether credit is being granted to form a viable economic unit that will provide a satisfactory living or to perpetuate an uneconomic farming unit. More important is the fact that even with reasonable help with credit and management, most farms in depressed areas cannot become economic units. Farms surveyed in the Ouachita Highlands of eastern Oklahoma (part of the Ozarks) averaged 220 acres (Back and Hurt, 1961). With good management and the most efficient allocation of resources among coventional products, specialty crops excluded, a 220-acre farm in that area would provide a net income of approximately $1,400. Thus, within current farm boundaries, there was no feasible approach that would bring incomes to satisfactory levels. Even a 720-acre farm composed of typical resources for the area but with above-average management would provide a net farm income of only $3,000. Two conclusions were apparent. First, farms must be expanded, and in the process over two-thirds of all farms needed to be consolidated with existing farms. Second, numerous farm operators needed substantial off-farm employment either on a full-time basis or part-time basis. These results are consistent with those of other studies (Booth, 1960; Tweeten and Walker, 1963).

The Nation Discovers Poverty: Programs of the 1960's

Under the Administration of President Kennedy, the Rural Development Program was reorganized and named Rural Areas Development in 1961. As with its predecessor, the new program assumed that the local community would provide the leadership and initiative for the development process. Like the former program, it was basically a planning and coordinating program, designed to focus some of the activities of existing agencies on alleviation of poverty.

The Rural Community Development Service was formed in February 1965 to allow the U.S. Department of Agriculture to provide leadership in rural area development programs. Technical action panels operated at local levels. Federal representation on the panel usually consisted of local officers of the Farmers Home Administration, the Soil Conservation Service, the Agricultural Stabilization and Conservation Service, and the Federal-State Extension Service.

The Rural Areas Development effort from 1961 to 1966 entailed organization and promotion of an estimated 20,000 projects, ranging from community facilities to industrial parks (U.S. Department of Agriculture, 1966, p. 70). The advent of the new program was not met with a significant budget increase; hence it was essentially a continuation of the former pilot project. Cochrane's statement about the Rural Development Program can also be applied to Rural Areas Development.

Two additional domestic economic development programs were initiated during the Administration of President Kennedy to combat poverty through reduction of unemployment. The Accelerated Public Works Program was designed to stimulate economic activity in depressed rural areas, primarily through improvements in social overhead. Such improvements in public facilities not only provided direct employment but also made depressed areas more attractive to industry. Congress appropriated $850 million in 1962 and 1963 for the program. It was estimated that 220,000 man-years of employment would be provided by the program in its first two and a half years of operation (Cochrane, 1965, p. 205).

The Area Redevelopment Administration was established in the Department of Commerce by the Area Redevelopment Act of 1961. The new agency provided (*a*) loans to support job-creating commercial and industrial enterprises, (*b*) grants and loans for public facilities, (*c*) technical assistance to bridge the knowledge gap, and (*d*) retraining programs to fit workers to new jobs. An estimated $126 million in loans and grants were made or approved in fiscal 1962 to finance enterprises and development projects. An estimated 65,000 jobs were created in rural areas under the program (White House, 1967, p. 112).

The Manpower Act of 1965 transferred the training provisions of the Area Redevelopment Act to the Manpower Development and Training Act. The Economic Development Administration absorbed other programs of the Area Redevelopment Administration.

ECONOMIC DEVELOPMENT ADMINISTRATION

The Area Redevelopment Administration claimed it had been instrumental in starting 1,487 community industrial development projects by 1965, and that it had stimulated investment of $260 million in rural areas. But an evaluation of its activities indicated that many projects were too small in scope and required too high an investment of talent and money per job created. One worthy objective in reconstituting the Area Redevelopment Administration as the Economic Development Administration in 1965 was to place greater emphasis on regional development plans. Top priorities for assistance went to those areas and districts which had high unemployment and low per-family incomes. Accomplishments of the Economic Development Administration in 1967 included initiation of 472 public facility development projects at a cost of $200 million, the initiation of training programs for 17,000 workers at a cost of $27 million, business loans to 63 firms in 55 areas at a cost of $51 million, technical assistance and research in 105 areas for 236 projects at a cost of $13 million, and planning grants totaling $6 million to establish over-all economic development plans in areas, districts, and regions (U.S. Department of Commerce, 1967).

The concept of a viable economic area was embodied in the designation of Economic Development Regions established under authority of the Public Works and Economic Development Act of 1965. By the end of fiscal 1967, five

Economic Development Regions had been designated: Upper Great Lakes (the northern regions of Minnesota, Wisconsin, and Michigan); New England; Coastal Plains (the eastern parts of North Carolina, South Carolina, and Georgia); Ozarks; and Four Corners (most of Utah, Colorado, Arizona, and New Mexico). An *Economic Development District* included at least two *Redevelopment Areas* with sufficient population and resources to foster economic growth. Each district included an *Economic Development Center* that contributed to the economic revitalization of each district's redevelopment areas. The redevelopment areas and center were eligible for a full range of economic assistance. In addition, redevelopment areas in the district were eligible for a 10 per cent bonus on grants for public works projects. Initial action in creating a district had to be taken by a state or by a state agency.

Technical assistance was provided by the Economic Development Administration to help distressed areas understand their problems and economic potential. Assistance took the form of (*a*) studies to identify area needs or to solve industrial and economic problems, (*b*) grants-in-aid amounting to 75 per cent of the costs of planning and administering local economic development programs, and (*c*) management and operational guidance for private firms.

In addition to Economic Development Districts, two other geographic groupings qualified for funding by the Economic Development Administration, following submission and approval of an over-all economic development program. These geographic groupings were the redevelopment areas mentioned above (composed of counties, labor areas, or large cities characterized by high unemployment or low family income) and multistate development regions, which were groupings of states or parts of states with economic problems too complex to be solved locally. The Secretary of Commerce was authorized to designate a multistate development region. Regional commissions were then formed for each region to assist the Secretary of Commerce in planning and coordinating economic development programs in the region.

The Public Works and Economic Development Act of 1965 also provided for low-interest, long-term loans to encourage and help private businesses establish plants in Redevelopment Areas. The loans allegedly were for projects that could not be financed through commercial banks or other private lending institutions. The loans could be made to private enterprises or local development companies formed to lease facilities to private firms. Loans covered up to 65 per cent of the total project cost and could run for 25 years at interest rates commensurate with federal borrowing costs. In some cases, the federal government provided guarantees up to 90 per cent of the unpaid balance of working capital loans obtained from the Economic Development Administration.

APPALACHIA PROGRAM

The Appalachian Regional Development Act of 1965 established an integrated federal-state development program for Appalachia—an area comprised of some or all of twelve states. A federal-state commission was established to formulate a comprehensive development plan. By 1967, steps taken by the commission had led to construction of highways that eventually will form a 2,350-mile network, the construction of hospitals, nursing homes, clinics, and health centers, and the construction of forty vocational and technical schools.

OPERATION MAINSTREAM AND NEW CAREERS

Public employment to cope with mass unemployment is not new. In the 1930's as many as 3.7 million were employed at one time under emergency programs of the federal government. Public service employment in 1967 totaled only 500,000 persons (National Advisory Commission on Rural Poverty, 1967, p. 19). Most of these persons were on educational or other projects not specifically designed to provide public employment. Two specific programs of public employment are described below.

Persons 22 years of age or over, unemployed and below the poverty income threshold, were eligible for public employment in Operation Mainstream. The program attempted to provide the chronically unemployed with permanent jobs at decent wages while improving towns and depressed rural areas. Projects included improving parks, rehabilitating housing, and extending educational, health, and social services. The program provided public employment for only 8,100 in 1967, with about half the funds going to rural areas.

New Careers was a program of public employment for the hard-core unemployed, designed mainly for urban areas—only 12 per cent of the funds went to rural areas. Projects were funded to provide only 2,706 work opportunities in 1967. The program was similar to Operation Mainstream, but placed greater emphasis on trainees taking over some of the routine tasks from "overworked" professionals in hospitals and other facilities.

MISCELLANEOUS PROGRAMS

The Commodity Distribution Program was authorized by the Agricultural Adjustment Act of 1949. This program increased the market for domestically produced food acquired under surplus removal and price support operations. Available foods were donated to nonprofit school lunch programs, summer camps for children, needy Indians on reservations, charitable institutions, and state and local welfare agencies. The Department of Agriculture delivered the food in carload lots to points designated by the state receiving agency.

During the year ending June 30, 1966, 1.8 billion pounds of food were donated by the federal government. State and local governments paid additional costs of storage and distribution. If a county or city demonstrated that it could not finance a food donation program, the Office of Economic Opportunity provided assistance for such activity under the Community Action Program, but such efforts were inadequate and poorly financed.

In 1959 the incidence of participation among counties in food donation programs was greater for those with high income than for those with low income (cf. U.S. Department of Agriculture, 1966, p. 35). Many counties did not have food welfare programs because local officials would not distribute the commodities provided free by the federal government. Secretary of Agriculture Freeman in 1968 was severely criticized for not being more aggressive in expanding food welfare programs to such counties. In April 1968 the Department of Agriculture extended food assistance directly to needy persons in counties where local officials declined to do so, and by September 1968 such local programs were operating in 480 of the 1,000 poorest counties in the country.

The Food Stamp Plan was introduced in the 1930's, terminated in 1943, and revived in 1961. The Plan authorized families to exchange a portion of their income for food stamps worth more than that income portion. The value of stamps received was designed to provide an adequate diet. Low income families spend a higher percentage of their income for food than do high income families. It follows that requiring a prescribed percentage of income to be exchanged for food stamps should lead automatically to participation and to welfare benefits for poor families. The program was designed to eventually be extended to all areas of the country that want it.

It is disturbing to note that in the mid-1960's the incidence of county participation in the Food Stamp Plan was greatest among counties with high median income per family (U.S. Department of Agriculture, 1966, p. 35).

The Consumer and Marketing Service of the U.S. Department of Agriculture administers both the food donation and food stamp programs. During May 1967 some 3.5 million persons in the U.S. took part in the Commodity Distribution Program and an additional 1.7 million persons took part in the Food Stamp Plan.

Reducing the minimum payment for food stamps, increasing the variety and quality of distributed foods, and extending coverage to more counties have materially improved Department of Agriculture food welfare programs since 1967. One-third of the nation's 1,000 poorest counties had no federal food welfare program in July 1967. This situation improved rapidly. Half of these 1,000 counties were taking part in the Food Stamp Plan by the end of 1968. The remaining half were taking part in the Commodity Distribution Program. By the end of 1968, 85 per cent of the nation's population lived in areas included in the federal food welfare programs. An estimated 6.1 million people were benefiting.

Federal funds and commodities assist primary and secondary schools in serving nonprofit lunches. Three out of four children were in schools affiliated with the program and an estimated 18 million children received lunches every day under the program in 1965–66 (National Advisory Commission on Food and Fiber, 1967, p. 165). States in which average income was low were compensated at a higher rate per school lunch than were states in which income was high. In addition, the Special Milk Program that dates to 1954 has for some years subsidized milk for children in public and private schools.

There have been indications that the school lunch programs do not reach the very poor: "About 30 per cent of all rural schools have no facilities for preparing lunches, and hence cannot participate. Less than one-third of all school children from families of less than $2,000 [annual income] receive either free lunches or lunches at reduced prices" (Clawson, 1967, p. 1231).

PROGRAMS OF TRAINING AND EDUCATION

Some of the most promising programs to raise incomes of poor people focus on training and education. Many of these programs were not designed specifically for the rural poor but have a sufficient impact on economically disadvantaged rural people to warrant their inclusion in this section.

ELEMENTARY AND SECONDARY EDUCATION ACT OF 1965

The Elementary and Secondary Education Act of 1965 offered federal help for rural areas to improve their educational facilities. Aid to deprived children was the largest program under the legislation, although the act also provided funds for libraries, supplemental educational centers, research, and for strengthening states' departments of education (U.S. Department of Agriculture, 1966, p. 24). Aid to states for deprived children was based on a formula applicable to all states. The allocation to each school district within each state was determined by the state's current expenditures per school child and the number of school-age children in the district who come from families with incomes under $2,000 a year or from families receiving over $2,000 a year under the program called Aid to Families with Dependent Children. The formula resulted in a regressive distribution of benefits. According to Zimmer (1967), the amount approved for allocation per child in 1965–66 was $85 in counties in the bottom 10 per cent (i.e., with the most rural poverty) and $246 per child in the upper 10 per cent (counties having the least rural poverty).

Funds for libraries and instructional materials were allocated among the states according to the enrollment in elementary and secondary schools. Distribution of funds to local districts was left to the states.

In fiscal 1966 nearly $1.2 billion was allocated to local educational agencies in over 17,000 school districts to assist in expanding and strengthening programs for educationally deprived children. About 2.5 million children benefited in the 1966 summer program and 8.3 million in the fall school session.

Title I funds were used for children from preschool levels through grade 12. Emphasis was on remedial reading and other such programs, but funds could be used for such diverse purposes as clothing, dental care, food, and equipment. A review of the Title I program reported a most disappointing finding: the failure of most schools to identify and attract the most seriously disadvantaged children (White House, 1967, p. 94).

Title II funds were used to purchase books and other instructional material. Title III funds were used to support "innovative" and "creative" projects in education.

VOCATIONAL TRAINING

Vocational training in rural areas traditionally has been in agriculture and home economics. Growing realization that many farm youth must take their place in nonfarm employment has led to greater emphasis on shop skills in vocational agriculture and to a series of new vocational training programs.

The Manpower Development and Training Act of 1962 provided federal support for vocational training for unemployed and underemployed workers. Members of farm families with less than $1,200 annual income were considered "unemployed" under the act, and were eligible for training allowances. Training was in farm or nonfarm skills, with monetary allowances for subsistence and transportation for those who needed such assistance while in training.

In 1966, an estimated 160,000 persons were enrolled in institutional training and 37,000 in on-the-job training (White House, 1967, p. 117). Only 2.5 per cent of the institutional trainees and 1.3 per cent of the on-the-job trainees were farm workers prior to training. Trainees of farm background were older and had less formal education than other trainees. Few of these farm workers received training in farm skills; most were trained for nonfarm occupations.

THE VOCATIONAL EDUCATION ACT OF 1963

Federal grants to states on a matching basis for vocational education were made under the Vocational Education Act of 1963. Eligible trainees included high school students (both dropouts and graduates), and adults who required retraining to hold or upgrade their jobs. Numerous types of nonagricultural technical education were included. Agricultural training under the act was not generally designed for persons who returned to the farm but included courses in related occupations such as the food processing, distribution, and service industries.

In 1965, 41 states built or authorized 125 area vocational-technical schools at a cost of $55 million in conjunction with the Vocational Education Act. An additional 1,100 such schools have been authorized and allegedly will be available by 1975. An estimated half-million adult rural people were reached by vocational courses under the act in fiscal 1965. Less than one-fourth of the training approvals were for rural residents, and most of the vocational schools were located in urban communities. Since 28 per cent of U.S. residents were rural, the incidence of training under the program was lower for rural than urban residents.

The Vocational Education Act provided about $118 million annually through fiscal 1966 and $225 million thereafter for grants to states on a matching basis. The act also provided $50 million in fiscal 1966 and $35 million thereafter for experimental work-study programs and for construction and operation of residential vocational schools (Bonnen, 1966a, p. 61).

SCHOOLING UNDER THE ECONOMIC OPPORTUNITY ACT OF 1964

Several vocational programs were offered under the Economic Opportunity Act of 1964. The programs were administered by the Office of Economic Opportunity and other federal agencies (Table 13.1). The Neighborhood Youth Corps program was established under Title I and provided paid-work experience for youth 16–21 years of age. Of 1,477 Neighborhood Youth Corps projects operating in fiscal 1966, more than a third were rural. Of the half-million enrollees, an estimated one-fourth were rural—roughly the same percentage as under the programs created by the Manpower Development and Training Act and the Vocational Education Act. The trainees of rural residence were largely from small towns rather than farms. The young people in the program remained in their home environment while gaining job proficiency through full-time work or while supplementing their income with part-time work in order to remain in school.

Amendments in the Neighborhood Youth Corps program authorized enrollment in the in-school programs at age 12 instead of 16, as previously required. This change was intended to reduce school dropouts among the disadvantaged. Also, amendments authorized the payment of out-of-school enrollees for time spent in counseling and training—services of special importance for dropouts (White House, 1967, p. 96).

The Job Corps was authorized by Title I of the Economic Opportunity Act and was established to provide youth characterized by low income, lack of

TABLE 13.1. Obligations by Office of Economic Opportunity, Fiscal Year 1966

Program		Obligations
		(Thousands of dollars)
Community Action Program		653,500
Upward Bound (224 institutions, 20,418 students)	27,986	
Legal service (157 projects)	27,512	
Foster grandparents (33 projects)	5,089	
Migrants (Title IIIB; 66 grants)	25,285	
Neighborhood multiservice centers	51,130	
Indian reservation projects (78 grants, 100 Indian tribes)	12,000	
Health centers (8 grants)	9,296	
Head Start:		
Summer (1,645 sponsoring agencies, 573,000 children)	97,000	
Full year (470 grants, 178,000 children)	83,000	
Job Corps (28,533 youths (25,927 males, 2,606 females) in 106 centers: 86 conservation, 8 men's urban, 11 women's urban, 1 special)		303,500
VISTA (1,053 volunteers)		15,900
Neighborhood Youth Corps; (1,477 projects, 528,000 authorized enrollment opportunities)		271,000
Adult Basic Education (HEW; 45 state plans approved, 9 state plans pending)		35,500
Work Experience (HEW):		112,400
147 projects, 38,261 trainees	53,487	
127 renewals, 46,559 trainees	58,913	
Rural loans:		
17,073 individual loans		27,264
391 cooperative loans		5,000
Small business loans (SBA)		17,000

SOURCE: Office of Economic Opportunity (1967, p. 9).

employment, and inadequate job preparation with some education, vocational training, and work experience. The youth were sent to urban training centers or rural conservation centers located, unlike those of the Neighborhood Youth Corps, often at some distance from the youth's neighborhood. The Job Corps and the Youth Corps together were authorized to spend over one-half billion dollars in fiscal 1966. More than 30,000 young men and women were enrolled in late 1966 in 106 Job Corps centers. A majority of these were conservation centers, but the number of urban centers was growing (Table 13.1).

Job Corps applicants were required to be young (16–21), undereducated, and jobless. Lack of motivation, unsatisfactory family background, and other special handicaps frequently characterized persons selected for the Corps. Despite such handicaps, follow-up studies showed that two-thirds of the former Corpsmen (including dropouts) were employed after training and at wages related to the length of stay in the Corps (White House, 1967, p. 97). Considering the backgrounds and personal problems of this previously hard-core unemployed group, the record of the Job Corps can be viewed with measured optimism. The Nixon Administration closed numerous conservation centers in 1969, and opened new urban centers which emphasized training in skills required by industry. The Job Corps was moved from the Office of Economic Opportunity to the U.S. Department of Labor.

The largest and perhaps most enthusiastically endorsed of the community action programs under Title II of the Economic Opportunity Act was Operation Head Start. Assistance was provided to preschool centers for children of limited opportunity who later entered kindergarten or first grade. The program involved teachers, parents, doctors, and social workers in an effort to overcome deficiencies that would lead to underperformance in school and society. The pupil-teacher ratio was very low, and costs ran about $1,000 per pupil per year. During fiscal 1966, 573,000 youngsters were enrolled in summer programs and 178,000 in full-year programs. In some cases, all-day care was provided so that the mothers could work and leave relief rolls. Only one-fifth of the 2.5 million youngsters 3–5 years old living in poverty were enrolled in the program in 1966.

Follow-up studies showed that in a traditional elementary school environment, the Head Start children lost the gains achieved. This was because the primary schools were not designed to build on the special progress made in preschool programs. It was also because our middle-class teaching methods were only slowly being revised and oriented to compensate for the lack of verbal and cognitive skills and of functional discipline that characterizes children of the poor. Programs were needed to improve instruction in all grades of primary schools in poverty areas and to bring more youngsters into Head Start at an early age. Head Start programs included few farm children and needed to be expanded in depressed rural farm areas. The Head Start program was placed under the Department of Health, Education, and Welfare in 1969 by the Nixon Administration.

In addition to project Head Start, the Community Action Program supported projects operated by welfare agencies, schools, churches, and other groups to deal with problems of inadequate job opportunities, housing, education, and health (Table 13.1). Neighborhood centers operated under the program provided employment services, day-care for children of working mothers, legal services, and health services. An estimated 100,000 poor were employed in the program itself in fiscal 1967. Specialized job training was provided for an estimated 25,000 under the program in the same year (White House, 1967, p. 95). The operation of the neighborhood centers and other aspects of program were largely confined to the cities. The Community Action Program had total obligated expenditures of $653 million in fiscal 1966.

The Adult Basic Education Program was established under Title IIB of the Economic Opportunity Act of 1964. The program was for persons of age 18 and over who lacked the basic skills necessary to qualify for better jobs or for occupational training. Remedial programs included instruction in reading, writing, and arithmetic. Title IIB was repealed by section 315 of the Elementary and Secondary Education Act. Title III of the latter act authorized a program generally similar to Title IIB of the 1964 act. Powers of the Director of the Office of Economic Opportunity under Title IIB were delegated to the Secretary of the Department of Health, Education, and Welfare.

Title III of the Economic Opportunity Act included financial assistance for migrants and other seasonal farm employees and their families. Projects included accelerated school programs to shorten the school year for children of migrants, adult education in literacy and other basic skills, remedial summer school programs for youth, vocational training for adults, and day-care centers for preschool children. An estimated 150,000 workers and their dependents had been served in twenty-seven states under the program by the end of 1965 (cf. U.S. Department of Agriculture, 1966, p. 26).

Title V of the Economic Opportunity Act of 1964 contained a Work-Experience Program for the needy and unemployed, including part-time and seasonal farm workers, who were receiving public assistance. For fiscal 1966, $112 million was obligated to support community work and training projects and to simultaneously create work experience, income, and training for the needy. The Work-Experience Program provided job experience and training for 84,820 unemployed heads of families and other persons on public assistance in fiscal year 1966. The projects were conducted by state and local government welfare agencies with financing from the federal government. Those who were illiterate first completed a basic education program before receiving experience in an occupation. The length of training under the Work-Experience Program averaged about nine months, after which the trainees were placed on a job, referred to the programs of the Manpower Development and Training Act for further training, or returned to the welfare rolls. Nearly 12,000 enrollees in the Work-Experience Program who had previously received general assistance or aid to families with dependent children became self-supporting between October 1963 and December 1964, saving an alleged $1.8 million per month in public assistance (White House, 1966, p. 70). While work-experience projects were unavailable to most farm families, the projects were of benefit to seasonal farm workers who were supported by public assistance part of the year.

MISCELLANEOUS SCHOOLING PROGRAMS

Numerous programs in addition to those listed above were available to residents of impoverished rural areas. The Upward Bound Program under the

Office of Economic Opportunity was a national precollege program of intensive education designed to motivate secondary students, handicapped by cultural and educational deficiencies, to attend college or otherwise reach their academic potential (Table 13.1).

A number of programs financially assisting disadvantaged youth to attend college were available under the Higher Education Act of 1965. The 1965 act also provided for a National Teachers Corps. The corpsmen were generally graduate students at a university who provided supplementary teaching in elementary or secondary schools in areas with a large proportion of disadvantaged pupils. In isolated rural areas, an experienced teacher would be provided to supplement the local school program.

VISTA (Volunteers in Service to America) was another program under the Office of Economic Opportunity. Following a six-week training period, the volunteers usually went out in teams for a period of one year to work with the disadvantaged in, for example, Job Corps camps, migrant worker communities, or Indian reservations. The volunteers, who often performed teaching assignments, received only $50 per month in addition to board, room, and health care.

STATE AND LOCAL PROGRAMS TO FINANCE INDUSTRIAL DEVELOPMENT

LOCAL INDUSTRIAL DEVELOPMENT BONDS

States and local governments rely on three basic programs to finance industrial development (Stinson, 1967). The most popular is the local industrial development bond. A plant for a new firm is constructed with funds obtained from a municipal bond issue. The plant is leased to the new firm at an annual rate necessary to retire the bonds, after which the title to the plant is usually transferred from the local government to the firm. The advantages to the firm are that capital is obtained at low cost, because interest payments on municipal bonds are tax-free, and that property taxes usually are not charged during the time the title to the plant is held by the local government.

Two types of development bonds are used. One is the *general obligation bond*, usually characterized by liability of the community for any unpaid balance (should a firm default on payments), by statutory debt limitations, and by exemption from local property tax on plants so financed. In 1966 there were an estimated forty-three such bond issues totaling $20 million in ten states, eight of them in the South.

A more popular type is the *local revenue bond*, with an estimated ninety-four issues totaling $485 million in 1966. At least thirty-one states in 1966 used this system to finance industrial development. The local government is not required to retire local revenue bonds if the firm leasing a plant defaults. Because such bonds are not bound by statutory debt limitations, large issues can be floated by small communities. The general obligation bond has advantages for small firms with unestablished credit ratings; the local revenue bond has advantages for large, established firms which desire low cost financing.

STATE INDUSTRIAL FINANCE AUTHORITY

A second method for financing industrial development is the *state industrial finance authority*. Under the Pennsylvania Plan, the state industrial development authority is authorized to make loans out of the state general revenue fund to local nonprofit development corporations for 40 per cent of industrial facility costs in return for a second mortgage on the facility. Under this plan, financing is free from federal taxes like municipal bonds and does not require local subsidy through exemption from property tax. In addition to Pennsylvania, Kentucky and Arkansas used the plan in 1966. Pennsylvania had the only sizable program, however, with 576 loans totaling $104 million outstanding at the end of 1966.

The Oklahoma Plan operates similarly to the Pennsylvania Plan, except that bonds rather than state general revenue fund money are used to support local industrial development. Hence, financing is not limited by shortages of general revenue funds. The Oklahoma Plan was used in Oklahoma, New York, Maryland, New Hampshire, and Alaska in 1966. By the end of 1966, 295 loans had been made totaling $39 million, about half of this amount in one state, New York.

LOAN GUARANTEE

Under a third financing method, a *loan guarantee plan*, the local industrial development corporation is financed solely through private sources and decides what facilities will receive assistance. The "standard" rate of interest is charged, but the rate tends to be low because of reduced risk—the state insures repayment of up to 90 per cent of the loan in return for a small service charge. Five New England states and Delaware used loan guarantee systems in 1966. A total of 105 loans, some dating back to 1959, for a total of $61 million had resulted in no defaults as of 1967.

After reviewing several previous studies of the impact of taxes and public finance programs on local industrial development, Stinson (1968, p. 20) concluded "that there is reason to doubt that a decision based on the economics of different locations would be influenced by the tax costs of any particular location." Another study by the Advisory Commission on Intergovernmental Relations (1967) reached a similar conclusion. The principal reason for the conclusion that tax and financial inducements have had little impact on industrial location derives from the finding that these inducements in their current form had little impact on firm costs and returns. The studies must not be interpreted to mean that more substantial inducements, such as sizable tax write-offs, would not have a major impact on the location of new industry.

COSTS AND EFFECTS OF WELFARE PROGRAMS

A total of 3 million U.S. workers were unemployed in 1966. In rural areas alone, there were at least 2 million man-equivalent-years of underemployment; most of it is not included in the above figure on unemployment. Federal training opportunities existed for roughly 700,000 in 1966 and 1967 (Table 13.2). Federal training programs were not large enough to have a telling impact on national unemployment.

TABLE 13.2. Training Opportunities, Fiscal Years 1966–67

	Thousands of Trainees	
Program	1966	1967[a]
Manpower Development and Training Act Program		
Institutional training	160	125
On-the-job training and other	113	125
Job Corps[b]	10	31
Neighborhood Youth Corps[b]		
In school	106	125
Out of school	55	60
Summer	209	165
Work experience	64	46
Adult work program		25
Special impact		8

SOURCE: *Economic Report* (1967, p. 109).

[a] Estimates.

[b] These estimates differ from those in Table 13.1, partly because each position may be occupied by more than one person in the course of a training period. Trainees often do not occupy positions for the full period.

IMPACT OF WELFARE PROGRAMS ON AGRICULTURE

Funds for farm commodity programs averaged $4 billion annually in the 1960's. The benefits went to commercial agriculture, and largely eluded the really poor. Funds from all public programs for the poor in agriculture totaled only a few hundred thousand annually. Most of the programs to benefit the farm poor were part of national programs to help those in poverty, rural and urban alike.

Antipoverty programs in fiscal 1963 directly created 35,000 rural jobs and indirectly added another 35,000 due to multiplier effects (Cochrane, 1965, p. 213). This was a very small dent in total rural underemployment of at least 2 million man-years.

TOTAL NATIONAL WELFARE OUTLAYS

Social welfare expenditures in the United States totaled $100 billion in 1967. Fifty-four per cent was from federal sources and 46 per cent from state and local sources (Table 13.3). As recently as 1955, total social welfare expendi-

TABLE 13.3. Social Welfare Expenditures, by Source of Funds and Public Programs, 1959 and 1967

	1959		1967[a]	
	Federal	State and Local	Federal	State and Local
	(Millions of dollars)			
Social insurance	13,028	5,240	30,687	6,691
Public aid	2,082	1,916	5,399	3,502
Health and medical programs	1,435	2,618	4,164	3,950
Veterans programs	5,033	61	6,990	22
Education	513	16,095	5,233	30,400
Housing	128	28	285	90
Other social welfare	383	637	1,385	1,442
Total	22,601	26,594	54,142	46,097

SOURCE: U.S. Department of Commerce (1968, p. 277, and earlier issues).
[a] Preliminary data.

tures were only $32 billion, and the federal portion was 44 per cent. Thus all welfare outlays were rising rapidly, and federal outlays were increasing faster than state and local outlays. Funds for all welfare purposes comprised approximately two-fifths of all government expenditures for each year of the 1960's.

"Public aid" was focused on the poor and accounted for only 9 per cent of all welfare expenditures in 1967. Categories such as social insurance (37 per cent), education (36 per cent), and veterans programs (7 per cent) were not narrowly focused on the poor but accounted for 80 per cent of all so-called "welfare" expenditures in 1967. It follows that total social welfare expenditures ($100 billion) were a highly inflated measure to use in estimating the funds spent to alleviate poverty in the U.S.

FEDERAL WELFARE OUTLAYS

Measures of federal expenditures for welfare depend on the definition of welfare used. Table 13.3 includes a number of programs, such as Social Security, which benefit many people who cannot be classified as poor. Under a broad classification, federal outlays for welfare programs were $23 billion in 1959 and $54 billion in 1967. The portion most narrowly focused on poverty—public aid— totaled only $2.1 billion in 1959 and $5.4 billion in 1967.

Old Age, Survivors, and Disability Insurance (Social Security) benefits totaled $18 billion in 1965. Approximately one-third went to the poor and another two-fifths went to households which otherwise would have been poor (*Economic Report*, 1967, p. 140). Much of these benefits went to the aged. Still two-fifths of the aged were poor in 1965. Future changes in Social Security will reduce the number of aged actually in poverty. Better measures of poverty that account for assets will reduce the *recorded* number of aged in poverty.

PUBLIC ASSISTANCE AND THE ROLE OF THE STATES

In the decade preceding December 1968, nearly 3 million people were added to welfare roles, bringing the total to 9 million Americans receiving welfare (Welfare, 1968, p. 25). Excluding Social Security and other government insurance programs, the cost of welfare at all levels of government was $5.5 billion in 1968. Of this, the federal government paid slightly over half, the cities 12 per cent and the states a third. Aid to dependent children was the largest category, with 5.6 million recipients paid an average of $68 per recipient. Other sizable categories were aid to the blind (81,200 persons, $91 per recipient), aid to the disabled (670,000 persons, $81 per recipient), and general assistance (737,000 persons, $45 per recipient). Less than 1 per cent of the welfare recipients were able-bodied men, and welfare programs provided help for only one-third of the 27 million Americans classified in poverty in 1968 (Welfare, 1968, p. 25).

Nearly all Aid to Families with Dependent Children recipients were either children or women whose family responsibilities precluded work outside the home unless child care was provided. Until amended in 1967, the law required that such benefits be reduced $1 for each $1 of income earned by adult members of the household. This "penalty" discouraged all but the most determined from taking jobs, because earnings would not add to income. Under 1967 legislation, welfare recipients could earn up to $30 per month without loss of benefits. Beyond this level, welfare benefits were reduced $2 for each $3 of earned income. In addition, the 1967 legislation provided for day-care facilities and access to training for recipients. These changes led to more gainful employment in families receiving such assistance (*Economic Report*, 1968, pp. 144, 145).

Under past Aid to Families with Dependent Children programs, an unemployed father who could not provide for his family would sometimes desert his family to make it eligible for payments. A 1967 amendment made it possible for states to make federally aided payments to families with an unemployed father. By 1968, only twenty-one states had elected to join the unemployed parent program and only 60,000 families were benefiting. Unemployed beneficiaries were assigned either to training or to jobs with local public agencies.

These changes improved the program, but many faults remain. The program requires administrators to make difficult decisions, such as whether the mother should care for children or place them in day-care and go to work, and whether payments should be denied (with attendant trauma to children) to a family whose male head refuses to train or take a job. If payments are too high, the program encourages illegitimate births and participation by families that otherwise would have found a way to earn a living by productive employment. If payments are too low or requirements for participation too restrictive, the chances for breaking the intergeneration cycle of poverty through a better life for children may be sacrificed. These problems will not easily be resolved. A dilemma is that many people, who see real abuses of Aid to Families with Dependent Children, use the program to justify opposition to other promising welfare programs that could substantially reduce poverty.

Programs such as Aid to Families with Dependent Children are at odds with the enterprise creed, yet transfer payments can improve the home environment and intervene in a cycle of dependency that in some instances has lasted for generations. A study of second-generation welfare recipients in Mecklenburg County, North Carolina, of which Charlotte is the county seat, gives some basis for optimism (How about welfare kids? 1967, p. 10). Of 456 children in 100 families receiving payments from the program in 1955, only 1.9 per cent of those children who were adults in 1967 were on public relief, and only 10 per cent were unemployed in 1967—despite the fact that, of the 100 families in 1955, 33 were on welfare because the father had deserted the family, 25 families involved unwed mothers, 35 had disabled or deceased fathers, and 7 families had fathers in jail.

Wide variation exists among states in welfare assistance payments. States with a relatively high proportion of the very old and very young tend to have low incomes and the greatest need for welfare assistance. States with low per capita income tend to provide low average payments. Aid to Families with Dependent Children payments are larger, and the probability of being granted assistance is higher outside the South. For example, Mississippi offered $8.50 per person per month in 1968, while New York offered benefits of $71.75 (Welfare, 1968, p. 25). In 1960 Texas granted assistance to only 34 per cent of those who applied, while Massachusetts granted assistance to 80 per cent (Cloward and Piven, 1968, p. 32). Between 1960 and 1968, participants in the national program rose by more than 1.6 million persons, with almost half the increase taking place in only sixteen urban areas. The opportunity to obtain more favorable welfare assistance undoubtedly prompted some of the migration from the rural South to the urban North, with the attendant social disruption. A case can be made for the federal government to take over welfare assistance in order to distribute welfare funds more equitably among states and among recipients based on national norms of eligibility. Then generous states would not be penalized by inmigration for their benevolence, and state funds would be freed for other uses such as education.

Multiple regression analysis using data from all states reveals that states which are most rural tend to spend less per capita on welfare, have a lower rate of welfare recipients in relation to the number of eligible people, and have lower welfare payments per recipient. A reexamination of the allocation formula is called for. In some instances, for example, federal allocation of welfare funds for certain purposes is determined by the number of unemployed. Since rural farm people tend to be *underemployed* rather than *unemployed*, a revision of grant formulas to account for underemployment would create a more equitable fund distribution. Also many farm people are not yet adequately covered by programs such as Social Security and workmen's compensation.

Taxes in the U.S. have been in total slightly regressive over a considerable range of income (cf. Chapter 14, Table 14.8). Federal taxes are progressive, but do not completely offset the regressiveness of state and local taxes. Federal programs of taxes *and grants* promote a progressive redistribution of income among states (cf. Tweeten, 1968). For example, federal grants and taxes in 1962 redistributed $15 per capita to Alaska and $101 to Wyoming. At the other extreme, federal grants and taxes redistributed about $33 per capita away from residents of the more wealthy Connecticut and Delaware. In general, the poorer states such as West Virginia and Arkansas enjoyed a net gain from federal taxes and grants. These data fail to account for huge sums of nongrant federal spending for military, space, and research purposes. This spending is proportionately greatest in wealthy states such as California, Massachusetts, and New York. It is also important to emphasize that the progressive redistribution of taxes and grants *among* states does not mean that the federal monies are distributed equitably *within* each state.

SUMMARY AND CONCLUSIONS

Several inferences can be drawn from this study of the poverty programs:

1. One "law" of poverty programs is that benefits are regressive within the group at which they are aimed. Thus the well-to-do commercial farmers receive the major benefits from farm programs. Most programs focused specifically on

alleviating poverty give a disproportionately large share of the benefits to the "poor" who need help least. The reasons are quite obvious. The more aggressive, knowledgeable persons within a group eligible for public programs are most effective in obtaining funds from such programs as well as in deriving income from other sources. They are also more active vocally and in the voting booth, and hence are needed for the political propagation of the programs.

Administering poverty programs requires personnel and operating funds. Qualified people who have the education and leadership ability to administer poverty programs are able to receive good pay doing other jobs and can be attracted to administer poverty programs only with adequate salaries. Thus the administrative expenditures of poverty programs do not go to the poor.

To make public funds go far to raise incomes of persons in poverty, poverty funds should be allocated to give the highest return on investment. And the return is likely to be highest by investing in "poor" persons with basic resources and personal attributes required for success in the commercial world. But these attributes often mean that the person who received aid either has already achieved some monetary success even in the poverty environment, or he would have succeeded economically even without help in the form of public subsidies.

2. A combination of too many programs and too few funds have made federal efforts to relieve rural poverty imaginative and promising but often ineffective. The 1967 catalog of Federal Assistance Programs was 701 pages long (Office of Economic Opportunity, 1967). One point in favor of such diversification is that programs are so diffuse and numerous that an economy-minded Congress can hardly rid the country of them in one impetuous act. Another advantage is that income regressiveness within poverty programs can partially be circumvented by making poverty programs more specific and by sharpening their focus on individual groups.

3. A large number of the really poor people in the U.S., many of whom are legally eligible for help, do not receive assistance for various reasons, including racial discrimination. According to Clawson (1967, p. 1231), "It is estimated that no more than one-fourth of all poor participate in any of these Federal welfare programs." A compounding problem is that state and local taxes are regressive. Also, economically retarded states which are least able to care for the poor often have the highest percentage of persons needing help. A case can be made in the name of equity for the federal government to assume a larger role in providing standards of eligibility and funds for general welfare assistance programs.

4. One hypothesis is that the income regressiveness of poverty programs tends to be proportional to the number of administrative hierarchies involved. Poverty programs of the 1930's had some success because they were administered by organizations set up especially for that purpose. There was a return to traditional organizations and local leadership in the ineffective programs of the

two decades after World War II. The Economic Opportunity Act of 1964 represented a departure from the past system, with the Office of Economic Opportunity reporting directly to the President and by-passing many of the national, regional, and state channels so as to work directly with cities and local areas. Rivalries, political infighting, and promotion of narrow self-interests at the Cabinet, state, and regional level were thus often exchanged for similar behavior at the local level. Furthermore, the platitude that local people can best understand and work out their own problems is often incorrect. Without outside financial help and guidance, impoverished areas will have limited success in catching up with progressive areas. Attempts to let the poor who lack proper training administer programs will only increase administrative inefficiency.

The administration of poverty programs stands in need of much improvement. Two useful procedures for improving such programs would be to consolidate programs at top levels, thereby reducing duplication and competing government activities, and to place more administrative authority within regional development districts established within the states. The purpose of the latter procedure would be to increase local flexibility and place local decision making in the hands of professional administrators who know the situation and can recognize opportunities to stimulate the local economy. The local professional staff must be at least somewhat insulated from the exigencies of local politics.

5. Under most government programs to alleviate poverty, farm people receive a share of benefits considerably lower than the share of farmers in the population or their "fair" share based on need. Farmers undoubtedly have dissipated much of their political power on commodity programs. These do not benefit the poor, however. An increase in funds to ameliorate rural poverty can focus on enlarging programs that are part of a national intersector effort. Or they can focus on enlarging programs of the U.S. Department of Agriculture. The political power structure supporting agriculture is heavily oriented to commercial farmers, and the farm poor may have to look for help mainly to programs geared to the needs of nonfarmers.

Basic factors underlying the political impotence of the rural poor are: they have no effective political pressure group working for them; they are not prone to organize as are commercial farmers; they do not riot or use violence as do the urban poor; they either do not vote or exhibit insufficient switch-voting to attract the eyes and ears of politicians; and they do not have funds to make their case before the American people in newspapers, television, and other media.

Legislators with predominantly rural constituencies often have not supported effective poverty programs because some of their constituency would be lost by outmigration, because they feared federal control of schools (integration), and because the rural poor packed little political muscle.

In all likelihood the economically disadvantaged will remain the politically disadvantaged. Yet society increasingly recognizes that many urban problems are tied to the disadvantaged in rural areas, since the rural poor who migrate to urban areas take their deficiences with them. Out of this recognition may come adequate programs for rural areas supported by enlightened farm legislators and urban legislators who see the connection between the invisible rural poor and the highly visible urban poor.

There is talk of spending billions to rebuild the central cities. It would be unfortunate if such efforts only "gild the ghetto" and omit the two-thirds of the poor who reside outside the central city. Ghettos already are overcrowded. There is a need to move people from them and not cause them to attract millions of future migrants. Census data show that rural Negroes tend to migrate to the metropolitan cities of the North and Far West. The social cost of dealing with poverty would probably be less if more migrants would settle in cities of 10,000 to 250,000 and avoid the metropolitan ghetto. Failure to recognize the silent rural poor, merely because they are not adept at "public relations" (rioting), will only perpetuate past mistakes.

REFERENCES

Advisory Commission on Intergovernmental Relations. 1967. State-local taxation and industrial location. A-30. Washington.

Back, W. B., and Verner G. Hurt. 1961. Potential for agricultural adjustment in the Ouachita highlands of Oklahoma. Bulletin B-582. Stillwater, Okla., Agricultural Experiment Station.

Bonnen, James T. 1966a. Emerging public policy orientations. In *Policies Affecting Rural People*, Agricultural Policy Institute Series 20, Raleigh, North Carolina State University, pp. 59–76.

————. 1966b. Rural poverty: programs and problems. *Journal of Farm Economics* 48:452–65.

Booth, E. J. R. 1960. The potential for rural development in Cherokee County, Oklahoma. Bulletin B-548. Stillwater, Okla., Agricultural Experiment Station.

Clawson, Marion. 1967. Rural poverty in the United States. *Journal of Farm Economics* 49:1227–34.

Cloward, Richard, and Frances Piven. 1968. Migration, politics, and welfare. *Saturday Review*, Nov. 16, 1968, pp. 31–35.

Cochrane, Willard. 1965. *City Man's Guide to the Farm Problem*. Minneapolis: University of Minnesota Press.

Economic Report of the President. 1967, 1968. Washington: U.S. Government Printing Office.

How about welfare kids? 1967. *Stillwater* [Okla.] *News-Press*, Nov. 21, 1967, p. 10.

National Advisory Commission on Food and Fiber. 1967. *Food and Fiber for the Future*. Washington: U.S. Government Printing Office.

National Advisory Commission on Rural Poverty. 1967. *The People Left Behind*. Washington: U.S. Government Printing Office.

Office of Economic Opportunity. 1967. The quiet revolution. Washington, Executive Office of the President.

Poverty. 1968. *Time*, Nov. 22, 1968, pp. 16–17.

Stinson, Thomas. 1967. Financing industrial development through state and local government. Agricultural Economic Report No. 128. Washington, U.S. Department of Agriculture.

———. 1968. The effects of taxes and public financing programs on local industrial development. Agricultural Economic Report No. 133. Washington, U.S. Department of Agriculture.

Tweeten, Luther. 1968. Rural poverty. Processed Series P-590. Stillwater, Okla., Agricultural Experiment Station.

——— and Odell Walker. 1963. Estimating socio-economic effects of a declining farm population in a sparse area. *Regional Economic Analysis*. Raleigh, North Carolina State University, Agricultural Policy Institute.

U.S. Department of Agriculture. 1966. Rural people in the American economy. Economic Report No. 101. Washington: U.S. Government Printing Office.

U.S. Department of Commerce. 1967. Economic Development Administration: annual report. Washington: U.S. Government Printing Office.

———. 1968. *Statistical Abstract of the United States*. Washington: U.S. Government Printing Office.

Welfare. 1968. *Time*, Dec. 13, 1968, pp. 25–26.

White House and U.S. Department of Labor. 1966, 1967. Manpower report of the President. Washington: U.S. Government Printing Office.

Zimmer, John. 1967. Expenditures for public elementary and secondary education. *Journal of Farm Economics* 49:1204–08.

CHAPTER FOURTEEN

Rural Poverty: Prospective Programs

To be effective, programs to alleviate poverty must be focused. To have a focus, it is important to set priorities. To set priorities, it is necessary to use some criterion. The criterion suggested here is cost-effectiveness. The assumption is that programs which go farthest with a given input to raise the income level of poor people are most desirable and should receive first priority for public funds.

Cost-effectiveness refers to efficient use of available means to reach a given objective. It can be expressed in several ways. One of the simplest concepts applicable to poverty programs is the amount of public funds required to create jobs for the unemployed. Another concept is the local benefit-cost ratio, defined as the income generated in a depressed community per unit of public funds spent to promote economic progress. A third concept, the social benefit-cost ratio, includes public and private costs. Benefits in the form of income generated in the local community ideally should be adjusted for income lost in other areas. Income generated by publicly induced industrialization of a depressed area may mean loss of jobs to communities where some industry would have otherwise located.

The social benefit-cost ratio is used in this chapter to rank federal programs from most to least efficient in alleviating poverty. Public and private funds to raise incomes of the poor are severely limited. Thus the social benefit-cost ratio is a felicitous criterion, because it indicates which programs make limited funds go farthest to alleviate poverty. In many instances, adequate data are unavailable, and the ranking must necessarily be somewhat subjective. Hopefully, future research will provide a more rigorous basis for ranking programs.

Poverty programs, like fertilizer application, cannot elude the law of diminishing returns. Injection of public funds into a program that has high cost-effectiveness will eventually drive efficiency down to a point where other programs more efficiently utilize incremental public outlays. This principle plus uncertainty and the need to reach special groups lead to diversification of funds among programs.

Before setting program priorities, it is first necessary to separate persons in poverty into two categories—those who can be productively employed and those who cannot. The latter category of "unsalvageables" includes children, the severely disabled, the mentally incompetent, and the aged. For these, welfare grants or transfer payments are the most cost-effective way to reach a satis-factory level of income. Training programs and other means to make these people employable are often unsuccessful. Thus, one must subtract the salaries of highly paid teachers and administrators who unsuccessfully attempt to generate long-term earning power in these poor from welfare payments that would otherwise have gone to the poor. This results in low cost-effectiveness of most nongrant programs for the unsalvageable poor.

The distinction between the unsalvageable poor and the salvageable poor, who can become productive workers, is not always clear cut. Mothers with small dependent children in households with no male wage earner at first glance might be considered ineligible for outside employment and hence seem to be in the unsalvageable category. But the children can be placed in day-care centers which not only free the mother for employment but provide useful preschool education for the children. We now turn to priority measures to deal with the poor who are not boxed in.

FULL EMPLOYMENT

Public monies, in conjunction with induced private investment, go farthest to raise the income and well-being of the salvageable poor when spent on monetary and fiscal policies for full employment. Monetary policies for full employment entail comparatively little opportunity cost and hence have a high social benefit-cost ratio. The issue remains: Do such policies really help the poor, i.e., are the redistribution of benefits from such policies progressive or regressive? Because the poor tend to be "last hired and first fired," they are highly sensitive to changes in national employment. Furthermore, the success of nearly all positive policies directly focused on the rural poor depends on the availability of jobs. It does little good to provide job counselors, employment bureaus, and training centers if jobs do not exist.

National monetary policies to establish full employment are not by them-selves sufficient to alleviate poverty in a reasonable period. Once national unemployment is down to 3–4 per cent of the labor force, other programs become more efficient means to help the poor.

Fiscal policies for full employment can have widely different effects depending on where public funds and programs to stimulate employment are focused.

While the over-all social benefit-cost ratio may be high, the issue finally is one of specific policies. Hence the ranking of priority policies (below) is fundamentally a ranking of specific fiscal policies.

IMPROVING FACTOR MARKETS

Improving factor markets is ranked just behind national full employment as a cost-effective approach to reduce poverty. Ways to improve the functioning of factor markets include (*a*) reducing racial discrimination, (*b*) strengthening the public employment service, and (*c*) providing loans (or grants) to facilitate factor mobility.

Racial discrimination explains much of the high incidence of Negro poverty. Acceptance of racial equality and "color-blindness" by the American public would do much to improve the economic welfare of Negroes. But, even if by some miracle this idealistic situation would become a reality, problems of Negro poverty would not be over. It will take decades to acculturate many Negroes to the values discussed earlier consistent with economic progress, and it will take decades for them to accumulate the human and material assets necessary to compete successfully for high-wage jobs in society. Middle-class values which are highly conducive to economic progress are only marginally accepted by Negroes who are isolated by discrimination. Without assimilation of Negroes into society, acculturation of Negroes to values consistent with rapid economic progress is likely to remain an illusion. And assimilation of Negroes through integrated schools and housing remains an elusive target indeed, although federal legislation has provided a major impetus.

EMPLOYMENT SERVICES

The Wagner-Peyser Act of 1932 established the U.S. Employment Service. The 1,900 local employment offices throughout the country in 1966 were federally financed but were operated by the respective state employment services. The federal government provided funds and direction in the form of data on standards of operation of local agencies; it provided statistical and research work and maintained an interstate recruitment program. The states did the actual placement work.

About three-fourths of all hiring in the national job market took place without use of any employment agency, public or private (White House, 1965, p. 159). The public employment services in the early 1960's participated in about 15 per cent of new hiring in the nation. Studies show that unskilled laborers made most use of the public employment service (Secretary of Labor, 1966, p. 79). In 1964, 6.3 million nonagricultural placements were made, of which

2 million were of three days or less duration. Farm placements totaled 7.1 million, over half of these of short duration, reflecting the seasonal nature of farm activities.

Data reveal that farm people who move long distances relied mostly on friends or relatives for information and as a consequence were uncertain about the availability of jobs or facilities upon arrival. In an Indianapolis study, two-fifths of the Northern whites reported they knew that a particular job or kind of job was available for them when they moved to the city. In contrast, less than one-tenth of the Negroes and Southern whites reported this degree of assurance (Smith, 1956, p. 816). It is not surprising then that half of the farm migrants from the South to Indianapolis were dissatisfied to the extent that they were hoping or actively planning to return to farming (Smith, 1956, p. 820). High turnover rates, especially among Southern whites, discouraged employers from training workers.

The federal-state cooperative employment service made a number of changes to increase its effectiveness. These adaptations included testing and counseling programs, electronic data processing, intensive studies of labor supply and demand in local areas, and specialized employment centers. Migrant farm workers were fitted with a full schedule of jobs through the Annual Worker Plan. The federal-state employment service also improved liaison with programs of the Economic Opportunity Act and the Manpower Development and Training Act and with private groups to guide persons into jobs or training programs offering the greatest opportunities.

The Small Communities Program under the U.S. Department of Labor provided mobile employment service teams to serve rural areas in which the labor market was too small to justify a full-time employment office. The program not only provided the usual services of counseling and placement but also published comprehensive manpower resource reports to help the community attract new industry. The program appeared to be successful and may warrant expansion.

Still, the employment service has many shortcomings. Interarea recruitment is nominal and resulted in placement of only 155,000 workers in nonfarm jobs outside their home community in 1964 (White House, 1965, p. 161). There is no real national employment service—each state operates its employment service with considerable independence. Each state locates jobs and applicants within its borders. Since new jobs and applicants often are not located in the same state, the efficiency of the employment service is reduced accordingly. The present supply of trained counselors is totally inadequate. There are no employment offices located in many of the low-income rural counties. To remedy these faults, a major increase in public support for the employment service is essential. The matching of workers and jobs is becoming increasingly complex. Modern, nationwide, computerized information systems, systematic job counseling beginning at the high school level, and mobile, well-staffed employment teams for rural areas are a few of the needed improvements. Furthermore, there must be increasing interaction among the employment services and agencies and firms providing general welfare assistance, education, skill training, jobs, and moving assistance.

Assisting Labor Mobility

Labor mobility demonstration projects conducted under the Manpower Development and Training Act have tested and demonstrated ways to assist underemployed farm people who must move away from home to find suitable employment. With funds appropriated in 1964, grants of up to 50 per cent of moving expenses, loans up to 100 per cent, or a combination of grants and loans not to exceed 100 per cent of moving costs were provided to unemployed workers who needed to migrate to a new job. This type of assistance was not new—it was used by the Bureau of Indian Affairs after 1952, and by the Department of Health, Education, and Welfare to resettle Cuban refugees.

I computed preliminary measures of the returns to subsidized relocation with data from a study of 255 subsidized relocatees in Wisconsin and Michigan (Somers, 1968). The average expenditures for moving household belongings was $149 and for living expenses during the move was $86—a modest total moving outlay of $235 per relocatee. Relocatees before relocation in 1964 earned an average of $209 annually more than a control group of nonmobile workers (excluding incomes over $9,997). In a transition year, 1965, the average income difference between relocatees and nonmobile workers dropped to $144. Forgone earnings (an opportunity cost of moving) were estimated to be $209 − $144 = $65 per relocatee in 1965. Income of relocatees exceeded that of nonmovers by $430 after relocatees were better established in 1966. It is of interest that 67 of the 255 relocatees returned to the area from which they migrated within six months of their relocation.

Based on the direct costs of relocation given above, the net gain (loss in the transition year) in income (assuming arbitrarily that the 1966 differential will be maintained for ten years but that 30 per cent of the remaining relocatees will fall back each year to the 1964 nonmobile worker income relationship), the internal social rate of return on the investment in relocation (including the income forgone in the transition year) is 44 per cent. The present value of private costs and benefits, discounted at 6 per cent, was $113,883 for the group. This implies that the public could afford to subsidize each of the 255 relocatees by $439 to make each dollar of public investment generate a dollar of private income. The above estimates are crude and may err in being too conservative. More refined estimates built on additional follow-up of relocatees would likely show even higher returns to relocation.

Proper guidance, preparation, and financial assistance can induce hitherto immobile underemployed or unemployed workers to take jobs elsewhere. The initial projects indicate that training to provide special skills is often a prerequisite to useful relocation (White House, 1966, p. 138). While some reorientation would be required, the Farmers Home Administration could reach many farm people with loans and grants to help them train and locate for a nonfarm job.

EDUCATION

Education, as stated before, has a twofold effect on rural poverty. It increases skills of persons, potentially raising their level of farm management and their suitability for nonfarm jobs. Education also broadens the outlook of people, enhances their motivation and aspirations for higher income and living standards, and creates attitudes more nearly consistent with frictionless assimilation into a new environment. The central role given to attitudes in the liminal theory of economic stagnation singles out education as a key element in any program to alleviate poverty.

Much additional thought must be given to design of socially acceptable formal education to create attitudes of secular asceticism and functional activism. This subject deserves extended research in the future. A pilot project is underway in McAlester, Oklahoma, in the Ozarks region, to generate an entrepreneurial spirit in a group of sixty-five adult males by formal means. The assumption of the study is that an attitude corresponding with McClelland's "need for achievement" can be taught, and that this will in turn lead to business activity that will create new jobs (Behavioral Science Center, 1968).

The 65 trainees, along with a control group, were selected from among 200 small businessmen and prospective entrepreneurs nominated by local community leaders. Training sessions were conducted in late 1967 and early 1968 to create attitudes consistent with functional activism and to impart skills necessary to expand or launch a business enterprise. Training sessions, which lasted only a few days, cost $250 per trainee.

A follow-up study of McAlester trainees and similar programs made at Washington, D.C., showed that each dollar spent on the program was estimated to generate from $15 to $100 of new investment in just six months. The cost per new job created by the program was estimated to range from $100 to $300— a very favorable cost-effectiveness rating. Average increased profits the first six months ranged from a low estimate of $57 per trainee to a high of $900. Arbitrarily assuming that these would be annual profits in perpetuity, the rate of return on training investment ranges from 23 per cent to 360 per cent.

These results are highly promising but tentative. Many years will be required to fully evaluate to what extent the benefits of the program reach the poor. The preliminary results would appear to warrant extension of the plan in an attempt to train other persons, such as the poor who are initially less endowed with human and material resources and are less strategically located to make use of traditional entrepreneurship but who can profit from functional activism in less spectacular ways. Because the experiment is new and needs further evaluation, its cost-effectiveness ranking is not considered in the summary and conclusions of this chapter.

In the following paragraphs, the more direct economic effects of education are emphasized, particularly the impact of education on earnings and mobility of farm people. The 1959 Census data for farmers, farm managers, and farm laborers and foremen suggest certain relationships between earnings and education levels (cf. Tweeten, 1968, pp. 69–70).

1. A consistent positive relationship exists between education and income. In the 35–54 age bracket, the lowest-earning group of farmers had approximately an elementary education; the highest-income group had a median education slightly over the high school level.

2. The education level of farmers and farm managers was improving. The median education of the 18–34 age group was over twelve years for each except the lowest income bracket.

3. The heavy concentration of farm operators and hired workers in the lower education brackets helps to explain the prevalence of socially unacceptable, low farm income. Not all of the difference between the incomes of farm and nonfarm males can be explained by education, however. Comparing income of farm males with their nonfarm counterparts, after adjustments for education, age, and cost of living have been made, reveals that median farm income in 1959 of the average male farm worker with four years of high school fell short of his national counterpart as follows: age 20–21, $29; age 22–24, $218; age 25–29, $848; age 35–44, $1080; and age 55–64, $1654 (U.S. Department of Agriculture, 1966, p. 110). The discrepancy between incomes of farm and nonfarm males of the same age and education generally was greatest for the highest education and age brackets.

4. Judging by factory worker wage standards of approximately $5,000, on the average a 35–44-year-old farmer needed to be a high school graduate to earn a "parity" income. In age brackets below 45, incomes over $5,000 were associated with at least a median education of over twelve years.

5. Both educational levels and income levels were low for the farm laborers. Ironically, a given income appeared to require less education for hired workers than for farm operators. This conclusion in all likelihood does not hold for the higher income brackets which were not shown in the census data.

Table 14.1 contains estimates of the rate of return on investment in education for rural males residing in thirty low-income counties in seven Southern states (Alabama, Kentucky, Louisiana, Mississippi, North Carolina, Tennessee, and

TABLE 14.1. Social Rates of Return to Schooling for Rural Male White Household Heads (and Selected Rates for Male Nonwhite Household Heads) in Thirty Low-income Counties in the South, 1959.

Years of Schooling	Rate of Return, in Per Cent
Elementary	
1 through 8	26.0 (11.7)[a]
High School	
9 through 10	7.4
11 through 12	12.4
9 through 12	11.0 (7.2)[a]
College	
13 through 14	2.5
15 through 16	2.0
13 through 16	2.0

SOURCE: Preliminary estimates from Redfern (1969).

[a] Rates in parenthesis for nonwhite household head.

Texas). The thirty counties were characterized by low incomes, rurality, old populations, and high outmigration rates. Earnings were estimated from a sample of 1,012 rural households surveyed in 1959. Seventy-two per cent of the sample was white, the remainder nonwhite. One-third of the household heads were farm operators or managers, and one-tenth were farm laborers for foremen. The remainder were operatives (18 per cent), craftsmen or foremen (15 per cent), laborers (10 per cent), and others (14 per cent).

The earnings generated by schooling were lower in poor rural areas than in other rural areas. In fact, data from the low income rural communities showed a strong association between having at least a high school education and having at least a $3,000 (poverty threshold) family income. In contrast, data from the Census for U.S. farm males showed a strong association between having at least a high school education and having at least a $5,000 (factory worker standard) income.

Costs of education were lower in the low-income areas than in other rural areas, and compensated for lower returns. Thus, social rates of return on elementary education for white males in 1959 in the thirty low-income counties were found to average 26.0 per cent for elementary school and 11.0 per cent for high school (Table 14.1). This compares favorably with average rates of return computed for all rural white males in the nation of 22.7 per cent for elementary school and 12.4 per cent for high school. There is clearly no significant difference between social rates of return in low income-areas and in the U.S. as a whole at these schooling levels. However, a college education appears to have a low average payoff in low-income rural areas. The social rate of return was estimated to be only 2.0 per cent for rural white males in such areas, compared to 8.9 per cent for rural white males in the entire U.S.

Table 14.1 indicates that the social rate of return on elementary and secondary schooling are favorable for nonwhite males in poor rural areas although the rates are considerably lower than for rural white males. The internal rate of return may be defined as the interest rate that society could pay for funds invested in schooling and break even on the investment. Few uses of public funds give higher returns than the rates in Table 14.1, and schooling appears to be a promising, if roundabout, way to raise incomes of depressed communities.

Private rates of return on investment in schooling are computed from earnings and consider only costs of schooling borne by the individual. These rates, applicable to the decisions made by individuals, are not shown but are even higher and more attractive than those in Table 14.1. College education is likely to be a wise investment for the individual in a low-income area who values schooling as a consumption good and is mobile enough to go outside the low-income area if necessary to obtain higher earnings obtainable with a college degree (see Chapter 5).

The impact of education on the persistence of poverty and on employment is inherent in the estimated rates of return in Table 14.1 but is more clearly brought into perspective in Tables 14.2, 14.3, and 14.4.

Not only are the chances of being in poverty higher for persons with less education, but the chances of remaining in that category are also much higher (Table 14.2). Chances were only two out of five that a family with a head with

TABLE 14.2. Persistence of Families in Poverty, by Education Level of Family Head

Years of Education of Family Head	Families Classified in Poverty in 1962 Who Remained in the Same Category in 1963
	(*Per cent*)
Less than 8	79
8	72
9–11	64
12	53
13–15	54
16 or more	40

SOURCE: *Economic Report* (1965, p. 164).

TABLE 14.3. Unemployment Rates, by major Occupation Groups, Age, Sex, and Color, 1966

	1966 Unemployment[a]
	(Per cent)
Total	3.9
White-collar workers	
Professional and technical workers	1.3
Managers, officials, and proprietors (except farm)	1.0
Clerical workers	2.8
Sales workers	2.7
Blue-collar workers	
Craftsmen and foremen	2.8
Operatives	4.3
Nonfarm laborers	7.3
Service workers	
Private household workers	3.6
Other service workers	4.8
Farm workers	
Farmers and farm managers	.4
Farm laborers and foremen	4.1
Teenagers (14–19 years of age)	
Males	11.2
White	9.9
Nonwhite	21.2
Females	13.0
White	11.0
Nonwhite	31.1
Adults 20–44 years of age	
Males	2.6
White	2.3
Nonwhite	5.3
Females	4.6
White	4.0
Nonwhite	7.8
Adults 45 years of age and over	
Males	2.3
White	2.1
Nonwhite	4.2
Females	2.7
White	2.5
Nonwhite	4.4

SOURCE: *Economic Report* (1967, p. 102).

[a] Number of unemployed in each group as percentage of labor force in that group; data relate to persons 14 years of age and over.

sixteen or more years of education, in poverty in 1962, would be in that category in 1963. Chances were four out of five that a family with a head possessing eight years or less of education, in poverty in 1962, would be in poverty in 1963.

One can infer from Table 14.3 that the level of education is inversely related to the level of unemployment. The unemployment rate was 5.6 times as high among nonfarm laborers as among professional and technical workers in 1966. Partly because of inadequate education, the unemployment rate among nonwhite teenagers was 21.2 per cent despite the relatively full employment economy.

Underemployment is a better measure than unemployment of manpower nonutilization in farming and is high for persons with little education (Table 14.4). The rate of underemployment among farm males with one to four years of elementary school is approximately double the rate of those with four years of high school. Raising the level of schooling will reduce the amount of underemployment in farming, as people find better opportunities to use their labor outside of the sector.

TABLE 14.4. Underemployment of Rural Males, by Education, 1966

	Average Annual Unemployment Man-Equivalents			
	Percentage of the Civilian Labor Force[a]		Number	
Years of School Completed	Rural Nonfarm	Rural Farm	Rural Nonfarm	Rural Farm
	(Per cent)		*(Thousands)*	
Total	8.4	26.1[b]	708.2	817.7
No schooling	26.8	35.1	28.2	20.1
Elementary				
1–4	18.3	36.8	101.4	99.6
5–7	10.7	31.2	139.1	171.0
8	8.5	28.5	126.6	221.9
High school				
1–3	8.2	23.8	140.9	119.2
4	5.4	19.6	112.5	144.3
College				
1–3	4.5	17.2	26.4	27.1
4	6.1	23.2	20.2	13.2
5 or more	4.7	4.6	12.8	1.3

SOURCE: See Bachmura (1967, p. 163).

[a] The number unemployed divided by the total number of rural males in the respective group.

[b] These data indicate a lower percentage of excess labor in agriculture than other methods, because here the total resource adjustments that would accompany a movement to equilibrium are not taken into account.

TABLE 14.5. Percentage of the U.S. Population Voting for President in 1952 and 1956, by Age, Sex, and Education

	Education Completed					
	Non-South			South		
Age and Sex	Grade School	High School	College	Grade School	High School	College
Less than 34						
Male	60	78	88	19	55	81
Female	44	73	90	13	41	74
Ages 34–54						
Male	80	87	96	55	80	88
Female	71	85	91	22	56	82
Age 55 and over						
Male	87	93	100	63	71	82
Female	71	91	93	31	58	86

SOURCE: See Weisbrod (1963, p. 127).

Table 14.5, indicating that the incidence of voting increases with education, appears to digress from the main theme of this section. It is included because voting behavior influences public programs, which in turn influence earnings. Poor people often display voting behavior inimical to their apparent best interests. Many of the poor have little education, and data in Table 14.5 show that low education means a low incidence of voting. Taking some extreme examples from the table, Southern females over 34 years of age with a college education had three to four times the incidence of voting in the indicated elections as their counterparts with only a grade school education, although racial discrimination also figures in the percentages. In an election decided by popular vote, 1,000 women with a college education packed about four times the political muscle of 1,000 women with only a grade school education in the South.

A second voting characteristic of the poor is their tendency to display loyalty. Some poor counties in eastern Kentucky, for example, consistently vote Republican, others consistently vote Democratic in national elections. Such voter loyalty leads not to political favors but to being ignored by national legislators and by Presidents who must concentrate on winning over the swing voter.

If a group wished to be by-passed by special development programs sustained by power politics, it would be difficult to think of characteristics more consistent with that goal than failure to vote, blind loyalty to a person or party, and failure to join organizations. Additional education will help to change these patterns. Political support for area development programs that reach the poor may follow.

EDUCATION AND MOBILITY

Education may not be very profitable to the local community if the local resource base offers few favorable job opportunities or if individuals leave who have absorbed the local investment in education. Considering risks involved and the shortage of individual capital and a small tax base, it should not be surprising that many local communities have little enthusiasm for a greatly expanded program of education. Individuals who profit most from education are likely to be those who leave the local community. The fact that some of the capital invested in education at considerable sacrifice is lost—and the fact that communities are understandably unwilling to see individuals leave the community—help to explain reluctance to invest adequately in education in poverty areas.

Statistics show a heavy reverse flow of migrants back to disadvantaged areas. One study found that 40 per cent or more of those who took nonfarm jobs received a lower income than in their farm employment. Not surprisingly, a high proportion of these people ended up in some kind of farm job and composed the predominant portion of the backmovers into agriculture (Hathaway, 1968, p. 9). This reverse flow undoubtedly is prompted in no small part by inadequate education and by attitudes inconsistent with smooth integration into urban society. The results of a number of local migration studies are summarized in a 1967 study (Tweeten, 1967). The results are conflicting. Some studies show that

TABLE 14.6. Percentage of U.S. Population 25–64 Years of Age Living Outside Region of 1955 Residence in 1960, by Age and Education

Age in Years	Years of Schooling							
	Elementary			High School		College		
	1–4	5–7	8	1–3	4	1–3	4 or More	Total
25–29	5.8	8.1	9.9	10.6	12.4	19.1	27.6	13.8
30–34	4.7	5.9	6.7	7.1	7.9	11.9	18.2	8.8
35–39	3.8	4.4	4.9	5.4	6.6	10.1	13.5	6.9
40–44	3.0	3.3	3.6	4.1	5.2	8.1	10.4	5.1
45–49	2.5	2.6	2.9	3.4	4.2	5.8	7.5	3.8
50–54	2.2	2.3	2.6	3.0	3.7	4.6	5.9	3.2
55–59	2.0	2.1	2.5	3.1	3.6	4.1	5.0	2.9
60–64	1.8	2.9	2.7	3.3	4.0	4.2	4.9	3.1
Total	2.8	3.5	3.8	5.3	6.8	9.6	13.7	6.2

SOURCE: U.S. Census (see Hines and Tweeten, 1968).

migration is highest among the least educated. While local studies show conflicting results about who migrates, census data provide more clear-cut conclusions.

U.S. Census data for 1960 in Table 14.6 permit us to reexamine the push-pull theories of migration. One contention is that the aphorism "last hired, first fired" applies to the least educated among regions as well as over time. Those with least education are most influenced by depressed economic conditions within a region, and these individuals are *pushed* by declining job opportunities from depressed regions to more prosperous regions. Using the farm example, the full renter, sharecropper, and hired farm laborer are least educated and have the least economic "bargaining power," hence are most likely to be pushed to employment elsewhere. Support for the push theory would be apparent in high migration rates among regions for the least educated.

Another contention is that the most educated are best fitted by skills and attitudes for successful employment and assimilation into more prosperous regions. These individuals would be *pulled* from a slow growing region to more lucrative jobs elsewhere. This theory would be supported by high migration among regions of the most educated.

Data in Table 14.6 clearly show that mobility is greater among young than old adults. For persons with four years of high school in 1960, 12.4 per cent of those 25–29 years of age lived outside of the region of their 1955 residence. But only 3.7 per cent of those 50–54 years of age lived outside their 1955 region of residence in 1960.

The data in Table 14.6 support the pull theory. Within a given age bracket, migration rates tend to be high among those with most education. The highest migration rates of all are found among individuals who are both young and highly educated. This suggests that the potential is likely to be large for redistributing benefits to other regions and away from the region where investment in schooling occurred.

VOCATIONAL EDUCATION

Vocational education has been said to be uniquely suited for upgrading skills and earnings of the poor. The following studies create a generally favorable outlook for the economic benefits of technical training. But the results sometimes conflict, and the relevance here of some of these studies may also be questioned because they report results not applicable to the poor.

A study of costs and benefits of a general high school education, high school vocational education, and post-high school vocational education in Worchester, Massachusetts, gave a largely pessimistic outlook for vocational training (Corazzini, 1966). The public per pupil costs of vocational education for males, whether at the high school or post-high school level, were 2.3 times those of a regular high school education. The size of the premium paid the vocational high school graduate relative to the regular high school graduate varied inversely with the size of the hiring firm. In the smaller firms the starting wage differentials were sufficient to equate present values of the two types of education for the graduate within six to twelve years. In the largest firms the starting wage differentials were not sufficient to equate the present value of extra costs and benefits at any rates of discount employed (Corazzini, 1966, p. 112). Data were only available on initial salary, but Corazzini argued that the starting pay differentials would *decrease* over time and perhaps would disappear within five years. If so, vocational education benefits would not cover costs.

Starting salaries for graduates of post-high school vocational-technical programs were, on the average, slightly higher than those of their vocational high school counterparts, but these wage differentials were not large enough to justify investing in post-high school vocational education (Corazzini, 1966, p. 115).

Any reasonable estimate of the contribution of vocational schools to reduction in dropout rates and to increased mobility of workers also could not justify the cost of the vocational school in Worchester. The author concluded that cash payments to employers who would then provide on-the-job training for workers would be a more efficient use of public funds for vocational education.

A New York City study of vocational education also reached pessimistic conclusions about the economic returns from vocational training (Taussig, 1968). A North Carolina study contains estimates of the rate of return on two years of post-high school technical education in the state (Carroll and Ihnen, 1966). The sample was forty-five high school graduates who did attend the technical school and forty-five "paired" high school graduates who did not attend the technical school. The estimated social rate of return on investment in technical education was 16.5 per cent if per capita real earnings would increase over time at the rate of 2 per cent per year. The social rate of return was reduced to 11.7 per cent when zero growth in the initial income advantage of the technical school graduates was assumed.

A 1969 study of 536 former vocational students at Oklahoma State Tech was based in some instances on twenty years of subsequent job history. Results indicated an over-all social rate of return on investment of 12 per cent (Shallah, 1969). The rate of return in the field of electronics was 6 per cent, diesel mechanics was 8 per cent, refrigeration mechanics was 12 per cent, and in food technology was 30 per cent. A Pennsylvania study found internal rates of return on technical-vocational education that averaged 20 per cent (Kaufman *et al.*, 1967).

Rates of return on investment in technical education were computed from data provided by 190 graduates of the Winona Area Technical School in Minnesota (U.S. Department of Labor, 1966). The school, located in a rural area, was selected to give insight into rates of return from training under the

Manpower Development and Training Act (MDTA). Median social rates of return based on 1960–65 graduates ranged from 9 per cent for the automotive repair technician program to 36 per cent for the general office clerk program. The average social rate of return over all fields was approximately 20 per cent.

The total cost per trainee at the Camp Kilmer Job Corps Center ranged from $6,412 to $18,750 (Cain and Somers, 1967, p. 43). To earn a 5 per cent return on total investment, former trainees would need to receive salaries from $7–$20 per week above salaries of persons with similar backgrounds but without the training. The target seemed to be potentially attainable based on a separate 1964–65 study of former MDTA trainees. The study revealed that Negroes on the average were earning $13 per week more than they earned on their pre-training jobs (Cain and Somers, 1967, p. 29). Whites, however, were earning only $4 more per week after training. While the above data on the Job Corps and the MDTA trainees are not comparable and one cannot make statements about absolute profitability, it is interesting to note that the investment in training of Negroes in this instance was relatively more profitable than investment in whites. It should be kept in mind that these were retraining programs, often dealing with hard-core unemployables who might be expected to have a low return on retraining investments.

An interview study of 1,379 workers in West Virginia in 1962 and a follow-up study in 1964 provided the basis for estimating rates of return on retraining courses sponsored by the Area Redevelopment Act and the Area Vocational Training Program (Cain and Stormsdorfer, 1967). The former was a federal program, the latter a program of the government of West Virginia. The social rate of return on investment in retraining was estimated to be 90 per cent for males and 64 per cent for females. Nontrainees, selected from the unemployed files at the local employment office, were the control group. Judging from data on education and work experience, it is doubtful that the control group adequately represented the earning of the retrained group if they had not been retrained.

Cain used two approaches to estimate the benefit-cost ratios from social investment in the Job Corps. One was based on improvements in educational attainment, coupled with Giora Hanoch's estimates of the relationship between education and income; the other was based on the 1967 survey of ex-corpsmen and persons who applied for the Corps but did not participate (Cain, 1967). Whether the "no-show" group was a realistic control group is questionable. Based on education gains, benefit-cost ratios ranged from .58 to 1.31 with a discount factor of 5 per cent. Based on wage gains and a control group of no-shows, the benefit-cost ratio was 1.04 with a discount factor of 5 per cent.

The uncertainties of the data were so great that even the "best" estimate, a 5 per cent rate of return on investment in the Job Corps, is none too reliable. Nonetheless, it is gratifying to note that a program basically contrived as a welfare measure to deal with hard-core poverty may have some positive net economic payoff.

SOME SUMMARY COMMENTS ON EDUCATION

I gave efforts to improve the amount and quality of primary and secondary education precedence over public investment in vocational education as a priority measure to alleviate poverty. There were two reasons for this. First, a good general education is the foundation for a successful vocational program. Second, reports conflict on the economic value of vocational education. It is nonetheless true that vocational education can often be a highly productive and rewarding activity, as some of the above case studies illustrate.

A continuing economic appraisal of vocational education is needed. Issues are the optimum combination of youth versus adult education, coordination of training with available jobs, use of public facilities versus paying industry to train workers, and the feasibility of portable vocational schools to bring training to the job demand (such as training workers for employment in a new factory).

From an efficiency and equity standpoint, a case can be made for improving the quality and amount of education in economically retarded rural areas. This incremental support should come largely from the federal government, and care must be taken to avoid a regressive distribution of funds. Data for 1966–67 reveal that about half the funds for elementary and secondary education comes from local sources and one-third from state sources. Since a high percentage of local graduates migrate from the area, the benefits of education tend to go with the migrants outside the community or state, while the costs are concentrated in the community. Without a redistribution of funds from the wealthy areas to poor areas of the nation, and from rich parts of individual states to the poor parts, the U.S. will continue to have underinvestment in the education of people in rural poverty areas.

There are now approximately thirty federal programs which can give vocational training to the disadvantaged. To improve administration and knowledge of available programs, the federal government should consolidate some of its efforts. This does not mean that concentration should be only on elementary and secondary schools. Programs must be diverse enough to reach the preschool child and adult, as well as youth.

INDUSTRY

Local industrialization is the most widely sought route to end rural poverty. Industrialization is appealing because it avoids confrontation with the distasteful prospect of outmigration, declining population, and area decay. Numerous areas and groups pursue aggressively the elusive industrialization which collectively they cannot achieve since there is not nearly enough industry to go around using current incentives. The most serious criticism of efforts to industrialize is that it diverts the attention of the community from the more basic priority of preparing young people for jobs and mobility.

A Case Study

Based on data obtained in 1961 and 1962, an Oklahoma study estimated tangible costs and benefits of successful community-sponsored efforts to attract industry (Saltzmann, 1964). Costs averaged $100,603 per community to attract industries with loans, facilities, and other concessions. Benefits from the industries brought in averaged $2,695,649 per community in the form of added payrolls, addition to real estate values, etc. The benefit-cost ratio for the communities averaged 26.8. Other research has also revealed high returns on subsidies to attract industry to communities (cf. Rinehart, 1963).

The Oklahoma communities, ranging in population from 1,500 to 13,000, received on the average a sizable payoff relative to the costs which they incurred. In the two communities where costs exceeded benefits, each industrial development corporation that attracted the industry was a nonprofit local organization. Two-thirds of the industrial development corporations in the eighteen communities were of the nonprofit type. The over-all record of achievement appeared to be no better for the profit-making industrial development corporations than for the nonprofit corporations.

Local benefit-cost ratios such as those given above can be misleading. The studies from which the ratios are estimated do not include communities that have unsuccessfully wooed industry, and only a few of the total social costs and benefits are included. The studies fail to measure the opportunity cost of not locating the industry elsewhere and the social cost of an industry that pays wages below what residents would have earned if they had gone elsewhere for employment in the absence of the new local industry. The full cost of additional construction and operation of city utilities, schools, churches, etc., was not included. An informative study of Clayton, Missouri, showed how introduction of labor-intensive industries such as textile and apparel can add more to tax roles (because of the influx of school age children) than they contribute (Hirsch *et al.*, 1964, p. 408).

Many locating industries in the Oklahoma study paid $1.35 or less per hour for labor. At 2,000 hours of employment per year, this would mean a $2,700 annual income—not enough to raise a one-breadwinner family above the poverty line. Such industry may only perpetuate poverty, although a case can be made for low-wage industries in some instances.

An excellent study of industrial firms that had recently located in the less industrialized regions of northern Louisiana gives substantial additional information on the impact of industrialization on employment, earnings, and other economic indicators (Hobgood and Tyner, 1968). The surveyed firms on the average paid wages well below the national average for the industry. They were located primarily on the basis of markets or resources (rather than state or local special inducements) and paid wages unrelated to capital-labor ratios.

The high local benefit-cost ratios and attractiveness of avoiding outmigration through industrialization could be expected to spawn numerous local development organizations. There were 14,000 such organizations in the nation in 1957, 68 per cent of them financed by private rather than public funds. Expenditures on promotion to attract industry nearly doubled from 1950 to 1957. More recent data would show a very large increase in the number of local development organizations and expenditures since 1957.

Unfortunately, many local development groups are unsuccessful and there are comparatively few high-wage industries attracted to depressed areas, which may have little more than "friendly people" to offer the prospective firm. For industry to become the powerful tool that it can be to raise incomes in depressed areas, the system of government program priorities and incentives for industry to locate must be revised.

DECENTRALIZATION

The classical position is that industry should be attracted to poverty areas where high ratios of labor to capital would make costs of labor low and returns on capital high. This presupposes that labor and capital are substitutes. But in many of the dynamic, growing, high-wage industries, skilled labor is an essential complementary input with capital in the form of plant and equipment. The return on capital operated with low-wage unskilled labor is high only if the unskilled labor is accompanied by skilled labor. And because depressed communities often possess little skilled labor, they are unable to entice firms to invest capital in plants and equipment.

Decentralization is indeed occurring. Between 1956 and 1966, U.S. manufacturing employment increased by 1,840,000 (11 per cent). Meanwhile, in the seven highly industrialized Northern states, manufacturing employment grew 37,000 (less than one-half of 1 per cent). During the same period, manufacturing employment grew 465,000 (26 per cent) in the West and 1,026,000 (33 per cent) in the South (Economic Report, 1968, p. 134). From 1962 to 1966, private nonfarm employment grew 5 per cent annually in nonmetropolitan counties and 4 per cent annually in metropolitan counties. The problem is to gain benefits of decentralization for depressed, declining rural areas. Large contiguous blocks of counties with declining population are found in Appalachia, in the northern portions of the Great Lakes states, in the Great Plains, and in the Southwest.

That economies of size attract industry is supported by the fact that employment in large metropolitan areas is growing at a rapid rate. But there are major disadvantages in large cities: social costs, which are not reflected in accounts of private firms. Crime, air pollution, and transportation congestion are only partly reflected in the private balance sheets that guide business location decisions. Of course, there are cultural advantages in the major population centers, but these mass benefits are perhaps overrated—they appeal especially to the comparatively few persons in top management. These people are also instrumental in making location decisions. But such persons after relocation are often pleasantly surprised to find advantages in living in less congested areas, advantages that compensate for the lack of museums, symphony orchestras, and opera. Somewhat tongue-in-cheek, one can blame the problem on unwarranted commitment to the urban way of life and call for a reverse "homesteads in reverse." The Homestead Act of 1862 brought people from the city to the country; "homesteads in reverse," proposed a century later by T. W. Schultz was a plea to move farm people to the city. "Reverse homesteads in reverse" would encourage people to move from the central city to communities of 10,000 to 250,000—not back to the farm.

In some industries there is a need to locate near other firms in the same business to keep abreast of industry trends and share in the local labor market for specialized industry skills. These economies external to the firm may rightly lead to location of head offices for garment makers, say, in New York City, but plants to do much of the "routine" production can be located elsewhere. Experience in Oklahoma and other states indicates that new plants in depressed areas frequently experience higher initial absenteeism and turnover than plants in larger cities. These problems are soon overcome, however, and the workers mature into a stable and productive labor force.

REDIRECTING INDUSTRY LOCATION

Industrialization of rural areas can be much more successful than in the past, and more rather than less effort should be made to attract industry to depressed rural areas along the lines suggested below.

The concept of a viable economic area rather than a functional economic area is especially important. A substantial number of firms will find sufficient factor and market economies in cities of 25,000 or more to locate efficient and profitable operations. For a development area to be viable, it is important that it includes either sufficient resources or markets to make it economically attractive to firms that potentially might locate. It has been shown that the majority of depressed rural areas are located within fifty miles of cities with populations of 25,000 or more. These growth nodes should be the focus of efforts to improve social overhead and to attract industry. The surrounding trade area of small towns and farms which must decline will have higher morale if they visualize themselves as part of a viable economic area with at least one expanding growth node.

The government should give financial support only to economic development corporations associated with designated depressed but *viable* economic areas. An area should be of size and potential to afford, with some government assistance, professional advice especially for economic planning and feasibility studies; it should have a reasonable probability of successfully attracting industry.

The federal government needs to change its policies toward industry. It is necessary for government to enlarge monetary inducements to attract industry to depressed areas and to abandon its policy of emphasizing loans to industries which cannot get credit from commercial sources. This latter policy leads to attraction of marginal, inexperienced, and unstable industries to developing areas because such firms are most likely to have difficulties getting commercial credit (cf. Yoho and Schmid, 1965).

A sizable subsidy program is likely to be seriously contested by large city political representatives who argue that decentralization of industry to more rural regions "robs Peter to pay Paul." Larger public monetary inducements to entice dynamic growth industries to locate in viable but depressed rural areas can be justified to the nonrural electorate as part of a national program to reduce the growth of slums, air pollution, crime, and transport problems in congested urban areas. By keeping rural migrants at home, such a policy shortens welfare and unemployment rolls in the large cities. The case for decentralization of industry also has favorable national defense and survival arguments.

A very large number of industries could reduce costs by locating plants in depressed rural areas. They have not done so because of inertia of past decisions, lack of knowledge, and attachment of management to the large-city way of life. A subsidy that would lead to location and lower costs for these industries in viable rural areas could be a social gain rather than a social cost. Furthermore, it may be argued that the current efforts of poor communities to attract industry with tax concessions and low-cost loans and facilities is unfair. It is regressive— the areas that pay these subsidies can afford them least. In the name of equity, a case can be made for the federal government assuming the costs of industry location now borne by the local communities.

Even a case for low-wage rural industry can be made: low wage industries use much female labor which has a low opportunity cost. Mothers have been found to be highly influential in determining aspirations and achievement of rural youth. Even at low wages, off-farm employment of mothers seems to give rise to awareness and creative tensions that lead to functional activism in children and to their escape from poverty. For men, nonfarm employment in a low-wage local industry is often an experiment for a part-time farmer. If satisfactory, the next step is a more complete break from the farm, relocation, and a job in an industry that pays a high wage.

The three principal factors considered by industry in plant location include (1) proximity to immobile factors of production including bulky raw materials and labor, (2) transportation costs and proximity to markets, and (3) economies of centralization or decentralization. The latter include external economies arising out of concentration of similar industries in an area.

Often firms find many locations which satisfy the three principal factors. Among locations that do satisfy, the final choice may be made on the basis of secondary factors, including (*a*) availability and cost of buildings and sites, (*b*) tax laws, (*c*) local infrastructure including schools, churches, recreation facilities, and cultural attractions, (*d*) living conditions, including housing, climate, air pollution, and population densities, and (*e*) other state and local incentives.

The three principal factors materially influence production costs and profits, and a community has limited control over them. While a final answer awaits definitive research, there appears to be little doubt that a large number of industries are not bound to large urban-industrial areas; these industries can profitably locate in less densely populated rural areas. Labor will have to be trained for expanded industry—it might as well be trained in depressed areas, possibly by "mobile" public vocational schools. The problem is getting industry (in the face of inadequate secondary factors, many of which require increased employment) to agree to the increased taxes required to finance social overhead.

Federal Inducements to Attract Industry

Low-interest loans, tax concessions, and direct grants have been used to attract industry to slow growing areas. The method discussed at some length earlier and used most frequently is loans. Loans are a rather weak inducement, however, and more powerful medicines—federal grants and tax concessions—warrant consideration.

One promising approach to attract industry to depressed rural areas is the investment tax credit. The magnitude of the tax credit would be a function of area unemployment rates (including, of course, farm underemployment). One suggestion is that the tax credit rate be equal to the unemployment rate, with no tax credit unless unemployment were over 10 per cent. No more than 25 per cent of new industry investment could be deducted from federal income tax if unemployment were 25 per cent or more. The tax credit would be 10 per cent of investment if the unemployment rate were 10 per cent.

There are many advantages to this program. It would be a powerful economic inducement to bring established, successful industries into depressed areas. It would pit the profit motive against other factors that have inhibited decentralization. The investment tax credit at once attacks the twin problems of too many people in the metropolis and too few jobs in depressed rural areas. To the extent that the investment credit encouraged industry to do only what it would profitably do in a more nearly perfect market, the incentives could be regarded as a productive investment rather than a subsidy or social cost.

The program would free personnel of the Economic Development Administration and other government agencies to concentrate on comprehensive economic planning, on feasibility studies of plant location, and on encouraging outmigration from areas where development is not feasible. The tax credit could be administered by existing government revenue agencies. The area and regional approach would continue to be the focus of development activity. It is expected that most industry attracted by the program would choose to locate in the development node cities of 25,000 or more population. There appear to be economies of city size between 25,000 and 250,000 population, but there are diseconomies due to congestion in large central cities. Development might best be encouraged in cities between these extremes.

The investment tax credit is a self-regulating device. Successful efforts to attract industry would reduce unemployment and eliminate the tax credit.

The tax credit would shift the burden of area economic development to the federal government and away from depressed areas which can ill afford such efforts. The exemptions of municipal bonds from federal income tax and of industry property from local taxes might be discontinued. The above changes might constrain overzealous local politicians from paying subsidies to industry that exceed the benefits derived.

Some crude estimates of the economic effectiveness of Economic Development Administration outlays can be made. In 1966 and 1967, the agency's loans to businesses totaled $94 million. This amount, directly combined with an estimated $81 million of private investment, led to a direct investment of $175 million. Based on an investment of $20,000 per worker, the investment created 8,750 jobs. An employment multiplier of 2.0 would place the primary and secondary job creation at 17,500 jobs. The result suggests that each job required $5,371 of government outlay. This estimate gives an upper limit to the cost-effectiveness. The lower limit can be estimated by considering that loans to business of $51 million in 1967 comprised only 19 per cent of the budget of the Economic Development Administration. Other expenditures for public facilities, planning, and other purposes may have been less cost-effective but contributed to the above employment. If the entire outlay of the agency is spread over 17,500 permanent jobs, the cost per job rises to $26,857. The true figure is somewhere between these extremes but is probably closer to the latter figure than to the former.

It has been estimated that the 7 per cent investment tax credit granted U.S. industry in recent years increased investment $1 for each $2 lost in tax revenue (cf. Larson, 1968). If a $20,000 investment is required per worker, and each new job in industry created one additional job through the multiplier effect, then each new job would "cost" the federal government $6,667. Thus the investment tax credit seems to be a more cost-effective approach than past programs of the Economic Development Administration.

Grants (cash subsidies) to attract industry have been little used in the U.S., but they have some obvious advantages. They can be specifically focused, their value can be known accurately in advance and hence can provide a solid planning target for firms, and grants can be a major benefit to firms in the difficult gestation period before production begins to generate receipts. By making grants proportional to investment, capital intensive firms are favored. By making grants proportional to the number of employees, labor-intensive firms are favored.

There are also obvious shortcomings in grants. They require Treasury expenses, which legislators facing a tight budget are reluctant to appropriate. They also invite abuse—a firm may receive payment, then fail to develop fully the planned facility. Finally, as with low-interest loans, there is a bias toward attracting capital-short, financially pressed companies rather than companies with established access to commercial credit.

The Canadian experience is instructive. That country shifted from tax concessions to grants, the latter allegedly a more powerful inducement to attract industry to slow growing regions (Parks, 1966). In 1966 a system of grants was introduced in Canada to encourage industrial development in designated areas of slow growth. Grants were made available to manufacturing and processing firms equal to one-third of the first $250,000 of capital investment, one-quarter of the next $750,000 and one-fifth of investment over $1 million—with a limit of $5 million per grant. The grants were not deductible from the capital against which allowances were claimed for tax purposes.

A recent review by N. M. Hansen of public programs in several countries to promote development through industrialization of depressed regions led to this conclusion:

> It is difficult to find any case where hot-house efforts to promote the development of large lagging regions have met with success. Moreover, recent American and foreign evidence concerning greater equality in the geographical distribution of manufacturing does not indicate any corresponding lessening of regional income differences or any relatively greater attractiveness of small towns or lagging regions. Recent growth in total national employment has been accounted for primarily by expanding tertiary activities, which have been located for the most part in metropolitan areas. Those industries that have tended to leave metropolitan areas have been characterized by relative stagnation or decline; they frequently seek cheap labor in areas with surplus agricultural population. Rapidly expanding sectors, on the

other hand, have favored already concentrated regions because of their numerous external economies of agglomeration. [Hansen, 1969, pp. 210–11]

Hansen (1969, p. 205) contended that it was not feasible to bring jobs to every depressed area, and outmigration was necessary. He criticized the Economic Development Administration and the National Advisory Commission on Rural Poverty for failure to recognize the need for programs to assist mobility out of depressed regions.

Clearly, more investigation of foreign and U.S. experience is needed to determine what approaches work best to create jobs. While it is clear that bringing jobs to people has previously been overrated relative to bringing people to jobs, still it appears that a tax or a grant system will work if there are sufficient monetary incentives.

FARM-NONFARM INTERACTION

Industrialization has mixed effects on farm income. Research indicates that industrialization often reduces income from the farm itself because farmers spend more of their effort at nonfarm work and less on farming. On many farms the increase in prices received for commodities due to proximity to a growing market does not compensate for lower labor input and production. But total earnings from farm and nonfarm sources tend to go up in the vicinity of an area that experiences an increase in nonfarm jobs.

After studying the development potential of the Memphis, Tennessee, economic area, Bachmura concluded that it was doubtful whether nonagricultural employment could be found for its emerging surplus farm population (Bachmura, 1959). Yet the Memphis area, with a sizable initial urban-industrial base, good location, and a subsidy program that had operated 20 years to support local industrialization (in the Mississippi section of the area), can be viewed as one of the more favorable growth areas in the South. If this area cannot absorb its farm migrants, there are probably few areas which can. In conclusion, local industrialization will be an alternative to mobility in only a few of the low-income rural areas unless area development programs are drastically revised.

INCOME AND EMPLOYMENT MULTIPLIERS

The economic repercussions on the farm and nonfarm economy following the introduction of new industry can be judged from income and employment multipliers. Multipliers show the impact of a change in a given economic sector on the entire economy. These multipliers for Oklahoma are high for agricultural processing and for manufacturing (Table 14.7). These sectors have high

TABLE 14.7. Income and Employment Multipliers, Oklahoma, by Sector

	Income		Employment	
Sector	State Only	Total	State Only	Total
Livestock and livestock products	2.81	3.02	2.82[a]	n.a.
Crops	1.40	1.52	2.82[a]	n.a.
Agricultural processing	4.32	4.92	2.82	3.35
Manufacturing	3.35	4.01	2.93	3.52
Transportation, communication, and public utilities	1.44	1.56	1.45	1.62
Finance, real estate, and insurance	1.46	1.61	1.55	1.71
Services	1.58	1.80	1.33	1.44
Wholesale and retail	1.28	1.37	1.32	1.40
Mining	1.57	1.72	2.56	2.94
Economy multipliers	2.13	2.39	2.00	2.28

SOURCE: Little and Doeksen (1968).

[a] Employment multipliers not available from above study. The multiplier 2.82 is taken from an estimate for southwestern Oklahoma (Olson and Walker, 1966).

linkages—they require a considerable amount of inputs, and their output entails considerable marketing costs before reaching consumers. Each $1.00 increase in farm income from livestock and livestock products in Oklahoma results in a $2.81 increase in income in the state and an additional 21 cents increase in income outside the state, giving a total multiplier of $3.02. Each $1.00 increment in crop income results in only a $1.40 increase in state income. Of the $1.40, $1.00 goes to crop producers and 40 cents goes to others who provide marketing and other services to crop producers.

On the average, state employment is increased by two workers when one worker is added to an economic sector. An Oklahoma study has estimated that an increase in farm employment by 100 workers leads on the average to 182 workers added to other sectors, hence the farm employment multiplier is 2.82 (Olson and Walker, 1966).

The multipliers in Table 14.7 indicate that location of an average manufacturing plant in Oklahoma employing 100 workers and paying $5,000 per worker per year would be expected to increase state employment by 293 workers. The population multiplier is 3.19, hence population would increase by 3.19 × 293 = 935 persons. The plant output (here assumed to equal the payroll) of $500,000 per annum would result in a total income increment of 3.35 × $500,000 = $1,675,000 in the state. These multipliers are averages—actual multipliers vary by plant and location. They also do not tell us much about the impact on agriculture of an increase in industrial activity.

The interdependence coefficients from an input-output matrix for Oklahoma show that each $1 increase in final output of manufacturing on the average requires a .3 cent increase in output of livestock and livestock products, a 1.0 cent increase in output of crops, a 16 cent increase in output of wholesale and retail services, and a 36 cent increase in output of mining (Little and Doeksen, 1968). An increase in the output of nonagricultural industries requires little increase in farm output. The provision of employment for farm workers can be an important factor in rural areas. While farm workers often possess fewer skills for industry than nonfarm workers and tend to be at a disadvantage when competing for nonfarm jobs, the location of new nonfarm jobs in rural areas does help farmers. Sometimes the effects are very indirect—farmers take over the unskilled jobs vacated by nonfarmers who moved to positions in the new firm or factory.

GUARANTEED EMPLOYMENT

Guaranteed employment by the federal government is ranked below subsidies to industry in cost-effectiveness to reduce poverty. This contention (as well as other rankings herein) depends partly on the time period and group being considered. For able-bodied workers with productivity below that of the minimum wage, public employment may be more cost-effective than tax concessions to locating firms as a means of raising income in the short run.

Both the National Advisory Commission on Food and Fiber and the National Advisory Commission on Rural Poverty placed their support behind federal programs to guarantee employment. The latter Commission (1967, p. 19) recommended "That the United States Government stand ready to provide jobs at the national minimum wage, or better, to every unemployed person willing and able to work."

According to a survey reported by the Commission (1967), most Americans favor establishing large-scale federal projects to give jobs to all unemployed: 66 per cent of the whites and 91 per cent of the Negroes interviewed in 1967 thought it a good idea. But is it? The efficacy of public employment depends on (a) the value of work which will be performed, (b) the extent to which workers will be attracted from private industry, and (c) the number of poor who can benefit from public employment.

Employment of the poor would be largely restricted to unskilled occupations. Frequently suggested activities would be to repair dilapidated housing, improve water and sewerage systems, assist personnel in schools and hospitals, and maintain and beautify parks and highways. Many of these jobs could be performed in home communities. But there are drawbacks. If the wage rate were equal to or exceeded the minimum wage, as recommended by the Poverty Commission, many workers would be bid away from more productive private employment, thereby reducing economic efficiency. Another problem is that a comparatively few welfare recipients can benefit from guaranteed public employment. Many persons on welfare are too old or too young, are disabled, or must take care of children at home. These groups constitute the serious, hard-core poverty problems. Hence guaranteed employment would frequently benefit those poor who need help least. Nevertheless, guaranteed employment has higher cost-effectiveness than welfare grants for some categories of the poor and can improve much neglected social overhead. The wage for such employment should be above the welfare grant provided by a guaranteed income and below the minimum wage.

Private Employment

The hard-core unemployed are shunned by private industry because of high costs of training, rapid turnover, and absenteeism. With at least 2 million rural unemployed or underemployed and average capital investments of $20,000 per worker for each productive, permanent job, the required public capital investment of $40 billion in jobs is both too great and too socialistic for the American public. An alternative to guaranteed public employment, and likely a more cost-effective approach, is guaranteed private employment through public support, in which the government takes bids from private firms to train and employ the hard-core unemployables in their plants.

In late 1967, Job Opportunities in the Business Sector (JOBS), was initiated to increase employment to the most deprived segments of the population through cooperation between private industry and government. The plan called for private industry to train and hire 100,000 of the disadvantaged during 1968 and the first half of 1969 at a federal cost of $350 million, or $3,500 per job created. A project of the National Alliance of Businessmen, JOBS demonstrated some early success. By November 1968, a reported 61,000 were at work for 12,000 firms at a total cost of $61 million to the federal government and some $120 million to the participating firms. The total federal cost was $1,000 per job created. It was estimated that the average JOBS trainee would pay the government's investment back in twenty months through his own taxes and his absence from the welfare rolls (Poverty, 1968, p. 16).

The JOBS approach appears to be more cost-effective than the industry location inducements discussed earlier. However, the program is focused on urban areas and is not effective in reaching rural people. A contemporary effort, the Concentrated Employment Program, was administered by the Department of Commerce and emphasized employment through local, state, and federal agencies of disadvantaged workers who were in rural and urban poverty (*Economic Report*, 1968, p. 147).

RECREATION

Many parts of the Ozark region and Appalachia are suitable for recreational development. Programs of reforestation and road improvements need to accompany efforts to improve the recreational value. Improved roads not only would provide easy access for tourists but also would enhance adjustment opportunities for area residents by improving communication with outside areas. The process of reforestation would provide some jobs, and public purchase of land for recreation sites would encourage adjustment of people now under-employed on marginal farms to more productive employment. Persons boxed in by lack of skills would need financial assistance to obtain job-training. Those boxed in by old age or disabilities would require transfer payments and could remain in the farm buildings even though the farmland is reforested.

It should be recognized that conversion of farmland to recreational uses is a very limited solution to problems posed by rural poverty. The rural nonfarm community would not necessarily benefit if the increased tourist trade was small in comparison to the reduced trade of farmers. Also, recreation activities tend to be seasonal and create problems of utilizing labor productively for the remainder of the year.

DIRECT GRANTS

Public assistance in the form of transfer payments ordinarily do not make federal funds go far to raise income of the salvageable poor. There are several forms of "direct payments": (a) payment in services or goods, such as food donation; (b) cash grants such as welfare payments and aid to dependent children; (c) partial grants such as unemployment, retirement, disability, and medical compensation, in which the government and the private sector or individuals share on an actuarial basis the cost of the program; and (d) a negative income tax. Some of these are more cost-effective than others.

It can be shown in theory that welfare payments in cash rather than in an equivalent dollar volume of specific goods or services places the individual on a higher indifference (satisfaction) curve. The case for payment in kind is that society knows better than the individual what is good for him. This is often true, in fact if not in theory. Tying welfare payments to education or to performance of work makes payments go farther to raise income but, as stated earlier, may give payments only to the particular "poor" who need assistance the least. There are many poor people who lack the physical and mental capacities not only to earn a socially acceptable income but even to qualify for welfare grants by the most token performance standards. For these, there are few alternatives to transfer payments. Efforts to train and create jobs for the aged and other hard-core unemployed may waste substantial administrative and teaching talent; thus direct grants are the most cost-effective means to raise the income of such persons. The earlier discussion indicated that there are still many of the needy to whom welfare assistance has not yet been extended.

EXTENDING SOCIAL LEGISLATION TO THE FARM

Substantial progress has been made in reducing the loss of dignity from welfare payments. Most notable is the case of Social Security and unemployment insurance, where the individual pays some part of the program. It is unfortunate that farm workers of all major groups on the labor force have been given the least protection under labor and social insurance legislation. They were excluded from workmen's compensation and unemployment insurance. The Labor Management Relations Act did not protect their right to organize and bargain collectively. They were largely excluded from the wage and hour provisions of the Fair Labor Standards Act and from most state minimum wage laws. Some additional social legislation undoubtedly should be extended to farm workers, but, as stated before, farm workers tend to receive low wages because they have inadequate human and material resources for earning a better living. Raising minimum wages above their low marginal value product would place more farm workers on welfare rolls and require further training and assistance. There already are too few training opportunities to fill present needs. Extension of minimum wages to hired farm workers must be accompanied by effective programs to prepare displaced workers for other jobs.

GUARANTEED ANNUAL INCOME

The numerous special programs designed to make government dollars go farther to raise the income of the poor are often messy and difficult to administer. Many of the poor are overlooked. To reduce the administrative nuisance and costs, to reduce scandal and attendant attacks on poverty programs by voters, and to get the poverty funds to those who need them, direct grants in the form of a guaranteed income have been suggested.

The National Advisory Commission on Food and Fiber (1967, p. 34) recommended that the public provide a minimal guaranteed annual income opportunity of $600 per qualified person for aged or disabled farm people, for survivors of agricultural workers, and for low-income rural workers as under employment compensation. The guaranteed income would be contingent upon able-bodied workers accepting needed training and would be terminated if the worker refused a reasonable job opportunity.

A widely heralded form of guaranteed annual income is the negative income tax or employment incentive payment. This type of program can take numerous forms. One is that a family of four be guaranteed an annual income of at least $1,600. The qualified family could earn up to $720 annually with no reduction in this minimum federal payment of $1,600. The family would remain eligible for payment until its over-all earnings (from sources other than welfare payments) reached $3,920 annually. For earnings above $720 per year, payments would be cut 50 cents for each additional dollar earned. The plan can be summarized by an equation: For annual earnings (E) from $0 to $720, the level of federal payments (P) is $1,600; for earnings between $720 and $3,920, the level of annual federal payments is:

$$P = \$1,600 - .5(E - \$720)$$

The total annual income is P + E. Thus the family of four would receive the following federal payments and total income for selected levels of earnings:

Earnings	Federal Payment (Dollars per year)	Total Income
None	1,600	1,600
720	1,600	2,320
1,000	1,460	2,460
2,000	960	2,960
3,000	460	3,460
3,920	0	3,920

One form of the plan would base federal payments only on the criteria of earnings and family size. A second form of the plan not only would gear payments to family size and income, but also would require able-bodied adult recipients (except mothers with children under six) to accept work or training if suitable jobs are available. One advantage of the first form is that all families, even those with able-bodied adults who refused to work, would be raised out of dire poverty. Children in poverty would not be penalized for failure of their parents to work and qualify for benefits. The second form of the plan would provide stronger inducements for employment but would be more difficult to administer because it would require difficult administrative judgments concerning the able-bodied.

Initially, a work incentive plan would require more federal dollars than would a flat guaranteed income to raise the income of the very poor. For the same total federal outlay, minimum payments to a family of four could be set at, say, $2,500 (rather than $1,600 as above) with a flat guaranteed income and for the same federal cost as the employment incentive plan. Some payments would go to the not-so-poor families earning over $3,500, using the above example of the negative income tax. But the incentive to work provided by the negative income tax would induce employment, and likely would have a higher long-term social benefit-cost ratio than other types of guaranteed income programs.

Grants ideally would be some fraction of the difference between income and a socially acceptable norm. The fraction would be less than one to maintain incentives for work. If the fraction were .5, say, then the net income of a family would be raised $50 by additional work that would add $100 of earnings and would reduce federal payments by $50. Income would always be higher for those who worked. This approach has been embraced widely by economic liberals and conservatives. The shortfall of income in the late 1960's was only $11 billion below the socially acceptable minimum among individuals and families over the country. Going to a guaranteed annual income or a negative income tax to eliminate poverty would remove many current welfare programs and would require a *net* increase in welfare outlays of $11 billion or more. Though a large expense, $11 billion was only 1.4 per cent of the 1967 gross national product.

But would this approach eliminate poverty? Though the approach is a good beginning, the answer is "no" if poverty, as was argued previously, is a state of body and mind as well as an economic condition. A guaranteed income may alleviate the symptoms rather than the causes. There are two conceivable ways to eliminate poverty: One is by using education (in its broadest sense) to create the proper attitudes and skills that will lead to adequate income levels. The other is to begin with a transfer payment to raise income to acceptable levels; then hopefully a middle class income will lead to "middle-class" attitudes and skills. There is no assurance that the latter approach will work, and with limited public funds it is better to concentrate on programs such as education and job creation, which make government dollars go farther to raise income levels. But as public funds become more available, it will be feasible to use a negative income tax or other transfer payment to raise the income of *all* in society to socially acceptable levels. The guaranteed annual income is one of the few programs that can totally eliminate the overt forms of poverty. It can reduce some of the overhead costs and some messy administration that have plagued past programs. These advantages suggest that some form of a guaranteed income is the direction that poverty programs will take in the future.

REDISTRIBUTION OF FEDERAL REVENUE TO STATES

Although redistribution of revenues to states is listed last among programs ranked by the social benefit-cost ratio criterion, the actual efficiency will depend on how the states use the payments. States may be less efficient than the federal government in disbursing poverty funds. Conflicts among power groups, lack of political muscle by the poor, and racial discrimination interfere with equitable use of funds. Furthermore, poverty programs that go through the fewest channels of government can be most equitable and efficient. These considerations certainly dampen enthusiasm for programs to redistribute taxes directly back to states, but such programs have substantial advantages, including a chance to promote a progressive redistribution of income among states and reduce the financial burden to low-income areas supporting good schools. As a stopgap measure before the guaranteed income becomes a reality, the Federal government can improve the income distribution by returning federal revenue to the states. This should be done by grants based on population and the shortfall of state per capita income below the national average. Every effort should be made to avoid returning revenue on the basis of the revenue paid by each state.

Studies of taxes in Oklahoma and other states reveal that state and local taxes are regressive. This finding is consistent with the data for the U.S. as a whole in Table 14.8. Total taxes as a proportion of income were 19.4 per cent

Table 14.8. U.S. Taxes as Percentage of Personal Income, 1958

Income bracket	State and Local Taxes			Federal Taxes			Total
	Property	Other	Total	Income	Other	Total	
Less than $2,000	7.4	6.6	14.0	2.3	5.1	7.4	21.4
$2,000–3,999	5.5	5.5	11.0	5.3	3.9	9.2	20.2
$4,000–5,999	4.9	5.0	9.9	7.0	3.6	10.6	20.5
$6,000–7,999	4.3	4.4	8.7	9.0	3.5	12.5	21.2
$8,000–9,999	3.8	4.1	7.9	8.4	3.3	11.7	19.6
$10,000–14,999	3.0	3.8	6.8	9.7	2.9	12.6	19.4
$15,000 and over	2.1	3.2	5.3	15.9	3.3	19.2	24.5
Average	3.8	4.2	8.0	9.6	3.5	13.1	21.1

SOURCE: See Weisbrod (1963, p. 94). Data include the estimated burden of corporate income tax.

for those in the $10,000–14,999 bracket and 21.4 per cent for those with income under $2,000. Even the progressive federal income tax is not sufficient to offset this regressiveness of state and local taxes in some states. The federal income tax is only mildly progressive, due to many loopholes such as capital gains, mineral depletion allowances, tax-free bonds, and "charitable" contributions. Closing of these loopholes and redistribution of income back to the states could do much to raise the level of living and education standards of poor areas. Some federal guidelines might be necessary to ensure that the state programs would help those who are most economically disadvantaged.

SUMMARY AND CONCLUSIONS

The ranking of poverty programs in this chapter was based on the proposition that those programs should receive priority which make limited public funds go farthest to raise incomes of the poor. The specific criterion was the social benefit-cost ratio, the increment in income of the poor per dollar of public and private investment.

TAILORING COST-EFFECTIVENESS TO SPECIFIC CATEGORIES OF THE POOR

There is a fundamental conflict between efforts to channel funds to the hard-core poor and efforts to increase the cost-effectiveness of poverty programs. The slogan "worst first" represented an attempt of the Economic Development Administration to give first priority to development of the most impoverished groups and areas. Efforts to bring industries and training to these groups and areas entailed low economic returns per dollar spent and were perhaps no more effective than welfare grants. On this basis, it should be recognized that *some* hard-core poverty can best be served by welfare grants—and many eligible people are not yet receiving assistance. Meanwhile, other approaches are more cost-effective among viable groups.

Ranking highest are programs of national full employment. Since the government has largely accepted and acted on this policy, little need be said of it. Ranking second are programs to improve factor markets, particularly labor markets. The federal-state cooperative employment service needs a substantial assist in funds and expertise and could significantly expand its operations in rural areas and across state lines. Efforts by public and private groups to reduce discrimination must be redoubled and can have a high economic payoff.

The third priority is education and training. Jobs, relocation subsidies, and knowledge of where job opportunities exist will do little good for people who do not qualify for available jobs. The past underinvestment in general education and skill training in poor rural areas has resulted in a disaster that will plague our great cities for years to come. The inertia of neglect can only be overcome with much more federal aid to education. The current programs are too fragmented and poorly financed to do the job. A substantial redistribution of federal funds back to the states for education of the disadvantaged offers one useful approach. Such a program has much appeal, because it could result in a progressive income redistribution.

Primary and secondary school quality must be raised in depressed rural areas by upgrading skills of current teachers, hiring better teachers, enriching the curriculum, and in some cases paying students to attend school. Vocational education also fills an important need but should succeed efforts to improve basic education. Improvements in general and vocational education can be pursued concurrently in instances where funds and general education have not lagged seriously. An intensive program of preschool education for 3–6-year-olds should receive an even higher priority than vocational or general schooling. Lastly, educational programs for adults round out the education priorities.

The fourth major priority is attracting industry to depressed rural areas with federal grants, loans, and tax concessions. It is suggested that substantial investment tax credits or grants be the principal tools to bring industry to viable cities in depressed rural areas and to encourage decentralization. The government is the largest single source of off-farm employment for farmers. There is considerable scope for the government not only to subsidize private firms locating in depressed areas but also to locate more of its activities in rural areas characterized by low income.

Guaranteed public employment is ranked fifth in cost-effectiveness. There are obvious opportunities for able-bodied workers who lack adequate skills to contribute to society by improving the rural landscape and social overhead. Even greater opportunities to improve skills and earnings for such persons may be opened by joint government-private industry efforts. Private industry would train and provide jobs, while the government would pay to industry the difference between training costs and earnings until the actual productivity of workers reached a socially acceptable level.

The top four priorities are considered to be within the current means of the country. The fifth priority, guaranteed public employment, may also be within current means. The sixth priority, a guaranteed annual income, may be attainable within the decade. A guaranteed annual income operated, perhaps, through the federal income tax structure could eliminate overt poverty. At the same time it would eliminate many current welfare programs that are difficult or impossible to administer satisfactorily. These troublesome programs continually jeopardize other poverty programs.

Two basic approaches to poverty can be used. One is to provide a minimum income and allow individuals to allocate the income to food, housing, education, and other uses as he sees fit. Another approach is to provide a specific public program offering food, another offering clothing, another health care, another education, and another housing. The latter approach provides the needy with what society deems to be basic essentials but requires substantial administrative machinery. An advantage of the negative income tax is that administration could be streamlined, and many special programs of housing, food distribution, and education could be eliminated. The additional cost of a guaranteed income—at least $11 billion per year—will be only 1 per cent of the gross national product in a few years and a small real cost to alleviate poverty.

OTHER CRITERIA FOR ESTABLISHING PROGRAM PRIORITIES

A second cost-effectiveness criterion is the local benefit-cost ratio associated with federal funds alone. The principal change from the above ranking would be to give programs of industrialization and family planning a much higher priority. If the loss in employment in other areas is ignored, federal programs to bring industrialization to depressed rural areas have very high benefit-cost ratios. If only state or local funds are considered, they too would have high benefit-cost ratios when only the local benefits of industrialization are considered. In short, this criterion does not reflect the real social benefits and costs but helps to explain much of the emphasis on industrialization through local development corporations.

A third cost-effectiveness criterion is the public funds required to create jobs for the disadvantaged. Of the comparisons reported in this chapter, public subsidies to private industry to train and employ the disadvantaged appear to require fewest public funds per job created. Tax incentives to attract industry to depressed areas would appear to require fewer funds per job created than the Economic Development Administration programs for industry location used in 1969. Public employment of the disadvantaged ranks lowest by this criterion in efficiency among the job-creating programs discussed in the chapter.

FAMILY PLANNING

No effort was made in the text to rank family planning as a cost-effective measure to raise income of poor people. Unfortunately, research is not yet available to appraise the efficiency of this publicly supported measure to help the poor. One can speculate, however, that help in family planning and birth control is a highly efficient means to alleviate poverty. Its impact is primarily long run. Every effort should be made to provide at public expense the means for birth control to the poor that are now available to middle-class families.

Consumer education to create more intelligent buying and consuming habits among the poor is another useful program that should not be overlooked. The cooperative extension service already has such programs; they could be expanded.

Research on the cost-effectiveness of public programs for the disadvantaged has been plagued by inadequate financing. Clearly more effort is needed, and the above list of priorities, of necessity, are subject to revision and await more definitive analysis.

REFERENCES

Bachmura, Frank. 1959. Man-land equalization through migration. *American Economic Review* 49:1004–17.

———. 1967. Manpower and well-being in rural areas. In *Agricultural Policy: A Review of Programs and Needs*, Washington, National Advisory Commission on Food and Fiber, pp. 133–72.

Behavioral Science Center. 1968. Business leadership training project, research report and evaluation. Boston, Sterling Institute.

458   *Foundations of Farm Policy*

Cain, Glen. 1967. Benefit-cost estimates for Job Corps. Washington, Office of Economic Opportunity (mimeo).

—— and Gerald Somers. 1967. Retraining the disadvantaged worker. In Cathleen Quirk and Carol Sheehan, eds., *Research in Vocational and Technical Education*, Center for Studies in Vocational and Technical Education, Madison, University of Wisconsin, pp. 27–44.

—— and Ernst Stormsdorfer. 1967. An economic evaluation of the government retraining of the unemployed in West Virginia. Preliminary report. Madison, University of Wisconsin, Department of Economics.

Carroll, Adger, and Loren Ihnen. 1966. Costs and returns of technical education: a pilot study. Raleigh, North Carolina State University, Department of Economics.

Corazzini, A. J. 1966. Vocational education, a study of benefits and costs. Princeton, N.J., Princeton University, Industrial Relations Section.

Economic Report of the President. 1965, 1967, 1968. Washington: U.S. Government Printing Office.

Hansen, Niles M. 1969. Regional development and the rural poor. *Journal of Human Resources* 4:205–14.

Hathaway, Dale. 1968. Statement to Senate Subcommittee on Government Research: The rural to urban population shift. National Manpower Conference. 90th Congress, 2nd Session. Stillwater, Okla., pp. 6–11.

Hines, Fred, and Luther Tweeten. 1968. Push-pull and schooling investment. *American Journal of Agricultural Economics* 50:1426–31.

Hirsch, W. Z., E. W. Segelhorst, and M. J. Marcus. 1964. Spillover of public education costs and benefits (II). Institute of Government and Public Affairs. Los Angeles, University of California.

Hobgood, William, and Fred Tyner. 1968. Development of new industry. D.A.E. Research Report No. 371. Baton Rouge, La., Agricultural Experiment Station.

Kaufman, J. J., E. W. Stormsdorfer, Teh-wei Hu, and M. L. Lee. 1967. An analysis of the comparative costs and benefits of vocational versus academic education in secondary schools. Preliminary report. OE 512. Washington, U.S. Office of Health, Education, and Welfare.

Larson, Robert E. 1968. Industrial development for rural poverty areas. Stanford, Calif., Stanford University (mimeo).

Little, Charles H., and Gerald A. Doeksen. 1968. An input-output analysis of Oklahoma's economy. Technical Bulletin No. T-124. Stillwater, Okla., Agricultural Experiment Station.

National Advisory Commission on Food and Fiber. 1967. *Food and Fiber for the Future.* Washington: U.S. Government Printing Office.

National Advisory Commission on Rural Poverty. 1967. *The People left Behind.* Washington: U.S. Government Printing Office.

Olson, Carl, and Odell Walker. 1966. Agricultural adjustments and area economic interrelationships. *Journal of Farm Economics* 48:1570–74.

Parks, A. C. 1966. Some stimulants to social and economic change. In G. R. Winter and W. Rogers, eds., *Stimulants to Economic Development in Slow Growing Regions*, Edmonton, University of Alberta, Department of Agricultural Economics, Chapter 10.

Poverty. 1968. *Time*, Nov. 22, 1968, pp. 16–17.

Redfern, Martin. 1969. Unpublished data on rates of return on education. Stillwater, Oklahoma State University, Department of Agricultural Economics.

Rinehart, James R. 1963. Rates of return on municipal subsidies to industry. *Southern Economic Journal* 29:297–306.

Saltzman, Raymond. 1964. Economic case studies of community sponsored efforts to develop industry. Tulsa, Okla., University of Tulsa, College of Business Administration.

Secretary of Labor. 1966. Manpower research and training under the MDTA. Washington: U.S. Government Printing Office.

Shallah, Salim. 1969. Unpublished data on rates of return on vocational education. Stillwater, Oklahoma State University, Department of Agricultural Economics.

Smith, Eldon. 1956. Nonfarm employment information for rural people. *Journal of Farm Economics* 38:813–27.

Somers, Gerald. 1968. Matching skills and jobs through relocation subsidies. In *Creating Opportunities for Tomorrow*, Agricultural Policy Institute, Raleigh, North Carolina State University, pp. 53–68.

Taussig, Michael. 1968. An economic analysis of vocational education in New York City high schools. *Journal of Human Resources* 3:59–87.

Tweeten, Luther. 1967. The role of education in alleviating rural poverty. Economic Report No. 114. Washington.

———. 1968. Rural poverty. Processed Series P-590. Stillwater, Okla., Agricultural Experiment Station.

U.S. Department of Agriculture. 1966. Rural people in the American economy. Economic Report No. 101. Washington: U.S. Government Printing Office.

U.S. Department of Labor. 1966. The role of technical schools in improving the skills and earning capacity of rural manpower. Washington, Office of Manpower Policy, Evaluation, and Research.

Weisbrod, Burton. 1963. *Spillover of Public Education Costs and Benefits*. St. Louis, Washington University.

White House and U.S. Department of Labor. 1965, 1966. Manpower report of the President. Washington: U.S. Government Printing Office.

Yoho, James, and Allan Schmid. 1965. Area development: observations on a failure. *Journal of Farm Economics* 47:468–70.

CHAPTER FIFTEEN

Foreign Trade and Aid in American Farm Products

Since colonial times, foreign markets for American farm products have been an important source of our nation's farm prosperity and economic growth. The failure of foreign markets, such as the failures of the 1920's and 1930's, leads to farm recession. Despite their importance, foreign markets have often been manipulated by U.S. policy-makers with seeming disregard for other countries or the long-term consequences of our policies. Economists have stressed the vital importance of foreign markets to the national economy (not just to any one group) and of the need to reduce barriers to world trade at home and in foreign countries. This chapter attempts to document the advantages of foreign trade, the importance of such trade to the U.S., and the progress made over the years to remove trade barriers. The chapter concludes with sections on foreign aid (emphasizing the food aspects) and on ways to improve the use of such aid.

THE MAGNITUDE OF U.S. AGRICULTURAL EXPORTS

Since the United States accounts for one-fifth of all agricultural commodities entering free world trade, it has a major stake in keeping trade channels open. In the year ending June 30, 1957, U.S. agricultural product exports totaled $4.7 billion, of which $1.9 billion were under government programs (sales for foreign currencies, barter, and donations). How different the picture a decade later—when exports totaled $6.8 billion, of which $1.6 billion were under government programs. Thus from 1957 to 1967, total exports expanded 3.7 per cent annually while commercial exports expanded 6.1 per cent annually.

Exports of agricultural products have comprised approximately one-fourth of all U.S. exports since the early 1950's; hence they play a major role in earning foreign exchange to offset outlays for imports. Total agricultural imports in 1966 were $4.5 billion, leaving a $2.3 billion net surplus of agricultural exports

(U.S. Department of Agriculture, 1967a, pp. 704 ff.). Supplementary imports, defined as those which compete with commodities produced domestically, have accounted for about half of all imports, although that percentage is growing. Agricultural exports are about three times as great in dollar volume as imports of agricultural products of the type produced domestically. It is apparent that agricultural exports contribute in a major way to our trade balance. Without an efficient agriculture, our balance of payments problems could be critical indeed.

EXPORTS BY COMMODITY

Table 15.1 shows trends in exports by individual commodity and for all agricultural commodities from 1961 to 1966. Wheat and wheat flour was by far the largest component of exports in 1961. By 1966, it was being challenged for first place by feed grain, with corn the principal component. The dollar volume shown in the table includes exports under government programs, which are a larger proportion for wheat than feed grain. Feed grain surpassed wheat in commercial sales by 1966 and was the number-one dollar earner of all U.S. export commodities, including industrial products.

The importance of cotton and tobacco, once the major farm exports, has declined until each is now surpassed in dollar export volume by grains, oilseeds, and animal products.

TABLE 15.1. Value of U.S. Agricultural Exports, by Commodity, 1961–66

	1961	1962	1963	1964	1965	1966
	(Millions of dollars)					
Wheat and flour	1,298	1,134	1,331	1,532	1,184	1,534
Feed grain	375	788	794	857	1,134	1,334
Milled rice	111	153	177	204	243	228
Cotton	875	528	577	682	486	432
Tobacco	391	373	403	413	383	482
Vegetable fat and oils	152	205	185	248	283	194
Oilseeds	367	429	506	609	687	802
Protein meal	48	90	125	144	187	232
Fruits and fruit preparations	272	286	276	279	313	315
Vegetables and vegetable preparations	124	149	173	158	155	176
Nuts and nut preparations	12	16	22	27	43	38
Animal products	634	490	677	840	787	726
Other	164	221	268	291	272	297
Total	4,823	4,862	5,514	6,284	6,157	6,790

SOURCE: U.S. Department of Agriculture (1967b, September, p. 43).

Farm product exports of $6.9 billion in 1968 comprised 16 per cent of all farm receipts. Farm exports as a proportion of farm receipts totaled 10 per cent in 1951 and 14 per cent in 1961, and hence have grown in relative importance as an outlet for farm production. Since about 7 per cent of world farm output finds its way into world trade, the U.S. is absolutely and relatively more heavily involved in world commerce in farm products than are other countries on the average.

The share of production exported varies considerably by commodities. In 1966, 65 per cent of the production of wheat (including flour equivalent), 68 per cent of the dried edible peas and 55 per cent of the rice (milled basis) were exported. The same year, 42 per cent of soybean production, 16 per cent of corn production and 37 per cent of the nonfat dry milk production were exported. As a 1959–61 average, 41 per cent of cotton production was exported. This percentage dropped to 21 per cent by 1966 and is an example of how export volume can change under new economic and institutional circumstances.

LEADING DOLLAR MARKETS FOR U.S. EXPORTS

Japan was the leading dollar market for U.S. agricultural exports in fiscal 1967 with nearly twice the dollar purchases of any other country (Table 15.2).

TABLE 15.2. Leading Dollar Markets for U.S. Farm Products, by Principal Countries of Destination, Year Ending June 30, 1967

	Sales for Dollars	
	(Millions of dollars)	*(Per cent)*
Japan	929	17.9
Canada	594[a]	11.4
Netherlands	471	9.1
West Germany	476	9.2
United Kingdom	434	8.4
Italy	215	4.1
Belgium and Luxembourg	179	3.4
Spain	153	2.9
France	148	2.9
Denmark	86	1.7
Other	1,503	29.0
Total	5,188	100.0

SOURCE: U.S. Department of Agriculture (1967b, November, pp. 14, 37).

[a] Includes estimated value of U.S. exports to Canada of grains and soybeans for finishing the loading at Canadian ports of vessels moving through the St. Lawrence Seaway ($116 million).

The United Kingdom, once the largest single foreign market for U.S. commodities, in the year ending June 30, 1967, ranked fifth—behind Japan, Canada, Netherlands and West Germany—in purchases. The European Economic Community (see note 1, below) comprises the largest single market bloc for U.S. farm exports. If it is joined by the United Kingdom and Denmark, and if Belgium and Luxembourg are counted as one importer, then seven of the top ten commercial importers of American farm commodities would be in the European Economic Community. These seven, which accounted for $2 out of each $5 of our commercial export earnings in fiscal 1967, are a vital concern in trade negotiations.

REASONS FOR TRADE

COMPARATIVE ADVANTAGE AND THE GAINS FROM TRADE

The fundamental proposition that participants benefit from exchange of goods and services underlies foreign trade. Figure 15.1 illustrates the concept of comparative advantage and the benefits of trade. The farm resources of the U.S. and Brazil will produce wheat and sugar in the combinations indicated by the respective production possibility curves P. In isolation, the highest societal indifference curve that can be reached with the given resources is I_0 in each country. The terms-of-trade line (not shown) in isolation, indicating the ratio of the price of sugar to the price of wheat, is tangent to the product transformation curves and the societal indifference curves I_0 at A. The slope of this price line is considerably steeper for the U.S. than for Brazil. The relatively high price for sugar in the U.S. and wheat in Brazil in Figure 15.1 reflects differences in production capabilities rather than in consumer preferences.

In isolation, quantities of sugar and wheat produced and consumed in the countries are W_i and S_i. The resources of the U.S. are better suited to produce wheat than sugar, and those of Brazil are better suited to produce sugar than wheat. Hence, even in isolation, with the same preferences reflected in similar indifference curves in each country, the U.S. consumes relatively much more wheat than sugar. The reverse is true for Brazil.

The U.S. is said to have a comparative advantage in wheat; Brazil in sugar. A nation is said to have an *absolute* advantage when it can produce a commodity at a lower cost (measured in hours of labor, or, more properly, in a weighted value-sum of inputs) per unit than can another country. The classical economists pointed out that one nation (say the U.S. in Figure 15.1) could have an absolute advantage in production of both wheat and sugar, and yet trade would be advantageous. It is only necessary to possess a *comparative* advantage, which can be illustrated by an example. Suppose the U.S. can produce a ton of

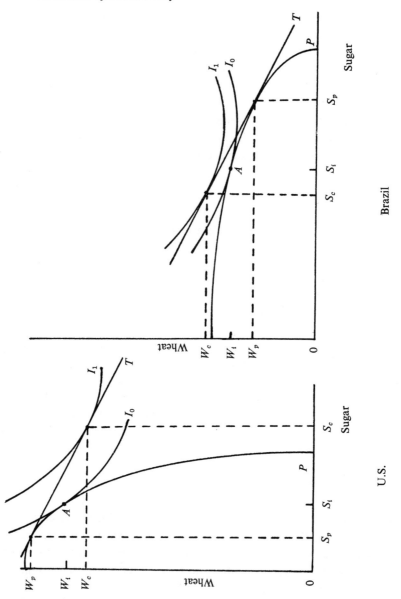

FIGURE 15.1. Production possibility curves and indifference curves for wheat and sugar in the U.S. and Brazil.

wheat with two hours of labor and a ton of sugar with six hours of labor. Suppose, further, that Brazil can produce a ton of wheat for five hours of labor and a ton of sugar for ten hours. Then, based on the classical concept, the U.S. is said to have a comparative advantage in wheat, and Brazil in sugar. The welfare of the two countries will be enhanced by the U.S. shipping wheat to

Brazil in return for sugar, although the U.S. has an absolute advantage in the production of both commodities.

The modern theory of comparative advantage is illustrated with the two production possibility curves *P* in Figure 15.1. If the curve for Brazil is rotated 180 degrees and placed on top of the curve for the U.S., it forms a pattern similar to that in Figure 16.3 in the next chapter. By making the two curves tangent at various points, different combinations of total sugar and wheat will be produced efficiently by the two countries. It is apparent that, because of the nature of the curves, the U.S. will tend to specialize in wheat and Brazil in sugar. The modern theory of comparative advantage, then, is based on the shape of the product transformation curves and hence on comparative production costs. Theory must also take into account the nature of consumer preferences and demand.

Trade results in greater specialization in production of wheat (W_p) in the U.S. and sugar (S_p) in Brazil. However, more wheat (W_c) is consumed in Brazil and more sugar (S_c) in the U.S. after trading than in isolation. The quantity $W_p - W_c$ is a net wheat export from the U.S. and a net import into Brazil. The quantity $S_p - S_c$ is the net sugar export from Brazil and a net import to the U.S. This trade enables each country to move from a lower indifference curve (I_0) in the absence of trade to a higher indifference curve (I_1) through greater specialization in production of what it does best. The new terms of trade, line *T*, would represent the same price ratio for both countries in the absence of trade barriers. It follows that tangency of the same price line to the product transformation curves and indifference curves in each country indicates equal marginal rates of substitution in consumption and production and a Pareto optimum (see next chapter). The case for freer trade among nations is much like the case for freer trade among regions within a nation; it depends on the assumptions of perfect competition. Unlike the analysis in the next chapter, the world trade model does not assume that resources are mobile among geographic entities.

The price line in reality does not have the same slope for each country because of transport costs and institutional impediments to trade, such as duties, quotas, export subsidies, and domestic price supports.

When one nation erects barriers to free trade, it is not necessarily to the advantage of another country to maintain a free trade policy. Also, inferences about the well-being of trading nations are hazardous because comparisons are required of marginal utility among nations as well as between producers and consumers. Finally, country *A* may have few qualms about erecting trade barriers which make it better off while other countries are made worse off and experience a much greater loss in utility than *A* gains. An impediment to this action of *A* is fear that other nations will reciprocate, erecting trade barriers that make *A* worse off. Thus, all the trading nations may find themselves worse off by individually pursuing trading policies that each nation, acting alone, finds advantageous.

COMPARATIVE PROFITS

Recognition that T in Figure 15.1 may differ among nations because of demand, transport, and institutional circumstances leads to rejection of comparative advantage based only on relative production costs as a basis for trade. The concept of comparative profits, which take into account consumer preferences, comparative production possibilities, and barriers to trade through costs and returns data, provides a more complete explanation of the basis for trade. A nation or region will emphasize production of those goods in which its profits are greatest. Country A may have higher profits in all potentially exportable commodities than does country B. But if the profit, which is the return to fixed resources, is highest in wheat among all commodities grown in A and is highest in sugar among all commodities grown in B when exposed to the world market, then A will export wheat to B and import sugar from B. One assumption is that comparative profit exists in export of at least one commodity.

Cynics argue that comparative advantage or comparative profits have little to do with world trade. In fact these concepts have a great deal to do with world trade and trade negotiations. They are the very foundation for trade, although the day-to-day bargaining more often is over institutional issues.

SUPPLY, DEMAND, AND TRADE

Figure 15.2 shows trade between the U.S. and foreign countries, given the domestic demand and supply curves in the U.S. (*a*), and in foreign countries taken as an aggregate entity in (*c*). The supply of U.S. exports is the amount by which domestic supply exceeds domestic demand $S_{US} - D_{US}$ at all possible prices, hence is the excess supply curve S_e in (*b*). The demand for U.S. exports is the amount by which foreign demand exceeds foreign supply $D_f - S_f$ at all possible prices, and hence is the excess demand curve D_e in (*b*). Export supply and demand intersect at an equilibrium price P_e, and Q_e is the quantity exported by the U.S. This does not allow for transport costs $P_f - P_{US}$. Transport costs lower the U.S. export demand by the amount of the cost—from D_e to D_e'. The equilibrium price is then P_{US} in the United States and P_f in the foreign market. Other barriers to trade such as foreign tariffs have an effect similar to transport costs in reducing the demand for U.S. exports. The exports from the U.S. are $Q_s - Q_d$ in (*a*); the same quantity as Q_e' in (*b*) and foreign imports $Q_d - Q_s$ in (*c*).

Export markets raise to P_{US} the domestic price of the commodity in the U.S. from the equilibrium price P_i in market isolation. The price P_f in the foreign market is lower than the market-isolated price P_i. With trade, the gain in producers' surplus exceeds the loss in consumers' surplus in the U.S. by the net

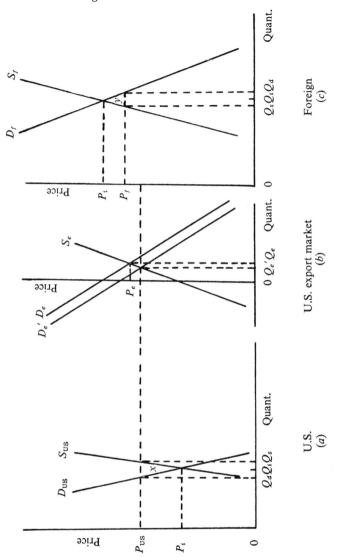

FIGURE 15.2. Domestic demand and supply curves (*a*), U.S. export demand and supply curves (*b*), and foreign demand and supply curves (*c*).

social gain represented by the triangle x in Figure 15.2 (see discussion of Figure 16.5 for definitions of terms). In the foreign market, the gain in consumers' surplus exceeds the loss in producers' surplus by the net social gain represented by the triangle y. Thus the public (made up of consumers and producers) in each trading area realizes a positive net gain from trade, but U.S. consumers are disadvantaged and foreign producers are disadvantaged in the example in Figure 15.2. These groups may resist freer trade. The losses focused on a few well-organized foreign producers may motivate such producers to press for barriers to curtail trade and cut off the widely dispersed consumer gains, though the consumers' gains in total outweigh producers' losses. A tariff equal to the price difference in isolation, P_t (foreign) − P_i (U.S.), stops trade even in the absence of transport costs.

The graphs in Figure 15.2 could be simplified by merely adding the foreign demand D_e' to the domestic demand D_{US} to form the total demand for U.S. farm products. Adding export demand would make total demand considerably more elastic than domestic demand alone. The total demand for U.S. products would intersect supply at P_{US}, giving the same equilibrium prices and quantities as before. The elasticity of demand for U.S. farm exports has been estimated (but not with much precision) to be −.5 in the short run, −2 in three years, and up to −6 in the long run (Tweeten, 1967). The same study estimated the elasticity of domestic demand for U.S. farm output at the farm level to be −.2 in the intermediate and long run. With inclusion of export demand, the estimated elasticity of total demand for U.S. farm output was raised to −.5 in the intermediate run and −1.1 in the long run.

ARGUMENTS FOR TRADE BARRIERS

Several reasons have been given to justify trade barriers. These include efforts to protect or promote national security, infant industry, balance of payments, and countervailing power.

Protection is said to be required for some items to maintain necessary domestic production when foreign supplies are cut off by drought, by political decree in peacetime, or by enemy attacks on shipping in wartime. Rather than depend on cheaper foreign sources, the reasoning goes, it is better to maintain domestic production as security, even at high cost. One weakness of this conclusion is that the pattern of wars have changed. Brush-fire wars of the Korean and Vietnam types do not cut off foreign supplies, and a major war using nuclear weapons would most likely be of comparatively short duration. In peacetime, diversification of supply sources and opportunities for substitution of one commodity for another should limit serious supply shortages.

The protect-infant-industry argument has validity where a domestic industry needs to grow to achieve external and internal economies of scale. Initially the industry is not competitive in world markets, but, with time, economies of scale and maturity of know-how reduce costs to competitive levels, eliminating the need for protection. This argument has particular appeal in developing nations, but it has little validity for dairy, beef, sugar, textile, steel, and chemical industries in the U.S.

Another rationale for trade barriers in the past has been to improve our balance of payments. This argument would have greater validity if exports were independent of imports, but efforts to curtail imports, such as the notorious Hawley-Smoot Tariff, lead to countermeasures by foreign countries to protect their trading position. Unless there is a real need, well recognized by other nations, to protect a balance of payments situation (and then only after domestic policies such as currency devaluation and curbs on inflation have been pursued) increasing trade barriers are not likely to be tolerated without reciprocal action on the part of foreign nations.

Proponents of trade barriers have reasoned realistically that unilateral reduction of trade barriers may not be in the interests of the U.S. and that countervailing trade barriers may be necessary. Out of such thinking has grown a theory of the second best (i.e., what kind and level of trade barriers are optimal for country *A*, facing a world of existing and mounting institutional barriers to free trade?). Such a theory must also account for the possibility of reciprocal action by other countries to counter increasing interference in trade on the part of country *A*.

Major support for trade barriers comes from domestic industries which want their price and income position protected from foreign competition. The fight for trade barriers is seldom waged in the name of maintaining or increasing income of the protected industry. Though this is the real reason, "good" reasons are officially stated, such as protection against dumping (goods sold here below the production cost in the exporting country), contributions to national defense, and balance of payments.

Seldom is the macro-micro inconsistency more apparent than in negotiations over trade barriers. Economists have repeatedly demonstrated—and history has supported—the contention that freer trade generates greater economic progress with but few exceptions. A major impediment to movement toward freer trade is that in reality it is not a Pareto optimum or Pareto better situation, since someone is made worse off. Removal of trade barriers is consistent with the new welfare economics, which stress greater efficiency irrespective of the distribution of the efficiency gains (see the next chapter). Given resources are able to produce more output—greater efficiency means that gainers theoretically can compensate the losers and make them no worse off than before the change. The problem is that compensation is seldom made. The gains are often widely dispersed over millions of consumers. The losses on the other hand are often rather narrowly focused on a few producers.

In the arena of pressure groups and power politics, millions of indifferent gainers are no match for the intense opposition generated by a few determined big losers. A small dollar loss to a group with high marginal utility of money, coupled with a large dollar gain to a group with low marginal utility of money, *may* represent a sizable *net* welfare loss from liberalized trade arrangements. The value judgment of most economists is that this is not usually the case, and they continue to press for freer trade. There is almost universal commitment among economists to the proposition that the U.S. (and the world) has far more to gain than to lose by multilateral reduction of trade barriers.

TOWARD FREER TRADE: HISTORICAL PERSPECTIVE

After World War I, American farmers and industry were committed to the protectionist policies under which they had prospered prior to the war. Protectionism had little impact on agriculture in the prewar period because farmers were net exporters, the world economy was relatively strong, and domestic prices were determined to a large extent by world markets. The drop in U.S. farm prices in 1921, following recovery of world agricultural production, brought new demands by U.S. farmers for protection from foreign competition. These demands were met to a considerable degree. Industry requested similar protection, which it received in the Tariff Act of 1922.

Unlike the prewar situation, Europe was now a debtor rather than creditor to the U.S. Europe reacted by increasing its own level of protection, especially for agricultural products. U.S. agriculture continued to be depressed in the 1920's. In 1929 a sharp drop in farm and industry exports led to demands for even greater protection. Again the demands were met in the Hawley-Smoot Tariff of June, 1930, creating the highest import duties in American history. Many trading nations reacted by increasing their levels of protection. In 1932, for example, the United Kingdom, then our largest customer for farm commodities, created legislation and Commonwealth agreements which required outsiders to pay a 10 per cent duty on farm products but allowed most agricultural products of Commonwealth countries to enter duty free.

Partly as a result of protectionist measures and countermeasures, the value of U.S. agricultural exports in 1930 fell to one-third of the average export value in 1925–29. Increased protectionism was clearly a disaster, but farm interests were reluctant to recognize that the U.S. could not expand exports without at the same time allowing expansion of imports.

THE TRADE EXPANSION ACT

The Trade Expansion Act of 1934, the reciprocal trade agreement program, represented a major change in policy. Under the act, the President was empowered to reduce Hawley-Smoot Tariff rates up to 50 per cent in return for reciprocal tariff reductions from foreign countries. Negotiations were largely bilateral, but the benefits of agreements were more widely dispersed through frequent application of the Most Favored Nation principle. This treatment applied, as a rule, to all countries the lowest rate of duty or other import charge granted to any country. In some instances, the policy discouraged signing of agreements, since a foreign supplier feared competition from other suppliers who would be granted similar concessions negotiated with the United States. Rising world political tensions and limited time permitted only a modest recovery of U.S. farm exports under reciprocal trade agreements before World War II.

The United States assumed the initiative after World War II, as it had done before the war, to promote freer trade among nations. Recognition of the tie between trade and development was apparent in creation of the Marshall Plan, the International Monetary Fund, and the World Bank.

Three steps were taken to reduce trade barriers. First, the President was granted authority by Congress to reduce the duty rates on imports. Second, efforts were pressed to negotiate among the principal trading nations common rules governing the use of tariffs and other measures regulating trade. Third, multilateral negotiations were pursued among principal trading nations to reduce duties and other charges on imports.

Comprehensive trading rules were incorporated in the draft charter of the International Trade Organization meeting in Havana in 1947–48. The comprehensive rules and proposed power of this body led to fears that its charter would not be ratified by Congress. Consequently, the trading nations sought a less binding trade agreement.

GATT

A set of trading rules, called the General Agreement on Tariffs and Trade (GATT) had earlier been agreed upon by several major trading nations meeting in Geneva in 1947. The General Agreement, a less comprehensive but similar set of trade rules to the draft charter of the International Trade Organization, did not require statutory changes in existing laws. A Protocol of Provisional Application was signed by the United States and other countries, with the intent that existing legislation in the countries of the signatories which violated rules of GATT would be revised (Zaglitz, 1967, p. 144). Revisions have been slow indeed.

GATT is the most comprehensive trade agreement in existence and is adhered to by more than seventy-five countries, including almost all the world's major trading countries. GATT rules can be condensed into five basic points (Worthington, 1967, pp. 2, 3):

1. Import and export duties are the only legitimate trade barrier consciously applied as a barrier. This outlaws quantitative restrictions on imports. Exceptions to the rule are allowed in emergency situations and for balance of payments or national security reasons. Exceptions can be used to protect a farm price support program if the program entails domestic production controls.

2. Import duties can be reduced and eliminated, or bound against increase, through negotiations.

3. Export subsidies should not be used to obtain more than a fair share of world trade.

4. All GATT members should be treated equally when measures are applied affecting imports or exports. This is the Most Favored Nation clause. A related National Treatment clause states that international regulations should not give favored treatment to domestically produced goods over imported competing goods.

5. Price and income support programs should not be used to increase exports from, or reduce imports into, the territory applying them. This principle has been widely ignored, particularly by the European Economic Community.

Several rounds of multilateral trade and tariff negotiations followed the signing of the General Agreement on Tariffs and Trade. The 1962 "Dillon Round" achieved an 8 per cent reduction in customs duties on $5 billion of global trade a year. Many of these adjustments were in industrial products; comparatively few concessions were made in agricultural products.

The sixth and most notable round of tariff reductions since World War II was the "Kennedy Round," which followed the passage of the Trade Expansion Act of 1962, replacing the Trade Expansion Act of 1934 and amendments. The negotiating authority under the Act was granted for five years, to June 1967, and empowered the President to reduce most import duties by 50 per cent of the rates in effect on July 1, 1962. The reductions, to be negotiated on a reciprocal basis, employed the Most Favored Nation concept—the reduced rates would be extended to countries outside of GATT with notable exceptions, such as the Communist Bloc.

The Kennedy Round, initiated by the United States, was particularly motivated by the need to maintain access to markets in the European Economic Community and the European Free Trade Association (see note 2, page 479). However, nearly all developed nations and a large number of developing nations participated in the negotiations.

The outcome of the extended negotiations was the signing by 43 nations of the most comprehensive tariff cuts in history. An estimated $40 billion of international trade was affected by the results. The tariff concessions obtained and given by the U.S. were estimated to cover approximately $7.5 billion of U.S. exports and $8 billion of U.S. imports. Tariff cuts among the principal negotiating countries averaged over 30 per cent on a large number of industrial products, including machinery, photographic equipment, automobiles and transport equipment, professional instruments and equipment, books and printed materials, fabricated metal products, and lumber and wood products (Zaglitz, 1967).

Negotiations on agricultural products were much more difficult than on industrial products and were encumbered by strong protectionist tendencies in the European Economic Community. Nevertheless, the U.S. obtained concessions on an estimated $852 million of farm product exports and in turn made concessions on an estimated import volume totaling over $600 million of non-tropical agricultural products. Liberalized trade arrangements in farm products with the countries of the European Economic Community and the European Free Trade Association were limited. Bindings of duty-free status on oilcake and meal, soybeans, cotton, hides, and skins had already been obtained in 1962 from the European Economic Community, which cut its tariffs in the Kennedy Round by an average of 25 per cent on such products as canned fruits and vegetables, juices, hops, nuts, raisins, and tobacco. But no significant tariff concessions were obtained for variable levy items, including grains, flour, rice, poultry, meat, and eggs. As of 1969, no concessions had been made in the GATT negotiations for about 45 per cent of U.S. exports to the European Economic Community.

The principal concessions in the Kennedy Round from the United Kingdom included 50 per cent tariff reductions or duty-free bindings on certain livestock products (including offals, hides, and skins), rice, and horticultural products (including certain canned fruits, raisins, lemons, carrots, and dried beans). The Scandinavian countries granted concessions on fruits and vegetables, tobacco, and oilcake meal. Some sizable reductions in tariffs on U.S. imports were obtained from Japan, Canada, and Switzerland.

The most disappointing feature of agricultural negotiations was their failure to increase the opportunity of grain exporters to compete in the grain markets of importing countries. American negotiators had limited success in using the European's desire for freer access of European industrial goods into the U.S. to gain freer access of U.S. agricultural products into Europe.

INTERNATIONAL COMMODITY AGREEMENTS

A product of the negotiations was the International Grains Arrangement, which replaced the old International Wheat Agreement. The Arrangement established minimum and maximum prices for international trade in wheat and committed several developed nations to share in programs to contribute 4.2 million metric tons of grain to needy countries. The minimum contributions in 1,000 metric tons for the major contributors were as follows: U.S. 1,890, European Economic Community 1,035, Canada 495, Australia 225, Japan 225, and United Kingdom 225. Other countries pledged smaller amounts. Foreign nations' pledges, which totaled only 85 million bushels of wheat-equivalent, could be given as wheat, coarse grains suitable for human consumption, or cash. The volume of aid committed under the International Grains Arrangement was small compared with U.S. wheat aid in recent years and represented a minor commitment of foreign countries to sharing this aid.

The Wheat Convention established the minimum price for no. 2 hard red winter wheat at $1.73 per bushel at American Gulf Coast ports. Wheat producers fought for decades, beginning with the McNary-Haugen Bills of the 1920's, for a two-price plan, featuring a higher price in the domestic market and a lower price in the elastic export market. It is an ironic twist that the International Grains Arrangement, which was strongly supported by some farm groups, led to a high export price and a considerably lower domestic market price. The price-fixing features of the Arrangement were put into effect in 1968, but proved to be unworkable.

Price-fixing for wheat above the equilibrium world market price was an intriguing product of the Kennedy Round, devoted in majority to freer trade. International commodity agreements are not new. They are particularly attractive to producers of commodities which are chronically in excess supply. The world demand is inelastic for each of a number of commodities traded in world markets. But because any one country frequently supplies only a small part of the total world production, its export demand tends to be elastic. For example, the elasticity of world demand for wheat may be $-.3$, but the U.S. export demand for wheat displays an elasticity of perhaps $-.5$ in the short run, -2.0 in the intermediate run, and an even greater absolute magnitude in the long run. These elasticities imply that, except in the short run, any attempt at pricing above world market prices by the U.S. alone will lead to greater loss of export volume than sellers will gain through higher prices; hence farm receipts from exports fall. It is clear that unilateral fixing of prices at high levels is not in the best interest of American farmers or our balance of payments. But receipts from exports can be increased through price fixing if other exporting nations practice production controls and maintain only their historic share of export sales.

International agreements in commodities exported mainly by developed nations have been restricted to wheat. More important have been international agreements in sugar, tin, coffee, and olive oil, exported mainly by developing nations and imported principally by developed nations. Only the agreements for wheat, coffee, and tin have operated with significant continuity. Exporters press for agreements to remove price fluctuation, to ensure markets, to raise prices above free trade levels, and in general to create an orderly market. Since developing nations produce and depend heavily for export earning on several commodities chronically plagued by problems of excess supply, commodity agreements can be of significant benefit to them. Developed countries, which are supposed to benefit by being assured of adequate supplies at reasonable prices, in fact receive few benefits from agreements in commodities which have tended to be chronically in oversupply. The developed countries can perhaps best justify such agreements as foreign aid, but such "aid" is distributed according to volume of sales, and the developing nations which need help most may have little to sell.

EXISTING TRADE BARRIERS

Free trade is a worthy ideal, but this section clearly shows that major institutional impediments to trade exist. Trading blocs have formed, or are being formed, which lean toward freer trade within the bloc while imposing formidable barriers to trade with outsiders. The blocs also command considerable bargaining power in trade negotiations.

DEVICES USED BY THE U.S.

The United States has used a number of devices to control imports of agricultural products and shape foreign trade to conform with domestic policies. These devices include export subsidies (including subsidized commercial exports as well as exports made under Public Law 480), import quotas, and tariffs. The domestic prices of several farm commodities have been held above the world price level, and quotas, tariffs, or government transfer payments to farmers have been needed to maintain and protect this structure. Foreigners argue that the higher domestic prices increase production and reduce domestic consumption, leaving a larger residual for "dumping" on foreign markets. American policy-makers argue that domestic production controls more than compensate for the price effect, and the quantity exported in commercial markets is reduced over what it would have been in the absence of both production controls and price supports. Hence American production control and price policies, it is reasoned, have held world prices above what they would have been without such programs.

Tariff rates for most farm products produced in this country are modest. Some tariffs are also of little relevance, such as those for soybeans and grains, which the U.S. exports in large volume. Although import quotas and export subsidies result in more protection than is apparent in tariff rates, still the important conclusion is that the degree of protection provided U.S. agriculture is not high compared to the protection found in other countries.

Johnson (1967) estimated the impact of changing the export subsidies and other trading practices on several U.S. commodities. With removal of tariffs, export subsidies, import quotas, and price supports, the domestic price of peanuts would fall to 6 cents or less per pound, about half the 1967 price. He suggested that tariffs be maintained at present levels but that import quotas and export subsidies be eliminated while paying peanut producers $50 per acre of "average" allotment for 10 years. Payments would continue even if the allotment were not utilized. The program would cost consumers and taxpayers no more than current programs.

In 1967 the domestic producer of raw sugar received a quota premium, tariff differential, and Sugar Act payments, which together provided the domestic producer 5.5 cents per pound over the world price, which was 2.2 cents per pound at the New York base point. The domestic producer received about three times the world price. Johnson (1967, p. 15) estimated the annual cost of of the sugar program to American consumers and taxpayers to be $544 million, or an average of $14,000 per farm producing sugar. Consumers and taxpayers could afford to pay American sugar producers and processors benefiting from the program several billion dollars to remove further subsidies and barriers on trade in sugar.

The U.S. has supported prices of dairy products but has not controlled production. The surpluses generated thereby have led to export dumping and other surplus disposal operations. Meanwhile, import quotas have been used to protect domestic prices. These quotas violate the General Agreement on Tariffs and Trade, which requires domestic production controls to accompany import quotas. The U.S. has requested and obtained waivers from General Agreement obligations, but each year must explain why quotas continue to be applied. In fiscal years 1964 and 1965, export subsidies comprised approximately one-third of the dollar volume of dairy product exports.

Milk production requires much labor. The high opportunity cost of labor in the U.S. gives rise to a comparative disadvantage in milk production. American producers can remain competitive in fluid milk and cream sales because transport and quality maintenance costs tend to insulate the market. The problem is manufactured milk products. Johnson (1967, p. 18) questions "whether there is any reasonable price for manufactured dairy products that would provide adequate returns for American farmers producing milk for these purposes." Hathaway (1958, p. 59) asks, "Why in the face of steadily increasing labor costs do we insist that manufactured dairy products and fruits and vegetables which can't be mechanized must be produced in the United States?"

Considerable progress has been made in recent years toward government programs consistent with freer trade in cotton. The same was true for tobacco until 1966, and for wheat prior to the International Grains Arrangement, ratified by Congress in 1968.

There are numerous legal devices available to the U.S. government for intervening in international commercial relations. One of the most prominent of these devices is Section 22. It was originally added to the Agricultural Adjustment Act of 1933 by the Act of August 23, 1935. It has since been drastically revised and amended by several acts of Congress. One reason for the popularity of Section 22 is its flexibility in the hands of the President. For example, the Secretary of Agriculture may report "emergency" conditions to the President and to the Tariff Commission. The latter must make an immediate investigation in such cases and report to the President in twenty-five days or less. The President, however, may take immediate action without waiting for the Tariff Commission report. Action under Section 22 can be taken regardless of any existing trade agreement or other international arrangement. Actions that can be taken by the President under Section 22 include (1) imposition of fees up to 50 per cent *ad valorem*, and (2) reduction of importation or warehouse withdrawal by up to 50 per cent of a representative period.

Section 22 was not used before September 1939. Until 1968, it had been used to control imports of only eleven different commodities or commodity groups. These include the following commodities and their products: wheat, cotton, milk, rye, barley, oats, almonds, filberts, peanuts, tung nuts, and flax. Commodities under import controls in 1967 included cotton, wheat, dairy products, and peanuts.

Section 22 is a necessary feature of programs designed to hold domestic prices above world price levels. There is some agreement that restrictions have been invoked only after a full and complete hearing of all interested parties— even exporting countries are allowed to testify. The surprising thing about Section 22, which gives the President such great power over trade in farm products, is that it has not been used to an even greater extent to control imports. Prudence has been used in handling complaints and in initiating action under the legislation (Hillman, 1967, p. 73).

Perhaps the most telling criticism of Section 22 and other such trade barriers is that they impart an air of hypocrisy to our strong statements calling for freer trade. When we practice what we ask other nations to abandon, our arguments lose strength. Nevertheless, flexible tools such as Section 22 can be an effective bargaining device. The very existence of the legislation and its potential application may dissuade other nations from erecting barriers to trade that would lead to reciprocal action on the part of the U.S.

SINO-SOVIET BLOC

U.S. exports to the Sino-Soviet Bloc increased from $1.8 million in 1953 to $351 million in 1964. This was a small part of the total U.S. exports, but the volume of trade with the bloc obviously grew rapidly.

While a complete embargo eliminates direct trade with mainland China, North Korea, and North Vietnam, trade in nonstrategic goods generally was permitted in 1967 with the Eastern European countries. The U.S. sales of wheat to Russia in 1964 were reduced by requiring that half the wheat be shipped in U.S. flag vessels. Other restrictions on credit and the "part cargo" stipulation that *some* of any given grain shipment to Eastern Europe be delivered to Western ports have hampered sales.

Under provisions of the General Agreement on Tariffs and Trade, the United States extends a Most Favored Nation policy to all countries except the

Sino-Soviet Bloc. Countries not eligible for such treatment do not receive duty reductions negotiated since the Reciprocal Trade Agreement Act, and duties are generally those that existed under the Tariff Act of 1930 (Goodman, 1967, p. 58).

EUROPEAN ECONOMIC COMMUNITY

The European Economic Community (EEC),[1] or Common Market as it is sometimes called, is, as a bloc, the largest outlet for U.S. exports, accounting for about half of all U.S. farm exports in the late 1960's.

The EEC, while gradually eliminating trade barriers among nations within the bloc, imposes a common external trade barrier. The variable levy system is the major instrument used by the EEC to protect domestic markets from foreign competition; it imposes a levy equal to the difference between the world price and the domestic support price. This tends to make EEC imports from other countries a perfectly inelastic demand within a considerable price range, with outside countries the residual supplier. To make matters worse, some of the proceeds from the levy are used to subsidize EEC exports, such as French wheat. The impact of the variable levy in the 1960's was not as disastrous to the U.S. as many economists predicted, partly because many farm commodities were not included but mainly because demand increased faster than supply of farm products in the EEC. The result was an increase of U.S. exports of grains and poultry (including eggs) to the EEC from $173 million in fiscal year 1957–58 to $669 million in 1965–66. Uniform grain prices went into effect in the EEC on July 1, 1967. This raised the price of wheat in France and gave incentives for the French to more fully utilize their sizable potential to produce wheat.

ASSOCIATED OVERSEAS COUNTRIES

The 18 African countries comprising the Associated Overseas Countries (AOC), as former colonies and trust territories of France, Belgium, and Italy, have received preferential treatment from the EEC. The AOC in July 1963 agreed to gradual elimination over a period of years of prices supported above world price levels. EEC tariffs on coffee, cocoa beans, vegetables and oils, and variable levies on sugar will eventually become binding on all outsiders, including the AOC.

THE UNITED KINGDOM

The United Kingdom in 1966 abolished all duties on imports from Ireland. It removed quotas on entry from Ireland of all agricultural commodities except

1. Including France, West Germany, Italy, Netherlands, Belgium, and Luxembourg.

main-crop potatoes, sugar, butter, bacon, and grain. In addition, the so-called "Commonwealth preferences" led to discrimination against the U.S. in exports to the U.K. of tobacco, canned fruit, oilseeds, and beans. Prior to 1968, tobacco from the Commonwealth countries entered the United Kingdom at a tariff advantage of 21.5 cents per pound. Before the Rhodesian incident in 1966, the share of U.K. tobacco imports from the Commonwealth increased steadily, mostly at U.S. expense. The U.S. share of canned peaches imported by the U.K. fell from 30 per cent in the early 1960's to 7 per cent in 1967. Similar trends, also due to Commonwealth preferences, are apparent for other canned fruits. Kennedy Round reductions in fruit and tobacco import duties by the U.K. may enable the U.S. to reverse some of the past trends.

EUROPEAN FREE TRADE ASSOCIATION

In contrast to the European Economic Community, the European Free Trade Association (EFTA)[2] has no uniform variable levy system nor common internal agricultural policy. Bilateral agreements reducing or eliminating trade barriers between members of EFTA are numerous, however. West German imports of Danish poultry, eggs, and meat fell off sharply following imposition of variable levies on these items in July 1962. For this reason, Denmark has looked for more trade concessions within EFTA. An agreement with the U.K. grants free access to Danish bacon, canned pork, and blue cheese (U.S. Department of Agriculture, 1968). Quotas may be applied on bacon, however.

JAPAN

Japan has replaced the United Kingdom as the country constituting the largest single market for U.S. farm products. Japan has made extensive use of bilateral trade agreements but is not a member of any preferential trade bloc. The country, whenever feasible, obtains its imports from countries which are or can become good customers for its exports. In 1966, Japan imported over 2 million metric tons each of corn, grain sorghum, and wheat from the U.S., and 1.8 million metric tons of soybeans.

The Japanese are aggressively pursuing more imports of rice from Taiwan, Burma, and Thailand; corn from South Africa, East Africa, and Thailand; and soybeans from Mainland China. Japan, with a lack of agricultural resources and with sharply rising industrial growth and income, constitutes a massive potential market for U.S. farm products. Whether trade preferences and development of agricultural production capacity in the countries mentioned above will constitute a competitive threat to the U.S. exports to Japan remains to be seen.

2. Including Austria, Denmark, Norway, Portugal, Sweden, Switzerland, and the United Kingdom. Finland is an associate member.

LATIN AMERICAN FREE TRADE ASSOCIATION

Members of the Latin American Free Trade Association (LAFTA)[3] move toward elimination of trade barriers among one another but individually maintain trade practices and barriers with nonmembers. Since LAFTA was formed in 1961, there has been a significant liberalization of trade among members in cotton, wheat, cocoa, sugar, cattle, and beef. These preferences, especially in wheat and cotton, have been reflected in reduced imports from nonmembers.

CENTRAL AMERICAN COMMON MARKET

The Central American Common Market (CACM),[4] like the European Economic Community, has free internal trade and common external tariffs for a number of agricultural products. The group also has variable levies on selected commodities. The U.S. share of CACM imports declined in the 1960's for those commodities covered by common tariffs and variable duties.

Latin American Presidents, meeting in 1967 in Punta del Este, agreed to establish progressively the Latin American Common Market beginning in 1970. The Common Market will be based on the two existing groups, LAFTA and CACM, with convergence by stages. The plan is to work progressively toward a system of common external tariffs and reductions of internal restraints on trade among countries within the common market.

UNITED NATIONS CONFERENCE ON TRADE AND DEVELOPMENT

Developing nations are eager to earn more foreign exchange through world trade but have been inhibited by excess supplies and low prices for the primary agricultural products which are their chief exports. Expansion of exports of these commodities is inhibited by the low-income elasticities of demand, by synthetics, and by trade barriers in developing countries. Import duties or quotas frequently are placed on coffee, tea, cocoa, and tobacco. The United Nations Conference on Trade and Development (UNCTAD) in 1964 heard the less developed countries call for more commodity agreements like those now in operation for coffee and wheat.

In the long run, the less developed countries will need to diversify and further process commodities if they are to adequately raise foreign exchange earnings. They are inhibited by progressively higher tariffs on the more processed commodities and by inability to achieve economies of scale. It has been proposed

3. Including Argentina, Bolivia, Brazil, Chile, Colombia, Ecuador, Mexico, Paraguay, Peru, Uruguay, and Venezuela.
4. Including Costa Rica, El Salvador, Guatemala, Honduras, and Nicaragua.

that industrial countries remove tariffs on all products of cottage industries, all semimanufactured goods, and all manufactured goods made primarily from raw materials from the less developed countries. These and other measures were discussed at the UNCTAD meeting in early 1968.

The U.S. has at least given lip service to extended market opportunities for the less developed countries and has indicated a willingness to drop the Most Favored Nation principle to provide preferential tariff advantages for all developing countries by the big industrialized countries. Elimination of protection on U.S. imports of shoes and textiles, for example, would provide a major impetus to economic development of less developed countries. The impact on the American shoe and textile industries would be great, and political interests representing these groups would be unlikely to accept such easing of trade restrictions. One argument favoring freer access of these countries to our markets is that the policy will reduce the need for foreign aid grants.

DEVELOPMENT OF U.S. FOREIGN ECONOMIC ASSISTANCE PROGRAMS[5]

With World War II, foreign economic assistance became a key tool in American foreign policy and a major factor in world affairs. Prior to the war, U.S. foreign economic assistance was given on an irregular basis, usually to provide relief for victims of natural disasters, and the amount of assistance was small.

On March 11, 1941, Congress passed the Lend-Lease Act providing an economic weapon for Great Britain and a few other nations' war efforts. From 1941 through 1945, the United States provided $50.2 billion in aid under this act (Benedict and Bauer, 1960, p. 28). Of this amount, $6.5 billion were spent on agricultural commodities.

Lend-Lease assistance was entirely a wartime arrangement, with no important carry-over of policy from it. Current economic assistance programs have their antecedents in the creation in 1942 of the Institute of Inter-American Affairs, a government agency responsible for providing U.S. technical assistance to Latin American countries (U.S. Department of State, 1966).

By the end of World War II, the United States had become involved in relief and rehabilitation in a large number of countries in Europe and Asia. Soon afterwards the Truman Doctrine led to large-scale military aid to Greece and Turkey. As the Cold War developed and the Marshall Plan was introduced to promote and accelerate war recovery in Western Europe, the volume of U.S. foreign assistance rose to unprecedented heights. The idea of aid for development

5. Per Andersen, Agricultural Economist, Centro Internacional de Agricultura Tropical, Colombia, is a coauthor of this section.

of poor countries emerged as a logical extension of economic aid under the Marshall Plan for reconstruction of war-damaged economies.

The United Nations Relief and Rehabilitation Administration program and the Marshall Plan were two of the most important programs of the immediate postwar period. Programs from the late 1940's to the present have been more concerned with economic assistance, not for war recovery but for purposes of promoting or accelerating economic development and reducing human miseries such as starvation and malnutrition in less developed nations.

UNITED NATIONS RELIEF AND REHABILITATION ADMINISTRATION

The United Nations Relief and Rehabilitation Administration (UNRRA) program was initiated in 1943. Its purpose was to provide food, clothing, shelter, and medical aid in the areas liberated from enemy occupation. After the war, UNRRA became an important supplier of aid in some of the severely disorganized countries such as Poland, Yugoslavia, and Greece.

However, UNRRA was soon replaced as the primary channel for U.S. aid. The new and more orderly procedures provided for various forms of transitional aid to war-devastated countries. The most important of these aid programs was undoubtedly an emergency loan to Great Britain in 1946 of $3.8 billion, or almost one half of the total aid given under these programs.

THE EUROPEAN RECOVERY PROGRAM

Soon after World War II it became clear that the war-damaged European countries needed external economic assistance if a quick recovery was to be obtained. This, along with recognition that a weak Europe might be an easy target for Communism, caused the United States to offer economic assistance to Europe on a scale never previously experienced in peacetime.

The main features of what was to become the European Recovery Program, or Marshall Plan, were outlined in 1947. The first appropriation under the program was made the same year, and in 1948 a four-year program was established.

The majority of the assistance was given in the form of U.S. commodities, including large shipments of wheat and other foodstuffs. No direct payment was to be made to the United States for these commodities. When received by European governments, the commodities were sold through regular trade channels. The funds obtained were placed in a trust account, held in the name of the recipient country, and could be released only on U.S. approval. The funds were generally released for long-term development projects in the countries. The economic assistance provided under the Marshall Plan totaled $13.2

TABLE 15.3. Foreign Assistance Commitments of AID and Predecessor Agencies, Fiscal Years 1949–66

	Marshall Plan 1949–51	Mutual Security Act 1952–61	Foreign Assistance Act 1962–66	Total 1949–66
	(*Millions of dollars*)			
Development loans[a]		1,987	5,821	7,808
Technical assistance and development grants	86	1,276	1,487	2,849
Supporting assistance	12,743[b]	11,462[c]	2,285[b]	26,490
Other assistance, including international organizations	331	1,834	1,916	4,081
Total	13,160	16,559	11,509	41,228

SOURCES: Price (1955, p. 162); Agency for International Development (1966, p. 60).

[a] This category covers loans for both projects and commodity programs designed to stimulate economic development; also Alliance for Progress loans to Latin America.

[b] These funds were used to provide economic aid directed primarily toward immediate political and security objectives—for example, economic assistance to a country engaged in a major defense effort. Direct military assistance was not included.

[c] During the period 1953–61, allocations made under supporting assistance programs were used jointly for economic and military assistance.

billion. The distribution of this amount among the various subprograms is shown in Table 15.3.

The apparent success of the sales for nonconvertible currencies, rather than outright grants or loans as a means of economic assistance in the European Recovery Program, undoubtedly was of great significance in structuring the later Public Law 480.

The Marshall Plan proved to be very successful in transforming the war-damaged economies of the European countries into highly productive economies with great potential for sustained growth. The success of the program undoubtedly promoted appeals for economic assistance by other foreign countries. Hope for results in the poor countries of Asia, Africa, and Latin America, similar to those obtained in Europe, undoubtedly was a major force behind the sizable foreign aid appropriations after 1952.

THE MUTUAL SECURITY ACT

The European Recovery Program was successful, not only in building the economies of the European recipient nations but also in restraining the spread of Communism. It may be argued that the success of the latter was due primarily to the former. It was believed that the economic and defense assistance programs were mutually supporting the cause of strengthening the Free World in its resistance to Communism. Therefore, major efforts were made in the U.S. Congress during 1950–51 to create a single legislative authorization under which the various U.S. foreign assistance programs could be gathered. The outcome was the Mutual Security Act of 1951.

The Mutual Security Act included all current assistance programs except the Export-Import Bank activities. The objective of the Act was "to maintain the security and promote the foreign policy of the United States by authorizing military, economic and technical assistance to friendly countries to strengthen the mutual security and individual and collective defenses of the free world" (Brown, 1953, p. 509). It is apparent that the foreign assistance authorized under the Mutual Security Act of 1959 primarily was aimed at strengthening the position of the United States towards the Communist Bloc, while economic development of the recipient countries *per se* was, at best, a secondary objective.

The portion of the foreign aid funds allocated to direct military assistance was very large during the early 1950's. Military assistance accounted for 32 per cent of the total foreign aid allocation in 1951. It increased to 53 per cent in 1952 and to about two-thirds in 1953, compared to 5 per cent in 1948–49 and about 16 per cent in fiscal year 1967 (Benedict and Bauer, 1960, p. 38; U.S. Senate, 1967, p. 334).

A small volume of surplus agricultural commodities moved under the Mutual Security Acts of 1951 and of 1952. Under the 1953 act, however, a special section was added providing for use of surplus agricultural commodities in foreign assistance. This Section 550 provided for sales of surplus agricultural commodities for local currencies in a manner similar to that developed under the European Recovery Program, except that the local currency funds obtained were to be deposited in the name of the U.S. Treasury rather than in the name of the recipient countries. The procedure used under Section 550 is identical to that used in the later Public Law 480. In addition to sale for local currency, Section 550 provided for a small amount of food aid as grants.

The provisions of Section 550 were continued by Section 402 of the Mutual Security Acts of 1954 to 1961. During this period the amount of food aid under Section 402 declined from $450 million in 1955 to $186 million in 1961. The decline in the amount of food aid under the Mutual Security Act was due to the establishment of Public Law 480 in 1954.

Until the Mutual Security Acts were replaced by the Foreign Assistance Act of 1961, they had provided for $16.6 billion in foreign aid (Table 15.3), some of which was for military assistance.

AGRICULTURAL TRADE DEVELOPMENT AND ASSISTANCE ACT

The Mutual Security Acts had opened the way for disposal of agricultural surpluses; and commodity stocks were mounting during 1953 and 1954. This situation, along with the real need for food and fiber in a large number of developing nations, pressed the U.S. Congress for a more extensive program of surplus food disposal to developing nations.

As an outcome of these pressures, the Agricultural Trade Development and Assistance Act, popularly known as Public Law 480, or PL 480, was enacted in 1954. Enactment of this law laid the foundation for what came to be the most extensive international transfer of agricultural commodities, on an aid basis, that the world has ever experienced. During twelve years, 1955–66, $15.7 billion of U.S. farm products were exported under PL 480 (Table 15.4). An

TABLE 15.4. U.S. Agricultural Exports, July 1, 1954, to December 31, 1966

Type of Export Program	Market Value (millions of dollars)	Per Cent of Govt Programs	Per Cent of Total Exports
PL 480:			
Sales for foreign currencies	10,190	57	17
Sales on long-term credit	561	3	1
Donations and disaster relief	2,724	15	4
Barter	2,220	12	4
Total PL 480[a]	15,719	88	26
Mutual security programs	2,179	12	3
Total export under government-financed programs	17,898	100	29
Total export outside government-financed programs	43,302	—	71
Total agricultural exports	61,190	—	100

SOURCE: U.S. Department of Agriculture (1967c and supplement).
[a] The sum of the components does not add to the total because of errors and leakages.

additional $2.2 billion were shipped under mutual security programs, making a total shipment under government-financed programs of $17.9 billion, or 29 per cent of all agricultural exports during this period.

PL 480 was originally scheduled to expire on June 30, 1957. However, the law has since continued to be extended by amendment. The various amendments to Public Law 480 have attempted to meet changing conditions, including changes in public attitudes since 1954. Some of these amendments are listed in the following discussion of individual Titles in PL 480.

TITLE I: SALES FOR FOREIGN CURRENCIES

Table 15.4 shows the total value of shipments under PL 480 and the distribution among the various programs. Sales for foreign currencies under Title I have been the major component of the PL 480 program measured by the quantities of commodities involved.

TABLE 15.5. Sales Agreements with Ten Major Recipients under PL 480, Title I, July 10, 1954 to June 30, 1966, and Fiscal Year 1966

	1954–66				Fiscal Year 1966	
	Market Value (millions of dollars)	Per Cent of Total	Population 1964 (millions)	Title I (1954–66) Dollars per Capita	Market Value (millions of dollars)	Per Cent of Total
India	3,513	31.2	471.6	7.45	686	66.0
Pakistan	1,064	9.4	100.8	10.56	25	2.4
United Arab Republic	845	7.5	n.a.	n.a.	41	4.0
Yugoslavia	625	5.6	19.3	32.38	0	
Korea	548	4.9	27.6	19.86	52	5.0
Brazil	546	4.8	79.0	6.91	0	
Turkey	544	4.8	31.1	17.49	19	1.8
Poland	520	4.6	31.2	16.67	0	
Spain	488	4.3	31.3	15.59	0	
Israel	324	2.9	2.5	129.60	24	2.3
Others	2,258	20.0			192	18.5
Total	11,275	100.0			1,039	100.0

SOURCE: Agency for International Development (1967, pp. 84 ff.)

It is apparent in Table 15.5 that India and Pakistan have been the major recipients of Title I aid; together, they received 40 per cent of the aid under Title I for the 1954–66 period. Major changes in the incidence of aid are also apparent. Yugoslavia, Poland, and Spain, which received substantial aid at some time in the 1954–66 period, received no Title I aid in fiscal year 1966. The United Arab Republic received substantial shipments before being dropped from the list of recipients.

Grains comprised 65 per cent of the market value of aid shipments under all types of U.S. government programs in the fiscal year ending June 30, 1967. Wheat was the largest single item, comprising 42 per cent of all farm commodities shipped under government programs in that fiscal year. Aid programs in fiscal year 1967 constituted the following percentages of the total U.S. export markets for the respective farm commodities: wheat, 50 per cent; rice, 44 per cent; cotton, 31 per cent; and dairy products, 83 per cent.

Public Law 480 was completely revised in 1966 by the Food for Peace Act. The law, as amended by the Food for Peace Act, continued to have four titles. However, the contents of the titles were greatly changed by the 1966 amendment. Title I of the 1966 Act authorized the President of the United States to negotiate and carry out agreements with friendly nations for the sale of agricultural commodities for foreign currencies or for *dollars* on *credit terms*.

Title I of the 1954 Act had dealt with sale for foreign currencies only. This title was the heart of the original PL 480 legislation. However, beginning with the introduction in 1959 of Title IV (sales on long-term credit), there has been a trend towards more emphasis on sales on dollar credit at the expense of sales for foreign currencies. The amendment of 1966, the Food for Peace Act, clearly specified that wherever feasible, sales for foreign currencies should be replaced by sales on dollar credit.

Sales of commodities under Title I are carried out through private trade channels within the framework of agreements between the United States government and the governments of the participating nations. The first step in the procedure is an application from a foreign country. This application as well as the surrounding conditions are carefully analyzed by the U.S. government in order to determine whether the application is a sound basis for an agreement.

A number of factors are taken into account in such an analysis: (1) the participating country's efforts to help itself towards a greater degree of self-reliance, including efforts to meet problems of food production and population growth; (2) the participating country's needs, economic status, and foreign exchange position; (3) the possible impact on dollar sales and other export programs; (4) the effect on export markets of other supplying countries; and (5) the relationship of the program to the foreign aid program and the foreign policy of the United States.

If the analysis indicates that sale for foreign currency is appropriate, negotiations concerning the content of an agreement takes place. An agreement between the U.S. government and a foreign country usually covers the quantity and price of commodities involved, the exchange rate between the foreign currency and the U.S. dollar, and the terms for the deposit and use of the foreign currency funds involved in the agreement.

After the agreement is completed, the actual trade transactions are handled by U.S. commercial exporters and importers or buying missions designated by the purchasing country. The U.S. exporters acquire the commodities, either from stocks owned by the Commodity Credit Corporation or from the domestic market, and transport them to the foreign country. The exporters are paid in dollars from the U.S. Treasury.

As the shipments are received, the recipient country's government deposits to the account of the United States government an amount of its own currency equivalent to the dollar amount due. The terms for the deposit and use of the foreign currency funds obtained from sales under Title I are usually included in each individual agreement under which the particular sale is carried out. Section 104 of PL 480, amended as of January 1, 1967, specifies a wide variety of purposes for which the foreign currency funds may be used.

By June 30, 1966, the United States had entered into agreements with recipients of Title I shipments, calling for the deposit of approximately $11.4 billion in the foreign currencies of 53 nations. Table 15.6 shows the use of the

TABLE 15.6. Uses of Foreign Currency, Agreements Signed July 1, 1954, through December 31, 1965, and Fiscal Year 1966

	(1954–65)		Fiscal Year 1966	
	Market Value[a] (millions of dollars)	Per Cent of Total	Market Value[a] (millions of dollars)	Per Cent of Total
Loans to foreign governments	4,714	44.9	604	61.6
Various uses by U.S. agencies	2,384	22.7	208	20.0
Grants for economic development	1,808	17.2	0	0.0
Common defense	1,003	9.5	141	13.6
Loans to private enterprises	595	5.7	50	4.8
Total	10,504	100.0	1,003	100.0

SOURCE: U.S. Congress (1966, pp. 136, 138); Agency for International Development (1967, p. 86).

[a] Including ocean transportation.

foreign currency funds provided by agreements signed from 1954 through 1965 and during the fiscal year 1966 for four major categories of uses. The largest outlet for these foreign currency funds has been as loans to foreign governments. Almost one-half of the total amount of funds was used for that purpose. The loans have been used to finance such projects as marketing and processing facilities, land reforms, and community development.

TITLE II

Title II of PL 480 authorizes the donation of U.S. agricultural commodities to meet famine or other urgent or extraordinary relief requirements, to combat malnutrition, to promote economic and community development in friendly developing countries, and for needy persons and nonprofit school lunch programs outside the United States. Such donations may be provided through friendly governments or through agencies, private and public, including international organizations.

Prior to the 1966 amendment, donations provided through certain agencies had been placed under Title III of PL 480. As of January 1, 1967, however, all donation programs under PL 480 were placed under Title II.

Provision for use of food donations as a direct self-help incentive was introduced by the 1966 amendment. This provision marked the beginning of a shift from straight relief to self-help programs utilizing food as part payment of wages for work on community development projects.

The estimated net export market value was $2.7 billion of donations under programs presently under Title II during the twelve-year period 1955–66. About $2 billion of this amount was donated through various U.S. relief agencies and international organizations, leaving $700 million for direct assistance from the U.S. government.

TITLE III

As mentioned above, certain donation programs were removed from Title III and included under Title II by the 1966 amendment. Left in Title III were provisions for barter transactions only. Under this provision the U.S. government is authorized to barter agricultural commodities for goods and services procured abroad for stockpiling.

Barter transactions have been used primarily to acquire foreign-produced strategic materials for government stockpiles. The program allegedly contributed to improvement of the U.S. balance of payments position by using agricultural commodities as payments for purchases which otherwise would have been paid in dollars.

During the period 1955–66, agricultural commodities valued at $2.2 billion were exported under the barter program (Table 15.4). Shipments under this program accounted for 12 per cent of government-financed exports and 4 per cent of the total U.S. agricultural exports during the period.

TITLE IV

Title IV was completely amended by the 1966 Food for Peace Act. Prior to this amendment, Title IV provided for sale of agricultural commodities on long-term dollar credit. PL 480 exports for long-term dollar credit totaled $561 million through 1966 (Table 15.4). This provision for credit sales was moved to Title I by the 1966 amendment, and Title IV now contains mainly general provisions and definitions. An interesting part of this title is Section 406, which provides for extensive development programs in the recipient countries' agricultural sector financed primarily by local currencies obtained through sale of Title I commodities. The section is an attempt to promote a greater degree of self-sufficiency in food production in the developing countries, a goal that is often expressed as one of the main objectives of U.S. foreign aid programs. Section 406 specifies a number of development programs for which the acquired foreign currencies may be spent, such as the agricultural extension service, research in tropical and subtropical agriculture, and youth exchange programs.

FOREIGN ASSISTANCE ACT

The original Foreign Assistance Act was enacted in 1961 to aid foreign countries and international organizations. The Act was later amended. The Foreign Assistance Act of 1967 consists of two parts: (1) an Act for International Development and (2) an International Peace and Security Act. The latter is concerned with military assistance and, therefore, falls outside the scope of this analysis.

The Act for International Development is probably the most important piece of legislation providing for foreign economic (nonfood) assistance since the Marshall Plan. The over-all objective of the act is to assist developing countries in achieving economic growth by means of loans, grants, and technical cooperation. The act also provides for investment guarantees to private entities by the U.S. government for investments in projects contributing to economic development in friendly countries.

The Foreign Assistance Act of 1961 emphasized the goal of economic progress and development in the poor countries for the sake of improving living conditions in these countries. A further extension of this line of thinking, the self-help criterion, was introduced by the 1967 amendment. The self-help criterion stresses that U.S. assistance be allocated among countries according to their own individual efforts towards development.

The Agency for International Development (AID) was established in 1961 to carry out the functions of the Foreign Assistance Act. The AID has responsibility for carrying out nonmilitary U.S. foreign assistance programs and for continuous supervision and general direction of all assistance programs under the Foreign Assistance Act. It also carries out certain functions under PL 480, primarily allocation of some of the local currency funds made available under PL 480.

Economic assistance under the Foreign Assistance Act through fiscal year 1966 totaled $11.5 billion (Table 15.3). The majority of the assistance was non-food, although a small volume of food assistance has been provided under AID programs, primarily as exports under the development loan program.

NEW DIRECTIONS FOR FOOD AID

Our food aid programs have been widely criticized, and the Food for Peace Act of 1966 was designed to correct some of this criticism. One charge is that food aid has depressed farm prices in recipient countries, and hence has discouraged private investment in agriculture. A related charge is that food aid has been more concerned with disposal of U.S. farm surpluses than with economic development in recipient countries. Furthermore, it is said that food aid has encouraged complacency in the recipient government, thereby retarding needed public investment in research facilities, roads, and other infrastructure essential for a more productive agriculture. The counter argument is that freeing of foreign governments from investing in agriculture has permitted investment in industry, which has in turn made possible greater industrial exports, which pay for food imports.

To blunt these and other criticisms, the Food for Peace Act of 1966 emphasized shifting from sales for "soft" foreign currencies to sales on long-term dollar credit. The 1966 act also encouraged aid only to those countries that invest in their own agricultural development. Critics reply that this is like using a case of whiskey to bribe an alcoholic to stop drinking. A third change in PL 480 stipulated that the 1966 act was to depart from the surplus concept. The U.S. would provide aid in commodities needed by aid recipients, not just commodities in surplus in the U.S. This permitted greater flexibility in aid programs and the ability to tailor commodity shipments more nearly to the needs of each country. This third revision also blunts misconceptions in the U.S. and foreign countries that food aid costs the U.S. Treasury nothing, since surplus capacity exists in agriculture. It also helps to blunt another misconception held by many Americans that surplus food is equal in its economic benefits, dollar for dollar, to aid in any other form.

EVALUATING BENEFITS AND COSTS OF AID

A number of studies have evaluated the benefits of food aid to recipient countries, including Colombia, Greece, India, Israel, Spain, and Turkey. The studies indicate that PL 480 has in fact promoted economic development, has averted starvation and malnutrition, and has subsequently opened commercial markets in some countries. These studies are all plagued by a serious shortcoming, however—they do not confront the fundamental economic issue of opportunity cost. What would have been the benefit to the recipient country of an equal dollar volume of aid in other forms, including fertilizer plants, irrigation equipment, plant scientists, and industrial know-how?

THE CASH-EQUIVALENT VALUE OF PL 480 AID

The aid component in PL 480 exports may be defined as the amount of unspecified cash aid that recipient nations would consider to be of equal value to the market value of food, feed, and fiber exported under PL 480. The results (Table 15.7) are from questionnaires completed by 88 persons who were knowledgeable and involved in issues of economic assistance and economic development. Most of the respondents were citizens of and living in the countries listed in the table. The majority were economists and political scientists in universities or government officials.

TABLE 15.7. Estimated Aid Components in PL 480 Food, Feed, and Fiber, by Country, 1964–66

	Grants (average value)	Grants (marginal value)	Grants, Foreign Currencies, and Credit (average value)
	(Per cent)		
India	90.6	73.1	53.1
Pakistan	100.0	100.0	—
Brazil	69.0	67.2	27.2
Korea	68.6	81.4	34.7
Turkey	65.4	70.6	24.6
Taiwan	70.3	68.4	12.9
Israel	85.9	80.5	52.9
Greece	84.3	77.9	22.5
Chile	80.9	78.4	31.7
Morocco	100.0	88.3	57.5
Congo	100.0	—	62.2
Colombia	70.9	73.1	28.6
Weighted average	79.4	76.9	43.2

SOURCE: Estimates from Andersen (1969, pp. 127, 153).

India would have been as well off for economic development with $100 of PL 480 aid (grant aid, valued at market prices) as with $91 of unspecified cash aid in the three-year period, 1964–66. The cash aid could have been used to buy fertilizer plants, technical assistance, irrigation equipment, or other items. India would have paid hard currency to import commercially a considerable quantity of food in the absence of PL 480 shipments. For that quantity, food aid was as good as cash aid. But beyond some level of cash purchases of food, India would have begun to purchase items not shipped under PL 480. Then unspecified aid begins to become more highly valued than an equal dollar volume of aid actually received. The last $100 dollars (market price) of PL 480 shipments to India could have been replaced with $73 dollars of unspecified cash aid. Brazil would have been as well off with a grant of $100 of PL 480 aid or $69 of cash aid on the average and $67 of cash aid at the margin.

Grants require no payments by recipient countries to the U.S. The aid component in grants is simply the cash equivalent. Sales for foreign currencies and credit require disbursements by recipients. These disbursements include the present value of down-payments, interest, and principal, plus the dollar spending displaced by nonconvertible currencies. Subtracting these from the "grant" aid component, the result is a substantially lower aid component shown in the last column of Table 15.7 for the actual combination of PL 480 aid. The trend to long-term credit aid has reduced the over-all average aid component. This is because the aid component on forty-year credit is zero and on twenty-year credit is negative if terms of the transactions are fulfilled (Andersen, 1969). Under twenty-year credit terms, there is a net transfer of resources from recipient countries to the U.S.—foreign aid in reverse. The average aid component in nonconvertible currencies was estimated to be 36.7 per cent of the face value.

Because the average aid component of grants was high for India, and because India received a low proportion of aid on long-term credit, the average aid component over all aid forms was 53.1 per cent in the 1964–66 period. The average aid components were also high for the Congo, Morocco, and Israel. Aid components were low for Turkey, Taiwan, Greece, and Colombia.

AN ECONOMIC EVALUATION OF PL 480

Table 15.8 summarizes estimates of the annual average cost, value, and social gain from all U.S. PL 480 aid in the three years, 1964–66. The reported annual average value of U.S. aid based on Commodity Credit Corporation costs was $1,569,400,000 during the period. The face value of the aid based on prevailing world market prices was slightly smaller; $1,473,700,000. As reported in Table 15.7, recipients would have found $79.40 of cash, unspecified aid to be equivalent in average value to $100 of food aid. The same average rate was used for all countries receiving aid as was found for the major aid recipients shown in Table 15.7.

The real value of food aid to the recipient countries would have been $1,173,100,000 per year if no disbursements were required. But disbursements were required. The present value of disbursement was higher when based on U.S. interest rates than when based on recipient country interest rates because of the greater opportunity cost of interest in the latter.

The cost of shipping was substantially higher on U.S. than on foreign vessels, and the U.S. paid the extra transport cost ($25.5 million per year). The cost to aid recipients of transportation was $258.9 million.

TABLE 15.8. Reported Value, Cash Equivalent, and Net Gain for Total
PL 480 Aid, 1964–66

	Per Cent of Face Value	Annual Average (millions of dollars)
Reported value	106.5	1,569.4
Face value (based on prevailing export prices)	100.0	1,473.7
Value to recipient countries	79.4	1,173.1
Disbursements required (U.S.)	29.2	430.6
Disbursements required (recipients)	28.4	418.6
Cost of transportation (paid by U.S.)	1.7	25.5
Cost of transportation (paid by recipients)	16.6	258.9
Cash equivalent value to recipients	33.6	495.6
Net gain to the U.S. from PL 480 vs. production control	.8	12.4

SOURCE: Estimates from Andersen (1969, p. 156). See text for explanation of data.

The value of aid to recipient countries, less the cost of disbursements and transportation, gives a total net value of U.S. food aid to recipient countries of $495.6 million annually in the 1964–66 period. This was only 34 per cent of the face value of aid. Transport costs were subtracted from the gross to arrive at this net value because other forms of aid would have required very much less transport cost per dollar of real aid. If transport costs are excluded under the assumption that they would accrue in equal magnitude under all forms of real aid, then the cash equivalent value of foreign aid was 48.1 per cent of the reported value of the aid.

Food aid was not the only alternative to maintain domestic farm income and promote foreign development. Cash grants and production control also could have provided the 1964–66 domestic farm income and foreign aid component. A cash grant of $495.6 million would have contributed equally to foreign aid. Domestic surplus production capacity could have been neutralized by dumping commodities in the ocean, by selling them in commercial markets, or by paying farmers not to produce them. The government cost would have been at least $681.1 million of the last-named alternative (production control of quantities shipped under PL 480) while leaving net farm income unchanged. Under the cash aid-production control alternative to PL 480, the U.S. government cost would have totaled an estimated $495,600,000 + $681,100,000 = $1,176,700,000. Under the PL 480 alternative the government cost was $1,569,400,000 for commodity purchases, plus $25.5 million for transport costs, less the present value of disbursements, $430,600,000, or $1,164,300,000. Thus the net gain to the U.S. from PL 480 rather than cash aid and production control was $1,176,700,000 − $1,164,300,000 = $12.4 million, or .8 per cent of the face value of PL 480 shipments. A net gain of zero would imply economic equilibrium on the average. Since the gain was small indeed from PL 480 versus the above alternative, it appears that the level of PL 480 was very nearly optimal on the average. The cash equivalent value of food aid was only about one-third of the face value of food aid. But at the same time food aid was cheaper to give than cash aid, because the American government would have had to pay farmers at least 43 cents not to produce each dollar of commodities that were exported under PL 480. Food "dollars" were cheap (57 cent) dollars.

Although aid shipments appeared to be near equilibrium on the average, the earlier analysis showed that considerable disequilibrium in the allocation of food aid existed at the margin among programs and recipient nations.

A PROPOSAL TO RAISE THE EFFICIENCY OF FOREIGN AID

Because food aid was heavily motivated by the desire to dispose of surpluses, and foreign economic development was a secondary consideration at least until recent years, it may be concluded that in fact the alternative to food aid often would have been no aid. Still, principles of economics apply in getting the maximum benefits from a given amount of federal funds. Of special concern here is the optimum amount of (*a*) food and nonfood foreign aid for maximum well-being of recipients from a given total aid appropriation and (*b*) the maximum contribution to net farm income from a total government outlay for farm price and income supports through voluntary production controls.

Data in Table 15.8 support the conclusion that on the average the United States has provided a proper balance of domestic farm production controls versus food exports to handle excess farm production capacity. The allocation has been less than optimum at the margin, however. An augmented market mechanism has been proposed that uses the equilibrating forces of the market to bring a more nearly optimum allocation (Tweeten, 1966).

The mechanism can be reduced to the single rule that foreign aid recipients should receive on each dollar's worth (market value) of food purchased in this country a discount equal to the cost to the U.S. Department of Agriculture of inducing farmers not to produce a dollar's worth of output with voluntary acreage-diversion programs.

Allowable purchases might be restricted to the set of items that would contribute most to economic growth in developing nations and would reduce the adverse effects on the U.S. balance of payments. The impact of food aid on our balance of payments can be important. This problem involves complex issues that cannot be treated definitively here, but certain issues are prominent. Because food aid is equivalent to cash foreign aid that must be spent for food in the

United States, such aid has a minimum short-run adverse impact on our balance of payments. Food aid has an adverse short-run effect on our gold balance to the extent that such aid replaces commercial purchases which countries would otherwise make in the United States. The long-run effect is adverse to the extent that food aid, compared with cash aid, delays economic development and commercial demand for our exports in a country. If U.S. balance of payments problems are severe, the stipulation might be that all purchases be from the United States. If items other than food are in excess in the United States, appropriate discounts might also be offered on these. Responsible governments might be free to use the aid money as desired. In other instances, the array of permitted purchases would be narrowed to whatever items would contribute most to economic development and eventual "weaning" of the recipient country from foreign aid. Additional features can be stipulated as necessary to establish terms and amount of repayment, if any.

SUMMARY AND CONCLUSIONS

Exports of agricultural products have comprised approximately one-fourth of all U.S. exports in recent years and totaled nearly $7 billion in 1967. One out of each five dollars earned by the farming industry came from exports. Farm exports are a major source of foreign exchange and help alleviate balance of payments problems. More than half the U.S. production of some commodities, including wheat, rice and dried edible peas, was exported in recent years.

The magnitude of foreign trade and advantages of freer trade demonstrated in this chapter point to the need for this country to strive to keep trade channels as free as possible from institutional barriers. This has been attempted, particularly during the period extending from the Reciprocal Trade Agreements Act of 1934 through the Kennedy Round of trade negotiations ending in 1967. While considerable progress has been made, many trade barriers remain. Furthermore, neo-Mercantilism remains a latent force among commodity groups in the U.S. and among foreign nations and trading blocs. Substantial efforts will be needed in the future to avoid rising levels of trade protection, especially in emerging world trading blocs!

Massive economic aid has been provided under various government programs to foreign countries. The largest amount of food aid has been under Public Law 480. The primary objective of PL 480, as it was enacted in 1954, was to establish a politically acceptable outlet for the mounting surpluses of certain agricultural commodities. A secondary objective of the law was to promote economic development in friendly nations. The objectives of PL 480, as amended by the Food for Peace Act of 1966, were stated somewhat differently. Unlike the former legislation, the new legislation gave precedence to the objectives of combating hunger and malnutrition and of encouraging economic development in developing nations, over the objective of surplus disposal. Furthermore, particular emphasis was placed on assistance to nations committed to improve their own agricultural production.

Public Law 480 originally contained three titles. Title I authorized the sale of U.S. surplus agricultural commodities to friendly nations with payment in the currency of the recipient nation. Title II authorized donations of agricultural commodities held in stock by the Commodity Credit Corporation (CCC) for famine and disaster relief in foreign nations. A 1961 amendment authorized, under Title II, donations of CCC-owned commodities for community development, school lunches, and other economic development purposes in foreign nations. Title III provided for the disposition of CCC-owned surplus commodities to carry out two separate programs: (*a*) donation programs administered by various government agencies or by recognized voluntary nonprofit charitable and relief organizations and (*b*) barter programs to obtain certain strategic materials as well as off-shore procurement of goods and services. The 1959 amendment of PL 480 added Title IV, which provided for the sale of commodities on long-term dollar credit. The 1966 Food for Peace Act moved provisions for long-term dollar credit to Title I.

Provision of unspecified cash aid grants of one-third the face value of actual PL 480 aid in the 1964–66 period would have contributed as much to economic progress in recipient countries as PL 480 aid, according to estimates in Table 15.8. But a dollar (face value) of PL 480 aid was much cheaper to the U.S. government than cash aid if the alternative was to pay farmers not to produce. Results reported in this chapter suggest that a nearly optimum combination of production controls and PL 480 aid existed from 1964 to 1966 on the average. Marginal conditions for an optimum were not met, however.

It is difficult for administrators to provide an efficient combination of food and nonfood aid and to provide an optimal combination of domestic production control and food exports as a way to handle excess domestic production capacity. An augmented price mechanism is suggested in this chapter to more efficiently make these allocations. The procedure is to provide all foreign aid in unspecified cash or credit form. The aid recipient may buy whatever it wishes (subject, perhaps, to certain restrictions discussed in the text). A discount would be offered on each dollar's worth of U.S. food (at the market price) that would be proportional to the cost to the U.S. government of paying our farmers not to produce a dollar's worth of the commodity.

REFERENCES

Agency for International Development. 1966, 1967. Operations report. Washington.

Andersen, Per. 1969. The role of food, feed and fiber in foreign economic assistance. Unpublished Ph.D. thesis. Stillwater, Oklahoma State University.

Benedict, Murray R., and Elizabeth K. Bauer. 1960. Farm surpluses, U.S. burdens or world assets? Berkeley, University of California.

Brown, William, Jr. 1953. *American Foreign Assistance.* Washington: Brookings Institution.

Foreign Trade and Agricultural Policy. 1967. National Advisory Commission on Food and Fiber Technical Papers, vol. 6. Washington.

Goodman, Richard J. 1967. East-west trade and U.S. trade policy. In *Foreign Trade and Agricultural Policy*, pp. 51–66.

Hathaway, Dale. 1968. World trade and United States agricultural policy. In George Capel, ed., *United States agricultural policy*, Agricultural Policy Institute Series No. 28, Raleigh, N.C., pp. 50–62.

Hillman, Jimmye. 1967. Section 22: description and present status. In *Foreign Trade and Agricultural Policy*, pp. 67–94.

Johnson, D. Gale. 1967. Agricultural trade and foreign economic policy. In *Foreign Trade and Agricultural Policy*, pp. 1–34.

Price, Harry. 1955. *The Marshall Plan and Its Meaning.* Ithaca, N.Y., Cornell University.

Tontz, Robert, ed., 1966. *Foreign Agricultural Trade.* Ames: Iowa State University Press.

Tweeten, Luther G. 1966. A proposed allocative mechanism for U.S. food aid. *Journal of Farm Economics* 48:803–10.

———. 1967. The demand for United States farm output. *Food Research Institute Studies* 7:343–69.

U.S. Congress. 1966. Food for peace, 1965. Washington: U.S. Government Printing Office.

U.S. Department of Agriculture. 1967a. *Agricultural Statistics.* Washington: U.S. Government Printing Office.

———. 1967b. Foreign agricultural trade of the United States. Washington: U.S. Government Printing Office.

———. 1967c. 12 Years of achievement under public law 480. ERS-Foreign 202. Washington.

———. 1968. Preferential trade arrangements of foreign countries. Foreign Agricultural Economic Report No. 41. Washington.

U.S. Department of State. 1966. The AID story. Washington.

U.S. Senate. 1967. Foreign Assistance Act of 1967. Hearings before the Committee on Foreign Relations. 90th Congress, 1st Session. Washington.

Worthington, Howard. 1967. A look ahead at agricultural trade policy. Annual Agricultural Outlook Conference. Washington.

Zaglitz, Oscar. 1967. Agricultural trade and trade policy. In *Foreign Trade and Agricultural Policy*, pp. 125–269.

CHAPTER SIXTEEN

Public Welfare and Economic Efficiency

Economics can be defined as the science of allocating scarce resources among competing ends to satisfy these ends as fully as possible. The definition raises several issues. The term "science" implies not only a meaningful classification of facts and a systematic body of knowledge but also a degree of precision and predictability. Whether economics can meet these requirements for a science is conjectural.

Of greater interest is the term "ends" in the definition. What ends or goals are to be achieved, and for whom? In farm management economics, the dilemma of alternative goals need pose no serious philosophic problems. The economist can hold out a profit-maximizing allocation of resources computed by linear programming, and the farm manager can take or leave it depending on his personal goals and financial circumstances.

Farm policies have a far-reaching impact not only on U.S. farmers and consumers but sometimes on the world. The individual farmer often must accept the policy that the majority of farmers or members of society voted to accept. The goal in broad terms may be defined as well-being, satisfaction, welfare, or utility in society. But there are problems in trying to maximize something as elusive as utility by a policy that affects many individuals, each with unique objectives in life. Welfare economics deals with such issues. It is a part of general economic theory that attempts to answer the question "What can the economist in his professional role of a scientist say about public policy?" The first section in this chapter outlines the origins of welfare economics and leads to criteria for making economic prescriptions. The last part of the chapter deals with perfect competition as a norm of efficiency and with factors that interfere with economic efficiency in society.

GENESIS OF WELFARE ECONOMICS

The judgments on welfare economics of political economists in the classical era entailed the Benthamite notions of cardinal utility (cf. Scitovsky, 1951). The so-called hedonistic concepts of gratification and the calculus of pleasure and pain continued from the classical into the neoclassical era. There was no contention that utility could be measured like pounds of butter or bushels of corn, but a less innocuous belief that economists could make sufficiently valid judgments of satisfactions to determine whether utility in society was increased by a public policy and hence whether that policy was desirable.

If public policies are undertaken that redistribute income, then to maximize utility, the optimum policy depends on the nature of the marginal utility functions of individuals. This is illustrated in Figure 16.1 for two individuals, I and II. Total utility in this two-person "society" is a maximum when the marginal utility of money for individual I is equal to that for individual II. Total income initially is X dollars possessed by individual II and is designated X_{II}. The optimum redistribution to maximize utility is X_I^* dollars to individual I and X_{II}^* to individual II, with the constraint that $X_I^* + X_{II}^* = X_{II}$.

The marginal utility curves in Figure 16.1 are idealized exaggerations of the shape of marginal utility curves. The set A of marginal utility curves imply that utility is independent of the level of income. This image might be regarded as a generalization from Alfred Marshall's statement (1890, p. 130):

> Or the real worth of a thing might be discussed with reference not to a single person but to people in general; thus it would naturally be assumed that a shilling's worth of gratification to one Englishman might be taken as equivalent with a shilling's worth to another, 'to start with,' and 'until cause to the contrary were shown'.

Marshall was of course referring to group rather than individual utility and to policies that would have comparatively small effect on the distribution of income. He recognized that marginal utility of money would differ among economic classes of people. If Figure 16.1A were revised to represent Marshall's position it would be for two groups rather than two individuals, each group composed of a random cross section of people, and each curve would be downward-sloping with a short flat segment, each segment of equal height, within which the income redistribution would be confined. Marshall (1890, p. 131) went on to conclude:

> On the whole however it happens that by far the greatest number of the events with which economics deals, affect in about equal proportions all the different classes of society; so that if the money measures

of the happiness caused by two events are equal, there is not in general any very great difference between the amounts of the happiness in the two cases.

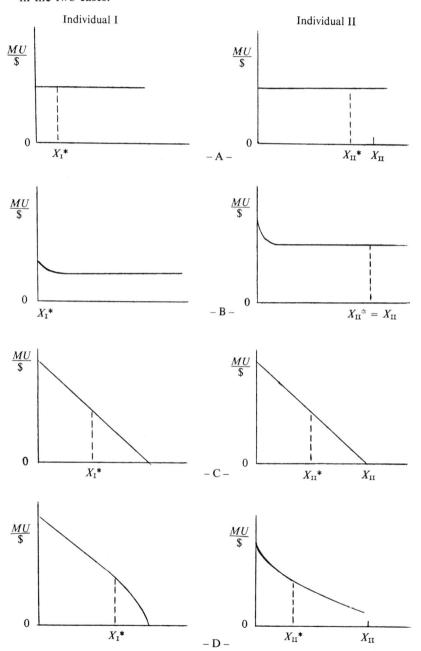

FIGURE 16.1. Images of the marginal utility (MU) of money and implications for optimum income redistribution X_I^* and X_{II}^*.

From the premise that the redistribution of income engendered by economic policies tended to be rather evenly distributed among classes, Marshall reasoned that the income would be transferred on the average among people with similar satisfactions as in A, hence total utility would be unchanged.

No *unique* redistribution of income maximizes utility in A. Or in other words, any distribution of income is consistent with maximum welfare, and the economist concerned with raising utility could be indifferent about the income distributing effects of alternative public policies.

The second set B of marginal utility curves in Figure 16.1 is consistent with a feudal interpretation. Individual II has greater capacity to enjoy income than individual I, therefore utility is maximized by allocation of all income to the second individual. More generally, an unequal distribution of income is optimum because some individuals or groups have a greater capacity than others to enjoy income. Feudal society could be content to concentrate income among the nobility, with little income for serfs.

The third set C of marginal utility curves ideally represents Marxist thinking. Marginal utility is declining, and all individuals have the same marginal utility function. The egalitarian consequence is that utility is maximized by a redistribution of income so that each individual has an equal amount.

The final conception (set D) of the marginal utility curves is considered to be most realistic. Marginal utility of money is declining, but the curve for each individual is unique. No curves are alike. This creates problems, because the "realistic" set D in Figure 16.1 is the only one for which the utility-maximizing income redistribution is not specified by a single rule of thumb such as: the redistribution makes no difference, income should be concentrated in one group, or income should be equal for all individuals. The prescription for an optimum redistribution of income for the modern set D calls for knowledge of cardinal utility for each individual. Though at X_I^* individual I has more income than individual II, redistributing a dollar from I to II reduces total utility. But for large income levels, individual II should have more income than individual I if total utility is to be maximized.

Virtually all economic policies, even those not explicitly intended to do so, entail some redistribution of income! And it is clear from Figure 16.1 that the change in total utility that attends economic policies that redistribute income depends on the nature of individual utility functions. Since interpersonal comparisons require cardinal measures of utility and are not reliable, it follows that the economist cannot know precisely whether a public policy adds to or detracts from total utility in society.

TOWARD A POSITIVE ECONOMICS

These considerations, coupled with the new formulations of economic theory based on the indifference curve analysis of Pareto (which permitted derivation of economic theories with use of ordinal rather than cardinal utility measures), led to rejection of interpersonal comparisons of utility. Lionel Robbins' *An Essay on the Nature and Significance of Economic Science* was a clear statement of the new philosophy in welfare economics. Robbins (1935, p. 30) says:

> Economics is not concerned at all with any ends *as such*. It is concerned with ends in so far as they affect the disposition of means. It takes the ends as given in scales of relative valuation, and enquires what consequences follow in regard to certain aspects of behavior.

If the economist is not to be concerned with judging ends such as utility, income, or freedom, not only is he to be neutral among ends but also he is to make no interpersonal comparisons of utility. Presumably Robbins' above assertion would be motivated by the fact that economists cannot make reliable appraisals of utility. But he goes on to conclude (1935, p. 142) that, even if economists *could* measure utility, and even if, "proceeding on this basis, we had succeeded in showing that certain policies *had the effect* of increasing social utility, even so it would be totally illegitimate to argue that such a conclusion by itself warranted the inference that these policies *ought* to be carried out."

Robbins' statement of positive economics leaves the economist basically concerned about specifying alternate means to reach ends *given* to him by Congress, the President, or his employer. He is to be a "social" engineer concerned with specifying alternative ways of reaching given goals. He is to be concerned with "what is," not with the normative economics of "what ought to be." For economics to be an objective science, the economist must not make value judgments that entail interpersonal comparisons of utility. He cannot take sides in policies that make some worse off, others better off. He can be a technician but not an advocate. In the role of economist, he can be an adviser but not a politician. He can maintain a political dialogue only as long as politicians are asking the questions.

Toward a New Welfare Economics

Because this philosophy of positive economics removed the profession of economics from the indeterminacy of utility measurement and moved it closer to the objectivity of a science, positive economics was widely accepted by the profession. But all was not well. If the economist were to have nothing to say about the merits of programs and policies that entailed interpersonal comparisons of utility, this virtually ruled out his education and policy role. Were not economists, because of their backgrounds, the appropriate persons to articulate value judgments on economic issues when lack of time, economic education, or imperfections in the political process precluded public involvement? Furthermore, the Great Depression was calling for economic prescriptions which positive economics was unable to voice (Scitovsky, 1951). And was not ruling out interpersonal utility comparisons in deference to the recognized indeterminacy depicted in Figure 16.1D really just tantamount to assuming naïvely that marginal utility functions are of the type A?

Many economists were not bound by the philosophy of positive economics, and Keynesian prescriptions were loudly proclaimed. What the profession sought was a new welfare economics to legitimatize intellectually their activity. Four criteria have been successively proposed to provide a rationale for policy recommendations when interpersonal comparisons of utility are ruled out by the indeterminate, modern view of utility shown in Figure 16.1D. The first is the Pareto criterion; an economic policy is desirable when it makes one or more individuals better off without making anyone worse off.[1]

The use of the Pareto criterion is illustrated in Figure 16.2 by an Edgeworth box for two individuals, I and II (cf. Reder, 1947). The initial distribution of two commodities A and B is $0_I a_I$ and $0_I b_I$ to individual I, and $0_{II} a_{II}$ and $0_{II} b_{II}$ to individual II. Indifference curves showing successively greater satisfactions to I are indicated by the solid lines 1, 2, and 3. The origin of the indifference curve mapping for II is in the upper right-hand corner, and successively higher levels of satisfaction for him are designated by broken line indifference curves 1, 2, and 3.

It is apparent that given the initial distribution of commodities at point S, I can be made better off while II is made no worse off by moving to point F—that is, II remains on the same indifference curve while I moves to curves denoting higher satisfaction levels. Point F is a Pareto optimum, defined as a position from which it is not possible to make someone better off without making someone else worse off. Also from point S, by moving along I's indifference curve to E, II can be made better off without making I worse off. The contract curve $0_I EFO_{II}$ is the locus of points of equal marginal rates of substitution between A and B for I and II—represented by tangency of an infinite number of indifference curves.

Given the initial distribution of commodities (resources) at S, any point on the contract curve between E and F is a Pareto optimum in the sense that it is not possible to make one party better off while the other is made no worse off. Any redistribution of A and B that falls in the area ESF or ERF is a "Pareto better," defined as a position that is an increase in utility for one individual

---

1. The terms "better off" and "worse off" refer here to satisfactions rather than the volume of goods and services. Because satisfactions are elusive, a common practice is to apply the Pareto criterion to the volume of goods and services. This procedure may err if external consumption diseconomies are present. Though the quantity of goods held by someone may remain unchanged, his satisfactions may decline sharply when he sees someone else receive more goods.

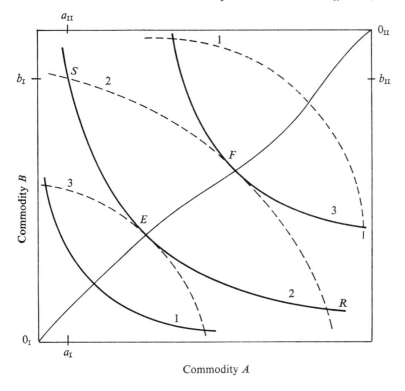

FIGURE 16.2. An Edgeworth box, showing indifference curves for individuals I and II.

without a decrease for the other. But utility can be increased for one without decreasing that of the other by moving to the contract curve. Given the initial point S, the actual ending location along EF depends on the relative bargaining power of the two individuals.

Any position on the contract curve from 0_I to 0_{II} is possible with some distribution of the total quantity of A and B designated by the dimensions of the "box" in Figure 16.2. A Pareto optimum represented by any given point along EF is not likely to maximize total utility. There is a third, vertical dimension not shown in the two-dimensional, horizontal figure which measures total utility to I and II from consuming A and B. The total utility surface may have one or more local maximums that lie along the contract curve. If there is one point that is the highest point on the utility surface, it is called the global maximum.

If the global maximum lies along $0_I E$, then beginning at, say, F and moving along the contract curve toward the global maximum the disutility of I from sacrificing simultaneously A and B is less than the utility gained by II. Rejection of cardinal utility means that we cannot determine the third, or utility, dimension in Figure 16.2. Any given Pareto optimum will rarely be the point of maximum total utility. But the point of maximum total utility will be *one* of the many possible Pareto optimums.

It is apparent from Figure 16.2 that the specific Pareto optimum allocation on which society settles depends on the initial distribution of commodities or resources. This is a major shortcoming of the criterion for public policy. If individual I begins with a very low amount of commodities *A* and *B*, the Pareto optimum along the contract curve may mean a very low level of utility for him alone and perhaps for I and II together. The Pareto optimum is also an inadequate criterion because there is virtually no public policy that does not require some to sacrifice while others are made better off.

The Kaldor criterion states that a given policy is desirable if those who gain from it can compensate the losers. Since the losers are made no worse off and the gainers are made better off, this criterion is essentially the Pareto criterion with a compensation principle added. Since it is stipulated that compensation be made payable only potentially (it would *not* be paid in practice), the Pareto criterion is not in fact met. The condition that compensation need not be made was dictated by practical considerations and justified by the contention that gains and losses are likely to be distributed somewhat randomly over time among members of society (Scitovsky, 1951). Students of public policy do not accept this contention, however.

The Hicks criterion is a modification of the Kaldor criterion and states that if those who lose from a public policy cannot bribe those who gain into not accepting the policy, then the policy is desirable. The Scitovsky criterion goes further and states that a policy is socially desirable if the gainers can potentially bribe the losers into accepting the change and if, in turn, the losers cannot bribe the gainers into not making the change.

EQUITY AND EFFICIENCY IN WELFARE ECONOMICS

The fundamental breakthrough of the new welfare economics was to separate the equity and efficiency components of policies. Equity here refers to the distribution of gains and losses, and efficiency refers to the real quantity of goods and services per unit of input. Public policies increasingly entail compensation, but for many policies compensation for loss is neither attempted nor made. And since there is an imperfect economic and political bargaining process between gainers and losers, the new welfare economics condenses to the issue that a policy is to be recommended if it either increases the real value of goods and services produced with given resources or reduces the resources required to produce a given output. Thus if social benefit-cost ratios are favorable, the policy meets the efficiency criterion and can be recommended.

There is also a question of how potential benefits should be measured. If only one commodity is involved, the measure can be technical efficiency. If more than one commodity is involved, aggregation problems arise. The procedure is generally to weight quantities by prices which in turn measure marginal utility (see the Appendix). If the marginal utility of money is different for gainers and losers, benefit-cost analyses will err as true measures of welfare. For example a publicly financed research program to increase productivity of agriculture might clearly pass the benefit-cost ratio (efficiency) criterion. Gainers potentially could use some of their consumers' surplus to compensate farmers for a lower producers' surplus (profit), and have some surplus left over. However, this bargaining process is not actually carried out between producers and consumers. Rather the analysis is worked out informally or on paper and compensation is not made. It is possible that the marginal utility of money to farmers is so great that the smaller dollar loss to farmers than the dollar gain to consumers represents a greater total utility loss to farmers than utility gain to consumers. Thus the total utility in society may be reduced.

PERFECT COMPETITION AS AN EFFICIENCY NORM

The efficiency concept is so important in welfare economics that it warrants further elaboration. Two types of efficiency are involved, technical and economic. Technical efficiency is involved in choices of production practices and mechanical input-output ratios. One chooses the practice that requires the least input to produce a given output or that produces the most output from a given input. However, economic efficiency is involved when more than one resource or product is introduced. The real cost of alternative inputs and the worth to consumers of several commodities must be estimated. Measures of output-input (benefit-cost) ratios thus entail problems of aggregation. To measure total real output, we wish to weight component quantities by marginal utilities. The analysis in the Appendix shows that under specified assumptions, product prices do this. To measure total real input we wish to weight input quantities by marginal products and marginal utilities. It can also be shown that factor prices do this.[2]

Perfect competition is generally used by economists as a norm for judging economic efficiency in the market. This section demonstrates that perfect competition is a Pareto optimum—it is the most efficient system possible under the following assumptions, if we are unable to make value judgments about the marginal utility of money.

2. In competition equilibrium $(dq/dx)P = P_x$, where q is product, x is factor, P is product price, and P_x is factor price. Hence, with the normalization of product price so that $P = 1$, the factor price equals the marginal product. It also follows that since $P = dU/dq$ (marginal utility), then $P_x = (dq/dx)(dU/dq) = dU/dx$.

1. The market is atomistic. There are many buyers and sellers so that actions of any one have no perceptible influence on price, and each market participant views his own actions as market-exogenous (the market influences him but he does not influence the market).

2. Resources and products are divisible. The assumption of divisibility is closely related to problems of scale, since a costly, lumpy input often gives rise to asset fixity that in turn may lead to a decreasing average cost curve for a firm.

3. There is absence of external economies and diseconomies of scale in production and consumption, and there is no divergence between private and social costs and benefits.

4. Knowledge of markets and production possibilities is complete, including the production function for developing new techniques. Individuals must be aware not only of the wages but also of the satisfactions associated with alternative employment opportunities.

5. Mobility of commodities and resources is perfect; markets are not restricted by institutional impediments. Firms have freedom of entry and exit.

Pareto Optimality in a Perfect Market

The physical Pareto optimum concept is illustrated in Figure 16.3 for two firms I and II producing two commodities A and B. The production possibility curves for the firms are designated respectively i and ii. By producing at point E, the bundle of resources used by firm I produce a_I and b_I of the commodities. The origin of the production possibility curve for firm II is in the upper right-hand corner. Producing at E, its output is a_{II} and b_{II}. The firms at E together produce A and B in quantities designated by the solid line dimensions of Figure 16.3. The same output would also be produced at H.

Neither E nor H is a Pareto optimum. More of B can be produced with the same resources without sacrificing A by shifting the production possibility curve ii straight up until it is tangent to i at F. The new origin for II is $0_{II}'$. Or more of A can be produced without sacrificing B by shifting ii directly to the right until ii is tangent to i at G. The new position of the origin for firm II is now $0_{II}''$. Thus points F and G, or any tangency point in between along i, represent Pareto optimums. And the locus of these points is a physical contract curve $FG = 0_{II}'0_{II}''$. There is no unique Pareto optimum—the actual outcome depends on the worth of having more A or B, on the production possibility curve, and on the initial distribution of resources. But the most efficient point, which is one, but probably not the only, Pareto optimum, will be at a tangency of the two production possibility curves, where the marginal rate of substitution in production of the two commodities for one firm is equal to the marginal

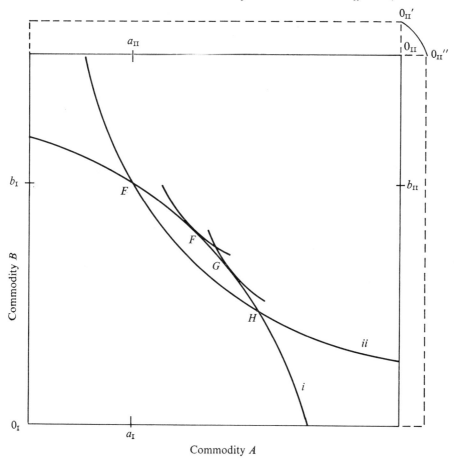

FIGURE 16.3. Production possibility curves—*i* for firm I and *ii* for firm II.

rate of substitution in production of the two commodities for the other firm.

The analysis in Figures 16.2 and 16.3 provide the basis for a heuristic proof that a perfectly competitive price economy is a Pareto optimum. From economic theory, it is known that to maximize utility under competitive market conditions, a consumer *i* equates the marginal rate of substitution of *A* for *B* to the price ratio as in the following equation:

$$-\frac{dB_i}{dA_i} = \frac{P_a}{P_b} \quad \text{(Consumption)} \tag{16.1}$$

If Equation (16.1) holds true for consumers *i* and *j* and each faces the same price ratio, then it is also true that the marginal rate of substitution of *A* for *B* is the same for all consumers:

$$\frac{dB_i}{dA_i} = \frac{dB_j}{dA_j} \quad \text{(Consumption)} \tag{16.2}$$

Hence, Equation (16.2) meets the condition for a consumption Pareto optimum along the contract curve in Figure 16.2.

It is also well known that under the assumptions of perfect competition, any firm i equates the marginal rate of substitution between products to the price ratio as in:

$$-\frac{dB_i}{dA_i} = \frac{P_a}{P_b} \qquad \text{(Production)} \qquad (16.3)$$

Since Equation (16.3) holds for firm j as well as firm i, and since both are confronted by the same price ratio, then

$$\frac{dB_i}{dA_i} = \frac{dB_j}{dA_j} \qquad \text{(Production)} \qquad (16.4)$$

holds for all firms, and the conditions for a production Pareto optimum in Figure 16.3 have been met.

Finally, since marginal rates of substitution in consumption and production are equal to the same price ratio, they must be equal to each other. The result

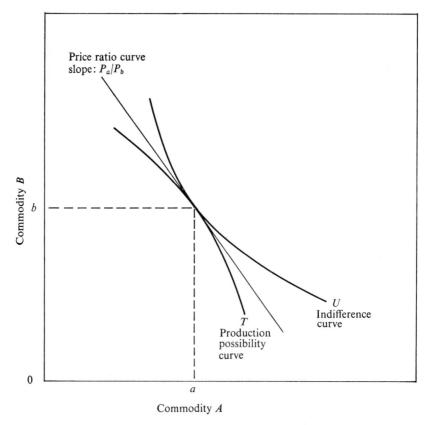

FIGURE 16.4. Societal indifference curve and production possibility curve.

is illustrated in Figure 16.4. A portion of the "societal" production possibility curve *T*, the indifference curve *U*, and the price ratio P_a/P_b are shown.

It is clear from the graph that production and consumption of any combination of commodities other than *a* and *b* mean attaining an indifference curve and utility level below *U*. Tangency of *T* and *U* to the price ratio line means a Pareto optimum for society under perfect competition. Any deviation from this point, where the marginal rates of substitution between two commodities in production and consumption are equal, would mean someone is made worse off. Thus if we do not make value judgments about the distribution of income attending the competitive equilibrium, the competitive equilibrium is as close to full economic efficiency as the economy can get. Qualifications to this conclusion will be discussed later.

It is necessary to add further marginal conditions for an equilibrium that is optimal. In addition to the conditions stated above (that the marginal rate of substitution between any two commodities be equal in production for all firms and in consumption for all consumers), it is necessary that:

1. The value of marginal product for any resource must be equal to its factor price in all uses, hence the value of marginal product must be equal in all uses of a given resource. If this condition holds, the marginal rate of substitution between any two factors will be equal in all production uses, and the marginal rate of substitution between any two products will be equal, as in Equation (16.4).

2. Given that the individual is free to allocate his personal resources between production and consumption, including leisure, he will employ his labor resource until, at the margin, the value of satisfactions from leisure just equals the monetary reward from work.

3. Assuming free access to a perfectly competitive bond market, producers and consumers can adjust their income streams over time. Consumers will adjust borrowing and lending until their marginal rate of discount on future versus present consumption is equal to the interest rate. And entrepreneurs will compete for funds until the marginal efficiency of capital is equal to the interest rate. Hence the marginal rate of discount on consumption between two periods is equal to the marginal efficiency of capital. And capital grows at the interest rate.

4. Second-order conditions of convexity, concavity, and stability must also be met (Reder, 1947; Henderson and Quandt, 1958).

It is again emphasized that the distribution of income under the competitive equilibrium is subject to the initial distribution of resources. Although there is no unique Pareto optimum and the competitive equilibrium does not likely represent the global maximum of potential utility, if there is a global maximum utility, it will be a Pareto optimum. Perfect competition does maximize total utility in society if the marginal utility curves are those in Figure 16.1A. If a totalitarian state were to force a nonprice allocation designed to maximize total utility, the allocation would also have to conform to a Pareto optimum of equimarginal rates of substitution.

AN ALTERNATE PROOF OF THE EFFICIENCY
OF PERFECT COMPETITION

CARDINAL MEASURES OF COMPETITIVE EFFICIENCY

Figure 16.5 illustrates the concept of consumers' and producers' surpluses based on industry demand and supply curves. A formal proof that demand and supply curves are measures of cardinal utility is presented in the Appendix. The analysis in the Appendix shows that the area beneath the supply curve is a measure of utility forgone by sacrificing other commodities to consume the particular commodity. The area beneath the demand curve is the direct utility derived from consuming the particular commodity. Hence, there is a net contribution to utility by producing and consuming the commodity up to the competitive equilibrium amount.

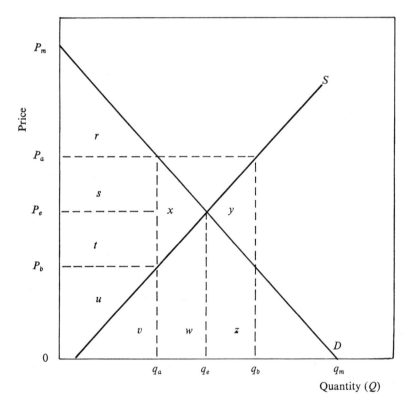

FIGURE 16.5. Industry demand and supply curves (*D* and *S*).

If a perfectly discriminating monopolistic seller utilized the entire demand curve, he would receive price p_m for the first unit, slightly less for the second, and nothing for the q_m unit (Figure 16.5). Adding these bits of revenue would be the same as integrating the area underneath the demand curve from 0 to q_m. The maximum revenue possible is represented by the entire area underneath the demand curve.

The supply curve may be viewed as the marginal cost curve. Integrating the area underneath the supply curve gives the total variable costs of producing a given quantity. Again employing the Pareto concept, producers are made no worse off as more Q is produced if they are paid variable costs—the area beneath the supply curve. It follows that the *net* gain in value of Q produced is represented by the area between S and D. This net increased gain is positive as we move from 0 out to q_e. The net value of goods produced is maximized at q_e and is the area composed of r, s, t, u, and x. If consumers are perfectly discriminating and pay only the marginal cost of each unit produced, the consumers' surplus would be this amount. And if producers act as a perfectly discriminating monopolist, the producers' surplus would be this amount. In practice there is generally only one price however, and the net value of goods produced is divided between producers and consumers. If price is p_e and output q_e, the consumers' surplus is r plus s and the portion of x above p_e. The consumers' surplus is the difference between the maximum amount consumers would pay for Q and what they are actually required to pay. The producers' surplus is the difference between what producers are actually paid and the minimum payment that would be required to have them produce Q. The producers' surplus is the return to fixed resources, or profit, and is the area composed of t and u plus the part of x below p_e.

The area x is the net value of goods forgone by a nonoptimum output q_a. Area y is the net value of goods forgone by a nonoptimum output q_b. If the dollar is assigned a fixed utility, the dollar volume in x or y becomes a measure of the utility forgone. Since perfect competition results in equilibrium price p_e and output q_e, it follows that perfect competition maximizes the net value of goods produced in society. And if the utility concept of Figure 16.1A is introduced, it maximizes total utility in society.

Given constant returns to scale, the supply curve becomes perfectly elastic in the long run and the producers' surplus vanishes. Hence the long-run consequence of economic activity is to maximize consumers' surplus.

Two Steps Forward and One Step Backward

The price mechanism operating in the framework of the perfectly competitive model is truly a remarkable allocative instrument. Under certain assumptions it represents a Pareto optimum. Under more rigid assumptions it leads to maximum welfare in society. Hence, in theory it can lead a complex economy requiring trillions of economic decisions to a "utopia." In the words of Adam Smith (1776, p. 400), each person "intends only his own gain, but he is in this . . . led by an invisible hand to promote an end which was no part of his intention." No wonder the price mechanism has become a prized institution in our society.

The logic of the perfectly competitive model is compelling, and the model remains an important norm. But economists recognize that the assumptions of the competitive model are not met. Some might even argue that the assumptions are so grossly and universally violated that the competitive model today has no relevance.

CRITIQUE OF THE PRICE SYSTEM

Examples are numerous of situations where the price mechanism does not result in a satisfactory allocation of resources, a proper determination of what, how, and when to produce, and a socially acceptable distribution of income. Even if the five assumptions listed earlier for a perfectly competitive market are met, some persons in society may have so few resources initially that a competitive market equilibrium will not bring them a socially acceptable income level.

The impact of monopoly can be observed in Figure 16.5. If supply S is the marginal cost curve for one large monopoly firm facing a demand D, profit will be maximized by output q_a and price p_a. The producer's surplus (profit) will be the areas s, t, and u, and consumers' surplus will be r. The net social cost or value of goods forgone due to monopoly pricing and output is the area x. Elements of imperfect competition in the resource market or product market will reduce output below competitive equilibrium q_e, and hence will reduce the net value of Q produced.

Failure to meet the second assumption of divisibility can lead to decreasing costs and nonmarginal cost pricing. Suppose a utility company installs a large generator that operates more efficiently at large than small loads. Marginal costs decline as output expands, and the supply curve in Figure 16.5 is downward sloping to the right. Pricing at the intersection of supply and demand resultsi n a negative producer's surplus. This would be an intolerable situation for a firm. If it has the choice between shutting down and producing at q_e, it would minimize losses by shutting down. However, because consumers' plus producer's surplus is positive ($r + s + t + u + x$ is positive) consumers can gain by compensating the firm for its losses and having it operate at q_e. Another approach would be to allow the firm to cover costs by monopoly pricing—but this would entail a social cost of *x*. Lumpiness of investment leads to a social cost through nonmarginal cost pricing in society.

Many industry studies show constant returns to size. Nevertheless, decreasing costs prevail at lower output, and constant costs may not be reached until one or a few firms can easily meet the demand for the commodity. Hence, in the case of the auto industry, the inefficiency caused by imperfect competition is small in comparison to the inefficiencies stemming from higher unit costs that would result from atomizing the industry.

The firms in an industry may experience decreasing costs due to external economies of scale as the industry grows. Skills and management are improved, resource and transportation facilities are more efficiently utilized, and markets developed. The "infant industry" argument is that government subsidies to industry are justified during this decreasing cost phase.

Indivisibility creates huge capital requirements that virtually preclude private enterprise for undertaking certain activities. The potential net social gain may be large, but capital requirements and uncertainties inhibit private firms from adequately investing in, for example, the atomic bomb development, vast radar warning systems, supersonic transport development, and some forms of agricultural technology.

Numerous examples can be found for differences between private and social costs. The social cost is greater than the private cost of automobiles because of smog and traffic congestion. Failure to meet assumption 3 leads to too much output and to a social cost (*y* in Figure 16.5) because the social cost curve lies above the private cost curve.

If left strictly to private firms, it is felt that cultural activities such as opera, symphony music, and public affairs TV presentations would be underproduced because the social benefits exceed the private benefits. The social benefits of well-kept yards, painted houses, and well-landscaped business establishments are likely to exceed private benefits.

The price system may not allocate optimally a collective good. A "collective good" is defined as a facility or service for which a charge on individual-use would entail a high "marketing" cost (relative to the value received from the good) or where "use" cannot be clearly defined (Dorfman, 1965, p. 4). An example is U.S. Department of Agriculture grading and inspecting of foods. A socialized armed forces is explained partially by this factor, but indivisibilities and external economies of scale are also important.

Some Application to Agriculture

If assumption 4 is violated, and knowledge is incomplete, the social cost curve also will lie above and to the left of *S*, which was defined as the supply based only on private costs. If farmers are unaware that better job opportunities exist elsewhere or underestimate the utility they would derive from a job in industry, then S does not represent the real social marginal cost of producing farm commodities. The result is too much farm output and a social cost such as y.

Institutional impediments may interfere with efficiency potentially attainable under perfect competition. If the government restricts resource use or places quotas on output in agriculture, output may be q_a in Figure 16.5. The producers' surplus is increased at the expense of consumers' surplus, and the net social cost is x. If the government supports farm price at p_a without production controls, then farm output is q_b and the net social cost is y. It is apparent that if there is no divergence between private and social costs, then the optimum farm income support program is one which leaves the competitive equilibrium quantity unaltered. In theory such a program could take the form of a free market complete with direct transfer payments to farmers. In practice it is difficult to keep the payments independent of supply, however.

Price supports and acreage restrictions might reflect deeper significance than a public concern for equity in agriculture. Lack of capital and uncertainty may limit the capacity of private firms to hold the degree of excess capacity in U.S. agriculture desired by the public to meet national and world emergencies. Stockpiling of agricultural capacity may mean that social benefits exceed private benefits of resources committed to agriculture. Use of direct transfer payments to support farm income without upsetting the competitive market equilibrium would be the wrong policy if society highly prizes excess capacity in agriculture.

A serious limitation arises in the application of the net social cost concept to farm programs requiring sizable government transfer payments to farmers. These may be regarded as transfers of surplus from consumers to producers in compensation for an unacceptably low farm income. In fact, however, it is not consumers of the specific commodity but all taxpayers who provide the transfer payment.

The public may judge that the sum of the areas r, s, t, u, and x to the left of demand and supply in Figure 16.5 (the total potential net gain) is divided inequitably between farmers and consumers, and a program to redistribute the net social gain may be initiated. Taxes or output restrictions redistributing income to farmers change output from q_e to q_a or q_b. The expense for personnel and equipment to administer the program is likely to be a social cost. The tax and subsidy may represent a social cost to the extent that the marginal utility of money is higher among taxpayers than among farmers. If marginal utilities of money are equal for taxpayers and farmers, then the social cost of a program that redistributes income by transfer payments through the U.S. Treasury will be small, provided output does not deviate appreciably from q_e. The fact that the income redistribution is approved by society may imply a higher marginal utility of money to farmers than to taxpayers—hence a conceivable utility gain from a tax-subsidy program.

National programs to redistribute income can shift the industry demand curve and, what is more likely, the supply curve. Farmers invest income supports in capital improvements and improved technology. The result may increase supply and bid resources away from uses more favored by society, thereby reducing utility. But purchase of capital representing improved technology may increase productivity and aggregate utility. The net effect on utility is unknown.

The exact validity of the social cost concept discussed above also requires equilibrium in perfectly competitive markets for all commodities other than Q (Figure 16.5). Given equilibrium in nonperfect markets for commodities other than Q (as for agriculture vis-à-vis other economic sectors), the net social cost in Figure 16.5 for Q will not necessarily remain valid (see Chapter 6).

Application of the net social cost concept to a number of wheat programs will be found in two publications: Tweeten (1965) and Tweeten and Tyner (1966).

RELEVANCE OF THE PRICE SYSTEM IN THE SCIENTIFIC AGE

In terms of the number of decisions made, as in allocation of consumer and producer purchases, the price system is king. But in terms of the decisions that determine economic growth, the price system is increasingly preempted by the political process and internal management decisions of firms and institutions. The same *principles* outlined above are still required for efficiency, however.

Agricultural output expanded one-third from 1950 to 1965 without increasing conventional farm inputs. Approximately half the increase in U.S. national income is explained by growth in conventional resources and by changes in scale, organization, and specialization (Denison, 1962). The unexplained increase can be attributed mainly to science and technology—to making conventional resources more productive through creation of knowledge by education and research. The knowledge industry lies to a considerable extent outside the price mechanism. Analytical tools of economic science are geared best to problems of allocation and growth where the price system operates. Our tools are blunt instruments in the research and education industries, where the price system holds limited sway. It is perplexing that, while we continue to search for the science of economics, we are called on to search for the economics of science.

There are several reasons why society has not deemed it desirable to leave education to the price system. Several assumptions of the competitive norm do not hold in this sector. Buyers (students or parents) are unable to judge adequately the quality of the product. Also the production process is so long, capital requirements so large, and the marginal value product so uncertain, that underinvestment seems likely if education is left strictly in private hands. Also social benefits exceed private benefits of education. The advantages that accrue to society from having an educated populace that can read laws and income tax regulations, can serve more effectively in the armed forces, and can contribute to culture and better health—not to mention other aspects of well-being engendered by education—are not reflected adequately in the price incentives faced by individuals.

Many of these factors also influence the public involvement in research. Farmers acting individually lack the entrepreneurial talents, capital, and scale to underwrite an adequate research program for agriculture. The production process by which basic inputs of education, imagination, and apparatus are turned into new knowledge is difficult to define—and to predict. Uncertainties are especially prominent in basic research, where there are potentially large economic payoffs from projects that private firms are unwilling to undertake.

Indivisibility is also important. Productive use of a fraction of the investment that went into the development of hybrid corn may not be feasible. And once technology is developed and released, much of the cost is sunk and marginal cost is low. If technology is to be released at marginal cost, zero in many cases, some provision must be made to recover the fixed cost. Arrow (1962, p. 617) states: "In a free enterprise economy, inventive activity is supported by using the invention to create property rights; precisely to the extent that it is successful, there is an underutilization of the information."

It was shown earlier that marginal cost pricing results in a Pareto optimum under static conditions, but extrapolation of the marginal cost pricing principle to the dynamics of firm growth raises several issues. One is the time element itself. The term "marginal" can be defined only in the context of a time interval. As the time interval is extended all costs become marginal even where indivisibilities exist, and marginal cost and average cost become synonymous in all-or-nothing production.

Marginal cost pricing made possible by public taxes is subject to considerable public scrutiny. The Pareto optimum that results may be deemed inappropriate in terms of the initial or final income distribution. In the case of U.S. land grant colleges, findings have in general been made available to the public at zero marginal cost. The consequent gains in farm productivity have resulted in a progressive redistribution of income among consumers—a bread tax in reverse. This is one reason why society backs the investment. But government aid for research to develop new technology that would benefit mainly the rich might meet resistance from society.

Marginal cost pricing makes no provision for covering overhead expenses and replacing fixed equipment. It provides inadequate price direction for additional capital that could be channeled to research. Thus the dynamic deficiencies of marginal cost pricing can outweigh the advantages (static Pareto optimum) of its use discussed above.

USE OF THE POLITICAL PROCESS TO CORRECT MARKET DEFICIENCIES

The political process is sometimes used by society to correct alleged or real deficiencies in the price mechanism, and to lend to a consensus of value judgments of what goals are to be achieved in society. In a perfectly competitive economy, the consumer is truly sovereign, since he "votes" with dollars for what to produce and in the long run reaps the net social gain. In the political process, votes are one per person and not proportional to dollars, hence a quite different allocation will evolve than under the price system. Of course it may be argued that power is somewhat proportional to income because those with money can spend it to advertise and sway other voters to their view.

It can be shown that even if the voting process is deemed to be appropriate, it is not necessarily consistent (Arrow, 1951). Suppose that individuals 1, 2, and 3 vote on policies X, Y, and Z as follows:

1	$X \to Y \to Z$	$X \to Z$
2	$Y \to Z \to X$	$Y \to X$
3	$Z \to X \to Y$	$Z \to Y$

The arrows are read "is preferred to." If there is a democratic vote on X versus Y, the majority (1 and 3) will favor it, so X is preferred. If there is a vote on Y versus Z, Y is favored by the majority (1 and 2). It would seem to follow that by this latter counting, since X is preferred to Y and Y to Z, then the majority would prefer X to Z. But this is not so; individuals 2 and 3 prefer Z to X. This example merely points up one of the difficulties of aggregating preferences through the voting mechanism. In a representative government, persons often are elected to the legislature based on two alternative issues such as X versus Y and Y versus Z. Problems arise however, when in the legislature they are called upon to decide issues such as X versus Z.

SUMMARY AND CONCLUSIONS

The search by economists for a basis on which to make policy recommendations has led to several criteria:

1: *Pareto criterion:* A policy A is preferred to policy B if, by changing from B to A, someone is made better off while no one is made worse off.

2: *Kaldor criterion:* A policy A is preferred to policy B if, by changing to A, those who gain can compensate those who lose and still be in a better position than under policy B.

3: *Hicks criterion:* A policy A is preferred to policy B if those who lose by changing to A cannot bribe those who gain into not making the change from B to A.

4: *Scitovsky criterion:* A policy *A* is preferred to policy *B* if those who gain by the change from *B* to *A* can compensate those who lose, and if simultaneously those who lose cannot bribe those who gain into not making the change from *B* to *A*.

Since it is recognized that practical considerations preclude compensation, the criteria fundamentally condense to a matter of economic efficiency. This is, in reality, not measured in utility but in value of output per unit of input. Compensation in dollar terms is feasible for policies that meet the efficiency criterion, but if the disutility of a dollar to the losers far exceeds the utility of a dollar gain to those who benefit, the conventional benefit-cost measures of efficiency fail.

Economists agree that the efficiency criterion alone is inadequate for public policy. It is argued that the economist must be concerned about who benefits and who loses. Public investment in new technology can leave a segment of society severely disadvantaged for extended periods. Also in many basic policy issues, efficiency questions may be dwarfed by equity considerations, as in problems of rural poverty and urban slums.

Some contend that professional economists are in a good position to make value judgments about questions of income distribution and other economic matters because they are well informed.[3] Thus there are two current positions on the use of value judgments in economics. One is that the profession should stick to positive economics but should carefully, if reluctantly, formulate value judgments in cases where an obvious need exists. The public is not likely to be fooled by a stance of pure objectivity. Greene (1963, p. 232) states, "I think you economists are trying to kid us when you say you just deal with pure facts and pure theory without an orientation of your own or building toward objectives you believe to be true." Even positive economics is not always consistent with the goal of preserving the usefulness of the policy economist. Sometimes outspoken objectivity and letting the facts speak for themselves terminates the dialogue before the learning process has really begun.

The second position is that positive economics has no modern-day applicability and that economics must regularly deal in value judgments. This view is formalized in the social welfare functions of Bergson and Samuelson (1947). However, economists holding this view also generally caution that the economist can go too far in formulating value judgments and can get so involved in politics that his objectivity is suspect and his usefulness as a professional economist is jeopardized. Economists holding this view caution that value judgments should be carefully formulated and explicitly stated. Unfortunately, an economist is insufficiently aware of his value judgments to articulate a meaningful compendium.

3. The serious student of welfare economics should read the excellent discussion of value judgments by Myrdal (1944, Appendix 2).

Thus the two positions—one that economists should only reluctantly make value judgments, the other that the economist must make value judgments but with care—generate much debate but converge to positions not very far apart. Both groups likely agree that an economist qua economist needs to strive for sufficient objectivity to be able to work with groups covering a considerable range of the political spectrum. Pursuit of objectivity (though full objectivity is never achieved) seems not an unreasonable price for the economist to pay for the license to educate and to practice his profession.

The study of welfare economics is a useful, maturing, and sobering influence for economists concerned with public policy, but it is clear from the above account of its genesis that there is no pot of gold at the end of the welfare economics rainbow. I. M. D. Little (1950, p. 272) best summarizes the situation: "Economic welfare is a subject in which rigor and refinement is probably worse than useless. Rough theory, or good common sense is, in practice, what we require."

Perfect competition as an efficiency norm was evaluated. Under strong assumptions, it was demonstrated that perfect competition maximizes utility in society. Under weaker assumptions (dropping the assumption of constant marginal utility of money) it was shown that perfect competition results in a Pareto optimum. The assumptions are so widely violated that the competitive model is only a crude norm for policy. In the dynamic setting of the actual world, atomistic competition never reaches an equilibrium. And even if it did, in the process it would make many worse off.

The above analysis of welfare economics and perfect competition can be attacked for placing too much emphasis on freedom and efficiency and too little on justice and security. Such emphasis can lead to making the price system an end rather than a means to more ultimate goals of society. Also relevant in this context is the statement of Colin Clark (1957, p. 1) that "economics must also take its place in the hierarchy of arts and sciences." Laws of economics co-ordinate and limit recommendations from the technical agricultural sciences. Economics must recognize its subordination however to the political process, ethics, and theology.

REFERENCES

Arrow, Kenneth. 1951. *Social Choice and Individual Values*. New York: Wiley.
———. 1962. Economic welfare and the allocation of economic resources for invention. In *The Rate and Direction of Inventive Activity*, National Bureau of Economic Research, Princeton: Princeton University Press, pp. 609–25.
Baumol, William J. 1965. In *Economic Theory and Operations Analysis*, Englewood Cliffs, N.J.: Prentice-Hall, Chapter 13.

Clark, Colin. 1957. *The Conditions of Economic Progress.* New York: St. Martin's Press.

Denison, Edward F. 1962. Education, economic growth and gaps in information. *Journal of Political Economy* 70:124–28.

Dorfman, Robert. 1965. Introduction. In Robert Dorfman, ed., *Measuring Benefits of Government Investments*, Washington: Brookings Institution, pp. 1–11.

Graaff, J. de V. 1957. *Theoretical Welfare Economics.* New York: Cambridge University Press.

Greene, Shirley E. 1963. Dialogue: role of the social scientist. In *Farm Goals in Conflict*, Center for Agricultural and Economic Adjustment, Ames: Iowa State University Press, pp. 232–34.

Henderson, J. M., and R. E. Quandt. 1958. *Microeconomic Theory: A Mathematical Approach.* New York: McGraw-Hill.

Hotelling, Harold. 1938. The general welfare in relation to problems of taxation and of railway and utility rates. *Econometrica* 6:242–69.

Lerner, Abba. 1944. *The Economics of Control.* New York: Macmillan.

Little, I. M. D. 1950. *A Critique of Welfare Economics.* Oxford: Clarendon Press.

Marshall, Alfred. 1890. *Principles of Economics*, 8th ed. (1920). New York: Macmillan.

Myrdal, Gunnar. 1944. *An American Dilemma.* New York: Harper & Row.

Reder, Melvin W. 1947. *Studies in the Theory of Welfare Economics.* New York: Columbia University Press.

Robbins, Lionel. 1935. *An Essay on the Nature and Significance of Economic Science*, 2nd ed. (1952). London: Macmillan.

Samuelson, Paul A. 1947. *Foundations of Economic Analysis.* Cambridge: Harvard University Press.

Scitovsky, Tibor. 1951. The state of welfare economics. *American Economic Review* 41:303–15.

Smith, Adam. 1776. *An Inquiry into the Nature and Causes of the Wealth of Nations*, vol. 1 (1933). London: Dent.

Tweeten, Luther G. 1965. Commodity programs for wheat. Technical Bulletin T-118. Stillwater, Okla., Agricultural Experiment Station.

———— and Fred Tyner. 1966. The utility concept of net social cost—a criterion for public policy. *Agricultural Economics Research* 18:33–42.

Appendix

Utility Measures from Industry Demand and Supply

The following analysis is methodological and is intended to illustrate the assumptions and possible uses and limitations of cardinal utility as a pedagogic device and as an added criterion for public policy. It is a mathematical development of the utility concept discussed in Chapter 16. Its real contribution—more important than the following demonstration that perfect competition leads to maximum utility—is to show the many explicit assumptions (often unrealistic) that are needed to reach the utopian conclusion.

The concept of social benefit is developed from individual consumer utility functions. Consider for a single consumer a domain of two commodities, q_1 and q_2, selling at constant prices P_1 and P_2, respectively. Given the utility function U associated with consumption of the two goods,

$$U = U(q_1, q_2), \tag{A.1}$$

the consumer's welfare function U^* is

$$U^* = U(q_1, q_2) + \lambda(Y_0 - P_1 q_1 - P_2 q_2). \tag{A.2}$$

The welfare function specifies total utility subject to the income restraint $Y_0 = P_1 q_1 + P_2 q_2$, with λ a Lagrangian multiplier.[1] To maximize utility, the derivatives with respect to q_1, q_2, and λ are computed and set equal to zero:

$$\frac{\partial U^*}{\partial q_1} = \frac{\partial U}{\partial q_1} - \lambda P_1 = 0 \tag{A.3}$$

1. Income can be regarded as the flow of goods and services from assets (resources) over a specified period, with the asset position remaining the same at the end as at the beginning of the period. Hence consumer utility is maximized, subject to the asset or resource distribution.

$$\frac{\partial U^*}{\partial q_2} = \frac{\partial U}{\partial q_2} - \lambda P_2 = 0 \tag{A.4}$$

$$\frac{\partial U^*}{\partial \lambda} = Y_0 - P_1 q_1 - P_2 q_2 = 0 \tag{A.5}$$

If Equation (A.1) were an explicit utility function, the marginal utilities in (A.3) and (A.4) would be specified, and Equations (A.3), (A.4), and (A.5) could be solved for λ and the utility-maximizing levels of q_1 and q_2.

The total derivative of Equation (A.1) with respect to q_1 and q_2 gives the following:

$$\frac{dU}{dq_1} = \frac{\partial U}{\partial q_1} + \frac{\partial U}{\partial q_2} \frac{dq_2}{dq_1}, \tag{A.6}$$

$$\frac{dU}{dq_2} = \frac{\partial U}{\partial q_2} + \frac{\partial U}{\partial q_1} \frac{dq_1}{dq_2}. \tag{A.7}$$

The first right-hand term is direct marginal utility, and the second is indirect marginal utility derived from changing consumption of the other commodity. Assuming that the marginal utility of q_1 is independent of q_2 and the marginal utility of q_2 is independent of q_1, the second right-hand terms in (A.6) and (A.7) drop out, and Equations (A.3) and (A.4), without being solved simultaneously, become

$$\frac{dU}{dq_1} = \lambda P_1 \tag{A.8}$$

and

$$\frac{dU}{dq_2} = \lambda P_2. \tag{A.9}$$

Assume that the marginal utility of money λ is constant and has arbitrarily been assigned the value 1. Constant utility of money units is likely to be approached only for small changes in consumption of q_1 or q_2, or if the commodity in question (q_1 for our purposes) represents a small part of the consumer's purchases. Given these assumptions, the marginal utility of consuming q_1 is measured by its price, i.e.:

$$\frac{dU}{dq_1} = P_1 \quad \text{or} \quad dU = P_1 dq_1. \tag{A.10}$$

The demand function (A.11) is formed by solving Equations (A.3), (A.4), and (A.5) for q_1:

$$q_1 = D(P_1) \quad \text{or} \quad P_1 = D^{-1}(q_1). \tag{A.11}$$

The demand quantity is a function of price P_1 (with P_2 and Y_0 fixed), as specified by the demand function (A.11). Substituting (A.11) for the demand price P_1 in

Equation (A.10), the integral from 0 to n is the total utility U from consuming n units of q_1:

$$U = \int_0^n D^{-1}(q_1)dq_1 \tag{A.12}$$

Since (A.11) becomes a marginal utility curve under the stated assumptions, the integral (A.12) measures total utility and is the area underneath the demand curve. The integral can be formed only if the demand function is continuously defined and touches the price axis. The assumption that price (and marginal utility) are finite, even for a quantity approaching zero, seems reasonable, especially if q_1 is not a necessity and if substitutes exist. Since the total utility from consuming q_1 is measured by the area beneath the demand curve from $q_1 = 0$ to $q_1 = n$, as n becomes larger the entire area beneath the consumer demand curve is included.

Equation (A.12) can be aggregated over all consumers to form the total demand and utility functions for q_1 if, for each consumer, the marginal utility of a given quantity of q_1 is independent of the quantities consumed by others (absence of external economies or diseconomies in consumption). If the independence condition is satisfied, and λ is homogeneous for all consumers, then the area beneath the *market* demand curve is a measure of utility gained— the total social benefit from consuming q_1.

Consumption of q_1 not only gives direct utility measured by (A.12), but also involves a cost of utility forgone by consuming q_1 rather than other commodities represented by q_2. To determine the forgone utility, it is necessary to specify a production function (A.13) for outputs q_1 and q_2 from the variable input x.[2] The private cost for a firm is the resource price P_x multiplied by the quantity, or $P_x x$. The firm profit π in (A.14) is maximized by equating derivatives of the expression (A.15) to zero in (A.16) through (A.19). The Langrangian multiplier is μ. Equations (A.13) to (A.19) are:

$$F(q_1,q_2,x) = 0 \tag{A.13}$$

$$\pi = P_1 q_1 + P_2 q_2 - P_x x \tag{A.14}$$

$$\pi^* = P_1 q_1 + P_2 q_2 - P_x x + \mu F(q_1,q_2,x) \tag{A.15}$$

$$\frac{\partial \pi^*}{\partial q_1} = P_1 + \mu \frac{\partial F}{\partial q_1} = 0 \tag{A.16}$$

$$\frac{\partial \pi^*}{\partial q_2} = P_2 + \mu \frac{\partial F}{\partial q_2} = 0 \tag{A.17}$$

2. Resources designated x are variable in the length of run considered. Other (fixed) resources will influence the productivity coefficients; hence the resulting marginal conditions and utility are subject to the initial distribution of assets in both production and consumption.

$$\frac{\partial \pi^*}{\partial x} = -P_x + \mu \frac{\partial F}{\partial x} = 0 \qquad (A.18)$$

$$\frac{\partial \pi^*}{\partial \mu} = F(q_1, q_2, x) = 0 \qquad (A.19)$$

Rearranging terms and dividing (A.16) by (A.17), (A.18) by (A.16), and (A.18) by (A.17), the respective results are:

$$-\frac{dq_2}{dq_1} = \frac{P_1}{P_2}, \quad \text{or} \quad P_1 = -\frac{dq_2}{dq_1} P_2 \qquad (A.20)$$

$$\frac{dq_1}{dx} = \frac{Px}{P_1}, \quad \text{or} \quad P_1 = \frac{dx}{dq_1} P_x \qquad (A.21)$$

$$\frac{dq_2}{dx} = \frac{Px}{P_2}, \quad \text{or} \quad P_2 = \frac{dx}{dq_2} P_x \qquad (A.22)$$

Equations (A.20) and (A.21) are two expressions of q_1 cost. Equation (A.21) indicates that P_1 is equal to the direct private cost of a small increment in q_1. $P_x dx$ is the increment in total cost associated with dq_1, hence $(P_x dx)/dq_1$ is the marginal cost. It is apparent that the supply price P_1 in the firm supply function may then be regarded as a measure of marginal cost.

P_1 viewed from the production or firm side in (A.20) is a measure of the opportunity cost or value of production (and consumption) forgone by producing additional q_1. The amount of production forgone dq_2, divided by an increment dq_1 and multiplied by the price P_2, is the value of production sacrificed. The two expressions of cost $-(dq_2/dq_1)P_2$ and $(dx/dq_1)P_x$ are equal.

Again assuming the marginal utility of money is unity ($\lambda = 1$), from (A.9) we derive $P_2 = dU/dq_2$. This expression for the marginal utility of q_2 is inserted into Equation (A.20) giving

$$P_1 = -\frac{dq_2}{dq_1} \frac{dU}{dq_2} = -\frac{dU}{dq_1} \quad \text{or} \quad dU = -P_1 dq_1. \qquad (A.23)$$

The relationship between supply price and quantity is specified by the supply function (A.24), found by solving Equations (A.16) through (A.19) for q_1:

$$q_1 = S(P_1) \quad \text{or} \quad P_1 = S^{-1}(q_1). \qquad (A.24)$$

After substituting (A.24) for P_1 in (A.23), the total utility forgone by production and consumption of q_1 is specified by integrating (A.23) over the range 0 to n:

$$U = -\int_0^n S^{-1}(q_1) dq_1. \qquad (A.25)$$

The integral is the area beneath the individual firm supply curve. It is a valid measure of total utility forgone only if the marginal utility of money is constant, the marginal cost curve is continuously defined, and there is no divergence between social and private cost.

Under competitive conditions and excluding external economies or dis-economies of scale in production,[3] the individual firm marginal cost (supply) functions can be aggregated to form the industry supply curve. The area beneath the industry supply curve is a measure of the total utility forgone or opportunity cost of producing and consuming q_1 rather than q_2 under the conditions stated above.

The total utility U_T, or net social gain from consumption and production of q_1, is the sum of the direct utility, Equation (A.12), and the utility forgone, Equation (A.25):

$$U_T = \int_0^N D^{-1}(Q_1)dQ_1 - \int_0^N S^{-1}(Q_1)dQ_1, \qquad (A.26)$$

where Q_1 and N indicate the commodities and units in the industry demand and supply relationships, respectively. To maximize U_T, we take the derivative with respect to Q_1 in (A.26) and set it equal to zero. The solution is the quantity at which the supply price and demand price (marginal utilities) are equal; that is, q_1 increases until the satisfactions achieved from consuming it just equal the satisfactions forgone by not consuming other commodities represented by q_2. Since this occurs only at the intersection of supply and demand, it follows that prices and quantities under perfect competition maximize utility, subject to the initial resource distribution.

Additional assumptions are that knowledge is complete, products and resources are mobile, and second-order conditions of convexity, etc., are met. Given these conditions, the equilibrium specified from Equation (A.26), with prices P_1 and P_2, represents a Pareto optimum.

Dividing Equation (A.8) by (A.9), the result is equivalent to (A.20):

$$-\frac{dq_2}{dq_1} = \frac{P_1}{P_2} \qquad (A.27)$$

The marginal rate of substitution of q_1 for q_2 in production for all firms and in consumption for all consumers equals the same price ratio, thus the marginal rates in production and consumption are equal to each other—a necessary condition for a Pareto optimum.

A two-commodity world of q_1 and all other commodities denoted by q_2 was considered above to simplify and shorten the analysis, but the results also apply when a larger group of commodities is included.

---

3. Some costs are external to the firm but internal to the industry. In the long run, many such costs are reflected in private accounts of the firm. More important is the dis-association between private and social costs (or returns) that do not become reflected in private accounts of the firm, even as the length of run increases.

Index